The Neurocognition of Language

The Neurocognition of Language

edited by

Colin M. Brown and Peter Hagoort

Neurocognition of Language Processing Research Group,
Max Planck Institute for Psycholinguistics,
Nijmegen, The Netherlands

OXFORD
UNIVERSITY PRESS

*This book has been printed digitally and produced in a standard specification
in order to ensure its continuing availability*

OXFORD
UNIVERSITY PRESS

Great Clarendon Street, Oxford OX2 6DP

Oxford University Press is a department of the University of Oxford.
It furthers the University's objective of excellence in research, scholarship,
and education by publishing worldwide in

Oxford New York

Auckland Bangkok Buenos Aires Cape Town Chennai
Dar es Salaam Delhi Hong Kong Istanbul Karachi Kolkata
Kuala Lumpur Madrid Melbourne Mexico City Mumbai Nairobi
São Paulo Shanghai Taipei Tokyo Toronto

Oxford is a registered trade mark of Oxford University Press
in the UK and in certain other countries

Published in the United States
by Oxford University Press Inc., New York

ISBN 0-19-850793-3

Printed in Great Britain by
Antony Rowe Ltd., Eastbourne

Preface

The subject of this book is the neurocognition of language. Both the functional organization of the human language system and its neural underpinnings are scrutinized. Our main motivation for putting this book together was triggered by the unprecedented increase in studies on the neural architecture of language functions in the last decade. Due to the rapid development of brain-imaging techniques it is now possible to measure brain activity related to language in action. This contrasts with the past where, in the absence of an animal model, we had to rely on the experiments of nature, in the form of brain lesions that led to language deficits. In this volume we attempt to combine state-of-the-art knowledge about speaking, listening, and reading with insights into the brain systems involved in these language functions. By reviewing and summarizing our understanding of the neural architecture of language in relation to its cognitive organization, and by discussing new approaches to bringing neural measures to bear on brain and language issues, we hope that the book will contribute to the advancement of a true cognitive neuroscience of language.

This book would not have been possible without the help of many friends and colleagues. First we want to thank a number of colleagues for their contribution to the review process of several chapters in this book: Jos van Berkum, Herb Clark, Eve Clark, Peter Indefrey, and Dick Stegeman. Second we thank Inge Doehring for her graphical support. Apart from designing the figures for the contributing authors from the Max Planck Institute for Psycholinguistics, she transformed all the other figures into a uniform format, thereby contributing substantially to the clarity of presentation and the aesthetics of the book. Finally we are tremendously grateful to Rian Zondervan, without whose secretarial support both our work on this book and that of the OUP staff would have been less joyful and more time consuming.

We also acknowledge the Netherlands Organization for Scientific Research (NWO) for its continuing financial support of our research.

Nijmegen, The Netherlands   C. M. B. and P. H.
July 1998

Contents

Section 3: The neurocognitive architectures of language

Contributors

Katrin Amunts   C. and O. Vogt Brain Research Institute, Heinrich Heine University, Universitätsstrasse 1, D-40225 Düsseldorf, Germany.

Irina N. Bogolepova   Brain Research Institute, Russian Academy of Medical Sciences, Per. Obukhas 103064, Moscow, Russia.

Colin M. Brown   "Neurocognition of language processing" Research Group, Max Planck Institute for Psycholinguistics, Wundtlaan 1, NL-6525 XD Nijmegen, The Netherlands.

Christian Büchel   Institute of Neurology, Welcome Department of Cognitive Neurology, 12 Queen Square, London WC1N 3BG, UK.

Charles Clifton, Jr.   Department of Psychology, University of Massachusetts, Amherst, MA 10003, USA.

Anne Cutler   Max Planck Institute for Psycholinguistics, Wundtlaan 1, NL-6525 XD Nijmegen, The Netherlands.

Kara D. Federmeier   Department of Cognitive Science D-015, University of California at San Diego, La Jolla, CA 92093-0515, USA.

Karl Friston   Institute of Neurology, Welcome Department of Cognitive Neurology, 12 Queen Square, London WC1N 3BG, UK.

Chris Frith   Institute of Neurology, Welcome Department of Cognitive Neurology, 12 Queen Square, London WC1N 3BG, UK.

Peter Hagoort   "Neurocognition of language processing" Research Group, Max Planck Institute for Psycholinguistics, Wundtlaan 1, NL-6525 XD Nijmegen, The Netherlands.

Peter Indefrey   "Neurocognition of language processing" Research Group, Max Planck Institute for Psycholinguistics, Wundtlaan 1, NL-6525 XD Nijmegen, The Netherlands.

Ray Jackendoff   Program in Linguistics and Cognitive Science, Brandeis University, Brown 125, Waltham, MA 02254-9110, USA.

Marta Kutas   Department of Cognitive Science D-015, University of California at San Diego, La Jolla, CA 92093-0515, USA.

Willem J. M. Levelt   Max Planck Institute for Psycholinguistics, Wundtlaan 1, NL-6525 XD Nijmegen, The Netherlands.

Lidia I. Malofeeva   Brain Research Institute, Russian Academy of Medical Sciences, Per. Obukhas 5, 103064, Moscow, Russia.

Lee Osterhout   Department of Psychology, NI-25, University of Washington, Seattle, Washington 98195, USA.

Charles A. Perfetti   Learning Research and Development Center, University of Pittsburgh, Pittsburgh, PA 15260, USA.

Cathy Price   Institute of Neurology, Welcome Department of Cognitive Neurology, 12 Queen Square, London WC1N 3BG, UK.

Michael D. Rugg   Institute of Cognitive Neuroscience, Department of Psychology, Alexandra House, Queen Square, University College London, Gower Street, London WC1E 6BT, UK.

Eleanor M. Saffran   Center for Cognitive Neuroscience, Temple University, 3401 N. Broad St., Philadelphia, PA 19140, USA.

Martin I. Sereno   Department of Cognitive Science D-015, University of California at San Diego, La Jolla, CA 92093-0515, USA.

Alexandra Sholl   Center for Cognitive Neuroscience, Temple University, 3401 N. Broad St., Philadelphia, PA 19140, USA.

Miranda van Turennout   NIMH, Laboratory of Brain and Cognition, Building 10, Room 4C104, 10 Center Drive MSC 1366, Bethesda MD 20892-1366, USA.

Harry B. M. Uylings   Netherlands Institute for Brain Research, Meibergdreef 33, NL-1105 AZ Amsterdam, The Netherlands.

Karl Zilles   C. and O. Vogt Brain Research Institute,   Heinrich Heine University, Universitätsstrasse 1, D-40225 Düsseldorf, Germany.

Section 1

Introductions

1 *The cognitive neuroscience of language: challenges and future directions*

Colin M. Brown and Peter Hagoort

1.1 Introduction

Does the brain hold all the answers to the questions that puzzle, intrigue, and delight us about human language? In some sense this has to be true: both the questions we pursue and the answers that we seek are to be found in the brain. Where else? Still, it is good to remind ourselves that not so long ago the study of the brain was deemed irrelevant for the study of cognition. In fact, it is rumoured that this still is received opinion in some corners of the world. And why not? After all, leaving aside (at our peril) neuro-psychological work for the moment, a great deal of what we know about the structure and functioning of the language system has come from research that has essentially ignored the fact that language is seated in the brain. And we should acknowledge that today, even after the explosive growth of ever more sensitive and revealing brain-imaging technology, a cognitive neuroscience approach to language has not as yet merged with linguistic and psycholinguistic research programmes.

There are, however, good reasons to believe that such a merger would be beneficial for our understanding of the language system. For example, neurobiological data can provide evidence on the neural reality of the representational levels that are dis-tinguished by competing language models, such as the disputed separation between syntactic and semantic knowledge. These issues can be addressed by positron emission tomography (PET) and functional magnetic resonance imaging (fMRI) research on the neural systems related to different kinds of linguistic knowledge. Such evidence is directly relevant for fundamental claims on the basic architecture of the language system. Neurobiological data are also relevant for long-standing debates on the domain specificity of language (for example on the putative existence of a dedicated verbal working-memory system, or of a dedicated system for recognizing speech sounds). In addition, various measures of neurobiological activity deliver fine-grained temporal information on the processing dynamics of language production and com-prehension. Such information is crucial for assessing the different claims of sequential and interactive processing models. In principle, then, we stand to gain a lot by taking a cognitive neuroscience perspective on language.

However, the field of language and brain research is at present quite fragmented, and has by no means reached maturity. In part this can be attributed to the separate histories of linguistics, psycholinguistics, and the neurosciences, which has not been conducive to cross-talk. Furthermore, cognitive neuroscience is still very much under development, with several conceptual, analytical, and neurophysiological issues not yet worked out. However, there has also been a certain unawareness, perhaps neglect even, of linguistic and psycholinguistic work by the neuroscience oriented disciplines. What we hope to achieve with this book, is to serve two sides of the emerging cognitive neuroscience community: those who have entered into the field of language from a more neuroscientific background, and those who are in the process of including a neurobiological perspective in their own work on language. Accordingly, this book includes an explication of the language system from a linguistic perspective, and state-of-the-art overviews of the cognitive architectures of speaking, listening, and reading. These foundational chapters reflect our belief that progress in the cognitive neuro-science of language is best achieved when our research questions are based on linguistic theory and psycholinguistic models, with a clear understanding and appreciation of the various factors that can affect comprehension and production. At the same time, given the complexities of brain-imaging work, neuroscience technology cannot be taken on board lightly by language researchers. Therefore, the book also presents theoretical and empirical discussion of language-related brain-imaging work, both as a review of our current knowledge, and as an explication of the specific problems that confront language researchers when they incorporate brain-imaging technology into their research.

The particular collection of chapters is motivated by several overarching themes that we see as being critical for the development of a cognitive neuroscience approach to language. These include the complexity of language, the mapping between measures of brain activity and the language system, and the issue of functional and anatomical variability.

1.2 Complexity

Despite the critical and central role that language plays in almost all aspects of human life, results from cognitive neuroscience research on language are not leading the field. Why is this? One obvious reason is that we lack an animal model of language. This severely limits our ability to investigate the neural foundations of language, excluding among others the standard neuroscientific repertoire of cell recordings, ablations, and the like, which have proven so fruitful in furthering our understanding in other areas.

A more fundamental reason emerges from the complexity of the human language system. Based on almost a century of linguistic and psycholinguistic research it is clear that language in action involves the activation, co-ordination, and integration of complex representational systems (such as for sound, orthography, grammar, and meaning), operating at millisecond speed. The chapter by Jackendoff introduces the various representational levels that need to be distinguished, and discusses their inter-relationships. The so-called blueprint chapters by Levelt, by Cutler and Clifton, and by Perfetti provide overviews of our current knowledge of the cognitive architectures for speaking, listening, and reading. Together, these four chapters present specific theories and working models of the representations and processes that define language. These chapters also describe a variety of variables that are thought to play a role during comprehension and production, discussing strengths and weaknesses of experimental paradigms and tasks, and mentioning several gaps in our current knowledge. In doing so, they set a large part of the scene for a cognitive neuroscience research programme on adult language comprehension and production.[1] Of course, various aspects of the models may turn out to be incorrect, and some of the variables and tasks may in fact be artifactual or irrelevant. Be that as it may, when we design brain-imaging experiments on language, a major concern should be the relationship between the chosen design and task(s), and the cognitive architecture of the language faculty, against the background of the accumulated linguistic and psycholinguistic knowledge. We think that it is fair to say that this concern has not always been carefully considered in the brain-imaging literature. For example, the common use of the verb-generation task as a presumed window on semantic aspects of the language system can be seriously questioned on both theoretical and empirical grounds (see the chapters by Levelt and by Price *et al.*). Likewise, the mapping of meaning in the brain on the basis of a comparison of brain activity elicited by undifferentiated, broad categories of word types runs the danger of underestimating the complexity of the semantics of language, as becomes clear from the discussion of semantic impairments in brain-damaged individuals in the chapter by Saffran and Sholl.

There is, moreover, another side to the brain-imaging and language complexity issue. Although, as we just noted, the complexity of language should not be under-estimated, it also needs to be met head on by the cognitive neuroscience community. The situation to date is that the large majority of PET and fMRI language studies have focused on single-word processing. This is perhaps understandable from the desire to perform a 'simple' experiment (although as various chapters in this book show, the presumption of simplicity is often unwarranted; for example, the search for 'words in the brain' cannot be lightly undertaken, as is discussed by Price *et al.* in their overview chapter on brain-imaging studies of lexical processing). However, language is much more than the processing of single words. Words are indispensable vehicles of com-munication, but the primary goal of speaking, listening, and reading lies in the message that is to be produced and understood. Message-level production and comprehension requires the activation and real-time co-ordination of several levels of linguistic and non-linguistic information. This complexity is central to the essence of language, and presents a major challenge to cognitive neuroscientists, which has to date basically not been taken up. There is one emerging area here, which is the work on event-related brain potentials and sentence processing (ERPs are components of the brain's electro-encephalographic activity, the EEG). Although still relatively modest in terms of the number of active research centres, ERP research on sentence-level syntactic and semantic processing is providing revealing data. This work is discussed in the chapter by Hagoort *et al.*, that also includes a review of PET and fMRI experiments on sentence processing. Almost all of this work is, however, limited to language comprehension. Research on the production of complex sentences awaits attention from psycholinguists and cognitive neuroscientists alike.

1.3 Mapping language in the brain

The cognitive neurosciences owe their sudden expansion to the increasing availability and sophistication of functional brain-imaging methods (we use the term 'functional brain-imaging' generically, to include all non-invasive measures of human brain activity). Part of the excitement that has accompanied these technical developments has been fed by the hope that they will provide a direct window on the brain/mind in action. There is some justification for this hope. PET and fMRI provide unrivalled possibilities to map language-related areas in the living, undamaged human brain, and ERPs (together with event-related fields, ERFs, the magnetic counterparts to ERPs, obtained from the magneto-encephalographic activity of the brain, the MEG) reflect neurophysiological activity at the millisecond level that can be reliable related to real-time cognitive processing. Together, these methods provide spatial and temporal data that can be directly applied to the general questions of the cognitive neurosciences: what is happening where and when in the brain? But next to their obvious value, it is important to appreciate the limitations and problems of brain-imaging methods. The chapter by Rugg discusses the strengths and weaknesses of PET, fMRI, ERPs, and ERFs. In addition, Rugg raises several general issues regarding the application of functional brain-imaging methods in cognitive neuroscience. Among these are the need to integrate spatial and temporal information, the problem of deciding what constitutes a real difference in brain activity (in particular, a difference that warrants the assumption of functionally distinct (sub)systems or operations), and the fundamental problem of moving from a neural correlate of cognition to a causal relationship between neural and cognitive activity.

Some of the issues that are raised by Rugg are taken up in the chapter by Kutas *et al.*, and the chapter by Büchel *et al.* Kutas and colleagues focus on the use of ERP and ERF data to understand language processes. The shapes and spatial distributions of electromagnetic activity provide a rich collection of ERP and ERF components that have been linked to different aspects of the language system. Kutas *et al.* discuss ways to compare and decompose the spatial distributions of electromagnetic data, and to map from spatial distributions to underlying neural generators. This mapping from surface recordings to neural tissue is often considered to be the Achilles heel of electromagnetic measurements: although ERPs and ERFs are unmatched in their temporal resolution, they lack spatial resolution. Kutas *et al.* critically discuss different kinds of neuronal localization approaches, from which it becomes clear that in fact substantial spatial information can be derived from electromagnetic data, given appropriate boundary conditions. This is one of the areas where much is to be expected from combining information from different brain-imaging measures. In particular the use of fMRI to constrain the solution space for electromagnetic localization procedures seems promising. Of course, this kind of combined approach critically assumes that we can sensibly relate the signals measured by fMRI and EEG or MEG, which is one of the issues discussed by Rugg. The combination of the millisecond precision of electromagnetic recordings with specific neuronal foci would be a big step towards answering the 'where' and 'when' questions.

The combination of 'where' and 'when' relates to another fundamental question on mapping language in the brain, namely the issue of interactions between brain regions. For a complex cognitive capacity such as language, it is beyond doubt that a variety of areas in the brain are going to be simultaneously active. Standard PET and fMRI analyses can reveal which areas of the brain were active during a particular period of time. However, a collection of activated areas does not by itself reveal which areas, if any, interacted. For this, we need to know two things. One, the functional connectivity, that is the temporal correlation between spatially remote neurophysiological events (which areas have correlated activity?). Two, the effective connectivity, that is the influence that one neuronal system exerts over another (which area modulates activity in another area?). This is the subject of the chapter by Büchel *et al.*, who introduce analytical procedures for characterizing both functional and effective connectivity. This is very much an emerging approach to the analysis of brain-imaging data, but it is an essential part of a cognitive neuroscience approach to language. If we are to succeed in our goal of tracking language in space and time in the brain, then elucidating the connectivity and interactivity of language-related cortical regions is of critical importance.

Amidst all the excitement that has been generated by the new brain-imaging technology, we run the risk of neglecting a fertile and prolific research area that has contributed, and is contributing, much to our knowledge of language in the brain. This is the neuropsychological tradition. The chapter by Saffran and Sholl shows how much information can be obtained from a detailed examination of the kinds of deficits that are associated with particular lesion sites. Their chapter is on the architecture of semantic memory, focusing on impairments in word meaning. The evidence that Saffran and Sholl review shows that semantic information is distributed over several areas in the brain, and that particular kinds of information can be localized to specific regions of the cerebral cortex. Interestingly, the lesion data indicate that areas outside the regions that are traditionally associated with language functions (i.e. the perisylvian cortex of the left hemisphere) are involved in semantic processing. In particular the inferotemporal cortex, possibly in both hemispheres, is clearly involved in the organization of meaning in the brain. As Saffran and Sholl point out, our knowledge of the functional and neural architecture of semantic memory that is being built up on the basis of lesion data, is finding support in brain-imaging experiments.

This converging evidence from brain-imaging and neuropsychological data highlights the importance of capitalizing on the combination of these two sources of information. Brain-imaging data can reveal which distributed areas of the brain are associated with the performance of a particular task, such as understanding a spoken sentence. However, these data do not indicate whether all of the active areas are essential to the task at hand. This is where neuropsychological data can provide critical information, by determining whether a damaged area was indeed crucial for the lost function (note that this still does not necessarily imply a direct relation between the damaged area and the proposed function). However, neuropsychological data do not reveal which other areas are normally involved in the impaired function. In short, the combination of brain-imaging and neuropsychological data provides the best basis for mapping language in the brain.

1.4 Anatomical and functional variability

In addition to the constraints, validations, and extensions that brain-imaging data can bring to cognitive models of language, it is a topic in its own right to investigate the neuroanatomy of language-related areas in the brain, and to unravel their connectivities. The human brain is the one and only organ to have developed a rich and varied system of verbal communication, and this raises questions about the neuroanatomy of this unique ability. Moreover, neuroanatomical knowledge can shed new light on the structure and functioning of the language system, in part by providing evidence on the morphological commonalities and differences among the cortical and subcortical areas that emerge in brain-imaging studies of language. The chapter by Uylings *et al.* is a good example here. These authors show that the classical, and not always uniform, definition of Broca's area needs to be reconsidered in the light of detailed anatomical information. It appears that several architectonically distinct areas have been subsumed under the heading of 'Broca's area'. This raises questions about the functionality of this cortical region, and is directly relevant for brain-imaging research that has linked a diversity of language operations to the overall region of Broca's area (see the review of the PET and fMRI literature in the chapter by Hagoort *et al.*).

An additional and critical contribution from detailed neuroanatomical work lies in assessing interindividual variability. It is now beyond any doubt that there is considerable variability among individual brains in the size and location of cortical areas. This also holds for the classically-defined Broca's area, as is demonstrated by the work of Uylings and his colleagues. The brain-imaging community still has to come to grips with these neuroanatomical differences. At present, the common approach is to map individual brain activations into a standardized brain atlas, and to define locations by reference to a co-ordinate system, usually the Talairach system. This approach does not define cortical regions as anatomical, cytoarchitectonic areas, and glosses over neuroanatomical variability between individuals. To some extent these issues can be resolved by fMRI measurements, where anatomical and functional information can be mapped for an individual brain. However, the basic problem of comparing subjects remains: we need to know whether one individual's foci of activity are located in anatomically the same or different areas of the brain as the foci obtained for another individual. One approach is to use a three-dimensional human brain database, incorporating detailed anatomical information from different brains, on the basis of which a probability map can be computed that takes variability in size and location into account (cf. Roland and Zilles 1994).

1.5 Future directions

In the preceding sections we have discussed some of the issues and themes that are central to the emerging field of the cognitive neuroscience of language. Although still a young effort, quite a lot has already been achieved, and several of the issues that are addressed in the chapters of this book point the way to future trends. In this final section, we want to draw attention to some challenges and future directions for research that are at present almost *terra incognita*, but that will hopefully receive some impetus from the theoretical and empirical work that the book presents.

The starting point for future directions lies in the need to take a more integrated approach towards language. This holds for our measurement and analytical procedures, and, most importantly, with respect to core characteristics of language in action (e.g. multiple activation of different knowledge bases, incremental and millisecond-level processing, integration among different representational systems and processing streams). An integrated approach requires considerable ingenuity in terms of experimental design (certainly with PET and standard fMRI measurements, that require blocked presentation of stimuli; event-related fMRI is more flexible in this respect, as are the ERP and ERF methods). In addition, it requires the combination of different measurement techniques, preferably in the same subject, and for some issues perhaps even at the same time.

The call for combined PET/fMRI and ERP/ERF measurements is often heard. It is thought that this kind of combination will help to overcome the spatial or temporal limitations of individual brain-imaging techniques. In principle this certainly is true, but we need to be aware that at present we have insufficient understanding of how the haemodynamic signals (measured by PET and fMRI) and the electromagnetic signals (measured by EEG and MEG) are related. This makes it difficult to determine the nature of the relationship between a particular component of the ERP/ERF signal and a haemodynamic response in a specific area of the brain (see the chapter by Rugg for further discussion). Nevertheless, an integrated spatiotemporal approach holds considerable promise. In the immediate future, progress can be made by devising experimental designs that allow the same stimuli and presentation procedures to be used in separate ERP/ERF and PET/fMRI experiments. For example, fMRI data can be used to constrain the solution space for neuronal source localization procedures based on ERP/ERF data. Analyses of effective connectivities in the fMRI data will help to identify the relations and constraints among activated cortical regions, some of which will be further defined by cytoarchitectonic data. If the experiment is appropriately founded in a model of the cognitive architecture, then by putting these different sources of data together we will be able to start building up a picture of the localization and the temporal dynamics of language in the brain.

There are other benefits to combining brain-imaging measures. One of these has received almost no attention in the literature so far. It concerns the use of ERPs as diagnostic tools for the evaluation of the processing activity measured by PET or fMRI. As is reviewed in part in the chapter by Hagoort *et al.*, ERPs have proven sensitive to distinct aspects of language processing. For certain components of the ERP waveform we now have a good understanding of their relationship to the language system (e.g. the N400 as an index of aspects of semantic processing, the P600/SPS of syntactic processing). This means that we can use ERP componentry to inform us about the processing impact of the language stimulation that we use to elicit a haemodynamic response. At the very least this provides an independent validation of the effect of the stimulation conditions during a PET or fMRI experiment. But it also opens the way to avoiding the use of extraneous task demands to evoke an overt response (such as judging the grammaticality or meaningfulness of a sentence). Often these tasks evoke additional processes that are not intrinsic to the processes that the experimenter is interested in, and that are moreover not well understood. This can considerably complicate the interpretation of the data. A grammaticality judgement task, for example, is by no means simple or focused on 'just grammar', but involves numerous representations and processes. ERP measurements can be helpful here, because reliable language-related ERP effects can be measured in the absence of additional task demands. For example, if subjects are instructed to listen attentively to sentences, without any further task, manipulating the semantic or syntactic context results in clear N400 or P600/SPS effects. The coregistration of PET/fMRI and ERPs can, therefore, open the way to language experiments that are less plagued by extraneous task demands.

The emphasis on more natural language experiments is related to another direction for future research, namely brain-imaging experiments with spoken language. The majority of imaging studies have focused on written language, following a long-standing bias in the psycholinguistic literature. This neglects the primacy of spoken compared to written language (despite its automaticity in most literate adults, reading remains an acquired skill, requiring explicit training). However, there is little reason for this neglect in a cognitive neuroscience research programme. The commonly used brain-imaging techniques are well suited for research on spoken language (although the noise generated by the current MR scanners does present some practical problems). Moreover, several decades of psycholinguistic work has provided a firm cognitive basis for research on spoken language comprehension, as is exemplified in the chapter by Cutler and Clifton. The time is more than ripe, therefore, for brain-imaging experiments in this area.

The situation is more complicated for language production research. Not because there is insufficient empirical and theoretical basis. Although language production has traditionally been less widely studied than comprehension, the chapter by Levelt presents a detailed cognitive model of speaking, together with convincing experimental support. The problems here are more practical in nature. Unlike listening or reading, speaking involves quite some facial movement, in particular of the jaw, lips, and tongue. And unfortunately, the standard brain-imaging techniques are quite susceptible to movement artefacts. For ERPs it is clear that substantial contamination can result (but possibilities to solve this by, for instance, digital filtering have been insufficiently explored). For ERF measurements less of a problem is claimed, although head movements under the MEG sensors remain very problematic. The extent of the problem in the case of PET and fMRI is unknown. Despite the frequent reaction in the brain-imaging community that speaking in the PET or MR scanner is out of the question, it is not clear how great the problem actually is. Certainly, if the position of the head relative to the registration device changes too much during the measurement, then this is very problematic. However, whether relatively small jaw, lip, and tongue movements create similar problems remains to be demonstrated. In fact, work within our own research group indicates that if subjects are asked to whisper, which naturally suppresses large articulatory movements, reliable and replicable PET and fMRI measurements can be obtained (e.g. Indefrey *et al.* 1998). A recent review of the PET and fMRI literature by Indefrey and Levelt (2000) indicates that in single-word production tasks reliable measurements can be obtained. It is, therefore, premature to rule out the use of the full battery of brain-imaging techniques in production research. But this clearly is an area where the more cognitively oriented work will have to be based on systematic investigation of the possibilities and limitations of the technology with respect to the act of speaking, in particular the production of full sentences.

A final and still very open area for future language research concerns neural plasticity, by which we mean the ability of the brain to compensate for damage by the reorganization of intact (sub)cortical areas. Aphasia is an obvious starting point for investigation here, although dyslexia and certain aspects involving language-learning impaired children also present interesting challenges. Another window on plasticity is the neural organization of language in deaf children and adults (cf. Neville *et al.* 1997). The general question with respect to aphasic patients concerns the role of non-damaged brain tissue in subserving the remaining language competence. Can intact brain tissue in part compensate for the loss of function in the damaged areas? This is a complicated issue, all the more so since brain damage as such does not have to directly involve language regions. Instead, damage could for example result in a limitation in the processing capacity (e.g. working memory) that is available for language, thereby indirectly leading to a language deficit. Progress in this area will critically depend on basing the research on a well-founded cognitive model of normal language processing, and on a firm understanding of the neurophysiological manifestations of normal and impaired language processing.

Not all of the areas for future research that we have discussed here are represented in the following chapters. In several cases that would have been premature. What we hope is that this book will help towards the further development of these exciting and challenging areas, and, more in general, towards the coming of age of a cognitive neuroscience approach to human language.

Acknowledgements

We thank Jos van Berkum and Miranda van Turennout for their helpful comments.

Notes

1. An obvious gap in the coverage of this book is language development, both in the first and in the second language learner. Although steps towards a more biologically-based understanding of language development are being taken (cf. Johnson 1993), this is even more an emerging field than research on brain and language in adults. We hope that with this book we will contribute to a more concerted and psycholinguistically motivated approach to the cognitive neuroscience of language, and thereby provide relevant information for developmental research.

References

Indefrey, P. and Levelt, W. J. M. (2000). The neural correlates of language production. In *The cognitive neurosciences* (2nd edn), (ed. M. Gazzaniga). MIT Press, Cambridge, MA.

Indefrey, P., Gruber, O., Brown, C. M., Hagoort, P., Posse, S., and Kleinschmidt, A. (1998). Lexicality and not syllable frequency determine lateralized premotor activation during the pronunciation of word-like stimuli: An fMRI study. *Human Brain Mapping*, 7, S4.

Johnson, M. H. (ed.) (1993). *Brain development and cognition: A reader*. Blackwell, Oxford.

Neville, H. J., Coffey, S. A., Lawson, D. S., Fischer, A., Emmorey, K., and Bellugi, U. (1997). Neural systems mediating American Sign Language: Effects of sensory experience and age of acquisition. *Brain and Language*, **57**, 285–308.

Roland, P. E., and Zilles, K. (1994). Brain atlases: A new research tool. *Trends in Neurosciences*, **17**, 458–467.

2 Functional neuroimaging in cognitive neuroscience

Michael D. Rugg

2.1 Introduction

This chapter is concerned with how different functional neuroimaging methods can be employed to study the functional organization and neural bases of cognitive functions such as language, and with the practical and conceptual limitations of these methods. Throughout the chapter, 'functional neuroimaging' will be used as a generic term to cover all of the methods currently available for the non-invasive measurement of brain activity in human subjects and not, as is more customary, to refer solely to those methods—positron emission tomography (PET) and functional magnetic resonance imaging (fMRI)—based on haemodynamic variables.

The cognitive neuroscience approach to the study of a complex cognitive ability comprises two principal goals: an understanding at the functional level[1] of the identity and organization of the 'elementary operations' (Posner and McLeod 1982) that underlie the ability, and an understanding of how these operations are instantiated in the nervous system. A distinctive feature of the cognitive neuroscience approach is that these goals are considered to be strongly interrelated (Rugg 1997), such that functional information can be used to inform and constrain neurobiological models, and vice versa. Given this conceptualization, it is natural that functional neuroimaging, which seemingly provides a direct means of investigating the neural activity that supports cognitive processing, should occupy a central role in cognitive neuroscience. This role is especially important for 'high-level' cognitive functions such as language, for which no animal models exist and for which, therefore, functional neuroimaging offers the only means for investigating their neural correlates.

Functional neuroimaging can be employed to study cognitive function in three ways which, while often conflated in practice, are nevertheless conceptually distinct. In one case, knowledge about the cognitive operation under investigation is assumed to be sufficiently advanced to allow a specification of the experimental manipulation necessary to 'isolate' it, and hence to permit its neural substrate to be identified. In the second case, the cognitive operations engaged by the experimental manipulations are the unknown; at issue is whether these manipulations are associated with distinct patterns of neural activity and, therefore, distinct cognitive processes. In the third case, knowledge about the neural correlates of a given cognitive operation are assumed to be known, and measures of these correlates are employed as a means of determining the circumstances in which the operation is engaged. These three applications of functional neuroimaging are discussed below in more detail.

2.1.1 Functional localization

This application of functional neuroimaging is predicated on the widely-held notion that the brain is 'functionally segregated' (Frith and Friston 1997), and that an important step in understanding the brain basis of cognition is to 'map' cognitive operations onto their functionally specialized neural substrates. This application of functional neuroimaging is closely related to the 'lesion deficit' approach, in which the neural bases of different cognitive functions are inferred from the loci of lesions that cause selective cognitive impairments. Functional neuroimaging studies are a valuable extension to the lesion deficit approach for four main reasons. First, they permit hypotheses derived from lesion studies to be tested in normal subjects. This is important because of the problems inherent in generalizing from small and possibly unrepresentative patient samples to the general population, and also because of the practical and logical difficulties surrounding the inferences that can be drawn about functional localization on the basis of lesion effects (e.g. Gregory 1961; Poeck 1983; Shallice 1988). Second, functional neuroimaging permits investigation of the function of brain regions that are only rarely, if ever, damaged selectively in humans, and therefore about which little can been learned from lesion studies. An example of one such region, germane to language, is the insula. Circumscribed lesions to this region are rare, but evidence from functional neuroimaging suggests that it may play a role in speech production (Price *et al.* 1996).

The third way in which functional neuroimaging can go beyond lesion data is in its capacity to provide information about the dynamics of neural activity. It is possible to address questions not merely about the localization of the neural activity associated with the engagement of a cognitive operation, but also about the way this activity evolves over time, and the nature of the interactions that take place between activity in different brain loci. Thus, it becomes possible to explore the role played by *functional networks* in the instantiation of cognitive functions. This opens the door to more complex conceptualizations of the mapping between cognitive operations and their underlying neural substrates than that which underlies the traditional lesion-deficit approach, with its assumption of a more or less one-to-one mapping between cognitive operations and individual functionally specialized neural populations (cf. Mesulam 1990; Frith and Friston 1997).

Finally, neuroimaging permits the systematic investigation of individual differences in functional localization. Brains differ markedly at both the gross anatomical and the cytoarchitectonic levels (e.g. Zilles *et al.* 1997), and there is every reason to expect that these differences will be reflected in individual variation in the mapping of cognitive functions onto their neural substrates. The study of such differences is likely to be of value in addressing questions such as whether, across individuals, the same cognitive operation can be instantiated in more than one way, and whether there is a relationship between the amount of tissue devoted to a particular operation, and the efficiency with which the operation functions. Such questions have long been part of the study of the neuropsychology of language (e.g. Rugg 1995), but are far from being settled.

2.1.2 Functional fractionation

Less recognized than its application to functional localization is the role that can be played by neuroimaging in identifying distinct cognitive operations. Historically, the fractionation of cognitive abilities into their constituent operations has been achieved in two logically interrelated ways. In studies of normal subjects, tasks hypothesized to rely upon functionally distinct operations are devised, and variables are sought, which have dissociative effects on the performance of these tasks. For example the finding that frequency of occurrence affected the processing of open-class but not closed-class words was taken as support for the proposal that the two word classes are processed in functionally distinct ways, reflecting their different syntactic roles (Bradley and Garrett 1983; but see Segui *et al.* 1987). A similar logic underlies the use of brain-lesioned patients to search for cognitive fractionations. Here it is the patient, rather than (or along with) specific experimental variables that provides the basis for task dissociations. For example the existence of a 'double dissociation' in patterns of preserved and impaired reading of irregular words and non-words (manifest in the syndromes of surface and phonological dyslexia) became a cornerstone of 'dual route' models of reading (Ellis and Young 1988). In neither normal subjects nor patients, however, is the mere demonstration of a task dissociation sufficient to support the inference that functionally distinct cognitive operations have been uncovered; such inferences also rest on the validity of several key assumptions, and, not infrequently, a commitment to a particular processing architecture or measurement model (Dunn and Kirsner 1988; Shallice 1988). The possibility of obtaining converging evidence from a method dependent on quite different assumptions is therefore an attractive prospect.

Functional neuroimaging provides such a method. It rests on the assumption (discussed in more detail in Section 2.3.2) that the mapping between a cognitive operation and its neural substrate, however complex, is invariant—in other words, it is assumed that a given cognitive operation is instantiated in a brain in only one way. Given this assumption, functional neuroimaging provides a means to separate and identify different cognitive operations in terms of their differing neurophysiological correlates; if two experimental manipulations give rise to qualitatively distinct patterns of neural activity, it can be concluded that they engaged functionally distinct cognitive operations. Of course, as with the purely behavioural methods described above, whether such a finding is of interest will depend to a large extent on how closely the two experimental manipulations are matched, and thus how closely the differences in their neural correlates can be linked to the cognitive function or functions at the focus of the study. For example, the significance for models of semantic representation of the finding (Martin *et al.* 1996) that naming pictures of animals and objects gives rise to different patterns of brain activation depends on how well the experimental stimuli were matched on such variables as their visual complexity.

2.1.3 Neural monitoring of cognitive function

In this third application of functional neuroimaging, neural measures are employed in order to identify the cognitive operations engaged by an experimental manipulation. By this means, it is possible to determine whether a particular task or class of experimental items recruit a specific cognitive operation without the need to obtain behavioural measures under what might be quite complex and assumption-bound experimental conditions. Furthermore, it permits cognitive processes to be monitored when direct behavioural measures would either be undesirable (e.g. during comprehension of continuous speech), or impossible (e.g. studies of the processing of unattended speech). This application of functional neuroimaging presupposes that one knows *a priori* the nature of the relationship between the cognitive operation of interest and its manifestation in the chosen measure of brain activity. In some cases, experiments can be designed so that this relationship can be left undefined. For example *any* differences in the neural activity elicited by unattended semantically primed and unprimed words would be evidence for the semantic processing of unattended input. In other cases, the validity of the assumed relationship is crucial (e.g. the use of the 'N400' component of the event-related brain potential as an index of the engagement of semantic rather than syntactic processing; Osterhout and Holcomb 1995).

2.2 Methods

In the following sections, the most important current functional neuroimaging methods are described briefly, and their principal strengths and weaknesses outlined. The methods fall into two broad classes, based upon haemodynamic and electrophysiological measures respectively. As will become apparent, the strengths and weaknesses of these different classes of method are to a large extent complementary, motivating efforts to find ways of combining the two kinds of data. The final section discusses some of the issues that such efforts must confront.

In what follows, technical information about data acquisition and analysis is either omitted or mentioned only briefly; such information is available from a number of authoritative recent sources, which are cited when appropriate.

2.2.1 Haemodynamic methods

These methods depend on the fact that there is a close coupling in the normal brain between changes in the level of activity of a neuronal population and changes in its blood supply, such that an increase in net activity is associated with an increase in blood supply, and vice versa (Raichle 1987). Neither the physiological mechanisms underlying the coupling between neuronal activity and blood supply, nor its functional significance, are well understood (Barinaga 1997). Nevertheless, its existence allows methods sensitive to haemodynamic variables such as regional cerebral blood flow (rCBF) to be used as indirect measures of relative neural activity. It is important to note that local haemodynamic effects occur only when changes in the activity of a neural population lead to a change in the overall metabolic demand of the population. Thus, a change solely in the *timing* of the activity of a set of neurons (e.g. from asynchronous to synchronous firing) will have little or no haemodynamic counterpart, despite the likely functional significance of such a change (e.g. Kreiter and Singer 1996).

Two methods for measuring the haemodynamic correlates of neural activity, positron emission tomography (PET) and functional magnetic resonance imaging (fMRI), are in common use at present. The rationale and application of each method is briefly outlined below. More detailed information about the physiological and technical bases of the two methods can be found in Toga and Mazziotta (1996), Frackowiak *et al.* (1997), and Frith and Friston (1997).

2.2.1.1 PET

PET is a method for the localization and quantitation of the radiation (arising from positron–electron annihilations) emitted from the body by certain classes of radioactive isotope (positron emitters). It permits the generation of three-dimensional images in which image intensity is proportional to the number of annihilation events detected during the scanning interval. In so called 'cognitive activation' studies, the events are produced by the decay of a short-lived isotope, usually $^{15}O_2$, which is introduced into the bloodstream and accumulates in different brain regions in proportion to the amount of blood flowing through each region. Thus, in a $^{15}O_2$ PET image of the brain, the intensity of the image at a given location is proportional to blood flow at that location, integrated over the interval taken to acquire the images (typically between 30 and 60 s, depending on the exact method employed). The short half-life of $^{15}O_2$ (~ 2 min) allows such images, which have a spatial resolution of approximately 5 mm, to be acquired at approximately 10 min intervals. Up to 12 images can be acquired from a subject without exceeding current radiation dosimetry guidelines.

The basic logic underlying the employment of PET to investigate the neural correlates of cognition is straightforward. Images are acquired from a minimum of two experimental conditions, designed so as to differ solely with respect to the cognitive operation(s) of interest, for example passively viewing a word versus naming it aloud. The two sets of images are then contrasted on a pixel-by-pixel basis so as to identify regions in which rCBF differed according to experimental condition, and these regions are taken to be those in which the two experimental conditions engendered differential neural activity (in the example above, the regions engaged by the requirement to overtly name visually presented words; Petersen 1993). Typically, the results of such contrasts are themselves depicted as images, in which intensity or colour is proportional to the significance level achieved by the test statistic employed to perform the contrast.

Much effort has been expended in the development of statistical methods for performing contrasts between PET images, and in extending these methods to deal with more sophisticated experimental designs and questions than those permitted by simple pairwise comparisons (Friston 1997). One of the most popular analytic approaches— 'statistical parametric mapping' (Friston *et al.* 1991)—takes the form of an implementation of the general linear statistical model, and permits one to construct and analyse experiments based on virtually any standard experimental design, including multifactorial and 'parametric' designs. Statistical methods have also been developed that allow PET data to be analysed in terms of the patterns of covariance existing within images, permitting the investigation of functional interactions between different regions (e.g. Friston *et al.* 1997; McIntosh *et al.* 1996).

Although until quite recently PET was the method of choice for localizing the neural correlates of cognitive function in normal subjects, it suffers from a number of drawbacks. Some of these drawbacks arise because of the length of time needed to acquire PET data (more than 30 s). This not only means that the temporal resolution of the method is very poor but, equally important, it seriously limits the experimental designs that can be employed. Specifically, it is impossible to employ anything other than blocked designs, in which for each scan a measurement is made over a succession of trials constituting a single experimental condition. This limitation has three undesirable consequences. First, it is difficult, if not impossible, to assess which experimental effects are stimulus-related (i.e. reflect changes in the neural activity time-locked to processing of the experimental stimuli), and which reflect more tonic, state-related changes in activity. In many situations this is a crucial distinction; one often wishes to draw conclusions about the neural activity associated specifically with the processing of experimental items rather than about 'background' neural activity. Second, blocked designs maximize the opportunity for subjects to adopt condition-specific 'sets' or strategies. The adoption of condition-specific sets is likely to enhance state-related differences between conditions, and may, in addition, modify stimulus-related effects relative to those that would be found in a randomized design. Third, blocked designs (as they are employed with PET) do not allow data from different experimental trials to be sorted and analysed *post hoc*. This difficulty is especially restrictive for any study in which the neural correlates of behavioural variability (e.g. accurate vs. inaccurate lexical decisions) are the focus of experimental interest.

The foregoing comments are not intended to imply that blocked designs are inherently inferior to randomized designs, such that the latter necessarily provide the more 'accurate' picture of the neural activity associated with a given experimental manipulation. Indeed, many real world situations are probably better captured in the laboratory by a blocked design (e.g. first vs. second language comprehension in bilingual individuals). Ideally, one would like to investigate the neural correlates of cognitive processing with both blocked and randomized designs, distinguishing effects that are insensitive to this manipulation from those which covary with it. To achieve this goal, however, it is necessary to measure brain activity on a trial-by-trial basis, something which cannot be accomplished with the PET method.

Other important drawbacks of PET stem from the limited number of scans (~ 12) that can be obtained from a single subject. This limitation restricts the number of experimental conditions that can be employed in a within-subjects design, and also means that it is almost always necessary to pool data across subjects to gain sufficient statistical power to detect the rather subtle effects that often accompany cognitive manipulations. Pooling requires that each subject's images be transformed into a 'standard' space and spatially smoothed, so as to reduce the influence of individual differences in brain anatomy and increase the degree to which experimental effects will overlap across subjects. The need to pool data across subjects has two consequences. First, the spatial resolution of across-subject data sets is lower than the theoretical resolution of the PET method, with the extent of the loss depending on the degree of smoothing. Second, there is no opportunity to investigate individual differences in patterns of task-related brain activation, and thus no means of addressing the kinds of issue discussed in Section 2.1.1. Indeed, the employment of across-subject pooling is predicated on the assumptions that individual differences in the data are both small and functionally inconsequential.

2.2.1.2 fMRI

Until recently, MRI was most well known for its role as a structural imaging method. A number of methods have been developed however that permit MRI to be used to image brain function as well as structure. Currently, the most important of these methods is 'blood oxygenation level dependent' (BOLD) imaging. The BOLD method (Ogawa *et al.* 1990) takes advantage of two fortuitous facts. First, the increase in blood supply triggered by increases in neural activity delivers more oxygen than is needed to meet metabolic demand. Somewhat paradoxically, therefore, the blood draining from a neuronal population is more richly oxygenated when the population is relatively active than when it is less active. Second, the magnetic susceptibility of deoxyhaemoglobin is greater than that of oxyhaemoglobin. Thus, an MRI signal sensitive to variations in susceptibility will reflect the ratio of deoxy- to oxyhaemoglobin in the blood and, other things being equal, serve as a measure of relative neural activity. Signals obtained from certain MRI measures (those sensitive to the 'T2*' parameter) fulfil this requirement, permitting MRI to be employed as a non-invasive method for indexing the haemo-dynamic correlates of changes in local neuronal activity. The speed with which fMRI data can be acquired, its spatial resolution, and its sensitivity to experimental effects, are highly dependent on variables such as the strength of the imposed magnetic field, scanner instrumentation, and the method used for data acquisition, variables which are all currently the subject of research and development. At the time of writing, acquisition times for single brain slices of less than 100 ms, with a spatial resolution of less than 3 mm, and a sensitivity to signal changes of less than 0.2%, are not untypical.

The fMRI technique has yet to be widely employed with experimental designs as sophisticated as those that can be employed with PET. One widely used design is the so-called 'box-car' procedure, in which blocks of two experimental conditions are alternated during a single run of data acquisition, and the resulting data analysed to

-egions in which signal intensity correlates reliably with experimental
... Such designs, which correspond to the simple pairwise contrasts discussed
-ove with respect to PET data, suffer from obvious limitations. There is, however, no
reason in principle why more complex designs cannot be employed, and the data
analysed within a framework similar to that developed for PET (Friston 1997).

Even with relatively simple blocked designs, fMRI offers a number of significant
advantages over PET. Among the most important of these is that because fMRI does
not involve the administration of ionizing radiation, the number of observations that
can be made on a single subject is essentially unrestricted. This opens the way to richer
and more powerful experimental designs (e.g. experiments involving multiple ses-
sions), and greatly enhances the possibility of obtaining reliable experimental effects at
the single-subject level, thus allowing the systematic study of individual differences in
the neural correlates of cognitive function (see Section 2.1.1). A second advantage of
fMRI over PET stems from its inherently greater spatial resolution. Together with the
capacity to collect large data sets from single subjects, this opens the way to considerably more fine-grained neuroanatomical studies than those possible with PET.
Finally, the speed with which fMRI data can be acquired ($\sim 3\,s$ for a whole brain
volume) confers a further advantage, even with blocked experimental designs. Fast
acquisition means that the length of trial blocks is flexible, and with no need to impose
an interval of $\sim 10\,min$ between successive blocks, these can be administered in
a counterbalanced order in the course of a single experimental run.

Against these advantages of fMRI over PET must be set some disadvantages.
Foremost among these is that whereas PET detects activity in all brain regions with
roughly equal sensitivity, this is not the case for fMRI, because of the degradation
suffered by the BOLD signal from regions that are affected by magnetic susceptibility
effects due to factors other than blood oxygenation. Such *susceptibility artefact* is most
marked in the vicinity of boundaries between air and bone. Because of their proximity
to the ear canals and the frontal sinuses respectively, basal temporal and orbitofrontal
regions are affected particularly badly. When these regions are of primary interest,
PET is likely to remain the technique of choice.

A second disadvantage of the fMRI method is that signal quality is degraded, and
artefacts introduced, by even quite small head movements. While methods for correcting the effects of small movements are in routine use, the movements associated
with overt speech, especially when it is time-locked to specific experimental conditions
or items, are more difficult to deal with, making it difficult to employ tasks involving
overt verbal responses. A final, more prosaic difficulty with the fMRI method is that
high speed MRI data acquisition produces an extremely noisy subject environment
($> 90\,dB$), not ideal for auditory studies.

As noted already, the majority of fMRI studies have employed simple variants of
the blocked experimental designs developed for use with PET. Such studies suffer from
exactly the same drawbacks—arising from the failure to obtain data on a trial-by-
trial basis—as those outlined for PET in the preceding section. The speed with which
fMRI data can be acquired means however that it is possible to obtain such data on a

trial-by-trial basis. The rapidly developing method of *event-related* fMRI (Buckner *et al*. 1996; Josephs *et al*. 1997) offers the prospect of haemodynamic studies directly analogous in design to those employed routinely in electrophysiological studies (see Section 2.2.2), and brings two major benefits over conventional blocked designs. First, trial-by-trial data collection allows the problems discussed in Section 2.2.1.1 to be overcome in a straightforward fashion. Using the event-related method and randomized experimental designs one can be confident that experimental manipulations are exerting stimulus-related rather than state-related effects, and data can easily be segregated *post hoc* on the basis of performance.

The other major advantage of the event-related technique is that it permits the time course of stimulus processing, as reflected by the event-related haemodynamic response, to be studied. Although such responses are much delayed and prolonged relative to the onset and duration of the neural activity that triggers them (Friston *et al*. 1994), reliable differences have nonetheless been reported in both their onset latency (Friston *et al*. 1998) and duration (Courtney *et al*. 1997). While the temporal resolution that can ultimately be achieved with fMRI has still to be determined, it seems likely to lie somewhere between 0.5 and 1 s (Friston *et al*. 1998); much poorer than the resolution that can be achieved with electrophysiological measures, but a considerable advance over that possible when trials are blocked.

While discussing issues of response timing, one undesirable property of haemodynamic measures should be mentioned. Because of the effect of the 'haemodynamic time-constant' (Friston *et al*. 1994), the magnitude of the haemodynamic response triggered by a change in neural activity increases as a function of the duration of the change (Boynton *et al*. 1996; Rosen *et al*. 1998). Thus, the haemodynamic response triggered by a task-related change in neural activity lasting, say, 100 ms would be smaller than the response triggered by an otherwise equivalent change in activity that lasted for 1000 ms. This means that the probability of detecting a haemodynamic signal is greater for sustained changes in neural activity than it is for transient changes.

Finally, two important, unresolved methodological issues concerning event-related fMRI should be noted. The first issue concerns the interpretation of regional differences in the time course of haemodynamic responses. Such differences may reflect regional variation in the time course of the neural activity elicited by experimental items. It is not possible, at the present time, however, to rule out the possibility that they merely reflect regional variation in the haemodynamic response function itself, and thus convey no information about the timing of the underlying neural activity (this problem does not, of course, extend to the situation in which the timing of haemodynamic responses from the *same* region are found to differ). The second issue concerns the implications for experimental design of the extended time course of event-related haemodynamic responses, which typically do not return to baseline until some 10 to 12 s poststimulus. Unless one is willing to employ interstimulus intervals (ISIs) greater than about 12 s, the responses elicited by successive stimuli will overlap, raising the concern that the responses will interfere with one another. Fortunately, the available evidence suggests that event-related changes in fMRI signals interact approximately linearly, permitting quite short ISIs ($\sim$ 2 to 4 s) to be employed without loss of sensitivity (Dale and Buckner 1997). Further work is required however to establish the generality of this important finding.

2.2.2 Electrophysiological methods

Unlike the haemodynamic methods described above, electrophysiological methods measure neural activity directly. The methods take advantage of the fact that, from a distance, some classes of neuron act like electrical dipoles (Wood 1987; Kutas and Dale 1997). While the currents associated with a change in the polarization of a single such neuron are too small to be detected non-invasively, this is not necessarily the case for a pool of neurons. If the members of the pool are oriented in roughly the same direction, and are polarized or depolarized synchronously, their individual dipole moments will summate and create an electromagnetic field (an 'open' field) that may be detectable from outside the head. The electrical component of such fields constitutes the electroencephalogram (EEG), and the magnetic component the magneto-encephalogram (MEG). At the present time, the great majority of electrophysiological studies of cognitive function employ time locked (event-related) measures of the EEG and MEG, known respectively as event-related potentials (ERPs) and event-related magnetic fields (ERFs); these measures are discussed in more detail in the following two sections.

2.2.2.1 ERPs

Picton *et al.* (1995), Rugg and Coles (1995), and Kutas and Dale (1997) provide between them a comprehensive introduction to the ERP method as applied to the study of cognitive function. Briefly, ERPs represent scalp-recorded changes in the ongoing EEG which are time locked to some external event such as the presentation of a word or the onset of a behavioural response. The magnitude of these changes is small in comparison to the amplitude of the 'background' EEG, which is in effect the noise from which the ERP 'signal' has to be extracted, and this necessitates the use of signal averaging to improve the signal-to-noise ratio of the event-related response. Thus, ERP waveforms represent the average of EEG samples obtained on a number of trials (typically, between 20 and 50) belonging to the same experimental condition. The averaged waveforms represent estimates of the time-locked neural activity set in train by the presentation of stimuli belonging to different experimental conditions. Differences between ERP waveforms derived from different conditions therefore represent differences in the neural activity engaged by the items belonging to each condition.

ERPs have proven useful in the study of cognitive function for several reasons. Because ERPs are a trial-based measure, they suffer from none of the problems discussed in Section 2.2.1.1. Randomized designs are the norm, and it is easy to obtain and compare records of brain activity associated with different classes of behavioural response. Moreover, neural activity associated with the processing of different classes of stimuli can be measured with a temporal resolution sufficient to track the neural correlates of cognitive processes in real time. Thus, upper-bound estimates of the time required by the nervous system to discriminate between different classes of stimulus (e.g. 'primed' and 'unprimed' words) can be made directly, merely by determining the latency at which the respective classes of ERP begin to differ reliably. Further, in the context of a well-developed theoretical framework, the onset, duration, and level of engagement of a hypothezised cognitive operation can be estimated and compared across experimental conditions by measuring the onset, duration, and magnitude of its putative ERP correlate. The benefits of the high temporal resolution of the ERP method have proven especially valuable when, combined with behavioural indices such as reaction time, they have been employed to understand fine-grained temporal properties of information processing (e.g. Van Turennout *et al.* 1997).

ERPs can also be used to investigate whether different experimental conditions engage functionally dissociable cognitive processes (see Section 2.1.2). If two experimental conditions are associated with qualitatively different patterns of scalp electrical activity, it follows that the generators of the two patterns of activity differed either in their loci within the brain, or in the relative strengths of their activation; either way, the two conditions are neurophysiologically dissociable. Thus, so far as one is willing to accept the assumption (Section 2.1.2) that experimental conditions that are neurophysiologically dissociable are also most likely to be functionally dissociable (see Section 2.3.2 and Rugg and Coles 1995 for discussion of this assumption), ERPs can be used to assess whether the cognitive operations engaged in different experimental conditions are functionally distinct.

The ERP method suffers from two drawbacks which impose quite serious limitations on its utility as a general functional neuroimaging method. One important drawback arises because, for three reasons, ERPs provide only a partial record of the neural activity engaged by an experimental item. First, because the strength of an electrical field declines quite quickly (as a square function) with the distance from its source, neural activity that is otherwise equivalent will be less readily detectable as its distance from the scalp increases. Thus, the ERP method is biased in favour of the detection of relatively superficial sources of neural activity. Second, as has already been noted, only neuronal populations configured so that their individual dipole moments summate (open-field configurations) will generate an electrical field that can be detected at a distance. In practice, this means that ERPs principally reflect the activity of neurons arranged in a laminar fashion (most notably, the pyramidal cells of the neocortex), and are 'blind' to activity in structures where cell orientation is random, such as the basal ganglia. Finally, even if configured as an open field, a neuronal population will only generate a detectable external field if its elements are activated (or deactivated) synchronously. If the neurons are activated asynchronously, their respective dipole moments will cancel and no field will be detected from a distance.

The second drawback to the ERP method arises from the fact that the localization of the sources of the neural activity generating a time-varying scalp electrical field is formidably difficult. Indeed, from a purely formal perspective, the problem of generator localization is ill-posed, and therefore insoluble (the infamous 'inverse problem'; see e.g. Hämäläinen *et al.* 1993). Headway with this problem is being made by combining methods for the inverse modelling of generators (see Picton *et al.* 1995 for a discussion of some of these methods) with constraints based on anatomical information, findings from lesion studies (e.g. Swick and Knight 1995), and, most recently, evidence from haemodynamic studies (e.g. Heinze *et al.* 1994; see Section 2.2.3). Nonetheless, methods for modelling the generators of diffusely distributed ERP effects typical of those found in cognitive studies are poorly developed, and progress has been slow. The poor spatial resolution currently achievable with ERPs limits the usefulness of the method for questions of functional localization, and hampers attempts to elucidate the functional significance of cognitive ERP effects. More often than not, such attempts must proceed without knowing where in the brain the effects are generated. It is important to emphasize, however, that unlike the problem of selectivity discussed in the preceding paragraph, there seems no reason in principle why the problem of ERP source localization cannot be overcome, and the spatial resolution of the method greatly improved.

2.2.2.2 ERFs

As already noted, event-related neural activity has both an electrical (ERP) and a magnetic (ERF) counterpart. Whereas the number of ERP studies of cognitive function can be numbered in thousands, only a handful of cognitive studies have employed ERFs. ERFs share many of the same strengths and weaknesses as ERPs, but the methods are nonetheless sufficiently distinct to justify their being regarded as complementary, rather than mutually redundant. A detailed description of the MEG/ERF method can be found in Hämäläinen *et al.* (1993).

For two reasons, ERFs provide an even more selective view of neural activity than do ERPs. First, the decline in the strength of a magnetic field as a function of distance is even more rapid than that for electrical fields, meaning that electromagnetic sources deep in the brain contribute less to ERFs than they do to ERPs. The second and more profound reason for the greater selectivity of the ERF method is that magnetic recordings are sensitive exclusively to fields arising from generators oriented *tangentially* to the scalp (i.e. with their dipole axes parallel to the immediately overlying scalp surface) and, unlike ERPs, are insensitive to radially oriented generators (when the dipole axis is perpendicular to the scalp). Because cortical pyramidal neurons are oriented perpendicularly to the cortical surface, ERFs therefore mainly reflect neuronal activity occurring within cortical sulci, and receive only a limited contribution from activity localized to cortical gyri. As gyral cortex constitutes approximately one-third of the cortical mantle, this is a quite serious limitation for the method.

That said, the fact that ERFs reflect a more limited range of neural sources than ERPs has its benefits. It means that ERFs can help constrain the interpretation of ERP data; experimental effects exclusive to ERPs are quite likely to arise from a either a deep or a radially oriented source. It also means that relative to ERPs, more constraints exist for generator localization—one knows the orientation of the generators of an ERF *a priori*.

Table 2.1   Strengths and weaknesses of electrophysiological and haemodynamic methods

	Strengths	Weaknesses
Electrophysiological	Direct measure of neural activity	Samples only partial and unknown fraction of activity
	High temporal resolution	Poor spatial resolution
	Easy to obtain data contingent on performance	
Haemodynamic	Homogeneous (PET) or near homogeneous (fMRI) sampling of task-related activation	Indirect measure of neural activity
	High spatial resolution	Poor temporal resolution
		Difficult (until recently) to obtain data contingent on performance
		Difficult (until recently) to distinguish state and stimulus-related effects

This advantage of the ERF method is magnified by another important difference between the magnetic and electrical components of neural activity. Because electrical fields are greatly affected by inhomogeneities in electrical resistance, they suffer from both spatial smearing and distortion as they flow through the highly (but inhomogeneously) resistive skull and scalp. The effects of this smearing and distortion complicate efforts to model their intracerebral sources (see Gevins *et al.* 1994 for one approach to the correction of these effects). By contrast, magnetic fields are unaffected by resistive boundaries. Together with their insensitivity to radial sources, this means that magnetic fields tend to be both simpler and less diffusely distributed over the scalp than their electrical counterparts, making them more amenable to source modelling procedures, albeit no less subject to the inverse problem.

2.2.3   Integrating haemodynamic and electrophysiological methods

Table 2.1 outlines the major strengths and weaknesses of the haemodynamic and electrophysiological methods discussed in the previous sections. As is clear from the table, the two classes of method are largely complementary to one another. In particular, haemodynamic methods offer excellent spatial resolution, making them the methods of choice for questions of functional localization. The temporal resolution of these methods, even when trial based, is poor however, making them of limited value for the study of the dynamics of cognitive processing. By contrast, because their temporal resolution is essentially unlimited, electrophysiological methods are well suited for studying the time course of cognitive processing. The poor spatial resolution of these methods means however that it is rarely possible to identify with confidence the regions responsible for the generation of electrophysiological data.

In light of the complementary strengths and weaknesses of haemodynamic and electrophysiological measures, it makes obvious sense to integrate the two kinds of data, thereby allowing the conjoint study of the loci and time course of the neural activity selectively engaged by a given cognitive operation. Progress towards this highly desirable goal is dependent on two important developments. One of these is the capacity to obtain haemodynamic and electrophysiological data under equivalent experimental conditions. In light of the rapid evolution of the event-related fMRI method, this is already feasible. In addition, it will be necessary to develop methods that allow haemodynamic data to be incorporated into procedures for modelling the sources of electrophysiological data. For the reasons outlined below, this is less straightforward than it might seem, as it is unlikely that haemodynamic and electrophysiological data will prove to be entirely isomorphic. None the less, progress in the development of such methods is encouraging (Dale *et al.* 1998).

A major problem for methods designed to 'coregister' haemodynamic and electrophysiological data is that even under the most favourable circumstances, one cannot be confident that a full integration of the two types of data will be possible. As summarized in Table 2.2, the preconditions for detecting the two classes of signal are different, and hence there are likely to be circumstances in which only one method is sensitive to changes in neural activity induced by an experimental manipulation. Among the most important of these differences are the insensitivity of electrophysiological methods to activity in neural populations that do not generate an open electromagnetic field, and the insensitivity of haemodynamic measures to changes in neural activity—in timing for example—which have little or no net metabolic consequence. Also noteworthy are the differing sensitivities of the two measures to transient changes in activity. Given good enough time locking, electrophysiological measures can detect task-related changes in neural activity lasting for only a few tens of milliseconds. While the limits of haemodynamic methods in this respect are not known, it is known that the magnitude of haemodynamic responses vary as a function of the duration of the underlying neural activity, making these methods less sensitive to transient than to sustained activity (see Section 2.2.1.2).

These and the other points summarized in Table 2.2 do not lessen the importance of performing convergent neuroimaging and electrophysiological studies, or of attempting to integrate the resulting data sets. They do however serve to emphasize the

Table 2.2   Preconditions for detecting electrophysiological and haemodynamic signals

Electrophysiological	Haemodynamic
Activation of a neural population must be synchronous	Neural activity need not be synchronous
Elements must be geometrically configured so as to produce an 'open-field'	Geometrical orientation of the activated neural population is irrelevant
Activity must be time-locked to some reference event	
But:	But:
Signal will be sensitive to changes in relative timing of activity as well as in relative magnitude	Signal amplitude influenced by the duration as well as the magnitude of a change in neural activity
Critical neural activity need not be extended in time	Changes in neural activity can only be detected if they alter net metabolic demand

difficulty of predicting whether, for any given experimental procedure, there will be overlap between the brain regions responsible for the effects detected by the two methods. The level of overlap that can generally be expected will become clear only after a substantial number of studies have been conducted.

2.3 Functional neuroimaging: general considerations

In this final section some more general issues regarding applications of functional neuroimaging in cognitive neuroscience are discussed. These issues are relevant to all of the methods described in the previous sections. The discussion borrows heavily from Rugg and Coles (1995), who cover much of the same ground from the narrower perspective of the ERP method alone.

2.3.1 Null results

The first issue concerns the constraints on interpretation that arise from the asymmetry between what can be concluded on the basis of positive and negative findings in a functional neuroimaging study. These constraints may appear to be obvious, but they are neglected surprisingly frequently. If an experimental manipulation gives rise to a reliable effect on some neuroimaging measure, it can be concluded that the manipulation engendered differential brain activity. The absence of an effect does not, however, permit the opposite conclusion. Differences in brain activity may well have occurred, but beyond the sensitivity of the method employed to search for them (though not necessarily that of some other method). To draw strong conclusions on the basis of a null effect, it is therefore not sufficient to determine that two experimental conditions have statistically indistinguishable effects on some neuroimaging measure. In addition, it is necessary to have a strong pre-experimental hypothesis that predicts the likely effect size if the null hypothesis is invalid, and an experimental design of sufficient power to detect an effect of this size should it exist.

2.3.2 Functional dissociation

The next issue relates to the employment of functional neuroimaging measures as a means of establishing functional dissociations, as described in Section 2.1.2. Two points are worthy of discussion. First, as was noted in Section 2.1.2, this application of functional neuroimaging is predicated on the assumption that the relationship between cognitive operations and their neural substrates is invariant, in other words, that there is a one-to-one relationship between a given cognitive operation and the pattern of neural activity that instantiates it. While this assumption may at first glance appear to be no more than a corollary of materialism (i.e. that mental phenomena are caused exclusively by the physical activity of the nervous system), this is not the case. The view that the same cognitive function can be instantiated in multiple ways is equally compatible with materialism. If this view is correct, it would follow that physiological data cannot be used to adjudicate between functional models of cognition, an argument advanced forcibly by Mehler *et al.* (1984). In fact, there is little reason at present to believe that cognitive functions are instantiated in the brain in multiple ways, and thus no reason at the moment to question the invariance assumption. In principle, the assumption is however open to empirical refutation.

The second point about using functional neuroimaging data to differentiate functional states centres on the question of the criteria that should be adopted when deciding whether such data signify the existence of functionally distinct processes, rather than the same process(es) active to differing degrees. It is generally (and usually implicitly) assumed that effects that differ from one another solely in terms of their magnitudes signify variations in the 'degree' or 'level' of the engagement of a common cognitive operation (or set of operations), and not the engagement of different operations. This may be a reasonable assumption, but it is unproven. (It also raises the interesting question of just what it means to talk about differences in the level of engagement of a cognitive operation.)

Even if the foregoing assumption is granted, it remains unclear just how different two experimental effects must be qualitatively before the conclusion that they signify the engagement of functionally distinct operations is justified. Should one treat *any* statistically reliable difference between two ERP scalp distributions, or between the loci of two haemodynamic effects, as functionally significant, however subtle the differences might be? Arguably, this question can only be given a principled answer with the accumulation of more knowledge about how cognitive operations are implemented in the brain (including, e.g., information about the size of functionally homogeneous regions of cortex—the 'grain size' at which functions are mapped to the brain). In the absence of such information, functional statements based on small differences in patterns of neural activity, even if these are reliable, are perhaps best regarded as tentative if not supported by converging evidence. Caution is even more warranted when such findings are obtained on data that have been pooled over subjects, when individual differences may interact with experimental effects to give rise to differential patterns of activity in the averaged data that do not exist in the data from any single subject.

2.3.3 Functional significance

The final issue to be discussed concerns the problem of how to establish the causal significance of a functional neuroimaging effect. This issue is crucial: a functional neuroimaging effect can only be informative about how cognitive processing is instantiated in the brain if the functional role of the neural activity reflected by the effect can be identified.

The first problem that attempts to relate measures of neural activity to cognitive function have to confront is that functional accounts of cognition can take a number of different forms. Accounts differ in their levels of analysis and abstraction, as well as in their assumptions about such basic questions as whether cognition can be modelled without commitment to some kind of 'symbolic' processing architecture (compare, e.g., Seidenberg and McClelland 1989, and Pinker and Prince 1988). Attempts to assign functional significance to task-related variations in neural activity must therefore tackle two issues. First, given the nature of the neural activity in question, what functional level of description is most appropriate for an attempt to assign functional significance to the activity? For example, within Marr's (1982) scheme, should the description be articulated at the 'computational' or 'algorithmic' level? Second, within what framework should the description be articulated? While functional models based upon differing processing architectures and assumptions are sometimes thought of as complementary rather than competitive, it seems unlikely that all functionally plausible models are equally amenable to elucidation by the physiological measures derived from functional neuroimaging.

The most fundamental difficulty, however, in determining the functional significance of neuroimaging data stems from their 'correlational' nature. Such data are typically obtained from studies in which the independent variables are experimental manipulations of cognitive function, and the dependent variable is one's chosen measure of neural activity. Such studies provide information about the neural *correlates* of one or more cognitive operations, but offer no means for determining which of these correlates are *necessary* for those operations to take place. For example, findings from PET studies (Price *et al.* 1996) demonstrate that passively listening to words is associated with activation in both posterior ('Wernicke's area') and anterior ('Broca's area') regions of the left hemisphere, despite the 'classical' view that the role of the latter region is in speech production. These findings do not in themselves contradict that view, however, as they leave open the possibility that Broca's area activation reflects the engagement of operations 'downstream' of those required for speech comprehension, rather than operations supporting comprehension *per se*.

In order to establish the functional significance of the neural activity identified by functional neuroimaging studies, it is necessary to establish a *causal* relationship between that activity and the cognitive operation(s) with which it is correlated. To do this requires a reversal of the standard functional neuroimaging experiment, such that the neural system(s) thought to instantiate a cognitive operation are manipulated, and the functional consequences of the manipulation are observed. With respect to the example given in the previous paragraph, this would amount to selectively disrupting the function of Broca's area during passive listening to words, and determining whether comprehension of the words was affected. For obvious reasons methods for conducting such studies in human subjects are limited. Two reversible methods, which can be applied to normal subjects, are pharmacological manipulations, which allow one to target specific neurochemical systems, and transcranial magnetic stimulation, which shows promise as a means of temporarily disrupting fairly circumscribed regions of cortex (e.g. Flitman *et al.* 1998).

The most important way, however, in which the functional consequences of the selective disruption of neural activity can be determined in human subjects is through the study of the effects of brain lesions. If neural activity in a given brain region is necessary for the instantiation of a given cognitive operation, the destruction of the region should result in its impairment. Thus, despite the advantages for functional localization of functional neuroimaging over the lesion-deficit method (see section 2.1.1), evidence from lesion studies will continue to play a key role in understanding how cognitive functions are instantiated in the brain.

In sum, as hypotheses from functional neuroimaging studies about the neural substrates of different cognitive functions become more numerous and specific, the importance of other methods for investigating the neural basis of cognition will increase rather than diminish. Without the contribution of these methods, it is difficult to see how the data derived from functional neuroimaging studies, which are inherently correlational, can be employed to draw strong conclusions about the functional significance of the neural activity reflected in those data.

Finally, it is important not to lose sight of the fact that existing functional neuroimaging methods provide only crude information about the neurophysiological properties of the neural activity that they detect, and give no information at all about the dynamics of the activity of individual or small populations of neurons. It therefore seems likely that, for a considerable time to come, it will be necessary to rely on invasive studies in experimental animals to gain knowledge about what neurons actually do when they process information. The lack of a suitable animal model imposes obvious limitations on this approach for the study of language, and may prove an insurmountable barrier to a full understanding of its neural basis. Together with other methods for investigating the neural basis of cognition in humans, the methods of functional neuroimaging should however permit substantial progress to be made towards this goal.

Acknowledgements

The author's research is supported by the Wellcome Trust. This chapter was written while the author was a visiting scientist at the Max Planck Institute of Cognitive Neuroscience, Leipzig. The comments of David Donaldson, Chris Frith, and Astrid Schloerscheidt on a previous draft are gratefully acknowledged.

Notes

1. By this is meant the development of theories of cognitive function framed in terms of abstract information processing operations, without reference to their physiological basis.

References

Barinaga, M. (1997). What makes brain neurons run? *Science*, **276**, 196–8.

Boynton, G. M., Engel, S. A., Glover, G. H., and Heeger, D. J. (1996). Linear-systems analysis of functional magnetic-resonance-imaging in human V1. *Journal of Neuroscience*, **16**, 4207–21.

Bradley, D. C. and Garrett, M. F. (1983). Hemisphere differences in the recognition of closed and open class words. *Neuropsychologia*, **21**, 155–9.

Buckner, R. L., Bandettini, P. A., O'Craven, K. M., Savoy, R. L., Petersen, S. E., Raichle, M. E., *et al.* (1996). Detection of cortical activation during averaged single trials of a cognitive task using functional magnetic-resonance-imaging. *Proceedings of the National Academy of Sciences of the United States of America*, **93**, 14878–83.

Courtney, S. M., Ungerleider, B. G., Keil, K., and Haxby, J. V. (1997). Transient and sustained activity in a distributed neural system for human working memory. *Nature*, **386**, 608–11.

Dale, A. M. and Buckner, R. L. (1997). Selective averaging of rapidly presented individual trials using fMRI. *Human Brain Mapping*, **5**, 329–40.

Dale, A. M., Halgren, E., Lewine, J. D., Buckner, R. L., Marinkovic, K., Liu, A. K., *et al.* (1998). Spatiotemporal cortical activation patterns to word repetition revealed by combined MRI and MEG. (Submitted.)

Dunn, J. C. and Kirsner, K. (1988). Discovering functionally independent mental processes: The principle of reversed association. *Psychological Review*, **95**, 91–101.

Ellis, A. W. and Young, A. W. (1988). *Human cognitive neuropsychology*. Erlbaum, NJ.

Flitman, S. S., Grafman, J., Wassermann, E. M., Cooper, V., O'Grady, J., Pascual Leone, A., *et al.* (1998). Linguistic processing during repetitive transcranial magnetic stimulation. *Neurology*, **50**, 175–81.

Frackowiak, R. S. J., Friston, K. J., Frith, C. D., Dolan, R., and Mazziotta, J. C. (1997). *Human brain function*. Academic Press, London.

Friston, K. J. (1997). Imaging cognitive anatomy. *Trends in Cognitive Sciences*, **1**, 21–7.

Friston, K. J., Frith, C. D., Liddle, P. F., and Frackowiak, R. S. J. (1991). Comparing functional (PET) images: The assessment of significant change. *Journal of Cerebral Blood Flow and Metabolism*, **11**, 690–99.

Friston, K. J., Jezzard, P., and Turner, R. (1994). Analysis of functional MRI time-series. *Human Brain Mapping*, **1**, 153–71.

Friston, K. J., Büchel, C., Fink, G. R., Morris, J., Rolls, E., and Dolan, R. J. (1997). Psychophysiological and modulatory interactions in neuroimaging. *NeuroImage*, **6**, 218–29.

Friston, K. J., Fletcher, P. C., Josephs, O., Holmes, A., Rugg, M. D., and Turner, R. (1998). Event-related fMRI: Characterizing differential responses. *NeuroImage*, **7**, 30–40.

Frith, C. D. and Friston, K. J. (1997). Studying brain function with neuroimaging. In *Cognitive neuroscience* (ed. M. D. Rugg), pp. 169–95. Psychology Press, Hove.

Gevins, A., Le, J., Martin, N. K., Brickett, P., Desmond, J., and Reutter, B. (1994). High-resolution EEG-124-channel recording, spatial deblurring and MRI integration methods. *Journal of Electroencephalography and Clinical Neurophysiology*, **90**, 337–58.

Gregory, R. L. (1961). The brain as an engineering problem. In *Current problems in animal behaviour* (ed. W. H. Thorpe and O. L. Zangwill), pp. 307–30. Cambridge University Press.

Hämäläinen, M., Hari, R., Ilmoniemi, R. J., Knuutila, J., and Lounasmaa, O. V. (1993). Magentoencephalography—theory, instrumentation, and applications to noninvasive studies of the working human brain. *Reviews of Modern Physics*, **65**, 413–97.

Heinze, H. J., Mangun, G. R., Burchert, W., Hinrichs, H., Scholz, M., Munte, T. F., *et al.* (1994). Combined spatial and temporal imaging of brain activity during visual selective attention in humans. *Nature*, **372**, 543–6.

Josephs, O., Turner, R., and Friston, K. (1997). Event-related fMRI. *Human Brain Mapping*, **5**, 243–8.

Kreiter, A. K. and Singer, W. (1996). Stimulus-dependent synchronization of neuronal responses in the visual cortex of the awake macaque monkey. *Journal of Neuroscience*, **16**, 2381–96.

Kutas, M. and Dale, A. (1997). Electrical and magnetic readings of mental functions. In *Cognitive neuroscience* (ed. M. D. Rugg), pp. 197–241. Psychology Press, Hove.

McIntosh, A. R., Bookstein, F. L., Haxby, J. V., and Grady, C. L. (1996). Spatial pattern-analysis of functional brain images using partial least-squares. *NeuroImage*, **3**, 143–57.

Marr, D. (1982). *Vision*. Freeman, San Francisco.

Martin, A., Wiggs, C. L., Ungerleider, L. G., and Haxby, J. V. (1996). Neural correlates of category-specific knowledge. *Nature*, **379**, 649–52.

Mehler, J., Morton, J., and Jusczyk, P. W. (1984). On reducing language to biology. *Cognitive Neuropsychology*, **1**, 83–116.

Mesulam, M.-M. (1990). Large-scale neurocognitive networks and distributed processing for attention, language, and memory. *Annals of Neurology*, **28**, 597–613.

Ogawa, S., Lee, T. M., Kay, A. R., and Tank, D. W. (1990). Brain magnetic-resonance-imaging with contrast dependent on blood oxygenation. *Proceedings of the National Academy of Sciences of the United States of America*, **87**, 9868–72.

Osterhout, L. and Holcomb, P. J. (1995). Event-related potentials and language comprehension. In *Electrophysiology of mind: Event-related brain potentials and cognition* (eds M. D. Rugg and M. G. H. Coles), pp. 171–215. Oxford University Press.

Petersen, S. E. (1993). The processing of single words studied with positron emission tomography. *Annual Review of Neuroscience*, **16**, 509–30.

Picton, T. W., Lins, O. G., and Scherg, M. (1995). The recording and analysis of event-related potentials. In *Handbook of neuropsychology* (ed. J. C. Boller and J. Grafman), **10**, pp. 429–99. Elsevier, Amsterdam.

Pinker, S. and Prince, A. (1988). On language and connectionism: Analysis of a parallel distributed processing model of language acquisition. *Cognition*, **28**, 73–193.

Poeck, K. (1983). What do we mean by 'aphasic syndromes?' A neurologist's view. *Brain and Language*, **20**, 79–89.

Posner, M. I. and McLeod, P. (1982). Information processing models: In search of elementary operations. *Annual Review of Psychology*, **33**, 477–514.

Price, C. J., Wise, R. S. J., Warburton, E. A., Moore, C. J., Howard, D., Patterson, K., *et al.* (1996). Hearing and saying. The functional neuroanatomy of auditory word processing. *Brain*, **119**, 919–31.

Raichle, M. E. (1987). Circulatory and metabolic correlates of brain function in normal humans. In *Handbook of physiology: The nervous system* Vol. 5 (eds F. Plum and V. Mountcastle), pp. 643–74. American Physiological Society, Baltimore.

Rosen, B. R., Buckner, R. L., and Dale, A. M. (1998). Event-related fMRI: Past, present, and future. *Proceedings of the National Academy of Sciences of the United States of America*, **95**, 773–80.

Rugg, M. D. (1995). La difference vive. *Nature*, **373**, 561–2.

Rugg, M. D. (1997). Introduction. In *Cognitive neuroscience* (ed. M. D. Rugg), pp. 1–9. Psychology Press, Hove.

Rugg, M. D. and Coles, M. G. H. (1995). The ERP and cognitive psychology: Conceptual issues. In *Electrophysiology of mind: Event-related brain potentials and cognition* (ed. M. D. Rugg and M. G. H. Coles), pp. 27–39. Oxford University Press.

Segui, J., Frauenfelder, U. H., Laine, C., and Mehler, J. (1987). The word-frequency effect for open-class and closed-class items. *Cognitive Neuropsychology*, **4**, 33–44.

Shallice, T. (1988). *From neuropsychology to mental structure*. Cambridge University Press.

Swick, D. and Knight, R. T. (1995). Contributions of right inferior temporal-occipital cortex to visual word and non-word priming. *NeuroReport*, **7**, 11–16.

Toga, A. W. and Mazziotta, J. C. (1996). *Brain mapping: The methods*. Academic Press, London.

Van Turennout, M., Hagoort, P., and Brown, C. M. (1997). Electrophysiological evidence on the time course of semantic and phonological processes in speech production. *Journal of Experimental Psychology: Learning, Memory, and Cognition*, **23**, 787–806.

Wood, C. C. (1987). Generators of event-related potentials. In *A textbook of clinical neurophysiology* (ed. A. M. Halliday, S. R. Butler, and R. Paul), pp. 535–67. Wiley, Chichester.

Zilles, K., Schleicher, A., Langemann, C., Amunts, K., Morosan, P., Palomero-Gallagher, N., *et al.* (1997). Quantitative analysis of sulci in the human cerebral cortex: Development, regional heterogeneity, gender difference, asymmetry, intersubject variability and cortical architecture. *Human Brain Mapping*, **5**, 218–21.

3 *The representational structures of the language faculty and their interactions*

Ray Jackendoff

3.1 Introduction

In studying the neurocognition of language, it is reasonable to inquire about what sorts of information the brain is processing during language perception and production. Linguistic theory, which can be taken as the study of this information, has revealed a great deal more to the organization of language than meets the eye (or ear). While there always has been (and continues to be) lively dispute about many aspects of this organization, I think it is fair to say that a strong implicit consensus has developed among linguists with respect to many important phenomena, despite the variety of theoretical frameworks in which these phenomena have been described. I take it as my task in this chapter to present some of the broad outlines of this consensus, and to try to show its relevance for an approach to language through the lens of cognitive neuroscience.

Since the 1960s, scientific thinking about language has been dominated by the framework of generative grammar, originated by Noam Chomsky (e.g. Chomsky 1965, 1975). Most alternative positions that have achieved any popularity during this period have arisen either as offshoots of the Chomskyan framework or in reaction to it.[1] And in fact, much in the past thirty years of research in linguistics, language acquisition, psycholinguistics, and neurolinguistics has substantiated and sharpened the major claims of the Chomskyan programme (including the important biological and neuropsychological claims of Lenneberg 1967).

In the past few years, I have attempted to step back and re-examine the foundations of generative linguistic theory, retaining the parts that have proven themselves and revising other (often unspoken) assumptions that in retrospect have turned out to be problematic. The goal is to develop a framework in which to understand findings in linguistics and in disciplines that depend on linguistic theory, with an eye to identifying issues for productive continuing research.

In particular, one difficulty with traditional generative-transformational grammar is that it has not always lent itself to useful interpretation in processing terms. Although some linguists maintain that the character of formal grammars written by linguists need have nothing to do with how language is processed (thus excusing this opacity of traditional generative grammar with respect to processing), I disagree. Along with a substantial minority of practitioners, I believe that a correct formal grammar will have something useful to say to theories of processing. And in fact, over the past two decades a number of different multi-representation, 'constraint-based' theories of grammar have developed somewhat independently; to some extent these prove more congenial to thinking about processing. Such approaches include Head-Driven Phrase Structure Grammar (HPSG) (Pollard and Sag 1987, 1994), Lexical-Functional Grammar (LFG) (Bresnan 1982; Dalrymple *et al.* 1995), Autolexical Syntax (Sadock 1991), Role and Reference Grammar (RRG) (Foley and Van Valin 1984; Van Valin and LaPolla 1997), Multidimensional Categorial Grammar (Bach 1983; Oehrle 1988), Construction Grammar (Fillmore and Kay 1993; Goldberg 1995), and Autosegmental Phonology (Goldsmith 1976); a similar architecture is proposed for musical structure (though involving quite different representations) by Lerdahl and Jackendoff (1983). Jackendoff (1997), building in part on proposals in Jackendoff (1987), works out a functional architecture for linguistic structure that is a generalization of these approaches.

The present chapter sums up some aspects of this synthesis, and shows where it diverges from standard generative grammars. I will be particularly concerned here to speak of consequences of the framework for the status of language in the brain.[2]

3.2 The foundational observations

We begin by rehearsing the basic observations that underpin the Chomskyan framework. Whatever revisions one makes to the rest of the theory, one must answer to these observations.

3.2.1 Combinatoriality

The first observation, and most crucial for all else that follows, is the combinatoriality of language: the fact that, from a stock of words and phrases stored in long-term memory, a speaker can build up an indefinitely large number of utterances of indefinite length. The principles which combine pieces stored in memory are themselves not arbitrary; they are quite elaborate and differ from one language to the next. Consequently, a speaker's brain must instantiate (i) a *lexicon*, the repertoire of memorized words and phrases, and (ii) a set of principles of combination, or a *mental grammar*, that permits novel utterances being perceived or produced to be related to items stored in the lexicon. The functional architecture of the language faculty must therefore specify the lexicon and mental grammar, and in particular the way these work together to enable the speaker to construct utterances.

It is an open question exactly how a mental grammar is to be instantiated in the brain. Here are the two most plausible options. (i) The rules of grammar are (in some sense) explicit in the brain, and the language processor 'refers to them' in constructing and comprehending utterances. On this interpretation, rules of grammar are 'declarative'. (ii) The rules of grammar are partial descriptions of the processor itself; that is, they are 'procedural'.

In the constraint-based frameworks mentioned above, a rule of grammar is conceived of as a fragment of grammatical structure stored in long-term memory. Collections of fragments are assembled into sentences by means of a general operation called *unification*; parsing can be construed as identifying all the fragments that serve as parts of a heard utterance. Thus this approach sees rules as directly invoked or recovered in the course of processing. Such a conception of rules contrasts with the movement, deletion, and adjunction rules of standard generative grammar, which are taken to be only 'metaphorically' related to processing.

Under any of these interpretations, it is still hard to know exactly what a description of language in grammatical terms means in real brain terms. I suspect a proper answer awaits better understanding of the brain itself. Although neuroscience has by now learned a great deal about coarse brain localization of function, about the functioning of individual neurons and small collections of neurons, and about the effects of neurotransmitters on brain processes, it cannot yet tell us much about the details of language. The regularities of grammar fall somewhere in scale between neuronal cell assemblies and imageable tracts of brain tissue, a scale about which little is known at present (except perhaps in early vision). The fact that we haven't any idea how something as elementary as a speech sound is neurally instantiated suggests that it is premature to demand a reduction of the formal apparatus of linguists' grammars to neural terms. Rather, for the time being, I think we must regard linguistic analyses as descriptions of the functional regularities of linguistic perception and behaviour, and take it as a challenge for future research to discover how these regularities play themselves out in terms of the detailed architecture and functioning of the brain.

Two more observations on combinatoriality. First, the construction and comprehension of novel and arbitrarily complex utterances in real time places important design demands on a processor. In particular, understanding an utterance requires imposing a set of structured relations on the long-term memory elements out of which it is built. This property, I believe, raises interesting problems for theories of working memory. We will get to specifics of this point in Section 3.12. Second, although it is sometimes said that combinatorial properties are unique to language, this is clearly not the case. Understanding novel visual fields in terms of the location and movement of familiar and unfamiliar objects requires construction of an indefinitely large number of spatial configurations, probably hierarchically arranged. And planning of actions at any time scale from immediate motor activity to reconfiguring one's life goals also requires construction of indefinitely many novel combinations out of known parts. So the generative character of language *per se* is just another instance of generative capacities found elsewhere in the brain. It is however unique in the nature of the elements being combined and consequently in many details of the principles of combination (for instance, it is hard to imagine a useful visual analogue to the principles of long-distance dependencies to be discussed in Section 3.8.2). These distinctive characteristics are of course what makes it language rather than some other faculty.

This is not to say that language shares *no* properties with other mental capacities. It is useful to invoke the analogy of physical organs. An account of the liver will share many parts with an account of the heart: for instance they both are made of cells with similar overall construction and metabolic properties. But at the same time they differ in many important particulars of organization and function. So it is, I suspect, with mental faculties: they inherit many properties from being built up out of assemblies of neur-. ones, but they differ in particulars of what sorts of information they process, learn, and store. The closest cross-faculty parallelism that I have encountered is in the sub-faculties that deal with rhythm in music and language respectively (Lerdahl and Jackendoff 1983; Jackendoff 1989). But these components, on detailed inspection, are not *identical*; they are homologous, rather like fingers and toes, with strongly parallel components that function somewhat differently.

3.2.2 Acquisition of language

The presence of a mental grammar in the brain of an adult speaker—and the fact that the speaker's mental grammar must differ from language to language—raises the problem of how the speaker acquires it. This problem is especially acute because adults' mental grammar is largely if not wholly unconscious, so they cannot teach it to children by instruction (as if the child could understand the instructions in any event). Rather, the child must construct the principles of combination internally on the basis of heard exemplars that the child assumes to be built on these principles. Since it is a fact that general-purpose intelligence is incapable of deriving these principles (evidence: linguists have as yet been unable to discover them in full, using general-purpose intelligence!), the only plausible explanation of their acquisition is that children are—in part—making use of special-purpose faculties adapted for language learning and not available for general-purpose problem solving.

The existence of a special-purpose human adaptation for language learning is now supported on a wide variety of grounds. Perhaps no single one of them alone would be thoroughly convincing, but collectively they add up to what strikes me (and many others) as a strong case.

1. In normal adult speakers, language functions are fairly reliably localized in the brain, suggesting an anatomical/functional specialization. This is not to deny the evidence of a certain amount of variation and plasticity, though probably no different than that for other cognitive functions.

2. Various genetic disorders can differentially affect language acquisition. For instance, Specific Language Impairment (Gopnik and Crago 1990; Gopnik 1999) disturbs acquisition of morphology but (often) spares intelligence. Williams Syndrome (Bellugi *et al.* 1993; Mervis *et al.* 1997) severely impairs general-purpose intelligence while sparing acquisition of many (though not all) aspects of mental grammar. Smith and Tsimpli (1995) report a severely retarded individual who however is an idiot savant at learning languages.

3. Signed languages have turned out to have all the grammatical properties of spoken languages except the vocal–auditory modality, including parallel patterns of

acquisition and parallel patterns of impairment due to brain damage (Klima and Bellugi 1979; Bellugi *et al.* 1989). This shows that grammatical competence is not simply a special organization of sound structure, but is modality-independent.

4.   Unlike many other kinds of learning, the ability for language acquisition falls off with increasing age. Though all normal individuals learn one or more languages fluently in childhood, adults differ greatly in talent at second language learning, and only the most exceptional rival children's ability. This is well known from common observation and has been documented more carefully by Newport (1990) and Klein and Perdue (1997), among many others. These studies include late *first* language acquisition of American Sign Language, which shows a pattern not unlike ordinary late second language acquisition; thus the phenomenon is not entirely the product of the language capacity being 'fixed' by a first language. The conclusion of Lenneberg (1967) was that there is a period in brain development when the capacity for language acquisition is available, and that later brain development impairs it differentially from general-purpose learning. (The cut-off need not be so sharp as is often imputed to advocates of a 'critical period' in order for this phenomenon to be telling.)

5.   Children have been found to create language-like systems in the absence of reliable linguistic input. Deaf children create 'home sign' systems that are more grammatically sophisticated than the gestures used by the parents (Goldin-Meadow and Mylander 1990). Children in a pidgin-speaking community collectively create from the grammatically rudimentary pidgin a much more heavily grammaticized creole within a generation (as documented for Hawaiian Creole in the early 1900s by Bickerton 1981). And in the last two decades, since the institution of schools for the deaf in Nicaragua, a Nicaraguan Sign Language has developed, with grammatical properties comparable to those of other sign languages (Kegl *et al.*, in press).

Each of these phenomena makes sense if normal children bring to the task of language acquisition one or more genetically determined brain specializations which lead them to expect a communication system in their environment that has the grammatical properties of human languages. These phenomena do not make sense if the learning of language is guided only by general-purpose intelligence.

In addition, of course, there is all the evidence amassed within linguistic theory itself for what is generally called Universal Grammar (UG). This is best understood, I think, as a description of the 'grain' of language, as it were: UG presents a range of possibilities for grammatical treatment of particular phenomena, and a measure of which possibilities are 'simpler' and which 'more complex'. Complexity here is to be understood not in some absolute information-theoretic sense, but in terms of difficulty for acquisition and in terms of predicted statistical distribution among the languages of the world.

The problem of determining what aspects of the language faculty are in place in advance of language acquisition has been one of the central concerns of linguistic theory since Chomsky's landmark *Aspects of the Theory of Syntax* (1965). No general-purpose learning procedure is up to the full measure of the task of acquiring language, the complexity of which has been severely underestimated by non-linguists (Elman *et al.* 1996 is a prominent recent example). Part of the point of the present chapter is to give the non-linguist reader a taste of that complexity.

Still, as discussed in the previous section, this is not to say that the language faculty does not partake of general aspects of mind. As a product of evolution, it must be largely the product of exploiting and specializing capacities that were present in the prehominid brain. But no one would claim that the bat's sonar capacity is just learned. All would concede that it evolved, and that it is a specialization of pre-existing faculties. A parallel story applies to language, I think.

It is conceivable, for instance, that UG is a repertoire of bits and pieces of linguistic structure out of which rules of grammar can be assembled. This view is particularly attractive in a constraint-based framework, in which rules of grammar are themselves fragments of linguistic structure that can be further assembled on-line into sentences. Under such a conception, the assembly of rules of grammar from UG might be a species of 'overlearned skill learning', as many have suspected. What would be special about language learning, then, would be the linguistic units in UG over which such learning takes place. Such an outcome would be an interesting mixture of language specialization with general-purpose capacity. (I present this only as an illustration of how the situation might work out; I am not yet prepared to endorse it.)

A species-specific brain specialization in turn requires a genetic specialization that leads to appropriate development of the brain. Since we don't know how genes can specify the development of something as simple as a fingernail, *and* we don't know how a brain can instantiate memory for linguistic units, again I think it is premature to ask how the fundamentals of mental grammar could be coded genetically—or to expect simple answers. (This despite the doubts of Elman *et al.* 1996 that something as complex and fine-grained as UG could be coded genetically: after all, other very complex behaviours in the animal world evidently have a genetic basis, so why not language learning?)

To sum up: the driving observations of the Chomskyan programme are (i) that the combinatoriality of language implies the existence of an unconscious mental grammar; and (ii) that the acquisition of mental grammar requires a genetically driven biological specialization for language. These observations must form the background for any investigation of mental grammar or of language processing. (See Pinker 1994 and Jackendoff 1994 as well as Chomsky 1965, 1975 for more longwinded expositions of these points.)

For purposes of studying language processing, it seems more important to characterize the linguistic structures that the mental grammar enables a speaker to compose than to work out the detailed rules of mental grammar themselves. This is because, however the rules of mental grammar are instantiated in the brain, the linguistic structures *must* be constructed in the course of perceiving and producing sentences. (In a constraint-based framework, where the rules *are* the fragments out of which structures are built, the two enterprises fall together more closely than in traditional generative grammar.) Consequently I will focus the discussion here on the nature of the linguistic structures about whose existence there is substantial consensus: phonological, syntactic, and semantic/ conceptual structure.

3.3 Phonological structure and its relation to syntax

In speech production, the brain must use phonetic representations to develop a set of motor instructions to the vocal tract. The motor instructions are not part of linguistic representations. Rather, phonetic representation is usually construed as the 'peripheral endpoint' of linguistic representation, and there is a non-trivial process of conversion from phonetics to motor instructions. Crucially, phonetic form does not uniquely encode motor movements. For example, the motor movements involved in speech can be modulated by concurrent non-linguistic tasks such as holding a pipe in one's mouth—without changing the intended phonetics. And although phonetic representation comes in discrete segments, the motor movements of speech are continuous and interleaved.

Similarly for speech perception: the process of phonetic perception is a non-trivial conversion from some sort of frequency analysis to phonetic form (if it were trivial, Haskins Laboratories would have been out of business years ago!). Of course, certain phonetic distinctions correspond to auditory distinctions. For instance, there is a (somewhat blurred) correspondence in linear order; the presence of auditory noise is a reliable sign of affrication or aspiration; and so on. But other aspects of the auditory signal are irrelevant to phonetics, such as the speaker's voice quality, tone of voice, and (usually) speed of articulation. Likewise, certain phonetic distinctions are not marked by auditory distinctions, for instance the division into discrete phonetic segments, analysis into distinctive features (see Section 3.6), and the systematic presence of word boundaries.

Thus phonetic representation can be thought of as encoding idealized sequences of speech sounds, abstracting away from any particular speaker, neutral between use for perception or production, and most prominently, encoded as a sequence of discrete units rather than as a continuous smear of sound or movement.[4] I don't think anyone, even the most rabid opponents of generative grammar, denies the existence of this level of representation.

Phonetic representation is a subsystem of phonological structure (PS). Section 3.6 will illustrate some details of PS. For the moment let us consider its relation to syntactic structure. It used to be thought (Chomsky 1965; Chomsky and Halle 1968; Chomsky 1980, p. 143) that PS is simply a low level of syntactic structure, derived by erasing syntactic boundaries, so that all that is visible to phonological rules is the string of words. Hence PS (and therefore phonetics) could be thought of as derived essentially by a continuation of a syntactic derivation. But on current views, which are as far as I know nearly universally accepted among phonologists, the units of PS are such entities as segments, syllables, intonational phrases, and a metrical grid—*prosodic* units, as will be seen in section 3.6.

Prosodic units do not correspond neatly to the standard units of syntax. For instance, among prosodic units are syllables and feet (a foot, as in the terminology of poetry, is a unit consisting of a stressed syllable and one or more adjacent unstressed syllables, usually to the right). These units often cut across the boundaries of morphemes (stems, prefixes, and suffixes, which are syntactic units within words). Such a situation is seen in (1):

(1)   a. Phonological: [or + ga + ni][za + tion]
       b. Morphosyntactic: [[[organ]iz]ation]

English articles form a phonological unit with the next word (i.e. they cliticize), whether or not they form a syntactic constituent with it, as shown in (2):

(2)   a. Phonological: [abig][house], [avery][big][house]
       b. Syntactic: [[a][[big][house]]], [[a][[[very]big][house]]]

And intonational phrasing cuts across syntactic phrase boundaries, as seen in the old chestnut (3):

(3)   a. Phonological: [this is the cat][that ate the rat][that ate the cheese]
       b. Syntactic: [this is [the cat [that [ate [the rat [that [ate [the cheese]]]]]]]]

Consequently, the constituent structure of PS cannot be produced by simply erasing (or, alternatively, adjusting) syntactic boundaries. For instance, the intonational units of (3a) cannot be identified with any syntactic units such as NP (noun phrase) or VP (verb phrase), and the prosodic feet in (1a), *or-ga-ni* and *za-tion*, cannot be identified with any morphosyntactic category.

The upshot is that phonological structure is *constrained by* syntactic structure but not *derived from* it; some of its aspects are characterized by autonomous phonological principles whose structural descriptions make no reference to syntax. For instance there is a general preference for the intonational phrases of a sentence to be approximately equal in length (Gee and Grosjean 1983; Selkirk 1984; Jackendoff 1987, Appendix A; Hirst 1993, among others); this has considerable bearing on the phonological parsing (see 3a).

Stepping back from the details, it appears that phonological structure and syntactic structure are independent formal (or generative) systems, each of which provides an exhaustive analysis of sentences in its own terms.

The compositional system for syntactic structure contains such primitives as the lexical categories Noun, Verb, Adjective, and Preposition (or their feature decompositions), and functional categories (or features) such as Number, Gender, Person, Case, and Tense. The principles of syntactic combination include the principles of phrase structure, the principles of long-distance dependencies such as wh-movement and topicalization (see Section 3.8), the principles of agreement and case-marking, and so forth.

The compositional system for phonological structure contains such primitives as phonological distinctive features (e.g. voicing, point of articulation, stop vs. continuant), the notions of syllable, foot, word, and phonological and intonational phrase, the notions of stress, tone, and intonation contour. The principles of phonological combination include rules of syllable structure, stress assignment, vowel harmony, and so forth.

Given the coexistence of these two independent analyses of sentences, it is necessary that the grammar contains a set of *interface rules* that mediate between syntactic and phonological units. Like the principles that mediate between phonetic representation and auditory or motor coding, these create only partial correspondences. For example, phonological words usually correspond to syntactic words—but not always, as will be seen in Sections 3.6 and 3.7. And the linear order of phonological words corresponds to the linear order of syntactic words. On the other hand, nothing in phonology corresponds to the distinction among syntactic lexical categories. And nothing in syntax corresponds to phonetic content. For example, the syntactic features of the words *dog* and *cat* are identical—they are both just singular count nouns as far as syntax is concerned.

To sum up, phonological structure has its own principles of organization, distinct from those for the auditory and motor codes and from syntactic structure. It is connected to each of these by interface principles that establish partial correspondences. What might appear novel here is the independence of phonological structure from syntactic structure. This should not be too surprising to those who have paid any attention to research in phonology since 1975, but it has been sorely neglected by the mainstream tradition in syntax (and hence by the outside world, for whom 'linguistics' means 'syntax').

3.4 The independence of semantic/conceptual structure from syntax

Next let us consider semantic/conceptual structure (CS). By this term I mean a system of mental representations in terms of which reasoning, planning, and the formation of intentions takes place. Almost everyone assumes that there is some such system of mind, and that it is also responsible for the understanding of sentences in context, incorporating pragmatic considerations and 'encyclopaedic' or 'world' knowledge.

Whatever we know about this system, we know it is not built out of nouns and verbs and adjectives; everyone knows that rules of inference and the interaction of language with world knowledge cannot be built out of standard syntactic units. Rather, the units of CS are entities like conceptualized physical objects, events, properties, times, quantities, and intentions. These entities (or their counterparts in other semantic theories) are always assumed to interact in a combinatorial system. Unlike the combinatorial systems of syntax and phonology, this system is usually assumed to be purely relational, in the sense that linear order plays no role. The principles of combination in conceptual structure include at least the following:

1.   *Argument structure* or *thematic role marking*: an entity can serve as an argument of a function, for example being understood as the Agent or Patient of an action (as in *Lois* (Agent) *hugged Clark* (Patient)) or as a part of another entity (as in *a leg* (part) *of the table* (whole)).

2.   *Predication*: a property or identity can be ascribed to an entity, as in *the black cat* or *the philosopher Socrates*.

3.   *Quantification*: the reference of a description can be dependent on the identity and number of other characters. For instance, in *Every boy has a bicycle*, there is understood to be a correlation between the set of boys and a set of associated bicycles.

4.   *Information structure*: various entities in a situation can be foregrounded or backgrounded, as in the contrast between *It is Mary who saw Bill* and *It is Bill who Mary saw*, or in the difference between *Bill sold a book to Mary* and *Mary bought a book from Bill*.

5.   *Modality*: conceptualized individuals and situations may be identified as descriptions of reality, as hypothetical, as imaginary, as possible or impossible.

The relation of this system to syntax parallels exactly the relation between syntax and phonology: conceptual structures are not made out of syntactic units, but syntactic structure must be used to express conceptual structure. Therefore it is again necessary to posit a component of interface rules in mental grammar, the *SS–CS interface rules*, which mediate between syntactic and conceptual units.

Note that in one sense, semantic/conceptual structure is not a part of language *per se*; it is language independent (translation is meant to preserve semantics), and it can be expressed in a variety of ways, partly depending on the syntax of the language in question. Moreover, it is possible to imagine non-linguistic organisms such as primates and babies using conceptual structures to reason. On the other hand, semantic/conceptual structure *is* part of language in the sense that it serves as the format for the messages that language encodes into utterances; it is the aspect of central cognition most directly related to language. And the SS–CS interface rules are definitely part of language, as they are the vehicle by which conceptual structures are related to linguistic forms.

Some theories of language (e.g. Katz 1977; Talmy 1985; Smith and Medin 1981; Pinker 1989; Bierwisch and Lang 1989) split what I am calling semantic/conceptual structure into two components, which we may call *semantic structure* and *conceptual structure* (not necessarily the terms these authors would use). Although the split is characterized somewhat differently in each case, the motivation is roughly the same. Semantic structure encodes those aspects of meaning relevant to language; 'dictionary' meanings, the aspects of meaning that affect syntactic behaviour, and/or the aspects of meaning that are germane to analytic judgements. Conceptual structure is much more wild and woolly, involving the contribution of 'encyclopaedic' information, pragmatic context, and heuristic reasoning. In these theories, semantic structure is part of language, and conceptual structure is not.

I have argued (Jackendoff 1983) that such a division is in practice impossible to make; Lakoff (1987) offers arguments in a similar spirit. But if I am wrong, and the division proves necessary, it only makes the problem more complex: we need, instead of one system of SS–CS interface rules, a system to map between syntax and semantic structure and one to map between semantic structure and conceptual structure. For purposes of simplicity, therefore, I will assume that there is a unified system of semantic/ conceptual structure, and I will use the terms *semantics* and *conceptual structure* somewhat interchangeably. I leave it to advocates of the alternative to divide up the work of the SS–CS rules between their two interface components.

Although the existence of an SS–CS interface has been (often tacitly) acknowledged in linguistic theory, there has been constant pressure to minimize its complexity. For example, in the late 1960s, Generative Semantics sought to encode aspects of lexical meaning in terms of syntactic combination (e.g. deriving *kill* from the same underlying syntactic structure as *cause to become not alive*, to cite the most famous example). And within the recent Chomskyan tradition (Chomsky 1986a, 1995), the level of Logical Form is conceived of as being a direct syntactic encoding of the structure of meanings.

In my opinion, however, the evidence is mounting that the SS–CS interface has many of the same 'dirty' characteristics as the phonology–syntax interface.[5] Here are some reasons.

1. It is widely accepted that syntactic categories do not correspond one-to-one to conceptual categories. Rather, the mapping from conceptual category to syntactic category is many-to-many, as seen in (4).

(4)   Noun: Object (*dog*), Situation (*concert*), Place (*region*), Time (*Tuesday*), etc.

   Verb: Situation (including Action as a major subcase)

   Adjective: Property

   Preposition: Place (*in the house*), Time (*on Tuesday*), Property (*in luck*)

2. A wide range of thematic roles (conceptual codings of who did what to whom) can be expressed in terms of apparently identical syntactic structure, as seen with the direct objects in (5).

(5)   a. Emily threw the ball. (object = Theme/Patient)

   b. Joe entered the room. (object = Goal)

   c. Emma emptied the sink. (object = Source/Patient)

    d. George helped the boys. (object = Beneficiary)

    e. The story annoyed Harry. (object = Experiencer)

    f. The audience applauded the clown. (object = ???)

3.   Some syntactic distinctions are related only sporadically to conceptual distinctions. Consider grammatical gender. In the familiar European languages, grammatical gender classes are a hodgepodge of semantic classes, phonological classes, and brute force memorization. But from the point of view of syntax, we want to be able to say that, for whatever crazy reason a noun happens to be feminine gender, it triggers identical agreement phenomena in its modifiers and predicates.

4.   A wide range of syntactic distinctions can signal the very same conceptual information. A prominent example is the telic/atelic distinction (also known as temporally delimited/non-delimited distinction) (Verkuyl 1972, 1993; Dowty 1979; Declerck 1979; Hinrichs 1985; Krifka 1992; Jackendoff 1991, 1996). *Telic* events are events that have a clear endpoint, such as dying, eating up a cookie, and getting to the top of a mountain. *Atelic* events (also called activities or processes) lack an inherently defined endpoint; for instance sleeping, chewing a cookie, and skating along a river can go on indefinitely. Sentences expressing telic events occur with temporal adverbials that set the position of the already presumed endpoint, for instance *in an hour*, *by noon*. Sentences expressing atelic events occur with temporal adverbials that either measure the total length of the activity (*for an hour*) or bound it by establishing an endpoint (*until noon*). (Note 11 mentions some experimental evidence concerning the processing of these adverbials.)

   This distinction is of interest in the present context because it has no single syntactic reflex. Rather, it can be syntactically differentiated through choice of verb (6a), choice of preposition (6b), choice of adverbial (6c), and choice of determiner in subject (6d), object (6e), or prepositional object (6f). Hence the syntax-to-semantics mapping is far from straightforward. (In these examples, the felicity of the adverbial *in an hour* shows that the sentence is telic; the felicity of *for an hour* shows that it is atelic.)

(6)   a. John destroyed the cart (in/*for an hour). (Telic)

         John pushed the cart (for/*in an hour). (Atelic)

      b. John ran to the station (in/*for an hour). (Telic)

         John ran toward the station (for/*in an hour) (Atelic)

      c. The light flashed once (in/*for an hour). (Telic)

         The light flashed constantly (for/*in an hour) (Atelic)

      d. Four people died (in/*for two days). (Telic)

         People died (for/*in two days). (Atelic)

e. John ate lots of peanuts (in/*for an hour). (Telic)

   John ate peanuts (for/*in an hour). (Atelic)

f. John crashed into three walls (in/*for an hour) (Telic)

   John crashed into walls (for/*in an hour) (Atelic)

In short, the mapping between SS and CS is a many-to-many relation between structures made up of different sets of primitive elements.

3.5 The tripartite parallel architecture

Let us now integrate this. The distinctness of phonological, syntactic, and conceptual information leads us to conceive of the grammatical structure of a sentence as a triple of three structures ⟨PS, SS, CS⟩, plus a set of connections among their parts. The mental grammar that characterizes grammatical sentences thus consists of three independent combinatorial components, plus the interface components that establish the connections among them. Figure 3.1 sketches the layout of such a grammar.

There is a further, rather limited set of interface rules that relates focal and contrastive stress in phonology to the dimension of information structure (topic, focus, given vs. new information, etc.) in conceptual structure. In addition, as suggested earlier, phonological structure is connected through other sets of interface rules with auditory and motor information (see section 3.11).[6]

This conception of the mental grammar as a number of parallel interacting components is not the predominant view in the field. Rather, the mainstream Chomskyan tradition invests all generative power in the syntactic component and treats phonology and semantics as 'interpretive' components. However, many of the constraint-based frameworks cited in the introduction explicitly adopt a similar conception of parallel, mutually constraining structures. For example, in Autolexical Syntax (Sadock 1991), phonology and syntax fall into this relation. Shieber and Schabes (1991) set up parallel

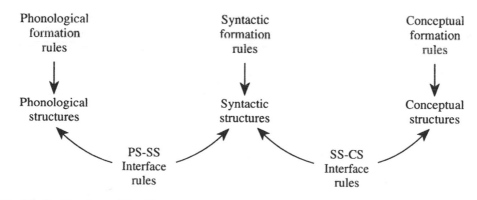

Fig. 3.1 The tripartite parallel architecture.

derivations in a Tree–Adjoining Grammar formalism, dealing with the syntax–semantics interface. Lexical–Functional Grammar (Bresnan 1982; Dalrymple *et al.* 1995) is based on two parallel mutually constraining subcomponents of syntax, constituent structure and functional structure. Role and Reference Grammar (Van Valin and LaPolla 1997) has parallel components of syntax and semantics, with parallel tiers of structure within each component. And of course the basic insight of Autosegmental Phonology was the separation of phonological structure itself into parallel and mutually constraining tiers such as segmental structure and prosodic structure (see the next section). Head-Driven Phrase Structure Grammar (Pollard and Sag 1987, 1994) can also be construed in this sense, although the formalism makes less of a fuss about distinguishing individual components from the interfaces among them. What I think is relatively novel in the present approach is the way it looks at a number of interfaces at once, and observes that they have similar structure. (I say 'relatively' because this parallel appears also in some versions of Categorial Grammar (Oehrle 1988), and in some sense way back in Lamb's (1966) Stratificational Grammar.)

This conception also abandons the assumption that the function of the grammar is *deriving* sentences. Rather, a large part of the grammar's function is in specifying or constraining the relationship between the three constituent structures. It may or may not be the case that the independent combinatorial components are stated in terms of traditional derivations—what I have proposed here does not bear on the question. However, it is worth noting that most of the constraint-based generative frameworks concur in formulating the grammar entirely in terms of constraints: the syntactic component, for example, is thought of as a set of constraints on well-formed tree structures rather than as a set of derivational principles.

A relatively recent trend in constraint-based theories has been the idea that constraints need not be rigid, but can be *violable* or *defeasible*. This appeared first, I believe, in semantics (Jackendoff 1983; Lakoff 1987); it has now become a fundamental assumption in the approach of Optimality Theory, particularly in phonology (Prince and Smolensky 1993) but also in syntax (Grimshaw 1997). It seems to me that such theories are moving in the direction of biological plausibility: a constraint that can be over-ridden by a more powerful constraint or by an ensemble of collectively more powerful constraints has a flavour reminiscent of the interaction of activation and inhibition in neural functioning.

3.6 An example

To make all this more concrete, let us look in some detail at the structure of a simple sentence (carefully selected to bring out various important points).

(7)   The little star's beside a big star.

Figure 3.2 gives a pretty fair articulation of the phonological structure and syntactic structure, though many particulars are still omitted. The gross articulation of conceptual structure is right, but much of the detail is unknown. I have also included a

Phonological structure

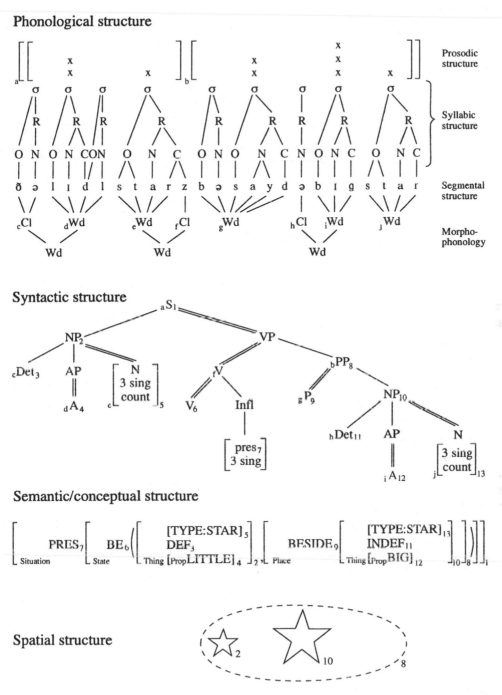

Syntactic structure

Semantic/conceptual structure

Spatial structure

Fig. 3.2 Structure of 'The little star's beside a big star'.

very sketchy articulation of a level of representation I have called spatial structure (SpS), the level at which this sentence can be compared with the output of the visual system.

3.6.1 Phonological structure

Begin with the phonological structure. It consists of four subcomponents or *tiers* (which might be thought of as even smaller parallel components). Down the middle is the *segmental structure*, the string of discrete speech sounds or phonemes, notated here in the phonetic alphabet. However, as is well known, the speech sounds are not actually unitary: they are composites, made up of a matrix of *distinctive features*. Figure 3.3 zooms in on the segmental structure of the word *star*, now broken into distinctive features. These features define the similarity space among speech sounds. Here is a classic example that illustrates their usefulness. The English regular plural

$$
\begin{bmatrix}
\text{+consonantal} \\
\text{-vocalic} \\
\text{-sonorant} \\
\text{-nasal} \\
\text{+continuant} \\
\text{-voiced} \\
\text{+anterior} \\
\text{+coronal}
\end{bmatrix}
\begin{bmatrix}
\text{+consonantal} \\
\text{-vocalic} \\
\text{-sonorant} \\
\text{-nasal} \\
\text{-continuant} \\
\text{-voiced} \\
\text{+anterior} \\
\text{+coronal}
\end{bmatrix}
\begin{bmatrix}
\text{-consonantal} \\
\text{+vocalic} \\
\text{+sonorant} \\
\text{-nasal} \\
\text{-high} \\
\text{+low} \\
\text{-front} \\
\text{-round}
\end{bmatrix}
\begin{bmatrix}
\text{+consonantal} \\
\text{+vocalic} \\
\text{+sonorant} \\
\text{-nasal} \\
\text{+continuant} \\
\text{+voiced} \\
\text{-anterior} \\
\text{+coronal}
\end{bmatrix}
$$

Fig. 3.3   The segmental structure of 'star', broken into distinctive features.

suffix has three pronunciations: 's' as in *cats*, 'z' as in *dogs*, and 'uhz' as in *horses*. The choice of which to use is determined by the distinctive features of the final sound of the word it is attached to. The (−voiced) sound 's' is used with words that end with a (−voiced) sound; the (+voiced) sound 'z' is used with words that end with a (+voiced) sound; and 'uhz' is used with words that end with the sounds 's', 'z', 'sh', 'zh', 'ch', or 'j', all of which have feature compositions close to those of 's' and 'z'. That is, the generalizations concerning use of the plural suffix fall out very naturally from the similarity space defined by the distinctive features. Hundreds of phenomena of this sort have been studied by phonologists. These features play a role in child language acquisition, in historical change, and in speech errors, as well as in the description of many dozens of languages. It is a scientific question what the right set of features is— one that is gradually being settled through phonological research.

However, phonological structure is more than a sequence of phonemes. It has a rhythmic organization indicated by the tree structures above the segmental structure in Fig. 3.2. The best-known part of this organization is the collection of speech sounds into syllables, indicated by σ. Now, syllables could be flat structures, like this:

(8)

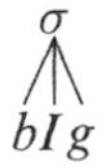

$$
\begin{array}{c}
\sigma \\
\bigwedge \\
b\,I\,g
\end{array}
$$

But in fact there are hierarchical distinctions inside the syllable. A syllable has to have one segment that functions as a *Nucleus*—the sonorous core around which the syllable is built. This is designated by *N* in Fig. 3.2. The nucleus is usually a vowel, but consonants with the distinctive feature (+sonorant) can also serve as syllabic nuclei. One of these is 'l', as in the second syllable of *little*, seen in Fig. 3.2.

The rest of the syllable's structure is optional. The nucleus and any following material (called the *Coda*) are grouped as the *Rime* (the part of the syllable that remains the same in rhymes). The material before the nucleus is grouped as the *Onset* (the part that remains the same in alliteration). These are indicated in Fig. 3.2 by *R* and *O* respectively. Notice also in Fig. 3.2 that the segment *d* in *little* is *ambisyllabic*: it serves both as coda of one syllable and onset of the next.

Above the syllabic structure is the *prosodic structure*, which has two components. The brackets indicate the organization of the syllables into *intonational phrases*; pauses in pronouncing the sentence can be inserted only between bracketed units. Within the brackets are the x's of the *metrical grid*, which indicates the relative stress of syllables. Syllables with no x's above them are unstressed; more x's indicate more stress, so that the word *big* receives the main stress of the sentence.

Looking now below the phonological string, we find the morphophonological structure—the grouping of the speech stream into words (indicated by *Wd*). Notice that the words *the* and *a* do not have the symbol *Wd* below them. As noted in Section 3.2, they are phonologically treated as *clitics*—phonological fragments that attach to adjacent words to form a larger Wd constituent. Finally, notice that the sound 'z' by itself also is a clitic, notated orthographically in sentence (7) by *'s*.

3.6.2 Syntactic structure

Consider next the syntactic structure. This is a tree diagram of the familiar sort. The largest constituent, S, divides into an NP subject and a VP predicate; the NP divides into a Determiner, a modifying AP, and a head N, which carries the features 3rd person count singular. (If this were a French or German sentence, the Det and A would also have number, and all constituents of NP would have grammatical gender as well.) The VP divides into a head V and a PP, the PP divides into Preposition and its NP object, and the NP divides like the subject NP. The V is attached to an Inflection which includes present tense plus 3rd person singular, to agree with the subject.

The way I have notated this tree differs from standard convention in two ways. First, it is customary to put the words of the sentence at the bottom of the tree. I have left them off because things like *the* and *star* are actually pieces of phonology, not syntax. All that can be represented of words in syntax is the part of speech (Det, N, etc.) and syntactic features such as 3rd person singular and present tense.

The other thing I have done is to notate some of the connections in the tree with double lines. These are connections between phrases and their heads. The idea is that phrases like NP, VP, AP, and PP are 'projections' of their heads—N, V, A, and P respectively. For example, there couldn't be a prepositional phrase with a noun as head or vice versa. So each phrase is to be thought of as a structural skeleton, indicated by

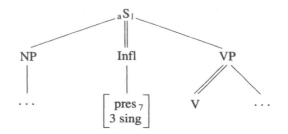

Fig. 3.4   An alternative syntactic structure for Figure 3.2.

the double lines, supplemented by modifiers, indicated by single lines. This is not a standard notation, but it makes more graphic an insight about syntactic structure that goes back at least to Zellig Harris in the 1940s and that was introduced into modern theory by Chomsky (1970) under the rubric of 'X-bar' theory (see also Jackendoff 1977).

In Fig. 3.2, I have continued the double line from V up beyond VP to S, in effect treating the sentence as a syntactic projection of the verb. This more or less reflects the traditional analysis. An important variant, originating in Chomsky (1986*b*), is shown in Fig. 3.4. Here the sentence is the projection of Inflection (Tense). Again, as in phonology, there is ongoing debate about the exact structure of this seemingly simple sentence. Nevertheless, everyone agrees that there is constituent structure of this sort, and that constituents have heads.

A further aspect of X-bar theory that has not been notated here is that syntactic categories such as Noun and Verb, like phonological segments, are treated as feature complexes rather than primitives. The most broadly accepted set (dating from Chomsky 1970) analyses Noun as $[+ N, -V]$ and Verb as $[-N, + V]$; Adjective is $[+ N, + V]$ and Preposition is $[-N, -V]$.

3.6.3 Conceptual structure

Next look at the conceptual structure. There is considerably less agreement here about the proper structure, and I have unabashedly given my version (which however omits the important independent tier of *information structure*, the foregrounding of topic and focus). The structure is a labelled bracketing, in which each pair of brackets surrounds a *conceptual constituent*. The label on a constituent designates it as belonging to a major conceptual type such as Situation, Event, State, Thing (Object), Place, or Property.

Two kinds of relations among conceptual constituents appear in this structure. The first is function–argument structure, notated as in (9).

(9) $[_X F([_Y \dots], [_Z \dots])]$

Here F is a function that maps a constituent of type Y and a constituent of type Z into a constituent of type X. A 2-place function is shown in example (9). BE is such a function in Fig. 3.2. There are also 1-place functions (such as BESIDE in Fig. 3.2) and possibly 3-place functions. The second kind of relation is modification, notated as in (10).

(10)
$$\left[\begin{array}{c} \cdots \\ [\text{Y} \cdots] \\ \text{X} \end{array} \right]$$

This is a constituent of type X, in which the inner constituent, of type Y, specifies a further characteristic of the outer constituent.

Using this notation, the conceptual structure in Fig. 3.2 says that there is a Situation in the present, consisting of a State. This State is one of a Thing being located in a Place; the function BE maps the Thing and the Place into this State.

Now look at the Thing that is the first argument of BE. It has three pieces of structure. The first designates the Thing as of the category STAR (which presumably has more internal articulation, not notated here; see Pustejovsky 1995 for a formal treatment of the conceptual structure of nouns). The second piece is a marker DEF, which means roughly that the identity of the object in question can be fixed by either the previous discourse or the context (if there were *two* little stars around, one couldn't say *THE little star*). The third piece is a modifying constituent of the type Property, which designates the object as having the characteristic LITTLE.

LITTLE has further internal structure, which again I have not formalized: basically it says that the overall size of the object in question is smaller than a pragmatically determined norm. This norm in turn may be chosen from (i) the average size of members of the category in question (here, stars), (ii) the average size of stars in the contextual environment (here, only two), (iii) the average size of all comparable objects in the contextual environment (as in *The star is little, the circle is big*), and perhaps others (Bierwisch and Lang 1989).

Turning to the rest of the conceptual structure in Fig. 3.2, the other Thing, *a big star*, works the same way as *the little star*. *A big star*, however, serves as the argument of a function BESIDE, which maps the Thing into a region or Place—the region in which the first Thing is located by the function BE. Again, I can give some detail of BESIDE: the region *beside* an object X is exterior to X, proximal to X, and in a horizontal direction from X (the Y is near but not beside the X in (11a)). In addition, no other object can come between X and an object next to it (the Y is near but not beside the X in (11b) as well).

(11)   a.   *Y*

                 X

            b.   *XZY*

Notice that these features of BESIDE must appear in some way also in spatial representation, so that 'beside-ness' can be verified in a visually presented array. I have notated the region 'beside the big star' very crudely in Fig. 3.2 by means of a dotted line that represents the approximate boundary of the relevant region.

3.7 Connecting the levels

Now we have all these structures, each belonging to a different form of representation—and each generated by its own set of formation rules (as in Fig. 3.1). But they cannot just exist independently: the relations among them created by the interface components have to be represented too.

I have notated correspondences between units of phonological structure and syntactic structure with pre-subscripts. For example, the phonological clitic *the* carries the pre-subscript c, which places it in correspondence with the initial Determiner in syntax. Similarly, correspondences between units of syntax and units of conceptual structure are notated with post-subscripts. For instance the initial Det in syntax is coindexed with the feature DEF in conceptual structure.

As with the representations themselves, many aspects of the correspondences notated in Fig. 3.2 are somewhat sketchy and imprecise; the details go beyond the scope of this chapter. Still, their general outline should be self-evident. An important feature of these correspondences—whatever their details—is that for the most part *they do not obtain between primitive elements of any of the levels—they are rather relations between composite units.* The primitive units of phonological structure such as distinctive features and syllables are completely invisible to syntax and meaning. Similarly, the word's syntactic category such as Noun or Verb (itself a composite of syntactic features) is invisible to phonology, as are various other primitive units of syntax, for instance *3rd person*. And the feature *3rd person singular* on the verb is a purely syntactic agreement feature that has no particular effect in conceptual structure.

Another thing to notice about these correspondences is that the units connected between phonology and syntax are not always the same units that are connected between syntax and conceptual structure. For example, the inflected verb (the upper V in Fig. 3.2) is connected to the phonology (subscript f), where it appears as the clitic z; but the bare verb and the inflection are connected separately to semantics (subscripts 6 and 7), where they are separate elements.

Generally speaking, the PS-to-SS mapping preserves linear order, while the SS-to-CS mapping tends to preserve the relative embedding of arguments and modifiers. In particular, the head of a syntactic phrase tends to map into the outermost function of the corresponding conceptual constituent. For instance, the preposition *beside*, the head of the PP, maps into the function BESIDE that governs the Place-constituent in Fig. 3.2.

In turn, some but not all parts of conceptual structure correspond to spatial structure—in Fig. 3.2, the two Thing-constituents and the Place. Other parts of conceptual structure are harder to represent directly in any spatial way. For instance, LITTLE and BIG raise the problem of how to notate relative size in spatial structure; definiteness (DEF) raises the problem of how to notate uniqueness. My impression is that these explicit pieces of conceptual structure encode information that is only *im*plicit in the spatial representation—so it is hard to see how to notate the relationship with a simple co-subscripting.

One aspect of this correspondence merits attention. The little clitic *z* in PS is of course the contracted verb *is*, which expresses the verb *be* in the 3rd person singular present tense, a smallish part of the syntactic tree. In turn, the verb *be* corresponds to the next-to-largest function in CS. The largest function in CS, present tense, appears as a feature of the verb *be* in syntax, and is not even an independent element in the phonology. So, by virtue of this two-step correspondence, elements of relative insignificance in PS can correspond to major organizing features of CS. (A similar situation arises in vision, where tiny features of a boundary can dramatically affect the three-dimensional interpretation of an array.)

A brief aside: the behaviour of Tense is a good illustration of the kinds of tensions that arise in syntactic theory. Tense has been notated in Fig. 3.2 as a feature on the verb, making it easy to match to phonology. But as a result it is more difficult to match to meaning, because it is necessary to say, exceptionally, that this feature inside of a verb (rather than the verb itself) maps to an outermost function in conceptual structure. We can improve the latter situation by adopting the alternative syntactic structure shown in Fig. 3.4, with Tense as the head of the sentence. This makes the mapping to conceptual structure a more canonical form, since now all syntactic heads map to outermost functions. But Fig. 3.4 creates a problem in mapping to the phonology, since the clitic *z* now must match two separate pieces of syntax at once, the Verb and the Tense. So changing the syntactic analysis to simplify one interface makes the other interface more complex.

A third possibility is to keep both interfaces simple by localizing the complexity in the syntactic component itself. This has been the standard approach in generative grammar. The idea is that the syntactic structure of our sentence contains two different trees. The form given in Fig. 3.2 is the 'surface structure', which interfaces easily with the phonology; and the form in Fig. 3.4 is the 'underlying structure', which interfaces easily with meaning. Then, internal to syntax, these two forms are related by a transformation that combines the underlying Inflection and Verb into the single unit found in surface structure. This approach was Chomsky's major innovation in *Syntactic Structures* (1957) and it has been a staple of syntactic analysis ever since.

Whichever of these three ways to deal with Tense proves correct, the point is that there is a mismatch between phonology and meaning, which has to be encoded somewhere in mental grammar. If this mismatch is eliminated at one point in the system, it pops up elsewhere. Much of the dispute in modern syntax has been over these sorts of mismatches and how to deal with them. (I don't think most linguists have viewed it this way, though.)

3.8 Two more important syntactic phenomena

For the sake of completeness, we step away from the overall architecture for a moment and briefly mention two syntactic phenomena that have been the focus of a great deal of research in linguistic theory and also in psycholinguistics and language acquisition: anaphora and unbounded dependencies.

3.8.1 Anaphora

The set of constraints on the use of anaphoric elements such as pronouns and reflexives has come to be called *Binding Theory* (not to be confused with the neuroscientist's notion of binding, to be taken up in Section 3.12). Some standard examples appear in (12) and (13).

(12)   a. Joe adores himself. (himself = Joe)

     b. Joe thinks that Fred adores himself. (himself = Fred)

     c. *Joe thinks that you adore himself.

(12a) shows that a reflexive pronoun in object position can co-refer with (or be *bound by*) an NP in subject position. (12b) shows that it must co-refer not just with any subject, but the subject of the same clause. (12c) shows that if the reflexive *cannot* be bound by the subject of its own clause—here because *you* and *himself* cannot co-refer—its use is ungrammatical (in English; certain other languages such as Japanese work differently).

(13)   a. Joe adores him. (him ≠ Joe)

     b. Joe thinks that Fred adores him. (him = Joe or 3rd party)

     c. Joe thinks that you adore him. (him = Joe or 3rd party)

     d. He thinks that Joe adores Fred. (he ≠ Joe or Fred)

     e. If you tickle Joe, he laughs. (he = Joe or 3rd party)

     f. If you tickle him, Joe laughs. (him = Joe or 3rd party)

(13a) shows that a simple pronoun in object position, by contrast with a reflexive, *cannot* co-refer with the subject of its clause. (13b,c) show that it can however co-refer with the subject of a higher clause—unlike a reflexive. (13d) shows that a pronoun cannot corefer with an NP in a subordinate clause on its right. However, (13e) shows that a pronoun *can* co-refer with an NP in a subordinate clause on its left. In (13f) the pronoun is, atypically, to the *left* of its antecedent; but this case is saved by the fact that the pronoun is in a subordinate clause.

Another sort of anaphoric element is the expression *do so*, which stands for a VP rather than an NP. Its relation to its antecedent resembles that of pronouns. Compare (14a–d) to (13c–f).

(14)   a. Fred impressed the boss without trying to do so. (do so = impress the boss)

     b. Fred did so without trying to impress the boss. (did so ≠ impress the boss)

     c. Without TRYING to impress the boss, Fred did so. (did so = impress the boss)

     d. Without trying to do so, Fred impressed the boss. (do so = impress the boss)

These examples make it clear that it is a complex matter to state the conditions under which an anaphoric element can corefer with an antecedent. In particular, the conditions crucially involve linguistic structure, and not just linear order. Thus it is no surprise that these conditions have been a constant preoccupation of linguistic research. The main lines of dispute are whether the linguistic structure involved in conditions on anaphora is syntactic structure alone (Chomsky 1981; Lasnik 1989), or whether semantic/conceptual structure plays a role as well or even instead (four independent approaches appear in Kuno 1987; Van Hoek 1995; Levinson 1987; Culicover and Jackendoff 1995).

3.8.2 Long-distance dependencies

In constructions like (15), the italicized elements are understood as having a role appropriate to the position marked by *t*. For instance, in (15a), *which movie* is understood as the object of the verb *saw*.

(15)   a. *Which movie* does Susan imagine that Sarah saw *t* last night?
          (Wh-direct question)

       b. John was wondering *who* Sarah decided she would go to the movies with
          t on Sunday.
          (indirect question)

       c. I didn't like the movie *which* you said that everyone was talking about
          t the other day.
          (relative clause)

       d. You may take *whichever sandwich* you find *t* on the table over there.
          (free relative)

       e. *That movie*, I wouldn't recommend that anyone consider taking their
          kids to *t*.
          (topicalization)

What is especially interesting about these cases is that the understood position can be within a subordinate clause, in fact deeply embedded within multiple subordinate clauses, as in (15e). For this reason, the relation between the italicized constituent and the understood position is called a *long-distance dependency*.

The analysis of such constructions within mainstream generative grammar is that the italicized constituent is actually *in* its understood position in underlying (deep) structure, and that it moves to the fronted position in the course of a syntactic derivation. The movement leaves behind an 'unpronounced pronoun' called a *trace*, which is indicated by *t* in (15). However, other generative frameworks, especially HPSG, have proposed analyses in which there is no movement, but instead the grammar directly establishes an anaphora-like relation between the italicized constituent and the trace (or a formal equivalent of the trace).

These constructions pose an interesting problem in that there are strong constraints on the structural position that an 'extracted' constituent can occupy in relation to its trace. For example, an 'extracted' constituent cannot be outside of a conjoined construction (16a), a relative clause (16b), an indirect question (16c), or a noun complement (16d) that the trace is inside of. These examples all involve direct wh-questions, but the same thing happens with all the constructions in (15).

(16)   a. **What* did Beth eat peanut butter and *t* for dinner?

    b. **Who* does Sam know a girl who is in love with *t*?

    c. **Who* does Betty know which professor flunked *t*?

    d. **What food* were you never aware of the fact that you shouldn't eat *t*?

As with anaphora, it has been a preoccupation of linguistic research for three decades (starting with Ross 1967) to characterize precisely the environments from which 'extraction' is possible. Again, one of the issues is whether the criteria are completely syntactic or partially semantic as well (Van Valin 1994; Culicover and Jackendoff 1997). But the overall outlines of the phenomenon are clear. Moreover, experimental work has shown that traces are 'recovered' in the course of sentence perception (Nicol *et al.* 1994): hearers must assign 'fronted' constituents a grammatical role in relation to a verb, and can be 'caught in the act' of doing so.

3.9 The lexicon

We next turn our attention to the lexicon, the store of words in long-term memory (LTM) from which the mental grammar constructs phrases and sentences.

What is a lexical item? It is widely agreed that a lexical item is to be regarded as a long-term memory association of phonological, syntactic, and semantic/conceptual features. Many have suggested that words for spatial concepts also carry with them some sort of image of a prototypical instance; in the approach suggested in Fig. 3.2 above, this would emerge as a spatial representation also linked to the lexical entry. (If a word is concerned with another sensory modality, for instance the word *acrid*, it will presumably be linked to a representation appropriate to that modality instead.)

In mainstream generative grammar, lexical items are taken to be inserted in their entirety into syntactic structure; their phonological and semantic features are interpreted later in the derivation by the appropriate components. A different scenario develops in the tripartite parallel approach. A lexical item, by virtue of having representations in each of the components of grammar, serves as part of the linking between the multiple structures. For example, (17) shows the material in the lexical entry for *star*.

(17)   Word corresponds to   N   corresponds to [Thing TYPE: STAR] corresponds to ☆
          | |
        /star/   ⌈count⌉
                            ⌊sing ⌋

This example lacks prosodic information. The reason is that prosodic information appears to be computed on-line (Levelt 1989), so it does not need to be stored in LTM.

The proper way to regard (17) is as a small-scale ensemble of interface rules. It lists a small chunk of phonology, a small chunk of syntax, and a small chunk of semantics, and it shows how to line these chunks up when they appear in parallel phonological, syntactic, and conceptual structures. It thus makes it possible for the interface components to establish the subscripts *e, j, 5,* and *13* in Fig. 3.2. A well-formed sentence, then, requires proper matching of the structures through the lexical entries of its words.

In short, *the function of lexical items is to serve as interface rules, and the lexicon as a whole is to be regarded as part of the PS–SS and SS–CS interface components.* On this view, the formal role of lexical items is not that they are 'inserted' into syntactic derivations, but rather that they establish the correspondence of certain syntactic constituents with phonological and conceptual structures.

This immediately leads to an attractive understanding of lexical access in sentence processing. In sentence comprehension, perception of a phoneme sequence leads to activation of a lexical item's phonological representation (or in Levelt's (1989) terminology, its *word form*). The activation of the word form leads in turn to activation of its syntactic structure and meaning (together called its *lemma*), so that the processor can use these to help construct the other structures. Similarly, in sentence production, selection of a lexical meaning as appropriate for the intended utterance activates the associated syntactic structure, so that the word can be integrated into the phrasal organization. In turn, the meaning and syntactic structure together (the lemma) activate the phonological structure (word form) so that a pronunciation may be initiated.

Notice that under this view it is not necessary to confine the lexicon to word-sized constituents. Lexical items are simply long-term memory associations of structures from the three components. There is no bar to storing such associations for larger-scale items such as idioms, or for smaller-scale items, such as the English regular plural affix (see the next section). Thus we dissociate the notion of 'lexical item'—a stored association of phonological, syntactic, and conceptual structures—from the notion of 'word'—a particularly significant unit of size in grammatical structure. Indeed, as we saw earlier, the notion of 'word' comes apart into 'phonological word', a prosodic unit, and 'syntactic word', a unit in syntax. Stereotypically, lexical items are both phonological words and syntactic words. But this need not be the case. For instance, *the* is a syntactic word but phonologically a clitic; the idiom *kick the bucket* is syntactically a three-word VP and phonologically two words and a clitic.

We should also recognize that there are 'defective' lexical items, which have phonology and semantics but no syntax. Examples are *yes, hello, ouch, hooray,* and many expletives. These can be used on their own as meaningful utterances, but they cannot be combined with other words into sentences (except of course in direct quotes, where anything goes). The lexicon also contains nonsense phrases such as *fiddle-de-dee* which even lack semantics.

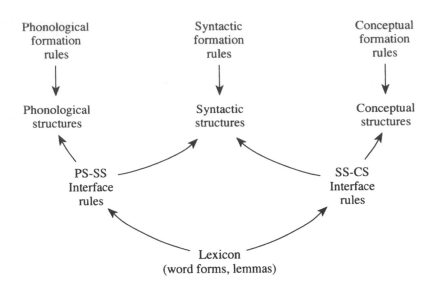

Fig. 3.5   The tripartite architecture, incorporating the lexicon.

The architecture of the grammar thus ends up looking like Fig. 3.5. Just to forestall misunderstanding, I should point out that the lexicon is not the only source of PS–SS and SS–CS correspondences. Among PS–SS correspondences are those dealing with the relation of prosodic and syntactic constituency, discussed briefly in Section 3.3. Among SS–CS correspondence are the rules telling how to relate syntactic relations such as verb-to-object to conceptual relations such as Action-to-Patient, how to relate the meanings of adjectives to those of the nouns they modify, how to determine scope of quantification from syntactic constituency, and so forth. All these rules go beyond the structures placed in correspondence by single lexical items.

3.10   Regular versus irregular morphology

In this framework, morphology is to be viewed as the continuation of phonological, syntactic, and conceptual structure down into the organization of words. So, for example, a suffix like the English regular past tense is a linking between a phonological structure -$(\partial)d$, a syntactic realization of verb inflection, and the conceptual structure PAST TIME. In other words, a regular affix can be regarded simply as a lexical item smaller than a word, and its attachment to stems is governed by principles of combination not unlike those that combine words into phrases.[7]

Irregular morphology, however, leads to further complexity. A typical situation arises with the clitic *'s* in Fig. 3.2. In semantics and syntax, this is made up of BE and present tense, two independent units (or lemmas[8]) linked by subscripts 6 and 7 in Fig. 3.2. However, their combination in syntax links to a single phonological unit (or word form), with subscript *f*. This is a standard sort of case that exemplifies the distinction between lemmas and word forms: the phonology–syntax connection (choice of word form) has to be established separately from the syntax–semantics connection (choice of lemma). For instance, if the two lemmas BE and present tense happened to link to a verb with the agreement feature (1st plural), the complex would link to the word form *are* rather than to the word *is* or the clitic *'s*. In general, then, irregular morphology prevents a simple linkage of the three structures, because it conflates two or more syntactic units into a single phonological unit.

This widespread situation raises a problem in the standard architecture, where one is required to insert all of a lexical item's features into initial syntactic structures. How does one know whether to insert *sing* or *sang*, for instance, if this depends on later stages in syntactic derivation such as the formation of a question (*Did she sing?*) versus a declarative (*She sang*)? There have been basically two responses. One is to assume that *all* inflectional forms are inserted into the syntactic derivation, and then the wrong ones are discarded when the surface integration of inflection is established. (This approach is advocated in Halle (1973) and Jackendoff (1975), for instance.) The other response is to say that lexical insertion inserts only syntactic and semantic features into initial syntactic structures; then, later in the derivation, after inflectional features have been established, the grammar 'goes back to the lexicon' and picks up the proper phonological realization. (This latter view is most recently represented in the theory of Distributed Morphology of Halle and Marantz (1993); it is in essence the approach of Levelt (1989), in which the lemma plus inflectional diacritics activate the proper word form.)

Because of these problems of irregular forms, most theorists have assumed for the sake of uniformity that regular inflectional forms are stored and accessed the same way. (This includes LFG and HPSG, where inflectional forms are explicitly determined by 'lexical rules'.) At the same time, it is recognized that there is something wrong with the idea of storing all regular inflectional forms. In English it is not such a severe problem, since verbs have only a few inflectional forms; but in many other familiar European languages, a verb typically has dozens of forms. Still worse are languages with rich agglutinative morphology such as Turkish or Navajo, where the number of verb forms can run into the tens of thousands. Hankamer (1989) calculates that a full listing of the inflectional possibilities for Turkish words would likely run into tens of billions of forms.

The upshot is that we are forced to posit an inhomogeneity in the way inflectional forms are produced by the language faculty. The irregular forms must be stored in long-term memory: the speaker must know that the word in question is inflectionally irregular and what the forms in question are (e.g. is it like *sing–sang* or like *sting–stung?*). On the other hand, although some regular forms *may* be stored in long-term memory, in general most must be produced on-line from a stem stored in LTM combined with appropriate affixes, which are also stored independently in LTM, as suggested at the beginning of this section.

A pair of examples from English derivational morphology points up this inhomogeneity more clearly. First consider the formation of denominal verbs, such as *shelve* (*books*), *saddle* (*a horse*), *butter* (*the bread*), and *dust* (*the furniture*). Although there are many of these in the language, they are not entirely productive: one knows that the process cannot be arbitrarily extended to allow forms like *table (*the dishes*) ('put the dishes on the table') or *mustard (*the bread*) ('put mustard on the bread'). Moreover, the forms that *do* exist show a certain degree of specialization in their semantics. One cannot saddle a horse by putting a saddle on the horse's head, and one cannot speak of putting a saddle on a table as saddling the table; saddling is a very specific action. Likewise, one cannot butter bread by just putting a stick of butter on the bread. And dusting the furniture is not putting dust *on* the furniture, but rather taking it off. Thus there is clear evidence of the forms being learned individually.[9]

This situation may be contrasted with a process called 'expletive infixation', used in non-standard speech register to emphasize a focused word in an emotional fashion (McCarthy 1982). It converts, for example, *Susquehanna* and *manufacture* into *Susque-goddam-hanna* and *manu-goddam-facture*. This process can be applied to any word of the proper stress pattern (roughly, secondary stress followed by unstressed syllable followed by primary stress), and it places the infix before the primary stressed syllable. There are no irregularities of meaning. The idea that infixed word forms are learned and stored seems absurd, especially since the hallmark of this usage is its creativity and spontaneity. Rather, what appears to be stored in LTM is the expletive and the prosodic template that it uses to combine freely with other stored forms. The actual composition of infixed forms is performed on-line. A similar if less vivid case is the Dutch diminutive *-tje*, which seems to suffix to just about any noun at all. The English *-ly* ending that forms adverbs from adjectives likewise is fully productive: if one were to hear a new adjective *zart* in the context *she has a very zart smile*, one would feel confident in saying *she smiled very zartly*.

Thus it is necessary to admit two distinct ways that word formation can take place: through free combination of regular affixes with stems, and through learning of irregular word forms. The English past tense is a regular process of combination overlaid with a couple of hundred irregular cases, a not atypical situation in morphology.

The existence of this inhomogeneity in morphology has of course been the subject of intense dispute during the past decade in psycholinguistics, computer science, and cognitive neuroscience. In particular, the connectionist tradition (e.g. Rumelhart and McClelland 1986; Plunkett and Marchman 1993; Elman *et al.* 1996) has argued for a single associationist system embracing both regular and irregular forms. The inhomogeneous solution has been advocated most strenuously by Pinker and associates (e.g. Pinker and Prince 1988, 1991; see also Jaeger *et al.* 1996). The arguments concern the nature of child learning versus the nature of neural network learning, and responses to regular versus irregular inflectional forms in various psycholinguistic and brain-imaging tasks. I do not wish to go into those arguments here. Suffice it to say that (i) as Pinker and Prince stress, the associationist solution is appropriate for the irregular forms but not for the regular forms; (ii) on purely linguistic grounds, an associationist solution will not scale up to the complexity of languages with more complex systems of regular inflection. Rather, regular inflection appears to be of a piece with the processes of free on-line combination that are characteristic of phrasal grammar.

3.11 Representational modularity

The account advocated here of the relationship between phonology, syntax, semantics, and the lexicon fits naturally into a larger hypothesis of the architecture of mind that might be called 'Representational Modularity' (Jackendoff 1987, Chapter 12; Jackendoff 1992, Chapter 1). The overall idea is that the mind, seen as an information-processing system, operates in terms of some finite family of representations or 'languages of the mind'. Each of these 'languages' has its own proprietary set of primitives and principles of combination, so that it defines an infinite set of expressions along lines familiar from generative grammar. However, these languages are formally incommensurate with each other, and communication between a pair of languages must be mediated by interface rules that relate partial representations in each of the languages.

This view of modularity differs in a number of respects from Fodor's (1983). Modularity as conceived here is a property not of a particular faculty (such as language or vision), but of a particular representation: we can regard syntax as processed by one 'representation module' and phonology by another. In addition, it is useful to think of each set of interface rules as constituting an 'interface module'. An interface module, instead of dealing with the well-formedness of a single format of representation, deals with the relation of a pair of formats—it has its feet planted in both, and forms the bridge between them. Still, it is modular, in that it is 'bi-domain-specific': for example, the PS–SS interface has no access to semantics or pragmatics. A faculty such as the language faculty can then be built up from the chaining of a number of representation modules and interface modules.

Fodorian modularity gives no account of the relationship between the 'shallow representations' produced by the language perception module (presumably syntactic structure) and the 'central representations' that serve thought; thus Fodor leaves it entirely unclear how the language faculty actually serves the purpose of communicating thought. By contrast, Representational Modularity makes explicit provision for an interface module that carries information from syntax to conceptual structure.

The language faculty is embedded in a larger system of similar interfaces. For instance, phonetic information is not the only information picked up by auditory perception. Rather, the speech signal seems to be picked up simultaneously by four or more independent interfaces: in addition to phonetic perception (the auditory-to-phonology interface), it is used for voice recognition, affect (tone-of-voice) perception, and general-purpose auditory perception (birds, thunder, bells, etc.). Each of these processes converges on a different representational 'language'—a different space of distinctions. At the same time, phonological structure takes inputs not only from the auditory interface, but also from a number of different interfaces with the visual system, including at least those involved in reading and sign language. Figure 3.6 lays out these representational formats and their interactions; each arrow or double arrow stands for an interface module.[10]

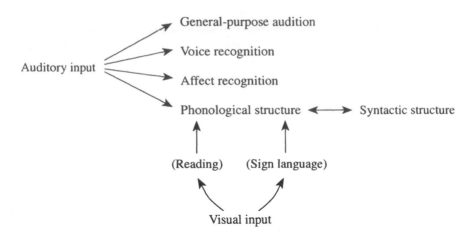

Fig. 3.6 Modules that interact with auditory input and phonological structure.

On the other end of the language faculty, CS interacts through interface rules with information proprietary to the visual system and visual imagery, as already indicated in Fig. 3.2 by the provision of Spatial Structure. Jackendoff (1987, Chapter 8) and Landau and Jackendoff (1993) characterize this level as a central level of cognition, responsible for encoding the shape, layout, and motion of objects in a format compatible with vision, haptic (touch) perception, and action.

There is abundant evidence for similar organization within the visual system, deriving more from neuropsychology than from a theory of visual information structure (Marr 1982 is the main example of the latter). It hardly needs saying here that numerous areas in the brain encode different sorts of visual information, and they communicate with each other through distinct pathways. For the most part there is no straight 'derivation' from one visual level to another; rather the information encoded by any one area is influenced by its interfaces with numerous others.

I emphasize that Representational Modularity is a hypothesis about the overall architecture of the mind, to be verified in terms of not only the language faculty but other faculties as well. So I do not wish to claim for it any degree of inevitability. Nevertheless, it appears to be a plausible way of looking at how the mind is put together, with preliminary support from many different quarters.

An architecture embodying Representational Modularity has useful consequences for theories of processing. Consider that in speech perception, a signal received by the brain in auditory format must give rise to representations in conceptual format ('thoughts' or 'meanings'); in speech production, representations in conceptual format must give rise to signals to the motor system. The tripartite architecture claims that these conversions are not direct, but rather involve passing through representations in phonological and syntactic formats.

Now consider what is involved in 'passing from one representational format to another' in the course of processing: principles must be invoked that tell the processor how a constituent in the input format determines or constrains the choice of constituents in the target format. But these principles are precisely the interface rules; there should be a fairly direct relation between the interface rule components of the grammar and the components of the processor that construct one form of representation on the basis of another. In other words, the interface components of the competence theory seem close to directly usable as components in a processor. Hence I find a rather close relation between the spirit of the present architecture and Levelt's (1989) multistage theory of speech production (even if the way the theories match up in detail calls for a certain amount of negotiation).[11]

On the other hand, I find the processing counterpart of the generative systems (or representational modules) of the competence theory to be somewhat less clear at the moment. In particular, the notion of spreading activation does not appear to lend itself to an appealing account of rule-governed free combination of elements into larger structures. And indeed, although Levelt's (1989) model uses spreading activation to interface between formats, it uses rather conventional symbolic buffers for building up composite syntactic and phonological structures.[12]

The modular architecture suggested here does not require each module to do its work entirely before passing its results on to the next module in the chain. Rather, the system can be thought of as performing 'opportunistic' or 'incremental' parsing of the sort widely assumed in current processing theories: any piece of information that one module can pass on to the next will be used in building partial structures, which in turn can be passed back to constrain further processing in the previous stage (Marslen-Wilson and Tyler 1987; Jackendoff 1987, Chapter 6; Levelt 1989). Thus, for example, lexical access in speech perception, through phonological structure, leads immediately to construction of partial structures in both syntax and semantics, which can therefore constrain each other in parallel. If enough structure can be constructed to pass something useful on to Spatial Structure, that too can play a role in providing feedback to the syntactic parsing process, as in the experiments of Tanenhaus *et al.* (1995).

3.12 The binding problem and short-term memory

Our analysis of *The little star's beside a big star* offers an interesting perspective on some current discussions in neuroscience. I am going to briefly lay a few of these on the table, for what ideas they may stimulate.

First, consider what happens in the perception or production of this sentence. All of these mental representations must be constructed and connected with each other. This amounts to an instantiation of what has come to be known as the *binding problem* (not to be confused with linguists' Binding Theory, in section 3.8.1).

In the discussions I have encountered, the binding problem is usually stated this way: we have found that the shape and the colour of an object are encoded in different regions of the brain. How is it, then, that we sense a particular shape and colour as attributes of the same object? The problem becomes more pointed in a two-object situation: if the shape region detects a square and a circle, and the colour region detects red and blue, how does the brain encode that one is seeing, say, a red square and a blue circle rather than the other way around? In fact, under time pressure, subjects can mismatch the features of multiple perceived objects (Treisman 1988). A proposal that has gained a certain popularity (Crick and Koch 1990; Singer *et al.* 1997) is that the different representations are phase-linked: the neurons encoding red and square fire in synchrony, and those encoding blue and circle do as well, but out of phase with the first pair.

However, the binding problem presented by linguistic representations is far more massive than this simple description (and, I suspect, more characteristic of the problems really faced by the brain). In our trivially simple sentence there are four independent structures, each of which has multiple parts that must be correlated, as notated by the structures in Fig. 3.2; and in addition, the four structures must be correlated with each other, as notated by the subscripts in Fig. 3.2. Consider just the prepositional phrase. To characterize it properly, the following relationships must be encoded:

a. It is of the type PP.

b. It is a part of the VP.

c. It follows V.

d. It has P and NP as parts.

e. It corresponds to the Place-constituent in conceptual structure.

f. It corresponds to the phonological constituent *beside a big star*.

For the object of the preposition:

a. It is of the type NP.

b. It is a part of PP.

c. It follows P.

d. It has Det, AP, and N as parts.

e. It corresponds to a particular Thing-constituent in conceptual structure.

f. It corresponds to the phonological constituent *a big star*.

How effectively can firing synchrony can be scaled up to deal with such an interlocking web of relationships? In particular, if the PP is synchronized with its parts, and its parts are synchronized with *their* parts, the whole tree structure is temporally unresolvable. More generally, is there sufficient bandwidth in the temporal resolution of neural firing to distinguish all the parts of the sentence from one another? To me, this casts considerable doubt on the feasibility of solving the binding problem in terms of temporal synchrony alone—even if temporal synchrony is indeed an important part of the solution. (Singer *et al.* merely speculate on the possibility of scaling their analysis in terms of synchrony up to hierarchically structured relations; though see Shastri and Ajjanagadde (1993) for a proposal.)

A second question arises here: the binding of the three independent structures with each other is mediated in part by lexical items, which therefore should be conceived of as long-term memory bindings of pieces of information. But binding through synchronous firing has generally been conceived of as temporary. Is there a way that long-term synaptic weights (the binding mechanism usually attributed to associative memory) lead to synchronous firing in working memory? Or is some other as yet unknown mechanism of binding at work here?

Another point concerning the lexicon concerns lexical retrieval, the process of using or recognizing a word in a sentence. It is often assumed that lexical retrieval involves no more than activating the word in long-term memory (LTM). However, consider yet again the sentence in Fig. 3.2, in which there are two occurrences of the word *star*. If the first occurrence simply activates the lexical entry, what can the second occurrence do? It cannot just activate the word a second time, since the word has to remain activated the first time in order for the sentence to receive a full interpretation. The second occurrence cannot just activate the word more strongly, because that leaves the two occurrences indistinguishable. In particular, the first occurrence is bound to *little* and the second to *big*, so binding to both simultaneously would lead to the concept of a little big star, a contradiction.

A more old-fashioned computational approach to lexical access supposes that the accessed word is copied from LTM into a buffer in short-term memory (STM)—in this case in two different places in STM. (And indeed Levelt's model so supposes.) This approach meets the objections raised in the previous paragraph, as it keeps the two occurrences of *star* distinct. On the other hand, how is it implemented neurally? The neural network approaches with which I am familiar do not allow for the possibility of 'copying' information from one 'register' to another.

It is worth pointing out that this problem occurs at every level of representation. For example, in phonological structure, if the detection of the sound *s* consists simply of activating an *s*-node, what happens in a word with more than one such sound, say *Sisyphus* or *sassafras*?[13]

A final question raised by lexical representation concerns the organization of spatial structure. Figure 3.2 gives a very rudimentary picture of the spatial configuration that might be envisioned in hearing the sentence. But think about what spatial structure might be associated with the lexical entry of the word *star* (in the sense of a geometrical figure, not a celestial object or a media celebrity), such that the spatial configuration in Fig. 3.2 could be constructed in order to check the truth of the sentence against a presented visual scene. A stereotypical five-pointed star such as I've drawn in Fig. 3.2 does not fall in any natural way out of popular theories of shape such as Marr's 3D model or Biederman's (1987) geons. Evidently some enrichment is necessary to deal with this shape.

Worse is the problem of providing a spatial representation that will suffice for identifying stars with four, five, six, seven, or more points. How is an indefinite multiplicity of points to be encoded in spatial structure? (This is parallel to the old problem of how animals with varying numbers of legs can fall under a visual image for the word *animal*.)

The same problem, only more general, arises from another syntactic structure and interpretation associated with the phonological structure of our by now tired example: *the little stars beside the big star (. . . are painted red)*. Here the clitic *-s* designates plural instead of the contracted verb *is*. The problem is: what should appear in spatial representation to correspond to plurality? No particular number of tokens will do; evidently some non-iconic device must be added to encode this property.

More generally, in recent years there has been a great deal of work on the semantics of spatial expressions in language (Haviland and Levinson 1994; Bloom *et al.* 1995). It seems to me that a major bottleneck in proceeding with this work is the absence of an adequate theory of high-level visual representations—the output of the visual system with which the output of spatial expressions in language must be compared, in order to achieve object identification and categorization on the basis of linguistic input. Work on language is constantly running against problems like this one of indefinite multiplicity, about which visual theorists have (as far as I know) had nothing much to say. Another such example is the concept of force, which appears again and again in linguistic expressions to encode the distinction between *hit* and *touch*, the notion of *leaning against* something, the notion of *support*, and so forth. So far, there has been no corresponding theory of the perception of force (except for perhaps Michotte (1954), who deals with dynamic but not static forces, I think).

3.13 Summary

The fundamental goals of generative grammar are (i) to characterize the formal structure of the mental system underlying language use, and (ii) to characterize the formal structure of the innate basis that enables the child to achieve linguistic competence. Without abandoning these fundamental goals, we have arrived at a somewhat different picture of the system than the mainstream Chomskyan view. In particular, the independent richness of the structures for phonology, syntax, and semantics gives rise to a tripartite parallel architecture, rather than the mainstream architecture in which syntax is the predominant generative capacity. This leads to a need to characterize the interface components that mediate between these structures, components largely neglected in the generative literature.

It leads as well to a view of the grammatical system that is much more heavily constraint-based than the mainstream approach. The multiple components are related by constraints rather than derivations from underlying to surface form (or from D-structure to PF and LF). At the moment I have left open whether the individual components have derivational structure or whether they too are purely constraint-based (as in many of the constraint-based frameworks cited in section 3.1).

The lexicon is now to be viewed as part of the interface components. Lexical items, rather than being inserted into syntactic structures and interpreted phonologically and semantically, play an integral role in establishing the connections between the three parallel structures. This approach permits us easily to integrate into the lexicon items smaller than words, such as regular affixes, and larger, such as idioms.

All of these changes, I believe, lead to a more realistic connection of linguistic theory with theories of processing and brain function. It is characteristic of the brain to operate in terms of multiple mutually constraining systems of this sort; moreover, the lexicon and other interface principles can be seen to play a direct role in the perception and production of sentences. On the other hand, the richness and interconnectedness of linguistic structure presents numerous challenges of interest to theories of brain processing.

A more general final point: I do not think that language is unusual among mental systems in its structural complexity. I would suspect that, in particular, vision, spatial orientation, and the formulation of action are of commensurate complexity. The only difference is that for language we have a rich theory of the structure of the mental information involved, whereas in these other areas we do not (see my complaint about high-level vision in the previous section). I would therefore hope that an appreciation of the challenges for neuroscience that are posed by language would not be confined to linguists, psycholinguistics, and neurolinguists alone.

Acknowledgements

I am grateful to Edgar Zurif, Victoria Fromkin, Susan Curtiss, Marcel Kinsbourne, and an anonymous referee for comments and assistance in bringing this chapter into its final form.

Notes

1. Offshoots include approaches to be cited shortly. Approaches in opposition include Cognitive Grammar (Lakoff 1987; Langacker 1987), Functional Grammar (Givon 1995), and connectionist approaches (Rumelhart and McClelland 1986; Elman *et al.* 1996).
2. I offer this analysis here with some ambivalence, as a handbook article is supposed to sum up the state of the art rather than presenting a personal view. I will take care to state when I deviate from mainstream understanding of the issues.
3. There has been considerable criticism of Gopnik's early work, in particular claims that SLI of the sort she describes is frequently accompanied by other impairments. Her more recent work, e.g. Gopnik (1999), answers many of these criticisms through more extensive testing of a broader population of SLI individuals speaking a number of different languages.
4. To continue a theme of the previous section: it may well be that action schemas in general are mentally encoded in discrete segments, which are converted into continuous and interleaved motor instructions. If so, the mapping from phonetics to motor instructions would be just a special case, involving specifically linguistic action schemas. But, as far as I know, this remains to be shown by future research.
5. An advocate of a distinction between semantic and conceptual structure might be able to keep the syntax–semantics interface clean. But then all the 'dirtiness' will fall into the semantics–conceptual interface, and my arguments here will apply to that interface instead.
6. Some colleagues have expressed a worry that within the parallel model the interface rules are (so far) imprecise: 'they are too unconstrained; they can do anything'. What I have tried to show here, though, is that interface rules are conceptually necessary in order to mediate between phonology, syntax, and meaning. It is an unwarranted assumption that they are to be minimized and that all expressive power lies in the generative (combinatorial) components. Rather, the empirical issue that constantly arises in such an architecture is the balance of power among components. Since the interface rules are part of the grammar of the language, they must be acquired by the child, and therefore they fall under all the arguments for Universal Grammar. In other words, interface rules, like syntactic and phonological rules, must be constrained so as to be learnable. Thus their presence in the architecture does not change the basic nature of the problem.
7. This is not to say that the principles of combination within words are the same as those for phrases. For instance, in phrasal syntax, it is common for there to be variations in word order. But this *never* happens in morphosyntax: one never finds variations in the permissible order of affixes on a stem.
8. Here I deviate a little from Levelt's usage. He would regard past tense not as a separate lemma, but as a 'diacritic' on the lemma BE.

9. This is not to say that the similarities among them do not lend the class coherence. This coherence is what makes learning a new member of the class easier than learning an altogether new word.

10. Fodorian modularity, as far as I can see, makes no provision for reading and sign language, cases in which visual input 'gets into' the supposedly informationally encapsulated phonology module. Here these inputs reach phonology via different interface modules from that used in spoken language, but observing the same overall architecture. It should be added, of course, that the interface module for reading—while it certainly behaves in processing like a module in Fodor's sense—can hardly be thought of as innate.

11. This conception leads directly to a hypothesis that more complex processing at an interface could lead to greater processing load. Piñango, Zurif, and Jackendoff (1999) test one such case, involving the telicity judgments discussed in Section 3.4. For example, a sentence like (i) is interpreted as repeated jumping, even though repetition is mentioned nowhere in the sentence.

(i) The boy jumped until the teacher told him to stop.

The standard analysis (see references in section 3.4) is that the word *until* is used semantically to bound a continuing process. *The boy jumped*, however, denotes a completed action. In order to obtain compatibility, the action of jumping is 'coerced' into repeated jumping, a continuing process. Adding this extra sense of repetition induces extra complexity into the SS–CS correspondence. Sentences like (i) were compared experimentally with sentences like (ii), where no coercion is necessary, since singing is a continuing action.

(ii) The boy sang until the teacher told him to stop.

Processing load was measured after the word *until*, using a dual-task interference paradigm. And indeed, the sentences like (i) registered significantly greater load than those like (ii).

   This is, of course, only a preliminary result, calling for many further experiments. I mention it here because it was suggested precisely by the hypothesis that the interface modules are directly involved in processing, which in turn is a consequence of the proposed architecture for the language faculty.

12. Note that Elman's (1993) so-called connectionist parser is not a parser at all. It simply attempts to predict the next word of incomplete sentences, choosing from a limited vocabulary and a limited number of grammatical constructions. See Marcus 1998 for discussion of its limitations.

13. I think this argument—the need to distinguish in STM multiple tokens of the same type—is the gist of one of Fodor and Pylyshyn's (1988) arguments against connectionism. But it is a little hard to tell.

References

Bach, E. (1983). On the relation between word-grammar and phrase-grammar. *Natural Language and Linguistic Theory*, **1**, 65–90.

Bellugi, U., Poizner, H., and Klima, E. S. (1989). Language, modality, and the brain. *Trends in Neurosciences*, **12**, 380–8.

Bellugi, U., Wang, P. P., and Jernigan, T. L. (1993). Williams syndrome: An unusual neuropsychological profile. In *Atypical cognitive deficits in developmental disorders: Implications for brain function* (eds S. Broman and J. Grafman). Erlbaum, Hillsdale, NJ.

Bickerton, D. (1981). *The roots of language*. Karoma, Ann Arbor.

Biederman, I. (1987). Recognition-by-components: A theory of human image understanding. *Psychological Review*, **94**, 115–47.

Bierwisch, M., and Lang, E. (1989). Somewhat longer—much deeper—further and further: Epilogue to the dimensional adjective project. In *Dimensional adjectives: Grammatical structure and conceptual interpretation* (ed. M. Bierwisch and E. Lang), pp. 471–514. Springer, Berlin.

Bloom, P., Peterson, M. A., Nadel, L., and Garrett, M. F. (eds) (1995). *Language and space*. MIT Press, Cambridge, MA.

Bresnan, J. (ed.) (1982). *The mental representation of grammatical relations*. MIT Press, Cambridge, MA.

Chomsky, N. (1957). *Syntactic structures*. Mouton, The Hague.

Chomsky, N. (1965). *Aspects of the theory of syntax*. MIT Press, Cambridge, MA.

Chomsky, N. (1970). Remarks on nominalizations. In *Readings in English transformational grammar* (ed. R. Jacobs and P. Rosenbaum), pp. 184–221. Ginn and Co., Waltham, MA.

Chomsky, N. (1975). *Reflections on language*. Pantheon, New York.

Chomsky, N. (1980). *Rules and representations*. Columbia University Press, New York.

Chomsky, N. (1981). *Lectures on government and binding*. Foris, Dordrecht.

Chomsky, N. (1986a). *Knowledge of language*. Praeger, New York.

Chomsky, N. (1986b). *Barriers*. MIT Press, Cambridge, MA.

Chomsky, N. (1995). *The minimalist program*. MIT Press, Cambridge, MA.

Chomsky, N. and Halle, M. (1968). *The sound pattern of English*. Harper and Row, New York.

Crick, F. and Koch, C. (1990). Towards a neurobiological theory of consciousness. *Seminars in the Neurosciences*, **2**, 263–75.

Culicover, P. and Jackendoff, R. (1995). *Something else* for the binding theory. *Linguistic Inquiry*, **26**, 249–75.

Culicover, P. and Jackendoff, R. (1997). Syntactic coordination despite semantic subordination. *Linguistic Inquiry*, **28**, 195–217.

Dalrymple, M., Kaplan, R. M., Maxwell, J. T., and Zaenen, A. (ed.) (1995). *Formal issues in lexical-functional grammar*. CSLI Publications, Stanford.

Declerck, R. (1979). Aspect and the bounded/unbounded (telic/atelic) distinction. *Linguistics*, **17**, 761–794.

Dowty, D. (1979). *Word meaning and Montague grammar*. Dordrecht, Reidel.

Elman, J. L. (1993). Learning and development in neural networks: The importance of starting small. *Cognition*, **48**, 71–99.

Elman, J. L., Bates, E. A., Johnson, M. H., Karmiloff-Smith, A., Parisi, D., and Plunkett, K. (1996). *Rethinking innateness: A connectionist perspective on development*. MIT Press, Cambridge, MA.

Fillmore, C. and Kay, P. (1993). *Construction grammar coursebook*. Copy Central, University of California, Berkeley.

Fodor, J. A. (1983). *Modularity of mind*. MIT Press, Cambridge, MA.

Fodor, J. A. and Pylyshyn, Z. W. (1988). Connectionism and cognitive architecture: A critical analysis. *Cognition*, **28**, 3–71.

Foley, W. and Van Valin, R. D. (1984). *Functional syntax and universal grammar*. Cambridge University Press.

Gee, J. and Grosjean, F. (1983). Performance structures: A psycholinguistic and linguistic appraisal. *Cognitive Psychology*, **15**, 411–58.

Givon, T. (1995). *Functionalism and grammar*. Benjamins, Amsterdam.

Goldberg, A. (1995). *Constructions: A construction grammar approach to argument structure*. University of Chicago Press.

Goldin-Meadow, S. and Mylander, C. (1990). Beyond the input given: The child's role in the acquisition of language. *Language*, **66**, 323–55.

Goldsmith, J. (1976). *Autosegmental phonology*. Ph.D. thesis, MIT. Indiana University Linguistics Club, Bloomington.

Gopnik, M. (1999). Some evidence for impaired grammars. In *Language, logic, and concepts: Essays in memory of John Macnamara* (ed. R. Jackendoff, P. Bloom, and K. Wynn). MIT Press, Cambridge, MA.

Gopnik, M. and Crago, M. B. (1990). Familial aggregation of a developmental language disorder. *Cognition*, **39**, 1–50.

Grimshaw, J. (1997). Projection, heads, and optimality. *Linguistic Inquiry*, **28**, 373–422.

Halle, M. (1973). Prolegomena to a theory of word-formation. *Linguistic Inquiry*, **4**, 3–16.

Halle, M. and Marantz, A. (1993). Distributed morphology and the pieces of inflection. In *The view from Building 20* (eds K. Hale and S. J. Keyser), pp. 111–76. MIT Press, Cambridge, MA.

Hankamer, J. (1989). Morphological parsing and the lexicon. In *Lexical representation and process* (ed. W. D. Marslen-Wilson), pp. 392–408. MIT Press, Cambridge, MA.

Haviland, J. B. and Levinson, S. C. (ed.) (1994). *Spatial conceptualization in Mayan languages*. Special issue of *Linguistics*, **32** (4/5).

Hinrichs, E. (1985). *A compositional semantics for aktionsarten and NP reference in English*. Ph.D. thesis, Ohio State University.

Hirst, D. (1993). Detaching intonational phrases from syntactic structure. *Linguistic Inquiry*, **24**, 781–8.

Jackendoff, R. (1975). Morphological and semantic regularities in the lexicon. *Language*, **51**, 639–71.

Jackendoff, R. (1977). *X-Bar syntax: A study of phrase structure*. MIT Press, Cambridge, MA.

Jackendoff, R. (1983). *Semantics and cognition*. MIT Press, Cambridge, MA.

Jackendoff, R. (1987). *Consciousness and the computational mind*. MIT Press, Cambridge, MA.

Jackendoff, R. (1989). A comparison of rhythmic structures in music and language. In *Phonetics and phonology*, Vol. 1 (ed. P. Kiparsky and G. Youmans), pp. 15–44. Academic Press, New York.

Jackendoff, R. (1991). Parts and boundaries. *Cognition*, **41**, 9–45.

Jackendoff, R. (1992). *Languages of the mind*. MIT Press, Cambridge, MA.

Jackendoff, R. (1994). *Patterns in the mind*. Basic Books, New York.

Jackendoff, R. (1996). The proper treatment of measuring out, telicity, and perhaps even quantification in English. *Natural Language and Linguistic Theory*, **14**, 305–54.

Jackendoff, R. (1997) *The architecture of the language faculty*. MIT Press, Cambridge, MA.

Jaeger, J., Lockwood, A., Kemmerer, D., Van Valin, R., Murphy, B., and Khalek, H. (1996). A positron emission tomographic study of regular and irregular verb morphology in English. *Language*, **72**, 451–97.

Katz, J. J. (1977). A proper theory of names. *Philosophical Studies*, **31**, 1–80.

Kegl, J., Senghas, A., and Coppola, M. E. V. Creation through contact: Sign language emergence and sign language change in Nicaragua. In *Comparative grammatical change: The intersection of language acquisition, Creole genesis, and diachronic syntax* (ed. M. DeGraff). MIT Press, Cambridge, MA. (In press.)

Klein, W. and Perdue, C. (1997). The basic variety (or: Couldn't natural languages be much simpler?). *Second Language Research*, **13**, 301–47.

Klima, E. S. and Bellugi, U. (1979). *The signs of language*. Harvard University Press, Cambridge.

Krifka, M. (1992). Thematic relations as links between nominal reference and temporal constitution. In *Lexical matters* (eds I. Sag and A. Szabolcsi), pp. 29–54. CSLI Publications, Stanford.

Kuno, S. (1987). *Functional syntax*. University of Chicago Press, Chicago.

Lakoff, G. (1987). *Women, fire, and dangerous things*. University of Chicago Press, Chicago.

Lamb, S. (1966). *Outline of stratificational grammar*. Georgetown University Press, Washington.

Landau, B. and Jackendoff, R. (1993). 'What' and 'where' in spatial language and spatial cognition. *Behavioral and Brain Sciences*, **16**, 217–38.

Langacker, R. (1987). *Foundations of cognitive grammar*, Vol. 1. Stanford University Press, Stanford.

Lasnik, H. (1989). *Essays on anaphora*. Kluwer, Dordrecht.

Lenneberg, E. H. (1967). *Biological foundations of language*. Wiley, New York.

Lerdahl, F. and Jackendoff, R. (1983). *A generative theory of tonal music*. MIT Press, Cambridge, MA.

Levelt, W. J. M. (1989). *Speaking: From intention to articulation*. MIT Press, Cambridge, MA.

Levinson, S. (1987). Pragmatics and the grammar of anaphora. *Journal of Linguistics*, **23**, 379–434.

Marcus, G. F. (1998). Rethinking eliminative connectionism. *Cognitive Psychology*, **37**, 243–82.

Marr, D. (1982). *Vision*. Freeman, San Francisco.

Marslen-Wilson, W. D. and Tyler, L. (1987). Against modularity. In *Modularity in knowledge representation and natural-language understanding* (ed. J. L. Garfield), pp. 37–62. MIT Press, Cambridge, MA.

McCarthy, J. (1982). Prosodic structure and expletive infixation. *Language*, **58**, 574–90.

Mervis, C. B., Morris, C. A., Bertrand, J., and Robinson, B. F. (1997). Williams syndrome: Findings from an integrated research program. In *Neurodevelopmental disorders: Contributions to a new framework from the cognitive neurosciences* (ed. H. Tager-Flusberg). MIT Press, Cambridge, MA.

Michotte, A. (1954). *La perception de la causalité*, 2me édition. Publications Universitaires de Louvain.

Newport, E. (1990). Maturational constraints on language learning. *Cognitive Science*, **14**, 11–28.

Nicol, J., Fodor, J. D., and Swinney, D. (1994). Using cross-modal lexical decision tasks to investigate sentence processing. *Journal of Experimental Psychology: Learning, Memory, and Cognition*, **20**, 1220–38.

Oehrle, R. T. (1988). Multi-dimensional compositional functions as a basis for grammatical analysis. In *Categorial grammars and natural language structures* (ed. R. T. Oehrle, E. Bach, and D. Wheeler), pp. 349–90. Kluwer, Dordrecht.

Piñango, M., Zurif, E., and Jackendoff, R. (1999). Real-time processing implications of enriched composition at the syntax-semantics interface. *Journal of Psycholinguistic Research*.

Pinker, S. (1989). *Learnability and cognition: The acquisition of argument structure*. MIT Press, Cambridge, MA.

Pinker, S. (1994). *The language instinct*. William Morrow, New York.

Pinker, S. and Prince, A. (1988). On language and connectionism: Analysis of a parallel distributed processing model of language acquisition. *Cognition*, **26**, 195–267.

Pinker, S. and Prince, A. (1991). Regular and irregular morphology and the psychological status of rules of grammar. In *Proceedings of the seventeenth annual meeting of the Berkeley Linguistics Society* (ed. L. A. Sutton, C. Johnson, and R. Shields), pp. 230–51. Berkeley Linguistics Society.

Plunkett, K. and Marchman, V. (1993). From rote learning to system building: Acquiring verb morphology in children and a connectionist net. *Cognition*, **48**, 21–69.

Pollard, C. and Sag, I. (1987). *Information-based syntax and semantics*. CSLI Publications, Stanford.

Pollard, C. and Sag, I. (1994). *Head-driven phrase structure grammar*. University of Chicago Press.

Prince, A. and Smolensky, P. (1993). *Optimality theory: Constraint interaction in generative grammar*. Rutgers University Center for Cognitive Science, Piscataway, NJ.

Pustejovsky, J. (1995). *The generative lexicon*. MIT Press, Cambridge, MA.

Ross, J. R. (1967). *Constraints on variables in syntax*. Ph.D. thesis, MIT.

Rumelhart, D. and McClelland, J. (1986). On learning the past tenses of English verbs. In *Parallel distributed processing*, Vol. 2 (eds J. McClelland, D. Rumelhart, and the PDP Research Group), pp. 216–71. MIT Press, Cambridge, MA.

Sadock, J. M. (1991). *Autolexical syntax*. University of Chicago Press.

Selkirk, E. O. (1984). *Phonology and syntax: The relation between sound and structure*. MIT Press, Cambridge, MA.

Shastri, L. and Ajjanagadde, V. (1993). From simple associations to systematic reasoning: A connectionist representation of rules, variables, and dynamic bindings using temporal synchrony. *Behavioral and Brain Sciences*, **16**, 417–50.

Shieber, S. and Schabes, Y. (1991). Generation and synchronous tree adjoining grammars. *Journal of Computational Intelligence*, **7**, 220–28.

Singer, W., Engel, A. K., Kreiter, A. K., Munk, M. H. J., Neuenschwander, S., and Roelfsema, P. R. (1997). Neuronal assemblies: Necessity, signature, and detectability. *Trends in Cognitive Sciences*, **1**, 252–60.

Smith, E. and Medin, D. (1981). *Categories and concepts*. Harvard University Press, Cambridge.

Smith, N. and Tsimpli, I.-M. (1995). *The mind of a savant*. Blackwell, Oxford.

Talmy, L. (1985). Lexicalization patterns: Semantic structure in lexical forms. In *Grammatical categories and the lexicon* (ed. T. Shopen), pp. 57–149. Cambridge University Press, New York.

Tanenhaus, M. K., Spivey-Knowlton, M. J., Eberhard, K. M., and Sedivy, J. C. (1995). Integration of visual and linguistic information in spoken language comprehension. *Science*, **268**, 1632–4.

Treisman, A. (1988) Features and objects: The fourteenth Bartlett Memorial Lecture. *Quarterly Journal of Experimental Psychology*, **40A**, 201–37.

Van Hoek, K. (1995). Conceptual reference points: A cognitive grammar account of pronominal anaphora constraints. *Language*, **71**, 310–40.

Van Valin, R. D. (1994). Extraction restrictions, competing theories and the argument from the poverty of the stimulus. In *The reality of linguistic rules* (eds S. D. Lima, R. L. Corrigan, and G. K. Iverson), pp. 243–59. Benjamins, Amsterdam.

Van Valin, R. D. and LaPolla, R. J. (1997). *Syntax: Structure, meaning, and function.* Cambridge University Press.

Verkuyl, H. (1972). *On the compositional nature of the aspects.* Reidel, Dordrecht.

Verkuyl, H. (1993). *A theory of aspectuality: The interaction between temporal and atemporal structure.* Cambridge University Press.

Section 2

The cognitive architectures of language

4 Producing spoken language: a blueprint of the speaker

Willem J. M. Levelt

4.1 Design by evolution

The ability to speak is one of the basic ingredients of human life. We are social animals, deeply caring for the cohesion of our closest kin and for harmony in our daily personal contacts. From this perspective, the copious time idled away on chatting and gossiping is well spent. In all cultures, human bonding is largely achieved and maintained through speech. This is, clearly, species specific. Our closest relatives in nature, the Old World primates, regulate much of their bonding by way of grooming. And they don't stint on it, just as we don't stint on conversation: there are baboons that spend no less than 20% of their waking day on grooming. Dunbar (1996) showed that the amount of time devoted to social grooming is directly related to group size. How much time should *Homo sapiens* be spending on grooming if we had continued that linear trend? That depends on estimations of our typical group size. Hunter–gatherer societies are characteristically partitioned in clans of about 150 persons; in a clan all members know one another. The same number seems to hold for the first agricultural settlements. On this estimate, we should be grooming about 40% of our waking day in order to maintain group cohesion. That would be excessive, especially for an ape with so little fur. Dunbar argues that here the other pre-existing communicative system, the vocal one, began to accumulate increasing functionality in the management of social cohesion, ultimately developing into language. Speech, after all, is so much more effective in transmitting the intentions and motivations that shape our social mesh than is grooming. Chatting is not limited to dyads; it can be practised in larger groups. Talking is information sharing. The 'aboutness' of language enables us to jointly attend to the current state of coalitions and conflicts, to the intentions and deceptions of those present or absent. And, inherited from the old vocal call systems, the prosody of speech is richly expressive of emotion. We can only guess what the many inter-mediate evolutionary steps have been that bridge the enormous gap between the vocal call systems of Old World primates and the speech/language ability of our species. But there have been two landmark developments. First, the development of supralaryngeal articulation under neo-cortical control. As Ploog (1990) and Müller-Preuss and Ploog (1983) have shown, primate call systems are largely controlled by caudal midbrain structures; they are directly expressive of the animal's emotion, such as fear, aggression, alarm, contact seeking. The only neocortical input is from the (limbic) anterior cingulate gyrus. The latter makes calling marginally conditionable, as Sutton *et al.* (1974) have demonstrated in macaques; amplitude and duration of innate calls are to some extent malleable. Speech, however, is fully under neocortical control. Larynx, pharynx, tongue, and lip movements in speech are controlled by left and right primary motor cortex, which is an evolutionary novelty. In addition, the function of the supplementary/premotor area became vastly expanded as a repository of articulatory gestural programmes.

The old call system is largely one of phonation, involving the modulation of vocal fold activity. This prosodic–emotional call system became overlaid with a rich supralaryngeal system of modulation in the time/frequency domain, involving pharynx, tongue, oral and nasal cavities, and lips. MacNeilage (1998) argued that this articulatory control developed from pre-existing ingestion-related cyclicities such as chewing, sucking, licking, which attained communicative significance as tongue and lip smacks, etc. The resulting ability to articulate in rhythmic, syllabic patterns is at the heart of all spoken languages. It allows us to pack an elaborate code of temporally overlapping distinctive information from multiple sources (such as glottis, pharynx, velum, and oral cavity) into the time/frequency domain (Liberman 1996).

This first landmark development involves the evolution of a rich species-specific articulatory system, which can function under intentional control. The old vocal system is not lost, but integrated. Prosody keeps being expressive of emotion, controlled by the limbic system. But, in addition, we have direct control over the voice from the larynx motor area. It not only allows us to sing, but also to do such things as feigning emotion in speech.

The second landmark development in evolution is one of social competence. The emergence of Theory of Mind. One of the most noticeable differences between human brains and those of other primates is the much larger relative size of neocortex in man. Still, there is no obvious ecological variable (such as size of territory) that can account for this difference. Dunbar (1996) found one surprisingly reliable predictor of relative neocortex volume: group size. The human data nicely fit the general log/log trend. This invites the interpretation that a major function of neocortical expansion in hominids has been to refine social competence. And, indeed, the vast neocortical areas in our brains dedicated to person recognition (face, voice), to the recognition of intention (facial expression), and to the processing of speech and language seem to support that interpretation. How has *Homo sapiens* dealt with the ever growing social complexity of its clan? It was not enough to interpret actions of group members as intentional, as goal directed. This ability we share with chimpanzees. But in order to make intentional behaviour predictable and malleable, we developed the ability to interpret that behaviour as caused by beliefs, wishes, hopes, that is in terms of mental states that we attribute to the agents around us. In Premack and Woodruff's (1978) terms, we acquired a 'Theory of Mind' (ToM). Since Wimmer and Perner's (1983) germinal paper on this issue, a flood of research has demonstrated that already at the age of four, but probably earlier, children do attribute beliefs, wishes, and fears to others in order to explain and predict their behaviour. In contrast, chimpanzees show no more than rudiments of this ability (see Bogdan 1997 for a review). ToM allows us to build up complex knowledge structures about our social environment. Over and above registering Who did What to Whom, we encode such complex states of affairs as 'A knows that B did X', 'A believes B did X', 'A hopes B does X', 'A fears that B does X', 'A erroneously believes that B did X', but also 'A believes that B knows X', 'A doesn't know that B hopes X', and so on. And we act on such knowledge, as appears from our remarkable ability to cheat, feign, mislead, and lie.

These two landmark developments are still reflected in the ontogenesis and design of our speech producing system (Levelt 1998). There is, on the one hand, the innate articulatory system. It begins to mature around the seventh month, when the infant utters its first exemplars of repetitive and alternating babbles. Babbles are simple syllables and initially they are not specific to the mother tongue. In fact, even deaf children have a short, transient babbling period. But in the next four or five months, children build up a quite elaborate syllabary, that is increasingly tuned to the syllable repertoire of the native language (De Boysson-Bardies and Vihman 1991; Elbers 1982). On the other hand, there is the very early development of social competence. Like the perception of causality (Leslie and Keeble 1987), the perception of intentionality already matures during the first year of life and, as mentioned above, ToM is up and running by the age of four (Premack and Premack 1995). But what is most remarkable is that these two competences initially mature independently. The elaborate system of social and physical knowledge that the infant acquires during the first year of life simply doesn't interact with the maturation of the syllabary. Babbles are, initially, devoid of any meaning. It is purely articulatory–motor activity, reinforced by auditory feedback. The initially diffuse state of this articulatory system appears from the floundering of arms and feet that accompanies all babbling. It takes months before these motor systems become independently controllable. There is, apparently, enormous plasticity here. As Petitto and Marentette (1991) have shown, deaf children of deaf, signing parents develop 'hand babbling' during roughly the same period. In the absence of auditory feedback, gestural feedback stimulates the adjacent motor system to take over.

It is only around the age of 12 months that first, hesitant links are created between the articulatory and meaning systems. First spoken words are probably 'borrowed' from already established meaning relations in the auditory domain. As Elbers (1982) has shown, first spoken words are usually pre-existing babbles that resemble already meaningful spoken words in the infant's perceptual repertoire.

Even after the two systems become increasingly linked during the second year of life, their further development is controlled by system-internal pressure in the first place. When the articulatory system has acquired some 50 different proto-words, the child slowly but surely gets overwhelmed by keeping ever more similar articulatory patterns apart. The fascinating solution is to 'phonologize' the initial lexicon (C. Levelt 1994).

The child begins to focus on initial, final, and middle parts of proto-words, freely varying their place and manner of articulation. This creates a rich segmental/featural bookkeeping system which allows us to keep apart unlimited amounts of spoken word patterns. In other words, the articulatory system becomes bipartitioned into something like the original syllabary, a repository of articulatory–motor gestures, and a generative phonological coding system for keeping the record.

Similarly, the semantic system begins to get overtaxed during the third/fourth year of life. The child's initial multiword utterances easily express the focused semantic relations (who does what to whom, who possesses what, etc.) by word order; usually a functor word plus one or two argument terms will do. But inevitably, the child's messages become ever more complex. The emergence of ToM probably plays a major role here. There is, first, an increasing awareness of what information is shared with the interlocutor and what not. Not only focused, but also non-focused arguments may need expression; the child's utterances become less elliptical. Second, there is increasing similarity of semantic roles to be expressed in the same utterance. To express *A thinks that B knows X*, the roles of A and B are very similar; they are not easily mapped on the old agent/action type word order. The, again fascinating, development here is the 'syntactization' of semantics. Semantically similar roles are all mapped onto a very lean system of syntactic categories (nouns and verbs, and their modifiers, adjectives, adverbs to start with), and each word gets a (language-specific) syntactic frame, specifying how semantic roles should be assigned to various syntactic functions and allowing for the expression of recursive states of affairs that are so typical for social conceptualizations. Like the articulatory system, the semantic system becomes bipartitioned. Syntax develops as 'the poor man's semantics' for the child to systematize the expression of semantic roles, just as phonology is 'the poor man's phonetics', a lean system for keeping track of the subtle infinitude of articulatory patterns.

These two bipartitioned processing systems play drastically different roles in speech generation. The semantic/syntactic system is there to map the conceptualization one intends to express onto some linear, relational pattern of lexical items ('lemmas'), a 'surface structure', for short. The function of the phonological/phonetic system is to prepare a pattern of articulatory gestures whose execution can be recognized by an interlocutor as the expression of that surface structure, and hence of the underlying conceptualization. I will call it the 'articulatory score'. Although the skilled adult speaker normally shows fluent co-ordination of these two underlying systems, the rift between them never disappears entirely, as I will discuss in subsequent sections.

4.2 The blueprint

The pair of bipartitioned systems emerging from evolution and ontogeny form the core of the adult speech producing apparatus. They figure centrally in the 'blueprint of the speaker depicted in Fig. 4.1. From top to bottom the processing components (rectangles) perform the following functions:

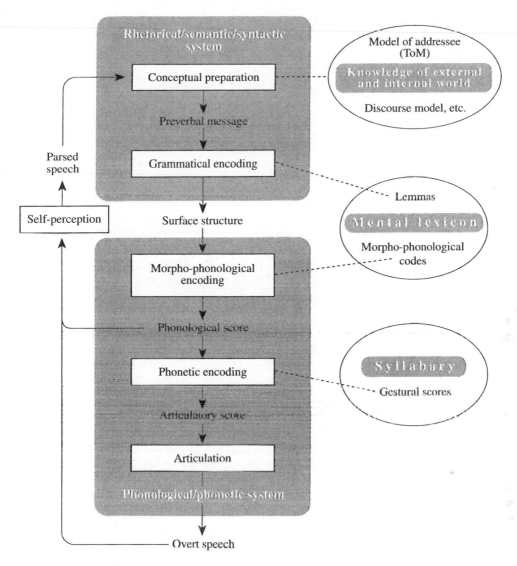

Fig. 4.1 A blueprint of the speaker.

Conceptual preparation Alone, or interactively with the interlocutor, the speaker generates a message, whose expression may affect the interlocutor as intended. Messages are conceptual structures of the kinds described above. In preparing a message, we exercise our social competence, minding the knowledge shared with our interlocutors, directing their attention to what is new or relevant, etc. This is accomplished by skilfully accessing various knowledge sources (knowledge sources are diagrammed as ellipses). The ultimate message is a conceptual structure, consisting of lexical concepts, that is concepts for which there are words in the language.

In this respect the message is more specific than just any conceptual structure. Not all concepts that we can entertain are lexical (think of a dead tree). But a message must eschew those, because it must be expressible in words. This is captured in the term 'preverbal message'.

Grammatical encoding   The lexical concepts in the message will activate the corresponding syntactic words ('lemmas') in the mental lexicon. Their selection makes the syntactic frames available that should correspond to the semantic functions and arguments in the message. In grammatical encoding, the speaker uses this lexical–syntactic information to build up the appropriate syntactic pattern, the 'surface structure'. And this is roughly done incrementally, that is 'from left to right'. This completes the processing of the first core system.

Morpho-phonological encoding   As soon as a lemma is selected, its form code becomes activated. The speaker gets access to the item's morphological and phonological composition. This is the basic material for building up phonological words. In particular, it is used to generate a word's syllabification in its syntactic context. For instance, the word *comprehend* is syllabified differently in the phrase *I-com-pre-hend* than in the phrase *I-com-pre-hen-dit*. In phonological encoding, the 'phonological score' of the utterance—its syllabified words, phrases and intonation pattern—is built up incrementally, dogging the steps of grammatical encoding.

Phonetic encoding   Each of the syllables in the phonological score must trigger an articulatory gesture. Here we finally reach the repository of syllabic gestures that the infant began to build up by the end of the first year of life. Sometimes new or infrequent syllables have to be composed, but mostly speakers can resort to their syllabary. Phonetic encoding is the incremental generation of the articulatory score of an utterance.

Articulation   The execution of the articulatory score by the laryngeal and supra-laryngeal apparatus ultimately produces the end product: overt speech.

Self-perception   When we speak we monitor our own output, both our overt speech and our internal speech. This output monitoring involves the same speech comprehension system that we use for listening to others (see Cutler and Clifton, Chapter 5). If we notice trouble in the speech we are producing, in particular trouble that may have communicative consequences, we can stop and correct ourselves.

This blueprint has a dual function. It is, first, a way of framing of what can be called a basic consensus in the language production literature. There is not much disagreement among researchers about the existence of such mechanisms as grammatical or phonological encoding. Neither is there much disagreement about the general flow of information from component to component. In particular, the notion of *incremental production* (Fry 1969; Garrett 1976; Kempen and Hoenkamp 1987) is generally accepted. It says that the next processing component in the general flow of information can start working on the still incomplete output of the current processor. A processing component will be triggered into action by any *fragment* of its characteristic input. As a consequence, the various processing components are normally simultaneously active, overlapping their processing as the tiles of a roof. When we are uttering a phrase, we are already organizing the content for the next phrase, etc. There are, certainly, many disagreements about details of the organization. This holds in particular for the amount and locus of feedback and interaction among components. But this doesn't affect the consensus on the general architecture of the system.

The second function of the blueprint is to frame a research programme. The ultimate aim of this research programme is to explain how we speak. The agenda can be read from the blueprint. We will have to produce and empirically test working models of the various functions performed by the speaker. How does grammatical encoding work? How does morpho-phonological encoding work? And so on. Also we will have to produce accounts for how the various processing components co-ordinate their activities in the generation of fluent speech. One thing should be clear about this research programme. Its advance will be measured by how well we succeed in producing empirically viable working models for smaller or larger aspects of the main processing components involved.[1]

In the following sections, I will discuss the various component functions in the above order, without losing sight of the ultimate purpose of the system, to map communicative intentions onto fluent speech.

4.3 Conceptual preparation in context

It is one thing to claim that language evolved for the management of cohesion in ever larger groups of humans, but quite another thing to specify in detail how that function is exercised in actual language use. In fact, that problem is horrendously complex, just as complex as the myriad linguistic transactions we perform in modern society. It cannot be the purpose of a working model to account for this complexity, just as it cannot be the purpose of a theory of thermodynamics to predict the weather. Still, advances in the analysis of language use provide an important sounding board for theories of speech production. The one major recent publication on language use, Clark (1996), analyses language use as a form of joint action. Participants in joint activities are aware of some goal of the activity and of their common ground. (In the above terms: they exercise their ToM to monitor the mutually shared state of information.) A production model should at least be 'on speaking terms' with core aspects of the QJ;co-ordination of action, such as details of turn-taking, managing politeness, inviting or initiating repair. A speaker's decision *what* to say, in our terms the speaker's *message*, should be understandable in terms of the current state of joint action.

The recent advances in the analysis of language use are, regrettably, not matched by similar advances in working models of conceptual preparation. In fact, the situation is hardly different from the state of affairs sketched in Levelt (1989). The progress has mostly been in the engineering of natural language generation, the development of models for artificial text generation (see, for instance, Pereira and Grosz 1994). Here I will only present a bare minimum of machinery that should go into the development of any working model, relating to the two core processes in the conceptual generation for speech: *macroplanning* and *microplanning*.

4.3.1 Macroplanning

This is the process by which the speaker decides what to say next. A working model will, of course, not deal with speakers' potential topics of discourse (see the *Encyclopaedia Britannica* for a short list). It will rather implement general principles of how subsequent moves within and between participants are sequenced. The central notion here is *discourse focus*. Given the communicative intention, the speaker will focus attention on something specific to be expressed (the 'current focus'). In moving to the next focus, the speaker's ToM is at work. The speaker will, normally, try to guide the intended focus shift of the interlocutor. Focus shifting is attention management at two levels. First, the speaker will monitor whether what should be said for realizing the communicative intention will be said. Second, the speaker will monitor whether the interlocutor is following the speech act.

The management of attention can be represented by the combination of a 'focus tree' (McCoy and Cheng 1991) and a stack. An overly simple example is presented in Fig. 4.2. When a speaker has as a goal to inform an interlocutor about the layout of the figure in the left panel, starting at the star, his focus tree may develop as shown in the right panel (in fact, it *will* develop that way, as numerous experiments have shown, cf. Levelt 1989). The ensuing text will, for instance, be:

> There is a star at the bottom. It has a line connection straight up to a triangle. From the triangle there is to the left a line to a square. Back to the triangle, there is a connection to the right to a circle. And the circle connects straight to the right to a diamond. That's it.

The focus tree has STAR at the top, the first focus of the speaker. The speaker's attention then moves to TRIANGLE. The speaker formulates how the triangle is placed with respect to the star. Now, the speaker has a choice, turning to the square or to the circle. The square is attended to first, but the speaker should keep in mind that a return must be made to the triangle. Hence, TRIANGLE is put on the stack. After mentioning the square, there are from there no further connections to attend to.

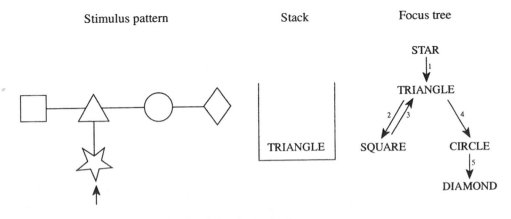

Fig. 4.2 Focus tree and stack for the description of a visual pattern.

The stack pops up TRIANGLE, and the speaker proceeds by describing the right branch of the figure.

What kind of principles govern the construction of focus trees? They are well-known for the description of networks such as the example case here (and much more complex ones). For that domain focus shift follows just three principles: *connectivity* (focus as the next item one that is connected to the currently focused item), *stack* (in the absence of a connecting item, turn to the top of the stack), and *simplest first* (if there is a choice, attend to the simplest item first). It is easy to see that the above description is predictable from these three principles. The working model can be found in Levelt (1982). Other types of discourse involve more and different principles, but hopefully it is a finite set (see especially Hovy 1994). As in the example, it is often the case that attention moves over a set of subgoals that must be fulfilled in order to realize the 'grand' communicative intention. Also, we will normally make an effort to guide the attention of our listeners in such a way that they can make the corresponding connections. For instance in the above description the phrase *Back to the triangle* is essential given the state of the listener's mental model—it was not yet known that TRIANGLE had become stacked. In fact, speech partners often intrude for clarification, redirecting attention to other parts of the focus tree, or inviting the growing of entirely new branches.

4.3.2 Microplanning

Conceptual preparation involves more than deciding what to say and in what order. Each bit of information needs further shaping in order to be formulated. Remember that the message is a particular kind of conceptual structure. In order for it to be expressible in words, its terminal elements must be lexical concepts. Also, it should incorporate the kind of semantic relations that are expressible in language, in particular function/argument and modification relations. Many conceptual structures don't have these properties. If they are focused for expression, we must somehow cast them in propositional form. Let us consider another spatial example, the state of affairs depicted in Fig. 4.3. Assume we intend to inform an interlocutor about this scene. Here are two of many possible descriptions:

(1)   There is a house with a tree to the left of it.

(2)   There is a tree with a house to the right of it.

In the first description, the position of the tree is related to that of the house; in the second description it is the other way round. But notice that the spatial scene itself is entirely neutral with respect to what should be related to what; it is the speaker's free choice to do it one way or another. The important point here is that *some* choice should be made. The speaker *must* take some perspective on the scene in order to express it in language. It should be cast as a propositional relation and the two options discussed here are LEFT (TREE, HOUSE) and RIGHT (HOUSE, TREE). The speaker may have pragmatic reasons for taking the one perspective rather than the other. For instance, a previously described scene showed a house with a man to the left of it.

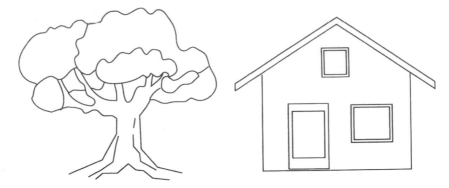

Fig. 4.3   Two different conceptualizations of a visual scene.

In that case description (1) is more appropriate to focus the listener on the difference with the previous scene (and the speaker will stress 'tree').

But there is more to perspective taking. There is also freedom in the choice of the lexical concepts that go into the propositional relation. That is easily demonstrated from still another description of the same scene:

(3)   There is a house with a tree to the right of it.

How can both (1) and (3) be veridical descriptions of the same scene? Does 'left' mean 'right'? No, it doesn't. The difference is in the kind of perspective the speaker takes. For description (1) the speaker takes so-called 'deictic' perspective, which is a relation between the perceiving speaker, the relatum (the house), and the referent (the tree). From the speaker's vantage point, the tree is to the left of the house. But for description (3) the speaker takes 'intrinsic' perspective. The relatum (the house) has an intrinsic orientation. It has, in particular, a front and a right and a left side. The tree is on the house's right side and this holds independently from the speaker's point of view. Hence, the same spatial relation between relatum HOUSE and referent TREE can be veridically expressed in terms of two converse lexical concepts, LEFT and RIGHT. And again, the speaker may have good pragmatic reasons for taking one or the other perspective (see Levelt 1996 for a full analysis).

In considering this example, we have not been dealing with a peculiar property of the terms 'left' and 'right', or of spatial descriptions in general. Rather, the example demonstrates an entirely general property of conceptual preparation for speech. Whatever the information to be expressed, there is always perspective taking. The information must be cast in propositional form (see below) and in terms of pragmatically appropriate lexical concepts. I can express the same kinship relation as *John is Peter's father* or as *Peter is John's son*; it will depend on what I want to focus as the new information for my listener. Also, I can refer to the same person as *my brother*, *my neighbour*, *my colleague*, etc., depending on whichever of my relations to the referent I want to highlight for my listener. Perspective taking is at the very core of all conceptual preparation for speech (Clark 1997).

What exactly is the propositional format of a message? There are various proposals in the literature (see, for instance, Levelt 1989; Zock 1997; Kempen 1999). The choice largely depends on the details of one's computational theory, which is not at issue in this chapter. But the information that goes into a message is essentially of four kinds, which can be exemplified from the speaker preparing the following utterance: *Poor Peter believes that the committee selected him*. This utterance is, first, about particular referents, namely Peter and the committee. The message should specify the referents and link them to the relevant 'state of affairs', that is in the discourse model. Second, there is some predication made about these referents (in particular that Peter believes something, namely that the committee selected him, Peter). We call this 'argument structure'. Arguments fulfil 'thematic roles' in the predication. Peter, for instance, is the *experiencer* of believing, and the *patient* of selecting. Other roles are *agent* (the one who causes something to happen), *actor* (the one who does something), *theme*, *source*, and *goal* (as in *the ball rolled from the chair to the table*), etc. Third, there may be specifications or modifications in a message. In the example message, Peter is further specified or modified as being pitiful or poor. An important kind of specification is quantification. A speaker could, for instance, refer to some apples or to all cows. Fourth, each message has a *mood*. It can be declarative, imperative, or interrogative. It is declarative when the speaker intends to assert something; it is imperative when the speaker wants to express the desirability of some state of affairs, and it is interrogative when the speaker wants to invite the interlocutor to provide some specific information. There is more that goes into a message (cf. Levelt 1989 for a fuller treatment), but this suffices for the present purposes. So, for *Poor Peter believes that the committee selected him*, the underlying message is something like this:[2]

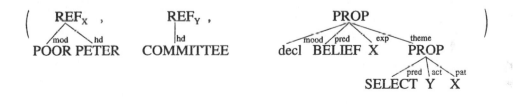

It says that there are two referents (X and Y), which are the arguments or thematic roles in a complex declarative proposition, where the predicate BELIEF has as experiencer X (*poor Peter*) and as theme argument the proposition that Y (*the committee*) selects X (*poor Peter*).

One final aspect of microplanning should be mentioned. Conceptual preparation is not language-independent. Languages differ, first, in their range of lexical concepts. Tzeltal, for instance, has no lexical concepts for LEFT and RIGHT, but only a superordinate concept TRAVERSE. A Tzeltal speaker's perspective taking for expressing a scene such as the one in Fig. 4.3 will therefore be different from that of a native Dutch or English speaker. Second, languages differ in the conceptual information that is *obligatorily* expressed. In a tense-marking language, such as English, the speaker must always think of the temporal properties of a state or event before expressing it. It is not enough for a speaker of English to prepare the above example message, because grammatical encoding will block on tense assignment. Should it become *Poor Peter believed the committee selected him* or *Poor Peter believes the committee selected him* or *Poor Peter believes the committee will select him*, etc? The speaker should mark the prevailing temporal relations (such as 'past') in the message, whether or not it is of any communicative significance. Speakers of Chinese or Javanese do not carry that conceptual burden, because their languages are not of the tense-marking kind. Slobin (1987) usefully called these language-dependent aspects of conceptual preparation 'thinking for speaking'.

4.4 Grammatical encoding

The blueprint in Fig. 4.1 depicts three properties of grammatical encoding: it takes preverbal messages as input, it produces surface structures as output, and it has access to the mental lexicon. Surface structures are syntactic in nature. They have a 'left-to-right' ordering of syntactic words ('lemmas' for short, such as nouns or verbs) that is incrementally generated from the emerging preverbal message. These lemmas are not evenly spread, but tend to be grouped in smaller or larger phrases. If a phrase contains a tensed verb, we call it a clause. Languages differ markedly in the kinds of syntactic relation they encode in a surface structure, but 'subject of' or various kinds of 'object of' are popular. One should not forget that syntax is the poor man's semantics. There are obviously different ways in which similar thematic role structures can be mapped onto a small number of syntactic relations. Also, languages differ in how they encode syntactic relations. Some languages, such as English, prefer to encode them in terms of phrasal relations and order relations within a sentence. Other languages prefer to mark lemmas in the surface structure for their syntactic function. Neither order nor hierarchy matter much, which leaves these features of surface structure available for pragmatic functions (such as directing the hearer's attention to particular elements in the sentence).

Whatever the differences between languages, the generation of surface structure is, for a large part, lexically driven. This means that in grammatical encoding a major operation is this: a lexical concept in the message (for instance SELECT in the above example) activates the corresponding lemma (*select*) in the mental lexicon. Upon its selection, the lemma's syntactic properties become available for further syntactic construction. The syntax of the lemma *select* is something like this:

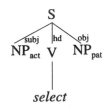

It says that *select* is a verb that should be the head of a sentence; it should have a subject NP and an object NP. Also, it specifies how these NPs should correspond to the thematic roles in the concept SELECT: the subject NP should link to the *actor* role in the message and the object NP to the *patient* argument.

Each lemma is the terminal node of such a syntactic tree and grammatical encoding consists of connecting these retrieved syntactic trees to form a surface structure that matches the input message. In a way grammatical encoding is like solving a set of simultaneous equations. Each lemma requires particular syntactic constraints from its environment and the emerging syntactic structure should simultaneously satisfy all these constraints.

But the mental lexicon contains more than just single-word lemmas. Some lexical concepts, or rather 'idiom concepts' map onto idioms of one kind or another. Idioms such as *to throw in the towel* are encoded by going from a single concept to a complex idiom lemma with its own syntactic properties. For instance, *to throw in the towel* is a verb lemma, but it doesn't allow for passivization (Jackendoff 1997). Probably, the amount of idiom and collocation in the mental lexicon is of the same order of magnitude as the number of words (a good source on idiom is Everaert *et al.* 1995).

Given that grammatical encoding is largely lexically driven (in this broader sense), I will first discuss lemma selection and then turn to further syntactic composition.

4.4.1 Lemma selection

Recent years have seen important progress in the theory of lemma access. Levelt (1989) still painted a bleak picture of inadequate theories, that all run into the so-called *hyperonym problem*. When the semantic conditions are met for selecting some lemma (for instance *horse*), the selection conditions are also met for selecting all of its hyperonyms (such as *mammal, animal*). But that hardly ever happens. Roelofs (1992, 1993) proposed a new model of lemma selection that does not run into this problem, and that also accounts for a wide range of old and new reaction time results. Meanwhile the computational model, now called WEAVER, has been extended to incorporate morpho-phonological encoding as well (Roelofs 1997*a,b*). Together, these developments have given us a new handle on the production lexicon. A comprehensive statement of this new theory of lexical access and its empirical foundations can be found in Levelt *et al.* (1999). Here I will present a small fragment of the production lexicon as modelled in WEAVER and then discuss how lemma selection is handled in the model. In later sections, other aspects of word production will also be discussed in reference to this fragment.

Figure 4.4 presents the lexical item 'select' in the lexical network. At the top, conceptual level the central node represents the lexical concept SELECT with its two thematic role slots X and Y for the one who selects and the entity selected. The semantics of the concept is represented by the set of labelled relations to other concepts in the network (both lexical and non-lexical ones). For instance, SELECT has CHOOSE as a superordinate concept (to select is to choose from among a number of similar entities), and has ELECT (to select by some democratic procedure) as a subordinate concept. The lexical concepts in the network are connected to the next stratum in the network, the lemma stratum. The concept node SELECT, for instance, is connected to a node at the lemma stratum that represents the lemma *select*. Its syntactic properties are represented by labelled connections to various nodes at this level. The network shows, for instance, that *select* is a transitive verb with two syntactic arguments x and y onto which the thematic roles X and Y should be mapped. In addition, it has a set of (variable) diacritic features (tense, aspect, number, and person) that can get fixed in various ways during grammatical encoding. At this level there are also nodes for all other lemmas, such as for *choose* and *elect*.

Lemma selection is modelled as follows. In the conceptual network, the target concept is in a state of activation. Its activation spreads to all semantically related concepts (for empirical evidence, see Levelt *et al.* 1991). Each active lexical concept also spreads part of its activation down to 'its' lemma, down in the lemma stratum. Lemma selection now becomes a probabilistic affair. During any smallest interval in time the probability of selecting the target lemma is its degree of activation divided by the total activation of all active lemmas in the stratum. This is called 'Luce's rule'. This probability allows one to compute the expected selection latency, which is the prediction tested in reaction-time experiments. An important property of the original model is that it will not make selection errors. The reason is that selection of any lemma must meet the condition that it entertains the correct sense relation to the conceptual level. If *examine* happens to win out by Luce's rule, it will not be selected, because its sense relation is not to SELECT.

The typical reaction-time experiment to test the model is one of picture naming. The subject names a picture of an action (such as a man drinking water) or of an object (such as a dog). But at some moment during the trial a distractor word is presented, either visually (in the centre of the picture) or acoustically as a spoken word. The distractor can be semantically related to the target word (for instance *eat* when the target word is 'drink', or *horse* when the target word is 'dog'), or it can be an unrelated word (such as *work* or *chair*, respectively). These distractors are supposed to activate 'their' lemmas in the lexical network and hence to reduce the Luce ratio. And indeed, reaction latencies are typically longer when there are distractors in the experiment. But the model further predicts that interference should be larger for semantically related distractors than for unrelated ones. Another prediction is that the difference will be maximal when picture and (visual) distractor coincide in time, diminishing with increasing stimulus onset asynchrony. The model gives an excellent fit both for the classical picture/word interference data of Glaser and Düngelhoff (1984) and for myriad new data obtained in further experiments (Roelofs 1992, 1993).

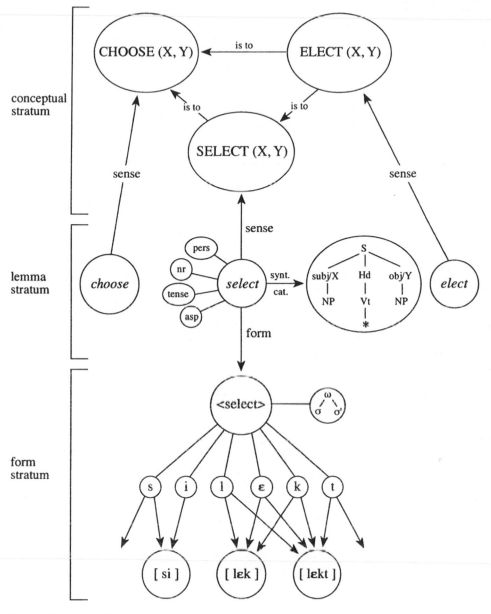

Fig. 4.4   Fragment of a lexical network.

4.4.2 Syntactic composition

As lemmas become available, triggered by the message, syntactic composition will be initiated. It consists essentially in coupling the syntactic fragments that come with the lemmas. This process is called 'unification'.[3] Let us consider how the syntactic fragments underlying *the committee selected him* are unified. Three lemmas are active here, *select*, *committee*, and *him*. Here are their syntactic tree fragments:

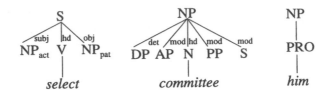

The tree fragment for *select* was introduced above. It has the node S as a root, and two NP nodes as feet. The syntactic fragment for *committee* is typical for any full noun. It has NP as the root node, which means that it must become the head of a noun phrase, and it has several feet. It allows, in particular, for a determiner phrase (in the present case the determiner will be the definite article *the*, whose selection I won't discuss here—but see Levelt 1989, p. 236 ff.). It can combine with an adjectival phrase (AP), as in *the big committee*, with a prepositional phrase, as in *the committee of the school*, and with a relative clause, as in *the committee that runs the soccer club*. The fragment for *him* is also head of an NP. How does the lemma *him* get triggered by the message? Remember that it refers back to referent X, POOR PETER. In the message, one of the occurrences of argument X will be marked as 'in focus'. That will tell the grammatical encoder that it should select a reduced, pronominal lemma for that occurrence of the lexical concept. Schmitt (1997) demonstrated experimentally that the full noun lemma does get selected in the process of pronominalization. In her model, the 'in focus' feature makes the connected pronoun lemma 'take over'.

Unification now consists in connecting roots to feet. In the example, the root node of *committee* can unify with the first NP foot of *select*. Similarly the root node of *him* can unify with the second NP foot of *select*. Feet that don't receive a unification get trimmed. If all this is done for our example, the following syntactic structure emerges:

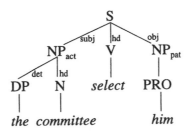

But how come that the NP fragment of *the committee* doesn't attach to the second NP foot of *select*? This is because of the linkage between syntactic functions and thematic roles. In the message COMMITTEE is the thematic actor role. The syntax of *select* requires that the subject NP expresses the actor. Also notice that *him* is the accusative pronoun, not *he* or *his*. When a pronoun unifies with an NP, it inherits the case of that NP. The object NP of *select* carries accusative case.

As everything else in speech production, the generation of syntax is an incremental process. As soon as one or a few fragments of the message, lexical concepts, become available the lemmas get selected and unification begins. The resulting syntax is, therefore, to some extent determined by the order in which lexical concepts come available. Highly accessible concepts tend to come first. In turn, they tend to 'claim' prominent syntactic positions. In particular human and animate referents are often the salient actors or agents in a message. For most verb lemmas these map onto the subject function (as in the *select* example). Less salient or less accessible concepts tend to end up with less prominent syntactic functions, such as direct object, indirect object, or oblique object. For more extensive reviews of grammatical encoding, see Levelt (1989) and Bock and Levelt (1994).

4.5 Morpho-phonological encoding

As lemmas become selected and positioned in the emerging surface structure, their morpho-phonological codes become available to the second main system involved in speech production, a system specialized in generating articulatory scores. Remember that in ontogeny the infant's articulatory system, the beginning syllabary, gets overtaxed when more and more protowords are acquired. The 'phonologization' of the articulatory memory codes solves this problem by providing the child with a discrete generative bookkeeping system for accessing the ever more similar articulatory codes. In the mature speech-producing system the articulatory score is accordingly generated in two steps. The speaker first uses the discrete memory codes to generate a 'phonological score', a score in terms of discrete segments and features, with phonological syllables as its basic units and with a simple hierarchy in terms of phonological words and phrases. Then these syllables are given gestural shape in their phrasal context, usually by retrieving their gestural scores from the old syllabary. It is at this second step that the limbic system still exerts direct control over speech generation. In this section we will consider the first, discrete step in the process.

4.5.1 Generating phonological words

Phonological words are the domains of syllabification. These domains may be larger or smaller than lexical words. For instance, most compound words syllabify per morpheme. Take *popart*, which is syllabified as *pop-art*, respecting the integrity of its morphemes 'pop' and 'art'; here the second /p/ is syllable-final and not aspirated. Compare this to the monomorphemic word *coupon*, which is syllabified as *cou-pon*, with the syllable-initial *p* aspirated. But the domain of syllabification is larger in so-called 'cliticization'. For instance, in the utterance *They will select us for the*

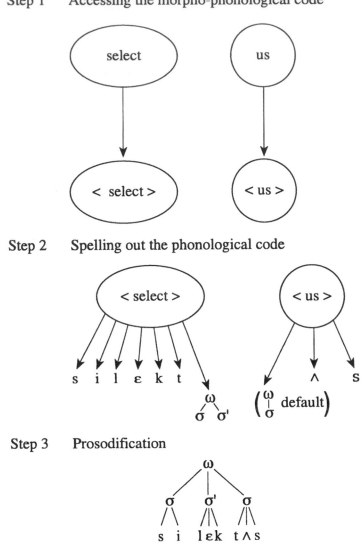

Fig. 4.5   Three steps in morpho-phonological encoding.

competition, the phrase *select us* is syllabified as *se-lec-tus*, ignoring the lexical boundary between *select* and *us*. I will use this latter example to discuss the generation of phonological words in stress-assigning languages such as English or Dutch.

Figure 4.5 presents a schema of phonological word generation. It involves three operations. First, as soon as a lemma gets selected for grammatical encoding, it spreads its activation to its morpho-phonological code in the lexicon. If the word is multimorphemic, such as 'popart', all morphemes get activated (namely both ⟨pop⟩ and ⟨art⟩). In the case of a monomorphemic word, such as 'select', the morpho-phonological code addressed is a single morpheme, ⟨select⟩ in this case. Second, the phonological code is spelled out. This involves two kinds of information. There is a spell-out of each morpheme's segments. For ⟨select⟩ the spelled out segments are /s/, /ɪ/, /l/, /ɛ/, /k/, and /t/. For ⟨us⟩ they are /ʌ/ and /s/. And there is a spell-out of a word's metrics, except when the metrics has default value. The spelled-out metrics consists of the word's number of syllables and the position of the stressed syllable. For ⟨select⟩ the metrics is σσ'. For ⟨us⟩ the metrics is just σ, but it is not spelled out because it is default metrics. What is default metrics? For stress-assigning languages a word has default stress if stress is on the first full-voweled syllable. For instance, the following words have default stress in English: *post, photo, marzipan*, but also *arrest, cadaver, potato*, whose first vowel is pronounced as a schwa. This has been called default metrics (by Meyer *et al.*, in preparation, see also Levelt *et al.* 1999) because most word tokens produced are of that type (85 per cent for English, 91 per cent for Dutch). Third, the spelled-out segments are incrementally grouped into syllables that attach to the spelled-out or composed metrics of the phonological word. It is only at this level of processing that (phonological) syllables appear in speech production. Syllables are not stored in the mental lexicon, because they are highly context-sensitive. For instance, the stressed part of the word 'select' will be syllabified as *lect* in *they will select Peter*, but as *lec* in *they selected Peter* or in *they will select us*. This context-sensitivity has the clear function to create optimally pronounceable utterances (imagine how hard it would be to say *they-se-lect-ed-Pe-ter*).

Let us now consider these three steps in somewhat more detail.

4.5.1.1 Accessing the morpho-phonological code

The first step in phonological encoding is most interesting from the neuroscience per-spective. It involves 'bridging the chasm' between two evolutionary distinct systems that come to meet during the first few years of life. There are several phenomena in adult speech production that still betray the underlying rift. A first such phenomenon is the so-called word-frequency effect. The phenomenon, discovered by Oldfield and Wing-field (1965), is that pictures with low-frequency names (such as *broom*) have longer naming latencies than ones with high-frequency names (such as *boat*). Wingfield (1968) showed that this was a genuine effect of lexical access; the latency differences didn't show up in picture recognition tests. With the development of a more detailed theory of lexical access (as exemplified in Fig. 4.4), it became important to find out at which stage of lexical access the word-frequency effect is generated. In a series of experiments, Jescheniak and Levelt (1994) showed that the effect is entirely due to word form access. The main problem in that study was to distinguish between the levels of lemma selection and of word form access as possible loci for the word frequency effect. A core experiment involved the production of homophones. Homophones are different words that sound the same. For most dialects of English high-frequency *more* and low-frequency *moor* are homophones. In our theory, their lexical analysis would be this:

(4)

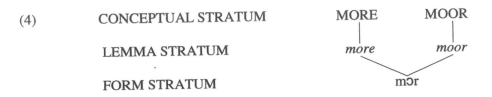

CONCEPTUAL STRATUM		MORE	MOOR
LEMMA STRATUM		more	moor
FORM STRATUM			mɔr

Now consider the latency of generating low-frequency *moor*. If the word-frequency effect resides at the lemma level, low-frequency *moor* should have a relatively long naming latency (i.e. as compared to the latency of high-frequency *more*). If, however, the word-frequency effect arises in accessing the word's phonological code /mɔr/, *more* and *moor* should have the same naming latency and, paradoxically, low-frequency *moor* should behave as a high-frequency item, because it inherits the accessing speed of its high-frequency twin *more*. In the reaction-time experiments the latter, quite non-trivial result was obtained. Hence, the word-frequency effect arises precisely in the speaker's effort to 'cross the rift' from the semantic/syntactic system to the phonological/articulatory system. In this connection it is particularly relevant that at least part of the word-frequency effect is in fact an age-of-acquisition effect (Carroll and White 1973; Morrison *et al.* 1992; Snodgrass and Yuditsky 1996; Brysbaert 1996). Crossing the rift is apparently easier for words that were acquired early, in part independently of their frequency of usage. These early, more stable connections were established in a brain with great plasticity.

Another well-known phenomenon also emerges at this step. It is the so-called tip-of-the-tongue (TOT for short) phenomenon. It can, at any time, happen in spontaneous speech that one suddenly blocks on a name of a person, plant, animal, instrument, or whatever. One knows that one knows the name, and one can even be aware of the word's beginning, stress pattern, or number of syllables. Again, the question is whether the effect arises at the lemma level or at the level of form access. Levelt (1989) pointed out that if TOT is a problem in accessing the word's form information, the speaker should have accessed the word's lemma. For gender-marking languages such as Dutch or Italian this means that in a TOT state the speaker might have access to the grammatical gender of a target noun. This is because gender is a lemma-level syntactic property of a noun. Viggliocco *et al.* (1997), in an elegant series of experiments, have shown that the prediction is borne out for Italian speakers; the finding was replicated by Caramazza and Miozzo (1997).

A related phenomenon in pathology is anomia. Anomic patients are handicapped in naming objects and they frequently enter TOT states when they speak. Badecker *et al.* (1995) tested an Italian patient who could hardly name any pictured object. But in all cases the patient knew the grammatical gender of the blocked target word. Anomia, or at least this particular kind of anomia, is a rupture of the apparently still somewhat fragile connection between the two main underlying systems in speech production. Of course, the TOT state in both healthy and anomic speakers is an 'off-line' state. After apparent trouble in on-line word access, the speaker is asked to ruminate about the lost word's gender or phonology. We do not know what exactly is involved in these metalinguistic processes; it is certainly premature to draw strong conclusions about the on-line process from whatever emerges in the off-line, metalinguistic state. The only way to find out whether lemma information (such as gender) is retrieved before word-form information (such as word initial segments) is to measure on-line. That is what Van Turennout *et al.* (1998) did in their study of lateralized readiness potential manifestations (LRPs) of gender and phoneme access in retrieving a picture's name. That study showed unequivocally that gender access precedes phoneme access, even in situations where that is disadvantageous to task performance.

All examples so far concerned the access of monomorphemic word forms. But what when a word is multimorphemic, such as *popart*? The present state of our theory is that all multimorphemic words have multiple morpho-phonological codes at the form level. Here are three examples, a compound, a derivation, and an inflection:

(5)　　LEMMA STRATUM　　*popart*　　　　*postal*　　　　*select*ₚᵣₒ𝑔ᵣ

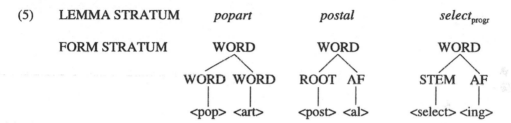

Notice that what is accessed from the lemma is not just a pair of morphemes, but an entire morphological structure to which the morphemes are attached. Levelt (1989, p. 321) called this 'morphological spell-out'. A decade ago the main evidence for the reality of such morphological structures in speech generation came from speech errors. For instance, in the exchange error *I hate rainn**g on a hitch**y day* (Shattuck-Hufnagel 1979), the stem *rain* and the root *hitch* got exchanged, leaving the affixes in place. But recently, Roelofs (1996*a,b*) began to study the generation of morphological structure by means of reaction-time experiments. In particular, he demonstrated that a word's morphemes are phonologically encoded in incremental fashion (e.g. first *pop*, then *art*). In addition, Janssen, Roelofs and Levelt (submitted) have shown that the spelled-out morphological structure functions as a frame to which the successive morphemes get attached. This holds at least for inflectional morphology, which specifies frames with slots for number and tense affixes.

4.5.1.2 Spelling out the phonological code

After having successfully traversed the Rubicon, the speaker can now begin to spell out the phonological codes of the monomorphemic or multimorphemic words that are involved in generating the phonological word. As mentioned above, the code consists of two parts, a segmental and a metrical code. In phonological speech errors, segmental errors (such as in *if you can change the p**i**rst part* in which /p/ is anticipated) are by far the most frequent. In the following, I will treat segments as basic units of spell-out. It should be added, though, that speech errors can involve consonant clusters, in particular when they are phonologically coherent (Berg 1989), such as in *steady state* sto*wel*. Therefore, Dell (1986) proposed that occasionally whole consonant clusters are spelled out. How 'phonologically complete' are spelled-out segments? Stemberger (1983, 1991*a,b*) and others have provided evidence that spelled-out segments can be phonologically underspecified or rather *abstract*. For instance, in one (of many) error induction experiments, Stemberger (1991*a*) showed that on target word pairs such as *sole foe* subjects more frequently erred in the direction of producing *fole* than in producing *soe*. Alveolar /s/ is phonologically unspecified for place. But in spelling out /f/ the marked place feature [labial] comes available. The 'unspecification' of /s/ cannot be inherited by /f/, but the [labial] specification of /f/ can be inherited by /s/, creating the error /f/. Whatever the precise characteristics of underspecification or 'abstractness' of spelled-out segmental units, they come with their contrastive features (the codes that the child develops during phonologization). This accounts for the robust finding that target segments and errors tend to share most of their distinctive features—such reflecting the underlying storage code.

The spell-out of segments can be primed. Schriefers *et al.* (1990) showed this by picture/word interference experiments. Here is an example. The subject has to name a picture of a sheep. At some moment during the trial, beginning with picture onset or a bit earlier or later, the subject hears a prime word. The prime can be phonologically related to the target (*sheet*) or unrelated (*nut*). A major finding was that naming latencies were shorter when the prime was related than when it was unrelated. The explanation is that the related prime (namely *sheet*) activates the corresponding segments in the target word's phonological code (/ʃ/ and /i:/), accelerating their spell-out. Meyer and Schriefers (1991) showed that not only begin-related primes (such as *sheet* for target 'sheep'), but also end-related primes (*deep* for 'sheep') facilitated the naming response. The same held for bisyllabic target words where either the first or the second syllable was shared with the prime (for instance *tailor* and *noble* for target 'table'). The gain in speed of spell-out is 'cashed in' later, during phonetic encoding, as will be discussed below.

Turning now to the spelling out of the metrical code, it should first be noticed that the code proposed above is rather lean. In the tradition of speech-error based research, the metrical code or 'frame' was supposed to be syllabified, with dedicated slots for onset, nucleus, and coda of each syllable in the word (see Levelt 1989 for a review of this position). The major argument for this view was the syllable position effect; in speech errors syllable onsets tend to exchange with syllable onsets, nuclei with nuclei, and codas with codas. If spelled-out segments would be marked for their slots in the frame (i.e. onset, nucleus, coda), they would automatically end up in the right syllable position, even in the case of error. But there are good reasons for not jumping to this conclusion. First, the syllable position constraint may be an epiphenomenon. Most segment errors (about 80 per cent in English) are word onset errors and word onsets are syllable onsets. Of the remaining 20 per cent a large part can be explained by the simple circumstance that when a consonant moves into the nucleus position the syllable will usually be unpronounceable (hence, that error will not occur). Finally, the above mentioned feature similarity between error and target will increase the probability that an error ends up in the same syllable position as the target. Vowels are more similar to vowels than to consonants, and syllable-final consonants are more similar to syllable-final consonants than to syllable-onset consonants.

The second reason is that a marking of spelled-out segments for their target position in a syllable will quite regularly interfere with phonological word encoding. How should the /t/ in ⟨select⟩ be marked? Marking as syllable-final would be alright for the encoding of *Whom do we select?*, with the syllabification *se-lect*. But it goes wrong for *They will select us*, with the syllabification *se-lec-tus*. Syllable positions are too variable and context dependent to be fixed codes in memory. Béland *et al.* (1990) suggested, as one of a few possible alternatives, that there is no frame whatsoever. And indeed, one should seriously consider whether a phonological word's metrical structure wouldn't automatically emerge from concatenating successive segments into (weak or strong) syllables. This might in particular work for a language such as French, which has word-final stress across the bank. There are, however, empirical arguments (Roelofs and Meyer 1997; Levelt *et al.* 1999) to assume that for stress-assigning languages such as Dutch and English, the spelled-out metrical frame does play a role.

4.5.1.3 Prosodification
The final step in phonological word construction is the incremental generation of its syllabic and metrical structure. How does this work for the phonological word *select us* in the utterance *They will select us*? Spell-out of the two lexical elements *select* and *us* left us with the following ingredients: two ordered sets of segments: /s/, /i/, /l/, /ɛ/, /k/, /t/ and /ʌ/, /s/, and one non-default metrical pattern for *select*: σσ'. That *select* and *us* should form one phonological word, that is *us* should cliticize to the head word *select* is syntactically conditioned in the surface structure. The procedure consists in incrementally attaching the ordered string of spelled-out segments to syllable nodes, either nodes in the non-default spelled-out metrical frame, or new nodes to be created on-line. This is, in short, the course of action for the present example (for more detail, see Levelt and Wheeldon 1994):

(1)   (2)   (3)   (4)   (5)   (6)

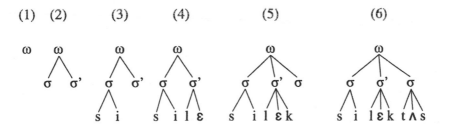

First, (1) the phonological word root ω is set up. Then (2) the spelled out metrics of *select* is attached to this root. In case there is no spelled-out metrical pattern, that is in the default case, a first syllable node is attached to the root. More specifically, a condition for opening a new syllable node is that there is a (further) vowel coming up; the system can look ahead up till the next vowel. Next (3) /s/ is attached to the leftmost syllable node, followed by /i/. Then (4) /l/ is to be attached, but attachment of a consonant is syllable-initial by default (this is called the 'maximization of onset' rule). Hence, it should attach to the next syllable. In case there would be no next syllable node, that is in case of default metrics, a new syllable node is opened. This is allowed because there is a further vowel in the offing. The new vowel element /ɛ/ will as a nucleus attach to the same syllable. Then (5) /k/ is up for attachment. Default attachment of a consonant is to syllable onset. A new syllable node is created in view of the upcoming vowel /ʌ/ down the line. However, /k/ cannot be attached to the syllable onset position, because /kt/ is not a legal syllable onset in English (it violates the so-called sonority gradient rule). Hence /k/ attaches as offset to the current syllable. Next (6) /t/ will attach as onset to the next syllable, followed by vowel /ʌ/. No new syllable node can be set up to attach the final consonant /s/ to, because there is no further vowel in the offing and /s/ attaches as offset to the current syllable.

The example shows how successive phonological syllables are created on the fly as successive segments attach to syllable nodes. Syllable nodes have either been spelled out or they are newly created every time a further vowel is coming up. Spelled-out segments are not *a priori* marked for syllable positions. For instance, the example shows that though consonants have a predilection for syllable-onset positions, they may well end up in syllable-final position depending on the prevailing context.

What is the evidence for this incremental prosodification process? There are, in particular, two claims in the theory. The first one is that the process is incremental, segment by segment, syllable by syllable. The second is that it makes use of spelled-out metrical information in case the metrics is not default. The evidence for these two claims stems from a host of experiments by Meyer and Roelofs. It is, however, beyond the scope of the present chapter to review that work in detail. The reader is referred to the comprehensive review in Levelt *et al.* (1999).

This completes our consideration of morpho-phonological encoding. The output of this complex process is a phonological, syllabified word. Usually, the phonological word is part of a larger utterance, as in the worked-out example above; the phonological word *select us* appears in the larger utterance *They will select us*. We will now turn to this larger context.

4.6 Generating utterance prosody

Phonological words are parts of phonological phrases, and phonological phrases are parts of still larger units, intonational phrases. In the following we will consider the production of phonological and intonational phrases, respectively. These are complex issues, deserving extensive treatment, but at the same time relatively little is known about the underlying generating process. For both types of phrase I will address just two points: what kind of unit is the phrase, and can it be incrementally generated?

4.6.1 Generating phonological phrases

Any sentence-like utterance is a concatenation of metrical units that are called phonological phrases. The first such phrase starts at the beginning of the utterance and ends right after the first lexical head of a noun phrase (NP), a verb phrase (VP), or an adverbial phrase (AP). The next phonological phrase begins just there and ends after the next such lexical head, and so recursively; any remaining tail after the last lexical head is added to the last phonological phrase. Here is an example (from Nabokov's *Bend Sinister*):

> *Claudina[1]/ was standing[2]/ quite still[3]/ in the middle[4]/ of the dining room[5]/ where he had left her[6]/.*

In the surface structure of this sentence we have the following heads of NP, VP, or AP: *Claudina* (head of NP), *standing* (head of VP), *still* (head of AP), *middle* (head of NP), *dining room* (head of NP), *he* (head of NP), *left* (head of VP), and *her* (head of NP). However, *he* and *her* are anaphors; they are not 'full' lexical heads. Each full lexical head ends a phonological phrase, except for the last one, *left*. Here the remaining tail (*her*) is added to the last phrase. Phonological phrases are metrical units in utterance production, phonological output packages, as Bock (1982), Garrett (1982), and Van Wijk (1989) have suggested.

A characteristic property of this metrical unit is its so-called 'nuclear stress'; the head word in a phonological phrase receives more stress than any of the others. That can be quite informative for the listener, because these heads-of-phrase are the syntactic 'pegs' for the sentence's interpretation. But a few qualifications are necessary. First, nuclear stress can be overridden by focal stress. For instance, in the third phrase above, *quite still*, the speaker can focus *quite*, which will then receive more stress than *still*. Second, phonological phrases are rather 'soft' packages. Selkirk (1984) and others have argued that boundaries between phonological phrases vary in depth and that speakers often blend adjacent phonological phrases with shallow borders into larger ones. In the example it would be quite normal for a speaker to pronounce *in the middle of the dining room* as a single phonological phrase. In other words, phonological phrase boundaries are break *options* rather than breaks.

Time and again we have discussed that we speak incrementally; a processing component will be triggered into action by any *fragment* of its characteristic input. The characteristic input for the generation of utterance prosody is the growing surface structure. How far should the speaker minimally look ahead in the surface structure to generate a phonological phrase? Not very far. When a new phrase begins, the speaker can process lemma after lemma without any look ahead. As soon as a head-of-phrase lemma appears, nuclear stress should be assigned and normally the phrase should be completed. The one complication is the tail. Coming to the end of a sentence, the speaker should not open a new phonological phrase after the last lexical head word. That means that there must be so much surface structure in the window that the appearance of a new lexical head word can be excluded. Levelt (1989) argues that that is a very short stretch. This being said, it does not mean that speakers *cannot* or *will not* look ahead further than a lemma or two. In fact, they probably often do, as will be discussed in the next section.

4.6.2 Generating intonational phrases

An intonational phrase is characterized by its pitch movement, and pitch movement is produced by the vocal tract. As we have seen, the vocal tract is the 'old' system in primate sound communication. Our closest relatives in evolution can phonate but hardly articulate. Their phonation, moreover, is emotional in character; it is under the control of the limbic system. Although our phonation has further evolved as a voluntary system under the control of the cortical face area and the supplementary motor area, our dorsal midbrain area (around the anterior sulcus cinguli) that, just as in other mammals, mediates vocal fold movements, has not lost its old connection to the limbic system. Although emotion can be expressed at all levels, from the semantic to the prosodic, the most immediate expression of emotion in speech is through pitch movement. The voluntary control of pitch movement makes it possible for us to feign emotion in our intonation, but the reverse is much more common; what we can hide in our wording is easily given away in our intonation.

The intonational phrase (IP) is a sense unit. It consists of one or more phonological phrases and often spans the whole utterance. It is characterized by its pitch contour. The intonational meaning of an IP is largely carried by what is called its *nuclear tone*. The nucleus of an IP is the syllable that receives the most prominent *pitch accent*. This pitch movement is the beginning of the nuclear tone. The tone ends at the last syllable of the IP with a *boundary tone*. These two pitch movements can be several syllables apart, or they can be made on the same (final) syllable of the IP. Figure 4.6a and b show these two cases for the sentences *They've a bear* and *They've a polar bear, I believe*, for instance uttered in response to the question *Isn't that a very small zoo?* This tone is called the 'fall–rise'. It begins slightly up at the nuclear syllable, drops over that syllable, only to rise up again at the final, boundary syllable. This tone expresses some reservation. There is a contrast to an apparent opinion that the speaker disagrees with. Compare this to the tone in Fig. 4.6c, which is called 'high–fall'. It could be a response to the question *What's their largest animal?* The tone starts high up from the preceding tune and drops all the way to the base level, just to stay there without further boundary movement. This is a very common tone. It expresses seriousness in a matter-of-fact way. It is typically used for declarative statements. The two parts of the tone fulfil different functions. The nuclear pitch movement is a focusing device, drawing the listener's attention to the one focused word in the IP. In addition it expresses illocutionary force, such as matter-of-factness, reassurement, opposition, etc. The boundary tone has a different kind of illocutionary function. It either rounds up, or it signals non-finality. Non-finality is probably universally expressed in a rising boundary tone. This is clearest in rising question intonation. But it also works in the Fig. 4.6a and b examples. The listener is invited to correct his opinion, and indeed a connecting move like *Oh, I didn't know that* would be appropriate. In these cases, rising intonation

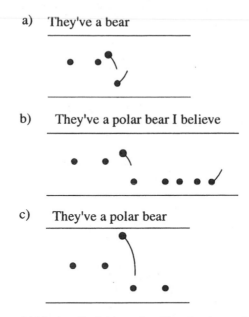

a)   They've a bear

b)   They've a polar bear I believe

c)   They've a polar bear

Fig. 4.6   Three nuclear tones: (a) fall–rise with pitch accent and boundary tone on the same syllable; (b) fall–rise with pitch accent and boundary tone on different syllables; (c) high–fall. (Levelt, W. J. M. (1989). *Speaking: From intention to articulation.* MIT Press, Cambridge, MA, reproduced by permission.)

invites the interlocutor to make some move. But a speaker can also use a rising, non-final boundary tone to signal that there is more to come, that the utterance is not yet finished. This is particularly clear in so-called 'listing intonation', for instance when the speaker instructs: *I want you to buy a box of beer* (rise), *a bag of ice* (rise), *and a bottle of Chardonay* (fall). The first two IPs here signal that there is more to come, only the third and last one rounds up the instruction. A steady or falling boundary tone (see also Fig. 4.6c) signals completeness; the case is closed. Each language provides a small number of basic tones, each with its own illocutionary meaning. We discussed two English tones here ('fall–rise' and 'high–fall'), but there are more of them (see Levelt 1989; Cruttenden 1986).

The generation of the nuclear tone doesn't require much look-ahead on the part of the listener. Nuclear pitch movement is made on the stressed syllable of the focused element. That lemma is marked as such in the surface structure. That information can be used as soon as it comes up for phonological encoding. The boundary tone is always at the IP's final syllable, which needs a one-syllable look-ahead to be spotted by the speaker. However, intonation can become much more euphonious when the speaker is early aware of upcoming foci. In euphonious speech, successive focusing pitch movements are often connected by a single pitch contour, for instance in an utterance like *I hópe to be présent at your birthday*. Here the pitch accents on *hope* and *present* can be made as two rise–falls, but also as a rise on *hope* and a subsequent fall on *present*.

The latter so-called 'hat-pattern' sounds a lot better. Empirical evidence for such larger stretches of intonational planning can be found in Blaauw (1995).

4.7 Phonetic encoding and articulation

The output of phonological encoding is a *phonological score* (see Fig. 4.1). The phonological score is an incremental pattern of phonological syllables, metrically grouped and marked for the tones they are participating in. This score must be phonetically realized. Remember that the purpose of the phonological/phonetic system is to prepare a sequence of articulatory gestures. These are patterns of syllabic gestures with their roots in the syllabary that began to develop by the end of the first year of life. These gestural scores have to be addressed by phonological codes and they have various free parameters to be set, both local and global ones, such as duration, amplitude, pitch movement, key, and register (see below).

How are gestural syllable scores addressed or constructed? Languages differ substantially in the number of syllables they use. Chinese and Japanese have no more than a few hundred syllables. Speakers of languages such as these have intensive experience with the articulation of all of their language's syllables. Hence, it is not far-fetched to assume that all of these syllables are stored as gestural scores, maybe in the supplementary motor area, which is the repository of frequently used motor routines (Rizzolatti and Gentilucci 1988). But what about languages such as English or Dutch that use more than 12 000 different syllables? Would the native speaker have them all

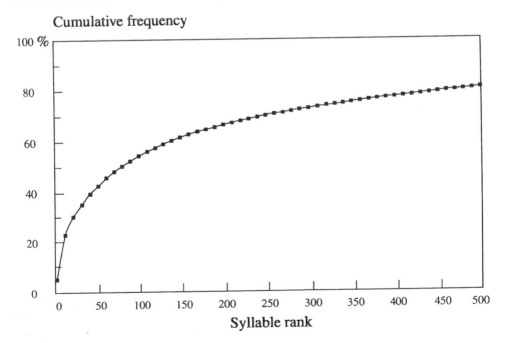

Fig. 4.7   Cumulative frequency distribution of the 500 most frequent syllables of English.

stored as motor routines? We don't know, but there are some relevant statistics that can qualify the question. Figure 4.7 shows the cumulative statistics of syllables used in running English texts. The figure shows that an English speaker produces 50 per cent of his speech with no more than 80 very high-frequent syllables (such as /ə/, /rɪ/, /ðə/, /tu:/, /lI/) and no less than 80 per cent with just 500 different syllables. The question need not be whether all odd 12 000 syllables are stored as gestures, but whether the small number of frequently used syllables are. That would do most of the work. The other syllables may or may not be stored. In the latter case one would need a mechanism that can compute new syllabic gestures.

Addressing a gesture in the syllabary begins during segmental spell-out (see section 4.5.1). Each spelled-out segment, for instance the first /l/ of *select* (see Fig. 4.4), activates all syllables in the syllabary that contain the segment. For instance, /l/ not only activates the phonetic gestural score [lɛk], but also [lɛkt], [lɪst], [bɔ:l], [əʊld], etc. Similarly, /ɛ/ activates not only [lɛk], but also such syllables as [lɛkt], [tɛn], etc. Because the three spelled-out segments /l/, /ɛ/, and /k/ will all activate [lɛk], it will accumulate a relatively high degree of activation. Still, its selection must wait till the phonological syllable /lɛk/ has been created in the incremental syllabification process. Only then the system can establish whether the highly activated syllable score [lɛk] is indeed the correct target. This will be so when the phrase *select us* is constructed, as we have seen, but not when *Whom do we select?* is being generated (see Roelofs 1997 for more details). It was noted in section 4.5.1 that the production of a word can be facilitated by presenting the speaker with an auditory prime, any segment or syllable of the target word. This speeds up the spell-out of the corresponding segments. But that, in turn, speeds up the activation of the target gestural scores in the syllabary. It is, eventually, at this level of phonetic encoding that the priming of segmental spell-out is 'cashed in'. The word's phonetic syllables come faster available, speeding up the spoken response.

A syllable's stored gestural score is still a rather abstract entity. It specifies which articulatory goals have to be successively achieved (Browman and Goldstein 1992), such as a tongue tip closure of the oral cavity at the onset of [lɛk]. There are also parameters to be set, such as for amplitude and pitch movement. They, in turn, depend on the metrical and intonational properties of the larger phrase. In *They'll select us*, for instance, [lɛk] will carry the main accent in the phonological word. Hence it will be stressed, which will be realized in the settings for the amplitude and duration of the vocal part of the gesture. Also, [lɛk] will be the nucleus of the intonational phrase. Depending on the nuclear tone, parameters for its pitch movement will be set (for instance high start, full fall).

Apart from such local settings of gestural parameters, there are also global settings, in particular for *key* and *register*. Key is the range of movement in a phonological phrase. The same pitch movement can be made with a relatively small pitch excursion or with sweeping, full-octave range of movement. This choice of key not only depends on whether the speaker wants to foreground or background the phrase's information for the interlocutor, it is also under emotional control, larger keys expressing more ego-involvement in what is said. Register is the pitch level of the baseline of intonation, the 'fall-back pitch' of intonational phrases. Whether desired or not, a high register universally expresses vulnerability, helplessness, or special deference. The origin of that impression may be the child's very high speech register. The articulatory score for an utterance is complete when all of these free parameters have been set.

In this chapter I will not go into the intricacies of articulation. A major theoretical and empirical issue is how the abstract gestural tasks are executed by the laryngeal and supralaryngeal systems. The same articulatory task can be performed in many different ways. Producing [l] in [lɛk] can be entirely realized by tongue tip movement. But the oral closure can, in part, be brought about by lifting the jaw, thereby pushing the tongue upward. Similarly lip closure in pronouncing [pɪt] can be realized by moving the upper lip, the lower lip, the jaw, or all three to some extent. In other words, there are many more degrees of freedom than there are articulatory tasks in the execution of a syllabic gesture. Theories differ in how they handle this reduction problem. Usually there is some kind of economy principle involved; how can the task be performed with a minimum of effort? For reviews of these matters, see Levelt (1989) and especially Kent *et al.* (1996).

4.8 Self-monitoring

There is no more complex cognitive–motor activity than speaking. The semantic/syntactic system has to map states of affairs in various modalities onto syntactically organized strings of lemmas. These come at a speed of two to three per second in normal conversation. The phonological/phonetic system must map this abstract surface structure onto the high-speed articulatory movements (10–15 consonants and vowels per second) that generate overt speech. Much can go wrong here, as appears from various kinds of speech errors that we make. But most surprising is how little goes wrong. Although error statistics differ, most of us do not make many more errors than about one per thousand words. The effort of keeping control is more apparent from hesitations, dysfluencies, and fresh starts that abound in normal speech. We are continuously monitoring what we produce or what we are about to produce. How is this monitoring system organized?

Let us return once more to the two systems that underlie our speech production, the semantic/syntactic system and the phonological/phonetic system. Both systems are subject to self-monitoring, but probably in different ways. Here is an example of self-monitoring within the former system, resulting in self-repair (from Schegloff 1979):

(6)   Tell me, uh what—d'you need a hot sauce?

The speaker probably started out saying *what do you need?*, but then decided to rather issue a yes/no question. This led to interruption of the original utterance and a fresh start. As Levelt (1989, p. 460) puts it: 'The speaker can directly monitor the messages he prepares for expression, and he may reject a message before or after its formulation has started'. There has never been serious doubt that the conceptual system is as much involved in the production as the perception of speech; it is a shared system. Nobody ever proposed that the message is first conceptually produced and then (more or less incrementally) conceptually parsed or perceived as a way of self-monitoring. But the story is less obvious for the control of syntactic operations, as in the following case (from Levelt and Cutler 1983):

(7)   What things are this kid—is this kid going to say incorrectly?

Opinions differ about the question whether our systems for generating syntax and for syntactic parsing are shared or different. Levelt *et al.* (1999) opted for sharing: 'the perceptual and production networks coincide from the lemma level upwards'. That paper dealt with the generation of words, but consistency may require to extend the claim to all processing within the concept/lemma domain. Kempen (1997) provided further arguments in support of the shared system claim. Still, the issue is at present unsettled.

Almost certainly not shared is the phonological/phonetic system. It simply cannot be the case that the neuromotor system that generates spoken-word gestures is identical to the neuroacoustic system that parses the auditory speech signal. Certainly, there will exist important connections between these systems, as Liberman has time and again claimed. It may in particular be the case that it is the listener's business to detect the articulatory gestures that produced the acoustic wave (Liberman 1996). But the neural substrate for acoustic/phonetic analysis is primarily the left temporal lobe (Démonet *et al.* 1992), whereas the phonetic generation of speech is largely controlled by the motor and premotor areas of the frontal lobe and the left central gyrus of the insula (Dronkers, 1996). Hence, for the speaker who made the error *unut* in (8):

(8)   A unut—a unit from the yellow dot.

and corrected it, the most likely route of self-monitoring was through the speech perception system. The speaker either heard the error in listening to his own overt speech or there was some internal representation, let us call it 'internal speech', that the speaker had been attending to. Levelt (1983) called this feedback mechanism the 'perceptual loop', which has an external branch (via overt speech) and an internal one (via internal speech). McGuire *et al.* (1996) provided support for this perceptual loop hypothesis by showing in a PET study that the monitoring of self-generated speech involves the temporal cortices, engaging areas concerned with the processing of externally presented speech.

Still, the notion of 'internal speech' is notoriously vague. What kind of representation is the inner voice that we can attend to in self-monitoring? The choice is essentially given in the previous sections. There are three alternatives. The internal representation monitored for in the internal loop can be (i) the spelled-out phonological code—see Fig. 4.5, step 2; (ii) the phonological score—see Fig. 4.5, step 3; or (iii) the articulatory score—see section 4.7. Wheeldon and Levelt (1995) developed a self-monitoring task for distinguishing between these three alternatives. In the task the (Dutch) subject was given a target segment (or string), for instance the consonant /l/. The subject would then hear an English word (example: *hitch hiker*) whose translation equivalent in Dutch was known to the subject (for the example, the translation equivalent is *lifter*). The task was not to overtly produce the Dutch word in response to the English word stimulus, but merely to check whether the Dutch translation equivalent contains the target segment and, if so, to push the response button. In this task, the subject supposedly checks the internally generated Dutch response word for the presence of the target segment. Figure 4.8, left upper panel, presents average response latencies when monitoring for segments that can be in syllable-onset position of the first or second syllable in bisyllabic words. The detection latencies for targets in these two positions differ by about 110 ms.

Is the speaker monitoring whatever there is in the articulatory buffer, that is the articulatory score (as proposed by Levelt 1989)? This can be tested by filling the buffer with different materials during the execution of the experimental task. Following Baddeley *et al.* (1984), we had the subject count aloud during execution of their detection task. The right upper panel of Fig. 4.8 gives the results for this condition. Response latencies were, of course, somewhat longer and the difference between monitoring for the two target segment positions was somewhat reduced, but a substantial, highly significant effect remained. Hence, the internal speech monitored must involve a representation different from the articulatory score. How to distinguish between the two remaining alternatives? Remember that the spelled-out phonological code is not yet syllabified; the phonological word, however, is syllabified. Hence, we tested whether internal speech monitoring is syllable-sensitive. Subjects were now given consonant/vowel (CV) or consonant/vowel/consonant (CVC) targets to monitor. For instance, the target could be /ma:/ for one block of trials and /ma:x/ for another block. For the Dutch internal response word *ma-gen* ('stomachs') the former target coincides with the first syllable, whereas for the word *maag-den* ('virgins') the latter target coincides with the first syllable. Still both targets occur in both words. The subjects' reaction times are presented in the lower panel of Fig. 4.8. It shows a full cross-over effect. Subjects are much faster when the target coincides with the first syllable than when it doesn't. In other words, the subjects monitored a syllabified representation. This excludes alternative (i) above, the spelled-out phonological code, and the conclusion is that internal self-monitoring runs on the phonological score, the string of syllabified phonological words.

Given the evidence for an internal perceptual loop in phonetic/phonological self-monitoring, it is hard to imagine that the system would use this loop exclusively for detecting word form trouble. It would always have to stop the perceptual parse at some phonological level of processing. But speech perception is reflex-like and it will rush forth into the syntactic/semantic domain. So even if there exists a self-contained monitoring facility within the semantic/syntactic system of the type Kempen (1999) proposes, then the feedback loop presented in the blueprint of Fig. 4.1 will keep contributing to semantic/syntactic self-monitoring as well.

4.9 Conclusion: relevance for brain-imaging research

Nothing is more useful for functional brain-imaging than an explicit processing theory. The subtraction method, and variants thereof, require the theoretical isolation

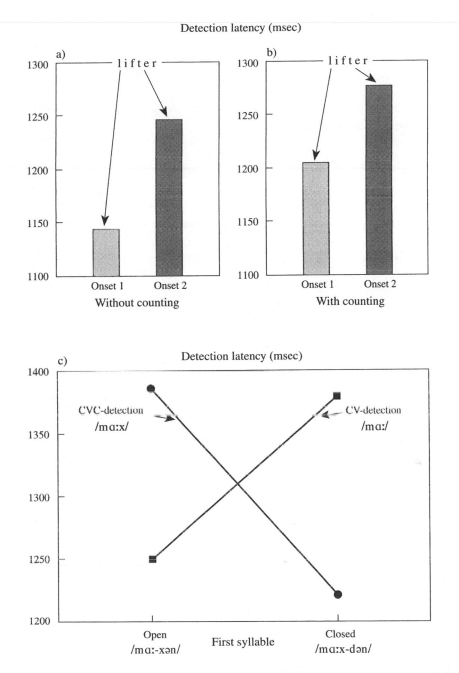

Fig. 4.8 Latencies for monitoring targets in internal speech: (a) syllable-initial consonant targets in bisyllabíc words; (b) same, but with concurrent counting aloud; (c) CV and CVC targets that either do or do not correspond to the word-initial syllable.

of particular processing components that are involved in the execution of a task. But intuition doesn't suffice here. The componential processing analysis of any complex task is a research programme in itself. The present chapter exemplifies this for speaking tasks. A quarter century ago only a small minority of the components discussed in the previous sections had been recognized at all, let alone been analysed as a modular process. Now, there is little disagreement about the major building blocks of the functional architecture of speaking and there is a wealth of detail about the component processes involved in the generation of words. Word production tasks used in brain-imaging research vary greatly, ranging from overt picture naming to silent word reading. All of these tasks incorporate some subset of the core processing components in word production that have been discussed in the present chapter, but they differ from task to task. This allowed Indefrey and Levelt (in press) to perform a meta-analysis of the word production findings in the imaging literature, which converged on a surprisingly consistent picture of the cerebral network subserving the generation of words. In addition, we now have reasonable timing estimates of successive functional steps in the process of word generation. These timing windows can with profit be used in the analysis of MEG or EEG activation patterns during the execution of word production tasks, as demonstrated by Levelt *et al.* (1998).

Notes

1. The present blueprint differs from the one in Levelt (1989, p. 9) rather in the partitioning of components than in their character and order of processing. In the original blueprint, grammatical and phonological encoding were grouped together as components of the formulator. That partitioning still makes sense from a linguistic perspective; they are the two components involved with purely linguistic representations. In the present version I rather stressed the evolutionary, developmental, and processing distinction between the symbolic and the form processors. The roots of phonetic encoding, such as the repository of frequently used syllabic gestures (now called the syllabary), were all there in the 1989 theory, but it does make sense to partition the many newly discovered phenomena of what was originally called phonological encoding under two separate rubrics: phonological and phonetic encoding, which involve rather different kinds of processes.
2. The formalism used here is a much slimmed down version of Kempen's (1999) proposal.
3. Again, I am roughly following Kempen's (1999) 'Performance Grammar', but there is no room here to do justice to the extent and detail of his treatment.

References

Baddeley, A., Lewis, V., and Vallar, G. (1984). Exploring the articulatory loop. *Quarterly Journal of Experimental Psychology*, **36A**, 233–52.

Badecker, W., Miozzo, M., and Zanuttini, R. (1995). The two-stage model of lexical retrieval: Evidence from a case of anomia with selective preservation of grammatical gender. *Cognition*, **57**, 193–216.

Béland, R., Caplan, D., and Nespoulous, J.-L. (1990). The role of abstract phonological representations in word production: Evidence from phonemic paraphasias. *Journal of Neurolinguistics*, **5**, 125–64.

Berg, T. (1989). Intersegmental cohesiveness. *Folia Linguistica*, **23**, 245–80.

Blaauw, E. (1995). *On the perceptual classification of spontaneous and read speech.* OTS Dissertation Series.

Bock, J. K. (1982). Towards a cognitive psychology of syntax: Information processing contributions to sentence formulation. *Psychological Review*, **89**, 1–47.

Bock, K. and Levelt, W. (1994). Language production. Grammatical encoding. In *Handbook of psycholinguistics* (ed. M. A. Gernsbacher), pp. 945–84. Academic Press, New York.

Bogdan, R. (1997). *Interpreting minds: The evolution of a practice.* MIT Press, Cambridge, MA.

Browman, C. P. and Goldstein, L. (1992). Articulatory phonology: An overview. *Phonetica*, **49**, 155–80.

Brysbaert, M. (1996). Word frequency affects naming latency in Dutch when age of acquisition is controlled. *The European Journal of Cognitive Psychology*, **8**, 185–94.

Caramazza, A. C. and Miozzo, M. (1997). The relation between syntactic and phonological knowledge in lexical access: Evidence from the 'tip-of-the-tongue' phenomenon. *Cognition*, **64**, 309–43.

Carroll, J. B. and White, M. N. (1973). Word frequency and age-of-acquisition as determiners of picture naming latency. *Quarterly Journal of Experimental Psychology*, **25**, 85–95.

Clark, E. V. (1997). Conceptual perspective and lexical choice in language acquisition. *Cognition*, **64**, 309–43.

Clark, H. H. (1996). *Using language.* Cambridge University Press.

Cruttenden, A. (1986). *Intonation.* Cambridge University Press.

De Boysson-Bardies, B. and Vihman, M. M. (1991). Adaptation to language: Evidence from babbling and first words in four languages. *Language*, **67**, 297–318.

Dell, G. S. (1986). A spreading-activation theory of retrieval in sentence production. *Psychological Review*, **93**, 283–321.

Démonet, J.-F., Chollet, F., Ramsay, C., Cardebat, D., Nespoulos, J. L., and Wise, R. (1992). The anatomy of phonological and semantic processing in normal subjects. *Brain*, **115**, 1753–68.

Dronkers, N. F. (1996). A new brain region for coordinating speech articulation. *Nature*, **384**, 159–61.

Dunbar, R. (1996). *Grooming, gossip and the evolution of language.* Faber and Faber, London.

Elbers, L. (1982). Operating principles in repetitive babbling: A cognitive continuity approach. *Cognition*, **12**, 45–63.

Everaert, M., Van der Linden, E.-J., Schenk, A. and Schreuder, R. (eds) (1995). *Idioms: Structural and psychological perspectives*. Erlbaum, NJ.

Fry, D. (1969). The linguistic evidence of speech errors. *BRNO Studies of English*, **8**, 69–74.

Garrett, M. F. (1976). Syntactic processes in sentence production. In *Psychology of learning and motivation*, Vol. 9, (ed. G. Bower), pp. 231–56. Academic Press, New York.

Garrett, M. F. (1982). Production of speech: Observations from normal and pathological language use. In *Normality and pathology in linguistic performance: Slips of the tongue, ear, pen, and hand* (ed. A. W. Ellis), pp. 19–76. Academic Press, New York.

Glaser, W. R. and Düngelhoff, F.-J. (1984). The time course of picture-word interference. *Journal of Experimental Psychology: Human Perception and Performance*, **10**, 640–54.

Hovy, E. H. (1994). Automated discourse generation using discourse structure relations. In *Natural language processing* (eds C. N. Pereira and B. J. Grosz), pp. 341–86. MIT Press, Cambridge, MA.

Indefrey, P. and Levelt, W. J. M. (2000). Language production. In *The cognitive neurosciences*, 2nd edn (ed. M. Gazzaniga). MIT Press, Cambridge, MA.

Jackendoff, R. (1997). *The architecture of the language faculty*. MIT Press, Cambridge, MA.

Janssen, D.P., Roelofs, A. and Levelt, W.J.M. (submitted). Inflectional frames in language production.

Jescheniak, J. D. and Levelt, W. J. M. (1994). Word frequency effects in speech production: Retrieval of syntactic information and of phonological form. *Journal of Experimental Psychology: Learning, Memory, and Cognition*, **20**, 824–43.

Kent, R. D., Adams, S. G., and Turner, G. S. (1996). Models of speech production. In *Principles of experimental phonetics* (ed. N. J. Las), pp. 3–45. Mosby, St. Louis.

Kempen, G. (1999). Grammatical performance in human sentence production and comprehension. (Book manuscript.)

Kempen, G. and Hoenkamp, E. (1987). An incremental procedural grammar for sentence formulation. *Cognitive Science*, **11**, 201–58.

Leslie, A. and Keeble, S. (1987). Do six-month-old infants perceive causality? *Cognition*, **25**, 267–87.

Levelt, C. C. (1994). *The acquisition of place*. Holland Institute of Generative Linguistics Publications.

Levelt, W. J. M. (1982). Linearization in describing spatial networks. In *Processes, beliefs, and questions* (eds S. Peters and E. Saarinen), pp. 199–220. Reidel, Dordrecht.

Levelt, W. J. M. (1983). Monitoring and self-repair in speech. *Cognition*, **14**, 41–104.

Levelt, W. J. M. (1989). *Speaking: From intention to articulation*. MIT Press, Cambridge, MA.

Levelt, W. J. M. (1996). Perspective taking and ellipsis in spatial descriptions. In *Language and space* (eds P. Bloom, M. A. Peterson, L. Nadel, and M. F. Garrett), pp. 77–108. MIT Press, Cambridge, MA.

Levelt, W. J. M. (1998). The genetic perspective in psycholinguistics. Or where do spoken words come from? *Journal of Psycholinguistic Research*, **27**, 167–80.

Levelt, W. J. M. and Cutler, A. (1983). Prosodic marking in speech repair. *Journal of Semantics*, **2**, 205–17.

Levelt, W. J. M. and Wheeldon, L. (1994). Do speakers have access to a mental syllabary? *Cognition*, **50**, 239–69.

Levelt, W. J. M., Schriefers, H., Vorberg, D., Meyer, A. S., Pechmann, Th., and Havinga, J. (1991). The time course of lexical access in speech production: A study of picture naming. *Psychological Review*, **98**, 122–42.

Levelt, W. J. M., Roelofs, A., and Meyer, A. S. (1999). A theory of lexical access in speech production. *Behavioral and Brain Science*, **22**, 1–38.

Levelt, W. J. M., Praamstra, P., Meyer, A. S., Helenius, P., and Salmelin, R. (1998). An MEG study of picture naming. *Journal of Cognitive Neuroscience*, **10**, 553–67.

Liberman, A. (1996). *Speech: A special code*. MIT Press, Cambridge, MA.

MacNeilage, P. F. (1998). The frame/content theory of evolution of speech production. *Behavioral and Brain Sciences*, **21**, 499–511.

McCoy, K. F. and Cheng, J. (1991). Focus of attention: Constraining what can be said next. In *Natural language generation in artificial intelligence and computational linguistics* (eds C. L. Paris, W. R. Swartout, and W. C. Mann), pp. 103–24. Kluwer, Dordrecht.

McGuire, P. K., Silbersweig, D. A., and Frith, C. D. (1996). Functional neuroanatomy of verbal self-monitoring. *Brain*, **119**, 101–11.

Meyer, A. S. (1990). The time course of phonological encoding in language production: The encoding of successive syllables of a word. *Journal of Memory and Language*, **29**, 524–45.

Meyer, A. S. (1991). The time course of phonological encoding in language production: Phonological encoding inside a syllable. *Journal of Memory and Language*, **30**, 69–89.

Meyer, A. S. and Schriefers, H. (1991). Phonological facilitation in picture-word interference experiments: Effects of stimulus onset asynchrony and types of interfering stimuli. *Journal of Experimental Psychology: Learning, Memory, and Cognition*, **17**, 1146–60.

Morrison, C. M., Ellis, A. W., and Quinlan, P. T. (1992). Age of acquisition, not word frequency, affects object naming, not object recognition. *Memory and Cognition*, **20**, 705–14.

Müller-Preuss, P. and Ploog, D. (1983). Central control of sound production in mammals. In *Bioacoustics—A comparative study* (ed. B. Lewis), pp. 125–46. Academic Press, London.

Oldfield, R. C. and Wingfield, A. (1965). Response latencies in naming objects. *The Quarterly Journal of Experimental Psychology*, **17**, 273–81.

Pereira, F. C. N. and Grosz, B. J. (eds) (1994). *Natural language processing*. MIT Press, Cambridge, MA.

Petitto, L. A. and Marentette, P. F. (1991). Babbling in the manual mode: Evidence for the ontogeny of language. *Science*, **251**, 1493–6.

Ploog, D. (1990). Neuroethological foundations of human speech. In *From neuron to action* (eds L. Deecke, J. C. Eccles, and V. B. Mountcastle), pp. 365–74. Springer, Berlin.

Premack, D. and Premack, A. J. (1995). Origins of human social competence. In *The cognitive neurosciences* (ed. M. S. Gazzaniga), pp. 205–18. MIT Press, Cambridge, MA.

Premack, D. and Woodruff, G. (1978). Does the chimpanzee have a theory of mind? *Behavioral and Brain Sciences*, **1**, 515–26.

Rizzolatti, G. and Gentilucci, M. (1988). Motor and visual-motor functions of the premotor cortex. In *Neurobiology of neocortex* (ed. P. Rakic and W. Singer), pp. 269–84. Wiley, Chichester.

Roelofs, A. (1992). A spreading-activation theory of lemma retrieval in speaking. *Cognition*, **42**, 107–42.

Roelofs, A. (1993). Testing a non-decompositional theory of lemma retrieval in speaking: Retrieval of verbs. *Cognition*, **47**, 59–87.

Roelofs, A. (1996a). Serial order in planning the production of successive morphemes of a word. *Journal of Memory and Language*, **35**, 854–76.

Roelofs, A. (1996b). Morpheme frequency in speech production: Testing WEAVER. In *Yearbook of morphology* (eds G. E. Booij and J. van Marle), pp. 135–54. Kluwer, Dordrecht.

Roelofs, A. (1997a). Syllabification in speech production: Evaluation of WEAVER. *Language and Cognitive Processes*, **12**, 657–93.

Roelofs, A. (1997b). The WEAVER model of word-form encoding in speech production. *Cognition*, **64**, 249–84.

Roelofs, A. and Meyer, A. S. (1997). Metrical structure in planning the production of spoken words. *Journal of Experimental Psychology: Learning, Memory, and Cognition*, **24**, 1–18.

Schegloff, E. (1979). The relevance of repair to syntax-for-conversation. In *Syntax and semantics*, Vol. 12 (ed. T. Givón), pp. 261–88. Academic Press, New York.

Schmitt, B. (1997). Lexical access in the production of ellipsis and pronouns. Unpublished Ph.D. thesis, Nijmegen University.

Schriefers, H., Meyer, A. S., and Levelt, W. J. M. (1990). Exploring the time course of lexical access in speech production: Picture-word interference studies. *Journal of Memory and Language*, **29**, 86–102.

Selkirk, E. (1984). *Phonology and syntax*. MIT Press, Cambridge, MA.

Shattuck-Hufnagel, S. (1979). Speech errors as evidence for a serial order mechanism in sentence production. In *Sentence processing: Psycholinguistic studies presented to Merrill Garrett*. (eds W. E. Cooper and E. C. T. Walker), pp. 295–342. Lawrence Erlbaum, Hillsdale.

Slobin, D. (1987). Thinking for speaking. In *Berkeley Linguistics Society: Proceedings of the Thirteenth Annual Meeting* (eds J. Aske, N. Beery, L. Michaelis, and H. Filip), pp. 435–45. Berkeley Linguistics Society.

Snodgrass, J. G. and Yuditsky, T. (1996). Naming times for the Snodgrass and Vanderwart pictures. *Behavioral Research Methods, Instruments, and Computers*, **28**, 516–36.

Stemberger, J. P. (1983). *Speech errors and theoretical phonology: A review*. Indiana University Linguistics Club.

Stemberger, J. P. (1991a). Radical underspecification in language production. *Phonology*, **8**, 73–112.

Stemberger, J. P. (1991b). Apparent anti-frequency effects in language production: The addition bias and phonological underspecification. *Journal of Memory and Language*, **30**, 161–85.

Sutton, D., Larson, C., and Lindemann, R. C. (1974). Neocortical and limbic lesion effects on primate phonation. *Brain Research*, **71**, 61–75.

Van Turennout, M., Hagoort, P., and Brown, C. M. (1998). Brain activity during speaking: From syntax to phonology in 40 milliseconds. *Science*, **280**, 572–4.

Van Wijk, C. (1987). The PSY behind PHI: A psycholinguistic model for performance structures. *Journal of Psycholinguistic Research*, **16**, 185–99.

Vigliocco, G., Antonini, T., and Garrett, M. F. (1997). Grammatical gender is on the tip of Italian tongues. *Psychological Science*, **8**, 314–7.

Wheeldon, L. R. and Levelt, W. J. M. (1995). Monitoring the time course of phonological encoding. *Journal of Memory and Language*, **34**, 311–34.

Wimmer, H. and Perner, J. (1983). Beliefs about beliefs: Representation and constraining function of wrong beliefs in young children's understanding of deception. *Cognition*, **13**, 103–28.

Wingfield, A. (1968). Effects of frequency on identification and naming of objects. *American Journal of Psychology*, **81**, 226–34.

Zock, M. (1997). Sentence generation by pattern matching: The problem of syntactic choice. In *Recent advances in natural language processing*. (eds R. Mitkov and N. Nicolov), pp. 317–52. Amsterdam, Benjamins.

5 Comprehending spoken language: a blueprint of the listener

Anne Cutler and Charles Clifton, Jr.

5.1 Introduction

The listener can be thought of as a device for conversion of acoustic input into meaning. The purpose of this chapter is to provide an outline, necessarily superficial but we hope not fragmentary, of the course of this conversion process. Language comprehension is the most active area of psycholinguistics, and while word recognition has been more intensely studied than sentence understanding, and comprehension in the visual mode has attracted more research effort than listening, there is nevertheless a vast body of relevant literature to which a single chapter cannot hope to do true justice.

Figure 5.1, the blueprint of the listener, sketches the account which we will flesh out in the following sections. The process of listening to spoken language begins when an auditory input is presented to the ear. The manner in which auditory information is initially processed—the psychoacoustic 'front end'—will not form part of our account; the initial processing of the auditory input with which we will be concerned is the speech decoding process. Here the listener first has to separate speech from any other auditory input which might be reaching the ear at the same time, then has to turn it into some more abstract representation in terms of which, for instance, a particular sound can be accorded the same representation when uttered in different contexts, at different rates of speech, or by differing speakers. These operations are discussed in Section 5.2.

The next stage is segmentation of the (continuous) signal into its component parts. However, the computations involved in segmentation do not form a separate stage which must be traversed before, say, word processing can begin. In Fig. 5.1 this is represented by the overlapping of the boxes: segmentation results in large part from the processing operations involved in word recognition and utterance interpretation. Nevertheless there is abundant evidence that listeners also use aspects of the spoken input—explicit segmentation cues, as they are referred to in Fig. 5.1—to determine word and syntactic boundaries. This evidence is described in section 5.3.

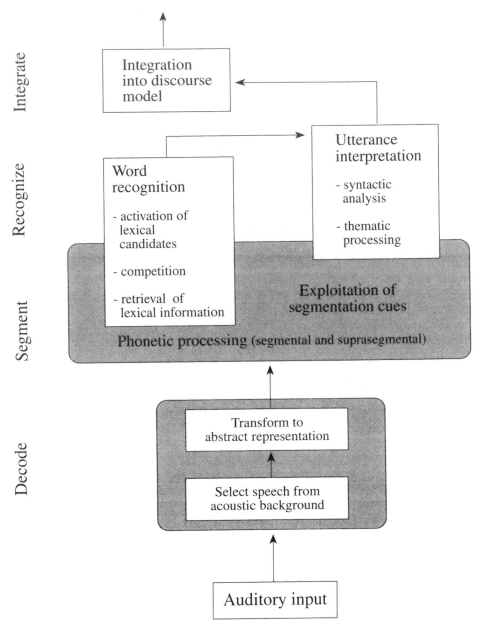

Fig. 5.1 A blueprint of the listener.

The process of lexical activation is the topic of section 5.4. Twenty years of lively research on the recognition of spoken words have led to a new generation of models in which multiple activation of word candidates, with ensuing competition between candidate words, is the core mechanism of recognition. We summarize the evidence regarding what type of information plays a role in initial activation of lexical candidates, and whether both matching and mismatching information are relevant. We also pay particular attention to a problem peculiar to auditory as opposed to visual word recognition, namely the relative weight of segmental versus suprasegmental information.

What information is retrieved from the lexicon is the topic of section 5.5, which discusses evidence concerning word semantics and morphology. Further evidence concerning retrieval of the syntactic relationships in which a word can occur, and the thematic roles it can adopt within a semantic structure, is examined in section 5.6, where we describe how the sequence of words which is the output of the processing so far is syntactically and thematically interpreted. We show how this interpretation process is incremental, is as near as possible to immediate, and is sensitive to a wide variety of lexical, pragmatic, discourse, and knowledge-based factors. The problems that the sequential, one-time-only nature of the auditory input pose for the listener may be solved by specialized characteristics of the human sentence processing system. This section also discusses the ways in which prosodic information can constrain the comprehension process.

As Fig. 5.1 shows, utterance interpretation as described so far is not the end-stage in the listener's process of extracting the speaker's message from the auditory input. The utterance must be related to its discourse context in a wide sense, beyond the computation of, for example, thematic relationships. Further, beliefs about the speaker, and about the speaker's knowledge, need to be taken into account, as well as a range of sociolinguistic factors involved in conversational interaction. These again go beyond the scope of our account.

In our final section 5.7, however, we consider another topic of considerable generality, namely the architecture of the entire device which we have called the listener. Among the central issues in language comprehension research are the extent and nature of interaction among distinct components of processing, such as those outlined in Fig. 5.1, as well as whether all aspects of this processing system are based on common underlying principles or whether different aspects of the system call for different operating principles and different representational vocabularies.

5.2 Decoding the signal

Speech, as Alvin Liberman and his colleagues (Liberman *et al.* 1967) so memorably declared, is a code. The listener has the key, and can unravel the code to reveal the message it contains. But the unravelling operation is one of fearsome complexity.

Even this operation cannot begin before the speech signal itself has been identified, of course. Speech is presented as sound waves to the ear of the listener; but it does not command an exclusive acoustic channel. The sound waves reaching the ear carry any other noise present in the listener's environment just as efficiently as speech-related noise. Thus the listener's first task is to separate speech from other auditory input reaching the ear at the same time.

Picking out a speech signal from background noise exploits the periodic nature of speech signals; noise is aperiodic and a regular structure stands out against it. Perceiving speech against a background of other sounds which, like speech, have a regular structure is less simple. However, the human auditory system can exploit grouping mechanisms which effectively assign acoustic signals to putative sources according to, for example, their frequency characteristics (see Bregman 1990 for a review).

Having isolated the part of the incoming noise which corresponds to the speech signal, the listener can then begin the decoding. The task is now to transform a time-varying input into a representation consisting of discrete elements. Linguists describe speech as a series of phonetic segments; a phonetic segment (phoneme) is simply the smallest unit in terms of which spoken language can be sequentially described. Thus the word *key* consists of the two segments /ki/, and *sea* of the two segments /si/; they differ in the first phoneme. The first phoneme of *key* is the same as the second phoneme of *ski* /ski/ or *school* /skul/ or *axe* /æks/, the third phoneme of *back* /bæk/ or *ask* /ask/, or the last phoneme of *pneumatic* /njumætɪk/.

The structure of the phonemes themselves can be further described in terms of linguistic units: distinctive features are based on articulatory factors, and allow us to describe the phoneme /k/, for example, as a velar voiceless stop consonant. That is, the place of articulation for /k/ is velar (the back of the tongue touches the soft palate); its manner of articulation is a stop (it involves a closure of the vocal tract); and it is not voiced (there is no vibration of the vocal folds during the articulation of /k/). It contrasts only in place of articulation with /t/ (alveolar) and /p/ (bilabial); only in manner with no other sound in American or southern British English, but with the velar fricative /x/ or the velar ejective /k'/ in some languages, and only in voicing with /g/, which is the same as /k/ except that articulation of /g/ involves vocal fold vibration. However, note that the articulatory features are not sequentially present; phonetic segments provide the finest-grained sequential description.

It is these phonetic segments which are present in speech only in an encoded form. Note that the linguistic description of phonetic structure does not imply a claim that this level of description constitutes an explicit representation which listeners have to construct in order to understand speech; such a description is necessary purely to capture the underlying distinctive linguistic contrasts. We will return later to the issue of whether explicit phonemic representations form part of the speech recognition process; for the present discussion, the statement 'recognizing the phoneme /k/' should be taken as equivalent to 'discriminating the word whose phonetic description includes /k/ from words containing contrasting phonemes'—for example *key* from *see*, *tea*, *pea*, or *he*.

The number of different acoustic realizations in which a particular phoneme can be manifested is potentially infinite. The acoustic realization is of course partly determined by any background noise against which it is presented. But is also to a substantial extent determined by the speaker. Different speakers have different voices. Children's vocal tracts are much smaller than those of adults; women's vocal tracts tend to be smaller than those of men. The larger the vocal tract, in general, the lower the fundamental frequency, and thus the pitch, of the voice. Voices also change with age. Further, even a single speaker can have varying voice quality due to fatigue, hoarseness, illness and so on. The amplitude, and hence the perceived loudness, of speech signals, varies with speaker–listener distance, and with vocal effort. Emotional state can affect voice pitch (tension tightens the vocal folds and raises pitch), and can also, of course, affect the amplitude of the voice. Thus there is a very large range, both of amplitude and of frequency, across which the acoustic realization of a given phonetic segment can vary. Finally, the timing of segments is also subject to considerable variation, since rate of speech is another important variable affecting the realization of segments (and one to which listeners are highly sensitive; Miller and Liberman 1979; Miller 1981).

In addition to all these sources of variability affecting the realization of phonetic segments, the segments themselves are not discretely present in the speech waveform. Segments overlap, and vary as a function of the context (surrounding segments) in which they occur. They are coarticulated—that is, speakers do not utter one segment discretely after another, but, as described by Levelt, they articulate words, phrases, utterances as fluent wholes; the smallest articulatory segment for which some degree of invariance could be claimed is, as Levelt (this volume) points out, the syllable. Thus the properties of the signal which are relevant for the perception of one segment flow seamlessly into, and to a great extent overlap with, the properties relevant for adjacent segments. Coarticulation effects can in fact stretch across several segments. For instance, the /s/ segments at the beginning of *strew* versus *street* are uttered differently due to anticipatory coarticulation of the vowel: lip-rounding for /u/, lip-spreading for /i/. Again, listeners are sensitive to these contextual effects, in that experimenter-induced mismatches in coarticulatory information impair processing in a wide range of phoneme and word recognition tasks (Streeter and Nigro 1979; Martin and Bunnell 1981, 1982; Whalen 1984, 1991; Marslen-Wilson and Warren 1994; McQueen *et al.*, in press).

Variation as a function of context can indeed result in completely different forms of the acoustic information to signal the same phoneme; thus /k/ before /i/ as in *key* is quite different from /k/ before /u/ or /ɔ/ as in *coo* or *caw*, and /k/ in initial position, as in cab /kæb/ or *keep* /kip/, is very different from /k/ in word-final position, as in *back* /bæk/ or *peak* /pik/. Moreover, the same acoustic form can signal different phonemes in different phonetic contexts; thus the noise burst appropriate for /k/ in /ka/ will signal /p/ in /pi/, and, more dramatically, the form of /p/ in *speak* is essentially identical to the form of /b/ in *beak*. In other words, there is no one-to-one mapping of acoustic realization to phonetic identity.

A spectrogram is a visual representation of an auditory signal. It displays frequency (on the vertical axis) against time (on the horizontal axis), with greater energy represented by, for instance, darker shading. Figure 5.2 presents, in its top panel, a

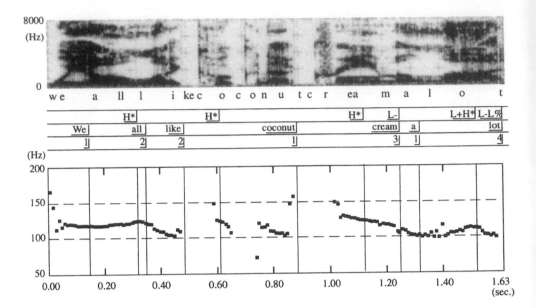

Fig. 5.2 Visual representation of the utterance 'We all like coconut cream a lot', spoken by a male speaker of American English. The top panel is a spectogram, which shows frequency (from 0 to 8000 Hz) on the vertical axis against time (0 to 1.63 s) on the horizontal axis. The lower panel traces the pitch contour (fundamental frequency in Hz) of the utterance. The middle panel is a prosodic transcription using the ToBI (Tones and Break Indices) system.

spectrogram of the utterance *We all like coconut cream a lot*, spoken by a male speaker of American English. At various points in the spectrogram clear horizontal striations can be seen, indicating concentration of energy in particular frequency bands. These frequency bands are the formants: the resonant frequencies of the speaker's vocal tract. The more steady-state portions of the speech signal, in which the formant structure clearly appears, are the vowels. Sometimes, as can be seen in Fig. 5.2, the vowels remain steady; these are the monophthongs (single vowels), as in *nut* and *lot*. Other vowels are double (diphthongs), and show clear movement—for example in *like*. Semivowels, as their name suggests, are sounds which are between consonants and vowels; they show formant structure moving into the vowel that follows them. At the beginning of Fig. 5.2 the semivowel /w/ can be seen, and the speaker has also inserted a semivowel /j/ between *we* and *all* (the movement from about 0.12 to 0.18 seconds).

This insertion—effectively converting the string *we all* into homophony with *we yawl*—shows that sounds can occur in the signal even though they are not part of the representation which the speaker encodes. No semi-vowel would have been inserted if the utterance had begun *Kids all*. . . . Similarly, sounds can be omitted or assimilated (the /k/'s at the end of *like* and the beginning of *coconut* have effectively become one sound), or can surface as other sounds (the final consonant of *coconut* and the initial consonant of *cream* have similarly merged into, effectively, one long /k/). These are effects of the coarticulation processes described above.

And, of course, it is very clear that the different phonemes in terms of which the utterance may be described are not discretely represented in the signal. Likewise, although the utterance shown in Fig. 5.2 consists of seven words, it is not easy to see in the visual representation where one word ends and the next begins. There is a clear gap in the signal at about 0.5–0.55, the boundary between *like* and *coconut*. But this gap appears almost identical to the gap at 0.66–0.71, and that latter gap falls in the middle of *coconut*. The gaps in both cases are stop closures—they are caused by the fact that the manner of articulation of /k/ involves a brief closure of the vocal tract; when the vocal tract is closed, no sound emerges, and there is a brief gap in the signal. This gap is acoustic evidence for a stop; it has no relevance to the segmentation of the signal into lexical units. At the boundary between *we* and *all* (approximately 0.12), and *all* and *like* (approximately 0.32), the speech signal is unbroken, and one phonemically determined pattern flows smoothly into the next; the same is true at the boundary of *cream* and *a* (approximately 1.22), and *a* and *lot* (approximately 1.33). Speech reaches the listener as a continuous stream, and, as we shall see in Section 5.3 below, this has important consequences for the operations involved in comprehension.

Finally, we return to the question of what units are explicitly represented during listening. Some decades ago, psycholinguists expended much research effort on investigating this question. The phoneme, as the smallest unit in terms of which the phonological form of utterances can be sequentially described, naturally exercises an intuitive appeal as a candidate 'unit of perception' in terms of which access to stored lexical representations could be achieved. Foss and Gernsbacher (1983), Marslen-Wilson and Welsh (1978), Pisoni and Luce (1987) are examples of models incorporating a phonemic level of representation in word recognition. However, the lack of one-to-one mapping between acoustic form and the phoneme led some researchers to reject the phoneme as a candidate perceptual unit. Thus Mehler *et al.* (1981) and Segui (1984) proposed obligatory intermediate representations in the form of syllables, and other models exist in which the intermediate representations are in the form of stress units (a stressed syllable plus optionally one or more unstressed syllables; Grosjean and Gee 1987), demisyllables (i.e. a vowel plus a preceding syllabic onset or a following syllabic coda; Fujimura and Lovins 1978; Samuel 1989), or diphones (i.e. effectively the stretch of speech from the midpoint of one phoneme to the midpoint of the next, capturing thus all the information relevant to contextual effects on phonemic realization, cf. Klatt 1979; Marcus 1981).

A radically different solution to the problems caused by lack of invariance in the acoustic signal was to postulate that the listener could in some manner reconstruct the true invariant underlying any given phoneme, namely the speaker's intended phonetic gestures. Although the /k/ sounds in *key* and *caw* are acoustically different, they both involve a burst of air produced with the back of the tongue in a given relationship to the velum (soft palate). The earliest version of such an approach, the Motor Theory of Speech Perception (Liberman *et al.* 1967) proposed invariant motor commands underlying the articulatory gestures corresponding to phonetic units, but in a later form of the theory (Liberman and Mattingly 1985) the invariant feature was proposed to be the more abstract intentional structures controlling articulatory movements. The heterogeneity and interdependence of gestural cues to a single phonetic unit however pose serious problems for the model (Klatt 1989).

More recently, there have been several related proposals which cast doubt on the necessity of phonemic representations in spoken-language recognition, or, in some cases, on the necessity for any intermediate representations at all. These proposals suggest that listeners are sensitive to various distinctive features of sounds (Elman and McClelland 1986); that there are no discrete units, but a continuous uptake of information relevant to the stored phonetic form of a word (Lahiri and Marslen-Wilson 1991; Marslen-Wilson and Warren 1994); or, most radically, that there are no single stored forms of words, but only a complete collection of memory traces of every earlier occurrence of words, against which incoming forms are compared for a process of recognition-by-analogy (Goldinger 1998). As a result, the theory of input representations for lexical access is currently once more a very active area.

5.3 Finding the constituent parts

The way in which spoken language differs most strikingly from written language, as we just saw, is that only in written text is clear information to be found (e.g. in spaces inserted between words) about the constituent units of which the text is composed. For a spoken message to be understood, however, the perceiver must find and recognize these discrete parts, because these are the jointly known and agreed building blocks of which the new message has been constructed by the speaker and can be reconstructed by the listener. In speech, words are not separated by discontinuities in the signal; they are uttered in a continuous stream, and coarticulation and other phonological assimilations may cross word boundaries. Likewise there is no necessary localized punctuation in speech to signal syntactic boundaries. Thus the listener's task involves computations with no counterpart for the reader (at least, for the reader of a text like this one).

As we foreshadowed in the introduction, the decisions which listeners eventually make regarding the constituent parts of incoming utterances may result to as great an extent from the word recognition and utterance interpretation processes themselves as from exploitation of explicit cues in the utterance form. Nevertheless, there is now a solid body of evidence that listeners can use aspects of the spoken form to determine word and syntactic boundaries. Prosodic structure—at one or another level—is closely involved in both. Listeners use the procedures which are summarized in this section, exploiting information included in the initial decoded representation of the utterance, to constrain aspects of both the lexical activation process (see section 5.4) and the interpretation process (see section 5.6).

To discover the constituent parts (such as words) of which continuous speech signals are composed, it would clearly be helpful if listeners were able to rely on explicit procedures which would enable them to locate where word boundaries are most likely to occur. Indeed, experimental evidence exists for explicit segmentation (i) into syllables: listeners detect target strings such as *ba* or *bal* more rapidly when the strings correspond exactly to a syllable of a heard word than when they constitute more or less than a syllable (Mehler *et al.* 1981; Zwitserlood *et al.* 1993); and (ii) at stress unit boundaries: recognition of real words embedded in nonsense bisyllables is inhibited if the word spans a boundary between two strong syllables (i.e. two syllables containing full vowels), but not if it spans a boundary between a strong and a weak syllable, since only the former is a stress unit boundary (Cutler and Norris 1988).

A striking outcome of the explicit segmentation research is that segmentation units appear to differ across languages. The evidence for syllables reported above comes from French and Dutch. Evidence of syllabic segmentation has also been observed in Spanish (Bradley *et al.* 1993) and Catalan (Sebastian-Gallés *et al.* 1992). Other tasks confirm the robustness of syllabic segmentation in French (Segui *et al.* 1981; Kolinsky 1992; Peretz *et al.* 1996). However, target detection does not show effects of syllabic segmentation in English (Cutler *et al.* 1986) or in Japanese (Otake *et al.* 1993). Cutler and Norris' (1988) observation that segmentation in English is stress-based, by contrast, is supported by patterns of word boundary misperceptions; for example, *a must to avoid* (in which only the second and last syllables are strong) is perceived as *a muscular boy* (Cutler and Butterfield 1992). Support also comes from evidence of activation of monosyllabic words embedded as strong syllables in longer words (e.g. *bone* in *trombone*; Shillcock 1990, Vroomen and de Gelder 1997).

This apparent asymmetry turned out to be in fact evidence of a deeper symmetry. Languages have many levels of structure, and one of these is rhythmic regularity. Yet rhythm is not the same for every language—there are several potential phonological levels at which regularity can be defined. (Such differences can be easily observed in the variation across poetic conventions used in different languages.) As it happens, the basic unit of language rhythm in French is the syllable, whereas the rhythm of English is stress-based. The most obvious reflection of this is in timing; syllables in French tend not to contract or expand, whereas in English unstressed syllables can be considerably compressed, and stressed syllables expanded, to maintain a perceived regularity in the occurrence of stress beats.

Given this parallelism, the evidence of stress-based segmentation in English and syllabic segmentation in French led to the hypothesis that the segmentation of continuous speech involved a universal strategy which exploited the rhythmic structure of speech input; apparent language-specificity in processing was simply due to different implementations of the rhythmic procedure for different language rhythms. Japanese offered a test case for the rhythmic hypothesis because it has a different kind of rhythm than the languages which had previously been tested. In Japanese, the unit of rhythmic regularity is the mora, a subsyllabic unit which can be a vowel, a vowel plus an onset, or a syllable coda. Thus the Japanese name *Honda* consists of three morae: *ho-n-da*; Japanese poetic forms are defined in terms of morae (seventeen morae in a haiku, for example).

Otake *et al.* (1993), and Otake *et al.* (1996a), using the fragment detection methodology that had been used by Mehler *et al.* (1981) and Cutler *et al.* (1986), found that

Japanese listeners indeed segmented speech most easily at mora boundaries. The targets were, for example, *ta* or *tan* in words such as *tanishi* or *tanshi*, each of which consists of three morae: *ta-ni-shi, ta-n-shi*. The target *ta* (which corresponds to the first mora of each word) was detected equally rapidly and equally accurately in both types of word. The target *tan* was hardly ever detected in *tanishi*, in which, in terms of mora structure, it is simply not present. Phonemes can constitute a mora by themselves: a nasal consonant in syllable coda position is moraic, and a vowel not preceded by a consonant is moraic; and Japanese listeners detect consonants and vowels significantly faster if they constitute a mora than if they do not. Thus /n/ is detected faster in *kanko* than in *kanojo*, and /o/ faster in *aoki* than in *tokage* (Cutler and Otake 1994; Otake *et al.* 1996*b*).

The rhythm of a language is a part of prosodic structure. This means that it represents a level of organization above the segmental level; it may be expressed in suprasegmental structure—timing, for instance—but it may also have segmental expression. In English this is so: the stress-based rhythm of English is defined in terms of the pattern of strong and weak syllables, and, as we saw above, strong syllables are defined as those containing full vowels, whereas weak syllables contain reduced vowels. English listeners are thus using segmental information—vowel quality—to drive their hypotheses about plausible word-boundary locations; yet the comparison with how such hypotheses are generated in other languages reveals that this behaviour arises because of the role of vowel quality in encoding rhythmic structure. Across languages, listeners exploit rhythm for lexical segmentation.

This is not the only heuristic which listeners can call upon in finding probable word boundary locations. There are language-specific effects such as the exploitation of vowel harmony information in Finnish (Suomi *et al.* 1997), and other general effects such as those based on phoneme sequencing constraints (McQueen 1998)—the sequence /mr/ cannot occur within a syllable, therefore there must be a syllable boundary between the two phonemes. Further, Norris *et al.* (1997) showed that recognition of real words embedded in nonsense strings is inhibited if the remainder of the string, once the word has been extracted, could not possibly itself be a word. English listeners in their study were presented with words like *egg*, embedded in nonsense strings like *fegg* and *maffegg*. In *fegg*, the added context /f/ is not a possible word of English—there are no English lexical items consisting of a single consonant. In contrast, the added context *maff* in *maffegg*, although it is actually not a word of English, might conceivably have been one—*mat*, *muff* and *gaff* are all English words. The listeners were faster and more accurate in detecting real words embedded in possible-word than in impossible-word contexts; in other words, they appeared to be able to rule out any candidate segmentation which would postulate, elsewhere in the input, a residue which was unparseable into words. Sections 5.4 and 5.5 will discuss in further detail how these effects feed into the process of recognizing words.

Words are the known constituent units of utterances, but there are higher levels of grouping of the words within any utterance as well. Section 5.6 will deal with the processing of syntactic and semantic structure. Cutler *et al.* (1997), reviewing the literature on the processing of prosodic structure, conclude that cues in the pitch contour of the utterance which signal a break, or cues in relative word prominence which signal an accent, can have an effect upon syntactic processing, by leading listeners to prefer potential analyses consistent with the prosodic information provided. But listeners cannot simply rely on the prosody of utterances to provide them with the necessary syntactic information or discourse-structure information—for the very good reason that prosodic structure is not directly isomorphic with these higher levels of utterance structure. Nevertheless, placement of sentence accent, or marking of a syntactic boundary via pitch movement, can result in marked effects in the speech signal, which in turn can be exploited by listeners even at the phonetic processing and word-recognition levels. For instance, the pitch movement associated with a boundary may be followed by a pitch reset, which will have the effect of ruling out coarticulation and hence make a boundary between words clearer, or the utterance of a word which is accented will be clearer and less likely to contain variant forms of the word's constituent phonemes. These effects are reviewed by Cutler *et al.* (1997).

5.4 Activating lexical representations

The recognition of spoken words differs from word reading not only in the lack of clear segmentation of the input into its constituent units, but also, and most clearly, in the temporal aspect of the input. Words do not arrive at the peripheral input stage all at once—they are presented over time, the beginning arrives first, the end arrives last. As Section 5.3 showed, listeners are adept at exploiting their knowledge of language phonology to circumvent the potential problems caused by the continuity and variability of speech signals; thus the task of recognizing spoken words might seem to be a matter merely of matching the incoming sequence to the stored word forms in the listener's mental lexicon.

Unfortunately there is another problem for the listener, and that is simply the size of the listener's vocabulary compared with the size of the set of phonetic components from which it is constructed. A listener's vocabulary contains tens of thousands of words (although of course the relevant measure here is not words as they are orthographically defined, in texts such as this one by spaces between the printed word forms; the relevant measure is sound-meaning mappings in the mental lexicon, and these will exist in comparable numbers for speakers of uninflected languages like Chinese, morphologically simple languages like English, or highly agglutinating languages like Turkish).

The words, however, are built up out of a repertoire of on average only 30–40 phonemes (Maddieson 1984). It requires only simple mathematics to realize that words are not highly distinctive. Any spoken word tends to resemble other words, and may have other words embedded within it (thus *steak* contains possible pronunciations of *stay* and *take* and *ache*, it resembles *state* and *snake* and *stack*, it occurs embedded within possible pronunciations of *mistake* or *first acre*, and so on). Computations of the amount of embedding in the vocabulary by Frauenfelder (1991; for Dutch) and

McQueen and Cutler (1992; for English) have shown that a majority of polysyllabic words have shorter words embedded within them. Moreover, these embedded words are most likely to appear at the onsets of their matrix words; Luce (1986) computed that, when frequency is taken into account, more than one-third of short words in English could not be reliably identified until after their offset (and experimental studies of the perception of incrementally presented words by Grosjean (1985) and Bard *et al.* (1988) have confirmed that this does form an actual problem for listeners). *Stay* could become *steak*, *steak* could become *stakehold*, and so on. So how do listeners know when to recognize *steak* and when not?

5.4.1 Concurrent activation and competition

The solution to this problem is a fundamental notion which is now accepted by nearly all researchers in the field of spoken-word recognition; candidate words compatible with (portions of) an incoming speech signal are simultaneously activated and actively compete for recognition. Concurrent activation has been a feature of all models of spoken-word recognition since Marslen-Wilson and Welsh's (1978) cohort model. Competition was first proposed in the TRACE model of McClelland and Elman (1986), and in the same form—competition via lateral inhibition between competitors—forms the central mechanism of the Shortlist model (Norris 1994). In other forms it is also found in the other main models currently available, such as the Neighbourhood Activation Model (Luce *et al.* 1990) and the re-revised cohort model (Gaskell and Marslen-Wilson 1997).

There is substantial evidence of activation of words embedded within other words (Shillcock 1990; Cluff and Luce 1990), and of simultaneous activation of partially overlapping words (Goldinger *et al.* 1989; Zwitserlood 1989; Marslen-Wilson 1990; Goldinger *et al.* 1992; Gow and Gordon 1995; Wallace *et al.* 1995). Although such evidence is consistent with the competition notion, it does not entail it. Inhibition of recognition as a function of the existence of competitors provides direct evidence. Taft (1986) observed that non-words which form part of real words are hard to reject. Priming studies by Goldinger *et al.* (1989) and Goldinger *et al.* (1992) suggested that recognition may be inhibited when words are preceded by similar-sounding words, the inhibition being presumably due to competition between the preceding word and the target. Direct evidence of competition between word candidates comes from a study by McQueen *et al.* (1994), who found that word-spotting latencies were significantly longer in nonsense strings which activated competing words; that is, *mess* was harder to find in *domess* (which could partially activate *domestic*) than in *nemess* (which activates no competitor). Similarly in Dutch *zee* (sea) is harder to spot in *muzee* (which can be continued to form *museum*) than in *luzee* (Donselaar *et al.* 1998). Norris *et al.* (1995) and Vroomen and de Gelder (1995) showed further that the more competing words may be activated, the more the recognition of embedded words will be inhibited.

As this last result emphasizes, analysis of patterns of competition depends crucially on precise knowledge of vocabulary structure. Studies of lexical structure have been revolutionized in recent years by the availability of computerized dictionaries; it is now easy to analyse the composition of the vocabulary in many languages, and arguments based on analyses of lexical databases have played an important role in theorizing about spoken-word recognition for the past decade (e.g. Marcus and Frauenfelder 1985; Luce 1986; Cutler and Carter 1987). It should be noted, however, that substantial corpora of spoken language, and the estimates of spoken-word frequency which could be derived from them, are still lacking; such spoken-word frequency counts as exist to date (e.g. Howes 1966; Brown 1984) are, for practical reasons, small in scale compared to written frequency counts.

Competition between candidate words which are not aligned in the signal provides a potential mechanism to achieve segmentation of the speech stream into individual words. Thus although the recognition of *first acre* may involve competition from *stay*, *steak*, and *take*, this will eventually be overcome by joint inhibition from *first* and *acre*. However, competition can also co-exist with explicit segmentation procedures of the type described above in section 5.3. When inter-word competition and stress-based segmentation are compared in the same experiment, independent evidence appears for both (McQueen *et al.* 1994). In section 5.3, we further described a prelexical effect in which listeners display sensitivity to the viability of stretches of speech as possible word candidates. When this Possible Word Constraint is incorporated in the Shortlist model, the model accurately simulates not only the experimental findings which motivated the constraint, but also a range of other experimental demonstrations of competition and explicit segmentation effects (Norris *et al.* 1997). In other words, such prelexical segmentation effects can be thought of as exercising constraints on the activation and competition process.

The way in which segmental information contributes to word-candidate activation has been the focus of much recent experimental attention. Connine *et al.* (1997) found that phoneme-monitoring for phonemes occurring at the end of non-word targets is faster the more similar the non-word is to a real word: /t/ was detected faster at the end of *gabinet* (which resembles *cabinet*) than at the end of *shuffinet* (which is less close to any existing word). This suggests that even partial information for a word, as present for instance in a non-word which resembles that word, will activate lexical information.

Marslen-Wilson and Warren (1994), following up the work of Streeter and Nigro (1979) and Whalen (1984, 1991) mentioned in section 5.2 above, examined the differential effects of subphonemic mismatch in words and non-words. They constructed three experimental versions of matched pairs of words and non-words like *job* and *smob*, by cross-splicing different initial consonant–vowel sequences (CVs) onto the final consonant of each item. The CV could either be from another token of the same word/non-word, from another word (*jog* or *smog*), or from another non-word (*jod* or *smod*). Marslen-Wilson and Warren performed lexical decision and phonetic decision experiments; in both of these tasks listeners were sensitive to a mismatch between CV and final consonant (e.g. a token of *job* in which the *jo-* had been taken from *jog* and therefore contained formant transitions into a velar place of articulation in the later part of the vowel). However, the effect of a mismatch on non-words was much greater when the CV came from a word than from another non-word, whereas for words, whether the CV came from another word or from a non-word had very little effect. McQueen *et al.* (in press) report similar studies manipulating the conditions under which these competition effects could be made to come and go.

All the results described in this section show that activation of lexical representations is a continuous process, based on whatever information is available. Even partial information (in partial words, for instance, or in non-words which in part overlap with real words) suffices to produce partial activation. Thus *domess* briefly activates *domestic*; *smob* briefly activates *mob* and *smog*. Activation of a lexical representation does not obligatorily require full presentation of the corresponding word form; the competition process, and its concomitant constraints, can so efficiently result in victory for words which are fully present in the signal, that concurrent activation of partially present words, or of words embedded within other words, is simply a low-cost by-product of the efficiency with which the earliest hints of a word's presence can be translated into activation.

5.4.2 Segmental versus suprasegmental information

The above studies showed clear evidence for continuous activation of potential candidate words based on the incoming segmental information. The discussion in section 5.2 above showed that there is controversy as to whether candidate-word activation proceeds via an explicit representation of phonetic segments; segmental information is encoded in the signal, and fully unravelling the code may not be necessary. However, the signal also contains suprasegmental information—variations in fundamental frequency, amplitude, and duration of the constituent parts, and this information may also be relevant to word identity.

Because Fig. 5.2 represents an utterance in English, it does not manifest suprasegmental contrasts with great clarity. The word *coconut* has a stressed first syllable and a weak second syllable, with a reduced vowel; orthography notwithstanding, the vowels in the two syllables are quite different. The first syllable is also nearly twice as long (from about 0.52 to 0.67) as the second (from 0.67 to 0.75, approximately). Other languages, however, offer more obvious contrasts. In the tone language Cantonese, for instance, a single CV syllable such as [si] can be realized with six different tones, and all possible realizations exist, with different meanings—some with multiple meanings, in fact. With tone 1 (high level) [si] means 'poem', with tone 2 (high rising) it means 'history', with tone 6 (low level) it means 'time', and so on. Tone distinctions are realized in the fundamental frequency contour of an utterance (F_0 height and F_0 movements), although tone and syllable duration do covary (Kong 1987; Kratochvil 1971), and tones may be distinguished by the timing of their movement within a syllable (Shen and Lin 1991). In Japanese, fundamental frequency distinctions also play a role in distinguishing between words; thus *ame* with a high–low (HL) pitch accent pattern means 'rain', *ame* with a LH pattern 'candy'.

Although stress is part of the acoustic realization of every polysyllabic word in English, there are remarkably few pairs of English words which are distinguished only by differences in suprasegmental structure: *FOREgoing* versus *forGOing*, *TRUSTy* versus *trustEE*, and a handful more (upper case here signifies stress). There are many more pairs like *SUBject/subJECT* or *REcord/reCORD*, which differ in segmental as well as in suprasegmental structure. The vowels in the latter word pairs, especially in the first syllables, are quite clearly different, just as are the first two vowels in *coconut* in Fig. 5.2. Stress in English is in fact expressed as much in the segmental structure of words (stressed syllables must have full vowels, while reduced vowels must be unstressed) as in the suprasegmental structure. Correspondingly, the segmental (vowel quality) distinctions involved in stress contrasts seem far more crucial to English listeners than the suprasegmental distinctions; cross-splicing vowels with different stress patterns produces unacceptable results only if vowel quality is changed (Fear *et al.* 1995). Studies of 'elliptic speech'—speech containing some systematic segmental distortion—showed that the manipulation which most inhibited word recognition was changing full vowels to reduced and vice versa (Bond 1981). Slowiaczek (1990) found that mis-stressing *without* resulting change in vowel quality had no significant effect on the identification of noise-masked words; and Small *et al.* (1988) and Taft (1984) found that such mis-stressing also had no effect on detection time for following phonemes. On the other hand, Bond and Small (1983) found that mis-stressed words *with* vowel changes were not restored to correct stress when listeners repeated a heard text at speed (indicating that subjects perceived the mis-stressed form and may not at all have accessed the intended word).

If, as this evidence combines to suggest, English listeners do not use suprasegmental information in activating word candidates, then pairs like *FOREgoing* and *forGOing*, distinguished only in suprasegmental structure, will be functionally homophonous: both *FOREgoing* and *forGOing* should be activated whenever either of them is heard. Indeed Cutler (1986) showed that listeners did not distinguish between these two word forms in initially achieving access to the lexicon.

The situation is quite different, however, in other languages. In tone languages, tonal information may be crucial for determining word identity. A categorization experiment by Fox and Unkefer (1985), using a continuum varying from one tone of Mandarin to another, confirms that listeners use tone to distinguish words: the crossover point at which listeners switched from reporting one tone to reporting the other shifted as a function of whether the CV syllable upon which the tone was realized formed a real word when combined only with one tone or only with the other tone (in comparison to control conditions in which both tones, or neither tone, formed a real word in combination with the CV). The lexical effect appeared only when the listeners were Mandarin speakers; English listeners showed no such shift, and on the control continua the two subject groups did not differ. Lexical priming studies in Cantonese also suggest that the role of a syllable's tone in word recognition is analogous to the role of the vowel (Chen and Cutler 1997; Cutler and Chen 1995); in auditory lexical decision, overlap between a prime word and the target word in tone or in vowel exercised parallel effects. On the other hand, there is evidence from a variety of experiments on the processing of Chinese languages that the processing of tonal information may be more error-prone than the processing of segmental information (Tsang and Hoosain 1979; Taft and Chen 1992; Cutler and Chen 1997). This suggests that suprasegmental information does constrain word activation in Chinese languages, but the effect of suprasegmental information may be weaker than that of segmental information.

Pitch accent in Japanese words can also be processed efficiently to constrain word activation at an early point in presentation of a word. Cutler and Otake (1999) presented Japanese listeners with single syllables edited out of bisyllabic words differing in accent pattern; listeners were able to determine, with great accuracy, whether the syllable came from a word in which it had high or low pitch accent. Interestingly, their scores were significantly more accurate for initial (80% correct) than for final syllables (68%). This suggests that pitch accent information is realized most clearly in just the position where it would be of most use for listeners in on-line spoken-word recognition. They then tested this suggestion in a gating experiment using pairs of Japanese words such as *nimotsu/nimono*, beginning with the same CVCV sequence but with the accent pattern of this initial CVCV being HL in one word and LH in the other. Fragments of the word extending no further than the first vowel (*ni-*) were sufficient to produce word guesses which correctly reproduced the initial accent patterns of the actually spoken words with a probability significantly above chance. Thus Japanese listeners can exploit pitch-accent information effectively at an early stage in the presentation of a word, and use it to constrain selection of lexical candidates. The strong dependence of pitch accent realization on dialect in Japanese, however, suggests that again, segmental information may be accorded priority in constraining word activation.

Thus both tonal information and pitch accent information are used by listeners in word activation, even though the evidence from English showed that stress information was not exploited in this way. Even in other stress languages, however, the situation turns out to differ from English. In Dutch, for example, mis-stressing a word can prevent lexical activation. The competition effect described above, in which *zee* (sea) is harder to spot in *muzee* (which can be continued to form *museum*) than in *luzee* holds only if *muzee* is, like *museum*, stressed on the second syllables. If *muzee* and *luzee* are stressed on the initial syllable then there is no longer a significant difference between them in detection time for *zee*, suggesting that there was in this case no competition from *museum* because it simply was not activated by input lacking the correct stress pattern (Donselaar *et al.* 1998). In Dutch, at least, there may be on-line directive use of stress information in lexical access, and this in turn suggests that the failure to find similar evidence in English may arise from the peculiar redundancy of purely prosodic cues to stress in English; stress information can nearly always be derived from segmental structure.

5.5 Retrieving lexical information

Once a word form has triumphed in competition over its rivals, what information does it bring with it from the lexicon for integration into the representation which the listener is forming of the utterance as a whole? Psycholinguistic research has lavished attention on some aspects of this question, while almost ignoring others. The experimental evidence on morphological and semantic information in the lexicon is summarized here; section 5.6.1 below discusses the syntactic and thematic information which may be made available by lexical retrieval.

5.5.1 Morphological structure

The stored forms of words in morphologically simple languages like English include considerable morphological detail; this conclusion can be drawn from the substantial literature investigating the role of morphological structure in word recognition. Recent models of the lexical representation of morphology have fallen into two general classes. On the one hand are models in which the stored representations consist of stems with the affixes with which they may combine; in such a model *count* would be stored as the head of an entry, and would be furnished with the prefixes *dis-*, *mis-*, *vis-*, *ac-*, and the suffixes *-s*, *-ed*, *-er*, *-able* etc. (see e.g. Caramazza *et al.* 1988; Marslen-Wilson *et al.* 1994). Contrasted with these are models in which full forms are separately represented but are linked with related forms (so that *count* and *counts* and *discount* and *counter* and *unaccountability* would all be stored forms, but linked to a common node; Schriefers *et al.* 1991; Baayen *et al.* 1997). McQueen and Cutler (1998), in a review of this literature, conclude that the evidence supports the latter type of model, with the additional specification that the links between morphological relatives are strong and that the stored word-forms do contain information about the morphological structure and relationships.

These relationships between morphologically complex words in English encode different types of linguistic connection. Thus inflection, for example of tense on verbs or number on nouns, as in *discount-ed* and *viscount-s*, contrasts with derivation, for example the addition of affixes especially to change word class, as in *account*, *account-able*, *accountabil-ity*. Yet it appears not to be linguistic relationships which determine the relative closeness of connections in the language user's lexicon. Instead, McQueen and Cutler (1998) conclude that the stored relationships are principally based on such factors as frequency of occurrence (*counts* is a more frequent form than *countering*) and semantic transparency (*count* and *counting* are more clearly related to one another than *discount* and *counter*).

The evidence thus suggests that in languages like English the recognition of any morphologically complex word will not involve obligatory decomposition of the word into its constituent morphemes, but that the full form will be activated by the incoming speech signal and will participate in the competition process as a whole. Importantly, however, the result of the recognition of a spoken word will be a form which brings with it information (such as word class and the fact of marking for tense, number, etc.) which can constrain the computation of the higher-level structure in which the word participates.

An important caveat must always be added, however, to the discussion of this body of research. English is in this instance not necessarily representative of the world's languages. Thus the model of access and retrieval which holds for English (and similar languages) does not necessarily hold for languages with different structure. Even within morphologically similar languages, Orsolini and Marslen-Wilson (1997) have proposed, different processing principles may be warranted. It is certainly conceivable that word recognition in Turkish and Finnish (languages with rich combinatorial morphology) might require affixes to be computed and accessed as separate entities, while word recognition in Chinese (a language with little affixal morphology) might provide little information which constrains the syntactic computation. There is not yet sufficient evidence to fill out the blueprint such that it would cover listeners in all languages.

5.5.2 Semantics

The meaning of a word is presumably above all what must be retrieved from the lexicon if the listener is to evaluate correctly the role that the word plays in the speaker's utterance. In fact research on precisely what becomes available in word meaning retrieval has more often been based on written input (see the chapter by Perfetti, this volume) than on spoken input. Much of the research described in section 5.4 above involves tasks which to a greater or lesser extent use meaning activation as a dependent variable (various forms of lexical decision; cross-modal priming). But while it seems relatively straightforward to envisage the meaning associated with the lexical representation of *egg* or *smog*, not all referential relations are so simple.

One of the semantic issues which has sparked as much attention in spoken-word recognition as in written-word recognition is the role of lexical ambiguity. The word *week*, for example, refers to a period of seven days. But exactly the same sequence of sounds encodes an adjective, meaning 'lacking in strength'. As in the reading domain, the principal questions concern whether both meanings are retrieved when an English-speaking listener hears [wik]; whether it matters that the two words differ in form class; and whether meaning retrieval depends upon degree of fit to the context of the rest of the utterance.

Studies with the cross-modal priming task have produced evidence for momentary simultaneous activation of all senses of an ambiguous spoken word, irrespective of relative frequency or contextual probability. Thus Swinney's (1979) original studies with this task showed that words such as *bug* facilitated the recognition of words related to both their senses, even when prior context was consistent with only one of the senses (a few syllables later, however, only the contextually appropriate sense remained active). Facilitation of words related to both senses occurred even when one reading of the ambiguous word was more likely simply because it had a higher frequency (thus *scale* primed both *weight* and *fish*; Onifer and Swinney 1981), and it occurred even when one reading was more likely because it had the word class required by the syntactic context (thus *week/weak* primed both *month* and *strong*; Lucas 1987). Tanenhaus and his colleagues (Tanenhaus *et al.* 1979; Seidenberg *et al.* 1982; Tanenhaus and Donnenwerth-Nolan 1984) also produced evidence for multiple-sense activation with a very similar task, and further support appeared from other kinds of listening experiments. Thus Lackner and Garrett (1972) presented listeners with two competing messages, and required them to attend to one and to paraphrase it. Speech in the unattended channel (which subjects could not report), resolved ambiguities in the attended utterances; subjects' paraphrases reflected either sense, depending on the available disambiguation, again suggesting availability of all senses. And the task of naming the colour of a visually presented word, which becomes harder if the word's meaning is activated, was also used to show that both meanings of a spoken ambiguous word were available to exercise this interference (Conrad 1974; Oden and Spira 1983).

Later experiments (Tabossi 1988*a*; Tabossi *et al.* 1987) found however that strongly constraining contexts could lead to only one sense being activated if that particular sense was highly dominant (e.g. the weight sense of *scale* in a sentence about weighing). But again, these contexts effectively primed the relevant sense via occurrence of a related word—contexts which forced one sense but did not prime it (e.g. *On the table stood a scale*) produced facilitation for all senses. The current picture is therefore that all meanings of an ambiguous word are potentially available, but that contextually inappropriate meanings may in many circumstances have no chance to play a role in the recognition process.

The same picture can potentially be constructed for the various senses in which even an unambiguous word can be interpreted. Tabossi (1988*b*) found that sentence contexts could constrain activation of different aspects of an unambiguous word's meaning; *hard* was primed after *The strong blow didn't crack the diamond*, but not after *The jeweller polished the diamond*. But other studies showed that all attributes may be momentarily activated when a word is heard, irrespective of their relative dominance and of their contextual appropriateness (Whitney *et al.* 1985). Shortly after word offset, however, attributes which are dominant and/or contextually appropriate are still active, but contextually inappropriate non-dominant attributes are not. Greenspan (1986) found that central properties of unambiguous words (e.g. that ice is cold) are activated irrespective of contextual appropriateness, but peripheral properties (e.g. that ice is slippery) may only be activated when appropriate. We will return to the issue of the relation between context and word meaning in section 5.7 below.

5.6 Interpreting the sequence

The comprehension process does not end with identifying words and their meanings. Determining what message a sequence of words conveys involves far more than simply adding together the meanings of the words. The sentence that contains them must be divided into its component parts, the relations between these parts must be determined and interpreted semantically, and the reference of the parts, their relation to ongoing discourse, and the truth or communicative force of the whole sentence or discourse must be determined. This process is guided by a language user's knowledge of the structure of his or her language, together with specific structural information made available by the particular words in a sentence. All this holds true whether reading or listening is involved.

We will first review what we take to be strong candidates for phenomena and processes common to reading and listening, focusing on data from reading experiments
(see Perfetti, this volume, for more thorough coverage). We will then turn to phenomena and processes that may be specific to interpreting a heard sentence.

5.6.1 Processes common to listening and reading

The past three decades of study of sentence and text comprehension allow some strong
conclusions. Readers and listeners often arrive at a semantic interpretation of a sentence in an apparently-incremental and nearly-immediate fashion. They do not wait
for the end of a clause or sentence, but instead (to a first approximation) their
understanding of a sentence seems to keep up with words as they are heard or as the
eyes land on them. The understanding that they arrive at honours grammatical
knowledge, even when it forces an unexpected or implausible interpretation.

While it is now clear that grammatical information must be used in sentence comprehension, researchers disagree about just what grammatical knowledge is used, at
least in the initial stages of analysing or 'parsing' a sentence. Some researchers argue
that a grammatical structure must be built first, in order to support semantic interpretation, and propose that only relatively global grammatical information (e.g. about
possible phrase structure configurations or templates and about the part of speech of
an individual word) is used to build such a structure (Frazier 1979; Frazier 1987;
Frazier 1989; Frazier and Rayner 1982). Other 'lexicalist' theorists place similar
emphasis on the creation of grammatical structures but suggest that a richer set of
information about the usage of individual lexical items guides their construction
(Abney 1989; Konieczny *et al.* 1997; MacDonald *et al.* 1994; Tanenhaus *et al.* 1990;
Tanenhaus *et al.* 1993). This richer information can include both grammatical information (about, e.g. the possible argument structures assigned by a verb) and extra-
grammatical information (about, e.g. the relative frequency of usage in different
constructions, or the plausibility of the different constructions). Theorists also differ in
their opinion about whether a single analysis is built and interpreted at a time, or
whether multiple analyses are built and allowed to compete with one another.

Some of these theoretical approaches have led to the identification of important new
phenomena of sentence comprehension. For instance, working in the phrase-structure
parsing tradition, Frazier and Rayner (1982) claimed that a preposition phrase (PP) in
the configuration V–NP–PP (e.g. *John hit the girl with the wart*) is initially taken as a
complement of the verb (V) rather than a modifier of the noun phrase (NP). The
example sentence is therefore read relatively slowly because it violates this initial
preference, which Frazier and Rayner claimed reflects a preference for the simplest,
most-quickly-constructed, syntactic analysis.

More recent work has made it clear that detailed lexical properties of verbs and
referential properties of noun phrases (as well as syntactic simplicity) affect comprehension very quickly (cf. MacDonald *et al.* 1994; Tanenhaus *et al.* 1993). This research
was stimulated by changes in linguistic theory over the past two decades that

accommodate substantial parts of syntactic functioning in the lexicon (including such approaches as Lexical Functional Grammar, Bresnan 1982; Head-driven Phrase Structure Grammar, Pollard and Sag 1994; and Pustejovsky's 1995 lexicalist approach). Psycholinguists have focused most on the argument structures and thematic structures made available by lexical items, usually verbs. The verb *cook*, for example, would allow argument structures with only an agent (the intransitive reading), or with both agent and theme (transitive reading). This information would become available upon retrieval of the word from the lexicon.

Marslen-Wilson, Tyler, and colleagues (e.g. Marslen-Wilson *et al.* 1988; Tyler 1989; Jennings *et al.* 1997) have provided evidence from listening experiments that verb-subcategorization information is available early in the process of sentence comprehension. They observed processing difficulty for sentences with subcategorization violations (e.g. *He slept the guitar*, compared for instance with the merely implausible *He buried the guitar*; the violation occurs because sleep cannot take a direct object). Subcategorization violations also caused greater difficulty than violations of selection restrictions (e.g. *He drank the guitar*; *drink* may take a direct object, but it must be something which can be drunk).

Spivey-Knowlton and Sedivy (1995) examined the effects of more detailed lexical information. They found that the advantage of a V complement interpretation (as observed by Frazier and Rayner 1982) seems to hold true only for action verbs. For perception and 'psych' verbs followed by an indefinite NP (e.g. *The salesman glanced at a customer with suspicion/ripped jeans*), modification of the NP is the preferred interpretation.

Properties of discourse as well as properties of lexical items also play a quick role in sentence comprehension. As one example, Trueswell and Tanenhaus (1991) showed that the classic *The horse raced past the barn fell* garden-path sentence (Bever 1970) no longer caused readers measurable difficulty when the temporal relations introduced by a discourse blocked the preferred main clause reading. Trueswell and Tanenhaus's subjects read sentences like *The student spotted by the proctor will receive a warning*. Normally, these sentences would be expected to be difficult, since a reader would initially take *The student* as the subject of *spotted*. However, if the discourse in which the sentence appeared specified a future time (*A proctor will come up and notice a student cheating*), this preference seemed to be replaced by a full willingness to take *spotted* as beginning a relative clause. The past tense interpretation of *spotted* was inappropriate for the future context, while the passive participle interpretation was acceptable.

5.6.2 Auditory sentence comprehension

One goal of a psycholinguistic theorist is to arrive at a model of a language user that explains how he or she can use the wide range of information provided by language in the course of understanding text or speech. Considering how people understand spoken as well as written language might seem simply to make the theorist's (and the listener's) task harder. More different types of information must be accounted for. But in fact, considering what might be special about the listener's task provides some new insights into what the language user's skills really are. Recent research, using ways of looking at how auditory language is processed, has turned up very informative phenomena about language comprehension. For an extensive review of this research, see Cutler *et al.* 1997; for concentrated presentations of a selection of recent research, see the special issues of the journals *Language and Cognitive Processes* (volume 11, 1996, numbers 1 and 2) and *Journal of Psycholinguistic Research* (volume 25, 1996, number 2) devoted to prosody and sentence processing. In the present brief survey, we will consider ways in which the auditory modality might be expected to present additional challenges to the listener as well as ways in which the auditory modality might carry additional useful information.

5.6.2.1 Added challenges to the listener

We assume, in the absence of clear evidence to the contrary, that the architecture of the system that interprets auditory sentences is the same as that of the system that interprets written sentences. It is true, though, that auditory presentation sets this system some extra challenges. One challenge has already been described extensively; in listening, the words are not physically set apart from one another as they are in reading. It is clear that a listener has some means of identifying candidate words in the speech stream (just as it is clear that a reader *can* read words printed without spaces between them, albeit at a generally substantial cost in reading time; Rayner and Pollatsek 1996). However, the uncertainties of segmenting the word stream might be expected to interact in interesting ways with the uncertainties of interpretation that have been identified in research on reading.

Another challenge comes from the evanescent nature of speech. A listener cannot listen back to what he or she has just heard in the way a reader can make a regressive eye movement. Some researchers have suggested that this difference may play a major role in sentence comprehension. Watt and Murray (1996) claim that since 'auditory input is fleeting and not readily available for 'reinspection'' (p. 293), a listener may delay structural commitments until the end of a constituent. A reader, who can look back to recover from an erroneous early commitment, can afford to make such commitments. There are some reasons to discount this claim. First, readers look back rather infrequently, about 10 to 15 per cent of the time (Rayner and Pollatsek 1989). Second, several researchers have reported garden-path effects in listening experiments, indicating that listeners do sometimes make an erroneous early commitment (Carroll and Slowiaczek 1987; Pynte and Prieur 1996; Speer *et al.* 1996).

It is possible to take the opposite perspective and view listening as more basic and somehow 'simpler' than reading. For most people, reading is, after all, developmentally parasitic on listening. Some researchers have even suggested that some reading phenomena can be understood by claiming that skilled readers create (perhaps via implicit subvocalization) an auditory representation of what they are reading. Creating an auditory representation may facilitate some aspects of comprehension

(Slowiaczek and Clifton 1980); creating the right auditory representation may block miscomprehension (Bader 1994).

This perspective is encouraged by the observation that humans are adapted through evolution to process auditory language, not written language. One must assume that our brains are well-tuned to extract information from an auditory signal, and that our language is adapted to the capacities of our auditory system. Exactly what the relevant capacities are, however, is far from understood, especially at the levels of parsing and sentence interpretation. One reasonable candidate is the existence of auditory sensory memory, which may be able to span a period of time on the order of one or a few seconds (Cowan 1984). Contrary to the suggestion discussed above, heard language may persist for a longer period of time than read language, permitting more effective revision of analysis. Another candidate is the facilitating effects of auditory structuring on short-term memory; imposing a rhythm on the items in a list to be remembered can facilitate their memory (Glanzer 1976; Ryan 1969). Beyond carrying the information needed to recognize words, the auditory signal is richly structured in its melody and rhythm, its prosody. This structuring can certainly affect memory for language (Speer *et al.* 1993), and could serve as a source of information that might guide the parsing and interpretation of utterances.

5.6.2.2 Prosody in auditory sentence comprehension

The prosody of an utterance plays many roles. It can help in resolving lexical and syntactic ambiguities. It can signal the importance, novelty, and contrastive value of phrases and relate newly-heard information to the prior discourse. It can signal the attitude and affect of a speaker toward his or her topic. We will review selected recent research on some of these topics. Before doing so, however, we will turn to the topic of how one might describe the prosody of an utterance.

We will treat prosody as the structure that underlies the melody and rhythm of a sentence. Much recent work aimed at examining how the auditory signal can convey information has assumed an explicit analysis of prosody, an analysis that developed out of work done by Pierrehumbert (1980) (cf. also Beckman and Pierrehumbert 1986; Beckman and Ayers 1993; Ladd 1996; Selkirk 1984). Pierrehumbert devised an elegant description of English prosody. In her scheme, an utterance is viewed as a shallow hierarchy of prosodic elements. For present purposes, the elementary prosodic unit is the phonological (or intermediate) phrase, a string of speech that must end with a phrase accent (high, H–, or low, L–), and must contain at least one pitch accent (which can be high or low, H* or L*, or bitonal, e.g. L + H*). One or more phonological (or intermediate) phrases constitute an intonation phrase, which must end with a boundary tone (high, H%, or low, L%). An utterance can contain one or more intonational phrases. The end of an intonational phrase is signalled by pausing, lengthening, and segmental variation in addition to the presence of a phrase accent and a boundary tone, where the combination of phrase accent and boundary tone can appear in any of several forms, such as a 'continuation rise' or the normal 'declarative' contour. An intermediate phrase is typically associated with a smaller amount of pausing and lengthening than an intonational phrase, and ends with a phrase accent but not a boundary tone. A pitch accent is associated with the stressed syllable of any word that receives focus-marking. The accent can be high or low, or moving, and generally falls on each word that is not treated as 'given' or predictable from context.

In our opinion, some explicit scheme for describing prosody must replace the vague, intuitive, and theoretically unmotivated descriptions psychologists have often used in the past. One such explicit scheme for coding the prosody of English sentences has developed out of the theoretical position sketched above. The scheme, called ToBI for 'Tones and Break Indices', is one that a researcher can learn with a reasonable amount of effort, since it is documented by a full training manual with examples (Beckman and Ayres 1993; Silverman *et al.* 1992; cf. Shattuck-Hufnagel and Turk 1996, for a brief introduction).

To see an application of ToBI analysis, consider Fig. 5.2 above. This acoustic representation of a sentence includes a pitch trace as well as an annotation of the pitch accents, phrase accents, boundary tones, and break indices (measures of the magnitude of a prosodic boundary) for the sentence *We all like coconut cream a lot.* This sentence contains just one intonational phrase and two phonological (intermediate) phrases. It has one maximal break (break index 4) at the end of the intonational phrase that ends the whole utterance, one substantial break at the end of the intermediate phrase within the sentence (break index 3), one less marked break (break index 2) after *all*, and a word-level break (break index 1) after each other word. The intonational phrase ends with a L% boundary tone preceded by a L− phrase accent and a L + H* pitch accent on *lot*. One acoustic reflection of the L + H* pitch accent can be seen in the pitch track at the bottom of the figure; the pitch of *lot* begins relatively low, but rises before falling again to the phrase accent and boundary tone. The remaining three pitch accents (on the stressed syllables of *all*, *coconut*, and *cream*) are simple H* accents, which are reflected in relatively high values of the pitch track.

Doing a ToBI analysis is not an automatic procedure. The elements of an analysis have neither invariant acoustic signals nor invariant syntactic associations that would unambiguously signal their identity. Nonetheless, training in the ToBI system does permit researchers to provide a rich, informative, and consistent description of the materials they are studying.

Once prosody has been described, psycholinguists can ask how it functions in language comprehension. Prosody can convey a speaker's attitude and emotion, it can help integrate a sentence into the proceeding discourse, and it can disambiguate otherwise ambiguous sentences. Consider the last function first. Some of the ambiguities that affect reading can disappear in listening. A typical student's first response to seeing the 'late closure' garden path sentence *Because John ran a mile seemed short* (Frazier and Rayner 1982) is that the possible misinterpretation would be blocked by speaking the sentence (or by putting a comma after *ran* in its written version). There are experimental demonstrations that speakers can provide cues that resolve such ambiguities as *The old men and women stayed home* (Lehiste 1973; Lehiste *et al.* 1976; were the women who stayed home old?). It is interesting that speakers may provide markedly more adequate cues when they are given clear reasons to do so—for example if the contrast they are supposed to disambiguate is made clear to them (Allbritton *et al.* 1996; Lehiste 1973; Wales and Toner 1979).

This observation means that a speaker has some options in what prosody to assign to an utterance, and reflects the important point that there is not a one-to-one mapping between syntax and prosody (Selkirk 1984, 1995; cf. Shattuck-Hufnagel and Turk 1996, for a review). A given syntactic structure can have multiple acceptable prosodic realizations, and a given prosody can be ambiguous between two or more syntactic structures. One can legitimately convey the same message by saying *The woman sent the gift to her daughter, The woman ^ sent the gift to her daughter,* and *The woman sent the gift ^ to her daughter* (intonational phrase breaks marked by '^'). Not all possibilities are legitimate, though. Selkirk (1984) notes that sentences like *The woman gave ^ the gift to her daughter* violate what she calls the 'Sense Unit Condition'. Conversely, one can convey either the message that the cop or the robber had a gun with the utterance *The cop shot the robber with a gun* (as well as several of its prosodic variants). While not all ambiguities can be eliminated prosodically, we can still legitimately ask what kinds of ambiguities can be resolved by what prosodic information, and we can ask how the processor uses this information.

One common goal of early work on prosody was to map out what sorts of ambiguities could be resolved in spoken language (e.g. Wales and Toner 1979). Success in reaching this goal was limited. It is not too much of a caricature to say that the basic conclusion was, if you want to get across a weird interpretation, say the sentence in a weird way. A more enduring suggestion of the early work is that some ambiguities of how the string of words could be broken up into phrases ('bracketing ambiguities', as *old men and women*) could be disambiguated prosodically, but alternative syntactic category membership of the words or phrases ('labeling ambiguities', as *visiting relatives can be a nuisance*) could not (Lehiste 1973).

This early work suffered from the lack of an adequate and explicit way of describing prosody, and it suffered from limitations of the then current syntactic analyses with their heavy emphasis on a distinction between deep and surface structure. However, it did point to important effects of the presence of prosodic boundaries at potential syntactic boundaries. It established the existence of acoustic correlates of major syntactic boundaries (e.g. lengthening and greater F_0 movement; Cooper and Paccia-Cooper 1980; Cooper and Sorenson 1981), and demonstrated that listeners can make use of these cues. In fact, some researchers interpreted the apparent limitation of prosodic disambiguation to bracketing ambiguities to suggest that prosodic boundaries provide the only prosodic information that is used in disambiguating ambiguous sentences (e.g. Lehiste 1973; Nespor and Vogel 1986). Price *et al.* (1991) present a particularly strong argument for this position, suggesting that only major intonational phrase breaks (in the ToBI system intonational phrase boundaries, as opposed to intermediate phrase boundaries) will successfully disambiguate strings like *Mary knows many languages you know.*

More recent work suggests that this claim is too strong. Speer *et al.* (1996) (cf. Kjelgaard and Speer, in press) studied sentences like (1).

(1)   a. Whenever the guard checks ˆ the door ˆ it's locked.

b. Whenever the guard checks ˆ the door ˆ is locked.

They found that placing either an intonational phrase boundary or a less salient pho-nological phrase boundary at one of the points marked by a ˆ effectively disambiguated the sentence. These sentences are sometimes referred to as 'late closure' ambiguities, because of Frazier's (1979) analysis of the preference for (1a) in terms of her late closure strategy. The ambiguous NP, *the door*, is preferentially taken as the object of the first, subordinate clause verb, *checks*. Speer *et al.*'s (1996) work shows that placing either kind of boundary in the appropriate position (after *the door* for (1a), before for (1b)) affects parsing preferences, when compared to placing the boundary in the other position.

Schafer *et al.* (1996) provided evidence that at least one kind of syntactic ambiguity can be disambiguated by placement of a pitch accent without changing the prosodic phrasing. They studied sentences like (2), in which the relative clause *that we bought yesterday* could legitimately modify either the first (2a) or the second noun (2b). They found that putting a H* pitch accent (indicated by upper case letters) on one of these two nouns made it more likely to be chosen as the host for the modifying relative clause.

(2)   a. We already have to repair the TIRE of the bicycle that we bought yesterday.

b. We already have to repair the tire of the BICYCLE that we bought yesterday.

Given that at least some aspects of prosody can effectively resolve syntactic ambi-guities, we can ask how they have their effect. One suggestion that was made earlier can be rejected. It might be that prosodic disambiguation is asymmetrical, so that a marked prosody can convey a marked structure but no prosody could disambiguate in favour of a normally-preferred structure. Speer *et al.*'s (1996) work used a baseline prosody, without a break either before or after the ambiguous NP (*the door*), as well as the two prosodic patterns shown earlier in (1). This baseline was judged to be equally appro-priate for either interpretation (*the door* as object of the first verb, or subject of the second). Using two different techniques (end-of-sentence comprehension time, and the time taken to name a visual probe that was a legitimate or an illegitimate continuation of the sentence; cf. Marslen-Wilson *et al.* 1992), Speer *et al.* reported both facilitation and interference as a result of different placements of a prosodic break, compared to the baseline condition.

Another question is whether prosody is used on-line to determine initial analysis, or simply after-the-fact to guide revision of an otherwise-preferred analysis that turned out to be grammatically or pragmatically inappropriate. Pynte and Prieur (1996) provide the most recent statement of the revision-support proposal as one of two possible accounts of their data on time taken to identify the occurrence of a target word in a prosodically-appropriate or inappropriate sentence. However, the proposal does not offer an attractive account of how prosody can disambiguate utterances that are fully ambiguous apart from prosody. Research on 'on-line' effects in auditory sentence processing may also provide evidence against the proposal. Marslen-Wilson *et al.* (1992) played their subjects an auditory string that, apart from prosody, was ambiguous between NP- and S-complement interpretations (3).

(3) The teacher noticed one girl from her class ...   WAS

The phrase *one girl from her class* is temporarily ambiguous between being the direct object of *notice* and the subject of a yet-to-appear complement sentence. Marslen-Wilson *et al.* measured the time to name a probe word (*was* in example (3)) when the string had been recorded with *one girl* ... as part of a sentence complement and when it had been recorded with *one girl* ... as direct object. Note that the word *was* fits with the sentence complement analysis (where *was* can play the role of verb to the subject *one girl* ...); it does not fit with the direct-object analysis. Times were faster when the probe word fit with how the sentence was recorded, strongly suggesting that the listener used prosody to help in analysing the structure of the sentence.

This evidence does not fully rule out Pynte and Prieur's (1996) revision-support account of prosody. Watt and Murray (1996) provide some methodological criticisms of the Marslen-Wilson *et al.* experiments and present data suggesting that they may be replicable only under severely constrained conditions. Further, it is not inconceivable that any effects observed using this task reflect revision processes invoked in trying to fit the probe word into the sentence. Clearly, better on-line research techniques are needed before the issue can be considered settled (cf. Ferreira *et al.* 1996, for further discussion).

Even if experimental evidence is not yet adequate to demonstrate conclusively that parsing decisions (not just parsing reanalysis processes) are guided by prosody, it is interesting to consider the possible ways in which prosody could guide parsing. One way, implicit in much early research, is for prosody to provide local cues. A prosodic break, for instance, could be a local signal to terminate a syntactic phrase (Marcus and Hindle 1990). An alternative hypothesis is that the listener constructs a full prosodic representation, presumably along the lines described by Pierrehumbert (1980), and this representation serves as one input to the parser (cf. Slowiaczek 1981, for an early precursor to this proposal; see Schafer 1996, for a careful examination of the hypothesis and comparisons with other hypotheses; see Beckman 1996, for an analysis of how the prosodic representation might be constructed from the speech signal).

Schafer (1996) presents some evidence in favour of the full prosodic representation hypothesis combined with the concept of 'visibility' (cf. Frazier and Clifton 1998), which claims that syntactic nodes within the current phonological phrase are more visible than nodes outside it, and hence preferred as attachment sites. She demonstrated fewer VP interpretations (47 vs. 64 per cent) of sentences like (4)—interpretations in which the prepositional phrase *with a mean look* is taken to modify the verb rather than the noun—when a phonological phrase (PPh) boundary intervened between *angered* and *the rider* (4a) than when it did not (4b; IPh denotes intonational phrase boundary).

(4)   a. (The bus driver angered L–)$_{PPh}$ (the rider with a mean look L–)$_{PPh}$ (L%)$_{IPh}$

    b. (The bus driver angered the rider with a mean look L–)$_{PPh}$ (L%)$_{IPh}$

This finding would not be predicted by a local cue mechanism, since the phonological phrase boundary did not occur at a point of ambiguity or a point where a phrase could be ended, even though it did contribute to the full prosodic description of the utterance (note, all content words except *driver* had a H* accent in Schafer's materials).

A full prosodic representation may play a role in interpreting sentences semantically as well as integrating them into discourses. In other research, Schafer (1996) presents evidence that intonational phrases (rather than phonological or intermediate phrases, which she claims play a role in parsing) are the domains within which semantic interpretation is completed. Listeners presented with an ambiguous word like *glasses* seem to have committed more fully to its preferred meaning when an intonational phrase boundary intervenes between the ambiguous word and its disambiguation than when a phonological phrase boundary does. The presence of the intonational phrase boundary increased the amount of disruption in end-of-sentence comprehension time when the utterance forced *glasses* to be analysed in its unpreferred (spectacles) sense.

While only a modest amount of research indicates that prosody plays a role in semantic interpretation, there is ample evidence that it figures importantly in how pragmatic factors affect the construction of a discourse interpretation. Prosody highlights the information in an utterance that is salient to the discourse as it has developed (Bolinger 1978). For instance, it is appropriate to place a pitch accent, signalling focus, on the phrase that answers a *wh*-question (thus, *GEORGE bought the flowers* but not *George bought the FLOWERS* appropriately answers the question *Who bought the flowers?*). Accented words, as well as words on which focus is appropriately placed, are identified faster (as measured by a phoneme-detection task) than non-accented words (Cutler and Fodor 1979; Cutler and Foss 1977), as well as being better remembered in their surface form (Birch and Garnsey 1995). They are taken as 'new' as opposed to 'given' (Chafe 1974; Halliday 1967). If a phrase that should be treated as given receives accent, comprehension can be disrupted; failing to place a pitch accent on a new phrase seems to disrupt comprehension even more (Bock and Mazella 1983; Nooteboom and Terken 1982; Terken and Nooteboom 1987). Going beyond the given/new contrast, placing a pitch accent on a phrase that selects between two contrasting possibilities in a discourse context can facilitate comprehension. Sedivy *et al.* (1995, see also Eberhard *et al.* 1995) showed that listeners who were told to select the *LARGE red square* selected it rapidly when the options were a large red square, a small red square, a large blue circle, and a small yellow triangle. The accent on *LARGE* was apparently interpreted as contrastive, allowing the listener immediately to select the one figure that contrasted with another in size.

The use of prosody in discourse interpretation is guided by the listener's knowledge of the prosodic structure of his or her language, not just by a crude principle such as 'important words are accented'. For instance, Birch and Clifton (1995) replicated Bock and Mazzella's (1983) finding of faster comprehension and higher prosodic acceptability judgements when focus fell on new information than the given information contained in the answer of a question–answer pair. They went further, though, by demonstrating that not every piece of new information in the focused phrase had to receive a pitch accent. Following a question like *What did Tina do when the neighbours were away?*, listeners were as quick and accurate at understanding the answer *She walked the DOG* , where only *dog* receives pitch accent, as the answer *She WALKED the DOG*, where both pieces of new information receive accent. This follows from Selkirk's (1984, 1995) theory of focus projection in English. According to this theory, an English listener's knowledge of language permits FOCUS to spread from a pitch-accented argument of a phrase (*the dog*) to the unaccented head of the phrase (*walked*), and then to the whole phrase. Since the whole phrase receives FOCUS (even without all being accented), the whole phrase can be treated as new information. And since this is a property of English language structure, it shows that the effects of prosody are mediated by the listener's knowledge of language structure, perhaps by the creation of a full prosodic representation.

We will close this section by mentioning briefly two other discourse roles of prosody. First, prosody is clearly relevant to the interpretation of anaphors. *Mary hit Sue and then she BIT her* is surely different from *Mary hit Sue and then SHE bit HER* (cf. Solan 1980). Further, as discussed by Cutler *et al.* (1997), there may be a close tie between unaccented words and anaphoric devices generally: both are used to refer to entities already introduced into the discourse. Finally, as also discussed by Cutler *et al.*, prosody can be used to impose structure on entire discourses. It can be used to signal, among other things, the introduction of a new topic or the end of an old one, or even the end of a speaker's turn.

5.7 The architecture of the listening system

The process sketched in Fig. 5.1 converts a spoken input to a representation of meaning. We have drawn it as encompassing various levels of processing, with a unidirectional flow of information from the input of sound to the output of utterance meaning. But the flow of information in the process of comprehension has been a fiercely disputed topic in psycholinguistics. Thus there is an abundance of experimental evidence pertaining to the question of autonomy versus interactivity of the various operations described in the preceding sections. In particular, the relationship of prelexical processing to lexical information, and of syntactic processing to information from the semantic and discourse context, have been the object of research attention.

Boland and Cutler (1996) have pointed out that current models of spoken-language comprehension can no longer be crudely characterized as in general interactive, or in general autonomous. Computational implementation, and refinement of model specification, has meant that it is necessary to consider the relationships between individual sub-components of each model; models may allow various degrees of interaction or autonomy and these may differ across processing levels. In this final section we consider the directionality of the flow of information in particular parts of Fig. 5.1.

5.7.1 Decoding, segmenting, and lexical processing

Space considerations prohibit even a summary of the enormous literature on the question of whether lexical information constrains prelexical processing. A recent review of this literature (Norris *et al.* 1998) concludes, however, that there is no necessity for models of this aspect of the listening process to include top–down connections—that is a reversal of the information flow, wherein lexical processing passes information back to affect the decoding processes etc. The literature in question contains numerous cases in which experimental findings have been held to warrant top–down information flow, but in which subsequent experimental or theoretical work has shown this claim to be unjustified.

One such case history concerns compensation for coarticulation (a shift in the category boundary for a particular phoneme distinction as a function of the preceding phonetic context). Elman and McClelland (1988) apparently induced such compensation from lexical information; the preceding phonetic context supplied in their experiment was in fact a constant token ambiguous between [s] and [ʃ], but it occurred at the end of *Christma** versus *fooli**. Listeners' responses to the phoneme following this constant token were shifted in the same direction as was found with the truly different phonemes at the end of *Christmas* and *foolish*. Elman and McClelland simulated their result in TRACE (a connectionist model of spoken-word recognition, see section 5.4.1) and attributed it to TRACE's feedback connections between the lexical and the phoneme level. Norris (1993), however, simulated the same experimental findings in a network with no feedback connections. Subsequent studies then showed that the contextual dependence of compensation for coarticulation apparently reflects listeners' knowledge of transitional probabilities (Pitt and McQueen, 1998). Thus, both empirical and theoretical arguments disproved Elman and McClelland's original claim.

Norris *et al.* (1998) have argued, furthermore, that top–down feedback from the lexical level to prelexical processing stages cannot even improve recognition performance. After all, the best word-recognition performance is achieved by selection of the best lexical match(es) to whatever prelexical representation has been computed. Adding feedback from the lexical level to the prelexical level does not improve the lexical level's performance, but merely confirms it. Indeed, simulations with TRACE have shown that the overall accuracy of the model is neither better nor worse if the top–down connections which the model normally contains are removed (Frauenfelder and Peeters, in press).

This is not to deny that top–down information flow can result in alteration of prelexical decisions. For instance, if the output of prelexical processing is the string of phonetic representations /s*i/ in which the * represents some unclearly perceived stop consonant, top–down activation from the lexicon (which contains the word *ski*, but neither *spee* or *stee*) might change the prelexical decision from uncertainty, to a certain decision that there had been a [k]. But if in fact there had not been a [k], because the speaker had actually made a slip of the tongue and said *spee* or *stee*, then the top–down information flow would, strictly speaking, have led to poorer performance by the prelexical processor, since it would have caused a wrong decision to be made about the phonetic structure of the input.

Thus top–down connections can clear up ambiguity in prelexical processing, but they do so at a potential cost; and more importantly, they do not result in an improvement of word recognition accuracy. There seems no need to build such connections into the blueprint of the listener.

5.7.2 Word recognition and utterance context

While the listener's knowledge of his or her lexicon may not directly feed into perceptual decisions of what segments are being heard, top–down influences may play a bigger role at higher levels of processing. The substantive context in which an ambiguous word, such as *bank* or *bug*, is heard clearly influences its interpretation. You do not think that a police agent is talking about insects if you hear him talking about putting a bug in a suspect's room. The interpretation of this observation, however, has shifted over the years. For a while, it was popular to suggest that a listener's context-based expectations played essentially the same role in word recognition as did perception of the physical signal (see Riesbeck and Schank 1978, for a particularly extreme statement of this position, extended to all of language comprehension). Experimental work reviewed earlier in this chapter (e.g. Swinney 1979) led to the opposite conclusion, that words were recognized (at least in the sense of the mental representations of all their senses being activated) regardless of context. Context was left the role of selecting from among the activated alternatives.

More recent work, also reviewed earlier, suggests that a strong enough context can effectively eliminate measurable activation of inappropriate word senses. Still, current theoretical opinion is sharply divided about the direction of information flow between the word recognition system and utterance-level processing. Some word recognition models (e.g. TRACE, McClelland and Elman 1986) assume that utterance context can activate mental representations of words directly, implying a top–down flow of information from higher-level processing to lexical processing. (Note, however, that the 1986 implementation of TRACE does not actually incorporate levels of processing above word recognition.) Other models (e.g. the Cohort model, Marslen-Wilson 1990, or Shortlist, Norris 1994) propose that the activation of words is immune from higher-level influence (although again, these models have not been implemented with utterance-level processing). In these models, as described in section 5.4.1, activation is automatic and may be initiated by partial information about a word; activated candidates are checked against current contextual representations, and early and powerful effects of context reflect the rapidity with which this check can lead to inhibition of inappropriate candidates.

No empirical data are as yet available to decide this issue. In line with the conclusion of section 5.7.1, it might therefore seem unnecessary at this point to build top-down information flow into the blueprint of the listener's word recognition system.

5.7.3 Syntactic and semantic processing

A similar theoretical contrast exists concerning how meaning and plausibility might influence the extraction of a message from a sentence. Here, though, as noted by Boland and Cutler (1996), some theoretical positions in which context and plausibility select from among several alternative structural analyses are termed 'interactive', while theories of word recognition that make a similar claim were termed 'autonomous'. This is partly because of Frazier's (1979, 1987) garden-path theory of parsing, which claims that a single structural analysis of a sentence is constructed on the basis of speed and economy, and later evaluated against context. In this context, a theory in which multiple candidates are allowed to compete with one another is interactive.

In Frazier's original theory, only a very limited amount of grammatical information was assumed to be used in constructing the initial analysis of a sentence. Recent work has expanded the range of grammatical information that seems to play an immediate role in initial sentence processing, most notably to include prosodic information. Prosody may be used to create a full prosodic representation of a sentence, developed in parallel with a mutually-constraining syntactic representation (cf. Frazier 1990, for an architecture that would permit this), or it might be viewed as another informational constraint in a constraint-satisfaction model such as that of MacDonald *et al.* (1994).

The question of the relation between syntactic and higher-level processing, however, still occasions much debate. Perhaps new advances will shortly be made here with new techniques. Electrophysiological studies of listening to spoken sentences, for instance, show clearly separable effects of violations of grammaticality and violations of semantic structure (Friederici 1998; Hagoort and Brown, in press). This suggests at least that comprehension models should incorporate appropriate distinctions between syntactic and semantic processing.

Currently, however, models are concerned to account for the many research results of the past decade showing that semantic context and plausibility, but also frequency of usage, are taken into account very quickly during parsing. Some models focus on how these factors may guide decisions among alternative syntactic structures. Tanenhaus *et al.* (in press) explicitly present their model as a model of such decisions, acknowledging that other theories must be devised to explain where the structures being decided among come from. MacDonald *et al.* (1994) suggest that the structures are simply projected from the lexical heads of phrases, a suggestion that has been criticized as inadequate by Frazier (1995). Other models (e.g. Frazier and Clifton 1996) focus more on the process by which structural analyses are initially constructed and less on how eventual selections are made. A compromise model was proposed by Boland (1997), involving constraint-based selection in combination with parallel autonomous generation of alternative structures. However, no completely satisfactory theory of how syntactic and extra-syntactic information are co-ordinated in comprehending language is in our opinion as yet available. As Boland and Cutler (1996) concluded, the field has moved beyond a simplistic modular/ interactive contrast, but the more refined models which are now needed have not as yet been formulated and tested. The coming few years should prove exciting and productive for researchers involved in investigating spoken-language comprehension.

Acknowledgements

We thank Brechtje Post for the ToBI transcription in Fig. 5.2, and James McQueen for helpful comments on the text.

References

Abney, S. (1989). A computational model of human parsing. *Journal of Psycholinguistic Research*, **18**, 129–44.

Allbritton, D:, McKoon, G., and Ratcliff, R. (1996). The reliability of prosodic cues for resolving syntactic ambiguity. *Journal of Experimental Psychology: Learning, Memory, and Cognition*, **22**, 714–35.

Baayen, R. H., Dijkstra, T., and Schreuder, R. (1997). Singulars and plurals in Dutch: Evidence for a parallel dual route model. *Journal of Memory and Language*, **37**, 94–117.

Bader, M. (1994). *The assignment of sentence accent during reading.* Paper presented at the CUNY᾿ Sentence Processing Conference, March, 1994, New York City.

Bard, E. G., Shillcock, R. C., and Altmann, G. T. M. (1988). The recognition of words after their acoustic offsets in spontaneous speech: Effects of subsequent context. *Perception and Psychophysics*, **44**, 395–408.

Beckman, M. (1996). The parsing of prosody. *Language and Cognitive Processes*, **11**, 17–67.

Beckman, M. E. and Ayers, G. M. (1993). *Guidelines for ToBI labelling, version 2.0.* Ohio State University.

Beckman, M. E. and Pierrehumbert, J. B. (1986). Intonational structure in Japanese and English. *Phonology*, **3**, 255–309.

Bever, T. G. (1970). The cognitive basis for linguistic structures. In *Cognition and the development of language* (ed. J. R. Hayes), pp. 279–352. Wiley, New York.

Birch, S. and Clifton, C., Jr (1995). Focus, accent, and argument structure. *Language and Speech*, **33**, 365–91.

Birch, S. and Garnsey, S. M. (1995). The effect of focus on memory for words in sentences. *Journal of Memory and Language*, **34**, 232–67.

Bock, J. K. and Mazzella, J. R. (1983). Intonational marking of given and new information: Some consequences for comprehension. *Memory and Cognition*, **11**, 64–76.

Boland, J. E. (1997). The relationship between syntactic and semantic processes in sentence comprehension. *Language and Cognitive Processes*, **12**, 423–84.

Boland, J. E. and Cutler, A. (1996). Interaction with autonomy: Multiple output models and the inadequacy of the Great Divide. *Cognition*, **58**, 309–20.

Bolinger, D. (1978). Intonation across languages. In *Universals of human language, Vol 2: Phonology* (ed. J. J. Greenberg.), pp. 471–524. Stanford University Press.

Bond, Z. S. (1981). Listening to elliptic speech: Pay attention to stressed vowels. *Journal of Phonetics*, **9**, 89–96.

Bond, Z. S. and Small, L. H. (1983). Voicing, vowel and stress mispronunciations in continuous speech. *Perception and Psychophysics*, **34**, 470–74.

Bradley, D. C., Sánchez-Casas, R. M., and García-Albea, J. E. (1993). The status of the syllable in the perception of Spanish and English. *Language and Cognitive Processes*, **8**, 197–233.

Bregman, A. S. (1990). *Auditory scene analysis: The perceptual organization of sound.* MIT Press, Cambridge, MA.

Bresnan, J. (1982). *The mental representation of grammatical relations.* MIT Press, Cambridge, MA.

Brown, G. D. A. (1984). A frequency count of 190,000 words in the London-Lund Corpus of English Conversation. *Behavior Research Methods, Instrumentation and Computers,* **16,** 502–32.

Caramazza, A., Laudanna, A., and Romani, C. (1988). Lexical access and inflectional morphology. *Cognition,* **28,** 297–332.

Carroll, P. J. and Slowiaczek, M. L. (1987). Modes and modules: Multiple pathways to the language processor. In *Modularity in sentence comprehension: Knowledge representation and natural language understanding* (ed. J. L. Garfield), pp. 221–48. MIT Press, Cambridge, MA.

Chafe, W. L. (1974). Language and consciousness. *Language,* **50,** 111–33.

Chen, H.-C. and Cutler, A. (1997). Auditory priming in spoken and printed word recognition. In *The cognitive processing of Chinese and related Asian languages* (ed. H.-C. Chen), pp. 77–81. Chinese University Press, Hong Kong.

Cluff, M. S. and Luce, P. A. (1990). Similarity neighborhoods of spoken two-syllable words: Retroactive effects on multiple activation. *Journal of Experimental Psychology: Human Perception and Performance,* **16,** 551–63.

Connine, C. M., Titone, D., Deelman, T., and Blasko, D. (1997). Similarity mapping in spoken word recognition. *Journal of Memory and Language,* **37,** 463–80.

Conrad, C. (1974). Context effects in sentence comprehension: A study of the subjective lexicon. *Memory and Cognition,* **2,** 130–8.

Cooper, W. and Paccia-Cooper, J. (1980). *Syntax and speech.* Harvard University Press, Cambridge, MA.

Cooper, W. and Sorenson, J. (1981). *Fundamental frequency in speech production.* Springer, New York.

Cowan, N. (1984). On short and long auditory stores. *Psychological Bulletin,* **96,** 341–70.

Cutler, A. (1986). *Forbear* is a homophone: Lexical prosody does not constrain lexical access. *Language and Speech,* **29,** 201–20.

Cutler, A. and Butterfield, S. (1992). Rhythmic cues to speech segmentation: Evidence from juncture misperception. *Journal of Memory and Language,* **31,** 218–36.

Cutler, A. and Carter, D. M. (1987). The predominance of strong initial syllables in the English vocabulary. *Computer Speech and Language,* **2,** 133–42.

Cutler, A. and Chen, H.-C. (1995). Phonological similarity effects in Cantonese word recognition. *Proceedings of the Thirteenth International Congress of Phonetic Sciences, Stockholm,* **1,** 106–9.

Cutler, A. and Chen, H.-C. (1997). Lexical tone in Cantonese spoken-word processing. *Perception and Psychophysics,* **59,** 165–79.

Cutler, A. and Fodor, J. A. (1979). Semantic focus and sentence comprehension. *Cognition,* **7,** 49–59.

Cutler, A. and Foss, D. J. (1977). On the role of sentence stress in sentence processing. *Language and Speech,* **20,** 1–10.

Cutler, A. and Norris, D. G. (1988). The role of strong syllables in segmentation for lexical access. *Journal of Experimental Psychology: Human Perception and Performance,* **14,** 113–21.

Cutler, A. and Otake, T. (1994). Mora or phoneme? Further evidence for language-specific listening. *Journal of Memory and Language*, **33**, 824–44.

Cutler, A. and Otake, T. (1999). Pitch accent in spoken-word recognition in Japanese. *Journal of the Acoustical Society of America.*

Cutler, A., Mehler, J., Norris, D. G., and Segui, J. (1986). The syllable's differing role in the segmentation of French and English. *Journal of Memory and Language*, **25**, 385–400.

Cutler, A., Dahan, D., and Van Donselaar, W. (1997). Prosody in the comprehension of spoken language: A literature review. *Language and Speech*, **40**, 141–201.

Donselaar, W. van, Koster, M., and Cutler, A. *Voornaam* is not a homophone: Lexical prosody and lexical access in Dutch. (Manuscript.)

Eberhard, K. M., Spivey-Knowlton, M. J., Sedivy, J. C., and Tanenhaus, M. K. (1995). Eye movements as a window into real-time spoken language comprehension in natural contexts. *Journal of Psycholinguistic Research*, **24**, 409–36.

Elman, J. L. and McClelland, J. L. (1986). Exploiting lawful variability in the speech wave. In *Invariance and variability in speech processes* (eds J. S. Perkell and D. H. Klatt), pp. 360–86. Erlbaum, NJ.

Elman, J. L. and McClelland, J. L. (1988). Cognitive penetration of the mechanisms of perception: Compensation for coarticulation of lexically restored phonemes. *Journal of Memory and Language*, **27**, 143–65.

Fear, B. D., Cutler, A., and Butterfield, S. (1995). The strong/weak syllable distinction in English. *Journal of the Acoustical Society of America*, **97**, 1893–904.

Ferreira, F., Anes, M. D., and Horine, M. D. (1996). Exploring the use of prosody during language comprehension using the auditory moving window technique. *Journal of Psycholinguistic Research*, **25**, 273–90.

Foss, D. J. and Gernsbacher, M. A. (1983). Cracking the dual code: Toward a unitary model of phonetic identification. *Journal of Verbal Learning and Verbal Behavior*, **22**, 609–32.

Fox, R. A. and Unkefer, J. (1985). The effect of lexical status on the perception of tone. *Journal of Chinese Linguistics*, **13**, 69–90.

Frauenfelder, U. H. (1991). Lexical alignment and activation in spoken word recognition. In *Music, language, speech and brain* (eds J. Sundberg, L. Nord , and R. Carlson), pp. 294–303. Macmillan, London.

Frauenfelder, U. H. and Peeters, G. Simulating the time-course of spoken word recognition: An analysis of lexical competition in TRACE. In *Symbolic connectionism* (eds J. Grainger and A. M. Jacobs). Erlbaum, NJ. (In press.)

Frazier, L. (1979). *On comprehending sentences: Syntactic parsing strategies*. Indiana University Linguistics Club, Bloomington.

Frazier, L. (1987). Sentence processing: A tutorial review. In *Attention and performance*, Vol. 12 (ed. M. Coltheart), pp. 559–86. Erlbaum, NJ.

Frazier, L. (1989). Against lexical generation of syntax. In *Lexical representation and process* (ed. W.D. Marslen-Wilson), pp. 505–28. MIT Press, Cambridge, MA.

Frazier, L. (1990). Exploring the architecture of the language system. In *Cognitive models of speech processing: Psycholinguistic and computational perspectives* (ed. G. T. M. Altmann), pp. 409–33. MIT Press, Cambridge, MA.

Frazier, L. (1995). Constraint satisfaction as a theory of sentence processing. *Journal of Psycholinguistic Research*, **24**, 437–68.

Frazier, L. and Clifton, C., Jr (1996). *Construal*. MIT Press, Cambridge, MA.

Frazier, L. and Clifton, C., Jr. (1998). Sentence reanalysis, and visibility. In *Sentence Reanalysis* (eds J. D. Fodor and F. Ferreira), pp. 143–76. Kluwer, Dordrecht.

Frazier, L. and Rayner, K. (1982). Making and correcting errors during sentence comprehension: Eye movements in the analysis of structurally ambiguous sentences. *Cognitive Psychology*, **14**, 178–210.

Friederici, A. D. (1998). The neurobiology of language processing. In *Language comprehension: A biological perspective* (ed. A. D. Friederici), pp. 263–301. Springer, Heidelberg.

Fujimura, O. and Lovins, J. B. (1978). Syllables as concatenative phonetic units. In *Syllables and segments* (eds A. Bell and J. B. Hooper), pp. 107–20. North-Holland, Amsterdam.

Gaskell, M. G. and Marslen-Wilson, W. D. (1997). Integrating form and meaning: A distributed model of speech perception. *Language and Cognitive Processes*, **12**, 613–56.

Glanzer, M. (1976). Intonation grouping and related words in free recall. *Journal of Verbal Learning and Verbal Behavior*, **15**, 85–92.

Goldinger, S. D. (1998). Echoes of echoes? An episodic theory of lexical access. *Psychological Review*, **105**, 251–79.

Goldinger, S. D., Luce, P. A., and Pisoni, D. B. (1989). Priming lexical neighbours of spoken words: Effects of competition and inhibition. *Journal of Memory and Language*, **28**, 501–18.

Goldinger, S. D., Luce, P. A., Pisoni, D. B., and Marcario, J. K. (1992). Form-based priming in spoken word recognition: The roles of competition and bias. *Journal of Experimental Psychology: Learning, Memory, and Cognition*, **18**, 1211–38.

Gow, D. W. and Gordon, P. C. (1995). Lexical and prelexical influences on word segmentation: Evidence from priming. *Journal of Experimental Psychology: Human Perception and Performance*, **21**, 344–59.

Greenspan, S. L. (1986). Semantic flexibility and referential specificity of concrete nouns. *Journal of Memory and Language*, **25**, 539–57.

Grosjean, F. (1985). The recognition of words after their acoustic offset: Evidence and implications. *Perception and Psychophysics*, **38**, 299–310.

Grosjean, F. and Gee, J. (1987). Prosodic structure and spoken word recognition. *Cognition*, **25**, 135–55.

Hagoort, P. and Brown, C. M. Semantic and syntactic effects of listening to speech compared to reading. *Neuropsychologia*. (In press.)

Halliday, M. A. K. (1967). *Intonation and grammar in British English*. Mouton, The Hague.

Howes, D. (1966). A word count of spoken English. *Journal of Verbal Learning and Verbal Behavior*, **5**, 572–604.

Jennings, F., Randall, B., and Tyler, L. K. (1997). Graded effects of verb subcategory preferences on parsing: Support for constraint-satisfaction models. *Language and Cognitive Processes*, **12**, 485–504.

Kjelgaard, M. M. and Speer, S. R. Prosodic facilitation and interference in the resolution of temporary syntactic closure ambiguity. *Journal of Memory and Language*. (In press).

Klatt, D. H. (1979). Speech perception: A model of acoustic-phonetic analysis and lexical access. *Journal of Phonetics*, **7**, 279–312.

Klatt, D. H. (1989). Review of selected models of speech perception. In *Lexical representation and process* (ed. W. D. Marslen-Wilson), pp. 169–226. MIT Press, Cambridge, MA.

Kolinsky, R. (1992). Conjunction errors as a tool for the study of perceptual processing. In *Analytic approaches to human cognition* (eds J. Alegria, D. Holender, J. Morais, and M. Radeau), pp. 133–49. North Holland, Amsterdam.

Kong, Q. M. (1987). Influence of tones upon vowel duration in Cantonese. *Language and Speech*, **30**, 387–99.

Konieczny, L., Hemforth, B., Scheepers, C., and Strube, G. (1997). The role of lexical heads in parsing: Evidence from German. *Language and Cognitive Processes*, **12**, 307–48.

Kratochvil, P. (1971). An experiment in the perception of Peking dialect tones. In *A symposium on Chinese grammar* (ed. I.-L. Hansson). Curzon Press, Lund.

Lackner, J. R. and Garrett, M. F. (1972). Resolving ambiguity: Effects of biasing context in the unattended ear. *Cognition*, **1**, 359–72.

Ladd, D. R. (1996). *Intonational phonology*. Cambridge University Press.

Lahiri, A. and Marslen-Wilson, W. D. (1991). The mental representation of lexical form: A phonological approach to the recognition lexicon. *Cognition*, **38**, 245–94.

Lehiste, I. (1973). Phonetic disambiguation of syntactic ambiguity. *Glossa*, **7**, 107–22.

Lehiste, I., Olive, J., and Streeter, L. (1976). Role of duration in disambiguating syntactically ambiguous sentences. *Journal of the Acoustical Society of America*, **60**, 1199–202.

Liberman, A. M. and Mattingly, I. G. (1985). The motor theory of speech perception revised. *Cognition*, **21**, 1–36.

Liberman, A. M., Cooper, F. S., Shankweiler, D. P., and Studdert-Kennedy, M. (1967). Perception of the speech code. *Psychological Review*, **74**, 431–61.

Lucas, M. M. (1987). Frequency effects on the processing of ambiguous words in sentence contexts. *Language and Speech*, **30**, 25–46.

Luce, P. A. (1986). A computational analysis of uniqueness points in auditory word recognition. *Perception and Psychophysics*, **39**, 155–8.

Luce, P. A., Pisoni, D. B., and Goldinger, S. D. (1990). Similarity neighborhoods of spoken words. In *Cognitive models of speech processing* (ed. G. T. M. Altmann), pp. 122–147. MIT Press, Cambridge, MA.

MacDonald, M. C., Pearlmutter, N. J., and Seidenberg, M. S. (1994). Lexical nature of syntactic ambiguity resolution. *Psychological Review*, **101**, 676–703.

Maddieson, I. (1984). *Patterns of sounds*. Cambridge University Press.

Marcus, S. M. (1981). ERIS—Context-sensitive coding in speech perception. *Journal of Phonetics*, **9**, 197–220.

Marcus, S. M. and Frauenfelder, U. H. (1985). Word recognition: Uniqueness or deviation? A theoretical note. *Language and Cognitive Processes*, **1**, 163–9.

Marcus, M. and Hindle, D. (1990). Description theory and intonation boundaries. In *Cognitive models of speech processing* (ed. G. T. M. Altmann), pp. 483–512. MIT Press, Cambridge, MA.

Marslen-Wilson, W. D. (1990). Activation, competition and frequency in lexical access. In *Cognitive models of speech processing* (ed. G. T. M. Altmann), pp. 148–72. MIT Press, Cambridge, MA.

Marslen-Wilson, W. D. and Warren, P. (1994). Levels of perceptual representation and process in lexical access: Words, phonemes and features. *Psychological Review*, **101**, 653–75.

Marslen-Wilson, W. D. and Welsh, A. (1978). Processing interactions and lexical access during word recognition in continuous speech. *Cognitive Psychology*, **10**, 29–63.

Marslen-Wilson, W. D., Brown, C. M., and Tyler, L. K. (1988). Lexical representations in spoken language comprehension. *Language and Cognitive Processes*, **3**, 1–16.

Marslen-Wilson, W. D., Tyler, L. K., Warren, P., Grenier, P., and Lee, C. S. (1992). Prosodic effects in minimal attachment. *Quarterly Journal of Experimental Psychology*, **45A**, 730–87.

Marslen-Wilson, W. D., Tyler, L. K., Waksler, R., and Older, L. (1994). Morphology and meaning in the English mental lexicon. *Psychological Review*, **101**, 3–33.

Martin, J. G. and Bunnell, H. T. (1981). Perception of anticipatory coarticulation effects. *Journal of the Acoustical Society of America*, **69**, 559–67.

Martin, J. G. and Bunnell, H. T. (1982). Perception of anticipatory coarticulation effects in vowel-stop consonant-vowel sequences. *Journal of Experimental Psychology: Human Perception and Performance*, **8**, 473–88.

McClelland, J. L. and Elman, J. L. (1986). The TRACE model of speech perception. *Cognitive Psychology*, **18**, 1–86.

McQueen, J. M. (1998). Segmentation of continuous speech using phonotactics. *Journal of Memory and Language*, **39**, 21–46.

McQueen, J. M. and Cutler, A. (1992). Words within words: Lexical statistics and lexical access. *Proceedings of the Second International Conference on Spoken Language Processing, Banff, Canada*, **1**, 221–4.

McQueen, J. M. and Cutler, A. (1998). Morphology in word recognition. In *The handbook of morphology* (eds A. Spencer and A. M. Zwicky), pp. 406–27. Blackwell, Oxford.

McQueen, J. M., Norris, D. G., and Cutler, A. (1994). Competition in spoken word recognition: Spotting words in other words. *Journal of Experimental Psychology: Learning, Memory, and Cognition*, **20**, 621–38.

McQueen, J. M., Norris, D. G., and Cutler, A. Lexical influence in phonetic decision-making: Evidence from subcategorical mismatches. *Journal of Experimental Psychology: Human Perception and Performance*. (In press.)

Mehler, J., Dommergues, J.-Y., Frauenfelder, U. H., and Segui, J. (1981). The syllable's role in speech segmentation. *Journal of Verbal Learning and Verbal Behavior*, **20**, 298–305.

Miller, J. L. (1981). Some effects of speaking rate on phonetic perception. *Phonetica*, **38**, 159–80.

Miller, J. L. and Liberman, A. L. (1979). Some effects of later-occurring information on the perception of stop consonant and semivowel. *Perception and Psychophysics*, **25**, 457–65.

Nespor, M. and Vogel, I. (1986). *Prosodic phonology*. Foris, Dordrecht.

Nooteboom, S. G. and Terken, J. M. B. (1982). What makes speakers omit pitch accents: An experiment. *Phonetica*, **39**, 317–36.

Norris, D. G. (1993). Bottom-up connectionist models of 'interaction'. In *Cognitive models of speech processing* (eds G. T. M. Altmann and R. Shillcock), pp. 211–34. Erlbaum, NJ.

Norris, D. G. (1994). Shortlist: A connectionist model of continuous speech recognition. *Cognition*, **52**, 189–234.

Norris, D. G., McQueen, J. M., and Cutler, A. (1995). Competition and segmentation in spoken word recognition. *Journal of Experimental Psychology: Learning, Memory, and Cognition*, **21**, 1209–28.

Norris, D. G., McQueen, J. M., Cutler, A., and Butterfield, S. (1997). The possible-word constraint in the segmentation of continuous speech. *Cognitive Psychology*, **34**, 191–243.

Norris, D. G., McQueen, J. M., and Cutler, A. (1998). Merging phonetic and lexical information in phonetic decision-making. (Manuscript.)

Oden, G. C. and Spira, J. L. (1983). Influence of context on the activation and selection of ambiguous word senses. *Quarterly Journal of Experimental Psychology*, **35**, 51–64.

Onifer, W. and Swinney, D. A. (1981). Accessing lexical ambiguities during sentence comprehension: Effects of frequency-of-meaning and contextual bias. *Journal of Verbal Learning and Verbal Behavior*, **17**, 225–36.

Orsolini, M. and Marslen-Wilson, W. D. (1997). Universals in morphological representation: Evidence from Italian. *Language and Cognitive Processes*, **12**, 1–47.

Otake, T., Hatano, G., Cutler, A., and Mehler, J. (1993). Mora or syllable? Speech segmentation in Japanese. *Journal of Memory and Language*, **32**, 358–78.

Otake, T., Hatano, G., and Yoneyama, K. (1996*a*). Speech segmentation by Japanese listeners. In *Phonological structure and language processing: Cross-linguistic studies* (eds T. Otake and A. Cutler), pp. 183–201. Mouton de Gruyter, Berlin.

Otake, T., Yoneyama, K., Cutler, A., and Van der Lugt, A. (1996*b*). The representation of Japanese moraic nasals. *Journal of the Acoustical Society of America*, **100**, 3831–42.

Peretz, I., Lussier, I., and Béland, R. (1996). The roles of phonological and orthographic code in word stem completion. In *Phonological structure and language processing: Cross-linguistic studies* (eds T. Otake and A. Cutler), pp. 217–26. Mouton de Gruyter, Berlin.

Pierrehumbert, J. B. (1980). The phonology and phonetics of English intonation. Unpublished Ph.D. thesis, MIT.

Pisoni, D. B. and Luce, P. A. (1987). Acoustic-phonetic representations in word recognition. *Cognition*, **25**, 21–52.

Pitt, M. A. and McQueen, J. M. (1998). Is compensation for coarticulation mediated by the lexicon? *Journal of Memory and Language*, **39**, 347–70.

Pollard, C. and Sag, I. A. (1994). *Head-driven phrase structure grammar*. CSLI, Stanford.

Price, P. J., Ostendorf, M., Shattuck-Huffnagel, S., and Fong, C. (1991). The use of prosody in syntactic disambiguation. *Journal of the Acoustical Society of America*, **90**, 2956–70.

Pustejovsky, J. (1995). *The generative lexicon*. MIT Press, Cambridge, MA.

Pynte, J. and Prieur, B. (1996). Prosodic breaks and attachment decisions in sentence processing. *Language and Cognitive Processes*, **11**, 165–92.

Rayner, K. and Pollatsek, A. (1989). *The psychology of reading*. Prentice-Hall, Englewood Cliffs, NJ.

Rayner, K. and Pollatsek, A. (1996). Reading unspaced text is not easy: Comments on the implications of Epelboim *et al.*'s (1994) study for models of eye movement control in reading. *Vision Research*, **36**, 461–70.

Riesbeck, C. K. and Schank, R. (1978). Comprehension by computer: Expectation-based analysis of sentences in context. In *Studies in the perception of language* (eds W. J. M. Levelt and G. B. Floris d' Arcais), pp. 247–94. Wiley, New York.

Ryan, J. (1969). Grouping and short-term memory: Different means and patterns of grouping. *Quarterly Journal of Experimental Psychology*, **21**, 137–47.

Samuel, A. G. (1989). Insights from a failure of selective adaptation: Syllable-initial and syllable-final consonants are different. *Perception and Psychophysics*, **45**, 485–93.

Schafer, A. (1996). Prosodic parsing: The role of prosody in sentence comprehension. Unpublished Ph.D. thesis. University of Massachusetts, Amherst.

Schafer, A., Carter, J., Clifton, C., Jr., and Frazier, L. (1996). Focus in relative clause construal. *Language and Cognitive Processes*, **11**, 135–63.

Schriefers, H., Zwitserlood, P., and Roelofs, A. (1991). The identification of morphologically complex spoken words: Continuous processing or decomposition? *Journal of Memory and Language*, **30**, 26–47.

Sebastian-Gallés, N., Dupoux, E., Segui, J., and Mehler, J. (1992). Contrasting syllabic effects in Catalan and Spanish. *Journal of Memory and Language*, **31**, 18–32.

Sedivy, J., Tanenhaus, M., Spivey-Knowlton, M., Eberhard, K., and Carlson, G. (1995). Using intonationally-marked presuppositional information in on-line language processing: Evidence from eye movements to a visual model. *Proceedings of the Seventeenth Annual Conference of the Cognitive Science Society*, 375–80. Erlbaum, Hillsdale, NJ.

Segui, J. (1984). The syllable: A basic perceptual unit in speech processing? In *Attention and performance X: Control of language processes* (eds H. Bouma and D. G. Bouwhuis), pp. 165–82 . Erlbaum, NJ.

Segui, J., Frauenfelder, U. H., and Mehler, J. (1981). Phoneme monitoring, syllable monitoring and lexical access. *British Journal of Psychology*, **72**, 471–77.

Seidenberg, M. S., Tanenhaus, M. K., Leiman, J. M., and Bienkowski, M. (1982). Automatic access of the meanings of ambiguous words in context: Some limitations of knowledge-based processing. *Cognitive Psychology*, **14**, 489–537.

Selkirk, E. O. (1984). *Phonology and syntax: The relation between sound and structure.* MIT Press, Cambridge, MA.

Selkirk, E. O. (1995). Sentence prosody: Intonation, stress, and phasing. In *Handbook of phonological theory* (ed. J. Goldsmith), pp. 550–69. Blackwell, Oxford.

Shen, X. S. and Lin, M. (1991). A perceptual study of Mandarin tones 2 and 3. *Language and Speech*, **34**, 145–56.

Shattuck-Hufnagel, S. and Turk, A. E. (1996). A prosody tutorial for investigators of auditory sentence processing. *Journal of Psycholinguistic Research*, **25**, 193–248.

Shillcock, R. C. (1990). Lexical hypotheses in continuous speech. In *Cognitive models of speech processing* (ed. G. T. M. Altmann), pp. 24–49. MIT Press, Cambridge, MA.

Silverman, K. E. A., Blaauw, E., Spitz, J., and Pitrelli, J. F. (1992). Towards using prosody in speech recognition/understanding systems: Differences between read and spontaneous speech. Paper presented at the Fifth DARPA Workshop on Speech and Natural Language, Harriman, NY.

Slowiaczek, L. M. (1990). Effects of lexical stress in auditory word recognition. *Language and Speech*, **33**, 47–68.

Slowiaczek, M. L. (1981). Prosodic units as language processing units. Unpublished Ph.D. thesis. University of Massachusetts, Amherst.

Slowiaczek, M. L. and Clifton, C., Jr (1980). Subvocalization and reading for meaning. *Journal of Verbal Learning and Verbal Behavior*, **19**, 573–82.

Small, L. H., Simon, S. D., and Goldberg, J. (1988). Lexical stress and lexical access: Homographs versus nonhomographs. *Perception and Psychophysics*, **44**, 272–80.

Solan, L. (1980). Contrastive stress and children's interpretation of pronouns. *Journal of Speech and Hearing Research*, **23**, 688–98.

Speer, S. R. and Kjelgaard, M. M. (1998). Prosodic facilitation and interference in the resolution of temporary syntactic ambiguity. (Manuscript.)

Speer, S. R., Crowder, R. G., and Thomas, L. M. (1993). Prosodic structure and sentence recognition. *Journal of Memory and Language*, **32**, 336–58.

Speer, S. R., Kjelgaard, M. M., and Dobroth, K. M. (1996). The influence of prosodic structure on the resolution of temporary syntactic closure ambiguities. *Journal of Psycholinguistic Research*, **25**, 249–72.

Spivey-Knowlton, M. and Sedivy, J. C. (1995). Resolving attachment ambiguities with multiple constraints. *Cognition*, **55**, 227–67.

Streeter, L. A. and Nigro, G. N. (1979). The role of medial consonant transitions in word perception. *Journal of the Acoustical Society of America*, **65**, 1533–41.

Suomi, K., McQueen, J. M., and Cutler, A. (1997). Vowel harmony and speech segmentation in Finnish. *Journal of Memory and Language*, **36**, 422–44.

Swinney, D. (1979). Lexical access during sentence comprehension: (Re)consideration of context effects. *Journal of Verbal Learning and Verbal Behavior*, **18**, 645–59.

Tabossi. P. (1988*a*). Accessing lexical ambiguity in different types of sentential contexts. *Journal of Memory and Language*, **27**, 324–40.

Tabossi. P. (1988*b*). Effects of context on the immediate interpretation of unambiguous nouns. *Journal of Experimental Psychology: Learning, Memory, and Cognition*, **14**, 153–62.

Tabossi. P., Colombo, L., and Job, R. (1987). Accessing lexical ambiguity: Effects of context and dominance. *Psychological Research*, **49**, 161–7.

Taft, L. (1984). Prosodic constraints and lexical parsing strategies. Unpublished Ph.D. thesis, University of Massachusetts.

Taft, M. (1986). Lexical access codes in visual and auditory word recognition. *Language and Cognitive Processes*, **1**, 297–308.

Taft, M. and Chen, H.-C. (1992). Judging homophony in Chinese: The influence of tones. In *Language processing in Chinese* (eds H.-C. Chen and O. J. L. Tzeng), pp. 151–172. Elsevier, Amsterdam.

Tanenhaus, M. K. and Donenwerth-Nolan, S. (1984). Syntactic context and lexical access. *Quarterly Journal of Experimental Psychology*, **36A**, 649–61.

Tanenhaus, M. K., Leiman, J. M., and Seidenberg, M. S. (1979). Evidence for multiple stages in the processing of ambiguous words in syntactic contexts. *Journal of Verbal Learning and Verbal Behavior*, **18**, 427–40.

Tanenhaus, M. K., Garnsey, S., and Boland, J. (1990). Combinatory lexical information and language comprehension. In *Cognitive models of speech processing* (ed. G. T. M. Altmann), pp. 383–408. MIT Press, Cambridge, MA.

Tanenhaus, M. K., Boland, J. E., Mauner, G., and Carlson, G. N. (1993). More on combinatory lexical information: Thematic structure in parsing and interpretation. In *Cognitive models of speech processing* (eds G. T. M. Altmann and R. Shillcock), pp. 297–319. Erlbaum, NJ.

Tanenhaus, M. K., Spivey-Knowlton, M. J., and Hanna, J. E. Modeling thematic and discourse context effects within a multiple constraints framework: Implications for the architecture of the language comprehension system. In *Architectures and mechanisms for language processing* (eds M. Crocker, M. Pickering, and C. Clifton). Cambridge University Press. (In press.)

Tanehaus, M. K. and Donenwerth-Nolan, S. (1984). Syntactic context and lexical access. *Quarterly Journal of Experimental Psychology*, **36A**, 649–61.

Terken, J. and Nooteboom, S. G. (1987). Opposite effects of accentuation and deaccentuation on verification latencies for Given and New information. *Language and Cognitive Processes*, **2**, 145–64.

Trueswell, J. C. and Tanenhaus, M. K. (1991). Tense, temporal context and syntactic ambiguity resolution. *Language and Cognitive Processes*, **6**, 303–38.

Tsang, K. K. and Hoosain, R. (1979). Segmental phonemes and tonal phonemes in comprehension of Cantonese. *Psychologia*, **22**, 222 4.

Tyler, L. K. (1989). The role of lexical representation in language comprehension. In *Lexical representation and process* (ed. W. D. Marslen-Wilson), pp. 439–62. MIT Press, Cambridge, MA.

Vroomen, J. and de Gelder, B. (1995). Metrical segmentation and lexical inhibition in spoken word recognition. *Journal of Experimental Psychology: Human Perception and Performance*, **21**, 98–108.

Vroomen, J. and de Gelder, B. (1997). Activation of embedded words in spoken word recognition. *Journal of Experimental Psychology: Human Perception and Performance*, **23**, 710–20.

Wales, R. and Toner, H. (1979). Intonation and ambiguity. In *Sentence processing: Psycholinguistic studies presented to Merrill Garrett* (eds W. E. Cooper and E. C. T. Walker), pp. 135–158. Erlbaum, NJ.

Wallace, W. P., Stewart, M. T., Sherman, H. L., and Mellor, M. D. (1995). False positives in recognition memory produced by cohort activation. *Cognition*, **55**, 85–113.

Watt, S. M. and Murray, W. S. (1996). Prosodic form and parsing commitments. *Journal of Psycholinguistic Research*, **25**, 291–318.

Whalen, D. H. (1984). Subcategorical mismatches slow phonetic judgments. *Perception and Psychophysics*, **35**, 49–64.

Whalen, D. H. (1991). Subcategorical phonetic mismatches and lexical access. *Perception and Psychophysics*, **50**, 351–60.

Whitney, P., McKay, T., Kellas, G., and Emerson, W. A. (1985). Semantic activation of noun concepts in context. *Journal of Experimental Psychology: Learning, Memory, and Cognition*, **11**, 126–35.

Zwitserlood, P. (1989). The locus of the effects of sentential-semantic context in spoken-word processing. *Cognition*, **32**, 25–64.

Zwitserlood, P., Schriefers, H., Lahiri, A., and Donselaar, W. van (1993). The role of syllables in the perception of spoken Dutch. *Journal of Experimental Psychology: Learning, Memory, and Cognition*, **19**, 260–71.

6 *Comprehending written language: a blueprint of the reader*

Charles A. Perfetti

6.1 Introduction

Reading is a language process that begins as a visual process. From a psycholinguistic point of view, reading is a *secondary* language process, partly derivative of primary spoken language processes. Thus, to understand the cognitive processes of reading one must refer to three general processing phases: (i) the visual; (ii) the processes that convert the visual input into something else (a linguistic representation); and (iii) the processes that then operate on the encoded representation.

In examining what cognitive research has learned about these reading processes, this chapter emphasizes the second and third processes. The initial visual processes, critical as they are, constitute only an initial input to the reader, and do not in themselves constitute a language process. The processes that operate on the encoded representations have a complementary character. They are likely to be shared with the language processes that are examined in other chapters in this volume, for example syntax (see Cutler and Clifton, Chapter 5). To this extent, the processes that are unique to reading are those that carry out the transcoding of the visual input into linguistic (phonological) forms, which then make a range of meaning and grammatical features available to a language comprehension process. However, these linguistically-based comprehension processes are not the end of the story, because they may be supplemented by highly generalized (non-linguistic) processes in both written and spoken language comprehension.

This approach to written language has the virtue of simplicity, because, by its coupling to spoken language processes, it does not require a theory of comprehension that is unique to reading in all its aspects. However, there are two additional considerations that imply limitations on the effectiveness of written language comprehension, relative to spoken language comprehension; one is that the written language comprehension processes can take advantage of general language processes only to the extent that the visual-to-linguistic transcoding processes are effective. The second is that the typical forms of written texts may place demands on comprehension that are not shared by spoken language. It is quite possible that additional comprehension strategies develop with literacy.

6.2 A blueprint of the reader

Following the lead of Levelt (1989) in his analysis of speech production, Fig. 6.1 shows a general schematic view or 'blueprint' of the reader. The blueprint represents the information sources that a reader would be expected to use in gaining comprehension of written language. The use of this information must be considered from two perspectives—from the view of the writing system that provides the units of reading and from the view of the cognitive processes that result in reading.

6.2.1 Writing system factors

Consider first the *writing system*, which determines in a general way how written units connect with units of language. It is traditional to consider writing systems as falling into one of three categories—*alphabetic*, *syllabic*, and *logographic*. Alphabetic systems, including English, Italian, and Korean, encode their language at the unit of the phoneme. Thus, the smallest unit of the writing system, the letter, corresponds to a meaningless unit of speech, the phoneme. Syllabic systems encode their language at the level of the syllable. Thus Japanese Kana, the most well known of the syllabic systems, has basic writing units that correspond to spoken syllables. Logographies are traditionally considered to be represented by Chinese, on the assumption that the basic units of the writing system, the character, corresponds to a word in the spoken language. Although this designation is reasonable, it is a bit misleading, because the characters themselves are typically compounds whose components often correspond to meaning (semantic radicals) and pronunciations (phonetics). Furthermore, the character nearly always corresponds to a single syllable in spoken language. Thus it may be more accurate to refer to Chinese as a morpho-syllabic (DeFrancis 1989) or even morpho-phonological system.

The writing system is of considerable importance in an account of reading processes. Because the writing system provides units that map onto one or more levels of the language—phonemic, syllabic, morphological, lexical—it will influence the process of identifying written words. Within the broad constraints provided by the writing system, there are further influences provided by the details of the *orthography*—the system that actually implements the writing system. In the case of alphabetic systems, which are the most common, we can distinguish among Roman, Cyrillic, Korean, Arabic, Hebrew, Greek, and other alphabets. These variations produce very salient visual differences in the forms of the scripts. Of perhaps more importance than this variation in alphabetic form, however, is variation in orthographic structure. For example, the 'Roman' alphabet is used in writing English, French, German, and Italian, among other languages. But the orthographies in these languages differ in transparency or 'depth' (Frost *et al.* 1987). Italian is highly transparent (or 'shallow') in that the spellings correspond reliably to the phonemes of words; English is less

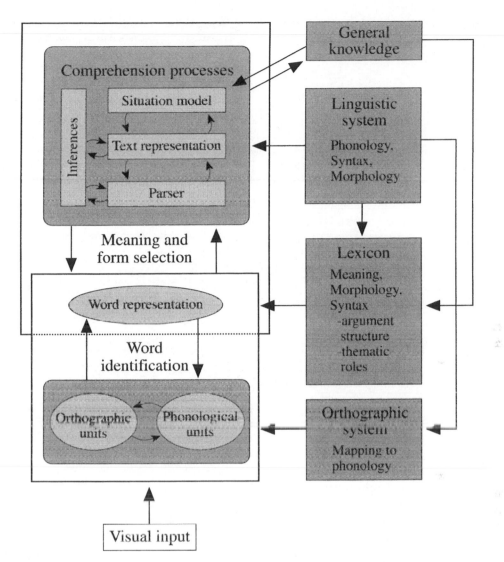

Fig. 6.1 A schematic blueprint showing the general components of reading. Arrows indicate flows of information or direction of influence. Linguistic knowledge informs the components of phonology, morphology, and syntax that are used in word reading and sentence comprehension. General (non-linguistic) knowledge informs the lexicon and the comprehension process. Word identification is represented as a process that establishes phonological–orthographic identities. Other views of word reading may not share this assumption. However, in most respects, the blueprint makes no commitment to a particular architectural assumption. In particular, whether bidirectional arrows are needed everywhere is an empirical question.

transparent in that its spellings do not as reliably map onto its phonemes. Thus, although the spellings of *chair* and *choir* differ in only one letter, their pronunciations differ in all but the final phoneme. The change in English pronunciations with identical spellings, however, sometimes preserves morphology, as when *national* preserves the root spelling of *nation* while altering the first vowel sound.

Figure 6.1 represents the influence of writing systems and orthographies at an abstract level. To instantiate the system for the case of English, we would merely substitute 'letters' for the orthographic units, and the relevant connection would be from letters to phonemes. The variable mapping between letters and phonemes would not be directly represented. Instead, we would enrich the size of the units in both the orthography and the phonology, from single letters through digraphs (*ch*), letter strings (*cho*), and even whole words (*choir*). At some large enough unit size, the mapping between spelling and pronunciations tends to stabilize, leaving only a handful of indeterminate pronunciations—for example *wind*, *lead*. These ambiguities remain at the level of word identification—is it the word *wind*, as in 'cold wind' or the word *wind* as in 'wind up'? One of the interesting characteristics of writing systems in general is that they produce relatively few of these ambiguities at the word level. In isolation, the relationship between written forms and spoken forms is more predictable than the relationships between forms and meanings, which tend to be more context dependent. Relatively strong form–form relationships may be one reason to expect phonology to be activated in reading in most writing systems (Perfetti and Zhang 1995*a*).

6.2.2 Elementary reading processes in a representation account

Given writing system factors, the process of reading can now be viewed from the perspective of the processes that convert the units of the writing system into mental representations, or understandings of printed messages. The comprehension of a printed message, must, to a considerable degree, depend on two major language-based components: (i) the identification of words and (ii) the engagement of language processing mechanisms that assemble these words into messages. The mechanisms provide contextually appropriate word meanings, parse word strings into constituents, and provide inferential integration of sentence information into more complete representations of extended text. As indicated in Fig. 6.1, these representations, to be clear, are not the result of exclusively linguistic processes, which must be complemented by a variety of general and specific knowledge sources.

It is visual word identification, however, that is the most distinctive process for reading. Elementary processes of word identification begin with a visual input, as shown in Fig. 6.1. The *visual input*—a string of letters—is handled by elementary perceptual processes that respond to various basic features (lines, angles, contours) and the relationships among them that define specific letters. The outcome of this process begins the reading process, the activation of *grapheme units* (individual and multiple letters), that constitute words. (It is important to emphasize that the interdependence of the elementary processes is an empirical matter, and the blueprint shows them as a series of processes as a convenience.) In traditional models of human cognition, the words are represented in a *lexicon*, the reader's mental representation of word forms and word meanings. Successful word reading occurs when visual input from a string of letters, activating one or more word forms in the lexicon, results in the word corresponding to the input letter string (rather than some other word) being

identified. Along the way, *phonological units*, including individual phonemes associated with individual letters, may also be activated. The phonological units may
increase the activation of word units, effectively bringing about their identification. It
is common to refer to such a process as 'phonological mediation', on the assumption
that the identification of a word has been mediated by a phonological recoding of the
graphic input. It is also common to represent two pathways, one from graphemic units
to meaning directly, and one from graphemic units to phonological units, and then to
meaning (the mediation pathway).

However, Fig. 6.1 indicates these two possibilities in a different way, rather
than as alternative pathways. The identification of a word involves the immediate
co-activation of graphemic and phonological constituents. Semantic activation
quickly begins as well and operates in a bidirectional mode from lexical representations
(the lexicon) to the elements of the orthography and phonology that are immediately
activated. In principle, it is possible for the graphemes to activate the word directly
without an intervening stage of phonological mediation, and the degree to which
phonological mediation occurs is an empirical question. Figure 6.1 represents a conclusion, based on one reading of the research, that phonological activation (orthographic–phonological coherence) will be immediate, even if, in some sense, it is not
decisively instrumental in every instance of identification. The output of the identification process is a word form and some of its associated meaning(s) and other information (grammatical form, argument structure, thematic range) that might be needed
for sentence comprehension. The comprehension of what is read is a process of
assembling words that are identified into phrases and sentences—parsing—and
building representations of text meanings. These processes take word identification as
input and will be taken up for discussion in a later section, after fuller examination of
the word identification component.

To emphasize one general point about the blueprint, the configuration of processes
into boxes and arrows is not a commitment to a cognitive architecture, but rather a
necessary and conventional manner of representing the sources of information that are
used during reading. Generally speaking, the bi-directionality of arrows indicates the
opportunities for important feedback information that goes from higher to lower
representational levels. The constraints on feedback (its effectiveness and timeliness) in
each case is an object of empirical investigation and there is no reason to assume that all
cases are equal in their constraints. For example the feedback from discourse-level
representations to syntactic representations is probably not as constraining as the
feedback from phonological representations to orthographic representations. More
generally, the blueprint allows for modularity of structures to the extent that some of
the feedback loops are ineffective.

6.2.3 Non-representational (emergent) accounts of identification

The description so far centres on processes of *activation*, but refers also to representations of words in the lexicon. There is an alternative description of the events of

word identification in which words are not represented permanently in the mind of the reader but rather emerge from the patterns of activation. There are several alternative descriptions of these emergent non-representational systems, including parallel distributed (PDP) networks and recurrent-network resonance models. PDP networks model word identification through activation that is sent across layers of graphic input units, 'hidden' units, and phonological output units (Seidenberg and McClelland 1989; Plaut *et al.* 1996). Words emerge from the distributed patterns of activation.

Resonance models, based on a dynamic systems framework, represent word identification as the stabilization of dynamic patterns that are continuously modified by interactions among inputs and various dynamic states resulting from prior experience (Van Orden and Goldinger 1994). In a resonance model, the identification of a word emerges as patterns of activity in a recurrent network move towards stabilization. One of the interesting features of the Van Orden and Goldinger (1994) model is that patterns of graphic–phonological activation stabilize more rapidly than do patterns of graphic–semantic activation. In effect, a word form becomes identified primarily through the convergence of orthography and phonology. Meaning is slower to exert an influence on the process.

Emergent models of identification, whether based on dynamic systems or PDP frameworks, offer significant contrasts with symbolic accounts of identification. To some extent the differences among the models are less in their empirical correctness, which is difficult to establish, than in their heuristic values. Thus, emergent accounts expose interestingly different ways to conceptualize language processes, including reading. One of these differences is the importance of feedback mechanisms in word reading. Such mechanisms are strongly implied by results that show effects of phonology-to-spelling consistency in reading (Stone *et al.* 1997). For example, the phonological unit /ob/ is always spelled *-obe* at the end of a one-syllable word, e.g. *probe*. By contrast, the phonological unit /ip/ is spelled inconsistently, sometimes *-eap* as in *heap*, sometimes *-eep* as in *deep*. Thus, Stone *et al.* (1997) found that a word such as *probe* is read more quickly than a word such as *heap* in a lexical decision task. Such results indicate that word reading models, whether their architecture is symbolic or emergent, need to include feedback from phonology to orthography as well as feedforward (orthography to phonology) connections. Models that describe emergent identification processes may seem especially compatible with the development of neurocognitive models of reading. Their ability to capture systems in states of change, whether through recurrent networks or layered networks of distributed information, may lend themselves to neurological modelling in a fairly natural way.

Nevertheless, there appears to be little, so far, that would favour one class of models over another just on cognitive behavioural grounds. Modelling systems are largely underdetermined by behavioural data, and the models are subject to fine tuning that can increase their ability to handle otherwise challenging results. However, some of the differences between symbolic and emergent accounts of word reading highlight important empirical questions about word identification, as illustrated in the next section.

6.3 Issues in word Identification

The foregoing provides general descriptions of word identification, with variation in descriptions being a matter of architectural frameworks. Needless to say, there are some interesting questions about the details of word identification processes that lie beyond this general description, and in some cases beyond the general consensus that underlies it. Some of these questions are highlighted by the alternative approaches— symbolic and emergent—described above. Others amount to important details that must be addressed by any system.

6.3.1 Routes to the lexicon

An enduring question, and one with obvious neurocognitive implications, has to do with whether there are two distinct pathways to the identification of words. Dual Route Theory embodies the hypothesis that there are indeed two routes: one route provides direct contact to a word representation from the graphic input. The second route converts graphemes, singly or in strings, into phonemes, which are used to access the word representations. The first route is sometimes referred to as the 'addressed' route, and the second, as the 'assembled' route. The addressed route is the direct look-up of an address; the assembled route is the assembly of the word's phonology as an intermediate step in the process.

Dual Route Theory, which was advanced by Coltheart *et al.* (1977) and elaborated in subsequent research (Besner 1990; Paap and Noel 1991), takes the following problem as central in word identification and solves the problem with the dual mechanism model: some words contain predictable spelling–sound correspondences, and some do not. Those that do, such as *safe*, can be read by converting the letters to phonemes, assembling the phonemes, and matching the assembled phonology with a lexical entry. But *safe* can also be read by an addressed mechanism, which simply looks up the lexical address of the letter string *s-a-f-e*. However, for the word *cafe*, the assembly process fails; by following the grapheme–phoneme correspondence rules for English, the assembly mechanism produces /kef/ instead of /kəfe/, an error. The only way to get the word right is to look up the spelling and produce the correct pronunciation. By itself this fact would not require two routes. A direct route could, in principle, be used for both *safe* and *cafe*. What seemed to force the need for the assembled route is the ability to pronounce non-words, such as *zate* or *tafe*. Because there is no word to look up, a process of assembly appeared to be necessary.

Additional data provided pillars for Dual Route Theory. One is the fact that in research on naming times for printed words, word frequency and word regularity interact; regularity affects the naming of low frequency words more than high frequency words (e.g. Seidenberg *et al.* 1984). Dual Route Theory handles this fact readily with the addition of two assumptions: that both pathways are activated in parallel and that the direct pathway is faster than the assembled pathway. Thus, for high frequency words, the direct pathway usually wins, even for regular words. For low frequency words, the direct route is a bit too slow, giving the assembled route a chance to compute the phonological form first. An irregular word must lag behind to wait for the direct route, because its irregularity creates noisy output along its assembled pathway. This general result has been replicated many times and has been studied by clever manipulations designed to modify the effectiveness of the two routes (Paap and Noel 1991). Additionally, patient data showing relatively selective impairment of either non-word reading (with high frequency word reading intact) or of irregular word reading (with non-word reading intact) have been argued to require the Dual Route Model (Coltheart *et al.* 1993). Brain lesions in such cases appear to have disturbed either only the assembled pathway or only the addressed pathway rather than produced a general impairment in word identification.

Although Dual Route Models handle such phenomena in a straightforward way, it turns out that single mechanism emergent models are also successful. In the case of word identification, the PDP models, armed with hidden layers and back-propagation algorithms that use feedback about correct pronunciations, can actually produce the major phenomena. In fact, the feedback mechanism allows the models to learn from exposure to printed words, which, with correct feedback, alters the weights assigned to graphic input–phonological output pairs (through the computational hidden units). Thus, as exposures to word forms come to reflect the actual frequency of their occurrence, the model learns to pronounce them correctly most of the time. Moreover, novel words and non-words are pronounced by using the same mechanism. This is achieved, in effect, by initially following whatever leads are provided by the network's learned connections, but then modifying the weight for a given form from its own feedback. In a series of simulations, Seidenberg and McClelland (1989) demonstrated impressive performance by a PDP network built from 400 graphic input units and 460 phonological units connected through 200 hidden units. It produced, in particular, the important frequency × regularity interaction. In effect, the phonological feedback for consistently pronounced letter patterns allowed 'regularity' to emerge with learning; and the high frequency established by specific word inputs was powerful enough to negate these regularity effects for high frequency words.

The only serious shortcoming of the single mechanism model was its relatively poor ability at reading pseudowords, which was demonstrated by Besner *et al.* (1990). Whereas human readers could read pseudowords accurately (around 80 per cent), the model could not. Seidenberg and McClelland (1990) argued that this failure reflected only the fact that the model had not been exposed to the number of words that a skilled reader would have been. With more exposure, pseudoword reading would have been better. More recent examples of PDP modelling have reported more success in pseudoword reading, an ability to model selective impairments, and additional performances that further narrow the gap between Dual Route Model and PDP successes (Plaut *et al.* 1996). (See Coltheart *et al.* (1993) for a detailed argument for the advantage of Dual Route Models over the earlier PDP models.)

At this point, an objective assessment of the Dual Route Model is that it continues to provide a good account of critical data in the field. But the PDP models are able to do quite well with a single mechanism and no explicit lexicon. The PDP models are powerful enough, in principle, to adapt their learning to a variety of data. The prospects for 'critical' behavioural experiments that can distinguish between single mechanism and dual mechanism models may be diminishing.

6.3.2 Phonological mediation[1]

Notice that in the Dual Route Model, phonology occurs only along the assembled route. Thus phonology appears to be an optional component of word identification, taken only when the assembled route is used. However, even when the addressed pathway is the one that brings about word identification, some assembly of phonology can occur. It just happens to be the 'wrong' phonology for word identification. In the single mechanism PDP models, phonology can be thought of as continuously occurring, as connections between graphic input units and phonological units (through a hidden layer) are activated.

Nevertheless, the role of phonology has remained controversial in word identification. Is it optional? Is it obligatory? Is it causal, mediating identification? Or 'post-lexical', resulting from identification? The results of research have been mixed and open to a variety of interpretations. As a general rule, tasks that limit the exposure of a letter string and mask its presentation may show phonology more reliably than tasks that do not (Berent and Perfetti 1995). For example, in backward masking paradigms, a word is presented briefly, 20–50 ms, and followed by a letter string mask. When the following mask is a pseudoword that shares the phonological form of the target, as in *rake* masked by *raik*, the identification of the target, which is adversely affected by the mask, is more likely than when the word is followed by a graphemic mask, for example *ralk*, that shares the same number of letters with the target but not as many of the phonemes. The graphic mask produces superior identification of the target compared with a control mask that does not share letters with the target (Perfetti *et al.* 1988; Berent and Perfetti 1995). Thus there are two effects, each suggesting that the identification of a word includes sublexical constituents: (i) abstract graphemic units (because letters shared between target and mask aid identification even when they are in a different font) and (ii) phonemic units (because phonemes shared between target and mask additionally aid identification). Similar effects are obtained when the presentation of the pseudoword precedes the target in a priming procedure (Perfetti and Bell 1991). (Priming in brief exposure situations can also be considered to be forward masking in that the 'prime' masks the following target word.) Because these brief exposure paradigms, both backward masking and priming, actually interrupt word processing, they can expose the partial products of the identification process—the sublexical units that are activated on the way to identification. Perfetti and Bell (1991) interpreted their effects as demonstrating phonemic processing within the first 40 ms of exposure to a word. Similar experiments in 'form priming' of lexical decisions and word naming produce evidence concerning the effects of graphic forms (Forster and Davis 1984, 1991). There is now considerable evidence from brief exposure paradigms that supports the conclusion that phonological as well as graphemic units are activated in the reading of alphabetic systems (Ferrand and Grainger 1992; Grainger and Ferrand 1994; Lukatela and Turvey 1990*a,b*).

Interestingly, the results from these brief exposure paradigms not only implicate sublexical orthography and phonology, they do so for high frequency as well as low frequency words and across variations in spelling-to-phonology consistency. This contrasts with the selective effect of regularity seen in word naming experiments. This difference between full exposure and brief exposure paradigms in their sensitivity to sublexical phonology was reviewed by Berent and Perfetti (1995). In explaining the differences between full and interrupted exposure to words, Berent and Perfetti proposed the Two Cycles Model of word identification, in which consonants and vowels are assembled from words in temporally distinct processing cycles. Although the linear string of letters may undergo serial left-to-right processing at the graphic input stage, the model assumes that the phonology is assembled non-linearly. Consonants (i.e. phonological consonants) are assembled in a first cycle and vowels (i.e. phonological vowels) are assembled in a second cycle. In effect, the model claims that consonants, which are more regular than vowels, always are assembled 'prelexically', that is prior to lexical access. Frequency, a lexical effect, and regularity effects arise at the second vowel cycle. Experiments that vary the stimulus-onset asynchrony (SOA) between target and mask, as well as the specific source of target–mask overlap (consonants vs. vowels), provide some support for this assumption.

It is not the case, however, that only brief exposure paradigms provide evidence for generalized sublexical phonology. Van Orden (1987) found a phonological interference effect when subjects were required to make category judgements. For example, when *rows* was presented as a foil for the category *flower*, decision times were longer and prone to errors. However, there may be some situations that do not produce this effect (Jared and Seidenberg 1991). Among other non-naming tasks that have provided evidence for automatic phonology in word identification are letter detection (Ziegler *et al.* 1997) and lexical decision (Stone *et al.* 1997). One of the most compelling classes of evidence comes from experiments with Serbo-Croatian, which is written in two different shallow othographies, one using the Roman and the other, the Cyrillic alphabet. These experiments, across a number of paradigms, produce results that can only be explained by the assumption that grapheme–phoneme connections are activated at every opportunity during simple word reading (Lukatela and Turvey, 1998).

The question of mediation implies more than phonological activity. It has referred traditionally to a causal relationship between the activation of a phonological form and some other identification event, especially the access of word meaning. It is one thing to discover sublexical phonology in word identification; it is another to demonstrate the instrumentality of this phonology. For this, Lukatela and Turvey (1991) and Lesch and Pollatsek (1993) developed semantic priming paradigms that expose phonological mediation. Semantic priming has been well demonstrated in naming, so, for example, presentation of *beach* would facilitate the naming time for the following target word *sand*. Phonologically mediated priming occurs when the prime is not *beach* but its homophone *beech*. *Beech* primes *sand* through the activation of its phonology, which in turn activates *beach*, and primes *sand* through its semantic link. Lesch and Pollatsek discovered that when the prime was exposed for 50 ms, followed by a pattern mask of 200 ms, the priming by the homophone was as large as the priming by the semantic associate, which they interpreted as demonstrating mediation—meaning access produced by phonology. But when the prime was presented for 200 ms, followed by a mask of 50 ms, mediated priming disappears as a spelling verification process occurs (Van Orden 1987).

There is an alternative to the traditional view of mediation as a causal event in access to word meaning. Rather than an instrument of access, phonology can be considered to be a *constituent* of identification (Perfetti and Zhang 1995*b*). The assumption is that the phonology always co-occurs with a word's graphic and meaning constituents, to constitute a three-constituent word identity. In a resonance model framework, which does not partition perception into discrete events such as implied by traditional mediation, Van Orden and Goldinger (1994) argue that mediation can be viewed as a process of stabilization in which word identity is 'negotiated' between sources of word form information. This rapid stabilization of a word's identity through phonology is enabled by the fact that orthography is more reliably mapped to phonology than it is to meaning.

6.3.3 The time course of graphic, phonological, and semantic activation

The mediation issue, especially when viewed as the stabilizing effect of rapid phonology on word identity, raises the question of the time course of activation of word constituents. The graphic, phonological, and meaning information sources that come together in the identification of a printed word become available over a very brief time period. The time to identify a printed word, as assessed in eye-tracking research, brings estimates of 200–300 ms (Rayner and Pollatsek 1989). On the other hand, in brief exposure paradigms with masked presentation to disrupt identification, 50 per cent thresholds are reached within 50 ms or so. Although such data may suggest that the visual system does not need very much time to initiate the process of word identification, visual transmission across areas of visual cortex requires more time than this, based on single cell recordings in non-human primates (Nowak *et al.* 1995). Thus, processing time estimates obtained in behavioural paradigms must be interpreted not as absolute neuroprocessing times, but as estimates of how quickly various information sources become available relative to others in specific processing tasks.

The question of when graphic, phonological, and semantic information becomes available is a difficult one to answer, dependent both on tasks and models. For example, the resonance model of Van Orden and Goldinger (1994) requires that phonological information immediately coheres with graphic information; there is no time at which the system has only graphic information. In a standard model, however, the process, which of course must begin with a graphic input, can take several courses. Partial graphemic information can activate both phonological and semantic information associated with candidate words, which can in turn feedback to graphic information. Interactions among levels (Plaut *et al.* 1996), rather than simple feedforward of information, suggest that, generally, there should be overlapping activation cycles of semantic and phonological information within a fully interactive system. However, the timing of specific events will be very sensitive to a wide range of factors: the printed frequency of a word, the spoken frequency of a word, its orthographic and phonological length, the consistency of its spelling, and its range of meaning possibilities. For example, a specific word meaning might be activated more quickly than phonological information for a word with high printed frequency, an inconsistent spelling pattern, and a single well-defined meaning. Phonological information should be more rapid for a word with low printed frequency, a consistent spelling pattern, and more varied meaning.

Research has identified the relative time course of orthographic and phonological word constituents in both brief exposure and full exposure paradigms. With lexical decision tasks, Ferrand and Grainger (1992, 1993) found orthographic facilitation with as little as a 17 ms prime exposure, with phonological facilitation emerging at around 50 ms. Perfetti and Bell (1991) found that subjects could use phonological information shared between a prime and target within 45 ms of prime exposure, only 10 ms of time lag relative to the use of shared graphemic information. No time lag between orthographic and phonological benefits was found in backward masking, with both benefits found within 35 ms. When words rather than pseudowords are used as primes, both facilitation and inhibition (reduced target identification) are produced. Tan and Perfetti (in press), examining the time course question in the backward masking paradigm with real word masks, found the earliest facilitative effect for graphic information coincided with phonological inhibition when both target and mask were presented for 28 ms. When the target was exposed for 42 ms, followed by a mask of 28 ms, both graphemic and phonological facilitation were obtained. Associative masks, on the other hand, began to inhibit target identification. Generally, with only slight variation across tasks, the picture seems to be that phonological information is rapidly available in word processing, only slightly later than orthographic information.

In non-alphabetic writing systems, studies of the time course of Chinese word components have not found evidence of semantic information prior to phonological information. Perfetti and Zhang (1995b) found that meaning judgements about pairs of Chinese characters produced phonological interference within 90 ms; judgements about pronunciation produced semantic interference within 140 ms. In primed naming tasks, where the time course is assessed according to various prime-target relations (graphic, phonological, semantic) graphic information is the first available, followed by phonological and then semantic (Perfetti and Tan 1998). Thus, whether in naming and or in non-naming judgements, the potential of the Chinese writing system to allow the by-pass of phonology in a direct-to-meaning process, does not prevent readers from encoding the phonology of printed words. In fact, the evidence from time course studies so far suggests it is semantics, rather than phonology, that is delayed at the character level. The stronger bonding of graphic and phonological forms, compared with graphic forms and meaning, may help explain this (Van Orden *et al.* 1990; Van Orden and Goldinger 1994; Perfetti and Zhang 1995*a,b*). Even Chinese may have more reliable mapping from visual form to phonological form (at the character level) than from visual form to meaning.

The time course of processing orthographic and phonological constituents of words is also a question amenable to temporally sensitive neurocognitive methods, specifically the recording of changes in event-related electrical potentials from the surface of the scalp. As discussed elsewhere in this volume, linguistic processes have been associated with specific ERP components, including the N400, a negative potential with an onset at about 200 ms after stimulus onset, which has been interpreted as an indicator of semantic analysis or of the integration required by prior context (Brown and Hagoort 1993). The more constraint the context puts on the target word, that is the more predictable the word is from the context, the lower the N400 amplitude. (For a review, see Kutas and Van Petten 1994.)

However, the N400 is sensitive not only to semantic events, but can be modulated by orthographic and phonological information and by the demands that tasks place on the use of this information. For example in rhyme judgements, the N400 is affected by both phonemic and orthographic similarity of the rhyming words; but in simple visual similarity judgements about word pairs, the N400 is affected only by orthographic similarity (Polich *et al.* 1983). Early effects of orthographic form are also seen when subjects make lexical decisions, with an early modulation of the N400 produced by orthographic overlap between successively presented primes and targets, even when the prime is a pseudoword (Doyle *et al.* 1996). As for phonological information, modulation of the N400 also has been reported during rhyme judgements to printed words, even when there is no orthographic overlap (e.g. *shoe chew*) (Rugg and Barrett 1987). Moreover, components other than the N400, both later and earlier, may be sensitive to phonological information. For example, one study of silent reading for meaning found that an earlier negative component (peaking around 200 ms after word onset) is associated with homophones (*hoar*) of a word (*bore*) that would have been sensible in that context, but not with words orthographically (*boat*) related (Niznikiewicz and Squires 1996). Thus, ERP results show sensitivity to the timing of orthographic and phonological processing, and do not appear to contradict a rapid phonology hypothesis. However, tracing the relative time course of events during word identification requires careful attention to tasks as well as to the separation of the orthographic, phonological, and semantic properties of words.

In summary, although the time course question is complex and presumably task dependent, experimental results are consistent with the rapid phonology hypothesis. Although one might expect semantic information to become available as quickly as phonological information, there is little evidence for this in the research. Such a result is surprising only if one assumes that there is a visual-to-meaning process that doesn't involve the primary linguistic (speech) system. On the view that primary speech processes remain functional in reading as well as in spoken language, there is no reason to assume that phonology is either by-passed or delayed in identifying words.

6.3.4 Word meanings and word forms

So far, I have treated word meaning as an unanalysed concept. However, multi-morphemic words, whose meanings reflect semantic composition from more than one morpheme, are very common. *Dislike*, for example, is related to *like* and *discredit*, and *undo* is related to *do* and *untie*. Certainly readers, like speakers and listeners, have implicit knowledge of these morphological relations. For reading, the question is whether some kind of morphological decomposition process accompanies printed word identification. One view is that words are represented as full forms without references to their morphological constituents (Butterworth 1983; Osgood and Hoosain 1974). An alternative view, more widely held, is that morphemes contribute to word reading. Whether words are decomposed into morphological components before or after word recognition is a further question (e.g. Fowler *et al.* 1985; Feldman 1994; Taft and Forster 1975; Taft 1992). Whether the morpheme is a unit of processing and mental organization is the question, and this question has proved difficult to answer in a simple manner. However, it appears that readers can be quite sensitive to the morphological structure of words under some circumstances.

6.4 Reading words in context

6.4.1 Word meaning activation and selection

Semantic information becomes available as words are read. However, words have many meanings, and the selection of a functional meaning depends on context. For example in a sentence such as *The men decided to wait by the bank*, the word *bank* is ambiguous. The question is how a reader selects the relevant meaning—the intended meaning—in any given sentence. Of course the general answer to the question is *context*. The meaning of a word in a particular instance is determined by the context in which it occurs. In the above example, where the context does not appear to constrain the meaning that *bank* can take, the process of meaning selection would appear to be indeterminate. The reader might select either the meaning 'financial institution' or 'side of a river' or both. We might expect that lacking a helpful context, the selection of word meaning will depend on statistical structures: the reader will tend to select the meaning that is the more common, in this case *bank* as 'financial institution', or at least the one more common in the experience of the individual (compare bankers with fishermen).

In more constraining contexts the situation becomes more interesting. Suppose one of the sentences below is encountered:

(1)   I pulled the fish up onto the bank.
(2)   I opened a checking account at the bank.

In (1) the riverside sense of *bank* becomes more likely than its financial sense, and, inversely for (2). The question is now whether the selection of the relevant meaning of *bank* occurs without notice of the irrelevant meaning. One possibility is that the selection of meaning is so strongly determined by the context—or what can be called the message level—that the word's meanings are selectively accessed; the one consistent with context is accessed and the one inconsistent with context is not (Glucksberg *et al.* 1986). This is the selective access model.

A second possibility, the multiple access model, is that the message level—the context—can assert no influence on the word level *at first*. On this account, the meaning selection process, which is determined by context, is preceded by a very brief general activation process, in which more than one meaning of a word is activated. This meaning activation process is automatic and very rapid (less than 250 ms), followed by a process that selects one of the meanings on the basis of consistency with message level information (Seidenberg *et al.* 1982; Kintsch and Mross 1985; Onifer and Swinney 1981). Thus, this account of autonomous activation + context selection is that both meanings of *bank* are initially activated regardless of the context, which then quickly selects from the activated meanings the one that fits the context.

A third possibility rests on limited multiple access that is controlled by the relative frequency of the word's meanings. The ordered search hypothesis assumes the most frequently used meaning of a word is always activated (Hogaboam and Perfetti 1975; Duffy *et al.* 1988; Neill *et al.* 1988). Reordered search adds the assumption that context can exert a short-lived re-ordering of the word's meanings (Duffy *et al.* 1988). Thus, on these accounts, the financial meaning of bank would be activated in both sentences (1) and (2), although it would be selected only in sentence (2). In an ordered search model, the contextual help provided for the less frequent river-bank meaning in (1) would not be sufficient to eliminate activation of the irrelevant dominant financial meaning. Refinements of the ordered search model are required to account for the fact that the relative frequency difference (meaning dominance) is a factor, as one would expect on the basis of a graded frequency (as opposed to all-or-none) assumption (Duffy *et al.* 1988).

The research surrounding these models has used a variety of procedures that vary in their potential for exposing the fine-grain temporal issues involved. Notice that the issue is never *whether* context exerts an influence, only *when* it does so. Lexical decision with cross-modal priming, in which the SOA between prime and target is varied, has been the most common method. One looks for whether a lexical decision target related to the unintended meaning of the word can be primed at very short SOA by the word in context. Eye-movement studies also provide a window on these issues by observing eye fixations on ambiguous words under various contextual conditions.

The research on these questions has grown quite large and resists simple summary conclusions. It does seem fair to say that whereas early research tended to support some version of multiple access (either ordered search or parallel activation versions), more recent research points to the possibility that context can exert a stronger and earlier influence under some situations (Kellas *et al.* 1991; Simpson and Krueger 1991; Tabossi 1988, 1991). Important in these results is the emphasis on properties of the context that can or cannot bring about sufficient constraint to allow selective access (i.e. no activation of the alternative meaning) to even a less frequent meaning.

Nevertheless, the overall pattern of results in this field cannot be taken to support a general process of prior meaning selection by context. Instead, as Simpson (1994) concluded in a review of the research, the overall pattern of results can be explained by assuming that all meanings are activated, but with the degree of activation sensitive to both the relative frequency of the meanings and the context.

6.5 Understanding sentences

To move from the word to the text can be a very large step. However, understanding sentences requires the identification of words. Eye movement studies estimate that over 80 per cent of the content words (as opposed to 'function' or grammatical words) in a text are fixated when a reader reads for comprehension (Carpenter and Just 1983). Although the length of a word plays a large role in the probability that it will be fixated, the general point is that substantial word reading is required to understand written texts. Obviously, word reading is only the beginning of the process. In insisting on this truism, we must be mindful that it does not imply that comprehension proceeds simply and unidirectionally from word identification to comprehension. The preceding section makes clear the possibility that what is obtained from a word—its meaning—at some point in the process is determined by the message context. Because word identification, now taken to include the semantic constituents of a word, is influenced at some point by context (again the issue is not whether but when), there must be some feedback between processes that represent messages and processes that select meaning for words.[2]

To represent the broad picture of reading comprehension, Fig. 6.1 shows the general sources of information that, combined with word identification, lead to comprehension. In general terms, comprehension occurs as the reader builds a mental representation of a text message. In this building process, lexical, syntactic, and inferential processes contribute, all in some degree of interaction with non-linguistic knowledge. The architectural question in reading comprehension research has been whether these interactions take place in a system that constrains their influence.

One approach to this architecture question has been to assume that the processes that interpret sentences to yield messages are constrained either by specific properties of processing components or by constraints in the direction of information flow among the components. Thus, the modularity thesis (Fodor 1983) is that there is a set of specialized processors, including language processors, that have characteristics that resist influence from other processing mechanisms. A syntactic processor would have access to restricted information about the forms of syntactic constituents—noun phrases, verb phrases, etc.—and would go about the business of building syntactic representations based on its specific, restricted sources of information. Its output—some form of constituent structure—would be constructed without interference from general knowledge that might be helpful in determining what the sentence is about. In effect, modularity prevents expectations about messages to influence the construction of syntactic forms. A similar analysis results from assuming that the processors, whether or not they correspond to modules, carry out their work in a feedforward fashion, in which lexical outputs provide input into syntactic processors, which, in turn provide input into semantic processors. This analysis leads to the hypothesis of an autonomous syntax as well as an autonomous lexicon (Forster 1979). Thus, one can expect autonomous processors within message construction, either as a consequence of essential characteristics of cognitive system modules or as a result of the organization among the processors. In either case, the important point for the blueprint of the reader is that there is little or no opportunity for general knowledge (expectations, discourse context, etc.) to have an influence on the operation of the syntactic processor (the parser).

The alternative architectural view is that interactions among sources of information are quite unconstrained (MacDonald *et al.* 1994) or, at least, that some non-syntactic information sources have an early influence on sentence parsing (Crain and Steedman 1985; Altmann and Steedman 1988). Thus, the general empirical question on which the interactive and the autonomous syntax hypotheses differ is whether the initial parsing decisions—understood roughly as a momentary attachment of the words (or mor-phemes) onto a syntactic structure—are independent of context. Although there are a number of both general and detailed proposals for how the parser works, the minimal attachment principle of Frazier (1979; Frazier and Rayner 1982) illustrates the architectural issue clearly, and has been a focus of empirical work. The principle assumes that a reader, like a listener, attaches every word as quickly as possible to a syntactic configuration that is built one-word at a time through sentence processing. There is no postponement of a syntactic decision. Nor are alternative structures built. Given this assumption, the minimal attachment principle is that, at any point in processing a sentence, the word (or morpheme) is attached to an accumulated syntactic configuration (or syntactic tree) so as to create the simplest attachment possible, consistent with syntactic constraints. Simplicity is a matter of the number of nodes in a syntactic tree that have to be established.

To illustrate, consider the sentences below from a study by Ferreira and Clifton (1986):

(3) The defendant examined by the lawyer *turned out* to be unreliable.
(4) The defendant who was examined by the lawyer *turned out* to be unreliable.

In both (3) and (4), the reader must interpret 'turned out' as a main clause verb phrase, that is *the defendant turned out* . . . However, in (3) the reader, in accord with a minimal attachment principle, takes 'examined' to be the main clause verb, that is *the defendant examined [something]* . . . This incorrect initial decision then leads to a problem when 'turned out' is encountered, because there is no open verb phrase slot for it. Thus, (3) is a garden-path sentence that produces a processing slow down in the critical (dis-ambiguating) region *turned out* compared with the same region in (4) (Ferreira and Clifton 1986; MacDonald *et al.* 1992). In (4) the occurrence of *that*, a relative pronoun, forces the parser to build the right attachments. In (3), the absence of *that* allows the parser to build either a main clause verb or a (reduced) relative clause when it encounters *examined*. The main clause attachment is syntactically simpler, because it requires no additional syntactic nodes to be established. The relative clause structure is more complex, because it requires a modifier node to be established at the initial noun phrase—something like *the defendant [the defendant examined by the lawyer]*, where the bracketed material is an additional node in the syntactic tree.

One can readily imagine other proposals for why a reader might have trouble with (3) and not (4), and some of these refer to the assignment of thematic roles (Pritchett 1988, 1992). These roles are filled by nouns in relation to the verbs. Thus, *examined* needs to assign roles to an examiner (an agent) and, in the verb phrase, to an examinee (a theme). Sentence (3) allows the first noun to be chosen as subject/agent, and leaves additional roles to be filled after the verb. There is evidence that the thematic roles defined by the verb play a part in parsing decisions (Frazier and Rayner 1982; Britt 1994; MacDonald *et al.* 1994). These and related syntactic issues are discussed elsewhere in this volume (Chapter 5, Cutler and Clifton; Chapter 9, Hagoort *et al.*). Here, it may be enough to conclude that the field is far from having established a clear consensus on exactly how all the sources of information that might be used in parsing actually do get used.

To return briefly to the central empirical question, however, it is whether the problems with a sentence such as (3) can be avoided in the right kinds of contexts. Can the processing difficulty be eliminated by a context that encourages the reader to immediately take the first noun, *the defendant*, as the object of *examined* rather than as its subject? Avoiding the incorrect assignment in this particular structure (the reduced relative clause) is very difficult and a number of studies have concluded this garden path reflects a very deeply embodied syntactically-based preference, whether minimal attachment or some other syntactic principle (Britt *et al.* 1992; Ferreira and Clifton 1986). However, some studies suggest the contrary, that the garden path—the momentary mistake in parsing that makes *the defendant* the subject rather than the object of *examined*—can be avoided by the use of some other information source: by properties of the initial noun itself—its meaning characteristics; by statistical properties of the verb and its past participle (*examine/examined*); and by the referential context provided by a previous discourse segment (e.g. MacDonald *et al.* 1982; Trueswell *et al.* 1994). Additionally, some results suggest that susceptibility to the garden path is a function of the reader's basic working-memory capacity, such that readers with large capacities can keep more than one parsing possibility in mind and then choose the needed one when later sentence information is read (Just and Carpenter 1992).

An example of how thematic roles and context interact is provided by Britt (1994), who varied the context and the verb type in post-nominal preposition phrases such as (5) and (6):

(5) He dropped the book on the war onto the chair.
(6) He put the book on the war onto the chair.

An important point about these sentences is that they produce garden paths that are much less severe than the reduced relative clauses illustrated in (3) and (4).

Both (5) and (6) tend to produce garden paths, in that readers' initial decisions lead to attaching the prepositional phrase *on the war* as part of the verb phrase, whereas it needs to be attached as part of the noun phrase. Britt found that this garden path could be overridden by a context that favours the noun phrase attachment; such a context specifies two books and constrains the situation so that only one of them—the one on the war—will be dropped. However, this context effect works only for verbs such as *drop* (5). Such a verb requires only one argument to be filled following the verb. This argument is filled by the theme role, the object that is dropped. Thus one must specify a dropped object in using *drop*, but need not specify the end state of the dropped object. (Notice that *John dropped* is incomplete but *John dropped the book* is not.) However, for verbs like *put* (6), two arguments must be filled following the verb: an object (theme) that gets put, and a location that specifies its end state. (Notice that *John put the book* and *John put on the floor* are both incomplete or ungrammatical.) The very same favourable context that avoids the garden path with *drop* fails to avoid it with *put*. Thus Britt's experiments suggest that the internal structure of a verb (its required arguments) is a more powerful determiner of parsing decisions in these structures than is the biasing effect of a discourse context.

The general question of how these various factors combine to determine parsing decisions remains very difficult. Again, one approach is to assume that parsing principles, derived from basic syntactic knowledge, control the first stages of comprehension and then are quickly (and usually beyond awareness) modified by other factors. An alternative account allows immediate use of all sorts of information, with no special processing provided by a syntactic analyser. For example the general proposal of MacDonald *et al.* (1994) is that a reader's parsing decisions are determined by the history of encounters with various forms and functions. All of these frequency-based considerations and more are assumed to be important: the semantic properties of a word, the relative frequency of a verb in a particular grammatical role (e.g. *examined* as a past tense verb vs. as a past participle), the relative frequency of specific nouns as fillers of thematic roles associated with verbs (e.g. *defendants* as an agent of *examine* relative to a theme (object of examination)), and the actual frequency of specific syntactic structures (main clauses with versus without reduced relative clauses). A reader is more or less likely to be garden pathed as a function of these frequency-based characteristics. To the extent that these characteristics support a particular parsing decision, that decision is more likely than some alternative.

The fundamental principles that guide parsing remain a source of disagreement.[3] Empirically, distinguishing among these principles turns on the timing of reading events, because the question is not whether context is used, but rather when it becomes available to the parser. While this question continues to be the object of research in studies that use self-paced reading and eye-tracking methods, which can provide reasonably good data on the time duration of reading events, temporally sensitive neurocognitive methods are also proving to be informative. Studies of event-related potentials (Hagoort *et al.* 1993; Neville *et al.* 1991; Osterhout *et al.* 1994) have discovered some distinct ERP components that are not associated with the N400 that has been linked to semantic processing. For example, Hagoort *et al.* (1993) found a positive component associated with syntactic violations of certain kinds, a component they called the 'Syntactic Positive Shift'. Osterhout *et al.* (1994) found a similar component associated with ambiguities that would lead to garden paths when they are processed by the minimal attachment principle. The convergence of results from several different studies may point to an ERP component sensitive specifically to processes that determine constituent structures.

Finally, it is interesting to note that most of these parsing results have been obtained with visual situations, and so apply most directly to reading. However, the reader has information in conventional print not available to the listener (and vice versa). Commas and full points, in particular, tend to disambiguate structures, and their role in helping the reader avoid parsing problems has been examined in a few studies (Adams *et al.* 1991; Mitchell and Holmes 1985). Interestingly, the use of punctuation is not sufficient, by itself, to avoid at least some of the syntactic preferences that lead to garden paths.

6.6 Comprehension beyond sentences

The reader uses sentences to build an understanding of a text, and for that larger purpose sentence comprehension is only part of the picture. The reader must combine the message of each sentence with the message accumulated up to that point on the basis of the prior text. This appears to complicate the comprehension process only slightly in requiring (i) individual sentence comprehension and (ii) integration across sentences. However, behind each of these is a complex picture that must accommodate a range of processes that assign discourse referents (the things referred to in the text) to the elements of sentences, and that establish higher-level representations that capture the gist of the text as a whole. These text-level processes must appeal significantly to sources of information that lie beyond the verbatim representation of the text—the reader's knowledge about the semantic domain of the text, the type of text (genre)—and to inferential processes that assist the integration of information.

6.6.1 Mental representations of text

The skilled reader has not one but many levels of representation for a text. The two most general are a model of what the text says (the text base) and a model of what the text is about (the situation model). In the influential framework of Van Dijk and Kintsch (1983; Kintsch 1988), the text base is a mental representation of the propositions of the text. The atoms of meaning are extracted from sentences, built up through the reading of the successive sentences of the text and supplemented only by inferences necessary to make the text coherent. The reader builds a situation model from the text base by combining knowledge sources through additional inference processes. Thus, a text base is essentially linguistic, consisting of propositions derived from sentences, whereas a situation model is essentially agnostic in its form of representation. It may well be linguistic—an elaborated set of propositions that includes inferences as well as propositions extracted from actual text sentences. However, it may also be fundamentally non-linguistic, a mental model that directly represents referential and spatial information in a non-propositional format (Johnson-Laird 1983). Indeed, it appears that when readers read texts that include descriptions of spatial information, they construct representations of the information that preserve both stated and inferable spatial information in the form of spatial analogues rather than in the form of propositions (Haenggi *et al.* 1995; Glenberg *et al.* 1994; Morrow *et al.* 1987). One of the most intriguing questions to which neurocognitive methods should be able to contribute is how the brain handles non-linguistic spatial analogue information when it is explicitly or implicitly part of a text.

To illustrate the distinction between a situation model and a text base, Perrig and Kintsch (1985) provided two texts that describe a fictitious town. One was written to encourage a *survey* representation and the other was encouraged to provide a *route* representation, as illustrated in (7) and (8) respectively:

(7)   North of the highway and east of the river is a gas station.
(8)   On your left just after you cross the river you see a gas station.

Readers who read the survey text, including (7), were better at drawing a map of the town; readers who read the route text were better at remembering the text itself. The implication is that the survey text encouraged the readers to make a spatial situation model at the expense of a strong propositional text base; and, inversely, the route model allowed a strong propositional text base, but a less accurate situation model.

The focus on spatial analogues in text has served the goal of trying to demonstrate a distinction between texts and situations, a distinction not easy to verify so long as readers can use propositional information for both texts and situations. The logic of some of the research is to demonstrate that readers are sensitive to information in a way consistent with a spatial representation but not with a linguistic sequential representation. For example Morrow *et al.* (1987) had subjects read a narrative that brought the reader from one room to another in a building and answer probe questions about whether two objects were in the same or a different room. Readers' decision times were a function of the distance between the current room location (according to where the narrative was at the time of the probe) and the room that contained the pair of objects. A linear distance function is readily explained if the reader has constructed a model of the situation based on a walk through the rooms; it is less readily explained on the assumption that the reader built only an ordered list of text propositions.

Nevertheless, spatial models are only one possible realization of the idea of a situation model. In reading a narrative, one might expect time, rather than only space, to organize the reader's model of the situation. Indeed, Zwaan (1996) has demonstrated that readers use time phrases in a narrative—phrases such as *an hour later* or *a moment later*—to build temporal models. Reading times slowed down when there was a time shift (one hour) compared to when there was no time shift (a moment), and information after a time shift was more available than information from before the time shift. More generally, Zwaan *et al.* (1995) argue that readers construct representations of stories along five dimensions—time, space, protagonist, causality, and intentionality. Their event-indexing model assumes that events and the intentional actions of characters are the focal points of situation models, which are updated during reading along some or all of these dimensions.

6.6.2 Inferences build situations

The reader, in order to get from a text to a situation, generally must go beyond the explicit text information by making inferences. Because texts are never fully explicit, there are rich opportunities for the reader to add information and make inferences about what is in the text. Generally, the difference between a text base and a situation model is one of inferences. Text bases appear to be semantically 'shallow', that is containing meaning representations generated with minimal inferencing machinery, perhaps only those inferences needed to maintain referential coherence. Situation models, by contrast, are semantically deep, containing situation-specific meanings that generate rich inferences.

The issue in text research has been when do what kinds of inferences occur? Readers appear to generate those inferences that maintain referential coherence when the inference is textually required (Corbett and Dosher 1978; Dell *et al.* 1983; Haviland and Clark 1974; Just and Carpenter 1987). The theoretical approach to text meaning developed by Kintsch, including the Construction–Integration Model (Kintsch 1988), assumes that readers establish referential coherence across sentences by connecting pronouns to noun-phrase antecedents in building a new proposition. For example an encounter with *it* leads the reader to establish a proposition containing the immediately available antecedent of the pronoun or, if it is not available in the immediately available propositions, to search for an antecedent in the memory for the text base. Readers seek to make what they are reading referentially coherent, so either a pronoun or a noun without a clear referent triggers a process to establish co-reference with something available from the text representation.[4] These co-referential inferences are considered minimal—needed not for an elaborated situation model but merely to make reading a text something different from reading a list of unrelated sentences. The question is what other kinds of inferences are made? And when?

Inferences that maintain causal coherence may also be made when needed (Keenan *et al.* 1984), although evidence is less strong on exactly when such inferences occur. On the other hand, for a whole range of elaborative inferences that a comprehender might be expected to make in establishing a situation model, the evidence is less strong. Most evidence does not support the assumption of early 'on-line' elaborative inferences (Corbett and Dosher 1978; McKoon and Ratcliff 1986, 1989, 1992; Singer 1979; Singer and Ferreira 1983), while some evidence suggests early inferences under restricted conditions (O'Brien *et al.* 1988). McKoon and Ratcliff (1989) suggest that inferences are encoded to different degrees of explicitness, with some, for example those that involve prediction of events, encoded only vaguely. Such less encoded inferences are readily made specific when required but are not specifically computed as part of comprehension. A related possibility is that elaborated inferences are not typically made as part of the text representation but can be observed in the situation model when readers are encouraged to attend to meaning (Fincher-Kiefer 1993). It is also possible that inferences required to maintain causal coherence among story elements are more likely to be made than other kinds of elaborative inferences (Trabasso and Suh 1993).

The possibility that all kinds of inferences are made routinely and automatically seems to have been clearly ruled out. Instead, it appears that readers are selective in drawing inferences, although the range of selectivity remains in question. The major theoretical issue in inferences can be captured by the contrast between the minimalist hypothesis (McKoon and Ratcliff 1992) and the constructionist hypothesis (Graesser *et al.* 1994). Whereas in the minimalist hypothesis only coherence-driven inferences are routinely made, with other inferences made only when task demands are right, the constructionist hypothesis is that a variety of inferences are made—those that address the reader's comprehension goals, those that explain why things occur, and those that establish global as well as local coherence.

It is difficult to draw clear conclusions about the inference question. The reader has to make some inferences just to keep the *text base* representation minimally coherent. And the reader is encouraged to make causal inferences just to keep the *narrative structure* (a situation model for a story) coherent. But other inferences, for example predictive inferences in which the reader might anticipate some event or some consequence of an action, are not required by considerations of coherence. Furthermore, they appear to require some effort and inferences of this 'forward' type, are especially subject to error. In fact, the search for robust inference drawing seems to be a search for active comprehension—understanding with learning—and the frustration of this search corresponds to the lament that many readers read passively, with minimal comprehension, rather than actively expending effort to connect and extend ideas in the text. To some extent, the large class of inferences that might separate the passive reader from the active reader can be viewed as under the control of individual reader and task variables. Thus, most readers can become more active readers, and hence inference generators, under the right circumstances. But under the mundane demands of typical experiments, there is little motivation to become an inference generator.

6.7 Individual differences in reading

The blueprint of the reader not only provides components for successful reading, it provides components that can fail and lead to problems in reading. When problems are relatively severe and occur without general intellectual problems, a child or an adult with reading difficulty is often categorized as having *dyslexia*, or specific reading disability. In many other cases, the reading problem may not lead to a label of specific reading disability. Although there may prove to be some important process deficits uniquely associated with specific reading disability, there are reasons at present to blur the distinction between specific and non-specific reading disability from a functional point of view. Individuals in these two categories seem to differ not so much in what their problem is, but in how they achieve in some other non-reading area. Indeed, the

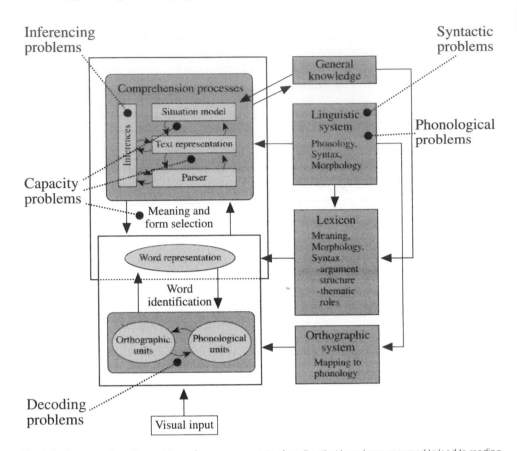

Fig. 6.2 Sources of reading problems. Some components of reading that have been assumed to lead to reading problems. The overall blueprint of the reader from 6.1 is shown in sketch form, with some potential sources of problems indicated. It should not be assumed that the indicated problems are equal in their empirical bases nor that they are mutually independent. Not represented are deficiencies in knowledge, which would have a pervasive negative effect in comprehension.

evidence that the two groups' reading problems have different causes is weak (Stanovich 1988; Stanovich and Seigel 1994).

Figure 6.2, based on Fig. 6.1, represents the components of reading that one could imagine might go wrong. A reader could have trouble with processing printed inputs, or more generally visual inputs of certain kinds. A reader might know relatively few words, or not be able to use the needed meaning of a word, thus limiting lexical processes. A reader might have defective phonological processes, which would limit word identification and memory for words. On the comprehension end, a reader could have syntactic difficulties, have insufficient conceptual knowledge to support understanding of many texts, could fail to generate inferences, or could have a lower than normal working-memory capacity; any of these would limit the reader's ability to construct a good model of the text (text base) or of the situation, or both. There are additional processes in which the reader monitors comprehension, staying alert to coherence problems in the text itself and checking the mental model he or she is building against some criterion of sensibility.

These various possibilities are by no means equiprobable, and research has provided information on the source of comprehension problems. The next sections summarize this information.

6.7.1 Problems in lexical orthographic–phonological processes

Readers who fail to read words fail to comprehend. Thus word-level problems are potentially the most important in creating reading failures, because they would lead both to specific reading disability, which by definition entails problems with reading words, and to comprehension problems. The second of these problems results when obstacles to reading words create a bottleneck in comprehension (Perfetti and Lesgold 1979). More generally, because skill in comprehension rests in part on the efficient execution of lower-level processes within the constraints of working memory, verbal efficiency theory (Perfetti 1985) assumes that readers who lack efficient word-coding procedures are at risk for comprehension failure. Thus, even when words are accurately read, slow or effortful reading is often associated with comprehension problems. One specific interpretation of the verbal efficiency hypothesis is that the working memory bottleneck that produces reading problems is phonological (Shankweiler and Crain 1986).

When lexical processes are severely defective, the reading problem is manifest more directly, not merely in comprehension but in obvious word reading difficulty. The theoretical locus of a word reading problem is in the process by which ortho-graphic and phonological information coheres to a word identity (see Fig. 6.2). Knowledge of letters and knowledge of phonemes that connect with letters in specific letter environments are necessary. A problem with either orthography or phonology produces lexical processing problems, and some research asks which of these sources is more important in any given case of reading failure. For example, in an ongoing study of familial aspects of dyslexia, monozygotic and dizygotic twins diagnosed as reading-disabled, are given tests that attempt to separate orthographic from pho-nological knowledge (Olson *et al.* 1990; Pennington 1990). For the phonological component, Olson *et al.* (1990) measure the time to read aloud pseudowords (both one- and two-syllable); for the orthographic component, they measure the time a reader takes to decide which of two homophonic letter strings is a real word, for example *rain, rane*. The assumption is that pseudoword reading reflects primarily phonological coding processes, whereas the word decision task requires knowledge about spelling patterns, independent of phonology. Both the phonological and orthographic component appear to have a significant heritable component (Olson *et al.* 1994).

The interdependence of orthographic and phonological knowledge is a difficult question. Research of Stanovich and West (1989) points to the possible independence of these two sources of knowledge, one primarily orthographic and one phonological.

They found that a measure of reading experience, the Author Recognition Test, was a strong predictor of word processing ability, even after accounting for phonological processing skill. In a factor analysis, this measure loaded on two separate knowledge factors, one orthographic and one phonological, derived from word processing tasks; however its larger loading was on the orthographic factor. (The phonological factor included decision times to select which of two letter strings was homophonic to a real word, *kake–dake*, and the times to name pseudowords.) Stanovich and West (1989) suggest that experience in reading leads to lexical knowledge that goes well beyond decoding. However, finding an orthographic knowledge factor that develops primarily with experience does not mean that this factor is independent of phonology. Although practice builds specific lexical knowledge, that is knowledge of specific words, there is no reason to suppose that this knowledge comes without assistance from phonology. Indeed, Share and Stanovich (1995) and Jorm and Share (1983) argue that it is only through phonology—in the form of decoding attempts to unfamiliar words—that the lexical representation for specific words can get established (see also Perfetti 1992).

Referring to orthographic and phonological knowledge sources in reading problems seems to invite a dual-route model of reading. The dyslexic reader can have either the orthographic or the phonological route disabled and thus be selectively impaired in either reading low frequency regular words and non-words (disabled phonological assembly route) or high frequency exception words (disabled direct access route). Such dissociations have been reported in a number of cases of reading disability and interpreted as evidence for dual-route models of word naming (Coltheart *et al.* 1993). However, single mechanism models can be adapted to account reasonably well for the emergence of differential orthographic and phonological deficiencies (Plaut *et al.* 1996). As in the case of the basic mechanisms of word reading, the apparent dissociation of word-specific orthographic information and word-general orthographic–phonological information in some cases of specific reading disability may not require qualitatively different mechanisms.

Whether conceived as arising from defects in single mechanisms that use phonological information immediately during word identification or from an impairment of a distinct processing route, phonological problems are pervasive among cases of specific reading disability. Phonological processing has indeed been assumed to be the central process deficiency that leads to both specific reading disability and non-specific low reading skill (Stanovich 1988). Moreover, phonological problems can arise at many levels critical for reading. In addition to problems that may be specific to the phonological component of written words, both more fundamental speech processing mechanisms and awareness of phonological structures are sources of phonologically-based reading problems. For example, phonemic awareness—the ability to become aware of speech segments as discrete meaningless pieces of the speech stream—is an obstacle to learning to read in an alphabetic writing system. Children come to schooling with only dim awareness that the speech system they use so well for speaking and listening can be decomposed into meaningless elements (phonemes). Children who do not become aware of phonemes are at risk for early failure in learning to read (see Liberman and Shankweiler 1991, for a review).

Finally, notice that phonological processing problems not only can be observed at different levels, they may have consequences throughout the reading process: learning to read words; remembering just read words (stored in memory in phonological form), and understanding phrases and sentences (processes operating on partly phonological representations).

6.7.2 Problems in processing lexical meaning

As summarized in the first section of this chapter, the selection of word meaning in context is typically assumed to be a two-stage process: (i) a general activation stage in which a lexical entry is accessed and its associated meanings non-selectively activated, and (ii), a few ms (100–400 ms) later, a selection stage in which the meaning appropriate for context is selected, or gains further activation, and meanings inappropriate for context are suppressed. Skilled and less skilled readers may differ in these meaning selection processes. Merrill *et al.* (1981) had children read sentences in which some attributes connected with a key word were emphasized over others. In *The girl fought the cat*, for example, the verb *fight* may emphasize *claw* more than *fur* among the attributes of *cat*. In a variation on the Stroop task, subjects named the colour of a key word (*fur* or *claw*) presented one second after reading the sentence. Interference is expected based on the activation of meanings of words whose colour must be named (Conrad 1974). Relative to control words, skilled readers showed slower naming times only for emphasized attributes, for example *claw* but not *fur*, whereas less skilled readers were slower for both kinds of attributes.

Although there are several possible explanations, one of some theoretical interest is that skilled readers more quickly establish a contextually-specific meaning than do less skilled readers, for whom both relevant and less relevant meanings remain activated for at least one second. On the other hand, because 'relevant' meanings in the Merrill *et al.* study are really attributes that result from elaborative inferences rather than distinct meanings, it may be that skilled readers were generating such inferences more than less skilled readers.

The first type of explanation, based on selecting a context-specific meaning, has been generalized by Gernsbacher (1990) as a difference in a suppression mechanism. This mechanism suppresses the activation of irrelevant information as a reader uses context to establish a comprehension framework. Less skilled readers, in this account, have deficient suppression mechanisms. To illustrate, Gernsbacher *et al.* (1990) had skilled and less skilled college readers decide whether a visually presented target word fit the meaning of a sentence. Gernsbacher *et al.* (1990) found that when the final word of the sentence was ambiguous, for example *spade*, there was a skill difference in the time to reject a target word related to the contextually inappropriate meaning of the ambiguous related word. For example, in *He dug with the spade*, the target word *ace* should be rejected as a fit to the meaning of the sentence; however, because *ace* is related to another meaning of *spade*, it should have some initial activation. Indeed, both skilled and less skilled comprehenders showed longer times to reject *ace* (relative to control sentences) when it appeared 100 ms after the sentence. When *ace* appeared 850 ms after the sentence, however, only less skilled readers showed longer times to reject it. Other studies with this population (Gernsbacher and Faust 1990) suggest that the use of context is not a general problem for less skilled comprehenders. Rather, less skilled readers have a problem specifically with the suppression of irrelevant information.

Whether or not ineffective use of context is a source of reading problems has become a complex issue. Pre-scientific beliefs on this question seemed to be that poor readers failed to use context in reading words. However, research on children's word identification led to the opposite result; less skilled readers use context in word identification at least as much and typically more than do skilled readers (see Perfetti 1985; Stanovich 1980, 1981). The understanding of this fact is that less skilled comprehenders are good users of context, which they rely on to identify words in compensation for weaker orthographic–phonological knowledge. However, Gernsbacher's work on meaning selection suggests a specific additional problem, one of using the semantic results of word identification.

6.7.3 Problems in processing syntax

Dyslexic children and even 'garden variety' poor readers—less skilled readers who do not necessarily meet all the criteria for specific reading disability—show problems handling various aspects of English morphology and syntax (Fletcher *et al.* 1981; Mann *et al.* 1984; Vogel 1975). The question is whether such problems, which are found across a wide age range, arise from some deficit in processing syntax or from some other source that affects performance on syntactic tasks.

Two hypotheses have been developed to account for problems observed in syntactic processing. On one account, syntactic problems, where they are observed, reflect a lag in the development of linguistic structures (Byrne 1981; Fletcher *et al.* 1981; Stein *et al.* 1984). Such an account, at first glance, seems consistent with the fact that syntactic deficits are observed in spoken language, not just written language. However, an alternative to a structural deficit was proposed by Perfetti and Lesgold (1977), who argued that the basic causes of less skilled comprehension were localized in working memory limitations. Problems in discourse comprehension, including syntactic problems, arise neither from intrinsic syntactic problems nor higher-level discourse structure problems, but from processing bottlenecks, partly, but not wholly, arising from lexical processing inefficiency.

There is by now evidence that at least some syntactic problems do result from processing deficiencies. Crain and Shankweiler (1988; also Crain *et al.* 1990) have argued that, on the structural deficit hypothesis, one should expect differential problems in syntax; the problems encountered by less skilled readers should not be just the ones that also cause problems for skilled readers. For example, object-relative clauses, such as (9) are generally more difficult than subject-relative clauses such as (10), even for skilled readers.

(9)   The girl that the boy believed understood the problem.
(10)   The girl that believed the boy understood the problem.

Using data of Mann *et al.* (1984), Crain and Shankweiler (1988) showed that third grade skilled and less skilled readers produced the same pattern of errors rather than different patterns of errors on subject- and object-relative clauses. Crain *et al.* (1990) also report garden-path data that they argue are inconsistent with a structural deficit hypothesis, again relying on identical error patterns across groups of skilled and less skilled readers in support of this conclusion.

A more direct demonstration that the processing load affects syntactic performance was also provided by Crain *et al.* (1990). They found that problems with understanding temporal clauses (*Push NP1 before/after you push NP2*) increased as assumed processing load increased, either by making the NP more complex (not affecting the clause structure) or by not satisfying certain presuppositions associated with normal use of these clauses.

The possibility that reading problems and spoken language problems (aphasia) arise from processing limitations rather than structural deficits has gained increasing support from research with adults (Carpenter *et al.* 1994). This research has revealed a strong correlation between working memory capacity and language processing. Especially relevant for syntax are data reported by King and Just (1991) on subject and object relatives similar to those in (9) and (10). Not only did low-span readers (low in working memory for language) have more problems with object-relative sentences than did high-span readers (high in working memory for language), the problems, as indexed in reading times on words, were most severe where the processing load was hypothesized to be the greatest: at the second verb in the object-relative sentence (see (9)). The generalization here is that reading difficulties are localized in sentences at points of high processing demands (syntactic complexity, for example), and readers with lower processing capacity have problems at these locations. The problem is not syntactic deficits but the processing capacity to handle complexity.

Another perspective on this issue is helpful—the opportunity for practice. Because some syntactic structures are more typical of written language than spoken language, the opportunity for practice is limited by the ability to read. Thus, continuing development of reading skill as a result of initial success at reading—and the parallel increasing failure as a result of initial failure—is undoubtedly a major contributor to individual differences in reading. Stanovich (1986) has discussed this rich-get-richer aspect of reading skill, borrowing, from Merton (1968) and Walberg and Tsai (1983), the Matthew metaphor: 'For unto every one that hath shall be given, and he shall have abundance: but from him that hath not shall be taken away even that which he hath' (Matthew XXV: 29). Seeing syntactic problems as Matthew effects places them intermediate to the syntactic deficit hypothesis and the processing capacity hypothesis. They can reflect either underdeveloped abilities—limited through restricted practice—or processing capacity—also limited through restricted practice with language.

6.7.4 Problems at the text level

What is the source of reading problems that are presented at the level of text comprehension specifically, as opposed to lexical or sentence levels? It is clear that at least some problems in comprehension can be explained by hypotheses that target lower level (lexical/phonological) processes within a limited processing-capacity working-memory system (Crain and Shankweiler 1988; Perfetti 1985; Carpenter *et al.* 1994). According to the blueprint of the reader, there are additional possibilities in the processing that builds mental models out of sentences. Readers must use knowledge outside of the text and apply inferences to the basic propositional content of the text, and these processes of knowledge use and inference generation can be the source of comprehension failure. (Note that simple lack of knowledge can also be the problem.)

The overall complexity of text comprehension (in terms of number of processes and possible interactions among them) implies corresponding complexity in the possibilities for comprehension failure. For example, some readers may be less likely to integrate sentences by establishing coreference, and, indeed, individual differences in coreferencing processes are found (Frederiksen 1981). Or some readers may be less successful in monitoring their text comprehension and thus fail to build coherent and accurate mental models (Ryan 1982). Additionally, because some knowledge of text content is helpful in all reading, individual differences in knowledge can produce individual differences in comprehension (Anderson *et al.* 1977; Spilich *et al.* 1979). However, low-knowledge readers can compensate for low knowledge with reading skill, at least to a limited extent (Adams *et al.* 1995). Readers who lack both content knowledge and reading skill have more serious problems; and the deleterious effect of low reading skill (and its motivational consequences) on learning through reading creates readers who lack knowledge of all sorts.

Among the several possibilities for problems, however, the one receiving the most attention is inferential processing. For example, Long and Golding (1993) conclude that skilled comprehenders are more able than less skilled comprehenders to make inferences about superordinate goals. More generally, Oakhill and Garnham (1988) summarize an array of evidence that suggests that less skilled readers fail to make a range of inferences in comprehension. Oakhill *et al.* (1997) conclude that this inference-making problem is general across spoken and written language, and even pictorial understanding. A general question of the hypothesis of specific comprehension deficits, including inferencing, is whether the observed differences in inferencing occur in the absence of problems in lower level abilities. Perfetti *et al.* (1996) suggest that although inference differences clearly have been established, they have generally not been established with procedures that assure the absence of lower-level lexical problems. Nevertheless, it appears that inferencing problems can arise for children who have no problems identifying words in context (Oakhill and Yuille 1986). Oakhill *et al.* (1997) further concluded that problems in inferencing observed in low skill readers are associated with reduced working memory capacity, providing an interesting integration of two lines of research that were initially quite separate. It seems safe to say that a specific inferencing disability, independent of other factors known to be critical for comprehension, remains unestablished.

In at least one study (Stothard and Hulme 1996), a careful attempt to delineate a group of less skilled comprehenders who show no problems in decoding and phonological processing has succeeded in showing distinctive types of comprehension problems: one type that occurs for children who also have decoding and phonological awareness problems and another type for those who do not have such problems. The latter group, which could be characterized as showing specific comprehension deficits, show problems in language processing generally and may be considered to have a comprehension-specific deficit, although not one necessarily independent of processing limitations.

Another example of a specific comprehension problem is comprehension monitoring, found to be ineffective among less skilled readers in a number of studies (Baker 1984, 1985; Garner 1980). The test for comprehension monitoring is typically whether the reader can detect (explicitly refer to) an inconsistency introduced into a short text. Low-skilled comprehenders have been found to be especially poor at detecting higher-level text inconsistencies, those that would interfere with the construction of a coherent model of the text content (e.g. whether successive paragraphs are on unrelated topics). However, it is not completely clear whether these higher-level differences are independent of the reader's ability to construct a simple understanding of the text, for example at the proposition level; some evidence suggests that poor comprehenders fail to accurately represent or weight the propositions in a text (Otero and Kintsch 1992). The general interpretive problem here is that comprehension monitoring, like inference making, both contributes to and results from the reader's text representation. This makes it difficult to attribute comprehension problems uniquely to failures to monitor comprehension, as opposed to more basic comprehension failures.

6.8 Summary

Comprehending printed language shares many of the processing resources used in spoken language processes. A 'Blueprint of the Reader' entails a set of interrelated elementary processes and momentary representations. Printed word identification is the central, recurring event in reading that is not shared directly with spoken language processes. However, word reading builds on spoken language processes, specifically requiring phonological connections to be established to printed forms (letter strings and words). One of the most important conclusions arising from research in this field over the last 20 years is the importance of automatic phonological processes in the identification of printed words. Reading comprehension processes build on the identification of words, rapidly extracting context-sensitive meanings, assembling strings of morphemes into syntactic structures (parsing), building basic meaning units (propositions), integrating basic meaning units within and across sentences, and inferring additional information required to build a general (non-linguistic) representation of the content of a text. How these various components interconnect—where interactions are unconstrained and where some information sources are privileged—is a major theoretical preoccupation of research on cognitive language processes, including reading. It is this architectural question, and in the individual differences that arise from different components of any candidate architecture, for which expectations are highest for increasing progress through cognitive and neurocognitive methods.

Acknowledgements

The author gratefully acknowledges Julie Van Dyke, Lesley Hart, Li Hai Tan, and Benjamin Xu for their input and assistance during the preparation of this chapter, which was supported in part by the Learning Research and Development Center of the University of Pittsburgh.

Notes

1. The term 'phonological' is widely used in the literature on reading, and will be used here. However, in most of its uses, what is referred to is the specification of the phonemes of a word, so 'phonemic' would be a more precise description. Note that 'phonological' can include suprasegmental information at the word level (syllabic stress in English; tone in Chinese) as well in phrasal units.

2. Whether semantic influences can operate quickly enough to affect the very beginnings of word identification is another matter. As reviewed in the section on word identification, the phonological activation of printed word forms appears to be so rapid and automatic, relative to semantic influences, that it seems better to say that meaning feedback operates as soon as it is available, but typically after some early cohering of phonological and orthographic information.

3. There are a number of proposals for how to conceptualize how parsing processes proceed and thus what causes garden-path phenomena. Minimal attachment remains the most general principle based on syntactic structures essentially independent of lexical factors. For other proposals within specific syntactic theoretical frameworks see Gibson (1991), Pritchett (1992), and Frazier and Clifton (1996). For a proposal outside the linguistic tradition with strong inter-active assumptions see MacDonald *et al.* (1992). For a hybrid proposal within a syntactic framework, see Perfetti (1990). And for a review of the theoretical and empirical issues, see Mitchell (1994).

4. Assigning coreference, for example assigning pronouns to antecedents, is clearly the joint function of syntactic information and referential information from the discourse. Thus, as in the case of syntactic attachment, the communication between a sentence processing mechanism and a model of the discourse becomes an issue. Garrod and Sanford (1994) conclude that contextual information is immediately integrated during sentence processing, at least when the text provides strong grounds for the reader to commit a specific referential assignment to an ambiguous pronoun. Referential assignment and constituent attachment both illustrate necessary comprehension processes that require a discourse–sentence processing interface.

References

Adams, B. C., Clifton, Jr, C., and Mitchell, D. C. (1991). Lexical guidance in sentence parsing. Poster presented at the meeting of the Psychonomic Society, San Francisco.

Adams, B. C., Bell, L. C., and Perfetti, C. A. (1995). A trading relationship between reading skill and domain knowledge in children's text comprehension. *Discourse Processes*, **20**, 307–23.

Altmann, G. and Steedman, M. (1988). Interaction with context during human sentence processing. *Cognition*, **30**, 191–238.

Anderson, R. C., Reynolds, R. E., Shallert, D. L., and Goetz, E. T. (1977). Frameworks for comprehending discourse. *American Educational Research Journal*, **14**, 367–81.

Baker, L. (1984). Spontaneous versus instructed use of multiple standards for evaluating comprehension: Effects of age, reading proficiency, and type of standard. *Journal of Experimental Child Psychology*, **38**, 289–311.

Baker, L. (1985). Differences in the standards used by college students to evaluate their comprehension of expository prose. *Reading Research Quarterly*, **20**, 297–313.

Berent, I. and Perfetti, C. A. (1995). A rose is a REEZ: The two-cycles model of phonology assembly in reading English. *Psychological Review*, **102**, 146–84.

Besner, D. (1990). Does the reading system need a lexicon? In *Lexical representation and processes* (ed. W. D. Marslen-Wilson), pp. 291–316. MIT Press, Cambridge, MA.

Besner, D., Twilley, L., McCann, R. S., and Seergobin, K. (1990). On the association between connectionism and data: Are a few words necessary? *Psychological Review*, **97**, 432–46.

Britt, M. A. (1994). The interaction of referential ambiguity and argument structure in the parsing of prepositional phrases. *Journal of Memory and Language*, **33**, 251–83.

Britt, A., Perfetti, C. A., Garrod, S., and Rayner, K. (1992). Parsing in discourse: Context effects and their limits. *Journal of Memory and Language*, **31**, 293–314.

Brown, C. and Hagoort, P. (1993). The processing nature of the N400: Evidence from masked priming. *Journal of Congitive Neuroscience*, **5**, 34–44.

Butterworth, B. (1983). Lexical representation. In *Language production, Vol II: Development, writing, and other language processes* (ed. B. Butterworth), pp. 257–94. Academic Press, London.

Byrne, B. (1981). Deficient syntactic control in poor readers: Is a weak phonetic memory code responsible? *Applied Psycholinguistics*, **2**, 201–12.

Carpenter, P. A. and Just, M. A. (1983). What your eyes do while your mind is reading. In *Eye movements in reading: Perceptual and language processes* (ed. K. Rayner), pp. 275–308. Academic Press, New York.

Carpenter, P. A., Miyake, A., and Just, M. A. (1994). Working memory constraints in comprehension: Evidence from individual differences, aphasia, and aging. In *Handbook of psycholinguistics* (ed. M. A. Gernsbacher), pp. 1075–1122. Academic Press, San Diego.

Coltheart, M., Davelaar, E., Jonasson, T. V., and Besner, D. (1977). Access to the internal lexicon. In *Attention and performance*, Vol. 6 (ed. D. Stanislav), pp. 532–55. Erlbaum, NJ.

Coltheart, M., Curtis, B., Atkins, P., and Haller, M. (1993). Models of reading aloud: Dual-route and parallel-distributed-processing approaches. *Psychological Review*, **100**, 589–608.

Conrad, C. (1974). Context effects in sentence comprehension: A study of the subjective lexicon. *Memory and Cognition*, **2**, 130–38.

Corbett, A. T. and Dosher, B. A. (1978). Instrument inferences in sentence encoding. *Journal of Verbal Learning and Verbal Behavior*, **17**, 479–91.

Crain, S. and Shankweiler, D. (1988). Syntactic complexity and reading acquisition. In *Linguistic complexity and text comprehension: Readability issues reconsidered* (eds A. Davison and G. M. Green), pp. 167–92. Erlbaum, NJ.

Crain, S. and Steedman, M. (1985). On not being led up the garden path: The use of context by the psychological syntax processor. In *Natural language parsing: Psychological, computational, and theoretical perspectives* (eds. D. R. Dowty, L. Karttunen, and A. M. Zwicky), pp. 320–58. Cambridge University Press.

Crain, S., Shankweiler, D., Macaruso, P., and Bar-Shalom, E. (1990). Working memory and comprehension of spoken sentences: Investigations of children with reading disorder. In *Neuropsychological impairments of short-term memory* (eds G. Vallar and T. Shallice), pp. 477–508. Cambridge University Press.

DeFrancis, J. (1989). *Visible speech: The diverse oneness of writing systems*. University of Hawaii, Honolulu.

Dell, G. S., McKoon, G., and Ratcliff, R. (1983). The activation of antecedent information during the processing of anaphoric reference in reading. *Journal of Verbal Learning and Verbal Behavior*, **22**, 121–32.

Doyle, M. C., Rugg, M. D., and Wells, T. (1996). A comparison of the electrophysiological effects of formal and repetition priming. *Psychophysiology*, **33**, 132–47.

Duffy, S. A., Morris, R. K., and Rayner, K. (1988). Lexical ambiguity and fixation times in reading. *Journal of Memory and Language*, **27**, 429–46.

Feldman, L. B. (1994). Beyond orthography and phonology: Differences between inflections and derivations. *Journal of Memory and Language*, **33**, 442–70.

Ferrand, L. and Grainger, J. (1992). Phonology and orthography in visual word recognition: Evidence from masked non-word priming. *Quarterly Journal of Experimental Psychology: Human Experimental Psychology*, **45A**, 353–72.

Ferrand, L. and Grainger, J. (1993). The time course of orthographic and phonological code activation in the early phases of visual word recognition. *Bulletin of the Psychonomic Society*, **31**, 119–22.

Ferreira, F. and Clifton, Jr, C. (1986). The independence of syntactic processing. *Journal of Memory and Language*, **25**, 348–68.

Fincher-Kiefer, R. (1993). The role of predictive inferences in situation model construction. *Discourse Processes*, **16**, 99–124.

Fletcher, J. M., Satz, P., and Scholes, R. J. (1981). Developmental changes in the linguistic performance correlates of reading achievement. *Brain and Language*, **13**, 78–90.

Fodor, J. A. (1983). *Modularity of mind: An essay in faculty psychology*. MIT Press, Cambridge, MA.

Forster, K. I. (1979). Levels of processing and the structure of the language processor. In *Sentence processing: Psycholinguistic studies presented to Merrill Garrett* (eds W. E. Cooper and E. C. T. Walker), pp. 27–85. Erlbaum, NJ.

Forster, K. and Davis, C. (1984). Repetition priming and frequency attenuation in lexical access. *Journal of Experimental Psychology: Learning, Memory, and Cognition*, **10**, 680–98.

Forster, K. and Davis, C. (1991). The density constraint on form-priming in the naming task: Interference effects from a masked prime. *Journal of Memory and Language*, **30**, 1–25.

Fowler, C. A., Napps, S. E., and Feldman, L. (1985). Relations among regular and irregular morphologically related words in the lexicon as revealed by repetition priming. *Memory and Cognition*, **13**, 241–55.

Frazier, L. (1979). *On comprehending sentences: Syntactic parsing strategies*. Indiana University Linguistics Club, Bloomington.

Frazier, L. and Clifton, C. (1996). *Construal*. MIT Press, Cambridge, MA.

Frazier, L. and Rayner, K. (1982). Making and correcting errors during sentence comprehension: Eye movements in the analysis of structurally ambiguous sentences. *Cognitive Psychology*, **14**, 178–210.

Frederiksen, J. R. (1981). Sources of process interactions in reading. In *Interactive processes in reading* (eds A. M. Lesgold and C. A. Perfetti), pp. 361–86. Erlbaum, NJ.

Frost, R., Katz, L., and Bentin, S. (1987). Strategies for visual word recognition and orthographical depth: A multilingual comparison. *Journal of Experimental Psychology: Human Perception and Performance*, **13**, 104–15.

Garner, R. (1980). Monitoring of understanding: An investigation of good and poor readers' awareness of induced miscomprehension of text. *Journal of Reading Behaviour*, **12**, 55–63.

Garrod, S. and Sanford, A. J. (1994). Resolving sentences in discourse context: How discourse representation affects language understanding. In *Handbook of psycholinguistics* (ed. M. A. Gernsbacher), pp. 675–98. Academic Press, San Diego.

Gernsbacher, M. A. (1990). *Language comprehension as structure building*. Erlbaum, NJ.

Gernsbacher, M. A. and Faust, M. (1990). The role of supression in sentence comprehension. In *Understanding word and sentence* (ed. G. B. Simpson), pp. 97–128. North-Holland, Amsterdam.

Gernsbacher, M. A., Varner, K. R., and Faust, M. E. (1990). Investigating differences in general comprehension skill. *Journal of Experimental Psychology: Learning, Memory, and Cognition*, **16**, 430–45.

Gibson, E. A. (1991). *A computational theory of human linguistic processing: memory limitations and processing breakdown*. D.Phil. thesis. Carnegie Mellon University. Available as a Center for Machine Translation technical report CMU-CMT-91-125.

Glenberg, A. M., Kruley, P., and Langston, W. E. (1994). Analogical processes in comprehension: Simulation of a mental model. In *Handbook of psycholinguistics* (ed. M. A. Gernsbacher), pp. 609–40. Academic Press, San Diego.

Glucksberg, S., Kreuz, R. J., and Rho, S. (1986). Context can constrain lexical access: Implications for models of language comprehension. *Journal of Experimental Psychology: Learning, Memory, and Cognition*, **12**, 323–35.

Graesser, A. C., Singer, M., and Trabasso, T. (1994). Construction inferences during narrative comprehension. *Psychological Review*, **101**, 371–95.

Grainger, J. and Ferrand, L. (1994). Phonology and orthography in visual word recognition: Effects of masked homophone primes. *Journal of Memory and Language*, **33**, 218–33.

Haenggi, D., Kintsch, W., and Gernsbacher, M. A. (1995). Spatial situation models and text comprehension. *Discourse Processes*, **19**, 173–99.

Hagoort, P., Brown, C., and Groothusen, J. (1993). The syntactic positive shift (SPS) as an ERP measure of syntactic processing. *Language and Cognitive Processes*, **8**, 337–64.

Haviland, S. E. and Clark, H. H. (1974). What's new? Acquiring new information as a process in comprehension. *Journal of Verbal Learning and Verbal Behavior*, **13**, 512–21.

Hogaboam, T. W. and Perfetti, C. A. (1975). Lexical ambiguity and sentence comprehension. *Journal of Verbal Learning and Verbal Behavior*, **14**, 265–74.

Jared, D. and Seidenberg, M. S. (1991). Does word identification proceed from spelling to sound to meaning? *Journal of Experimental Psychology: General*, **120**, 358–94.

Johnson-Laird, P. N. (1983). *Mental models*. Harvard University Press, Cambridge, MA.

Jorm, A. F. and Share, D. L. (1983). Phonological recoding and reading acquisition. *Applied Psycholinguistics*, **4**, 103–47.

Just, M. A. and Carpenter, P. A. (1987). *The psychology of reading and language comprehension*. Allyn and Bacon, Boston.

Just, M. A. and Carpenter, P. A. (1992). A capacity theory of comprehension: Individual differences in working memory. *Psychological Review*, **99**, 122–49.

Keenan, J. M., Baillet, S. D., and Brown, P. (1984). The effects of causal cohesion on comprehension and memory. *Journal of Verbal Learning and Verbal Behavior*, **23**, 115–26.

Kellas, G., Paul, S. T., Martin, M., and Simpson, G. B. (1991). Contextual feature activation and meaning access. In *Understanding word and sentence* (ed. G. B. Simpson), pp. 47–71. North-Holland, Amsterdam.

King, J. and Just, M. A. (1991). Individual differences in syntactic processing. *Journal of Memory and Language*, **30**, 580–602.

Kintsch, W. (1988). The role of knowledge in discourse processing: A construction–integration model. *Psychological Review*, **95**, 163–82.

Kintsch, W. and Mross, F. (1985). Context effects in word identification. *Journal of Memory and Language*, **24**, 336–39.

Kutas, M. and Van Petten, C. K. (1994). Psycholinguistics electrified: Event-related brain potential investigations. In *Handbook of psycholinguistics* (ed. M. A. Gernsbacher), pp. 83–143. Academic Press, San Diego.

Lesch, M. F. and Pollatsek, A. (1993). Automatic access of semantic information by phonological codes in visual word recognition. *Journal of Experimental Psychology: Learning, Memory, and Cognition*, **19**, 285–94.

Levelt, W. J. M. (1989). *Speaking: From intention to articulation*. MIT Press, Cambridge, MA.

Liberman, I. Y. and Shankweiler, D. (1991). Phonology and beginning reading: A tutorial. In *Learning to read: Basic research and its implications* (eds L. Rieben and C. A. Perfetti), pp. 3–17. Erlbaum, NJ.

Long, D. L. and Golding, J. M. (1993). Superordinate goal inferences: Are they automatically generated during comprehension? *Discourse Processes*, **16**, 55–73.

Lukatela, G. and Turvey, M. T. (1990*a*). Automatic and pre-lexical computation of phonology in visual word identification. *European Journal of Cognitive Psychology*, **2**, 325–44.

Lukatela, G. and Turvey, M. T. (1990*b*). Phonemic similarity effects and prelexical phonology. *Memory and Cognition*, **18**, 128–52.

Lukatela, G. and Turvey, M. T. (1991). Phonological access of the lexicon: Evidence from associative priming with pseudohomophones. *Journal of Experimental Psychology: Learning, Memory, and Cognition*, **17**, 951–66.

Lukatela, G. and Turvey, M. T. (1998). Learning to read in two alphabets. *American Psychologist*. **53**, 1057–72.

MacDonald, M. C., Just, M. C., and Carpenter, P. A. (1992). Working memory constraints on the processing of syntactic ambiguity. *Cognitive Psychology*, **24**, 56–98.

MacDonald, M. C., Pearlmutter, N. J., and Seidenberg, M. S. (1994). The lexical nature of syntactic ambiguity resolution. *Psychological Review*, **101**, 676–703.

Mann, V. A., Shankweiler, D., and Smith, S. T. (1984). The association between comprehension of spoken sentences and early reading ability: The role of phonetic representation. *Journal of Child Language*, **11**, 627–43.

McKoon, G. and Ratcliff, R. (1986). Inferences about predictable events. *Journal of Experimental Psychology: Learning, Memory, and Cognition*, **12**, 82–91.

McKoon, G. and Ratcliff, R. (1989). Assessing the occurrence of elaborative inference with recognition: Compatibility checking vs compound cue theory. *Journal of Memory and Language*, **28**, 547–63.

McKoon, G. and Ratcliff, R. (1992). Inference during reading. *Psychological Review*, **99**, 440–66.

Merrill, E. C., Sperber, R. D., and McCauley, C. (1981). Differences in semantic encoding as a function of reading comprehension skill. *Memory and Cognition*, **9**, 618–24.

Merton, R. (1968). The Matthew effect in science. *Science*, **159**, 56–63.

Mitchell, D. C. (1994). Sentence parsing. In *Handbook of psycholinguistics* (ed. M. A. Gernsbacher), pp. 375–409. Academic Press, San Diego.

Mitchell, D. and Holmes, V. K. (1985). The role of specific information about the verb in parsing sentences with local structural ambiguity. *Journal of Memory and Language*, **24**, 542–59.

Morrow, D. G., Greenspan, S. L., and Bower, G. H. (1987). Accessibility and situation models in narrative comprehension. *Journal of Memory and Language*, **26**, 165–87.

Neill, W. T., Hilliard, D. V., and Cooper, E. (1988). The detection of lexical ambiguity: Evidence for context-sensitive parallel access. *Journal of Memory and Language*, **27**, 279–87.

Neville, H. J., Nicol, J., Barss, A., Forster, K. I., and Garret, M. F. (1991). Syntactically based sentence processing classes: Evidence from event-related brain potentials. *Journal of Cognitive Neuroscience*, **3**, 151–65.

Niznikiewicz, M. and Squires, N. K. (1996). Phonological processing and the role of strategy in silent reading: Behavioral and electrophysiological evidence. *Brain and Language*, **52**, 342–64.

Nowak, L. G., Munk, M. H. J., and Bullier, J. (1995). Visual latencies in areas V1 and V2 of the macaque monkey. *Journal of Neurophysiology*, **4**, 1332–34.

Oakhill, J. and Garnham, A. (1988). *Becoming a skilled reader*. Basil Blackwell, New York.

Oakhill, J. and Yuille, N. (1986). Pronoun resolution in skilled and less-skilled comprehenders: Effects of memory load and inferential complexity. *Language and Speech*, **29**, 25–36.

Oakhill, J., Cain, K., and Yuille, N. (1998). Individual differences in children's comprehension skill: Toward an integrated model. In *Reading and spelling: Development and disorder* (eds C. Hulme and M. Joshi), pp. 343–67. Erlbaum, NJ.

O'Brien, E. J., Shank, D. M., Myers, J. L., and Rayner, K. (1988). Elaborative inferences during reading: Do they occur on-line? *Journal of Experimental Psychology: Learning, Memory, and Cognition*, **14**, 410–20.

Olson, R., Wise, B., Conners, F., and Rack, J. (1990). Organization, heritability, and remediation of component word recognition skills in disabled readers. In *Reading and its development: Component skills approaches* (eds T. H. Carr and B. A. Levy), pp. 261–322. Academic Press, New York.

Olson, R., Forsberg, H., and Wise, B. (1994). Genes, environment, and the development of orthographic skills. In *The varieties of orthographic knowledge 1: Theoretical and developmental issues* (ed. V. W. Beringer), pp. 27–71. Kluwer, Dordrecht.

Onifer, W. and Swinney, D. A. (1981). Accessing lexical ambiguities during sentence comprehension: Effects of frequency of meaning and contextual bias. *Memory and Cognition*, **15**, 225–36.

Osgood, C. E. and Hoosain, R. (1974). Salience of the word as a unit in the perception of language. *Perception and Psychophysics*, **15**, 168–92.

Osterhout, L., Holcomb, P. J., and Swinney, D. A. (1994). Brain potentials elicited by garden-path sentences: Evidence of the application of verb information during parsing. *Journal of Experimental Psychology: Learning, Memory, and Cognition*, **20**, 786–803.

Otero, J. and Kintsch, W. (1992). Failures to detect contradictions in a text: What readers believe versus what they read. *Psychological Science*, **3**, 229–35.

Paap, K. R. and Noel, R. W. (1991). Dual-route models of print and sound: Still a good horse race. *Psychological Research*, **53**, 13–24.

Pennington, B. F. (1990). Annotation: The genetics of dyslexia. *Journal of Child Psychology and Psychiatry*, **31**, 193–201.

Perfetti, C. A. (1985). *Reading Ability*. Oxford University Press, New York.

Perfetti, C. A. (1990). The cooperative language processors: Semantic influences in an autonomous syntax. In *Comprehension processes in reading* (eds D. A. Balota, G. B. Flores d'Arcais, and K. Rayner), pp. 205–30. Erlbaum, NJ.

Perfetti, C. A. (1992). The representation problem in reading acquisition. In *Reading acquisition* (eds P. B. Gough, L. C. Ehri, and R. Treiman), pp. 145–74. Erlbaum, NJ.

Perfetti, C. A. and Bell, L. (1991). Phonemic activation during the first 40 ms of word identification: Evidence from backward masking and masked priming. *Journal of Memory and Language*, **30**, 473–85.

Perfetti, C. A. and Lesgold, A. M. (1977). Discourse comprehension and sources of individual differences. In *Cognitive processes in comprehension* (eds P. A. Carpenter and M. A. Just), pp. 141–83. Erlbaum, NJ.

Perfetti, C. A. and Lesgold, A. M. (1979). Coding and comprehension in skilled reading and implications for reading instruction. In *Theory and practice in early reading*, Vol. 1 (eds L. B. Resnick and P. A. Weaver), pp. 57–84. Erlbaum, NJ.

Perfetti, C. A. and Tan, L. H. (1998). The time-course of graphic, phonological, and semantic activation in Chinese character identification. *Journal of Experimental Psychology: Learning, Memory, and Cognition*, **24**, 1–18.

Perfetti, C. A. and Zhang, S. (1995*a*). The universal word identification reflex. In *The psychology of learning and motivation*, Vol. 33 (ed. D. L. Medin), pp. 159–89. Academic Press, San Diego.

Perfetti, C. A. and Zhang, S. (1995*b*). Very early phonological activation in Chinese reading. *Journal of Experimental Psychology: Learning, Memory, and Cognition*, **21**, 24–33.

Perfetti, C. A., Bell, L., and Delaney, S. (1988). Automatic phonetic activation in silent word reading: Evidence from backward masking. *Journal of Memory and Language*, **27**, 59–70.

Perfetti, C. A., Marron, M. A., and Foltz. P. W. (1996). Sources of comprehension failure: Theoretical perspectives and case studies. In *Reading comprehension difficulties: Processes and intervention* (eds C. Cornoldi and J. Oakhill), pp. 137–65. Erlbaum, NJ.

Perrig, W. and Kintsch, W. (1985). Propositional and situational representations of text. *Journal of Memory and Language*, **24**, 503–18.

Plaut, D. C., McClelland, J. L., Seidenberg, M. S., and Patterson, K. (1996). Understanding normal and impaired word reading: Computational principles in quasi-regular domains. *Psychological Review*, **103**, 56–115.

Polich, J. M., McCarthy G., Wang, W. S., and Donchin, E. (1983). When words collide: Orthographic and phonological interference during word processing. *Biological Psychology*, **16**, 155–80.

Pritchett, B. (1988). Garden path phenomena and the grammatical basis of language processing. *Language*, **64**, 539–76.

Pritchett, B. (1992). *Grammatical competence and parsing performance*. University of Chicago Press.

Rayner, K. and Pollatsek, A. (1989). *The psychology of reading*. Prentice Hall, Englewood Cliffs, NJ.

Rugg, M. D. and Barrett, S. F. (1987). Event-related potentials and the interaction between orthographic and phonological information in a rhyme judgment task. *Brain and Language*, **32**, 336–61.

Ryan, E. B. (1982). Identifying and remediating failures in reading comprehension: Toward an instructional approach for poor comprehenders. In *Advances in reading research*, Vol. 3 (eds G. E. MacKinnon and T. G. Waller), pp. 224–62, Academic Press, New York.

Seidenberg, M. S. and McClelland, J. L. (1989). A distributed, developmental model of word recognition and naming. *Psychological Review*, **96**, 523–68.

Seidenberg, M. S. and McClelland, J. L. (1990). More words but still no lexicon: Reply to Besner *et al.* (1990). *Psychological Review*, **97**, 447–52.

Seidenberg, M. S., Tanenhaus, M. K., Leiman, J. L., and Bienkowski, M. (1982). Automatic access of the meanings of ambiguous words in context: Some limitations of knowledge-based processing. *Cognitive Psychology*, **14**, 489–537.

Seidenberg, M. S., Waters, G. S., Barnes, M. A., and Tanenhaus, M. K. (1984). When does irregular spelling or pronunciation influence word recognition? *Journal of Verbal Learning and Verbal Behavior*, **23**, 383–404.

Shankweiler, D. and Crain, S. (1986). Language mechanisms and reading disorder: A modular approach. *Cognition*, **24**, 139–68.

Share, D. L. and Stanovich, K. E. (1995). Cognitive processes in early reading development: Accommodating individual differences into a model of acquisition. *Issues in Education*, **1**, 1–57.

Simpson, G. B. (1994). Context and the processing of ambiguous words. In *Handbook of psycholinguistics* (ed. M. A. Gernsbacher), pp. 359–74. Academic Press, San Diego.

Simpson, G. B. and Krueger, M. A. (1991). Selective access of homograph meanings in sentence context. *Journal of Memory and Language*, **30**, 627–43.

Singer, M. (1979). Processes of inference during sentence encoding. *Memory and Cognition*, **7**, 192–200.

Singer, M. and Ferreira, F. (1983). Inferring consequences in story comprehension. *Journal of Verbal Learning and Verbal Behavior*, **22**, 437–48.

Spilich, G. J., Vesonder, G. T., Chiesi, H. L., and Voss, J. F. (1979). Text processing of domain-related information for individuals with high and low domain knowledge. *Journal of Verbal Learning and Verbal Behavior*, **18**, 275–90.

Stanovich, K. E. (1980). Toward an interactive-compensatory model of individual differences in the development of reading fluency. *Reading Research Quarterly*, **16**, 32–71.

Stanovich, K. E. (1981). Attentional and automatic context effects in reading. In *Interactive processes in reading* (eds A. M. Lesgold and C. A. Perfetti), pp. 241–67. Erlbaum, NJ.

Stanovich, K. E. (1986). Matthew effects in reading: Some consequences of individual differences in the acquisition of literacy. *Reading Research Quarterly*, **21**, 360–407.

Stanovich, K. E. (1988). Explaining the differences between the dyslexic and the garden-variety poor reader: The phonological-core variable-difference model. *Journal of Learning Disabilities*, **21**, 590–604.

Stanovich, K. E. and Siegel, L. S. (1994). Phenotypic performance profile of children with reading disabilities: A regression-based test of the phonological-core variable-difference model. *Journal of Educational Psychology*, **86**, 24–53.

Stanovich, K. E. and West, R. F. (1989). Exposure to print and orthographic processing. *Reading Research Quarterly*, **24**, 402–33.

Stein, C. L., Cairns, J. S., and Zurif, E. B. (1984). Sentence comprehension limitations related to syntactic deficits in reading-disabled children. *Applied Psycholinguistics*, **5**, 305–22.

Stone, G. O., Vanhoy, M., and Van Orden, G. C. (1997). Perception is a two-way street: Feedforward and feedback phonology in visual word recognition. *Journal of Memory and Language*, **36**, 337–59.

Stothard, S. and Hulme, C. (1996). A comparison of reading comprehension and decoding difficulties in children. In *Reading comprehension difficulties: Processes and intervention* (eds C. Cornoldi and J. Oakhill), pp. 93–112. Erlbaum, NJ.

Tabossi, P. (1988). Accessing lexical ambiguity in different types of sentential contexts. *Journal of Memory and Language*, **27**, 324–40.

Tabossi, P. (1991). Understanding words in context. In *Understanding word and sentence* (ed. G. B. Simpson), pp. 1–22. North-Holland, Amsterdam.

Taft, M. (1992). The body of the BOSS: Subsyllabic units in the lexical processing of polysyllabic words. *Journal of Experimental Psychology: Human Perception and Performance*, **18**, 1004–14.

Taft, M. and Forster, K. (1975). Lexical storage and retrieval of prefixed words. *Journal of Verbal Learning and Verbal Behavior*, **14**, 638–47.

Tan, L. H. and Perfetti, C. A. Phonological and associative inhibition in the early stages of English word identification: Evidence from backward masking. *Journal of Experimental Psychology: Human Perception and Performance*. (In press.)

Trabasso, T. and Suh, S. (1993). Understanding text: Achieving explanatory coherence through online inferences and mental operations in working memory. *Discourse Processes*, **16**, 3–34.

Trueswell, J. C., Tanenhaus, M. K., and Garnsey, S. M. (1994). Semantic influences on parsing: Use of thematic role information in syntactic ambiguity resolution. *Journal of Memory and Language*, **33**, 285–318.

Van Dijk, T. A. and Kintsch, W. (1983). *Strategies of discourse comprehension*. Academic Press, New York.

Van Orden, G. C. (1987). A ROWS is a ROSE: Spelling, sound, and reading. *Memory and Cognition*, **15**, 181–98.

Van Orden, G. C. and Goldinger, S. D. (1994). The interdependence of form and function in cognitive systems explains perception of printed words. *Journal of Experimental Psychology: Human Perception and Performance*, **20**, 1269–91.

Van Orden, G. C., Pennington, B., and Stone, G. (1990). Word identification in reading and the promise of subsymbolic psycholinguistics. *Psychological Review*, **97**, 488–522.

Vogel, S.A. (1975). *Syntactic abilities in normal and dyslexic children*. University Park Press, Baltimore.

Walberg, H. J. and Tsai, S.-L. (1983). Matthew effects in education. *American Educational Research Journal*, **20**, 359–73.

Ziegler, J. C., Van Orden, G. C., and Jacobs, A. M. (1997). Phonology can help or hurt the perception of print. *Journal of Experimental Psychology: Human Perception and Performance*, **23**, 845–60.

Zwaan, R. (1996). Processing narrative time shifts. *Journal of Experimental Psychology: Learning, Memory, and Cognition*, **22**, 1196–1207.

Zwaan, R., Langston, M., and Graesser, A. (1995). The construction of situation models in narrative comprehension: An event-indexing model. *Psychological Science*, **6**, 292–97.

Section 3

The neurocognitive architectures of language

7 The neural architecture underlying the processing of written and spoken word forms

Cathy Price, Peter Indefrey, and Miranda van Turennout

7.1 Introduction

To date, most brain-imaging studies on the neural architecture of language processing have focused on the word level. It is the aim of this chapter to review the available evidence for the involvement of cortical areas in single-word processing and to evaluate how far specific cortical activations can be linked to specific processing components. To this end, brief recapitulations of the processing components that are assumed by current psycholinguistic models may help to analyse the variety of paradigms used in brain-imaging work. A much more detailed account of state-of-the-art models of language production, comprehension, and reading, as well as the evidence justifying the functional distinctions made, is provided in section 2 of this volume.

The choice to study language processing at the level of single words is not arbitrary. While it is true that past the earliest stages of language acquisition, natural utterances as a rule comprise more than one word, a single word is nonetheless the smallest unit for speaking and comprehension, because it constitutes the smallest meaningful utterance. This means that the essential componentry necessary to transform a preverbal message into an acoustic speech signal and likewise the essential componentry necessary to analyse a perceived acoustic or visual signal for comprehension are already active at the single-word level. On the other hand, it should be kept in mind that models of single-word processing do not lend themselves to straightforward generalization of word processing in a sentence context. On the production side, this means, for instance, that the process of integrating a word's syntactic information into a syntactic representation of an intended sentence utterance is largely ignored. On the comprehension side, other central issues of psycholinguistic research, such as the identification of words in the continuous acoustic signal and context effects on word recognition are not considered.

Over the last few years, lesion studies and functional-imaging studies have revealed that the comprehension and production of spoken and written word-forms are sustained by a system of cortical and subcortical regions that are widely distributed, primarily across the left hemisphere of the brain (Mesulam 1990; Petersen *et al.* 1988, 1990; Wise *et al.* 1991). Further, this distributed language system is involved in the comprehension and production of words irrespective of whether processing is evoked from heard words (Wise *et al.* 1991; Démonet *et al.* 1992; Binder *et al.* 1997), seen words, or pictures of objects (Vandenberghe *et al.* 1996). The regions involved are predominantly left lateralized and include the dorsolateral prefrontal cortex, premotor cortex, the posterior auditory association cortex (Wernicke's area), the middle and inferior temporal cortices, the supramarginal and angular gyri in the posterior inferior-parietal cortex, the cerebellum, supplementary motor area (SMA), anterior cingulate, and the thalamus.

Within this network of diverse regions, however, there is clearly functional specialization at both the level of the cellular structure, and the processes that are being implemented. For instance, damage to the left posterior-superior-temporal cortex (Wernicke's area) results in impaired comprehension with less impairment in producing fluent, well articulated speech. In contrast, damage to Broca's area results in relatively intact comprehension but poor speech fluency, at least at the single-word level. A more detailed analysis suggests a complicated picture: speech perception is not always normal in patients with Broca's aphasia, and articulation of speech sounds is not normal in patients with Wernicke's aphasia (Caplan 1987; Blumstein 1995; see also Damasio and Geschwind 1984; Mesulam 1990).

While lesion studies can indicate functional specialization within the distributed language system, the conclusions that can be drawn are limited. This is because lesion studies can not indicate whether the association of the damaged region with the impaired function is direct or indirect (in the connections only). Further, lesion studies can not reveal whether the damaged region was originally sufficient to perform a function or whether it previously worked in co-operation with other connected regions. Functional-imaging studies are able to overcome the latter restriction by revealing distributed neural regions involved in a task. However, segregating the functions of the different regions has proved difficult with functional imaging, in part because the language system is so readily activated even when a task does not demand the involvement of a particular function (Sergent 1994; Frith *et al.* 1995; Price *et al.* 1996*c*). Responsiveness of the language system to word-like stimuli makes it difficult to select control tasks that do not themselves (partially) activate the process under investigation. Despite these difficulties, neuroimaging studies have successfully managed to subdivide the functions of different language regions. It is this functional specialization that we focus on in the following sections.

7.2 Word production

In describing the processing mechanisms underlying the transformation of a thought into speech, theories of speech production usually distinguish between conceptual, grammatical, and phonological processing levels (e.g. Bock and Levelt 1994; Dell 1986; Garrett 1980; Levelt 1989). Corresponding to the distinction between these levels, at least three types of word information are assumed to be represented: concepts, representing a word's meaning, lemmas, representing a word's syntactic properties, and word forms, incorporating a word's morpho-phonological characteristics. Although most models agree on the representational levels that have to be distinguished, there is disagreement about the nature of the representations and the interplay over time between the levels (see Caramazza 1997, for an overview). A standard experimental paradigm for studying word retrieval during speech production is the so-called picture-naming task (e.g. Glaser 1992). A picture of, for example, a table is presented visually and subjects have to say *table*. The plausible assumption behind this task is that it involves all stages of word production. The recognition of the picture and the activation of its associated concept trigger a retrieval process in the mental lexicon. At the conceptual level the concept node for *table* is activated in a conceptual network, where it is linked to other, semantically related nodes, such as *furniture*, or *chair*, all of which become activated to a certain degree. Following the model described by Levelt in Chapter 4, the activated concepts spread their activation to their corresponding lemmas, the lemma level being the first representational level in the lexicon. Lexical information on the syntactic properties of words, such as word class and grammatical gender, are retrieved at this level. The highest activated lemma, in our case *table*, is selected and its activation spreads to the corresponding word form on the second lexical level. The word form carries information on the phonemes of the word (/tcibl/) and information on its metrical structure ('two syllables, the first one stressed'). It is only by an additional process, phonological encoding, that these two sorts of information are brought together by assigning the phonemes to the metrical structure from left to right. The result of this process are two syllables with associated phonemes /tei/-/bl/. These are translated (or possibly retrieved from a syllable store) by phonetic encoding into a phonetic plan, a code which is understood and executed by the articulatory apparatus. The output of phonological encoding (the phonological word) provides the feedback (internal speech) speakers use to correct themselves before articulation.

The distinctiveness of the different processing levels has been demonstrated by various kinds of behavioural data, including speech errors (e.g. Garrett 1976), the tip-of-the-tongue phenomenon (see Brown 1991, for an overview), reaction-time data (e.g. Levelt *et al.* 1991; Schriefers *et al.* 1990), and neuropsychological data (see Garrett 1992, for an overview). Recently, dynamic measures of the real-time activation of the distinct types of word information during speech production have been obtained in a series of event-related brain potential (ERP) studies. These data will be described below. First, we will discuss neuroimaging studies of the brain areas that are involved in lexical retrieval during production.

7.2.1 Lemma retrieval and phonological encoding

Neuroimaging studies of speech production have mainly focused on two types of tasks: word generation and picture naming. In word-generation tasks, subjects are presented with an auditory or visual word (usually a noun) and asked to generate a semantically related verb, category exemplar, or synonym. In one variant of this task, called verbal fluency, subjects are given a visual or auditory cue such as a letter name or a category, and asked to generate as many words as possible associated with the cue. Obviously, the processes involved in this task include the levels of conceptualizing, lemma retrieval, phonological encoding, and articulation. However, in addition, word generation tasks involve a semantically, phonologically, or orthographically guided search for appropriate responses. The problematic aspect of the inclusion of an explicit search level is that it is unclear how subjects perform the search. They may use a variety of strategies involving additional cognitive components that are not part of natural language production. This makes it extremely difficult to attribute cortical activation observed during word generation to specific levels of word production.

The cognitive components that are involved in picture naming are more clear (see above), and therefore this task seems to be better suited to investigate whether separate stages of lexical access can be associated with separate cortical activations. However, only a few neuroimaging studies of picture naming have been reported, with inconsistent conclusions so far. When object naming is contrasted with baselines that control for object recognition, activation is observed in inferior temporal, inferior frontal, precentral, and subcortical cortices (Martin *et al.* 1996; Price *et al.* 1996*b*). However, the experimental designs did not allow for isolating regions specifically related to lemma activation.

Despite all difficulties that are associated with interpreting the results of neuroimaging studies on word production, we want to focus on two brain regions that possibly play an important role in lexical retrieval: the left posterior-temporal lobe (Brodmann's area (BA) 37; see Fig. 7.1), and the left frontal operculum. Price and Friston (1997) found these areas (together with the midline cerebellum) to be in common to reading, picture naming, letter naming, and colour naming, when articulation is controlled in the baseline condition. The left posterior-temporal region has also been found to be more active during word generation than during semantic judgements on heard words (Warburton *et al.* 1996), suggesting that, apart from semantic processing, it plays a role in lexical retrieval during production. Evidence from direct cortical stimulation and lesion studies also supports the role of the left basal temporal lobe in word production. For example, cortical stimulation of the basal-temporal region (including inferior temporal and fusiform gyri) in patients prior to surgery for epilepsy, results in a transient failure to produce words (Luders *et al.* 1986; Burnstine *et al.* 1990; Luders *et al.* 1991). Likewise, patients with lesions in the territory of the left posterior cerebral artery (usually occipital and inferior temporal lobe damage) are unable to read or name objects in response to visual presentation, tactile presentation, or verbal descriptions despite intact conceptual knowledge (De Renzi *et al.* 1987).

The other crucial word-production area that is always activated in concert with the posterior basal temporal region is the left frontal operculum. In the self-generated paradigms, however, the specificity of the frontal operculum signal is obscured by

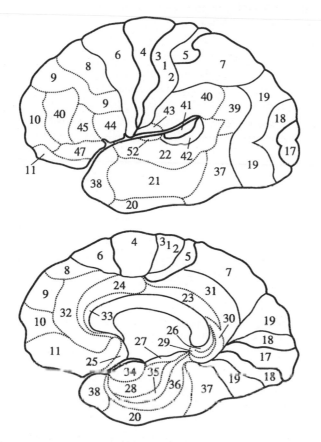

Fig. 7.1 Brodmann's areas of the cortex. Not all Brodmann numbers are listed in the figure. Areas with thick solid lines have histologically quite distinctive boundaries. Areas with less clear boundaries are marked by light solid lines. Areas that gradually merge into one another are marked by dotted lines. (From Kolb and Whishaw (1996). Copyright © 1996 W. H. Freeman and Company, reprinted by permission.)

extensive prefrontal activation which spreads from the frontal operculum, through the inferior frontal gyrus, the posterior part of the middle frontal gyrus, into the dorsal part of the precentral sulcus including BAs 44, 45, 46, and 47. Several functions have been attributed to these prefrontal regions including the initiation of strategies to identify the appropriate words from memory, attention to the task, and components of short-term verbal-working memory (Paulesu *et al.* 1993). Frith *et al.* (1991*a*,*b*) attributed involvement of the dorsolateral prefrontal cortex during word generation tasks to the exercise of will to perform a volitional act. In support of this claim they have shown that a similar region is activated when subjects perform another, non-verbal, willed act (Frith *et al.* 1991*b*). In contrast, Tulving *et al.* (1994) and Fletcher *et al.* (1995) have attributed left prefrontal activation to the encoding of novel verbal information into episodic memory. Tulving *et al.* (1994) further argue that once the task becomes familiar through practice, episodic memory encoding should cease and the left dorsolateral frontal activation should no longer be observed. This was indeed reported by Raichle *et al.* (1994) who demonstrated that activation in the left inferior frontal gyrus and SMA decreased with practice. Further studies are required to specify the precise role of the different prefrontal regions during self-generated word production tasks. However, within the context of word production, the common region is the left frontal operculum.

The left frontal signal during word production corresponds to that identified as being more active for naming pseudowords relative to regular and high frequency irregular words (e.g. Fiez *et al.* 1993; Herbster *et al.* 1997; Price *et al.* 1996*c*; Indefrey 1997; Hagoort *et al.* 1998). Details of these studies are described below. Importantly, these findings suggest that the left frontal operculum is involved in phonological processing. Its activation during word generation and picture naming might be related to the stage of lexical access in which the phonological form of a word is constructed.

In summary, the crucial word production areas appear to be the left posterior basal temporal cortex and the left frontal operculum. Additional experiments are required to obtain a more precise insight into the neuroanatomical structures that underlie the different stages of lexical access.

7.2.2 Phonetic encoding and articulation

In order for the phonological word-form to be articulated, it needs to be phonetically encoded into an articulatory plan. One possible candidate area for this phonetic encoding is the posterior part of Broca's area and the adjacent precentral sulcus (BA 44/6). This region is activated when repeating words is contrasted with listening to words, and lies 15–20 mm posterior to that associated with speech perception in BA 45 (Price *et al.* 1996*d*). Activity in BA 44 *per se* is not specific to speech production—it is also involved in preparing finger movements (Krams *et al.* 1998) and imaging movements (Stephan *et al.* 1995). It may be important for preparing intricate motor plans, including those required for speech. In addition to posterior Broca's area, articulation activates the bilateral sylvian sensorimotor cortex, anterior insular regions, the SMA, the basal ganglia, thalamic nuclei (particularly on the left), and the midline cerebellum (Warburton *et al.* 1996; Price *et al.* 1996*d*; Bookheimer *et al.* 1995). The primary sensorimotor activations include those areas controlling laryngeal, lingual, and facial muscles, but more dorsal regions are also involved. The dorsal activations may relate to the voluntary control of respiration (Ramsay *et al.* 1993), a necessary component of articulation.

7.2.3 The time course of lexical retrieval in speech production

In addition to identifying neuroanatomical structures that underlie speaking, a central issue in speech production research concerns the temporal dynamics of the different processing levels. The temporal co-ordination of the separate components is of crucial importance for the production of fluent speech. This becomes apparent when one considers the fast speech rate (on average, speakers produce two to three words per second; cf. Levelt 1989) and the high level of fluency that speakers are able to achieve. In order to produce such fluent speech the processing components of the production system need to be simultaneously active (Dell 1986; Kempen and Hoenkamp 1987; Levelt 1989). This means, for example, that a sentence does not need to be fully specified at one level before processing at the next level can start. However, in current models of speech production the notion of parallel activity is usually combined with a serial approach to lexical retrieval. This means that words are assumed to be retrieved from the mental lexicon in at least two steps. In the first step, a set of lemmas is activated by the conceptual input, and after some time the highest activated lemma gets selected. In the second step, the phonological form of the word is accessed, and a phonetic representation of the word is constructed. The two-stage approach to lexical access has been based on a variety of data from behavioural studies (e.g. Bock 1986; Garrett 1988; Kempen and Huijbers 1983; Levelt *et al.* 1991; Schriefers *et al.* 1990; Vigliocco *et al.* 1997), and from neuropsychological studies of patients with language impairment (e.g. Butterworth 1989; Garrett 1992; Miozzo and Caramazza 1997).

Recently, electrophysiological evidence has been provided on the temporal organization of the stages of semantic and phonological retrieval (Van Turennout *et al.* 1997). In this study, the main experimental task was picture naming. In addition subjects performed a go/no-go response task consisting of a semantic-phonological judgement on the name of the picture. The semantic task involved an animateness decision, and the phonological task involved a phoneme decision (e.g. does the name of the picture start with an /s/ or a/b/). During the performance of this task, ERPs were recorded. From the averaged electrophysiological activity time locked to picture onset, Lateralized Readiness Potentials (LRPs) were derived. The LRP is a brain potential that is directly related to the preparation for motor actions (Coles 1989; De Jong *et al.* 1988; Kutas and Donchin 1980). Prior work has shown that the LRP can be used as an index of response activation and that it is sensitive to even low levels of response activation that do not result in an overt response. Given these properties, the LRP was used in the go/no-go response task to detect the moments at which semantic and phonological information became available for response preparation. The results revealed that when the semantic judgement determined the response hand and the phonological judgement determined go/no-go, an LRP developed not only on go trials, but also on no-go trials on which no overt response was given. This means that semantic information was available to select the response hand before phonological information was available to distinguish between go and no-go trials. The presence of a no-go LRP proved to be independent of whether the go/no-go decision was based on the word-initial, or on the word-final phoneme of the word. Conversely, when the go/no-go decision was based on semantic information, an LRP was observed only on go trials, and not on no-go trials. These results strongly suggest that speakers retrieve the semantic properties of a word before they have access to its phonological form.

In another series of experiments, Van Turennout *et al.* (1998) investigated the time course of lemma retrieval and phonological encoding. Using the LRP go/no-go paradigm in combination with noun-phrase production, they found that speakers retrieve lemma and phonological information in a fixed temporal order. It was demonstrated that during noun-phrase production a word's syntactic gender, which is represented at the lemma level, is retrieved before its phonological properties and that the reverse is not possible: speakers cannot activate a word's phonology without having previously retrieved its syntax. (See Fig. 7.2.)

The data also provided estimations on the speed with which the phonological form of a word is built-up prior to articulation. Based on the time interval during which only lemma, and no phonological information, affected the LRP it could be estimated that after lemma selection it takes about 40 ms to construct the beginning of a word form. Furthermore, by comparing the duration of the no-go LRP in the word-initial and word-final phoneme conditions it could be estimated that for words consisting of an average of 4.5 phonemes, it takes about 80 ms longer to encode the end of a word than to encode its beginning. In conclusion, the electrophysiological data substantiate the idea that lexical retrieval proceeds from lemma retrieval to word-form encoding, and they suggest that it takes about 120 ms to build up a word form after its lemma has been retrieved.

7.3 Spoken-word processing

In listening, as compared to word production, the order of processing stages involving the stored knowledge of words is reversed. First, the lexical word form representing the sound of the word has to be selected on the basis of the acoustic input. Only then do the lemma and subsequently the word meaning become activated. Since lexical word forms have a phonological format, they cannot be accessed directly from the acoustic input. A prelexical phonological processing stage is required to convert the acoustic input into a phonological representation. Thus at least five processing components can be distinguished in single-word comprehension: (i) non-linguistic acoustic processing; (ii) prelexical phonological processing; (iii) lexical word form selection; (iv) lemma activation and (v) semantic–conceptual activation. Lemma activation as well as semantic–conceptual activation are processing stages which are shared with word production and written language processing, and are discussed in the respective sections of this chapter. Evidence on the cortical representations of the first three processing stages is discussed in this section. See Fig. 7.3 for a composite picture of cortical activity.

7.3.1 Non-linguistic acoustic processing

Areas associated with acoustic, but not phonological, processing should show equal activation for speech and non-speech input with respect to a silent baseline condition, or, conversely, should not show activation when speech and non-speech input are directly compared. This is indeed the case for the bilateral superior temporal gyri. When there is auditory input in the activation task and silence as the baseline, signals in bilateral superior temporal gyri are observed in Brodmann's areas 41, 42, and 22 (Wise *et al.* 1991; Binder *et al.* 1997; Price *et al.* 1992, 1996*d*). These signals are not detected

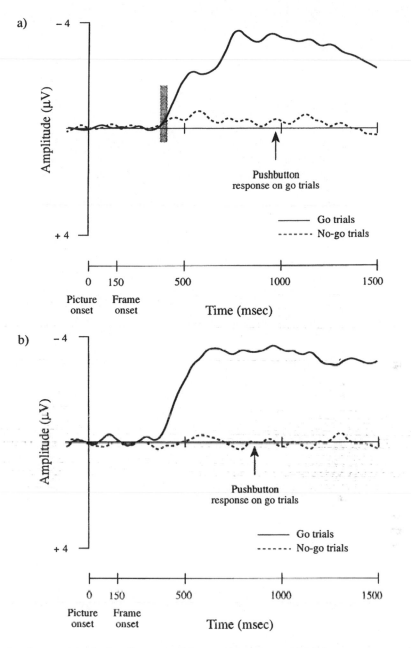

Fig. 7.2 Grand average lateralized readiness potentials on go trials and no-go trials in the noun-phrase production experiment. (a) The syntactic decision determined response hand, the word-initial phoneme decision determined whether a trial was a go or a no-go trial. Significant lateralization of the readiness potential was obtained both on go and on no-go trials from 370 ms after picture onset. The shaded area shows the time interval in which the go and the no-go LRPs were significantly different from the baseline, but not from each other. The presence of an LRP for no-go trials means that preparation of a syntactic response has started before phonological information is available to inform the motor system that a response should be withheld. The right border of the shaded area marks the moment (410 ms) at which phonological information leads to the termination of the syntactic response preparation on no-go trials. (b) The syntactic decision determined whether a trial was a go or a no-go trial, the word-initial phoneme decision determined the response hand. No significant lateralization of the readiness potential was obtained on no-go trials. (After Van Turennout *et al.* (1998). Copyright © 1998 American Association for the Advancement of Science, reprinted by permission.)

Spoken-word processing

Left   Right

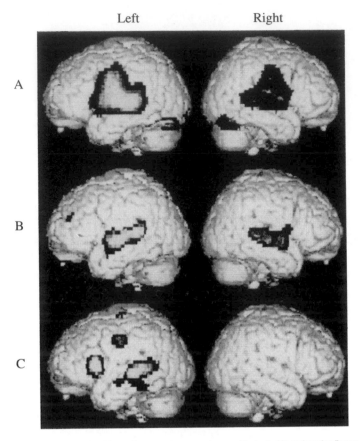

Fig. 7.3   The cortical regions involved in spoken-word processing are illustrated in red and yellow on models of the left and right side of the brain. The top row (A) shows the areas for repeating words relative to silent rest. The middle row (B) shows the areas for hearing words relative to silent rest. The bottom row shows the areas for repeating words relative to hearing reversed words (all data from Price *et al.* 1996).

when hearing words is contrasted to low-level acoustic input such as tones or reversed words (Binder *et al.* 1997; Howard *et al.* 1992; Démonet *et al.* 1992; Price *et al.* 1996*d*), implying equivalent activation in both conditions and a role for BA 41, 42, and part of 22 in low-level acoustic processing.

In the anterior region of Broca's area (the border of BA 45 and the anterior insula), Fiez *et al.* (1995) have reported increased activity during auditory detection tasks on stimuli with rapid temporal changes (e.g. words, syllables, and tone sequences), but not during auditory detection on steady-state vowels or during passive listening (Petersen *et al.* 1988, 1989; Fiez *et al.* 1995). The fact that tone sequences elicited responses in this area suggests specialization for detecting rapid temporal changes which is not specific

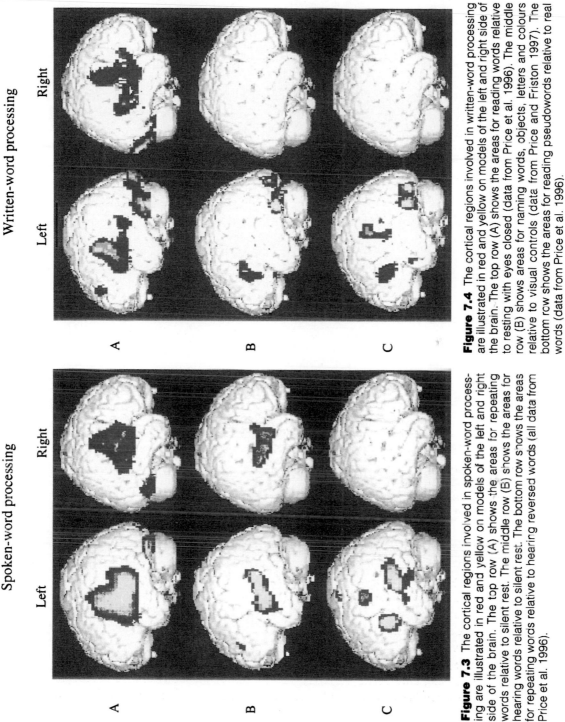

Spoken-word processing

Figure 7.3 The cortical regions involved in spoken-word processing are illustrated in red and yellow on models of the left and right side of the brain. The top row (A) shows the areas for repeating words relative to silent rest. The middle row (B) shows the areas for hearing words relative to silent rest. The bottom row shows the areas for repeating words relative to hearing reversed words (all data from Price et al. 1996).

Written-word processing

Figure 7.4 The cortical regions involved in written-word processing are illustrated in red and yellow on models of the left and right side of the brain. The top row (A) shows the areas for reading words relative to resting with eyes closed (data from Price et al. 1996). The middle row (B) shows areas for naming words, objects, letters and colours relative to visual controls (data from Price and Friston 1997). The bottom row shows the areas for reading pseudowords relative to real words (data from Price et al. 1996).

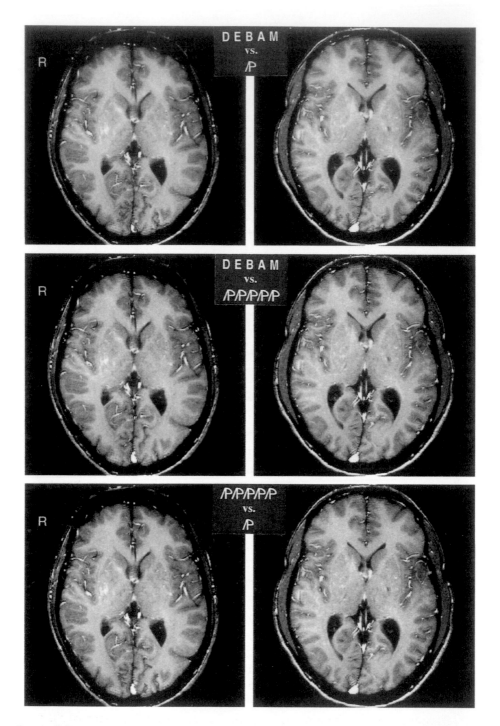

Figure 7.5 Functional MRI activations of medial occipital areas involved in visual processing of word-like stimuli relative to single false-font stimuli (top row). Activations are overlayed in red and yellow on horizontal anatomical MR slices (AC-PC oriented, z = +4) of two subjects. The activations disappear with length-matched non-linguistic control stimuli such as strings of false-fonts relative to single false-fonts. Almost identical activations reappear when strings of false-fonts are contrasted with single false-fonts (bottom row). (Data from Indefrey et al. 1997. Copyright 1997 Academic Press, reprinted by permission.)

for speech input. Other studies are not entirely consistent with Fiez's findings: activity in BA 45 has been observed during passive listening relative to (i) hearing reversed words which control for the acoustic input (Price *et al.* 1996*d*), and (ii) silent rest when the rate of heard word presentation is slow (Warburton *et al.* 1996; Price *et al.* 1996*d*). Clearly, further investigation is required to determine the different functions of this region.

7.3.2 Prelexical phonological processing

If auditory processing of speech sounds activates regions that are not involved in the processing of non-speech sounds, then specialization for a prelexical phonological processing stage would be demonstrated. The difficulty identifying such an area with functional imaging is that speech input will also trigger lexico-semantic processing. To avoid this confound, the candidate areas should be demonstrated to be insensitive to the lexical status of the stimuli, yet respond to phonemes, illegal non-words, pseudo-words, or words.

When acoustic input is controlled for, auditory word presentation results in left lateralized activity in the superior temporal sulcus and the middle temporal gyrus. These regions are posterior and ventral to those involved in acoustic analysis (see Binder *et al.* 1997). For instance, speech-specific activation in posterior temporal regions has been observed during hearing and repeating tasks (Howard *et al.* 1992; Price *et al.* 1992, 1996*d*) and when subjects make phonological judgements on heard syllables, words, or non-words (Zatorre *et al.* 1992; Démonet *et al.* 1992, 1994). In these studies, lexical effects cannot be excluded. However, left-lateralized posterior superior-temporal gyrus activation was also found in an interesting condition introduced by Mazoyer *et al.* (1993). They presented French subjects with a story spoken in an unfamiliar language (Tamil). This condition involves both acoustic processing and phonological processing of the phonemes that Tamil shares with French. But since the sounds of the words are unfamiliar they are unlikely to trigger lexico-semantic processing. The left lateralized activation reported in the posterior superior-temporal gyrus may therefore have a role in prelexical phonological processing.

Activation of the left posterior inferior-frontal region (Broca's area) has also been associated with phonological processing. Robust activation is detected during (i) phonological judgements on heard stimuli (Zatorre *et al.* 1992; Démonet *et al.* 1992, 1994); (ii) the retrieval of words (Petersen *et al.* 1988, 1989; Wise *et al.* 1991; Warburton *et al.* 1996); (iii) semantic judgements on heard words (Démonet *et al.* 1994; Warburton *et al.* 1996); and (iv) silent 'repetition' of non-words with three repetitions per stimulus (Warburton *et al.* 1996). Although a pre-lexical phonological analysis component is involved in most of the tasks used, the presence of additional task components certainly does not allow for an interpretation in terms of a role for Broca's area in phonological processing. All these tasks, for example, require auditory–verbal short-term memory to remember the auditory stimuli whilst phonological or semantic decisions are made, related words are retrieved, or whilst non-words are silently 'repeated' three times. Since activity in Broca's area increases during auditory–verbal short-term memory tasks (Paulesu *et al.* 1993), it may be that the observed activity is partly attributable to phonological rehearsal.

In summary, neuroimaging research supports the association of acoustic analysis with bilateral activity in the superior temporal gyri, and of phonological analysis from auditory input with left lateralized perisylvian activity focused around the superior temporal sulcus and the posterior middle-temporal gyrus. As discussed at the end of section 7.3.1, further experiments are required to verify the different roles of the regions in the vicinity of Broca's area.

More specific evidence on prelexical phonological processing in the left auditory cortex has been provided by recent ERP and magneto-encephalographic (MEG) studies. As discussed by Cutler and Clifton in Chapter 5 of this book, acoustic processing of speech sounds presumably proceeds in a categorical way. This means that listeners are better able to distinguish between acoustic differences in speech sounds that occur between phonetic categories than they are able to distinguish equivalent acoustic differences occurring within a phonetic category. Developmental studies have suggested that phonetic categories develop as a function of the native language during the first year of life. For example Werker and colleagues showed that 6-months old Canadian infants could discriminate between the English contrast [ba]–[da] as well as they could discriminate between the Hindi retroflex /d/ versus the dental /d/. This sensitivity changed when the children got older; at 12 months old, the infants only showed a sensitivity for the English speech contrast, and not for the Hindi contrast (Werker and Tees 1984; Werker and Lalonde 1988). Recent evidence for the existence of language-specific phoneme representations in adults' left auditory cortex has come from ERP and MEG studies (Dehaene-Lambertz 1997; Näätänen *et al.* 1997). In an ERP study, Dehaene-Lambertz (1997) presented subjects with acoustically deviant syllables within a series of identical syllables. The deviant syllables were either variants within the same phonetic category (for example, as in /ba/$_1$ /ba/$_1$ /ba/$_1$ /ba/$_5$), or belonged to a different phonetic category (for example, as in /da/$_9$ /da/$_9$ /da/$_9$ /ba/$_5$). The ERP component of interest was the mismatch negativity (MMN). The MMN is a negative component of the ERP, peaking at about 200 ms after stimulus onset. The MMN is thought to reflect the automatic detection of a stimulus that mismatches the traces of auditory stimuli kept in sensory memory (Näätänen 1990). Dehaene-Lambertz showed that although the acoustic differences between the standard and deviant tones were kept constant, deviants crossing the phonetic category borders elicited a much larger MMN than deviants belonging to the same phonetic category as the standard stimulus. Interestingly, this effect was shown to be specific to native-language processing; when series of Hindi syllables were presented to French subjects, neither deviants that crossed phonetic category borders, nor deviants from the same phonetic category induced a MMN. Similar to the findings by Dehaene-Lambertz, Näätänen *et al.* (1997) showed that in Finns the MMN amplitude was enhanced when the deviant stimulus was a phoneme prototype of Finnish (e.g. the phoneme best representing the Finnish vowel /ö/), relative to when it was a non-prototype (e.g. the Estonian vowel /õ/ that does not occur in Finnish), even though the non-prototype was acoustically closer to the standard stimulus. Importantly, in Estonians, the phoneme /õ/ did elicit an enhanced MMN, showing that the effect is indeed language specific. Based on MEG and EEG recordings, Näätänen *et al.* posited that the neural generator of the phonemic prototype effect is located in the left auditory cortex. A plausible interpretation of the MMN effects reported by Dehaene-Lambertz and Näätänen *et al.* is that prelexical phonemic codes, presumably located in the left auditory cortex, are used as recognition patterns for identifying speech sounds. From the latency of the MMN effects, it can be inferred that prelexical phonemic codes are identified within at most 200 ms after the onset of a speech sound.

7.3.3 Lexical word-form selection

Theoretically, in order to discriminate cortical activation associated with lexical word-form selection from sublexical phonological processes one would have to find areas that respond to lexical stimuli (words and potentially pseudowords) but do not respond to other language material, such as single speech sounds or illegal non-words, or tasks focusing on sublexical phonology (e.g. phoneme or rhyme detection). Furthermore, one would have to show that this area is not activated by processes which are subsequent to the successful retrieval of a lexical word form, for example lemma and conceptual activation. Such an area has not been identified as yet in neuroimaging. Clinical studies have suggested that the role of Wernicke's area is critical for auditory word representations but also for conceptual knowledge. However, Wernicke's aphasics do show semantic priming effects, indicating that at least partial access to word meanings is retained (Blumstein *et al.* 1982; Milberg and Blumstein 1981). The role of Wernicke's area is therefore more consistent with a semantic–lexical pole for the language network, associating word sound with word meaning (Mesulam 1990).

Several researchers have used ERPs to investigate the nature and organization of the lexical representations and processes that underlie speech comprehension. With respect to auditory word-form processing, only a few ERP studies have been published. These studies concentrated on phonological priming, and on phonological mismatch effects. The most important findings are the following. Praamstra *et al.* (1994) studied the electrophysiological effects of phonological priming using an auditory lexical decision task. They observed that in the latency range of 450–700 ms after target onset a negative peak occurred in the ERP signal. The amplitude of this peak was modulated by the phonological relatedness between the prime and the target: a reduced amplitude was observed for words that were preceded by a rhyming word (for example *house–mouse*) or by an alliterating word (for example *mouth–mouse*) relative to an unrelated word (for example *chair–mouse*). For pseudowords, such a reduction in amplitude was only observed in the alliterating condition but not in the rhyming condition. A plausible interpretation is that in the rhyming condition pseudowords started with illegal consonant clusters and therefore they were excluded immediately from lexical processing. For alliterating pseudowords additional lexical processing was required in order to reject them. The ERP effect observed by Praamstra *et al.* can be interpreted as a lexical word-form effect that occurs independently of the semantic status of an item. The latency of the peak was modulated by the position of the shared segments in prime and target: in the alliterating condition the ERP effect arose earlier than in the rhyming condition. This finding suggests that the time course of phonological processing can be reflected in ERP effects.

A slightly different approach was taken by Connolly and colleagues. Connolly and Phillips (1994) and Connolly *et al.* (1992) observed a phonological mismatch effect in the ERP signal when they presented subjects with words that violated their phonological expectancies. Connolly *et al.* showed that when the initial phoneme of a sentence-final word was not identical to the phoneme of the word that was highly expected on the basis of the context, a negative peak was observed in ERP signal (the phonological mismatch negativity, PMN). This peak occurred between 270 and 300 ms after the onset of the terminal word, and was claimed to be independent of the semantic N400 effect (a large-amplitude negative peak in the ERP signal at about 400 ms after stimulus onset. The amplitude of this peak can be modulated by semantic context). Connolly and colleagues argue that the PMN is not a manifestation of early phonological processing, because of its dependency on semantic context. Rather, it might reflect an intermediate stage in which both phonological and semantic information contribute to the process of word recognition.

Together, the ERP data on auditory word recognition suggest the existence of a lexical level of word-form processing that can be influenced by higher order semantic processing. When comparing the latencies of these phonological ERP effects with the latency of the MMN effects described earlier, it becomes clear that the lexical word-form effects occur later in the ERP signal than the prelexical phonemic effects. This delay might reflect differences in the time course of pre-lexical and lexical phonological processes during speech perception.

7.4 Written-word processing

In word reading, the lexically stored word knowledge has to be accessed from visual input. During the first visual processing stage, orthographic units are identified. The further processing can then, in principle, proceed in two different ways: on the basis of only the orthographic code, and by mapping orthographic to phonological units. In the former case, the lemma and subsequently the word meaning are retrieved via an orthographic lexical word form. In the case of orthography–phonology conversion, the resulting phonological representation allows for selection of a phonological lexical word form as in spoken word comprehension. Most notably, there is simultaneous processing of orthographic and phonological codes.

The extent to which the two codes are relied on, however, depends on a number of factors, such as the writing system, (alphabetic, syllabic, or logographic), the level of reading skill, and the kind of words read. Only the orthographic code of 'regular words' which conform to language-specific spelling-to-sound regularities can be pre-lexically converted into a phonological code, whereas 'irregular words', such as *colonel* rely on the orthographic code for lexical retrieval. Unknown or artificial words ('pseudowords'), for which no lexical entry exists, can be read out by directly feeding the output of orthography-to-phonology mapping into the production system. This sublexical pathway may also be used by patients who are able to read out texts in spite of a severe comprehension deficit (Patterson and Shewell 1987).

In summary, the following processing components can be distinguished in single word reading: (i) early (not language specific) visual processing, (ii) sublexical orthographic and/or phonological processing, (iii) lexical orthographic and/or phonological word-form selection, (iv) lemma activation, and (v) semantic conceptual activation. For reading aloud, two further processes are required, (vi) phonetic encoding and (vii) articulation. Particular kinds of written input, such as irregular words or pseudowords, depend on only a subset of these processes. See Perfetti, Chapter 6, for a comprehensive overview of the reading process.

The full network of regions subtending these processes can be identified by contrasting reading words with a low-level non-linguistic baseline (Bookheimer *et al.* 1995; Price *et al.* 1996a). For example, in the Price *et al.* (1996a) study, reading compared to a resting eyes-closed baseline activated: (i) visual and visual association areas, (ii) motor, premotor, and cerebellar areas, (iii) temporo-parietal areas, (iv) prefrontal areas and (v) subcortical areas. The respective roles of these regions will be considered below. See Fig. 7.4 for a composite picture of cortical activity.

7.4.1 Early visual processing

It is generally agreed that activations observed in bilateral occipital gyri (BA 18/19) during reading relate to early visual processing because they are not seen when viewing words is contrasted to viewing falsefont stimuli (letter-like forms of equivalent visual complexity to the words) (Price *et al.* 1994; Bookheimer *et al.* 1995). In contrast, there is not a consensus on the role of the left medial extrastriate cortex. This region was associated with visual word-form storage by Petersen *et al.* (1990) who observed activation during visual presentation of single words and pseudowords, but not consonant letter strings or falsefonts. The word-specific response has not been replicated in more recent studies (Howard *et al.* 1992; Price *et al.* 1994; Bookheimer *et al.* 1995), and the visual word-form interpretation has been further challenged by findings that the fMRI signals elicited in the medial occipital cortex by strings of falsefonts are largely identical to those elicited by pseudowords of the same length (Indefrey *et al.* 1997, see Fig. 7.5), suggesting a more elementary role for this area. The role of the left medial extrastriate region does nevertheless appear to differ from that of the surrounding occipital cortices: the latter show a linear dependency on the number of words presented per minute whilst responses in the left medial extrastriate cortex show a non-linear dependency (Price *et al.* 1996a). These findings support the view that within the occipital visual areas there are distinct functionally specialized areas.

An alternative interpretation of the differing responses in the medial extrastriate cortex during different task comparisons is that activity in this region is selectively modulated by attention. For example, activation in the medial lingual gyrus is enhanced when subjects explicitly name visual stimuli (words and objects) relative to

Written-word processing

Left   Right

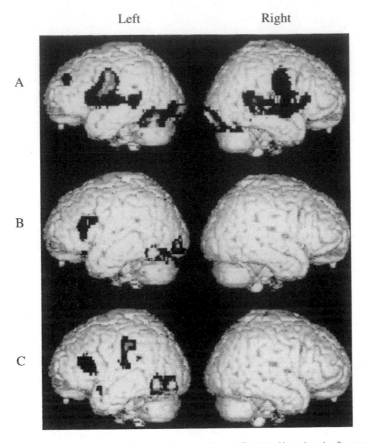

Fig. 7.4   The cortical regions involved in written-word processing are illustrated in red and yellow on models of the left and right side of the brain. The top row (A) shows the areas for reading words relative to resting with eyes closed (data from Price *et al.* 1996). The middle row (B) shows areas for naming words, objects, letters, and colours relative to visual controls (data from Price and Friston 1997). The bottom row shows the areas for reading pseudowords relative to real words (data from Price *et al.* 1996).

silent viewing of the same stimuli (Price *et al.* 1997*a*). Since the visual input remains constant, these results can be attributed to enhanced visual processing when an identification response is required. Higher attentional allocation to real words and pseudowords as compared to letter strings and falsefonts may also explain the results obtained by Petersen *et al.* (1990).

7.4.2 Prelexical orthographic processing
Evidence for specialized visual processing of orthographic features comes from intracranial recordings made directly from the cortical surface of patients undergoing

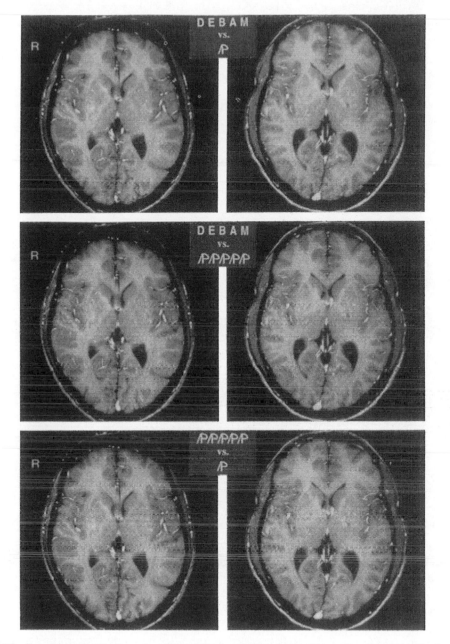

Fig. 7.5 Functional MRI activations of medial occipital areas involved in visual processing of word-like stimuli relative to single false-font stimuli (top row). Activations are overlaid in red and yellow on horizontal anatomical MR slices (AC-PC oriented, z=+4) of two subjects. The activations disappear with length-matched non-linguistic control stimuli such as strings of false-fonts. Almost identical activations reappear when strings of false-fonts are contrasted with single false-fonts (bottom row). (Data from Indefrey *et al.* 1997. Copyright © 1997 Academic Press, reprinted by permission.)

surgery for intractable epilepsy. In the posterior fusiform gyri, large negative field potentials with peak latencies near 200 ms (N200) were recorded to letter strings but not to other visually salient stimuli such as faces, objects, or checkerboards (Nobre *et al.* 1994). The prelexical nature of this early potential is suggested from the insensitivity of responses to lexical or semantic features: equivalent potentials were recorded from real words, pseudowords, and consonant letter strings. Similar specialization within the fusiform gyrus has also been demonstrated by f MRI studies (Puce *et al.* 1996), cortical stimulation studies (Luders *et al.* 1991), and lesion studies (Damasio and Damasio 1983).

7.4.3 Orthographic word-form access versus sublexical orthography-to-phonology conversion

After a prelexical graphemic representation of the written words has been established, dual pathway models allow for two ways to gain access to the lemma level. One is direct selection of the best matching orthographic word form in a visual input lexicon with subsequent lemma activation. The other is a translation of the graphemic representation to a phonemic representation with subsequent lexical access as described for spoken word comprehension. Clinical data suggest that the orthography-to-phonology conversion allows for the pronunciation of words even without lexical access (hence 'sublexical')—there are patients who are able to read out texts in spite of a severe comprehension deficit (Patterson and Shewell 1987). A number of ERP studies have revealed the involvement of phonological factors in visual word recognition. Rugg (1984) reported an N400-like effect for visually presented rhyming word pairs compared to non-rhyming word pairs, using a rhyme judgement task. This rhyme/non-rhyme effect was elicited by words as well as by orthographically legal pseudowords and occurred regardless of their orthographic similarity. Rugg and Barrett (1987) showed that the rhyme/non-rhyme effect is smaller for orthographically similar than for orthographically dissimilar words, implying an interaction between orthographic and phonological processing. In addition, Barrett and Rugg (1990) observed an N400-like effect for pairs of pictures that had rhyming names, compared to non-rhyming names. The effect was similar to the one observed for words, suggesting that this effect depends on phonological rather than orthographical processing of the visually presented materials.

Yet another type of evidence comes from ERP research that has used the repetition priming paradigm. A number of ERP studies have shown that repeating items in a list or in text, results in a sustained positive shift for the second presentation of the items compared to the first (e.g. Besson *et al.* 1992; Doyle and Rugg 1996; Rugg 1985, 1990; Smith and Halgren 1987; Van Petten *et al.* 1991). The effect is seen both for immediate repetition, and for repetitions with some six or more intervening stimuli. The onset of the standard visual–visual repetition priming effect can be as early as 250 ms, stretching over some 300 ms. This effect has been reported for both words and legal non-words, but not for illegal non-words. This indicates that the involvement of a word-like orthographic and/or phonological representation is a necessary precondition for the elicitation of a repetition effect. This is further supported by the finding that the repetition effect is sensitive to word frequency (with low frequency words showing the largest positive shift), clearly demonstrating the involvement of representations at the level of the mental lexicon. Importantly, the repetition effect has been observed for both within and across modality repetitions (e.g. Rugg *et al.* 1993), with some interesting differences in the latency of the onset of the effect. The Rugg *et al.* data showed that the repetition effect had a later onset when the first presentation was a spoken word and the second was written, than when both words were visually presented (the delay in onset was some 100 ms). The latency shift for this across-modality repetition can be interpreted as reflecting the activation of both orthographic and phonological representations during the processing of written words: for the auditory-visual repetition effect to come about, the letter string has to have been recoded into a phonological representation. These findings support the basic assumption of access to both orthographic and phonological form-representations during visual word recognition. Moreover, the overall pattern of results suggests that these representations are located at a lexical level.

Several neuroimaging studies have attempted to distinguish whether separate regions of the brain are involved in sublexical and lexical orthographic-to-phonological conversion. The issue has been addressed by contrasting different types of words that are thought to weight lexical or sublexical connections (Fiez and Petersen 1998; Price *et al.* 1996c; Herbster *et al.* 1997; Rumsey *et al.* 1997). For example, pseudowords (e.g. *froop*) have no direct connections between visual word-forms and phonological or semantic associations. They must therefore be assembled via sublexical spelling-to-sound associations (e.g. 'f', 'r', 'oo', 'p' becomes /f/,/r/,/uː/,/p/). In contrast, irregularly spelled words (e.g. *choir*) cannot be pronounced from the assembly of sublexical units but rely on association of the complete visual word-form with the corresponding phonological word-form. Words that abide with consistent orthographical and phonological associations can be read successfully via both direct (lexical) and indirect (sublexical) connections. In 1993, Fiez *et al.* published an abstract claiming that the most contrasting word types (i.e. pseudowords and low frequency irregularly spelled real words) both resulted in increased activation in the left frontal operculum relative to regularly spelled words (see Fiez and Petersen 1998). This result has been replicated in a study by Herbster *et al.* (1997). Other investigators, (Price *et al.* 1996c; Indefrey 1997; Hagoort *et al.* 1998) have also observed that pseudowords activate the left inferior-frontal cortex relative to regularly spelled or familiar irregularly spelled words. This suggests that the left inferior-frontal activation may be differentially involved in sublexical processing.

One interpretation offered by Fiez and Petersen (1998) is that when regularly spelled words are read, there is consistency between lexical and sublexical associations which produces a rapid pronunciation of the word, but when irregularly spelled words are read, lexical and sublexical associations compete, thereby delaying the offset of phonological encoding and the onset of articulation. The left inferior-frontal activation is more marked for low frequency irregular words than high frequency irregular words because the lexical retrieval processes are slowed down, thereby allowing more time for the sublexical route to come up with a competing regular phonological representation. However, the left frontal operculum is also activated in conjunction with the left posterior basal-temporal lobe (BA 37) and the midline cerebellum, during picture naming, letter naming, and colour naming (Price and Friston 1997). Since naming pictures and meaningless colour shapes can not be achieved by mapping sublexical orthographic codes to sublexical phonological codes, the left frontal operculum can not be exclusively involved in this process. See Fiez and Petersen (1998) for further discussion.

In another study that contrasted regularly spelled words and pseudowords, greater activation during pseudoword presentation than real word presentation was reported in the left inferior temporal and supramarginal gyri in addition to the left inferior-frontal cortex (Price *et al.* 1996*c*). These results were interpreted more generally in terms of pseudowords activating both lexical and sublexical processes more strongly than real words, because the phonological code is unfamiliar and because lexical representations are also activated in a search for a matching representation. Increased activation in the left supramarginal gyrus (BA 40) has also been reported for reading aloud pseudowords relative to irregularly spelled words (Rumsey *et al.* 1997); when Japanese subjects read Kana relative to Kanji (Law *et al.* 1991, see, however, Sakurai *et al.* 1992); and for reading relative to picture naming (Vandenberghe *et al.* 1996; Menard *et al.* 1996). In each of these contrasts, the activation condition involves sublexical processes relative to the baseline conditions, consistent with a specialized role for the left supramarginal gyrus in sublexical phonological processing. Further supporting evidence for this hypothesis is the finding that the left supramarginal gyrus is particularly active during tasks such as rhyming and syllable decisions that maximize sublexical processing (Paulesu *et al.* 1993; Price *et al.* 1997*b*)—see Price (1997*b*) for further discussion. In the reverse contrast (words relative to pseudowords) activation differences have been weak and inconsistent and therefore cannot be interpreted as reflecting orthographic lexical processing. A likely explanation is that pseudowords activate the visual word-form selection process as strongly as real words, and visual word-form activations immediately spread to lemma and conceptual representations.

In summary, the current status of neuroimaging supports the association of (i) visual analysis with posterior occipital activation, and (ii) sublexical processing with the left supramarginal gyrus and the left frontal operculum. There is, to date, no conclusive evidence as to the cortical areas subserving an orthographic input lexicon.

7.5 The semantic system

The meaning of words is implemented by a system of conceptual representations generally referred to as the semantic system. In the psychological literature there is debate as to whether a common semantic system is shared by different modalities or whether there are separate systems depending on the mode of input. Neuroimaging studies have provided evidence on a semantic system that is shared by written and spoken language (Vandenberghe *et al.* 1996). The organization of semantic knowledge is the focus of Chapter 8 by Saffran and Sholl. In this section, we describe the distributed set of regions associated with semantic processing and attempt to clarify the apparently contradictory views postulated by neuroimaging studies.

In contrast to neuropsychological studies which indicate that the temporal cortex is crucial for semantic processing, neuroimaging studies have found that the area that responds most strongly to semantic task demands is the left inferior-frontal cortex (BA 44, 45, 46, 47). A role for the inferior-frontal cortex in semantic processing was first suggested in the pioneering studies of Petersen *et al.* (1988, 1989). In subsequent neuroimaging paradigms, frontal activation has been associated with word generation tasks (Wise *et al.* 1991; Raichle *et al.* 1994; Buckner *et al.* 1995; Shaywitz *et al.* 1995; Warburton *et al.* 1996) and semantic decision tasks (Petersen *et al.* 1989; Kapur *et al.* 1994; Demb *et al.* 1995; Gabrielli *et al.* 1996; Warburton *et al.* 1996; Vandenberghe *et al.* 1996; Binder *et al.* 1997). The involvement of temporal and parietal cortices in the above studies has also been observed (Wise *et al.* 1991; Raichle *et al.* 1994; Shaywitz *et al.* 1995; Warburton *et al.* 1996; Vandenberghe *et al.* 1996; Binder *et al.* 1997). For instance when subjects make semantic decisions on words and pictures (relative to physical size decisions on the same stimuli), Vandenberghe *et al.* (1996) reported extensive left temporo-parietal activity which spread from the angular gyrus through the middle temporal gyrus and ventrally through the inferior temporal and anterior middle-temporal cortex, in addition to prefrontal activations. With the exception of the left anterior-temporal lobe, the same regions were reported by Binder *et al.* (1997) using f MRI during an auditory semantic task (relative to acoustic decisions on tone stimuli). The lack of signal in the anterior temporal lobe in the f MRI study by Binder *et al.* may relate to magnetic susceptibility artefacts in this region. Therefore we do not know as yet whether the anterior temporal lobe is specific to visual semantics. Nevertheless, the overlap of activation in the other temporal and parietal regions indicates a widely distributed semantic system shared by spoken words, visual words, and objects.

Whilst all the above neuroimaging studies of semantic decision have reported extensive left prefrontal activation, there is one condition where such activity is greatly diminished. This is when semantic decisions are contrasted to phonological decisions which require a judgement on the sound structure of the stimuli, (Démonet *et al.* 1992, 1994; Pugh *et al.* 1996; Price *et al.* 1997*b*). In this contrast, differences in prefrontal activation have either not been reported or have been limited to a small region in BA 47 and the medial superior-frontal cortex. In contrast, increased activation for semantic relative to phonological tasks remains in temporo-parietal cortices (BA 39, 20, 28) indicating that these extrasylvian temporal regions are specific to semantic processing and are the most likely correlates of stored semantic knowledge.

The absence of significant differences in inferior-frontal lobe activation in studies that have contrasted semantic and phonological decisions does not permit us to exclude a role for the frontal lobes in semantic processing. Areas where there were no significant changes could have been equally activated by implicit semantic processing during both tasks. Another possibility is that the prefrontal activity detected in semantic decision tasks relative to visual tasks, reflects increased involvement of phonological processing. Indeed, using several baseline conditions, Pugh *et al.* (1996) have demonstrated that phonological judgements on non-words increase activation in the inferior-frontal cortices, and that the same level of prefrontal activation is involved in semantic decisions. Further evidence for collateral activation of phonology during semantic tasks comes from behavioural and ERP studies (see above). For instance, Van Orden *et al.* (1988) and Coltheart *et al.* (1994) have demonstrated that when subjects are instructed to respond only to exemplars of a given category, they incorrectly accept words or non-words that sound like category exemplars (e.g. *rows* as a flower; *sute* as an article of clothing). However, the association of frontal activity with phonology may only apply to regions BA 44 and 45. Other regions (in particular BA 47 and BA 10) do appear to show effects specific to semantic tasks. One suggestion is that BA 47 is part of a semantic executive system that maintains and controls the effortful retrieval of semantic information from posterior temporal regions (Fiez 1997). Support for this theory is offered by priming studies on Broca's aphasics who have intact automatic semantic priming effects but abnormal strategic semantic priming effects (Hagoort 1997).

In summary, the majority of studies investigating semantic processing have reported left inferior-prefrontal activation. However, other studies that have controlled for phonological processing, short term memory, and willed action—cognitive functions which also activate the prefrontal cortices—have associated semantic processing with anterior and posterior extrasylvian temporal regions. It appears likely that the extrasylvian temporal areas are the sites of stored semantic knowledge whilst regions of the left inferior-frontal cortex exert an executive role in some semantic tasks. These conclusions rely heavily on neuropsychological data. As discussed above, damage to the frontal cortex does not generally impair performance on semantic matching tasks. In contrast, damage to extrasylvian temporal areas does impair semantic performance (Alexander *et al.* 1989; Mesulam 1990; Hodges *et al.* 1992). For example, patients with transcortical sensory aphasia have fluent speech with intact repetition but have a severe deficit in comprehension. These patients have lesions distributed in the left inferior-temporal lobe, the posterior inferior-parietal lobe (the junction of Brodmann's areas 39 and 19), the left thalamus, and the white matter connecting these regions (Alexander *et al.* 1989).

7.6 Final remarks

The aim of this chapter has been to structure the available evidence on neuro-anatomical correlates of single-word processing in terms of theoretically motivated functional processing components. If processing components are to be related to brain processes it is necessary to demonstrate their temporal dynamics as processing 'stages' and their possible spatial correlates in the form of neuronal populations subserving them. For this reason we have tried to combine both electrophysiological data and brain-imaging data.

Most task-control comparisons in brain-imaging studies, however, comprise more than one processing component. Thus, despite a relatively large number of studies on single-word processing, rarely has any activation reported for a single task-control comparison allowed for a unique interpretation in terms of specific processing components such as 'lexical word-form selection' or 'lemma activation'. It is the task of overview articles such as this to constrain the possible interpretations. One way to do this is to combine evidence across brain-imaging studies. Even if no one study has isolated a specific processing component it may well be that this processing component was the only one shared by a set of studies, making an interpretation across studies possible. We have tried to point out such commonalities across studies that shed light on the anatomical correlates of shared processing components (see Price and Friston 1997, for a statistical implementation of this logic, Indefrey and Levelt (in press), for a meta-analysis of brain-imaging studies on language production).

As a second way to constrain the possible interpretations of neuroimaging data we have taken into account independent evidence provided by neuropsychological data. To the extent that the interpretation of neuroimaging results relies on neuropsychological data, the role of neuroimaging in language studies might be questioned. However, the information gleaned from both kinds of technique is different. Neuroimaging reveals the distributed systems associated with a task. However, not all areas of the system may be crucial for task performance. In contrast, neuropsychological studies can determine that a damaged area was crucial for the lost function, but can not say what other brain regions were also necessary. In conclusion, it is the combination of data from both functional neuroimaging and neuropsychology that provides the most robust evidence for functional–anatomical links.

References

Alexander, M. P., Hiltbrunner, B., and Fischer, R. S. (1989). Distributed anatomy of transcortical sensory aphasia. *Archives of Neurology*, **46**, 885–92.

Barrett, S. E. and Rugg M. D. (1990). Event-related potentials and the phonological matching of picture names. *Brain and Language*, **38**, 424–37.

Besson, M., Kutas, M., and Van Petten, C. (1992). An event-related potential (ERP) analysis of semantic congruity and repetition effects in sentences. *Journal of Cognitive Neuroscience*, **4**, 132–49.

Binder, J. R., Frost, J. A., Hammeke, T. A., Cox, R. W., Rao, S. M., and Prieto, T. (1997). Human brain language areas identified by functional magnetic resonance imaging. *Journal of Neuroscience*, **17**, 353–62.

Blumstein, S. E. (1995). The neurobiology of the sound structure of language. In *The cognitive neurosciences* (ed. M. S. Gazzaniga), pp. 915–29. MIT Press, Cambridge, MA.

Blumstein, S., Milberg, W., and Shrier, R. (1982). Semantic processing in aphasia: Evidence from an auditory lexical decision task. *Brain and Language*, **17**, 301–15.

Bock, J. K. (1986). Meaning, sound, and syntax: Lexical priming in sentence production. *Journal of Experimental Psychology: Learning, Memory, and Cognition*, **12**, 575–86.

Bock, K. and Levelt, W. J. M. (1994). Language production: Grammatical encoding. In *Handbook of psycholinguistics* (ed. M. A. Gernsbacher), pp. 945–84. Academic Press, San Diego.

Bookheimer, S. Y., Zeffiro, T. A., Blaxton, T., Gaillard, W., and Theodore, W. (1995). Regional cerebral blood flow during object naming and word reading. *Human Brain Mapping*, **3**, 93–106.

Brown, A. S. (1991). A review of the tip-of-the-tongue experience. *Psychological Bulletin*, **9**, 226–45.

Buckner, R. L., Raichle, M. E., and Petersen, S. E. (1995). Dissociation of human prefrontal cortical areas across different speech production tasks and gender groups. *Journal of Neurophysiology*, **74**, 2163–73.

Burnstine, T. H., Lesser, R. P., Hart, J., Jr, Uematsu, S., Zinreich, S. J., Drauss, G. L., *et al.* (1990). Characterization of the basal temporal language area in patients with left temporal lobe epilepsy. *Neurology*, **40**, 966–700.

Butterworth, B. (1989). Lexical access in speech production. In *Lexical representation and process* (ed. W. D. Marslen-Wilson), pp. 108–35. MIT Press, Cambridge, MA.

Caplan, D. (1987). *Neurolinguistics and linguistic aphasiology: An introduction.* Cambridge University Press, New York.

Caramazza, A. (1997). How many levels of processing are there in lexical access? *Cognitive Neuropsychology*, **14**, 177–208.

Coles, M. G. H. (1989). Modern mind-brain reading: Psychophysiology, physiology, and cognition. *Psychophysiology*, **26**, 251–69.

Coltheart, V., Patterson, K., and Leahly, J. (1994). When a *rows* is a *rose*: Phonological effects in written word comprehension. *Quarterly Journal of Experimental Psychology*, **47A**, 917–55.

Connolly, J. F. and Phillips, N. A. (1994). Event-related potential components reflect phonological and semantic processing of the terminal word of spoken sentences. *Journal of Cognitive Neuroscience*, **6**, 256–66.

Connolly, J. F., Phillips, N. A., Stewart, S. H., and Brake, W. G. (1992). Event-related potential sensitivity to acoustic and semantic properties of terminal words in sentences. *Brain and Language*, **43**, 1–18.

Damasio, A. and Damasio, H. (1983). The anatomic basis of pure alexia. *Neurology*, **33**, 1573–83.

Damasio, A. and Geschwind, N. (1984). The neural basis of language. *Annual Review of Neuroscience*, **7**, 127–47.

Dehaene-Lambertz, G. (1997). Electrophysiological correlates of categorical phoneme perception in adults. *NeuroReport*, **8**, 919–24.

De Jong, R., Wierda, M., Mulder, G., and Mulder, L. J. M. (1988). Use of partial stimulus information in response processing. *Journal of Experimental Psychology: Human Perception and Performance*, **14**, 682–92.

Dell, G. S. (1986). A spreading-activation theory of retrieval in sentence production. *Psychological Review*, **93**, 283–321.

Demb, J. B., Desmond, J. E., Wagner, A. D., Vaidya, C. J., Glover, G. H., and Gabrieli, J. D. E. (1995). Semantic encoding and retrieval in the left inferior prefrontal cortex: A functional MRI study of task difficulty and process specificity. *Journal of Neuroscience*, **15**, 5870–8.

Démonet, J.-F., Chollet, F., Ramsay, S., Cardebat, D., Nespoulous, J.-D., Wise, R., *et al.* (1992). The anatomy of phonological and semantic processing in normal subjects. *Brain*, **115**, 1753–68.

Démonet, J.-F., Price, C. J., Wise, R., and Frackowiak, R. S. J. (1994). Differential activation of right and left posterior sylvian regions by semantic and phonological tasks: A positron emission tomography study. *Neuroscience Letters*, **182**, 25–8.

De Renzi, E., Zambolin, A., and Crisi, G. (1987). The pattern of neuropsychological impairment associated with left posterior cerebral artery territory infarcts. *Brain*, **110**, 1099–116.

Doyle, M. C. and Rugg, M. D. (1996). A comparison of the electrophysiological effects of formal and repetition priming. *Psychophysiology*, **33**, 132–47.

Fiez, J. A. (1997). Phonology, semantics and the role of the left inferior prefrontal cortex. *Human Brain Mapping*, **5**, 79–83.

Fiez, J. A. and Petersen, S. E. (1998). Neuroimaging studies of reading. *Proceedings of the National Academy of Sciences, U.S.A.*, **95**, 914–21.

Fiez, J. A., Tallal, P., Raichle, M. E., Miezen, F. M., Katz, W. F., and Petersen, S. E. (1995). PET studies of auditory and phonological processing: Effects of stimulus characteristics and task demands. *Journal of Cognitive Neuroscience*, **7**, 357–75.

Fletcher, P. C., Happe, F., Frith, U., Baker, S. C., Dolan, R. J., Frackowiak, R. S. J., *et al.* (1995). Other minds in the brain: A functional imaging study of theory of mind in story comprehension. *Cognition*, **57**, 109–28.

Frith, C. D., Friston, K. J., Liddle, P. F., and Frackowiak, R. S. J. (1991a). A PET study of word finding. *Neuropsychologia*, **29**, 1137–48.

Frith, C. D., Friston, K. J., Liddle, P. F., and Frackowiak, R. S. J. (1991*b*). Willed action and the prefrontal cortex in man: A study with PET. *Proceedings of the Royal Society of London—Series B: Biological Sciences*, **244**(1311), 241–6.

Frith, C. D., Kapur, N., Friston, K. J., Liddle, P. F., and Frackowiak, R. S. J. (1995). Regional cerebral activity associated with the incidental processing of pseudo-words. *Human Brain Mapping*, **3**, 153–60.

Gabrielli, J. D. E., Desmond, J. E., Demb, J. B., Wagner, A. D., Stone, M. V., Vaidya, C. J., *et al.* (1996). Functional magnetic resonance imaging of semantic memory processes. *Psychological Science*, **7**, 278–83.

Garrett, M. F. (1976). Syntactic processes in sentence production. In *New approaches to language mechanisms* (eds R. J. Wales and E. Walker), pp. 231–56. North-Holland, Amsterdam.

Garrett, M. F. (1980). Levels of processing in sentence production. In *Language production*, Vol. 1 (ed. B. Butterworth), pp. 177–220. Academic Press, London.

Garrett, M. F. (1988). Processes in language production. In *Linguistics: The Cambridge survey, Vol. III* (ed. F. J. Newmeyer), pp. 69–96. Cambridge University Press, Cambridge.

Garrett, M. (1992). Disorders of lexical selection. *Cognition*, **42**, 143–80.

Glaser, W. R. (1992). Picture naming. *Cognition*, **42**, 61–105.

Hagoort, P. (1997) Semantic priming in Broca's aphasia at a short SOA: No support for an automatic access deficit. *Brain and Language*, **56**, 287–300.

Hagoort, P., Indefrey, P., Brown, C., Herzog, H., Steinmetz, H., and Seitz, R. J. (1999). The neural circuitry involved in the reading of German words and pseudo words: A PET study. *Journal of Cognitive Neuroscience*.

Herbster, A. N., Mintun, M. A., Nebes, R. D., and Becker, J. T. (1997). Regional cerebral blood flow during word and nonword reading. *Human Brain Mapping*, **5**, 84–92.

Hodges, J. R., Patterson, K., Oxbury, S., and Funnell, E. (1992). Semantic dementia. *Brain*, **115**, 1783–806.

Howard, D., Patterson, K., Wise, R. J. S., Brown, W. D., Friston, K., Weiller, C., *et al.* (1992). The cortical localization of the lexicons: Positron emission tomography evidence. *Brain*, **115**, 1769–82.

Indefrey, P. (1997). PET research in language production. In *Speech production: Motor control, brain research and fluency disorders* (eds W. Hulstijn, H. F. M. Peters, and P. H. H. M. van Lieshout.), pp. 269–78. Elsevier, Amsterdam.

Indefrey, P. and Levelt, W. J. M. (2000). The neural correlates of language production. In *The cognitive neurosciences*, 2nd edn. (ed. M. Gazzaniga), MIT Press, Cambridge, MA.

Indefrey, P., Kleinschmidt, A., Merbolt, K.-D., Kruger, G., Brown, C., Hagoort, P., *et al.* (1997). Equivalent responses to lexical and nonlexical visual stimuli in occipital cortex: A functional magnetic resonance imaging study. *NeuroImage*, **5**, 78–81.

Kapur, S., Rose, R., Liddle, P. F., Zipursky, R. B., Brown, G. M., Stuss, D., *et al.* (1994). The role of the left prefrontal cortex in verbal processing: Semantic processing or willed action? *NeuroReport*, **5**, 2193–6.

Kempen, G. and Hoenkamp, E. (1987). An incremental procedural grammar for sentence formulation. *Cognitive Science*, **11**, 201–58.

Kempen, G. and Huijbers, P. (1983). The lexicalization process in sentence production and naming: Indirect election of words. *Cognition*, **14**, 185–209.

Kolb, B. and Whishaw, I. Q. (1996). *Fundamentals of human neuropsychology*. W. H. Freeman and Company, New York.

Krams, M., Rushworth, M. F. S., Deiber, M. P., Frackowiak, R. S. J., and Passingham, R. E. (1998). The preparation, execution and suppression of copied movements in the human brain. *Experimental Brain Research*, **120**, 386–98.

Kutas, M. and Donchin, E. (1980). Preparation to respond as manifested by movement-related brain potentials. *Brain Research*, **202**, 95–115.

Law, I., Kannao, I., Fujita, H., Miura, S., Lassen, N., and Uemura, K. (1991). Left supramarginal/angular gyri activation during reading of syllabograms in the Japanese language. *Journal of Neurolinguistics*, **6**, 243–51.

Levelt, W. J. M. (1989). *Speaking: From intention to articulation*. MIT Press, Cambridge, MA.

Levelt, W. J. M., Schriefers, H., Vorberg, D., Meyer, A. S., Pechmann, T., and Havinga, J. (1991). The time course of lexical access in speech production: A study of picture naming. *Psychological Review*, **98**, 122–42.

Luders, H., Lesser, R. P., Hahn, J., Dinner, D. S., Morrsi, H., Resor, S., *et al.* (1986). Basal temporal language area demonstrated by electrical stimulation. *Neurology*, **36**, 505–10.

Luders, H., Lesser, R. P., Hahn, J., Dinner, D. S., Morris, H. H., Wyllie, E., *et al.* (1991). Basal temporal language area. *Brain*, **114**, 743–54.

Martin, A., Wiggs, C. L., Ungerleider, L. G., and Haxby, J. V. (1996). Neural correlates of category-specific knowledge. *Nature*, **379**, 649–52.

Mazoyer, B. M., Tzourio, N., Frak, V., Syrota, A., Murayama, N., Levrier, O., *et al.* (1993). The cortical representation of speech. *Journal of Cognitive Neuroscience*, **5**, 467–79.

Menard, M. T., Kosslyn, S. M., Thompson, W. L., Alpert, N. M., and Rauch, S. L. (1996). Encoding words and pictures: A positron emission tomography study. *Neuropsychologia*, **34**, 184–94.

Mesulam, M.-M. (1990). Large scale neurocognitive networks and distributed processing for attention, language and memory. *Annals of Neurology*, **28**, 597–613.

Milberg, W. and Blumstein, S. E. (1981). Lexical decision and aphasia: Evidence for semantic processing. *Brain and Language*, **14**, 371–85.

Miozzo, M. and Caramazza, A. (1997). On knowing the auxiliary of a verb that cannot be named: Evidence for the independence of grammatical and phonological aspects of lexical knowledge. *Journal of Cognitive Neuroscience*, **9**, 160–6.

Näätänen, R. (1990). The role of attention in auditory information processing as revealed by event-related potentials and other brain measures of cognitive function. *Behavioral and Brain Sciences*, **13**, 201–88.

Näätänen, R., Lehtokoski, A., Lennes, M., Cheour, M., Huotilainen, M., Iivonen, A., *et al.* (1997). Language-specific phoneme representations revealed by electric and magnetic brain responses. *Nature*, **385**, 432–4.

Nobre, A. C., Allison, T., and McCarthy, G. (1994). Word recognition in the human inferior temporal lobe. *Nature*, **372**, 260–3.

Patterson, K. and Shewell, C. (1987). Speak and spell: Dissociations and word class effects. In *The cognitive neuropsychology of language* (eds M. Coltheart, G. Sartori, and R. Job), pp. 273–94. Erlbaum, London.

Paulesu, E., Frith, C. D., and Frackowiak, R. S. J. (1993). The neural correlates of the verbal component of working memory. *Nature*, **362**, 342–4.

Petersen, S. E., Fox, P. T., Posner, M. I., Mintum, M., and Raichle, M. E. (1988). Positron emission tomographic studies of the cortical anatomy of single word processing. *Nature*, **331**, 585–9.

Petersen, S. E., Fox, P. T., Posner, M. I., Mintum, M., and Raichle, M. E. (1989). Positron emission tomographic studies of the processing of single words. *Journal of Cognitive Neuroscience*, **1**, 153–70.

Petersen, S. E., Fox, P. T., Snyder, A. Z., and Raichle, M. E. (1990). Activation of extrastriate and frontal cortical areas by words and word-like stimuli. *Science*, **249**, 1041–4.

Praamstra, P., Meyer, A. S., and Levelt, W. J. M. (1994). Neurophysiological manifestations of phonological processing: Latency variation of a negative ERP component timelocked to phonological mismatch. *Journal of Cognitive Neuroscience*, **6**, 204–19.

Price, C. J. (1997). Functional anatomy of reading. In *Human brain function* (eds R. S. J. Frackowiak, K. J. Friston, C. D. Frith, R. Dolan, and J. C. Mazziotta), pp. 301–28, Academic Press, London.

Price, C. J. and Friston, K. J. (1997). Cognitive conjunctions: A new approach to brain activation experiments. *NeuroImage*, **5**, 261–70.

Price, C. J., Wise, R., Ramsay, S., Friston, K. Howard, D., Patterson, K. *et al.* (1992). Regional response differences within the human auditory cortex. *Neuroscience Letters*, **146**, 179–82.

Price, C. J., Wise, R. J. S., Watson, J. D. G., Patterson, K., Howard, D., and Frackowiak, R. S. J. (1994). Brain activity during reading: The effects of exposure duration and task. *Brain*, **117**, 1255–69.

Price, C. J., Moore, C. J., and Frackowiak, R. S. J. (1996*a*). The effect of varying stimulus rate and duration on brain activity during reading. *NeuroImage*, **3**, 40–52.

Price, C. J., Moore, C. J., Humphreys, G. W., Frackowiak, R. S. J., and Friston, K. J. (1996*b*). The neural regions sustaining object recognition and naming. *Proceedings of the Royal Society*, Series B, **263**, 1501–7.

Price, C. J., Wise, R. J. S., and Frackowiak, R. S. J. (1996*c*). Demonstrating the implicit processing of visually presented words and pseudowords. *Cerebral Cortex*, **6**, 62–70.

Price, C. J., Wise, R. J. S., Warburton, E., Moore, C. J., Patterson, K., Howard, D., *et al.* (1996*d*). Hearing and saying: The functional neuro-anatomy of auditory word processing. *Brain*, **119**, 919–31.

Price, C. J., Moore, C. J., and Friston, K. J. (1997*a*). Subtractions, conjunctions and interactions in experimental design of activation studies. *Human Brain Mapping*, **5**, 264–72.

Price, C. J., Moore, C. J., Humphreys, G. W., and Wise, R. J. S. (1997*b*). Segregating semantic from phonological processing. *Journal of Cognitive Neuroscience*, **9**, 727–33.

Pucc, A., Allison, T., Asgari, M., Gore, J. C., and McCarthy, G. (1996). Differential sensitivity of human visual cortex to faces, letter strings and textures: A functional magnetic resonance imaging study. *Journal of Neuroscience*, **16**, 5205–15.

Pugh, K. R., Shaywitz, B. A., Shaywitz, S. E., Constable, R. T., Skudlarski, P., Fulbright, R. K., *et al.* (1996). Cerebral organization of component processes in reading. *Brain*, **119**, 1221–38.

Raichle, M. E., Fiez, J. A., Videen, T. O., Macleod, A. K., Pardo, J. V., Fox, P. T., *et al.* (1994). Practice-related changes in human brain functional anatomy during non-motor learning. *Cerebral Cortex*, **4**, 8–26.

Ramsay, S. C., Adams, L., Murphy, K., Corfield, D. R., Grootnoonk, S., Bailey, D. L., *et al.* (1993). Regional cerebral blood flow during volitional expiration in man: A comparison with volitional inspiration. *Journal of Physiology*, **461**, 85–101.

Rugg, M. D. (1984). Event-related potentials and the phonological processing of words and non-words. *Neuropsychologia*, **22**, 435–43.

Rugg, M. D. (1985). The effects of semantic priming and word repetition on event-related potentials. *Psychophysiology*, **22**, 642–7.

Rugg, M. D. (1990). Event-related brain potentials dissociate repetition effects of high- and low-frequency words. *Memory and Cognition*, **18**, 367–79.

Rugg, M. D. and Barrett, S. E. (1987). Event-related potentials and the interaction between orthographic and phonological information in a rhyme-judgment task. *Brain and Language*, **32**, 336–61.

Rugg, M. D., Doyle, M. C., and Melan, C. (1993). An event-related potential study of the effects of within- and across-modality word repetition. *Language and Cognitive Processes*, **8**, 357–78.

Rumsey, J. M., Horwitz, B., Donohue, C., Nace, K., Maisog, J. M., and Andreason, P. (1997). Phonologic and orthographic components of word recognition: A PET-rCBF study. *Brain*, **120**, 739–59.

Sakurai, Y., Momose, T., Iwata, M., Watanabe, T., Ishikawa, T., Takeda, K., *et al.* (1992). Kanji word reading process analysed by positron emission tomography. *NeuroReport*, **3**, 445–8.

Sakurai, Y., Momose, T., Iwata, M., Watanabe, T., Ishikawa, T., and Kanazawa, I. (1993). Semantic process in kana word reading: Activation studies with positron emission tomography. *NeuroReport*, **4**, 327–30.

Schriefers, H., Meyer, A. S., and Levelt, W. J. M. (1990). Exploring the timecourse of lexical access in language production: Picture-word interference studies. *Journal of Memory and Language*, **29**, 86–102.

Sergent, J. (1994). Brain imaging studies of cognitive functions. *Trends in Neurosciences*, **17**, 221–7.

Shaywitz, B. A., Pugh, K. R., Constable, R. T., Shaywitz, S. E., Bronen, R. A., Fulbright, R. K., *et al.* (1995). Localization of semantic processing using functional magnetic resonance imaging. *Human Brain Mapping*, **2**, 149–58.

Smith, M. E. and Halgren, E. (1987). Event-related potentials during lexical decision: Effects of repetition, word frequency, pronounceability, and concreteness. In *Current trends in event-related potential research*, Suppl. 40 (eds R. Johnson, Jr, J. W. Rohrbaugh, and R. Parasuraman), pp. 417–21. Elsevier, Amsterdam.

Stephan, K. M., Fink, G. R., Passingham, R. E., Silbersweig, D., Ceballos-Baummann, A., Frith, C. D., *et al.* (1995). Imagining the execution of movements: Functional anatomy of the mental representation of upper extremity movements in healthy subjects. *Journal of Neurophysiology*, **73**, 373–86.

Tulving, E., Kapur, S., Craik, F. I., Moscovitch, M., and Houle, S. (1994). Hemispheric encoding/retrieval asymmetry in episodic memory: Positron emission tomography findings [see comments]. *Proceedings of the National Academy of Sciences of the USA*, **91**, 2016–20. (Comment in: *Proceedings of the National Academy of Sciences of the USA*, **91**, 1989–91.)

Vandenberghe, R., Price, C. J., Wise, R., Josephs, O., and Frackowiak, R. S. J. (1996). Semantic system(s) for words or pictures: Functional anatomy. *Nature*, **383**, 254–6.

Van Orden, G. C., Johnston, J. C., and Hale, B. L. (1988). Word identification in reading proceeds from spelling to sound to meaning. *Journal of Experimental Psychology: Learning, Memory, and Cognition*, **14**, 371–86.

Van Petten, C., Kutas, M., Kluender, R., Mitchiner, M., and McIsaac, H. (1991). Fractionating the word repetition effect with event-related potentials. *Journal of Cognitive Neuroscience*, **3**, 131–50.

Van Turennout, M., Hagoort, P., and Brown, C. M. (1997). Electrophysiological evidence on the time course of semantic and phonological processes in speech production. *Journal of Experimental Psychology: Learning, Memory, and Cognition*, **23**, 787–806.

Van Turennout, M., Hagoort, P., and Brown, C. M. (1998). Brain activity during speaking: From syntax to phonology in 40 milliseconds. *Science*, **280**, 572–4.

Vigliocco, G., Antonini, T., and Garrett, M. F. (1997). Grammatical gender is on the tip of Italian tongues. *Psychological Science*, **8**, 314–7.

Warburton, E., Wise, R. J. S., Price, C. J., Weiller, C., Hadar,U., Ramsay, S., *et al.* (1996). Studies with positron emission tomography of noun and verb retrieval in normal subjects. *Brain*, **119**, 159–80.

Werker, J. F. and Lalonde, C. E. (1988). Cross-language speech perception: Initial capabilities and developmental change. *Developmental Psychology*, **24**, 672–83.

Werker, J. F. and Tees, R. C. (1984). Cross-language speech perception: Evidence for perceptual reorganization during the first year of life. *Infant Behavior and Development*, **7**, 49–63.

Wise, R., Chollet, F., Hadar, U., Friston, K., Hoffner, E., and Frackowiak, R. S. J. (1991). Distribution of cortical neural networks involved in word comprehension and word retrieval. *Brain*, **114**, 1803–17.

Zatorre, R. J., Evans, A. C., Meyer, E., and Gjedde, A. (1992). Lateralisation of phonetic and pitch discrimination in speech processing. *Science*, **256**, 846–9.

8 Clues to the functional and neural architecture of word meaning

Eleanor M. Saffran and Alexandra Sholl

8.1 Introduction

Words and sentences are pointers to objects, states, and events, represented mentally in a format that we designate as semantic and/or conceptual. In truth, we know little about these representations, although they have been the target of a good deal of empirical research as well as much speculation. Some theorists, following the path set by formal semanticists, have argued for a unitary proposition-based format (e.g. Caramazza *et al.* 1990), while others, adopting an evolutionary perspective, have proposed that concepts are represented perceptually (Barsalou 1991). Still others have suggested that the conceptual system employs both of these formats, each for a different type of information (e.g. Jackendoff 1987; Paivio 1991; Warrington and McCarthy 1987; Shallice 1988a,b). The manner in which semantic information is organized in memory has also been controversial; proposed structures include hierarchies, feature lists, exemplars, family resemblances, schemata, and connectionist networks (for reviews, see Chang 1986; Komatsu 1992).

Cognitive psychologists have not yet resolved these issues using behavioural measures. In this chapter, we take a different approach, viewing the semantic system from the perspective of evidence drawn from two sources: semantic impairments in brain-damaged individuals, and neural correlates of semantic activity in normal subjects. Both lines of research are concerned with the architecture of semantic memory, from a functional as well as an anatomical perspective. The evidence we will review suggests that semantic knowledge is heterogeneous and distributed, and that different aspects of knowledge are subserved by different brain structures. In line with current usage, we will refer to these forms of knowledge as semantic properties or features.

The emphasis on semantic features reflects the nature of the current database. Neuropsychological studies of semantic deficits, as well as studies of brain activity patterns, have largely been concerned with object concepts—knowledge of tools, animals, foods, and the like—that we encounter directly in daily life as well as indirectly through other channels of communication. This is not to suggest that a semantics based solely on aggregates of properties could support all of the work that a semantic system is called upon to do. The features that are critical to object concepts are largely irrelevant to the meanings of abstract words. Moreover, the representations of concrete and abstract concepts are likely to differ substantially; whereas associative networks may be suitable for concrete concepts, which are open to modification by adding features, the meanings of abstract words are likely to have a more tightly structured organization (e.g. Breedin *et al.* 1994*b*). We also note that reasoning tasks—such as deciding whether a horse that has undergone surgery to make it look like a zebra is a horse or a zebra (Keil 1989)—cannot be performed simply by accessing the properties of the entities in question; the answer requires an understanding of basic principles of biology. Nevertheless, one can reasonably assume that mundane tasks—such as deciding whether a picture represents a horse or a zebra, distinguishing the habitats of horses and zebras, determining the functions typically performed by horses—can be carried out by calling up properties of the entities in question. There is evidence that rapid, automatic access to semantic features can account for semantic priming effects (McRae *et al.* 1997), and that loss of featural information underlies some of the semantic disturbances associated with neurological disease (e.g. Hodges *et al.* 1995).

Knowledge of an object embraces a wide range of properties, from its appearance (its shape, colour, texture, and size, as well as characteristics and relationships of its parts), the sounds (if any) that it makes, the things that it does or is used for (its functions), its origin (natural or man-made), its mode of locomotion (if any), and other types of information, sometimes referred to as encyclopaedic, such as an animal's food preferences and habitat. Although characteristic of a given object, these features may be learned at different times and in different ways, through direct experience via one or more sensory modalities, and/or through language. Given the range of object properties, it would be surprising if the representations of all of these attributes shared the same format. While there are proponents of such a view (e.g. the Organized Unitary Content Hypothesis (OUCH) of Caramazza *et al.* 1990), the neuropsychological and neuroimaging data that we will discuss suggest a more heterogeneous picture. We also believe that it is reasonable to posit some relationship between the manner in which information is acquired and the format in which it is stored. It is likely, for example, that the shape and other visual characteristics of an object are encoded visually, and that the manner in which an object is manipulated is represented sensorimotorically. Properties acquired through language (e.g. that a whale is a mammal) are likely to be entered in a propositional store. This general approach to semantic organization, in which knowledge of a concept is distributed over subsystems that bear a direct relationship to the channel through which information was acquired, is shared by a number of investigators who have examined this question from a neuropsychological perspective (e.g. Allport 1985; Damasio 1990; Gainotti *et al.* 1995; Shallice 1988*b*). A graphic rendering of such a model, taken from Allport (1985), is shown in Fig. 8.1. Below, we provide support for this approach, based in large part on the fractionation of semantic knowledge in patients with neurological disorders. We consider evidence

Non-linguistic attribute domains

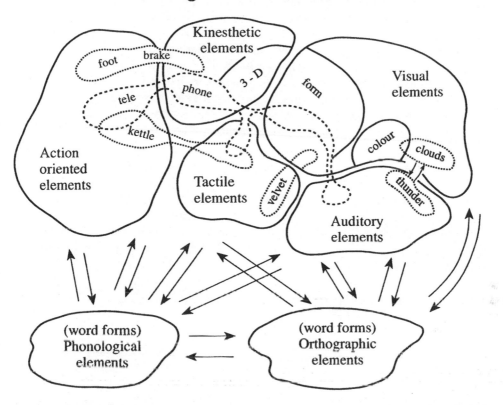

Fig. 8.1 A distributed model of conceptual information. (Reproduced from Allport (1985). Copyright © 1985 Churchill Livingstone, reprinted by permission.)

that links these breakdown patterns to specific areas of the brain, along with converging data from images of normal regional brain-activity patterns, obtained while subjects were performing semantic tasks.

8.2 Evidence from studies of semantic impairment

Contemporary neuropsychological research on the organization of conceptual knowledge began with the groundbreaking studies of Warrington (1975), which provided evidence for the selective impairment of semantic memory. Warrington's first subjects were three patients with progressive, degenerative diseases of the brain. At least two of them would meet recently proposed criteria for the disorder termed 'semantic dementia', manifested as a gradual loss of word retrieval and word comprehension, and semantic impairment on non-verbal tasks,[1] with other cognitive functions relatively spared (Snowden *et al.* 1989; Hodges *et al.* 1992). This disorder is associated with atrophic changes in the temporal lobes, particularly on the left

(Hodges *et al.* 1992). Note, however, that the superior temporal areas associated with the processing of auditory information, including speech, are spared. Phonological abilities are preserved, as are syntactic functions (e.g. Breedin and Saffran, 1998; Schwartz *et al.* 1979).

Warrington's case studies led to two important findings. First, there was evidence that appeared to reflect hierarchical breakdown in the semantic system. Patients had a tendency to lose specific information (e.g. whether or not elephants are native to Britain), while retaining information about category membership (e.g. that an elephant is an animal), although progression of the disease has been shown to compromise even this basic knowledge (e.g. Hodges *et al.* 1995). Severely impaired patients are likely to respond with superordinate terms (an animal, something you eat, etc.) in picture naming or naming to definitions tasks; in comprehension tasks, such as word–picture matching, they often choose category co-ordinates instead of the target item, and may lose this selectivity as the disease progresses. Examples of these behaviours are provided in Table 8.1. Such deficits are thought to reflect the pruning of specific semantic features that differentiate category members from one another (e.g. Hodges *et al.* 1995; Schwartz *et al.* 1979). In contrast, the ability to assign exemplars to categories is relatively robust because it is sustained by a wide range of characteristics. If one's knowledge of elephants is limited to the fact that they are living things that move, it follows that they must be animals.

Table 8.1   Examples of the loss of specific information
a) Evolution of naming responses (patient JL) from Hodges *et al.* (1995). Correct response: +; incorrect responses are in italics.

	9/91	3/92	9/92	3/93
horse	+	+	+	+
dog	+	+	+	*cat*
cow	+	+	+	*animal*
pig	+	*on farms*	*horse*	*horse*
deer	+	*horse*	*cow*	*vehicle*
rabbit	+	*cat*	*cat*	*cat*
mouse	*cat*	*cat*	*cat*	*animal*
monkey	*pig*	*cat*	*boy*	*animal*
bear	*dog*	*big animal*	*dog*	*dog*
lion	*dog*	*dog*	*dog*	*animal*

b) Evolution of picture-to-printed word matching responses (patient WLP) from Schwartz *et al.* (1979). Choices included matching word, semantic distractor, phonologically related distractor, and two unrelated words.

Month	Total errors (%)	Choice of semantic distractor (% of total errors)
3	39	85
15	44	90
24	55	74
27	65	61

Warrington's (1975) initial study included another important observation: that certain broad domains of conceptual knowledge could be more affected than others, and that patterns of impairment need not be homogeneous. One of the three patients, AB, demonstrated a striking loss of concrete concepts, with relative preservation of the meanings of abstract words. The others showed an advantage for concrete words.

8.2.1 Abstract versus concrete

The relative preservation of abstract concepts, observed in Warrington's (1975) patient AB, runs counter to the normal concreteness effect in language and memory tasks (e.g. Paivio 1991). This reversal is even more striking when it is considered that left hemisphere damage often magnifies the advantage for concrete words. Poorer performance on abstract words is observed in aphasics in general (e.g. Goodglass *et al.* 1969), and perhaps most dramatically in the syndromes of deep dyslexia and deep dysphasia. In oral reading tasks, deep dysphasic patients show a marked advantage for concrete over abstract words (e.g. Coltheart 1980*a*); in deep dysphasia, a concreteness advantage emerges in the repetition of single words (e.g. Martin 1996). Superior performance on concrete words is often attributed to the relative richness of the semantic representations of concrete concepts as well as their specificity of meaning (e.g. Jones 1985; Saffran *et al.* 1980); a *rose* is always a rose, but the meaning of an abstract word like *phase* varies with the context in which it is used (compare *phase of the moon* with *phase of infant development*). Although AB's pattern represents a rare departure from the usual advantage for concrete words, other such cases have been reported. Patients who have shown this reversal of the normal concreteness effect include SBY (Warrington and Shallice 1984), FB (Sirigu *et al.* 1991), DM (Breedin *et al.* 1994*b*), DRN (Cipolotti and Warrington 1995), RG (Marshall *et al.* 1996*b*), and EC (Carbonnet *et al.* 1997).

Only two of these studies, those of Breedin *et al.* (1994*b*) and Marshall *et al.* (1996*b*), focus on the advantage for abstract words. The subject of the Breedin *et al.* study was DM, a patient with a progressive semantic disorder (semantic dementia). DM demonstrated an advantage for abstract concepts across a range of tasks that included word definitions, synonymy judgement (in which the task involved selecting the two words of three that were closest in meaning), and a four alternative word picture matching task. His performance on the latter was particularly striking, in that the concrete word matches were simply depictions of the objects, whereas the abstract items required inferential processing (for example, the correct choice for the word *disparity* involved two mittens, one larger than the other). Whereas normal subjects performed better on the concrete words, DM showed the opposite pattern. DM's definitions of concrete words were striking for their lack of specificity, and, in particular, for a paucity of perceptual descriptors, characteristics noted in other patients who show an abstract word advantage (see examples in Table 8.2). In directly querying DM about the properties of objects, Breedin *et al.* found that DM was significantly more impaired on perceptual (e.g. *Does a whale have four legs?*) than non-perceptual

Table 8.2   Definitions of abstract and concrete words produced by patients with a superiority for abstract words (definitions are in italics)

AB (Warrington 1975)

Supplication	*Making a serious request for help.*
Pact	*Friendly agreement.*
Cabbage	*Eat it.*
Geese	*An animal' but I've forgotten precisely.*

SBY (Warrington and Shallice 1984)

Malice	*To show bad will against somebody.*
Caution	*To be careful how you do something.*
Ink	*Food—you put on top of food you are eating—a liquid.*
Cabbage	*Use for eating, material it's usually made from an animal.*

DM (Breedin et al. 1994b)

Try	*Try is to endeavour to accomplish something.*
Opinion	*Your concept or perspective.*
Ink	*Something that covers.*
Cheese	*Something sweet to eat.*

FB (Sirigu et al. 1991)

Society	*A large group of people who live in the same manner and share the same principles.*
Culture	*A way to learn life's customs, it varies from country to country.*
Duck	*A small animal with four legs.*
Thimble	*We often say sewing thimble.*

DRN (Cipolotti and Warrington 1995)

Vigorous	*Very forceful.*
Free	*Not restricted by anything.*
Leopard	*Some sort of animal . . . it is small like an insect . . . I think it flies.*
Giraffe	*I don't know . . . it is a sort of foreign term. . . . something to do with furniture.*

features (e.g. *Does a whale live in water?*). Breedin *et al.* attributed DM's reversal of the normal concreteness advantage to a loss of perceptual properties, which are critical components of the meanings of concrete words. Marshall *et al.* (1996*b*) reached a similar conclusion, based on the finding that their patient, DG, was selectively impaired on the perceptual characteristics of objects.

Of the cases in which an abstract superiority effect has been demonstrated, two, the patients reported by Warrington and Shallice (1984) and Sirigu *et al.* (1991), suffered the aftereffects of herpes simplex encephalitis, a pathogen that tends to invade inferior and medial temporal lobe structures, often producing an amnesic deficit as well as a semantic disorder. In addition to the involvement of medial structures such as the hippocampus, Sirigu *et al.*'s patient sustained extensive damage to anterior, inferior-temporal cortex bilaterally (see Fig. 8.2). Three of the patients meet the criteria for semantic dementia. Breedin *et al.*'s patient, DM, demonstrated hypometabolism of the anterior inferotemporal region, also bilaterally, but greater on the left (Fig. 8.3), and later showed bitemporal atrophy on MRI (Srinivas *et al.* 1997). The patient reported by Cipolotti and Warrington (1995) showed focal temporal lobe atrophy, greater on

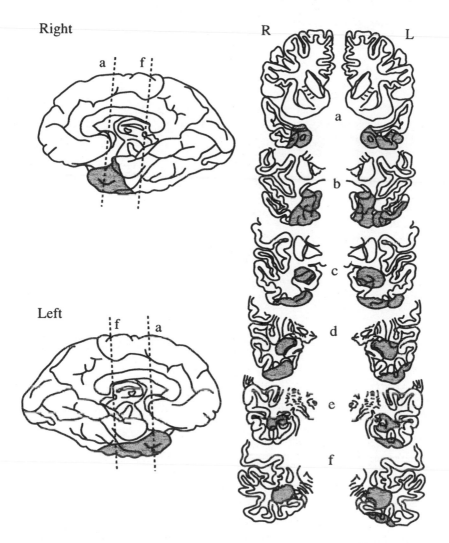

Fig. 8.2 Schematic reconstruction of MRI for Sirigu *et al*.'s (1991) patient. (Reproduced from Sirigu *et al*. (1991). Copyright © 1991 Oxford University Press, reprinted by permission.)

the left; localization within the temporal lobe is not reported. Lesion localization data were not available for Warrington's (1975) patient, AB, a presumptive case of semantic dementia, or for two others who suffered bilateral damage due to stroke (Marshall *et al*. 1996*b*) or anoxia (Carbonnet *et al*. 1997).

The indications of inferior anterior-temporal involvement in cases of abstract superiority suggest that this region of the cortex may support the representation of perceptual properties that are critical components of the meaning of referential terms. Breedin *et al*. noted that this area adjoins posterior areas of inferior temporal cortex that are involved in the visual processing of objects (for further discussion, see

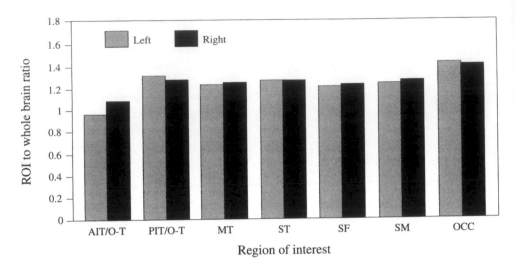

Fig. 8.3 Hypometabolism in the anterior inferior temporal lobes of Breedin *et al.*'s patient DM, as indicated by single-photon emission computed tomography (SPECT) co-registered with a structural MRI scan. AIT/OT = anterior inferior temporal and occipto–temporal; PIT/OT = posterior inferior temporal and occipito–temporal; MT = middle temporal; ST = superior temporal; SF = superior frontal; SM = supramarginal; OCC = occipital lobe. (Reproduced from Breedin *et al.* (1994*b*). Copyright © 1994 Psychology Press Limited, reprinted by permission.)

Sirigu *et al.* 1991; Srinivas *et al.* 1997). We will return to this point later on. In contrast, patients who exhibit deficits on abstract words (aphasics, deep dyslexics, deep dysphasics) have lesions affecting language areas of the left hemisphere. In the case of deep dyslexia, the lesions are typically large and extend posteriorly from Broca's area, located inferiorly in the lateral frontal lobe (Brodmann's areas 44 and 45), to other portions of perisylvian language cortex (e.g. Marin 1980). The lesion site in deep dysphasia, where patients have difficulty repeating abstract words, involves left temporoparietal cortex (e.g. Butterworth and Warrington 1995; Martin and Saffran 1992). Some investigators have invoked right hemisphere mechanisms to account for this pattern (Cardebat *et al.* 1994; Coltheart 1980*b*; Saffran *et al.* 1980); this hypothesis is based, in part, on the assumption that right hemisphere mechanisms provide more support for concrete than abstract words.

8.2.2 Category-specific semantic deficits

In addition to breakdown along the abstract–concrete dimension, there are deficits that involve certain broad categories within the domain of concrete objects. The impairment most often reported involves the disproportionate loss of knowledge of living things, including animals, fruits and vegetables. Also observed, although to this point less frequently, are cases in which patients are more impaired on man-made things—artefacts such as tools, for example. Both deficits are typically manifested in naming as well as comprehension tasks, and apply, in most cases, to pictorial as well as verbal materials. These two types of impairments are almost invariably associated with different lesion sites, the 'living things' impairment with inferior temporal lobe damage, often bilateral, and the 'artefacts' problem with unilateral left hemisphere lesions, in almost all cases involving frontal and parietal cortex[2] (see Saffran and Schwartz 1994, for review).

One cautionary note before we go on to describe these studies: perhaps more so than in other areas of neuropsychology, there are factors that predispose against consistency in the data. People's knowledge across categories can be expected to vary as a function of their experience and interests: some are particularly interested in sports, others in music; some may have limited exposure to implements used in food preparation, others to gardening tools.[3] People differ, as well, in the manner in which they acquire object concepts; some have direct experience with gardening tools, some only read about them or observe others use them. Not surprisingly, some investigators have demonstrated male–female differences for some categories of objects (Funnell and De Mornay Davies 1997). And, as in other neuropsychological studies, differences in the nature and extent of the lesions also contribute to variability across patients. These sources of variability are compounded by the fact that, almost without exception, this research has been carried out as single-case studies by different investigators, using different tasks and materials. In examining these data, then, it is important to focus on the consistency in the patterns across patients and not so much on the exceptions.

There are methodological concerns as well, particularly in the early studies but not limited to them. Although word frequency and the familiarity of objects are clearly important in evaluating semantic knowledge, these factors have not always been carefully controlled. Other significant variables include visual complexity and cross-item visual similarity. It is more difficult to distinguish among pictorial representations of living than non-living things (Gaffan and Heywood 1993), reflecting the greater perceptual similarity of exemplars within categories of living things (Humphreys *et al.* 1995) and the more extensive overlap of semantic features (McRae *et al.* 1997). There are two cases in which an apparent deficit for living things disappeared when materials across the two domains were matched for familiarity and visual complexity (Funnell and Sheridan 1992; Stewart *et al.* 1992), although attempts to control for these variables have not eliminated the deficit in others (e.g. Funnell and De Mornay Davies 1997; Farah *et al.* 1996; Sartori *et al.* 1993*b*). Most importantly, inadequate matching across domains is unlikely to account for the patients who demonstrate the opposite pattern—significantly greater impairment on artefacts (e.g. Warrington and McCarthy 1983, 1987; Sacchett and Humphreys 1992), which tend to be more familiar and less visually complex than living things, as well as perceptually more distinct from one another (e.g. Humphreys *et al.* 1995). There is one study in the literature in which two patients tested with the same materials showed opposite patterns; one was disproportionately impaired on artefacts and the other on living things (Hillis and Caramazza 1991). Examples of cases that illustrate the two types of deficits are provided in Table 8.3.

Table 8.3   Examples of patients disproportionately impaired on living or non-living things.

Patient	Task	Data (% correct)	Lesion site
Patients impaired on living things			
JBR (Warrington and Shallice 1984)	Definitions	Living: 8 Non-living: 79	Bilateral temporal
SBY (Warrington and Shallice 1984)	Definitions	Living: 0 Non-living: 52	Bilateral temporal
LA (Silveri and Gainotti 1988)	Picture naming	Living: 20 Non-living: 79	Bilateral frontotemporal greater on left
Felicia (De Renzi and Lucchelli 1994)	Picture naming	Animals: 33 Objects: 90	Bilateral frontal and inferotemporal
EW (Caramazza and Shelton 1998)	Picture naming	Animals: 33 Non-animals: 67	Left posterior frontal and parietal
Patients impaired on non-living things			
VER (Warrington and McCarthy 1983)	Word–object matching	Animals: 86 Objects: 63	Left frontoparietal
YOT (Warrington and McCarthy 1987)	Word–pix matching	Living: 87 Manipulable Objects: 58	Left frontoparietal
CW (Sacchett and Humphreys 1992)	Picture naming	Living: 95 Non-living + body parts: 35	Left frontoparietal
JJ (Hillis and Caramazza 1991)	Picture naming	Living: 92 Non-living + body parts: 45	Left temporal and basal ganglia

The interpretation of these deficits remains controversial. One possible account is that the brain organizes knowledge by semantic category.[4] An argument against this position is that the breakdown patterns rarely respect the usual taxonomic divisions (animals, plants, furniture, and so on). Patients impaired on animals are almost invariably impaired on fruits and vegetables, and on other types of foods as well; those impaired on artefacts are generally deficient on body parts (e.g. Saffran and Schwartz 1994). The OUCH hypothesis formulated by Caramazza *et al.* (1990) attempts to accommodate these findings within the framework of a model that locates correlated properties (e.g. shape and movement) in the same region of semantic space; consequently, damage localized to a particular region could impair performance on a range of objects that included these properties. However, compelling examples of correlated properties across the domain of living things are not provided. More recently, Caramazza and Shelton (1998) have dealt with the division between living and non-living by postulating an innate disposition for the representation of living things. Noting that infants learn to distinguish animals from other objects early in life, these authors suggest that there is a genetically-based commitment of neural tissue for the recognition of animals and plants, reflecting the significance of this knowledge for the survival of the species. In their view, the impairment on artefacts falls out in default: as artefact recognition must depend on other (uncommitted) neural mechanisms, impairments involving non-living things arise as a secondary consequence of the innate specialization for living things, and not as a result of special representational requirements for artefacts. This account may appeal to those who are comfortable with the leap from early learning to innate disposition. In addition to the difficulty of testing this hypothesis, the account generates little in the way of specific predictions, either with respect to the nature of semantic breakdown or the localization of semantic functions in the brain.

An alternative proposal, originally put forth by Warrington and her colleagues (Warrington and Shallice 1984; Warrington and McCarthy 1987), invokes a different principle for the organization of semantic information. This account rests on the assumption that different kinds of information are differentially weighted in the representations of living and man-made things: whereas animals, fruits and vegetables are largely distinguished by their physical characteristics, functional information plays a more significant role in the representations of man-made things. Support for this hypothesis was provided by Farah and McClelland (1991), who asked subjects to quantify the properties (visual or functional) that figured in dictionary definitions of living and man-made things. Visual descriptors figured much more heavily than functional features in the definitions of living (ratio = 7.7 : 1) than non-living (1.4 : 1) things. This finding was substantiated by Tranel *et al.* (1997*b*), who obtained ratings of characteristics of objects from several different categories (animals, fruits/vegetables, tools/utensils, etc.). Items within the fruits/vegetables and animal categories were rated as highly similar in visual form, while tools/utensils were judged as distinctive; these findings were supported by computer-generated measures of form overlap. In contrast, tools were rated high in manipulability and characteristic movement. Additional data come from a longitudinal study of patients with dementia of the Alzheimer type that revealed differences in the types of features that support correct naming. Lambon-Ralph *et al.* (1997) compared picture naming performance with semantic information generated to the name of an object, focusing on names that were lost as the patients' performance declined. The inability to retrieve names of living things was associated with the loss of sensory features, and the failure to retrieve artefact names with the loss of functional/associative properties. These findings provide support for the account put forward by Warrington and her colleagues, implicating the disproportionate loss of perceptual information in the impairment for living things, and the loss of functional knowledge in the impairment for artefacts.

Additional support for the idea that there are cross-category differences in the weighting of perceptual and functional characteristics comes from the co-occurrence of deficits on certain classes of objects. Patients impaired on animals tend to be impaired on foodstuffs, many of which are manufactured (e.g. sausage, crackers) although their ingredients may be derived from living things. Members of the food category serve the same function of satisfying hunger and sustaining life; what distinguishes a particular food is its colour, shape, texture, aroma, and taste. Several patients have demonstrated greater impairment on foods than animals (Arguin *et al.*

1996; Forde *et al.* 1997; Sheridan and Humphreys 1993), although most have shown the opposite pattern. It has been speculated that this variability reflects the salience of particular features (e.g. colour in the case of food; shape in the case of animals) and their differential impairment across patients (e.g. Warrington and McCarthy 1987; Sheridan and Humphreys 1993). Moreover, food is not the only (at least partially) man-made category that is problematic for patients impaired on living things. Several investigators have found that these individuals perform poorly on some non-living categories, such as musical instruments, where exemplars that serve similar functions are differentiated by perceptual characteristics such as form, the material they are made of, and the sounds they emit (e.g. Silveri and Gainotti 1988; Warrington and Shallice 1984). Noting that this finding could simply reflect a relative lack of familiarity with musical instruments, some researchers have focused on categories that were previously well-known to their patients. Forde *et al.* (1997) found that SRB, a patient impaired on living things, performed poorly when asked to name types of cars, a class of objects previously of great interest to him, and one where exemplars are largely distinguished by characteristics such as shape. Barbarotto *et al.* (1995) report a case study of an architect disproportionately impaired on living things who failed to recognize famous monuments (such as the Parthenon), and was unable to distinguish architectural styles across the centuries. As this was a case of semantic dementia, it could be argued that the patient was experiencing a general deterioration of his conceptual knowledge; nevertheless, his knowledge of legal procedures essential to the practice of architecture was remarkably spared.

If the 'living things' deficit reflects a loss of perceptual knowledge, patients who demonstrate this pattern should have particular difficulty with the perceptual properties of objects.[5] This question has been investigated in a number of patients, utilizing a range of tasks that include property verification, naming to definitions that emphasize perceptual or non-perceptual characteristics, comparison of the perceptual properties of two different objects, colouring and drawing tasks, priming with words that are perceptually or non-perceptually related to the target, and providing definitions for object terms.

Property verification tasks generally involve the presentation of a word (e.g. *tiger*) along with a characteristic that is either true (e.g. *has a striped coat; found in the jungle*) or false (e.g. *has a spotted coat; found on the farm*); some investigators have used a version in which several choices are offered. A number of different patterns have been reported in patients impaired on living things. Some have performed worse on perceptual than other properties, but only within the category of living objects (e.g. De Renzi and Lucchelli 1994; Farah *et al.* 1989; Hart and Gordon 1992). On non-perceptual properties of living things, some have scored at or near the level of control subjects (e.g. Basso *et al.* 1988; De Renzi and Lucchelli 1994; Hart and Gordon 1992; Sartori *et al.* 1993c), while others have been impaired on these properties as well (e.g. Sartori and Job 1988). And, as will be noted below, some patients are as poor at verifying non-perceptual as perceptual features (e.g. Barbarotto *et al.* 1995;

Caramazza and Shelton 1998; Funnell and De Mornay Davies 1997). The variability across patients no doubt reflects differences in the pre-morbid knowledge base and task difficulty, as well as the extent and generality of the semantic impairment. A number of these studies can be faulted, however, in that investigators failed to match across categories for the familiarity of the items and difficulty of the probes. This is particularly problematic, as living things tend to be less familiar, and perceptual probes of living things relatively difficult (e.g. Laws *et al.* 1995). One study that can be excepted from this criticism has been reported by Moss *et al.* (1997). These authors carried out a series of investigations on SE, a herpes encephalitis patient with a relatively mild impairment on living things. SE's performance on a carefully controlled property judgement task was comparable to that of control subjects, with the exception of perceptual properties of living things. Moss *et al.* also used priming paradigms to investigate this question. They tested SE on tasks that compared the effects of visually and non-visually related primes, as well as unrelated primes, on lexical decision for words representing living and non-living things. (For example, a visual prime for the word *fox* is *red*; a non-visual prime is *sly*.) SE's priming data were similar to those of control subjects, except for perceptual primes for living things, where the priming manipulation proved ineffective.

Patients impaired on living things have also performed worse on naming to definitions tasks where the definitions emphasized perceptual (for example, *large wild animal with long tusks, long ears, and long tail*) as opposed to other properties of the objects (*wild animal whose tusks are used for ivory*). Gainotti and Silveri (1996) report such data for LA, a patient impaired on living things and foodstuffs following about with herpes encephalitis (originally reported by Silveri and Gainotti 1988). LA had more success with functional than perceptual definitions for living things (43 per cent versus 6 per cent correct), and performed still better on non-living things, with no difference (58 per cent correct) between the two types of definitions (for other evidence of a similar nature, see Forde *et al.* 1997; Sirigu *et al.* 1991). In describing visual differences between pairs of named objects, where the pairs were matched for visual similarity across categories (e.g. ears of a cat versus those of a rabbit; a nail versus a screw), LA's performance was significantly worse on animals than artefacts (15 per cent versus 50 per cent correct), although considerably poorer than that of controls on both sets of materials (Gainotti and Silveri 1996). Forde *et al.*'s (1997) patient SRB showed a similar performance pattern on this task, as did De Renzi and Lucchelli's (1994). In providing definitions for object terms, some patients have given incorrect perceptual information. For example, Sartori *et al.*'s (1993c) patient, Giulietta, was much better at defining artefacts (15/17 judged correct) than living things (3/17 correct). Her definitions of living things included such attributions as a *bee* is 'the same colour as grass', a *penguin* is a 'four-legged animal', and a *turtle* 'has fur'.

Additional data in support of the perceptual deficit hypothesis come from drawing tasks, in which a number of patients have generated more adequate representations of artefacts compared with living things (e.g. De Renzi and Lucchelli 1994; Sartori *et al.*

1993*a,b*; Sheridan and Humphreys 1993), although familiarity and visual complexity were generally not controlled. When asked to draw a named animal, these patients typically provide a generic, four-legged representation that is much the same, irrespective of whether they are instructed to draw a horse or a chicken. Also relevant is the finding that patients impaired on living things have difficulty identifying the colour of objects, as in choosing a coloured pencil to colour a line drawing, deciding whether a drawing was coloured correctly, or identifying the colour of a named object (e.g. De Renzi and Lucchelli 1994; Gainotti and Silveri 1996). For example, Forde *et al.* (1997) investigated SRB's ability to determine whether living and non-living objects were coloured correctly. SRB performed significantly worse on living objects; and when objects were coloured incorrectly, had more difficulty naming the correct colour of living than non-living things (50 versus 91 per cent correct).

A number of the patients impaired on living things have performed poorly on object decision tasks, where they are required to discriminate between drawings of real and unreal objects. Some investigators have taken these findings to reflect loss of the structural descriptions that support visual object recognition (e.g. Forde *et al.* 1997; Sartori *et al.* 1993*b*; Silveri and Gainotti 1988); others have taken issue with this position, pointing out that this task may depend on access to semantic as well as structural information (e.g. Srinivas *et al.* 1997). It is also important to note that some patients impaired on living things have shown little impairment or even normal performance on object decision tasks (Breedin *et al.* 1994; Hart and Gordon 1992; Laiacona *et al.* 1997; Sheridan and Humphreys 1993; Sirigu *et al.* 1991).

The patients impaired on living things who performed poorly on object decision include ELM, who suffered bilateral temporal damage due to stroke (Arguin *et al.* 1996). ELM, who had difficulty naming animals (56 per cent correct) as well as fruits and vegetables (41 per cent correct), was only slightly impaired on non-biological objects (88 per cent correct). He performed at chance (59 per cent correct) in discriminating real from unreal but plausible animals (e.g. a deer head on a cow body), but very well (93 per cent correct) in discriminating real and unreal artefacts (e.g. a typewriter with a piano keyboard).[6] Probed for perceptual knowledge of living things, ELM performed at chance (45 per cent correct) on animals but much better (85 per cent correct) when queried about other properties of these objects. In these respects, ELM appears quite similar to two other patients reported in the neuropsychological literature: LH (Farah *et al.* 1989) and Michelangelo (Sartori and Job 1988; Sartori *et al.* 1993*a,b*).

By systematically manipulating the shapes of line drawings, Arguin *et al.* determined that ELM confused fruits and vegetables on the basis of combinations of shape characteristics (e.g. elongation + tapering). Thus, for example, a carrot and a cucumber were often mistaken for one another. The same line drawings were not subject to confusion when they were given artefact labels (e.g. tentpeg and cigar). Arguin *et al.* concluded that the problem with living things reflects the intersection of shape similarity with semantic similarity. They suggest that semantic knowledge interacts with structural properties (e.g. shape dimensions such as elongation and tapering) that are extracted separately, and helps to integrate these disparate pieces of information. In their view, ELM's impairment, and those of patients like him, arises from a deficit in the integration of shape information.

While these data are consistent with the hypothesis that the loss of knowledge of living things reflects a loss of perceptual features, exceptions to this pattern have been reported. Funnell and De Mornay Davies (1996) studied JBY, one of the herpes encephalitis cases originally described by Warrington and Shallice (1984). When tested on a property probe task, which contrasted perceptual versus other properties of 14 living and an equal number of non-living objects, no significant differences emerged either as a function of property type or category of object. Barbarotto *et al.*'s (1995) patient, the architect MF, performed normally on a property verification task for man-made objects but poorly on living things, with no significant difference between perceptual and associative characteristics. Caramazza and Shelton (1998) found no evidence of greater impairment on perceptual (0.67 correct) than associative/functional (0.74 correct) attributes in a patient (EW) disproportionately impaired on animals.[7] Laiacona *et al.* (1993) also observed equivalent performance on perceptual and non-perceptual characteristics of living things in two head injury patients with multiple lesion sites who were particularly impaired on animals. In another study from this group (Laiacona *et al.* 1997), two herpes encephalitis patients with 'living things' deficits were equally impaired on perceptual and other types of probes; the data are reported for a mixed set of living and non-living things with no breakdown of scores for the two categories. Lambon Ralph *et al.* (in press) have reported data for two patients, using materials that were well controlled for the relevant variables. One, a patient with Alzheimer's disease, was disproportionately impaired on living things; the other, a semantic dementia case, was disproportionately impaired on visual attributes. The first patient was no more impaired on perceptual than functional/associative properties, whereas the second was more impaired on artefacts than living things. Once again, the findings are contrary to the predictions of the perceptual deficit hypothesis.

The evidence that bears on the perceptual deficit hypothesis is mixed: there are positive findings (some that may be discounted due to methodological problems) as well as data that fail to support this account of the impairment on living things. Caramazza and Shelton (1998) have raised an additional concern: questioning the restriction of the perceptual loss to living things in almost all of the patients, they argue that this deficit should emerge with artefacts as well. But as De Renzi and Lucchelli (1994) have pointed out, the physical characteristics of man-made things are often closely related to their functions, and it may be that patients can generate perceptual properties for objects whose functions they know (also see Moss *et al.* 1997). Examples from Moss *et al.*'s items are illustrative. Perceptual probes for man-made things include 'a cannon is made of metal' and 'a blouse has sleeves'; in both instances, these characteristics are predictable from the functions served by the items. In contrast, there is no comparable rationale, or indeed any predictive basis at all, for the distinctive perceptual properties of living items, such as 'a rabbit has long ears' and 'a pumpkin is round'. It might be possible to control for this factor by choosing properties of artefacts that are not predictable from their functions, but to our knowledge this has yet to be done.

While acknowledging these weaknesses in the case for the perceptual deficit hypothesis, we are not moved to abandon this account of the 'living things' impairment, or the general approach to the organization of semantic knowledge in which it is framed. We note, first, a not inconsiderable amount of supportive data. With respect to the negative findings, the fact that some patients are as impaired on non-perceptual as perceptual properties of living things may not be as damaging as it might seem. If perceptual properties figure importantly in the representations of living things, loss of these features may so reduce activation of the conceptual representation that it becomes difficult to access other properties of the object. This is precisely the result obtained in computational studies, carried out on a model where perceptual characteristics are weighted more heavily for living than non-living things (Farah and McClelland 1991). There is also a striking association between deficit patterns that is also suggestive—although we cannot rule out an accidental relationship due to proximity of separate anatomical substrates. Of the seven reported cases that demonstrate an advantage for abstract words, five were disproportionately impaired on animals (EC, Carbonnet *et al.* 1997; DM, Breedin *et al.* 1994*b*; RG, Marshall *et al.* 1996*b*; FB, Sirigu *et al.* 1991; SBY, Warrington and Shallice 1984); relevant data for the other two cases were not provided. If Breedin *et al.* (1994*b*) are correct in their view that reversal of the normal concreteness effect reflects the loss of perceptual information (but see Plaut and Shallice 1993), the evidence of greater impairment for living things in this group of patients is, again, consistent with the perceptual deficit hypothesis.

The correspondences between knowledge type and lesion site are also suggestive. The brain regions most often implicated in the deficit for biological kinds include inferior and medial temporal cortex;[8] in many cases, the lesions are bilateral and are often located anteriorly. Anterior inferior-temporal cortex is proximal to areas concerned with visual object recognition, while medial areas of temporal neocortex constitute a convergence zone for projections from association areas of the cortex to the hippocampus. Inferotemporal cortex (IT, which includes Brodmann's areas 20 anteriorly and 37 more posteriorly) is an area that is seldom affected by cerebrovascular disease, which is the major cause of brain damage in adults. The majority of the patients who are disproportionately impaired on living things have suffered damage to inferior as well as medial temporal and frontal lobe structures as a result of herpes simplex encephalitis, which has an affinity for these areas of the brain. As to the other cases, several meet the criteria for semantic dementia (Barbarotto *et al.* 1995; Breedin *et al.* 1994*b*; Cardebat *et al.* 1996), although disproportionate impairment on living things is not a consistent feature of that syndrome. This neurodegenerative condition is the result of atrophic changes in the temporal lobes (e.g. Hodges *et al.* 1992), particularly in the left hemisphere, and IT is among the areas affected, albeit more selectively in some cases than others. A third cause is closed head injury (e.g. Farah *et al.* 1991), where the vulnerability of IT cortex reflects its proximity to the bony shelf that underlies it. As noted, vascular aetiologies are relatively infrequent, although a few such cases have been reported.

In monkey and in man, IT is the terminus of the 'what' or object recognition stream in vision, which appears to have a more posterior locus in humans than in other primates (Biederman *et al.* 1997). As already noted, IT is in close proximity to limbic structures that receive converging input from all sensory systems (for discussion of this point, see Gainotti *et al.* 1995). Some of the patients impaired on living things are significantly impaired on visual object decision tasks, a finding that is consistent with damage to more posterior areas of IT; these individuals generally perform better on verbal than on visually-based tests (e.g. Arguin *et al.* 1996; Sartori and Job 1988), which is not the case for all of the patients impaired on living things. One possible interpretation of the spectrum of deficits that disproportionately involve animals and foods is that patients are affected at different points in a network where visual (and other perceptual) information converges with other types of knowledge. In this vein, Srinivas *et al.* (1997, p. 506) have distinguished between three deficit patterns in patients with damage to IT:

> 'First, some patients perform poorly on object decision tests but appear to have preserved conceptual knowledge when tested with words rather than pictures (Sartori *et al.* 1993*a*; Arguin, Bub and Dudek, in press). There is a second group of patients that appears to have difficulty with object decision tests and tests of semantic knowledge regardless of whether pictures or words are used (Hodges *et al.* 1992, 1994). And there are other patients who perform well on object decision tests but are impaired on tests of semantic knowledge (Sirigu *et al.* 1991; Sheridan and Humphreys 1993). We speculate that these three different patterns may reflect damage to different areas in the inferior temporal region. Specifically, we hypothesize that patients with lesions limited to the anterior temporal cortex will demonstrate semantic deficits without impairment to structural descriptions (e.g. DM; Sirigu *et al.*'s patient, FB), whereas patients with posterior involvement and relative sparing anteriorly exhibit impairments to structural descriptions with relative preservation of semantic knowledge (e.g. Arguin *et al.*'s patient ELM). Patients with more extensive lesions of the IT will show deficits in both domains.' (p. 506)

Srinivas *et al.* point out that this hypothesis remains speculative, awaiting greater standardization of the object decision tests administered to patients, which have ranged considerably in difficulty, as well as more precise localization of the lesions of patients with category-specific deficits.

In another attempt to account for the variable findings in patients, Lambon Ralph *et al.* (1998) have suggested that damage to visual areas may not be sufficient to generate impairment disproportionate to living things; disruption of projections between association areas of the cortex may be required as well. With damage solely to visual components of meaning, the patient may continue to identify biological entities on the basis of functional-associative characteristics. With more substantial or extensive impairment, this distinction may disappear. Gainotti *et al.* (1995) raise another consideration, namely, the extent of uni- or bi-temporal involvement. They suggest that damage restricted to the left hemisphere may only affect verbal tasks, whereas bilateral lesions are likely to impede performance across modalities. In most herpes encephalitis cases, the pathology involves right as well as left temporal lobe structures, with a good deal of variability across patients. The extent of right and left temporal lobe involvement is also variable in other disorders (semantic dementia; traumatic brain injury) that sometimes yield deficits on living things. Again, investigation of these factors will depend on careful analyses of the loci of brain damage, as well as patterns of behaviour.

There is less to say about the deficit that underlies poorer performance on man-made things, where the database is more limited. The reported cases include the two described by Warrington and McCarthy (1983, 1987), and the patients of Behrmann and Leiberthal (1989), Hillis and Caramazza (1991), and Sacchett and Humphreys (1992). A patient marginally more impaired on artefacts than on living things has recently been reported by Silveri *et al.* (1997). The deficit is demonstrable in comprehension tasks, as well as in naming (in those patients who are not too aphasic to name). Other relevant data come from a study in which aphasic patients were asked to judge similarity in word meaning, selecting one word from a set of three that was least similar in meaning (e.g. *toad, frog, turtle*; *shears, pliers, scissors*). Using a battery that examined word similarity judgements across 16 categories, Breedin *et al.* (1994*a*) identified three aphasic patients who performed more poorly on tools than animals. The three aphasics were also deficient in judging the similarity of words referring to clothing, furniture, and body parts. Difficulty with body parts has been reported in other patients impaired on man-made things (Hillis and Caramazza 1991; Sacchett and Humphreys 1992). While body parts are highly familiar and clearly biological in origin as opposed to artefactual, each is distinguished by its function.[9]

All of the patients disproportionately impaired on artefacts have had significant aphasic impairments. As aphasics tend to be more impaired on abstract words (Goodglass *et al.* 1969), the impairment on artefacts could conceivably reflect the greater abstractness of functional as compared with perceptual components of meaning (e.g. Keil 1989). The locus of the lesions in these cases suggests another possibility. The two patients reported by Warrington and McCarthy were severely aphasic, reflecting large frontoparietal lesions due to stroke (Warrington and McCarthy 1983, 1987). Although not as aphasic, the same locus of damage and aetiology apply in Sacchett and Humphrey's (1992) and Behrmann and Leiberthal's (1989) patients, and in the cases identified by Breedin *et al.* (1994*a*). The lesion in Hillis and Caramazza's (1991) case, JJ, involved the left temporal lobe, as well as the basal ganglia, which have extensive projections to the frontal lobe. Detailed analyses of the lesions in these cases have not been carried out. However, the left frontoparietal areas reported as damaged either overlap, or are in close proximity to, those involved in sensorimotor functions, and it is possible that manipulability, and the attendant sensorimotor experiential component that tools and utensils afford, is heavily weighted in their semantic representations. Data from an ongoing study conducted by members of our research group (Buxbaum, Saffran and Sholl, in progress) offer support for this notion. We are attempting to tease apart functional knowledge and manipulability, using a task in which subjects choose the one of three object terms (or pictures) that is least similar on one of these dimensions. Thus far, patients impaired on tools, relative to living things, are performing worse on comparisons that involve manner of manipulation (e.g. *hatchet, baseball bat, hammer*) than on functionally-based comparisons (e.g. *lock, latch, pliers*). Another consistent finding is that these patients have difficulty performing gestures appropriate to object use (that is, they are apraxic). Other aphasics, neither disproportionately impaired on tools nor apraxic, have not demonstrated this pattern. These results are consistent with a distributed model of semantic knowledge, in which manipulability figures importantly in the representations of artefacts such as tools and utensils. Functional information may be less significant, although we cannot yet exclude this as a factor.

8.2.3 Impairments involving nouns or verbs

We have focused thus far on disorders that involve the semantic representation of nouns, concrete nouns in particular. Neuropsychology also provides evidence for impairments that are disproportionate to nouns in some cases and to verbs in others. Although verb retrieval is frequently impaired in agrammatic Broca's aphasics (e.g. Miceli *et al.* 1984, 1988; McCarthy and Warrington 1985), who typically have large left hemisphere lesions that extend from frontal cortex posteriorly, verb impairments have been described in other types of aphasics as well (e.g. Berndt *et al.* 1997; Breedin *et al.*, in press). In contrast, greater impairment on nouns than verbs is usually found in patients classified as anomic (e.g. Miceli *et al.* 1988; Zingeser and Berndt 1988). The lesion sites for noun and verb impairments also differ: most of the patients impaired on verbs have incurred damage to the left frontal and/or parietal lobes, whereas patients impaired on nouns typically have left temporal lesions (Daniele *et al.* 1994; Gainotti *et al.* 1995).

As verbs tend to be more abstract than nouns that refer to object concepts, it might be speculated that the breakdown occurs along the abstract–concrete dimension. Evidence along these lines has been obtained by Breedin *et al.* (in press), who have demonstrated an effect of the specificity of verb meaning in patients with verb impairments. The specificity factor is illustrated by the distinction between the verbs *hurry* and *go*; while *hurry* and *go* share components of meaning, *hurry* specifies the manner in which the action occurs (rapidly), while *go* does not. Of eight verb-impaired patients in their study, six (most of them agrammatic) showed a preference for more specific verbs in a story-retelling task. We also note that of the patients who have demonstrated an abstract superiority on nouns, the two who were tested on verbs demonstrated a verb/noun advantage (Breedin *et al.* 1994*b*; Marshall *et al.* 1996*b*). Abstractness is unlikely to be the whole story, however, as differences between nouns and verbs have persisted in studies that have controlled for imageability (e.g. Berndt *et al.* 1997). Some investigators have linked deficits that disproportionately involve nouns or verbs to modality-specific (phonological or orthographic) output lexicons (e.g. Caramazza 1997), on the basis of evidence that patients can be more impaired on nouns in one modality and on verbs in the other (in almost all cases, the oral modality for nouns and the written modality for verbs). It may be that the deficits reflect semantic factors in some cases, and principles of lexical organization in others.

8.3 Evidence from studies of normal brain activity

8.3.1 PET and fMRI

Until recently, the evidence that bears on the localization of functions in the human brain has come almost exclusively from the study of individuals with cognitive deficits associated with brain damage. This question can now be pursued in normal subjects, using new methods for the detection of patterns of brain activity as subjects engage in cognitive tasks. The methods most frequently used in research studies—positron emission tomography (PET) and functional magnetic resonance imaging (fMRI)—do not assess neuronal activity directly, but rely on the positive correlation between brain activity and local increases in blood flow that support that activity. A distinctive feature of these functional neuroimaging studies is the attempt to isolate brain regions associated with specific cognitive operations by subtracting the regional activity pattern associated with a control or baseline task from the pattern generated by the task of interest. So, for example, the baseline task for word reading might involve the presentation of complex but meaningless visual patterns; the increases in blood flow generated by this task would then be subtracted from the increases associated with reading, isolating the changes specific to the reading task. Although concerns have been raised with respect to the design and interpretation of functional-imaging studies (e.g. Nadeau and Crosson 1995; Poeppel 1996; for alternative approaches, see the chapter by Büchel *et al.*, this volume), these investigations have yielded useful information that largely converges with the evidence from studies of brain damage.

Semantic memory is presumed to underlie performance on any task that involves conceptual information, irrespective of the nature of the input (e.g. Kintsch 1980). In support of that assumption, a PET study by Vandenberghe *et al.* (1996) provides evidence for considerable overlap in the brain areas activated in semantic judgements for words versus pictures. These authors asked subjects to judge which two of three objects, presented either in written form or pictorially, were most closely related (e.g. *pliers*, *wrench*, *saw*), or were most similar in size (e.g. *pen*, *electric plug*, *pitcher*). The baseline task involved the matching of word or object stimuli for actual size. Judgements for pictures and words activated a common set of areas, including the temporoparietal junction (Brodmann's areas (BA) 19 and 39), portions of the inferior temporal lobe (BA 20, 37), left middle temporal lobe (BA 21), and left inferior frontal gyrus (BA 11, 47). Other studies that have examined activation patterns for semantic tasks have largely confirmed these findings (e.g. Démonet *et al.* 1992). Vandenberghe *et al.* note that IT cortex and the ventral frontal convexity are known to be involved in object recognition in monkeys and suggest that 'when primates acquired language, a pre-existing object-recognition system could have been adapted to attribute meaning to nouns' (p. 255).

Perani *et al.* (1995) conducted a PET study that compared recognition of animals and artefacts. Subjects were asked to determine whether two different drawings represented the same object. These data were evaluated against baseline tasks that involved texture, luminance, and shape discrimination. The animal discrimination task selectively activated occipital (BA 18, 19) and IT (BA 20 and 37) areas in both hemispheres. In contrast, the recognition of artefacts produced mainly left-sided activation, including the lingual (BA 18), middle occipital (BA 19), and para-hippocampal (BA 36) gyri, as well as dorsolateral frontal cortex (BA 45, 46). Note that these findings are largely consistent with the lesion data for category-specific impairments. Also using PET, Martin *et al.* (1996) examined activity patterns associated with the silent and oral naming of animals and tools against a baseline condition that involved the viewing of nonsense figures. These authors noted IT activation bilaterally for both types of objects; animal naming differed from tool naming in eliciting greater occipital activation, while tool naming selectively activated left middle temporal areas and the left premotor area. Martin *et al.* attribute the occipital activation to the greater perceptual similarity of exemplars within the animal category, which may have increased visual inspection time for these items. They note that the frontal area activated in tool naming was also active in a previous study in which subjects imagined grasping objects with their right hand. Grafton *et al.* (1997) conducted a PET study that examined activity patterns associated with tool examination, silent naming of tools, and silent naming of the manner in which they were used. The baseline task involved viewing of complex colour fractals. Simply observing tools activated left premotor cortex (BA 6). This area was also activated in silent tool naming, and even more so in the objectuse naming condition. Grafton *et al.* note that premotor cortex is also activated when monkeys view objects suitable for grasping. In a PET study of picture naming that focused on temporal cortex, Damasio *et al.* (1996) observed activation in IT for both animals and tools, more posteriorly for the latter. The authors claim that this activation reflects lexical as opposed to semantic processing, but their study does not provide a clear basis for this distinction.[10] In another recent PET study that examined activation patterns associated with silent word reading, left IT cortex (BA 20) was more extensively activated by concrete as compared to abstract words (Beauregard *et al.* 1997).

For the most part, these results converge with the findings for the category-specific deficits discussed earlier. In particular, there is evidence for the activation of IT cortex in semantic tasks, and some suggestion that anterior parts of this area are selectively activated in tasks that involve the names of animals. There is also confirmation of left frontal activation in verbal tasks that involve tools.

Functional-imaging studies have also revealed some differences in regions activated in noun versus verb retrieval. In particular, verbs appear to activate inferior frontal cortex more than nouns do (e.g. Martin *et al.* 1995). We have already noted that this area of the cortex is generally damaged in Broca's aphasics, who are likely to demonstrate verb impairments. As this region is in close proximity to cortical areas that subserve motor functions, it is tempting to speculate that there is a relationship between the anatomical substrates for verbs and the actions that they designate (see Gainotti *et al.* 1995 for discussion of this point), although there are many verbs that do not denote actions.

There is a good deal of evidence for the activation of left dorsolateral frontal cortex (BA 45, 46, and 47, in particular) in semantic tasks such as the generation of names of items within particular categories (e.g. animals), or of verbs given a noun (e.g. *sew* for *needle*). The frontal activation pattern was first interpreted to indicate that frontal cortex is the site of the semantic networks that underlie performance on such tasks (e.g. Petersen *et al*. 1988). This view has changed. It is now considered that prefrontal cortex is involved in the regulation of semantic functions—for example in conducting searches for semantic information stored elsewhere in the brain, and in maintaining the activation of semantic information in working memory (e.g. Gabrieli *et al*. 1996; Posner 1992).

8.4 Concluding remarks

The evidence we have reviewed in this chapter is consistent with the view that semantic information is distributed over a number of brain areas, and that particular kinds of information are localized to different regions of the cerebral cortex. It is noteworthy that at least part of this region—inferotemporal cortex, possibly in both hemispheres—lies outside the area that is usually considered to be committed to language function (that is, the perisylvian cortex of the left hemisphere), and that it abuts areas committed to sensory (especially visual) processing. Humans' ability to conceptualize—for example, to generalize across exemplars—is presumably continuous with that of sub-human species and must therefore pre-date the evolution of human language. Hence, it is not surprising to find some relationship between perception and conceptualization, particularly as perceptual characteristics are essential components of meaning, at least for concrete words.

In the neuropsychological literature, there has been considerable debate over the issue of modality-based versus modality-free semantics (see, for example, papers in *Cognitive Neuropsychology*, 1988, no. 5). The controversy has centred, in particular, on the question of whether there are distinct 'visual' and 'verbal' semantic systems, as opposed to a single system, accessed from all modalities, in which the representational format is amodal (e.g. Caramazza *et al*. 1990; Shallice 1988*a*).[11] Although we accept the distinction between visual and verbal that is implicit in the distributed model, we view these regions, each subserving a different form of representation, as extensively interconnected. Shallice (1988*b* pp. 302–303) has expressed a similar view:

'Instead of conceiving of the semantic system as a set of discrete subsystems (functions, sensory properties, and so on) it may be more useful to think of it as a giant distributed net in which regions tend to be more specialised for different types of process. For an object, these might include the representations of non-visible sensory features; knowledge related to relevant actions; knowledge related to what would be found near it; somewhat more abstract aspects, such as knowledge related to an object's function; and even more abstract operations, such as how it was manufactured. The specialisation could arise because of the different pattern of connections—outside the semantic system itself—used by each particular process. On a distributed network approach, such a developmental process can be viewed as one in which individual units (neurons) within the network come to be most influenced by input from particular input channels, and in turn, come to have most effect on particular output channels. Complementarily, an individual concept will come to be most strongly represented in the activity of those units that correspond to the pattern of input–output pathways most required in the concept's identification and use. The capacity to distinguish between members of a particular category would depend on whether there are sufficient neurons preserved in the relevant partially specialised region to allow the network to respond clearly differentially to the different items in the category.' (pp. 302–303)

A core assumption of this approach is that information is stored in memory in the form in which it is experienced (e.g. visual, kinaesthetic, linguistic/propositional). It is also assumed that the various types of information pertaining to a concept become linked via temporal co-occurrence. It may be possible, through selective damage to one subsystem or another, to isolate components from one another, so that, for example, information is available to verbal inquiry that is not accessible via visual input, or vice versa (for examples, see McCarthy and Warrington 1988, 1994; Warrington and McCarthy 1994). Under normal conditions, the subregions are tightly interconnected via reciprocal activation; hence, when properties of a concept are activated in one subsystem, properties entered in other systems are also activated. This model also allows for the enormous flexibility in processing that is another hallmark of semantic memory. Properties will be differentially accessed as a function of context. So, for example, if the scenario has to do with moving, the weight of a piano is likely to be the object's most salient feature, rather than its musical properties. We view a distributed model of this nature not only as most consistent with the evidence we have reviewed in this chapter, but also as a coherent approach to the evolution of conceptual capacities across species.

As we have noted, the data clearly need strengthening in some areas, and are only fragmentary in others. Despite these limitations, we have tried to build a case for a brain-centred approach to the question of semantic organization, incorporating evidence from semantic impairments and from studies of regional brain-activity patterns associated with the performance of semantic tasks. We hope we have succeeded in demonstrating that this represents a useful approach to a difficult set of issues in human cognition.

Notes

1. The little evidence so far available suggests, however, that object use is relatively preserved at a point where semantic dementia patients perform poorly on both verbal and pictorial semantic tests (Buxbaum *et al.* 1997). If substantiated, this finding would provide an additional source of support for the type of distributed model outlined above.

2. Deficits that disproportionately involve one or the other of these categories have also been described in patients with Alzheimer's disease (e.g. Gonnerman *et al.* 1997). Gonnerman *et al.* suggest that conceptual knowledge of living things is likely to be relatively spared early in the progression of the semantic impairment, due to intercorrelations among features within this class of objects; as the disorder progresses, living things are likely to be more severely affected than artefacts, due to the loss of distinguishing information. This progression has recently been the subject of computational modelling (Devlin *et al.* 1998). Since there is as yet little evidence that bears on these predictions, we have elected not to discuss this work here.

3. Returning to the topic of the previous section, superiority for abstract words might not emerge in a patient with a low educational level.

4. Computational modelling of the acquisition of semantic information yields a network in which properties shared by category members are represented across a common set of units, providing an existence proof for the principle of taxonomic organization (e.g. Ritter and Kohonen 1989). Some neuropsychologists have suggested a different form of categorical organization that is restricted to modality-specific subsystems. For example, McCarthy and Warrington (1994; Warrington and McCarthy 1994) have argued for category-based distinctions within separate domains of visual and verbal semantics, while Sartori and Job (1988) have suggested that the structural description system that supports visual object knowledge is organized along category lines.

5. It should be noted that, with the exception of tasks where subjects must judge whether objects are real or not (object decision), visual perceptual functions are unimpaired in these cases (e.g. De Renzi and Lucchelli 1994; Sartori *et al.* 1993*c*).

6. It could be argued that this task is open to strategies of the following sort: all animals have ears, eyes, tails, etc., but certain features are specific to particular artefacts. For example, piano keys are found on only a few kinds of musical instruments, and do not co-occur with typewriter features.

7. It should be noted that this patient's lesion spared the temporal lobes, which have been implicated in virtually all of the other reported cases with this pattern.

8. One contrary finding has been reported by Tippett *et al.* (1996), who examined the naming of living and non-living things in patients following anterior temporal lobectomy. Overall, the left temporal patients ($n = 17$) showed significantly better performance on living than non-living things. It may be that this pattern reflects the history of uncontrolled seizures that preceded surgical intervention.

9. Cases have been reported in which patients are specifically impaired on body parts, with other categories of objects remaining relatively preserved (e.g. Suzuki *et al.* 1997).

10. In the same paper, Damasio *et al.* report lesion localization data for patients impaired in naming and/or identifying (providing semantic information for) animals and tools. The lesion data overlap with the activated regions in the PET study, and Damasio *et al.* conclude that the impairment involves lexical processing. However, as Caramazza and Shelton (1998) point out, the deficits in these patients were not explored as thoroughly as those of the subjects of the case studies discussed earlier. In particular, Damasio *et al.* did not test for comprehension deficits, so it is not possible to exclude semantic loss. Furthermore, Damasio *et al.* used a different measure to identify category-specific deficits in their subjects; rather than computing differences in performance levels across categories as was the case for the other studies, they based their classification on deviations from the performance levels of normal controls.

11. The nature of the distinction between visual and other properties of objects has been articulated in a number of different ways. For example, Chertkow *et al.* (1992) have argued for a distinction between a component that identifies and differentiates visual exemplars and one that stores other types of information about objects. Riddoch *et al.* (1988) distinguish between a structural description component and another system that represents other properties in an amodal format.

References

Allport, D. A. (1985). Distributed memory, modular subsystems and dysphasia. In *Current perspectives in dysphasia* (eds S. K. Newman and R. Epstein), pp. 32–60. Churchill Livingstone, Edinburgh.

Arguin, M., Bub, D., and Dudek, G. (1996). Shape integration for visual object recognition and its implication in category-specific visual agnosia. *Visual Cognition*, **3**, 221–75.

Barbarotto, R., Capitani, E., and Laiacona, M. (1995). Slowly progressive semantic impairment with category specificity. *Neurocase*, **1**, 107–19.

Barsalou, L. W. (1991). Flexibility, structure, and linguistic vagary in concepts: Manifestations of a compositional system of perceptual symbols. In *Theories of memory* (eds A. F. Collins, S. E. Gathercole, M. A. Conway, and P. E. Morris), pp. 29–101. Erlbaum, Hove.

Basso, A., Capitani, E., and Laiacona, M. (1988). Progressive language impairment without dementia: A case with isolated category specific semantic defect. *Journal of Neurology, Neurosurgery and Psychiatry*, **51**, 1201–7.

Beauregard, M., Chertkow, H., Bub, D., Murtha, S., Dixon, R., and Evans, A. (1997). The neural substrate for concrete, abstract, and emotional word lexica: A positron emission tomography study. *Journal of Cognitive Neuroscience*, **9**, 441–61.

Behrmann, M. and Leiberthal, T. (1989). Category-specific treatment of a lexical-semantic deficit: A single case study of global aphasia. *British Journal of Disorders of Communication*, **24**, 281–99.

Berndt, R. S., Mitchum, C., Haendiges, A., and Sandson, J. (1997). Verb retrieval in aphasia: 1. Characterizing single word impairments. *Brain and Language*, **56**, 68–106.

Biederman, I., Gerhardstein, P. C., Cooper, E. E., and Nelson, C. A. (1997). High level object recognition without an anterior inferior temporal lobe. *Neuropsychologia*, **35**, 271–87.

Breedin, S. D. and Saffran, E. M. (1998). Sentence processing in the face of semantic loss: A case study. (Manuscript.)

Breedin, S. D., Martin, N., and Saffran, E. M. (1994a). Category-specific semantic impairments: An infrequent occurrence? *Brain and Language*, **47**, 383–6.

Breedin, S. D., Saffran, E. M., and Coslett, H. B. (1994b). Reversal of the concreteness effect in a patient with semantic dementia. *Cognitive Neuropsychology*, **11**, 617–60.

Breedin, S. D., Saffran, E. M., and Schwartz, M. F. Semantic factors in verb retrieval: An effect of complexity. *Brain and Language*. (In press.)

Butterworth, B. and Warrington, E. K. (1995). Two routes to repetition: Evidence from a case of 'deep dysphasia'. *Neurocase*, **1**, 55–66.

Buxbaum, L., Schwartz, M. F., and Carew, T. G. (1997). The role of semantic memory in object use. *Cognitive Neuropsychology*, **14**, 219–54.

Caramazza, A. (1997). How many levels of processing are there in lexical access? *Cognitive Neuropsychology*, **14**, 177–208.

Caramazza, A. and Shelton, J. R. (1998). Domain-specific knowledge systems in the brain: The animate–inanimate distinction. *Journal of Cognitive Neuroscience*, **10**, 1–34.

Caramazza, A., Hillis, A. E., Rapp, B. C., and Romani, C. (1990). The multiple semantics hypothesis: Multiple confusions? *Cognitive Neuropsychology*, **7**, 161–89.

Carbonnet, S., Charnallet, A., David, D., and Pellat, J. (1997). One or several semantic system(s)? Maybe none: Evidence from a case study of modality and category-specific 'semantic' impairment. *Cortex*, **33**, 391–417.

Cardebat, D., Démonet, J-F., Celsis, P., Puel, M., Viallard, G., and Marc-Vergnes, J-P. (1994). Right temporal compensatory mechanisms in a deep dysphasic patient: A case report with activation study by SPECT. *Neuropsychologia*, **32**, 97–104.

Cardebat, D., Démonet, J-F., Celsis, P., and Puel, M. (1996). Living/non-living dissociation in a case of semantic dementia: A SPECT activation study. *Neuropsychologia*, **34**, 1175–9.

Chang, T. (1986). Semantic memory: Facts and models. *Psychological Bulletin*, **9**, 199–220.

Chertkow, H., Bub, D., and Caplan, D. (1992). Constraining theories of semantic memory: Evidence from dementia. *Cognitive Neuropsychology*, **9**, 327–65.

Cipolotti, L. and Warrington, E. K. (1995). Semantic memory and reading abilities: A case report. *Journal of the International Neurospychological Society*, **1**, 104–10.

Coltheart, M. (1980*a*). Deep dyslexia: A review of the syndrome. In *Deep dyslexia* (eds M. Coltheart, K. E. Patterson, and J. C. Marshall), pp. 22–48. Routledge and Kegan Paul, London.

Coltheart, M. (1980*b*). Deep dyslexia: A right hemisphere hypothesis. In *Deep dyslexia* (eds M. Coltheart, K. E. Patterson, and J. C. Marshall), pp. 326–80. Routledge and Kegan Paul, London.

Damasio, A. R. (1990). Category-related recognition defects as a clue to the neural substrates of knowledge. *Trends in Neurosciences*, **13**, 95–8.

Damasio, H., Grabowski, T. J., Tranel, D., Hichwa, R. D., and Damasio, A. R. (1996). A neural basis for lexical retrieval. *Nature*, **380**, 499–505.

Daniele, A., Giustolisi, L., Silveri, M. C., Colosimo, C., and Gainotti, G. (1994). Evidence for a possible neuroanatomical basis for lexical processing of nouns and verbs. *Neuropsychologia*, **32**, 1325–41.

Démonet, J-F., Chollet, F., Rumsay, S., Cardebat, D., Nespoulous, J-L., Wise, R., Rascol, A., *et al.* (1992). The anatomy of phonological and semantic processing in normal subjects. *Brain*, **115**, 1753–68.

De Renzi, E. and Lucchelli, F. (1994). Are semantic systems separately represented in the brain? The case of living category impairment. *Cortex*, **30**, 3–25.

Devlin, J. T., Gonnerman, L. M., Anderson, E. S., and Seidenberg, M. S. (1998). Category-specific semantic deficits in focal and widespread brain damage: A computational account. *Journal of Cognitive Neuroscience*, **10**, 77–94.

Farah, M. J. and McClelland, J. (1991). A computational model of semantic memory impairment: Modality specificity and emergent category specificity. *Journal of Experimental Psychology: General*, **120**, 339–57.

Farah, M. J., Hammond, K. H., Mehta, Z., and Ratcliff, G. (1989). Category-specificity and modality-specificity in semantic memory. *Neuropsychologia*, **27**, 193–200.

Farah, M. J., McMullen, P. A., and Meyer, M. M. (1991). Can recognition of living things be selectively impaired? *Neuropsychologia*, **29**, 185–93.

Farah, M. J., Meyer, M. M., and McMullen, P. A. (1996). The living/nonliving dissociation is not an artifact: Giving an a priori implausible hypothesis a strong test. *Cognitive Neuropsychology*, **13**, 137–54.

Forde, E. M. E., Francis, D., Riddoch, M. J., Rumialati, R. I., and Humphreys, G. W. (1997). On the links between visual knowledge and naming: A single case study of a patient with a category-specific impairment for living things. *Cognitive Neuropsychology*, **14**, 403–58.

Funnell, E. and De Mornay Davies, P. (1997). JBR: A reassessment of concept familiarity and a category-specific disorder for living things. *Cognitive Neuropsychology*, **9**, 135–53.

Funnell, E. and Sheridan, J. (1992). Categories of knowledge? Unfamiliar aspects of living and nonliving things. *Cognitive Neuropsychology*, **9**, 135–54.

Gabrieli, J. D. E., Desmond, J. E., Demb, J. B., Wagner, A. D., Stone, M. V., Vaidya, C. J., *et al.* (1996). Functional magnetic resonance imaging of semantic memory processes in the frontal lobe. *Psychological Science*, **7**, 278–83.

Gaffan, D. and Heywood, C. A. (1993). A spurious category-specific visual agnosia for living things in normal humans and nonhuman primates. *Journal of Cognitive Neuroscience*, **5**, 118–28.

Gainotti, G. and Silveri, M. C. (1996). Cognitive and anatomical locus of lesion in a patient with a category-specific semantic impairment for living beings. *Cognitive Neuropsychology*, **13**, 357–89.

Gainotti, G., Silveri, M. C., Daniele, A., and Giustolisi, L. (1995). Neuroanatomical correlates of category-specific semantic disorders: A critical survey. *Memory*, **3**, 247–64.

Gonnerman, L. M., Andersen, E. S., Devlin, J. T., Kempler, D., and Seidenberg, M. S. (1997). Double dissociation of semantic categories in Alzheimer's disease. *Brain and Language*, **57**, 254–79.

Goodglass, H., Hyde, M. R., and Blumstein, S. E. (1969). Frequency, picturability and availability of nouns in aphasia. *Cortex*, **5**, 104–19.

Grafton, S. T., Fadiga, L., Arbib, M. A., and Rizzolatti, G. (1997). Premotor cortex activation during observation and naming of familiar tools. *NeuroImage*, **6**, 231–6.

Hart, J. and Gordon, B. (1992). Neural subsystems for object knowledge. *Nature*, **359**, 60–4.

Hillis, A. E. and Caramazza, A. (1991). Category-specific naming and comprehension impairment: A double dissociation. *Brain*, **114**, 2081–94.

Hodges, J. R., Patterson, K., Oxbury, S., and Funnell, E. (1992). Semantic dementia: Progressive fluent aphasia with temporal lobe atrophy. *Brain*, **115**, 1783–1806.

Hodges, J. R., Patterson, K., and Tyler, L. K. (1994). Loss of semantic memory: Implications for the modularity of mind. *Cognitive Neuropsychology*, **11**, 505–42.

Hodges, J. R., Graham, N., and Patterson, K. (1995). Charting the progression of semantic dementia: Implications for the organisation of semantic memory. *Memory*, **3**, 463–95.

Humphreys, G. W., Lamote, C., and Lloyd-Jones, T. J. (1995). An interactive activation approach to object processing: Effects of structural similarity, name frequency, and task in normality and pathology. *Memory*, **3**, 535–86.

Jackendoff, R. (1987). On beyond zebra: The relation of linguistic and visual information. *Cognition*, **26**, 89–114.

Jones, G. V. (1985). Deep dyslexia, imageability, and ease of predication. *Brain and Language*, **24**, 1–19.

Keil, F. C. (1989). *Concepts, kinds and cognitive development*. MIT Press, Cambridge, MA.

Kintsch, W. (1980). Semantic memory: A tutorial. In *Attention and performance VIII* (ed. R. S. Nickerson), pp. 595–620. Bolt, Beranek and Newman, Cambridge, MA.

Komatsu, L. K. (1992). Recent views of conceptual structure. *Psychological Bulletin*, **112**, 500–26.

Laiacona, M., Barbarotto, R., and Capitani, E. (1993). Perceptual and associative knowledge in category specific impairment of semantic memory: A study of two cases. *Cortex*, **29**, 727–40.

Laiacona, M., Capitani, E., and Barbarotto, R. (1997). Semantic category dissociations: A longitudinal study of two cases. *Cortex*, **33**, 441–61.

Lambon-Ralph, M. A., Patterson, K., and Hodges, J. R. (1997). A longitudinal study of naming and knowing in dementia of Alzheimer type. *Neuropsychologia*, **35**, 1251–60.

Lambon-Ralph, M. A., Howard, D., Nightingale, G., and Ellis, A. W. Are living and non-living category-specific deficits linked in impaired perceptual or associative knowledge? Evidence from a category-specific double dissociation. *Neurocase*. (In press.)

Laws, K. R., Humber, S., Ramsey, D., and McCarthy, R. A. (1995). Probing memory and associative semantics for animals and objects in normal subjects. *Memory*, **3**, 397 408.

Marin, O. S. M. (1980). CAT scans of five deep dyslexic patients. In *Deep dyslexia* (eds M. Coltheart, K. E. Patterson, and J. C. Marshall), pp. 407–11. Routledge and Kegan Paul, London.

Marshall, J., Pring, T., Chiat, S., and Robson, J. (1996*b*). Calling a salad a federation: An investigation of semantic jargon. Part I Nouns. *Journal of Neurolinguistics*, **9**, 237–50.

Martin, N. (1996). Models of deep dysphasia. *Neurocase*, **2**, 73–80.

Martin, N. and Saffran, E. M. (1992). A connectionist account of deep dysphasia: Evidence from a case study. *Brain and Language*, **43**, 240–74.

Martin, A., Haxby, J. V., Lalonde, F. M., Wiggs, C. L., and Ungerleider, L. G. (1995). Discrete cortical regions associated with knowledge of color and knowledge of action. *Science*, **270**, 102–5.

Martin, A., Wiggs, C. L., Ungerleider, L. G., and Haxby, J. V. (1996). Neural correlates of category-specific knowledge. *Nature*, **379**, 649–52.

McCarthy, R. A. and Warrington, E. K. (1985). Category specificity in an agrammatic patient: The relative impairment of verb retrieval and comprehension. *Neuropsychologia*, **23**, 709–27.

McCarthy, R. A. and Warrington, E. K. (1988). Evidence for modality-specific meaning systems in the brain. *Nature*, **334**, 428–30.

McCarthy, R. A. and Warrington, E. K. (1994). Disorders of semantic memory. *Philosophical Transactions of the Royal Society of London*, **B346**, 89–96.

McRae, K., De Sa, V. R., and Seidenberg, M. S. (1997). On the nature and scope of featural representations for word meaning. *Journal of Experimental Psychology: General*, **126**, 99–130.

Miceli, G., Silveri, M. C., Villa, G., and Caramazza, A. (1984). On the basis for the agrammatic's difficulty in producing main verbs. *Cortex*, **20**, 207–20.

Miceli, G., Silveri, M. C., Nocentini, U., and Caramazza, A. (1988). Patterns of dissociation in comprehension and production of nouns and verbs. *Aphasiology*, **2**, 351–8.

Moss, H. E., Tyler, L. K., and Jennings, F. (1997). When leopards lose their spots: Knowledge of visual properties in category-specific deficits for living things. *Cognitive Neuropsychology*, **14**, 901–50.

Nadeau, S. E. and Crosson, B. (1995). A guide to the functional imaging of cognitive processes. *Neuropsychiatry, Neuropsychology and Behavioural Neurology*, **8**, 143–62.

Paivio, A. (1991). Dual coding theory: Retrospect and current status. *Canadian Journal of Psychology*, **45**, 255–87.

Perani, D., Cappa, S. F., Bettinardi, V., Bressi, S., Gorno-Tempini, M., Matarrese, M., *et al.* (1995). Different neural systems for the recognition of animals and man-made tools. *NeuroReport*, **6**, 1637–41.

Petersen, S. E., Fox, P. T., Posner, M. I., Mintun, M., and Raichle, M. E. (1988). Positron emission tomographic studies of the processing of single words. *Journal of Cognitive Neuroscience*, **1**, 153–70.

Plaut, D. C. and Shallice, T. (1993). Deep dyslexia: A case study of connectionist neuropsychology. *Cognitive Neuropsychology*, **10**, 377–500.

Poeppel, D. (1996). A critical review of PET studies of phonological processing. *Brain and Language*, **55**, 317–51.

Posner, M. I. (1992). Attention as a cognitive and neural system. *Current Directions in Psychological Science*, **1**, 11–14.

Riddoch, M. J., Humphreys, G. W., Coltheart, M., and Funnell, E. (1988). Semantic systems or system? Neuropsychological evidence re-examined. *Cognitive Neuropsychology*, **5**, 3–25.

Ritter, H. and Kohonen, T. (1989). Self-organizing semantic maps. *Biological Cybernetics*, **61**, 241–54.

Sacchett, C. and Humphreys, G. W. (1992). Calling a squirrel a squirrel but a canoe a wigwam: A category-specific deficit for artifactual objects and body parts. *Cognitive Neuropsychology*, **9**, 73–86.

Saffran, E. M. and Schwartz, M. F. (1994). Of cabbages and things: Semantic memory from a neuropsychological perspective: A tutorial review. In *Attention and performance XV* (eds C. Umilta and M. Moscovitch), pp. 507–36. MIT Press, Cambridge, MA.

Saffran, E. M., Bogyo, L. C., Schwartz, M. F., and Marin, O. S. M. (1980). Does deep dyslexia reflect right hemisphere reading? In *Deep dyslexia* (eds M. Coltheart, K. E. Patterson, and J. C. Marshall), pp. 381–406. Routledge and Kegan Paul, London.

Sartori, G. and Job, R. (1988). The oyster with four legs: A neuropsychological study on the interaction between vision and semantic information. *Cognitive Neuropsychology*, **5**, 677–709.

Sartori, G., Job, R., and Coltheart, M. (1993*a*). The organization of object knowledge: Evidence from neuropsychology. In *Attention and performance XIV* (eds D. E. Meyer and S. Kornblum), pp. 451–66. MIT Press, Cambridge, MA.

Sartori, G., Miozzo, M., and Job, R. (1993*b*). Category-specific naming impairments? Yes. *Quarterly Journal of Experimental Psychology*, **46A**, 489–504.

Sartori, G., Miozzo, M., Zago, S., and Marchiori, G. (1993*c*). Category-specific form-knowledge deficit in a patient with herpes-simplex virus encephalitis. *Journal of Clinical and Experimental Neuropsychology*, **15**, 280–99.

Schwartz, M. F., Marin, O. S. M., and Saffran, E. M. (1979). Dissociation of language function in dementia: A case study. *Brain and Language*, **7**, 277–306.

Shallice, T. (1988*a*). Specialisation within the semantic system. *Cognitive Neuropsychology*, **5**, 133–42.

Shallice, T. (1988*b*). *From neuropsychology to mental structure*. Cambridge University Press.

Sheridan, J. and Humphreys, G. W. (1993). A verbal-semantic category-specific recognition impairment. *Cognitive Neuropsychology*, **10**, 143–84.

Silveri, M. C. and Gainotti, G. (1988). Interaction between vision and language in category-specific semantic impairment. *Cognitive Neuropsychology*, **5**, 677–709.

Silveri, M. C., Gainotti, G., Perani, D., Cappelletti, J. Y., Carbone, G., and Fazio, F. (1997). Naming deficit for non-living items: Neuropsychological and PET study. *Neuropsychologia*, **35**, 359–67.

Sirigu, A., Duhamel, J. R., and Poncet, M. (1991). The role of sensorimotor experience in object recognition: A case of multimodal agnosia. *Brain*, **114**, 2555–73.

Snowden, J. S., Goulding, P. J., and Neary, D. (1989). Semantic dementia: A form of circumscribed cerebral atrophy. *Behavioural Neurology*, **2**, 167–82.

Srinivas, K., Breedin, S. D., Coslett, H. B., and Saffran, E. M. (1997). Intact perceptual priming in a patient with damage to the anterior inferior temporal lobes. *Journal of Cognitive Neuroscience*, **9**, 490–511.

Stewart, F., Parkin, A. J., and Hunkin, N. M. (1992). Naming impairments following recovery from herpes simplex encephalitis: Category specific? *Quarterly Journal of Experimental Psychology*, **44A**, 261–84.

Suzuki, K., Yamadori, A., and Fujii, T. (1997). Category-specific comprehension deficit restricted to body parts. *Neurocase*, **3**, 193–200.

Tippett, L. J., Glosser, G., and Farah, M. J. (1996). A category-specific naming impairment after temporal lobectomy. *Neuropsychologia*, **34**, 139–46.

Tranel, D., Logan, C. G., Frank, R. J., and Damasio, A. R. (1997*b*). Explaining category-related effects in the retrieval of conceptual and lexical knowledge for concrete entities: Operationalization and analysis of factors. *Neuropsychologia*, **35**, 1320–39.

Vandenberghe, R., Price, C., Wise, R, Josephs, O., and Frackowiak, R. S. J. (1996). Functional anatomy of a common semantic system for words and pictures. *Nature*, **383**, 254–56.

Warrington, E. K. (1975). The selective impairment of semantic memory. *Quarterly Journal of Experimental Psychology*, **27**, 635–57.

Warrington, E. K. and McCarthy, R. A. (1983). Category-specific access dysphasia. *Brain*, **106**, 859–78.

Warrington, E. K. and McCarthy, R. A. (1987). Categories of knowledge: Further fractionation and an attempted integration. *Brain*, **100**, 1273–96.

Warrington, E. K. and McCarthy, R. A. (1994). Multiple meaning systems in the brain: A case for visual semantics. *Neuropsychologia*, **32**, 1465–73.

Warrington, E. K. and Shallice, T. (1984). Category-specific semantic impairments. *Brain*, **107**, 829–53.

Zingeser, L. B. and Berndt, R. S. (1988). Grammatical class and context effects in a case of pure anomia: Implications for models of lexical processing. *Cognitive Neuropsychology*, **5**, 473–516.

9   *The neurocognition of syntactic processing*

Peter Hagoort, Colin M. Brown, and Lee Osterhout

9.1 Introduction

Syntax matters. This is illustrated by the fact that we can parse sentences without understanding their meaning, as in *I knuster with my knesidon and strinpel like a criks* (after Cees Buddingh, *Het mes op de gorgel*, 1960). Although we don't know what *knuster* and *knesidon* mean, we can still determine that the former must be a verb and the latter a noun. Sentences made up (in part) of word-like elements with a legal orthographic form but bereft of meaning are often easy to structure in terms of grammatical categories such as subject, direct object, etc. It thus should come as no surprise that syntactic cues are seen as an integral part of language processing. That is, it is a nearly universally accepted notion in current models of the production and interpretation of multiword utterances that constraints on how words can be structurally combined in sentences are immediately taken into consideration during speaking and listening/reading. These constraints operate next to qualitatively distinct constraints on the combination of word meanings, on the grouping of words into phonological phrases, and on their referential binding into a mental model. Together, these constraints solve the 'binding problem' for language, or in other words how speakers and writers, listeners and readers bind single-word information into multiword utterances and complex messages.

Despite considerable agreement on the types of constraints that are effective during the formulation and the interpretation of sentences, exactly how these constraints are implemented in the overall design of the sentence processing machinery is still an issue of intense debate in psycholinguistics. Central in this debate is to what extent the operation of syntactic cues can be sealed off from the influence of other types of constraints during the on-line interpretation or formulation process. This focus on the contribution of syntactic cues is presumably a consequence of the 'syntactocentrism' of the Chomskian tradition within linguistics (Jackendoff 1997). As a result, in research on sentence-level processing the role of syntactic constraints has been at centre stage over at least the last two decades. This holds alike for neurolinguistic patient studies, recent brain-imaging studies, and psycholinguistic studies of sentence processing. Since this chapter discusses language processing beyond the single-word level, its focus is therefore on syntax.

A complete theory of the neurocognition of syntax has to specify how grammatical encoding (speaking) and parsing (comprehension) are organized and embedded in the overall process of speaking and listening/reading. However, this is not enough. In addition we need to specify which neural mechanisms enable and instantiate the combinatorial apparatus that is so central to natural language. Knowledge about the neural basis of syntax will furthermore help to sharpen our understanding of syntactic processing. At the same time, we need a sufficiently detailed analysis of syntactic processing to target our research on its neural underpinnings. Although it is early days for a truly cognitive neuroscience of syntax, it is possible to sketch some of its ingredients and the currently most relevant results. This is the task we set ourselves in this chapter.

First we will present the ingredients of a cognitive architecture of syntactic processing, with special attention to issues that are of relevance for studies on the neural architecture of syntax. Then we will discuss recent electrophysiological insights into syntactic processing, followed by a review of the relevant lesion literature and of recent brain-imaging (haemodynamic) studies with a focus on sentence processing. In the final section of this chapter we evaluate the current state of knowledge on the neuro-cognition of syntax and conclude with a few suggestions for future research. Since most sentence processing research investigates comprehension (reading/listening), and not production (speaking), we will mainly focus our discussion on comprehension.

9.2 Issues in syntactic processing

Each word form (*lexeme*) in the mental lexicon is associated with syntactic word information (Levelt 1989, and this volume, Chapter 4; Roelofs 1992, 1993). This latter type of information is referred to as *lemma* information. Lemmas specify the syntactic properties of words, such as their word class (Noun, Verb, Adverb, Adjective, Preposition, etc.). For nouns in gender-marked languages their grammatical gender is specified as well (e.g. *horse* in French has masculine gender, in Dutch it has neuter gender). Verb lemmas contain information on syntactic frames (the argument structures), and on the thematic roles of the syntactic arguments (the thematic structure). For instance the lemma for the verb *donate* specifies that it requires a subject-NP, and a direct object-NP, with the optional addition of an indirect object-PP (e.g. *John* ⟨subject-NP⟩ *donates a book* ⟨direct object-NP⟩ *to the library* ⟨optional indirect object-PP⟩). In addition, the mapping of this syntactic frame onto the thematic roles is specified. For *donate* the subject is the *actor*, the direct object the *theme*, and the indirect object the *goal* or *benefactive* of the action expressed by the predicate (for more details see Chapter 3 and the chapters in Section 2 of this volume).

In speaking, lemmas are activated on the basis of the preverbal message that the speaker intends to express. Here lemmas are the intermediary between the preverbal message and the articulation of an utterance. In listening and reading, the direction of processing is the reverse. Now lemma activation occurs on the basis of word form information. Despite this difference in the sources of lemma activation between production and comprehension, in both cases lemmas are crucial as triggers for further structure-building operations. These structure-building operations cluster words in syntactic phrases and assign these phrases their grammatical roles. An example of this clustering is given with a labelled bracketing notation in (1):

(1) [s [NP The little old lady] [VP bit [NP the gigantic pitbull terrier]]]

It is generally assumed that both in production and comprehension structure building is done incrementally and with no or very short delays relative to lemma activation. In speaking, the syntactic fragments that come with the lemmas are assembled into larger structures, a process labelled unification (Kempen 1997; Levelt, this volume). Through the incremental unification process the syntactic structure of the complete utterance is determined. In this way the speaker generates an abstract surface structure (grammatical encoding) that guides the retrieval of the sound patterns (morpho-phonological encoding) necessary for determining the articulatory gestures resulting in overt speech. A similar incrementality is characteristic for comprehension. Once a lemma is retrieved on the basis of the spoken or written input, the relevant lemma information is immediately inserted into the constituent structure built for the preceding lemmas. This on-line assignment of structure to an incoming string of written or spoken words is referred to as parsing. A crucial aspect of comprehension is that the sentence structure is often locally underdetermined (syntactic ambiguity). Since at many points in the input more than one structural assignment is possible, the incremental nature of structure building can result in a garden path, as is clear in the famous example of Bever (1970):

(2) The horse raced past the barn fell.

Sentence processing theories differ with respect to how much of the overall sentence structure is assumed to be present as precompiled syntactic fragments in memory (i.e. the lexicon). In some proposals (e.g. Kempen 1997; MacDonald *et al.* 1994) substantial pieces of syntactic structure are lexically specified. The overall sentence structure can then be seen to result from linking the syntactic fragments that are activated on the basis of lemma input. Other proposals (e.g. Frazier 1987; Frazier and Clifton 1996; Pritchett 1992) assume that lemmas trigger structure-building operations in some form of procedural memory, and that these operations assemble phrase structures on the fly.

Despite these differences, there is again almost universal agreement that usually the whole sentence structure cannot be retrieved from memory, but has to be built out of smaller fragments. This then requires that lemmas and syntactic fragments or partial products of structure building are kept active until all the relevant syntactic slots are filled. Computational resources are needed to run this process to its completion. That is, the lemma information and syntactic fragments or intermediate structure-building products have to be instantiated and integrated in working memory. Both storage and processing in working memory tax the available amount of computational resources

(Caplan and Waters, 1999; Gibson 1998; Just and Carpenter 1992). Differences in the amount of computational resources needed for structure building might explain why some sentences are harder to understand or need more processing time than others. For instance, across comprehension studies using a variety of dependent measures (e.g. reading times, lexical decision latencies, response accuracy to probe questions) it is consistently found that object-extracted relative clauses (3a) are more complex than subject-extracted relative clauses (3b) (e.g. Gibson 1998; King and Just 1991; Waters *et al.* 1987).

(3)   a. The reporter who the senator attacked admitted the error.
       b. The reporter who attacked the senator admitted the error.

Similarly, sentences with centre-embedded structures (4a) are notoriously harder to process than sentences with right-branching structures (4b).

(4)   a. The juice that the child spilled stained the rug.
       b. The child spilled the juice that stained the rug.

Despite different proposals about the relation between structural complexity and computational resources (see Gibson 1998, for an overview), a tight relationship seems to exist between structure-building operations and the resources that are necessary to support them. However, often the notion of computational resources lacks sufficient precision to determine in more detail how limitations in these resources affect grammatical encoding and parsing.

Apart from the overall agreement on the major components of grammatical encoding and parsing, there are also unresolved issues that have to be kept in mind when studying the neural architecture of syntactic processing. We will discuss the most relevant ones. Given the current bias of the field, all points relate to parsing, and only two (see 9.2.1 and 9.2.3) also relate to grammatical encoding.

9.2.1 A single versus a dual processor for grammatical encoding and parsing

Although the syntactic constraints are not different in speaking and listening/reading, nevertheless *prima facie* grammatical encoding is quite different from parsing. For one, word order is given in parsing, but has to be computed in grammatical encoding. Furthermore, structural indeterminacy has to be faced continuously in parsing, whereas in the formulation process structure is incrementally determined by the pre-verbal message, the lemma input, and the syntactic constraints.

Despite the seemingly relevant differences between parsing and grammatical encoding, there are arguments in favour of a single processor account, and architectures have been proposed that handle both grammatical encoding and parsing in a unified manner (Kempen 1999; Vosse and Kempen 1999). One argument is parsimony; it is more parsimonious to assume that the lexical building blocks for syntactic processing such as lemmas and, if present, syntactic fragments are not doubly, but singly represented. Moreover, intuitively there seems to be a fairly strong correlation between sentence structures that speakers find hard to produce and sentence structures that listeners find difficult to understand. The reason why more complex structures are often less frequent than more simple constructions might be exactly because they seem to cause the same problem for the formulator as for the parser. Finally, with a few exceptions, the overwhelming majority of agrammatic aphasics show strong correlations between impairments in grammatical encoding and parsing.

However, the presence of those exceptional cases of patients with a syntactic production deficit without a concomitant comprehension impairment (Kolk *et al.* 1985; Miceli *et al.* 1983; Nespoulous *et al.* 1992) can be taken as an argument *against* a single processor account. Rare as these cases might be, the fact that impairments in grammatical encoding can be dissociated from impairments in parsing, suggests that there is no necessary connection between syntactic processing in production and comprehension.

In short, whether the processing machinery for grammatical encoding and parsing is the same or different, is still an open issue. Although this issue is obviously relevant for research on the neural architecture of syntactic processing, it has hardly been explicitly addressed.

9.2.2 A modality-specific parser versus a modality-independent parser

One of the clear differences between reading and listening to speech is the prosodic information that is encoded in the speech signal but not in writing. The phonological and intonational phrasings of an utterance contribute to the assignment of a syntactic structure to a sentence. Given the contribution of speech-specific information to parsing, we cannot exclude the possibility that the parsing operations in listening are qualitatively different from the ones in reading. This would imply modality-specific parsers for reading and listening. Alternatively, the parsing operations could be modality-independent, with an extra source of information that the general parser works with in the case of speech. This latter view is explicitly or implicitly assumed in most models of language comprehension (see Cutler and Clifton, Chapter 5 this volume, for more detail).

9.2.3 General versus dedicated working-memory support for structure building

As we discussed above, syntactic operations require working-memory resources. There is an ongoing debate in the literature with respect to the specificity of these resources. Just and Carpenter and their colleagues (e.g. Just and Carpenter 1992; Just *et al.* 1996*a*) have advocated the view that all aspects of language processing are supported by a common general verbal working memory. Caplan and Waters (e.g. Caplan and Waters 1996, in press; Waters and Caplan 1996) claim that parsing is subserved by a dedicated working-memory system. A major reason for postulating a separate parsing buffer comes from neuropsychological data. Patients have been described who show a co-occurrence of a severe reduction in their working-memory capacity and a preservation of the capacity to formulate and/or understand syntactically complex sentences (e.g. Butterworth *et al.* 1986; Caplan and Waters 1990, in press; Martin 1993; Waters *et al.* 1991). To date the issue of a general versus a dedicated resource system for parsing has not yet been settled.

9.2.4 Structural precedence versus all cues are equal

One of the central issues in research on sentence-level comprehension is what sources of information contribute to the structure that is initially assigned to an incoming string of words. As was discussed above, at many points in a sentence its structure is underdetermined. That is, more than one structure can be assigned on the basis of particular lemma information, as is clear in the following example:

(5)   The teacher sees the boy and the girl...

After reading (or hearing) *girl* the sentence can continue in two structurally different ways, affecting the structural role that has to be assigned to the noun *girl*, as is exemplified in (6a) and (6b):

(6)   a. [$_S$ The teacher [$_{VP}$ sees [$_{NP}$ the boy and the girl] during their holiday]]
      b. [$_S$ The teacher [$_{VP}$ sees the boy]] and [$_S$ the girl [$_{VP}$ sees the teacher]]

In (6a) the string *the boy and the girl* forms the object-NP of the sentence. In (6b) *the girl* is not part of the object-NP, but it is the subject of the second clause. Which structure has to be assigned becomes clear only after the noun *girl*. However, there is pretty solid evidence that even in the absence of sufficient information for determining the structure, there will be a preference when encountering the noun *girl* to assign it one structural role rather than the other. In this particular case the structure of (6a) is preferred over the one in (6b), presumably on the basis of differences in syntactic complexity (Frazier 1987; Frazier and Rayner 1982) or differences in frequency of occurrence of the alternative structures (Mitchell 1994; Mitchell *et al.* 1995).

The bias for one structure over the other can be modulated or overwritten by the preceding discourse or by lexical information in the sentence context, as is clear in (7):

(7)   The teacher buys the ticket and the girl...

In this sentence the context induces a strong expectancy for a structure where *girl* starts a second clause. This is due to the semantics of the verb *buy* which goes together easily with an inanimate object but not so easily with an animate object. However, some sentence-processing models claim that independent of this type of contextual information, in first instance a structure is assigned exclusively on the basis of structural principles, which is then passed on to the semantic interpreter for evaluation (cf. Frazier 1987). The semantic interpreter can reject this structure, resulting in the subsequent assignment of an alternative structural option. Other models, in contrast, claim that there is no such priority for purely structural information in computing a syntactic structure, but that all relevant sources of information are immediately taken into consideration when assigning syntactic structure to an incoming string of words (e.g. Garnsey *et al.* 1997; Tanenhaus and Trueswell 1995). Over the last few years there has been increasing evidence in favour of this latter class of so-called constraint-based parsing models. That is, pragmatic, semantic, and syntactic information all seem to play an immediate role in determining the structure of an utterance, at least in cases of syntactic ambiguity.

9.2.5 Structural output versus semantic output

So far, we have tacitly assumed that both in language production and in language comprehension there is a processing level that generates a syntactic output. In models of speaking, this assumption is widely accepted (cf. Bock 1990, 1995; Bock and Levelt 1994; Dell 1986; Garrett 1980). To produce grammatically well-formed utterances the speaker has to order the lemmas and specify their grammatical functions in accordance with the syntactic constraints of the language. The abstract surface structure thus generated is the frame for the insertion of morpho-phonological information (see Levelt, Chapter 4 this volume). The situation is different in comprehension. In comprehension the listener or reader wants to derive the message of the speaker or the text. One can imagine that in this case all information is used and combined in a direct mapping of word information onto an overall interpretation, without an intermediate level of syntactic structure. This is exactly what some constraint-based models of sentence interpretation propose (cf. Bates and Goodman, 1997; Bates *et al.* 1982; McClelland *et al.* 1989). In these models pragmatic, semantic, and syntactic cues all immediately contribute to constrain the interpretation space of a given utterance and to settle it in a state of equilibrium that underlies the derived message. In the most parsimonious version of such a model all relevant cues are handled by a unified sentence processor that takes the lexical information as input and derives the interpretation by the operation of frequency-based co-occurrence constraints of all the cues that are available in the input (cf. Elman 1990). As of yet, no completely worked out version of such a model that adequately deals with most of the fundamental observations in sentence processing is around. Nevertheless, on the basis of its general architectural principles the prediction for the neural architecture is that no syntactic processor can be isolated in the brain. We will have more to say about this issue in the next section.

Note that it is not an inherent feature of constraint-based models that no syntactic output is generated. Although constraint-based parsing models often make a connection between the interactive conspiracy of all available cues and the absence of separate semantic and syntactic components, this is by no means a logical or necessary connection. Thus although all constraint-based models agree that all relevant sources of information immediately and jointly contribute to sentence interpretation, in some of these models the joint contribution of the relevant cues results in a syntactic output (e.g. McRae *et al.* 1998; Tanenhaus *et al.*, in press). In short, whether or not sentence-level comprehension requires an intermediate level of the computation of sentence form (syntax) is still a matter of considerable debate.

The issues discussed above have been the subject of experimental research and computational modelling in the psycholinguistics of sentence processing. Until now, these issues have not been central to brain-imaging studies on sentence-level processing. Only ERP studies of recent years have started to investigate the central claims of different parsing models. It is to the electrophysiological evidence on parsing that we will first turn.

9.3 The microvolts of syntax: electrophysiological evidence

The discussion of ERP effects related to parsing can only be put in the right perspective against the background of another set of ERP effects that are sensitive to different aspects of sentence processing. Historically speaking, the discovery by Kutas and Hillyard (1980) of an ERP component that seemed especially sensitive to semantic manipulations marks the beginning of an increasing effort to find and exploit language-relevant ERP components. Kutas and Hillyard observed a negative-going potential with an onset at about 250 ms and a peak around 400 ms (hence the N400), whose amplitude was increased when the semantics of the eliciting word (i.e. *socks*) mismatched with the semantics of the sentence context, as in *He spread his warm bread with socks*. Since 1980, much has been learned about the processing nature of the N400 (for extensive overviews, see Kutas and Van Petten 1994; Osterhout and Holcomb 1995). It has been found that most word types (e.g. nouns, verbs, etc.) in the language elicit an N400 (cf. Kutas 1997). As such the N400 can be seen as a marker of lexical processing. The amplitude of the N400 is most sensitive to the semantic relations between individual words, or between words and their sentence and discourse context. The better the semantic fit between a word and its context, the more reduced the amplitude of the N400. This is illustrated in Fig. 9.1, where waveforms are shown for words that vary in a very subtle way in their degree of semantic fit with the context (Hagoort and Brown 1994). ERPs to sentences of the following types were compared (the critical words are in italics):

(8)   a. The girl put the sweet in her *mouth* after the lesson.
      b. The girl put the sweet in her *pocket* after the lesson.

Independent behavioural evidence indicates that it is easier to fit semantically *mouth* into this sentence context than *pocket* (Hagoort and Brown 1994). As can be seen in Fig. 9.1, the N400 amplitude to *mouth* is smaller than the N400 amplitude to *pocket*.

Modulations of the N400 amplitude are quite generally viewed as directly or indirectly related to the processing costs of integrating the meaning of a word into the overall meaning representation that is built up on the basis of the preceding language input (Brown and Hagoort 1993; Osterhout and Holcomb 1992). This holds equally when the preceding language input consists of a single word, a sentence, or a discourse.

The N400 is usually largest over posterior scalp sites with a slight right hemisphere preponderance in reading but shows no laterality effects with spoken input. Intracranial recordings have suggested an N400 generator in the anterior fusiform gyrus (Nobre *et al.* 1994, but see Kutas *et al.*, Chapter 12 this volume).

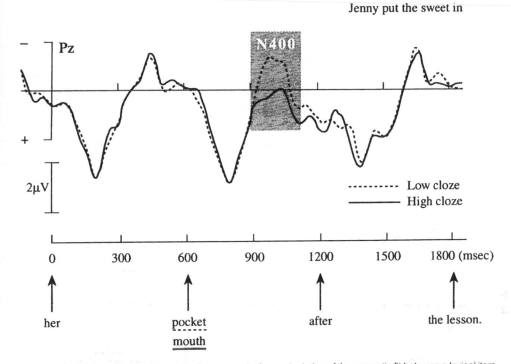

Fig. 9.1 Modulation of the N400-amplitude as a result of a manipulation of the semantic fit between a lexical item and its sentence context. The grand average waveform is shown for electrode site Pz (parietal midline), for the best fitting word (High Cloze; solid line), and a word that is less expected in the given sentence context (Low Cloze; dashed line). The sentences were visually presented word by word, with an interval (SOA) of 600 ms. In the figure the critical words are preceded and followed by one word. The critical word is presented at 600 ms on the time axis. Negativity is up on the y axis in this and all other figures. (Adapted from Hagoort and Brown (1994). Copyright © 1994 Erlbaum, reprinted by permission.)

Jackendoff (1997; Chapter 3 this volume) has argued for a tripartite architecture of the language faculty, in which conceptual/semantic structures, phonological structures, and syntactic structures are crucial in language processing. In relation to language, the N400 amplitude modulations have been reliably linked to the processing of conceptual/semantic information. In recent years, much ERP research has been devoted to establishing ERP effects that can be related to the other two qualitatively distinct types of information that are involved in understanding language.

Relatively little is known about phonological ERP effects. Some studies (Praamstra *et al.* 1994; Rugg 1984*a,b*; Rugg and Barrett 1987) have reported ERP effects to manipulations of phonological structure that are reminiscent of N400 effects in terms of their polarity and latency. For instance, Praamstra *et al.* (1994) reported a reduction in the amplitude of an N400-like component when a target word shows rhyme overlap with a preceding prime, compared with the ERP waveform to a target word with no phonological overlap with the preceding prime. The issue of whether the scalp topography of these effects is identical to the topography of the semantic N400 effects is not yet completely settled. Other studies have reported phonological ERP effects that are both earlier (Hagoort and Brown, in press) and functionally dissociable from the classic N400 effects (Connolly and Phillips 1994).

In the remainder of this section we will focus on ERP correlates of syntactic processing. Two issues will be central to our discussion of syntax-related ERP effects. The first one is what these effects imply for the functional components of syntactic processing. The second issue concerns the inferences that they allow with respect to the neural architecture of the parser.

9.3.1 ERP evidence for functional components of syntactic processing

A first distinction should be made between lexical-syntactic effects and syntactic effects beyond the lexical level. Lexical-syntactic effects concern the activation of lemma information that specifies the syntactic features of lexical items. This lemma information is the crucial input for the computation of sentence structure.

So far, ERP studies have mainly tested the distinction between two broad classes of words, namely closed-class (or function) words and open-class (or content) words. The category of closed-class words contains, among others, articles, conjunctions, and prepositions. The category of open-class words contains nouns, verbs, and adjectives. Broadly speaking, the distinction between open- and closed-class words can be seen as a basic reflection of the separation between semantics and syntax. The open-class words are the main bearers of meaning in the language, providing the building blocks for the overall sense that is contained in a spoken or written sentence. In contrast, the closed-class words are relatively devoid of meaning. However, they serve an important role in that they provide crucial information for the computation of the syntactic relations that hold among the open-class words of a sentence.

A series of ERP studies (Brown *et al.* 1999; King and Kutas 1998; Neville *et al.* 1992; Nobre and McCarthy 1994; Osterhout *et al.* 1997a; Pulvermüller *et al.* 1995) investigated the ERP profiles for open- and closed-class words. All studies reported early differences between these two word classes around 280 ms after word onset. At this latency closed-class words showed an increased negativity that was most prominent over left anterior electrode sites (see Fig. 9.2).

In some studies, this N280 component was only seen to closed-class words (Neville *et al.* 1992; Nobre and McCarthy 1994). In these studies the open-class words elicited an N400 with a posterior distribution. This qualitatively distinct ERP componentry to closed- and open-class words was seen as evidence for separate brain systems subserving the processing of these two word classes. Other studies, however, failed to find this qualitative distinction, and observed the same componentry to open- and closed-class words, with, however, a longer latency for the open-class words (see Fig. 9.2; Brown *et al.* 1999; King and Kutas 1998; Osterhout *et al.* 1997a).

Usually word length and word frequency are confounded with the word class distinction, with closed-class words being shorter and more frequent than open-class words. Some studies have found that these variables account for most of the variance

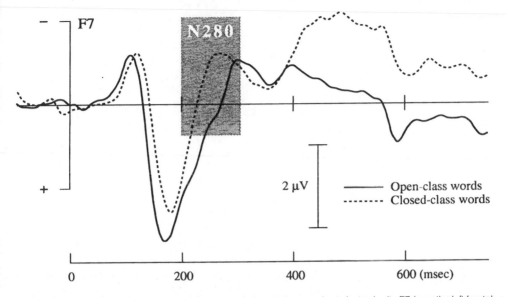

Fig. 9.2   The averaged ERP waveforms for open- and closed-class words at electrode site F7 (over the left frontal cortex). The ERP data were collected while subjects read a simple, fairytale-like story, presented word by word with an interval (SOA) of 800 ms. The open-class waveforms (solid line) were averaged over nouns (202), adjectives (86), and verbs (151). The closed-class waveforms (dashed line) were averaged over articles (212), prepositions (115), and conjuncts (71). Although the waveforms already diverge at around 200 ms (the P200), this difference is either seen as resulting from the upcoming negativity of the closed class items, or from prelexical processing. The closed-class words show a negative peak (N280) that is earlier than the negative peak for the open-class words. In addition, the closed class items show an increased negative shift in the later part of the waveform, between 400 and 800 ms. (Adapted from Brown, Hagoort, and ter Keurs 1999.)

between the ERPs to open- and closed-class words (King and Kutas 1998; Osterhout *et al.* 1997*a*). However, other studies only found an effect of word class, and failed to find a differential effect of length and frequency (Brown *et al.* 1999; Neville *et al.* 1992; Nobre *et al.* 1994).

Since the results of current studies differ with respect to the issue of whether the same or different ERP components are elicited by open- and closed-class words, it is too early to conclude that the processing of these two word types is subserved by the same or different neural tissue. However, independent of this latter issue, the conclusion must be that some of the syntax-relevant word class information is available for further processing in less than 280 ms. Whether this syntax-relevant word-class information emerges from length and frequency parameters, or directly from word-class specifications, is still unclear. Moreover, whether the time course estimation of word-class retrieval generalizes to other types of lemma information, such as the grammatical gender of a noun or the syntactic frame of a verb, also remains to be seen.

Once lemma information has been retrieved during comprehension, syntactic (and possibly other) constraints conspire to structure the linear string of lemmas into a hierarchically organized constituent structure. Two classes of ERP effects have been reported in relation to postlexical structure building operations. The first class of ERP effects are modulations of a negative-going potential with a frontal maximum. The amplitude modulations of this potential are usually referred to as the LAN (Left Anterior Negativity; Friederici *et al.* 1996; Kluender and Kutas 1993). The second class of ERP effects are modulations of a positive-polarity component which is referred to as the P600/SPS (cf. Coulson *et al.* 1998; Hagoort *et al.* 1993; Osterhout and Holcomb 1992; Osterhout *et al.* 1997*b*).

In addition to ERP studies on assigning lemmas to constituent structures, a limited number of ERP studies have addressed the processing of so-called filler-gap relations (Garnsey *et al.* 1989; Kluender and Kutas 1993; McKinnon and Osterhout 1996; Mecklinger *et al.* 1995). Filler-gap dependencies occur in sentences where constituents have been moved from one location to another. The moved constituent is the filler, its original location is known as the gap (Fodor 1978). Filler–gap dependencies exist in sentences with so-called wh-words such as *who* and *which*. For instance, in the sentence *The little old lady did not remember which dog she had bitten*, the filler *dog* has been extracted and moved up front from the object position after the verb *bitten*, leaving a postulated gap after this verb. Dependent upon the exact details of the studies, different types of ERP effects have been observed in relation to establishing filler–gap relations (e.g. Garnsey *et al.* 1989; Kluender and Kutas 1993). We will not discuss these studies here, but refer to Osterhout and Holcomb (1995) for an overview.

9.3.1.1   Left anterior negativities

A number of studies have reported negativities that are different from the N400, in that they usually show a more frontal maximum (but see Münte *et al.* 1997), and are usually larger over the left than the right hemisphere. Moreover, *prima facie,* the conditions that elicit these frontal negative shifts seem to be more strongly related to syntactic processing (but see below) than to semantic integration. Usually, LAN effects occur within the same latency range as the N400, that is between 300 and 500 ms post-stimulus (Friederici *et al.* 1996; Hagoort and Brown, in press; Kluender and Kutas 1993; Osterhout and Holcomb 1992; Münte *et al.* 1993; Rösler *et al.* 1993). But in some cases the latency of a left-frontal negative effect is reported to be much earlier, somewhere between 125 and 180 ms (Friederici *et al.* 1993; Neville *et al.* 1991).

The LAN effects are to be distinguished from the N280 that we discussed above with respect to the processing of closed- versus open-class words. The N280 is an ERP component that is seen in an averaged waveform to words of one or more types. For instance, in the averaged waveform for closed-class words one can easily identify a component with a maximal amplitude at around 280 ms (see Fig. 9.2). The left-anterior negativity, however, refers to the amplitude *difference* between two conditions. It is identified by comparing the averaged waveforms of two conditions. That is, in one condition one sees an increased negativity in comparison with another condition. This negative increase is usually largest over left frontal sites.

In some studies LAN effects have been reported to violations of word-category constraints (Friederici *et al.* 1996, Münte *et al.* 1993; Rösler *et al.* 1993). That is, if the syntactic context requires a lemma of a certain class (e.g. a noun in the context of a preceding article and adjective), but in fact a lemma of a different class is presented (e.g. a verb), early negativities are observed. Friederici and colleagues (e.g. Friederici 1995; Friederici *et al.* 1996), have tied the early negativities specifically to the processing of word-category information. This, however, seems unlikely in the light of the fact that similar early negativities are observed with number, case, gender, and tense mismatches (Hagoort and Brown in press; Münte and Heinze 1994; Münte *et al.* 1993). In these violations the word category is correct but the morphosyntactic features are wrong.

Before discussing the functional interpretations of LAN effects, we have to point to one worrisome methodological aspect of many studies reporting these effects. This is that they are picked up to words in sentence-final position. For various reasons, presenting the critical words in sentence-final position can impact the overall morphology of the ERP waveform and by consequence complicate the comparison with results obtained to words in other than sentence-final positions. It is well known in the reading-time literature that apart from local effects, the sentence-final words are often strong attractors of global processing factors related to sentence wrap-up, decision, and response requirements (e.g. Mitchell and Green 1978; Schriefers *et al.* 1995). For example in sentences that subjects judge as unacceptable, final words seem to elicit an enhanced N400-like effect, regardless of whether the unacceptability is semantic or syntactic in nature (Hagoort *et al.* 1993; Osterhout and Holcomb 1992, 1993). Osterhout (1997) found that syntactic anomalies were more likely to elicit a noticeable anterior negativity when placed at the end of the sentence than when embedded within the sentence. The ERP effects of the local violation and the more global ERP effects of sentence processing thus tend to overlap most strongly in sentence-final position, thereby affecting the resulting ERP waveforms for the local effect particularly in this position. Cross-study comparisons would thus be made easier if words that realize the critical experimental manipulation were not in sentence-final position.

The functional interpretation of LAN effects is not yet agreed upon, partly for the methodological reasons given above, partly because its antecedent conditions are not yet sufficiently clarified. As indicated above, one possibility is that this effect is specifically syntactic in nature. Along these lines, it has been proposed that LAN effects are functionally related to matching word-class information against the requirements of the constituent structure derived from the earlier lemmas in the sentence (Friederici 1995). The word-class information might have some temporal precedence over other lexical information in generating a syntactic structure for the incoming string of words (Friederici *et al.* 1996). However, as we argued above, this would explain only a subset of the reported LAN effects.

LAN effects have also been related to verbal working memory (Kluender and Kutas 1993; Coulson *et al.* 1998). Such an account is compatible with the finding that both lexical and referential ambiguities seem to elicit very similar frontal negativities (Hagoort and Brown 1994; Van Berkum *et al.* 1997; see also King and Kutas 1995). These cases refer to the processing of words with more than one meaning (e.g. *bank*) and to the processing of nouns that have more than one antecedent in the preceding discourse. Such ambiguities are clearly not syntactic in nature, but can be argued to tax verbal working memory more heavily than sentences in which lexical and referential ambiguities are absent. This account denies a special relation of LAN effects to syntactic processing, but relates them to the general resource requirements for language comprehension.

It is, however, also unlikely that all frontal negativities that are reported can be subsumed under a verbal working-memory account. For instance, the frontal negativities elicited by morphosyntactic violations (Münte *et al.* 1993) are difficult to account for in terms of working memory.

A third possibility is that under the heading of LAN effects more than one type of effect has been subsumed, which we have not yet been able to separate due to similarity in distribution and latency and a limited understanding of the antecedent conditions. The few reports of very early LAN effects have recently led to the claim that this effect might be at least functionally different from the 'standard' LAN effects in the 300– 500 ms latency range (Friederici 1995; Friederici *et al.* 1996). The early effects are now sometimes referred to as ELAN (Friederici *et al.* 1998). Since research on LAN/ELAN effects has started only very recently, we can expect that some of these issues will be clarified in coming years.

9.3.1.2 P600/SPS

A relatively more stable finding than the reported LAN effect in terms of reproducibility and establishing the antecedent conditions are the later positivities, nowadays referred to as P600/SPS (Coulson *et al.* 1998; Osterhout *et al.* 1997*b*).

One of the antecedent conditions of P600/SPS effects is a violation of a syntactic constraint. If, for instance, the syntactic requirement of number agreement between the grammatical subject of a sentence and its finite verb is violated (see (9), with the critical verb form in italics), a positive-polarity shift is elicited to the word that renders the sentence ungrammatical (Hagoort *et al.* 1993). This positive shift starts at about 500 ms after the onset of the violation and usually lasts for at least 500 ms. Given the polarity and the latency of its maximal amplitude this effect was originally referred to as the P600 (Osterhout and Holcomb 1992) or, on the basis of its functional characteristics, as the Syntacic Positive Shift (SPS) (Hagoort *et al.* 1993).

(9)   *The spoilt child *are* throwing the toy on the ground.

An argument for the independence of this effect from possibly confounding semantic factors is that it also occurs in sentences where the usual semantic/pragmatic constraints have been removed (Hagoort and Brown 1994). This results in sentences like (10a) and (10b) where one is semantically odd but grammatically correct, whereas the other contains the same agreement violation as in (9):

(10)   a. The boiled watering-can *smokes* the telephone in the cat.
     b. *The boiled watering-can *smoke* the telephone in the cat.

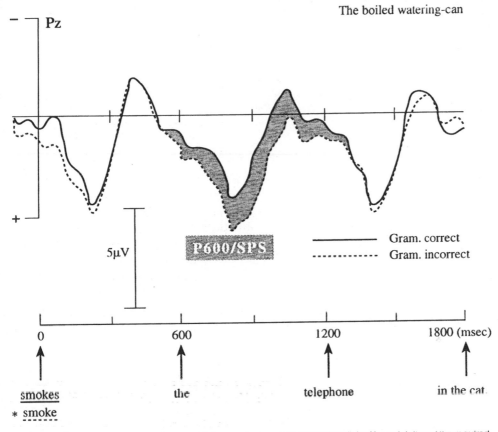

Fig. 9.3 ERPs to visually presented syntactic prose sentences. A P600/SPS is elicited by a violation of the required number agreement between the subject-noun phrase and the finite verb of the sentence. The averaged waveforms for the grammatically correct (solid line) and the grammatically incorrect (dashed line) words are shown for electrode site Pz (parietal midline). The word that renders the sentence ungrammatical is presented at 0 ms on the time axis. The waveforms show the ERPs to this and the following two words. Words were presented word by word, with an interval (SOA) of 600 ms. (Adapted from Hagoort and Brown (1994). Copyright © 1994 Erlbaum, reprinted by permission.)

If one compares the ERPs to the italicized verbs in (10a) and (10b), a P600/SPS effect is visible to the ungrammatical verb form (see Fig. 9.3). Despite the fact that these sentences do not convey any coherent meaning, the ERP effect of the violation demonstrates that the language system is nevertheless able to parse the sentence into its constituent parts.[1]

Similar P600/SPS effects have been reported for a broad range of syntactic violations in different languages (English, Dutch, German), including phrase-structure violations (Hagoort *et al.* 1993; Neville *et al.* 1991; Osterhout and Holcomb 1992), subcategorization violations (Ainsworth-Darnell *et al.* 1998; Osterhout and Holcomb 1992; Osterhout *et al.* 1994), violations in the agreement of number, gender, and case

(Coulson *et al.* 1998; Hagoort *et al.* 1993; Münte *et al.* 1997; Osterhout 1997; Osterhout and Mobley 1995), violations of subjacency (McKinnon and Osterhout 1996; Neville *et al.* 1991), and of the empty-category principle (McKinnon and Osterhout 1996). Moreover, they have been found with both written and spoken input (Friederici *et al.* 1993; Hagoort and Brown, in press; Osterhout and Holcomb 1993).[2]

Already in the first P600/SPS studies (Hagoort *et al.* 1993; Osterhout and Holcomb 1992) it became clear that syntactic violations are not the only antecedent condition of this ERP effect. The other way to elicit this effect is closer to normal sentence processing, since it occurs in sentences that are grammatically correct. It relates to the issue of structural indeterminacy. In on-line sentence comprehension, as one goes along structuring words as they come in, at many points in a sentence the words can be grouped into constituents in more than one way (see example (5)). At these points of indeterminacy, there will nevertheless be a temporary preference (or increased level of activation) for one structure over its alternative(s). Later incoming words can either support the preferred structure, or provide evidence that an alternative option has to be assigned. This latter case involves extra processing costs. Dependent on the particulars of the proposed parsing model the extra processing costs are ascribed to rejection of the initial structure and the necessary reassignment operations (Frazier 1987), or to inhibition of the higher activated structure and increase in activation for the initially less-activated structure (Tanenhaus and Trueswell 1995). It turns out that the word in the sentence that signals this change in preference/activation also elicits a positive shift reminiscent in latency and polarity of the P600/SPS. An example can be seen in a recent study by Hagoort *et al.* (forthcoming), in which the following sentence pairs were compared (the original sentences were in Dutch):

(11)   a. The sheriff saw the indian and the cowboy noticed the horses in the bushes.
        b. The sheriff saw the indian, and the cowboy noticed the horses in the bushes.

The comma after the noun *indian* in sentence (11b) marks the end of the first clause and signals that after the connective *and* a new clause follows. This is different from sentence (11a). Once *the indian and the cowboy* has been read, the sentence can continue as it does, but it could also have continued in a structurally different way. The alternative structure takes the string *the indian and the cowboy* together as one complex noun phrase in the role of the direct object of the verb *see*. Sentence (12) is an example of this alternative structure:

(12)   The sheriff saw the indian and the cowboy after lunch time.

In other words, up until reading *cowboy* the sentence is syntactically ambiguous, in that the final structure among the alternative options cannot yet be determined. In the absence of information that unambiguously determines the structure (i.e. the verb following the noun *cowboy*), one alternative is preferred or more highly activated. This preference is presumably determined by either syntactic simplicity (go for the simplest structure; Frazier 1987) or the frequency of the different possible syntactic structures

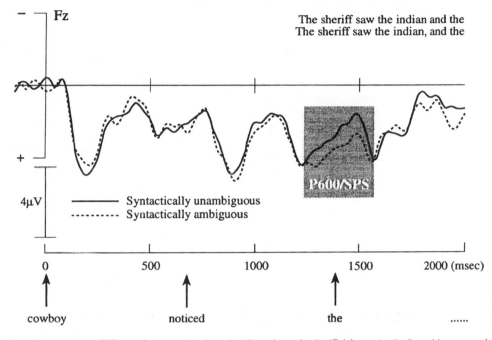

The sheriff saw the indian and the
The sheriff saw the indian, and the

Syntactically unambiguous
Syntactically ambiguous

0   500   1000   1500   2000 (msec)

cowboy   noticed   the   ......

Fig. 9.4 Averaged ERP waveform over the frontal midline electrode site (Fz) for syntactically ambiguous and unambiguous sentences. Sentences were presented visually, word by word with an interval (SOA) of 686 ms. In the ambiguous condition (dashed line), the sentences were initially syntactically ambiguous (see text). At the point of disambiguation (at 686 ms in the figure) the sentence continued with a grammatically correct but non-preferred reading. In the unambiguous control condition (solid line), the same sentence was presented with the addition of a comma, dictating that only the non-preferred reading was possible. In the figure the disambiguating word is preceded and followed by one word.

(go for the most frequent structure; Mitchell 1994; Mitchell *et al.* 1995). In both cases the conjoined-NP structure is preferred over the sentence-conjunction. If this preference exists, one should find a processing cost at the following verb which indicates that a conjoined-NP analysis can no longer be maintained and that the sentence-conjunction analysis is the right one instead. Figure 9.4 shows that indeed a P600/SPS is obtained to the verb *noticed* in the syntactically ambiguous sentence (11a) compared to its unambiguous counterpart (11b). Similar P600/SPS effects of syntactic ambiguity have been reported for English (Osterhout *et al.* 1994) and German (Friederici *et al.* 1996).

The presence of P600/SPS effects to subtle but pervasive phenomena like structural indeterminacy and structural preference has been used to address some of the central issues in the parsing literature. One such issue is whether non-syntactic sources of information immediately contribute to structure-building operations. One of these sources of information is lexical in nature (Trueswell *et al.* 1993). Another possibly relevant source is the discourse context in which sentences are normally embedded (Altmann 1988; Altmann and Steedman 1988; Crain and Steedman 1985; Ni *et al.* 1996).

Whether lexical information guides parsing was investigated in another condition of the Hagoort *et al.* (forthcoming) study. The same structural ambiguities were tested as in (11a,b). This time, however, the semantics of the main verb preceding the two nouns connected by *and* went together with an animate but not with an inanimate object. Nevertheless, if the structural analysis is initially only determined by syntactic cues, the lexical-semantic verb bias should not help. So, the structural preference for a con-joined-NP analysis over a sentence conjunction analysis should also hold in (13a), resulting in a P600/SPS to the main verb of the second clause (*varnishes*). If, in contrast, lexical-semantic information is used immediately during structural analysis when reading the second noun of the coordinate structure, it is immediately clear that this noun (*skipper*) cannot be inserted into a conjoined-NP analysis and thus has to be the subject of a second clause. This predicts that the ERPs for the main verb of the second clause (in italics) are identical in (13a) and (13b).

(13)   a. The helmsman repairs the mainsail and the skipper *varnishes* the mast of
          the battered boat.
       b. The helmsman repairs the mainsail, and the skipper *varnishes* the mast of
          the battered boat.

The ERP results showed no difference between sentences of type (13a) and (13b), indicating that semantic constraints are used immediately and in parallel with syntactic constraints during the assignment of a constituent structure to an incoming string of words.

In another experiment that addressed the influence of lexical information on par-sing, Osterhout *et al.* (1994) had subjects read sentences of the following type (the critical word for the ERP comparisons is in italics):

(14)   a. The doctor hoped the patient *was* lying.
          (pure intransitive verb)
       b. * The doctor forced the patient *was* lying.
          (pure transitive verb)
       c. The doctor believed the patient *was* lying.
          (intransitively biased verb)
       d. The doctor charged the patient *was* lying.
          (transitively biased verb)

These sentences can be distinguished in terms of the lemma information associated with the main verb in each sentence. In this case the specific lemma information concerns the subcategorization properties of the verbs. For sentences (14a) and (14b) these properties fully determine the role of the following noun phrase (*the patient*). Specifically, the intransitive verb *hope* in (14a) does not allow a direct object-noun phrase, unambiguously indicating that the noun phrase is the subject of an upcoming clause. The lemma information of the transitive verb *force* in (14b) specifies that it requires a direct object, implying that in this case the same noun phrase must be assigned the direct object role. Sentence (14b) becomes ungrammatical at the auxiliary verb, since the sentence-final phrase *was lying* prohibits the necessary direct object role for the preceding noun phrase.

The verbs in (14c) and (14d) can be used both with and without a direct object. This introduces temporary syntactic ambiguity upon encountering the following noun phrase, since *the patient* might be acting as the direct object of the verb, or as the subject of a forthcoming clause. However, although both *believe* and *charge* can be used transitively and intransitively, one is more often used intransitively (*believe*), the other more often transitively (*charge*). This induces different lexically specified sub-categorization preferences for these two verbs.

The question is whether these lexical preferences rapidly influence the assignment of structure to the sentence. According to so-called depth-first serial parsing models (Frazier 1987; Frazier and Rayner 1982), in the first instance the simplest structure is always assigned in case of ambiguity. Since the direct object analysis is syntactically simpler than the subject-of-a-clause analysis, there should be an initial preference for the first structure independent of the lexically specified preferences associated with the particular verbs. Alternatively, constraint-based parsing models predict that these lexically-specified preferences immediately influence the syntactic analysis (Trueswell *et al.* 1993). Given the different verbal preferences, this model predicts that the subject role will be correctly assigned to the noun phrase in (14c) since the verb *believe* 'prefers' to be used without a direct object. In (14d) initially the same noun phrase will be erroneously assigned the direct object role, since the verb *charge* 'prefers' to be used transitively, that is with a direct object. This should show up as a parsing problem at the auxiliary verb in sentences like (14d).

In summary, a depth-first parser predicts syntactic anomaly/preference effects at the auxiliary verb in sentences like (14b), (14c), and (14d). A constraint-based parser predicts such effects only in sentences like (14b) and (14d).

Osterhout *et al.* (1994) presented these types of sentences (for details see Osterhout *et al.* 1994), and compared the ERP waveforms to the auxiliary verb (*was*) in each sentence type. Figure 9.5 summarizes the results. As expected, the syntactic violation in (14b) elicited a large P600/SPS, that was maximal over parietal sites. More important-ly, auxiliary verbs that followed transitively biased verbs (14d) also elicited a P600/SPS, although with a smaller amplitude than for the outright violation. ERPs for auxiliary verbs in sentences with an obligatorily intransitive verb (14a) and sentences containing a verb with an intransitive bias (14c) did not differ from each other and did not elicit a P600/SPS.

As in the Hagoort *et al.* study (forthcoming), these data show that lexical preferences can immediately guide the structural analysis of a sentence. Recently, P600/SPS effects have been observed in a study investigating whether discourse information had an immediate effect on the structural analysis of a following sentence (Van Berkum *et al.* 1999). The pattern of effects indicated that discourse information also immediately co-determines the structural analysis, at least in cases where more than one structure (i.e. a relative clause vs. a complement clause) could be legally assigned.

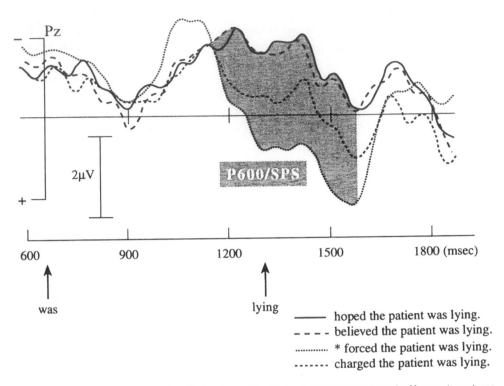

Fig. 9.5   Averaged ERP waveforms from Pz (parietal midline) to the final three words in each of four sentence types (see text): intransitive (solid line), transitive (dotted line), intransitively biased (medium-dash line), and transitively biased (small-dash line). The critical auxiliary verb starts at 0 ms on the time axis as marked by the arrow. Sentences were presented visually and word by word, with an interval (SOA) of 650 ms. (Adapted from Osterhout *et al.* (1994). Copyright © 1994 American Psychological Association, reprinted by permission.)

Importantly, the influence of non-syntactic cues might be restricted to a situation of syntactic indeterminacy, such as when the input allows more than one syntactic analysis. If no alternative analysis is possible, the P600/SPS to a syntactic violation is found not to be affected by an additional semantic violation (Hagoort and Brown 1997). This suggests that when the syntactic analysis is fully determined by the lemma input, syntactic processing is relatively independent of non-syntactic cues.

9.3.1.3   Topographical aspects of the P600/SPS

An important, but often complex aspect of ERP data is the similarity or dissimilarity across experiments in the topographical distribution of the scalp-recorded potentials (cf. Kutas 1997). Especially for the longer latency components related to higher cognitive functions, it is most likely that a distributed ensemble of neural generators is contributing to the recorded surface potentials. That is, a particular language-relevant ERP effect (e.g. an N400 or a P600/SPS effect) is almost certainly based on the concerted action of a number of brain areas. Some of these areas subserve the core aspects of a cognitive function, others might be related to the input channel (auditory, visual) that triggers a cognitive function (e.g. parsing). This often complicates the functional interpretation of topographical differences. Answering the question when a topographical difference is central (i.e. different processing components involved) or peripheral (e.g. resulting from the attentional modulation of core processes) with respect to the core aspects of a cognitive function is far from trivial. This also holds for the P600/SPS effects.

Although syntactic violations and syntactic preferences both elicit a positive shift within about the same latency range, there are nevertheless clear topographical differences between these two cases, and sometimes even between different types of ambiguity. Generally speaking, the P600/SPS to syntactic violations shows a posterior maximum, whereas the syntactic preference effects are more equally or more frontally distributed. Furthermore, it has been reported that for syntactic violations the initial phase (500–750 ms) of the P600/SPS has a fairly equal scalp distribution, whereas the second phase (750–1000 ms) shows a clear parietal maximum (Hagoort and Brown, in press). It thus could be that the P600/SPS is not one effect but a family of effects, with the (additional) contribution of different generators in the early and late phase of the effect, related to functionally different states of the parser. A tentative hypothesis is that the processing costs associated with overwriting the preferred or most activated structure results in a more frontally distributed P600/SPS, whereas a structural collapse as in outright syntactic violations results in a more posterior P600/SPS.

Recently, a few studies have claimed that the P600/SPS belongs to the family of classical P300 effects (Coulson *et al.* 1998; Gunter *et al.* 1997; Münte *et al.* 1998). This claim is based on the finding that the amplitude of the P600/SPS is sensitive to the probability of a syntactic violation. The less probable such a violation, the larger the amplitude of the P600/SPS. However, the crucial aspect for answering the question of whether the P600/SPS is a member of the P300 family is not whether probability has an effect on the amplitude of the positive shift. It is unlikely that only one brain response is sensitive to probability, and hence it does not follow that just because the P300 is probability-sensitive, any ERP effect that shows a similar sensitivity to probability is therefore a P300. Secondly, since the ERP waveform is often a composite of more than one underlying process, the increase of the positive shift to a syntactic violation as a function of the probability of such a violation does not necessarily imply that the probability effect can be ascribed to the same underlying neural generators as the syntactic violation effect. This, for instance, would be difficult to argue for if the effects of violation and probability were additive. According to Helmholz' superposition rule, if the scalp-recorded ERP effects of syntactic violations and of probability differences are additive, one is entitled to assume that the generators of the violation effect and the generators of the probability effect are non-overlapping. Osterhout *et al.* (1996) showed that the syntactic violation effect and the probability effect are additive, indicating that the generators of the syntactic violation effect are most likely not the standard P300 generators. Finally, as we have discussed above, in interesting cases of syntactic processing the distribution of the P600/SPS is very different from the posteriorly distributed classical P3b component. So far convincing evidence for the claim that the P600/SPS is generated by the classical P300 generators is lacking (for a more extensive discussion, see Osterhout and Hagoort 1999).

However, more importantly, unless one wants to make claims about the language-specificity of the P600/SPS (a claim that, at present, cannot be made for any of the language-relevant ERP components), not much hinges on the outcome of the P600/SPS versus P300 debate. As holds for the other language-relevant ERP effects, how directly or indirectly they are related to the actual processors that operate on the input is unknown (Rugg and Coles 1995). But this does not limit the value of ERPs for the study of the neurocognitive machinery underlying language functions. As long as under conditions of linguistic input different ERP effects can be shown to supervene on the processing of different types of linguistic information (e.g. phonological, syntactic, conceptual/semantic), these effects can be exploited to study the segregation and interaction of the different knowledge types, and to make inferences about the similarity versus dissimilarity of the concomitant brain states.

9.3.2 The implications of ERP effects for the neural architecture of parsing

Inferences about the neural basis of cognitive processing from scalp-recorded surface potentials are complicated by a number of issues (for an in-depth discussion, see Kutas *et al.*, Chapter 12 this volume; Rugg, Chapter 2 this volume; Rugg and Coles 1995). A first complication is the impossibility to uniquely determine the location of the neural generators responsible for the surface potentials on the basis of only the information of the surface recordings. This so-called inverse problem severely restricts the localization value of ERPs in the absence of independent neurophysiological constraints on the brain areas that might be involved in generating the language-relevant ERP effects.

A second complication is that we do not know whether the cognitive processes that we are interested in are directly or only indirectly reflected in the ERP effects. This complication has its parallel in PET and fMRI where it is often unknown whether an area with an increased haemodynamic response is the source of the cognitive operation or the site where it has its effect. With respect to ERPs, with their millisecond time-course resolution, we face the problem that if the scalp-recorded potential is only indirectly related to the cognitive operation under investigation, the time course of the ERP is displaced in time relative to the time course of the cognitive operation by an unknown amount. This implies that the latency of an ERP effect reflects the upper bound on the estimation of the time course of a cognitive operation (Rugg and Coles 1995). The time of the cognitive operation might have preceded the moment where it started to manifest itself in its ERP index.

Related to this second complication is that it is unclear and unlikely that the language-relevant ERP effects that we discussed are also language-specific. That is, presumably other domains of cognitive processing also drive all or a subset of the neural generators that elicit the language-relevant scalp-recorded potentials. For instance, structural violations in music also seem to elicit P600/SPS effects (Patel *et al.* 1998), and semantic violations in the form of pictures elicit N400 effects that are not unlike the N400 effects with linguistic input (Ganis *et al.* 1996). However, again this does not limit the usefulness of ERPs, provided that the right experimental controls are carried out. What is important is that under conditions of language input the behaviour of the different ERPs can be causally linked to the different constituting elements of the neurocognitive machinery for language.

With these provisos in mind, can we nevertheless claim anything of interest about the neural basis of syntactic computations? The answer is yes, under the reasonable assumption that the generators of the language-relevant scalp-recorded potentials supervene on the spatiotemporal aspects of the neural machinery that subserves language processing. This implies that if two states of the neural machinery for language are identical, they cannot give rise to ERP effects that are qualitatively distinct (i.e. different in polarity or topography), provided that the experimental design controls for the contribution of non-language variables such as, for instance, attention. Finding qualitatively distinct ERP effects can thus be seen as an indication of the processing and/or representational uniqueness of the underlying component of the neurocognitive machinery.

The observation that qualitatively distinct ERP effects are elicited (directly or indirectly) by semantic integration processes and syntactic structure building operations thus suggests that these aspects of language processing have a non-identical spatiotemporal neural profile. This difference favours a view in which semantic and syntactic processes have processing and/or representational uniqueness relative to each other. The neural basis of syntactic computations can therefore not be collapsed into a general-purpose language processor that operates only on the co-occurrence frequencies of the word input, or in which semantic and syntactic factors do not result in clearly different states in the processing/representational landscape (cf. Tabor and Tanenhaus 1998). The claim for the uniqueness of semantic and syntactic processes and/or representations is further supported by the finding that in severely agrammatic aphasics a dissociation between P600/SPS and N400 effects can be obtained. That is, under certain syntactic violation conditions, the P600/SPS disappears but the N400 effects remain (Wassenaar *et al.* 1997).

In conclusion, although the inverse problem prevents strong claims about the location of the generator ensembles of language-relevant ERP componentry, nevertheless the nature and the differential sensitivity of this componentry places constraints on the neural organization of language functions. On the basis of the ERP data one can best characterize this organization as a dynamic coalition of multiple areas of relative specialization. The boundary conditions of the current ERP evidence thus favour independent but partially interactive semantic and syntactic processors. In contrast to single-processor models of sentence processing, the ERP evidence predicts that networks for syntactic and semantic processing are at least partially segregated in the brain.

With respect to the functional organization of sentence processing, the ERP evidence suggests that the syntactic processor (parser) is influenced by lexical-semantic and pragmatic information most clearly when the lemma input and the syntactic

constraints leave room for structural indeterminacy. If, however, the syntactic information allows only one structure to be assigned, semantic influences on parsing are
limited or absent (Hagoort and Brown 1997; for supportive evidence from reaction-
time research, see O'Seaghdha 1997).

9.4 Brain areas and syntax: evidence from lesions and PET/fMRI

Although ERP evidence provides some insights in the fractionation of the neural
machinery for language, for more precise assignments of syntactic functions to brain
structure we have to turn to other methods. Evidence on the brain areas involved in
syntactic processing comes from two sources. These are lesion studies and brain-
imaging studies. Ideally these two sources of evidence should allow us to determine the
areas that are necessary (lesion data) and sufficient (brain-imaging data) for grammatical encoding operations during speaking and parsing operations during language
comprehension. However, as we shall see, the picture that emerges from this literature
is not yet clear. A number of different factors might be responsible for the inconsistencies in the results of lesion and brain-imaging studies. Among these factors are
(i) the use of designs that insufficiently single out syntactic operations from other
sentence-level processes, or from task-related cognitive operations; (ii) the failure to
distinguish between grammatical encoding (cf. Levelt, Chapter 4 this volume) and
syntactic parsing (cf. Cutler and Clifton, Chapter 5 this volume; Perfetti, Chapter 6
this volume), which might operate under quite distinct processing requirements;
(iii) interindividual variability (both anatomical and functional) which might be substantially larger for abstract linguistic operations than for sensory and motor functions
(Bavelier *et al.* 1997; Caplan 1987).

   In this section we will first summarize the results from lesion studies, followed by an
overview of the current PET/fMRI data. We will then come back to the claims that can
be made on the basis of the available evidence.

9.4.1 Lesion studies

The classical Wernicke–Lichtheim neural model of language and its revival by
Geschwind (1965) focused completely on the processing of words. It was not until the
beginning of the seventies that the sentence came back on stage as a central unit of
analysis (for the historical roots of a reorientation from word aphasiology to sentence
aphasiology in the beginning of this century, see De Bleser 1987). It is in this period that
left-anterior brain damage, in particular Broca's area, became associated with syntactic impairments in all language modalities. Broca's area is usually taken to
encompass Brodmann areas 44 and 45 (see Uylings *et al.*, Chapter 10 this volume).
Although classically Broca's aphasia was seen as mainly affecting speech output,
studies carried out in the seventies have shown that Broca's aphasics are not only
impaired in syntactic encoding, but also in exploiting syntactic information during
sentence interpretation (Caramazza and Zurif 1976; Heilman and Scholes 1976; Von
Stockert and Bader 1976; Zurif *et al.* 1972). On the basis of these studies, Broca's area

came to be seen as crucially involved in both grammatical encoding and parsing operations. Modality-independent grammatical knowledge was thought to be represented in this area (Zurif 1998). However, since then the pivotal role of Broca's area in syntactic processing has faced a number of serious problems. Studies that correlated aphasic syndromes with site of lesion led to the conclusion that the relation between Broca's area and Broca's aphasia is not as straightforward as once believed, for a number of reasons.

First, lesions restricted to Broca's area often do not seem to result in lasting aphasic (including agrammatic) symptoms (Mohr *et al.* 1978). According to Mohr *et al.*, involvement of adjacent frontal-opercular areas, the parietal operculum, and the insula are also required for a long-lasting Broca syndrome.

Secondly, large-scale correlational studies found a substantial number of exceptions to the general rule that left frontal lesions go together with Broca's aphasia (Basso *et al.* 1985; Willmes and Poeck 1993). Basso *et al.* (1985) correlated cortical lesions as revealed by CT scans with aphasiological symptomatology for a group of 207 patients. They reported a substantial number of exceptions (17 per cent) to the classical associations between lesion site and aphasia syndromes. Among these exceptions were patients with lesions restricted to left-anterior areas, but with a fluent aphasia of the Wernicke type (seven cases), as well as non-fluent Broca's aphasics with posterior lesions and sparing of Broca's area (six cases). Willmes and Poeck (1993) investigated the CT lesion localization for a group of 221 aphasic patients with a vascular lesion in the territory of the middle cerebral artery. Their results were even more dramatic. The conditional probability of an anterior lesion given a Broca's aphasia was not higher than 59 per cent, whereas the probability that an anterior lesion resulted in a Broca's aphasia was only 35 per cent.

Thirdly, impairments in syntactic processing have also been reported in Wernicke's aphasics with posterior lesions (e.g. Heeschen 1985), indicating that other areas might be crucial for syntax as well.

Fourthly, cases have been reported of patients in which an impairment in grammatical encoding was observed without a concomitant impairment in parsing (Kolk *et al.* 1985; Miceli *et al.* 1983; Nespoulous *et al.* 1992). These findings suggest that brain areas involved in grammatical encoding might not necessarily be the same as the ones involved in parsing.

In addition, more recent studies indicate that the syntactic deficit in Broca's aphasics is probably more limited than was believed in the seventies. Many agrammatic patients with Broca's aphasia show a relatively high sensitivity to syntactic structure in tasks such as judging the grammaticality of sentences (Linebarger *et al.* 1983). With respect to their language output, recent analyses indicate that the telegraphic style of agrammatic aphasics follows the syntactic regularities of elliptic utterances, and therefore shows syntactic competence at least to some degree (Kolk and Heeschen 1992).

In summary, the view that a central syntactic deficit is the distinguishing feature of Broca's aphasia and that Broca's area therefore is a crucial area for grammatical encoding and parsing is difficult to maintain in the light of more recent neurolinguistic studies and lesion studies correlating Broca's aphasia with the concomitant lesion sites.

However, there are good reasons to consider all this evidence as not really decisive with respect to the role of Broca's area in syntactic processing. One major reason is that the characterization of the language disorder in lesion studies usually is based on clinical impressions (Mohr *et al.* 1978) or clinical aphasia test batteries (Basso *et al.* 1985; Willmes and Poeck 1993), which are often insufficient to determine the degree and specificity of the syntactic impairment. The classification of aphasic patients in terms of a limited set of syndromes is insufficient guarantee that core language operations are singled out according to articulated cognitive architectures for speaking, listening, or reading (cf. Shallice 1988). Willmes and Poeck (1993, pp. 1538–39) therefore rightly conclude that

> '. . . localization studies along the traditional lines will not yield results that lend themselves to a meaningful interpretation of impaired psychological processes such as aphasia. Small-scale in-depth studies lend themselves better to characterizing the functional impairment in an information-processing model.'

In recent years a small number of such in-depth studies have appeared (Caplan *et al.* 1985, 1996; Dronkers *et al.* 1998; Vanier and Caplan 1990). In these studies, aphasic patients were selected on the basis of specific tests of their syntactic abilities. In both Caplan *et al.* (1985) and Caplan *et al.* (1996) patients were tested on a series of sentence types that required them to process a range of syntactic structures. These studies showed that the task performance for the different sentence types did not differ between patients with anterior (Broca's area) and patients with posterior lesions. The size of the lesion within the perisylvian area also did not correlate with the syntactic task performance. The lesion analysis of 20 agrammatic aphasics in Vanier and Caplan (1990) suggests that this conclusion not only holds for sentence comprehension but also for sentence production. Caplan *et al.* (1996) give two possible explanations for these results. One possibility is that syntactic processing is fairly strictly localized, but the exact site can vary quite substantially between individuals within the borders of the left perisylvian area including the insula (Caplan 1987; Vanier and Caplan 1990). The other possibility is that the syntactic machinery is organized as a distributed neural network in which several regions of the left perisylvian cortex are critically involved.

In contrast to the lesion studies by Caplan and colleagues, Dronkers *et al.* (1998) recently reported a fairly focused common area of lesion in aphasic patients with syntactic impairments in parsing. Dronkers *et al.* reconstructed and compared the area of full lesion overlap in nine patients with syntactic impairments in comprehension with a group of 12 patients who were aphasic but without syntactic comprehension problems. A straightforward relation between structure and function requires, in their view, that all patients with a specific deficit share one or more lesions sites, and, crucially, all patients without this deficit are not lesioned in the identified sites (Dronkers *et al.* 1998). Following this criterion, they identified the anterior portion of

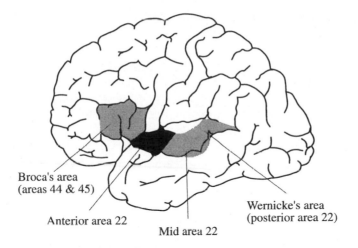

Fig. 9.6 Area of 100 per cent lesion overlap (in black) in aphasic patients with a morphosyntactic processing deficit. The data are from the Dronkers *et al.* study (see text). The numbers indicate Brodmann areas.

the superior-temporal gyrus as the only area meeting their stringent criteria for assignment of function to structure (see Fig. 9.6). This area lies anterior to the primary auditory cortex, and posterior to the temporal pole. It comprises part of Brodmann area 22.

The anterior-temporal area is not classically associated with syntactic functions. The authors hypothesize that especially the reciprocal connections of this temporal lobe area to areas relevant for memory in parahippocampal, perirhinal, and hippocampal regions might explain its role in supporting 'specialized aspects of memory dedicated to linguistic structure' (p. 29). The classical Broca's area was found to be lesioned in eight of the nine patients with syntactic impairments, but also in three of the twelve patients without syntactic problems.

Although not directly isolating syntactic functions, data from a PET study (Mazoyer *et al.* 1993) and a 4 Tesla fMRI study on sentence processing (Bavelier *et al.* 1997) are compatible with the syntactic involvement of the anterior parts of the superior-temporal gyrus, although in these studies the temporal pole was clearly part of the activated area as well.

The findings in the Dronkers *et al.* study are clearly suggestive for a role of the left-anterior superior-temporal gyrus in the neural circuitry for parsing. Despite its absence in the list of classical language areas, future brain-imaging research might be able to confirm the role of this area in syntactic processing. At the same time, it is unlikely that this area is the only one with a syntactic function. The stringency of the criteria that were used in the Dronkers *et al.* study almost certainly led to an underestimation of the number of areas involved in syntactic processing. Moreover, a closer inspection of the patients' impairment profiles suggests that one cannot exclude the possibility that the impairments in the patients with the anterior-temporal lesions were not solely related to syntactic processing, but implicated other sentence-level processes as well. The precise contribution of this area to syntactic processing is, therefore, yet to be determined.

Lesion data are also available on syntactic processing at the single-word level. This concerns lemma retrieval, more in particular the access to grammatical word-class information. Especially Caramazza and colleagues (Caramazza and Hillis 1991; Hillis and Caramazza 1995; Rapp and Caramazza 1997) have made some interesting claims on the basis of dissociation patterns in neuropsychological patients with lesions in the left perisylvian cortex. On the basis of a few single-case studies, these authors have claimed that grammatical word-class information is linked to word-form information, and thus independently represented for orthographic and phonological word-form representations. They reported a patient with a parietal lesion who had a specific impairment in the oral reading of verbs, a patient with a frontotemporal lesion and a specific impairment in the written production of verbs (Caramazza and Hillis 1991), and a patient with left frontal and temporoparietal strokes who made far more errors on nouns than verbs in speech, but showed the opposite pattern in reading (Hillis and Caramazza 1995). These data led them to believe that orthographic and phonological form-level representations are organized by grammatical category, and that separate brain structures subserve the processing of verbs and nouns. The multimodal, form-related representation of grammatical word-class is usually not assumed by psycho-linguistic models on language production and language comprehension (see Chapters 4, 5, and 6 of this volume). Moreover, the number of cases are too few, and the reported lesions not focal enough to make any substantial claims about the brain areas involved.

The distinction between the processing of nouns and verbs, however, is supported by other neuropsychological evidence. One source of evidence comes from the general observation that fluent aphasic patients who tend to have more posterior (temporal) lesions usually have more difficulty naming nouns than verbs. Non-fluent Broca's aphasics who more often have a frontal lesion, show a stronger tendency for naming difficulties in verbs than nouns (Miceli *et al.* 1988). Damasio and Tranel (1993) propose on the basis of a number of cases they studied, that the processing of nouns is subserved by left anterior and middle temporal regions, whereas left frontal regions are crucially involved in the processing of verbs. Minimally, these results lend support to the claim that neural representations for specific types of lemma information are differentially distributed within the left perisylvian cortex.

9.4.2 Haemodynamic studies

PET and fMRI studies on language have mainly focused on single-word processing. Only a very limited number of brain-imaging studies investigated sentence-level processes. Most of these studies looked at the activation patterns associated with sentence comprehension (Bavelier *et al.* 1997; Caplan *et al.,* 1998; Just *et al.* 1996*b*; Mazoyer *et al.* 1993; Nichelli *et al.* 1995; Stowe *et al.* 1994; Stromswold *et al.* 1996). Only one study (Indefrey *et al.* 1996) contained a sentence production component. Only one study presented the sentence materials auditorily (Mazoyer *et al.* 1993). In all other studies, subjects were given written input. In several of the studies it is difficult to disentangle activations due to syntactic processes from those related to sentence-level semantics and phonology. In some studies this is not possible at all, since the designs of these studies did not aim at isolating syntactic operations from other sentence-level processes (Bavelier *et al.* 1997; Mazoyer *et al.* 1993). However, inasmuch as anything can be said on the basis of these studies about areas that are crucial for parsing, the left inferior-frontal gyrus including Broca's area is reported in five studies (see Fig. 9.7). In contrast to what the lesion data seem to suggest, on the whole the recent brain-imaging data are not incompatible with the classical picture of Broca's area involvement in syntactic processing.

Four studies manipulated the syntactic complexity of the presented sentence materials (Caplan *et al.* 1998; Just *et al.* 1996; Stowe *et al.* 1994; Stromswold *et al.* 1996). Stowe *et al.* had subjects read sentences that were presented word by word. Three types of sentences were used: (i) long, syntactically complex sentences; (ii) short sentences that were syntactically ambiguous; (iii) short, unambiguous sentences. The subjects were instructed to read the sentences carefully and be prepared to answer questions about the sentences at the end of the scanning session. The regional cerebral blood flow (rCBF) in these sentence conditions was compared with the rCBF in a resting condition in which subjects looked at an empty screen. Having a resting condition as the control state is now known to be far from optimal, since the resting condition itself elicits a complex pattern of activations and deactivations that might affect the results of the subtraction (cf. Shulman *et al.* 1997). For the syntactically

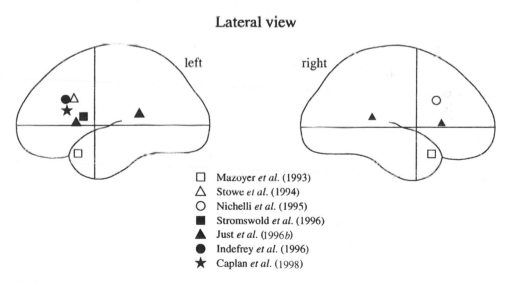

Lateral view

□ Mazoyer *et al.* (1993)
△ Stowe *et al.* (1994)
○ Nichelli *et al.* (1995)
■ Stromswold *et al.* (1996)
▲ Just *et al.* (1996*b*)
● Indefrey *et al.* (1996)
★ Caplan *et al.* (1998)

Fig. 9.7 A summary of brain activations reported in PET/fMRI studies on syntactic processing. The reported areas of syntax-related activations are projected onto a left and right lateral view of the brain. (Data of Bavelier *et al.* (1997) are not included because of individual subject variation.) (Adapted from Hagoort and Indefrey (1997). Copyright © 1997 Bohn, Stafleu, van Loghum, reprinted by permission.)

complex sentences and for the ambiguous sentences the authors report a number of activations, including Broca's area on the border of the Brodmann areas (BA) 44 and 45. Activation in Broca's area was also seen in a direct comparison between ambiguous and unambiguous sentences. The authors select this area among other areas of increased rCBF as the one that is most directly related to syntactic processing. Their argument is that the activation in Broca's area fits best with the results of the classical lesion literature on syntax-relevant areas. There clearly is some circularity involved in this line of reasoning, and, as we have seen, the lesion data are not at all conclusive about the role of Brocas area.

Stromswold *et al.* (1996) contrasted sentences that were comparable in terms of their propositional content, but differed in syntactic complexity (e.g. *The child spilled the juice that stained the rug* versus *The juice that the child spilled stained the rug*). Half of these sentences contained a semantic anomaly. The task of the subjects was to judge the acceptability of the sentences. A direct comparison between the structurally complex and the less complex sentences resulted in activation of Broca's area, more in particular the pars opercularis.

Caplan *et al.* (1998) repeated part of the design of the Stromswold *et al.* (1998) study, using the same sentence materials. In the repeated experiment, increased activation was again observed for the centre-embedded sentences in Broca's area, more specifically in the rostral part of the pars opercularis (BA 44). Additionally, medial-frontal activations were observed in the anterior cingulate gyrus and the immediately superior medial-frontal gyrus. Although the exact same comparison for the identical sentences as in the Stromswold *et al.* study resulted in activation in the pars opercularis, the exact location of the rCBF increase was not identical to the Stromswold *et al.* study, but was higher and more anterior than in this earlier study. Factors related to subject variation between studies might account for this regional activation difference within Broca's area.

A variation in syntactic complexity was also used in the fMRI study by Just *et al.* (1996b). In one condition subjects read simple active sentences (e.g. *The reporter attacked the senator and admitted the error*), in a second condition they read sentences in which the subjects of the matrix clause and the subordinate clause were identical (e.g. *The reporter that attacked the senator admitted the error*). Finally the condition with the most complex sentences consisted of a matrix and a subordinate clause that had different grammatical subjects (*The reporter that the senator attacked admitted the error*). These sentence were presented together with a probe question (e.g. *The reporter attacked the senator, true or false?*) that the subjects had to answer via a push-button response. The authors found an increasing number of activated voxels in relation to the increase in syntactic complexity in both Broca's and Wernicke's area as well as in their right hemisphere homologues.

In contrast to the previous three studies, Nichelli *et al.* (1995) did not manipulate the syntactic complexity of their materials, but varied the task. In all conditions subject read the same story, that was presented visually, word by word. In the syntactic condition, subjects had to perform a syntactic error-detection task by indicating when an occasional syntactic error had occurred. In the control condition, they had to detect words that were written in a different font. The syntactic error-detection task resulted in activation of the right inferior-frontal gyrus, the cingulate gyrus, and the left pre-central gyrus.

Mazoyer *et al.* (1993) compared three conditions that had a syntactic component with two conditions that did not. These latter two conditions were a list of words and a story in Tamil, a language unknown to the French monolingual speakers in this study. Listening to a story in French, to a series of sentences consisting of pseudowords, and to semantically anomalous sentences all had in common the presence of a syntactic structure detectable for the French subjects. Subjects were required to listen attentively to the speech stimuli. Bilateral temporal pole activation was the prime candidate for being involved in syntactic processing, although the authors admit that other sentence-level processes could also be responsible for this temporal pole activation.

Bavelier *et al.* (1997) performed an fMRI study at 4 tesla while subjects read sentences in a word by word presentation, where a word followed the presentation of the previous word after a delay of 600 ms. The activations due to sentence reading were compared to the activations induced by consonant strings that were presented in the same way as the sentences. After each run, subjects were given a recognition memory task for the presented materials. Although the design of this study does not allow the isolation of syntactic processing, it nevertheless contains a number of relevant results. Overall, activations were distributed throughout the left perisylvian cortex, including classical language areas (Broca's area, Wernicke's area, angular gyrus, supramarginal gyrus), but also left prefrontal areas and the left anterior-temporal lobe. At the individual subject level these activations were in several small, local, and distributed patches of cortex. Moreover, the precise pattern of activation varied quite substantially between individuals. For instance while Broca's area was activated in every subject, the precise localization of the activation with respect to the main sulci of Broca's area varied significantly between subjects. Similar between-subject variation in the distribution of language-relevant patches of cortex has been reported in electrical stimulation studies (e.g. Ojemann 1991). Bavelier *et al.* report that for a non-language visual stimulation task the activated areas were much less patchy, containing more significantly activated contiguous voxels than the activations related to sentence reading. If the patchy pattern of activations and the substantial differences between subjects in the sentence reading condition of this study reflect an underlying difference between the neural organization of language and the neural organization of sensory processing, this might well, at least in part, explain the lack of consistency in lesion and brain-imaging studies on higher sentence-level processing.

To date, the only study that had a grammatical encoding component next to a parsing component in its design is Indefrey *et al.* (1996; 1998). These authors required subjects to read sentences consisting of pseudowords and function words in German (e.g. (*Der Fauper*) (*der*) (*die Lüspeln*) (*febbt*) (*tecken*) (*das Baktor*)). Some of these sentences contained a syntactic error (i.e. *tecken*, which does not agree in number with its preceding subject *Fauper*). In one condition, subjects had to detect this error (parsing) and to produce the sentence in its correct syntactic form (*Der Fauper, der die Lüspeln febbt, teckt das Baktor*). This latter part requires grammatical encoding. In a second condition, subjects only judged the grammaticality of the input string while reading out the string as it was presented. A third condition required them to give phonological acceptability judgements for strings consisting of the same pseudowords and function words as before, but this time without syntactic structure and with an occasional element that violated the phonotactic constraints of German. All these conditions were compared with a control condition in which subjects had to read out unstructured strings of pseudowords and function words. All syntactic conditions resulted in activation of the inferior frontal sulcus between (and partly including) the dorsal part of Broca's area and adjacent parts of the middle frontal gyrus (see Fig. 9.8). Both acceptability judgement tasks (syntactic and phonological) showed activation ventral of Broca's area, in the pars orbitalis of the inferior frontal gyrus and the orbital gyrus, as well as in the right hemisphere homologue of Broca's area. These results suggest that the right hemisphere activation also found in some other studies (Just *et al.* 1996*b*; Nichelli *et al.* 1995) might be due to the error detection component. The common syntactic processing component seems to be subserved more by the left frontal areas.

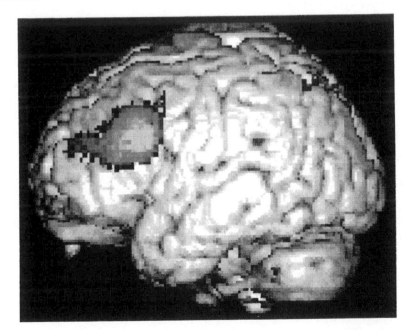

Fig. 9.8   The results of an SPM-conjunction analysis projected onto a left lateral view of the brain, separating the activated areas for syntactic processing from areas active during non-syntactic tasks (i.e. pseudoword pronunciation and phonological acceptability judgement). The area of greatest rCBF difference between syntactic and non-syntactic tasks is shown in yellow. (From Indefrey *et al.* 1998).

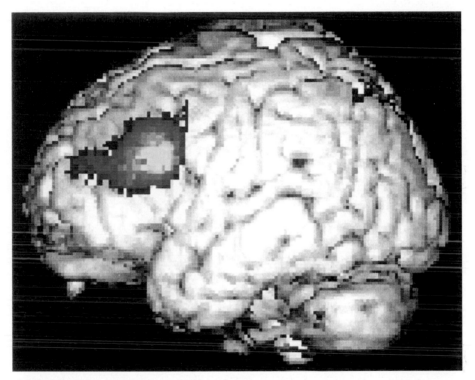

Figure 9.8 The results of an SPM-conjunction analysis projected onto a left lateral view of the brain, separating the activated areas for syntactic processing from areas active during non-syntactic tasks (i.e. pseudoword pronunciation and phonological acceptability judgement). The area of greatest rCBF difference between syntactic and non-syntactic tasks is shown in yellow. (From Indefrey *et al.* 1998).

9.4.3 Conclusion

The combined evidence from lesion studies and haemodynamic studies results in a complicated picture. It is clearly impossible to single out one area that is dedicated to parsing and grammatical encoding operations. As was already discussed in the context of the ERP evidence, it is most likely that both parsing and grammatical encoding are based on the concerted action of a number of different brain areas with their own relative specialization. These relative specializations can be the memory requirements for establishing long-distance structural relations, the retrieval of a verb's argument structure and other lexical–syntactic information, the use of implicit knowledge about the structural constraints in a particular language for grouping words into phrases, etc. All these operations are important ingredients of grammatical encoding and parsing. At the same time, they are clearly quite distinct and therefore are most likely not all subserved by one and the same area. Depending on which of these ingredients is manipulated in a particular study, different areas might be involved.

Some haemodynamic studies (Caplan *et al.* 1998; Just *et al.* 1996*b*; Stromswold *et al.* 1996) manipulated the syntactic complexity. Syntactic complexity effects are probably intimately linked to a memory system that is required for computations on and temporary storage of chunks of syntax-relevant information. Other studies manipulated the presence of syntactic cues. For instance, in the study of Mazoyer *et al.* (1993) listening to syntactically structured input was compared with listening to input that subjects could not interpret syntactically because they lacked the knowledge about the syntactic constraints of the language (Tamil). It is possible that the difference in results between this study and studies manipulating syntactic complexity is due to the fact that they capitalized on different central components of parsing. Similar differences probably contribute to the mixed results of lesion studies.

Altogether, it appears that a series of areas in the left perisylvian cortex contribute to syntactic processing, each with its own relative specialization. What these specializations are is to be determined in studies that single out the relevant syntactic variables.

In addition, there might well be (restricted) individual variation in the organization of the syntactic processing networks in the brain, adding to the complexity of the neural architecture of syntax (cf. Bavelier *et al.* 1997).

9.5 What to conclude and where to go?

The picture emerging from the literature is that syntactic processing is subserved by a network of areas in the left perisylvian cortex, where each area has its own relative specialization. The detailed distribution of these areas presumably varies between individuals to a larger extent than areas involved in sensori-motor functions. Broca's area has been found to be especially sensitive to the processing load involved in syntactic processing. It thus might be a crucial area for keeping the output of structure-building operations in a temporary buffer (working memory). At the same time one has to realize that Broca's area probably consists of a number of morphometrically separate areas (Uylings *et al.*, Chapter 10 this volume). Broca's area might thus be too crude a structure for the right grain size of function to structure mappings.

Temporal cortex, including anterior portions of the superior-temporal gyrus, are presumably involved in morpho-syntactic processing. The retrieval of lemma information such as word class (noun, verb, etc.) supposedly involves left frontal and left temporal regions (Damasio and Tranel 1993; Hillis and Caramazza 1995).

Electrophysiological data collected in the last few years have been most informative with respect to the cognitive architecture of the parser. These data are compatible with a sentence processing model in which processing/representational uniqueness is attributed to syntactic versus other sentence-level processes. In addition, electrophysiological data provide relevant time-course information. ERP evidence suggests that lemma retrieval occurs within 300 ms. Semantic and syntactic integration seems to occur within a time range between 300 and 600 ms, where crosstalk between these processes is possible under certain conditions.

Progress in our understanding of the neural architecture of language is clearly handicapped by the lack of an animal model. Moreover, the individual variation in the organization of the language cortex might be partly responsible for the lack of consistency in the results of lesion and brain-imaging studies. But in addition, the notions of sentence-level processing that were used in lesion and brain-imaging studies have often been too crude to allow real progress in our understanding of the neural architecture. Operational definitions of sentence processing or of syntactic processing have not always been sufficiently informed by psycholinguistic processing models of language. This has sometimes limited the contribution of these studies to our understanding of the neural underpinning of language functions. For instance, in the case of syntactic processing, one has to make at least a distinction between grammatical encoding and parsing, and within each of these further distinctions have to be made between lemma retrieval, morpho-syntactic processing (i.e. the processing of the morphemes specifying the syntactic features, such as tense and number that are required by the syntactic context), the establishment of syntactic relations across word groups (e.g. long-distance dependencies), and the working memory involved in keeping the output of syntactic computations in temporary storage.

However, the good news is that models of language production and comprehension have become detailed enough in the last decade to enable quite specific questions about the neural architecture of syntactic processing. Recent ERP studies have already contributed substantially to our understanding of the processing characteristics of syntactic processing. With the rapid developments in brain-imaging technology, the absence of an animal model for language will be compensated through *in vivo* measurements of brain activity in the most syntactic animal of all. Although a cognitive neuroscience of language is only beginning to see the dawn of light, no doubt our current limited understanding of the neurocognition of language is the prelude to fundamental discoveries in the years to come.

Acknowledgements

We are thankful to the following colleagues for their comments on an earlier version of this chapter: Jos van Berkum, Kay Bock, David Caplan, Peter Indefrey, Gerard Kempen, Don Mitchell, Patrick O'Seaghdha, Mick Rugg, David Wilkins. We are grateful to Nina Dronkers for providing Fig. 9.6.

Notes

1. Interestingly, but for reasons that are not fully clear, a recent study failed to find a P600/SPS to the same agreement violations as in the Hagoort *et al.* (1993) and Hagoort and Brown (1994) studies in sentences consisting of pseudowords (Münte *et al.* 1997).

2. It is often seen as a surprising finding that the latency of the N400 is earlier than the latency of the P600/SPS. This surprise is based on the assumption that in the cognitive architecture of language comprehension the computation of a syntactic structure provides necessary input for the semantic interpretation process. The parser delivers candidate representations for semantic interpretation and for integration with prior discourse and expectations. However, as is argued by Bever *et al.* (1998), this is by no means the only possibility. There are good reasons to claim that semantic analysis takes place before a full syntactic structure is computed. According to Bever *et al.* a correct syntactic structure is assigned only after an initial semantic analysis of the input. Although this is clearly a minority view and although there might be other reasons for the observed latency difference between the N400 and the P600/SPS, the ERP evidence on the latency of 'semantic' and 'syntactic' integration effects is certainly not incompatible with this proposal.

References

Ainsworth-Darnell, K., Shulman, H., and Boland, J. (1998). Dissociating brain responses to syntactic and semantic anomalies: Evidence from event-related potentials. *Journal of Memory and Language*, **38**, 112–30.

Altmann, G. T. M. (1988). Ambiguity, parsing strategies, and computational models. *Language and Cognitive Processes*, **3**, 73–97.

Altmann, G. T. M. and Steedman, M. (1988). Interaction with context during human sentence processing. *Cognition*, **30**, 191–238.

Basso, A., Lecours, A. R., Moraschini, S., and Vanier, M. (1985). Anatomoclinical correlations of the aphasias as defined through computerized tomography: Exceptions. *Brain and Language*, **26**, 201–29.

Bates, E. and Goodman, J. C. (1997). On the inseparability of grammar and the lexicon: Evidence from acquisition, aphasia, and real-time processing. *Language and Cognitive Processes*, **12**, 507–84.

Bates, E., McNew, S., MacWhinney, B., Devescovi, A., and Smith, S. (1982). Functional constraints on sentence processing: A cross-linguistic study. *Cognition*, **11**, 245–99.

Bavelier, D., Corina, D., Jezzard, P., Padmanabhan, S., Clark, V. P., Karni, A. *et al.* (1997). Sentence reading: A functional MRI study at 4 Tesla. *Journal of Cognitive Neuroscience*, **9**, 664–86.

Berkum, J. J. A. van, Brown, C. M., and Hagoort, P. (1999). Early referential context effects in sentence processing: Evidence from event-related brain potentials. *Journal of Memory and Language*, **40**, (in press).

Bever, T. G. (1970). The cognitive basis for linguistic structures. In *Cognition and language development* (ed. J. R. Hayes), pp. 277–360. Wiley, New York.

Bever, T. G., Sanz, M., and Townsend, D. J. (1998). The emperor's psycholinguistics. *Journal of Psycholinguistic Research*, **27**, 261–83.

Bock, K. (1990). Structure in language: Creating form in talk. *American Psychologist*, **45**, 1221–36.

Bock, K. (1995). Sentence production: From mind to mouth. In *Speech, language, and communication* (eds J. Miller and P. Eimas), pp. 181–216. Academic Press, San Diego.

Bock, K. and Levelt, W. J. M. (1994). Language production: Grammatical encoding. In *Handbook of psycholinguistics* (ed. M. A. Gernsbacher), pp. 945–84. Academic Press, San Diego.

Brown, C. M. and Hagoort, P. (1993). The processing nature of the N400: Evidence from masked priming. *Journal of Cognitive Neuroscience*, **5**, 34–44.

Brown, C. M., Hagoort, P., and ter Keurs, M. (1999). Electrophysiological signatures of visual lexical processing. *Journal of Cognitive Neuroscience*. **11** (In press).

Butterworth, B., Campbell, R., and Howard, D. (1986). The uses of short-term memory: A case study. *The Quarterly Journal of Experimental Psychology*, **38A**, 705–37.

Caplan, D. (1987). *Neurolinguistics and linguistic aphasiology: An introduction.* Cambridge University Press.

Caplan, D. and Waters, G. S. (1990). Short-term memory and language comprehension: A critical review of the neuropsycological literature. In *Neuropsychological impairments of short-term memory* (eds G. Vallar and T. Shallice), pp. 337–89. Cambridge University Press.

Caplan, D. and Waters, G. S. (1996). Syntactic processing in sentence comprehension under dual-task conditions in aphasic patients. *Language and Cognitive Processes,* **11**, 525–51.

Caplan, D. and Waters, G. S. (1999). Verbal working memory and sentence processing. *Behavioral and Brain Sciences.* (In press)

Caplan, D., Baker, C., and Dehaut, F. (1985). Syntactic determinants of sentence comprehension in aphasia. *Cognition,* **21**, 117–75.

Caplan, D., Hildebrandt, N., and Makris, N. (1996). Location of lesions in stroke patients with deficits in syntactic processing in sentence comprehension. *Brain,* **119**, 933–49.

Caplan, D., Alpert, N., and Waters, G. S. (1998). Effects of syntactic structure and propositional number on patterns of regional cerebral blood flow. *Journal of Cognitive Neuroscience,* **10**, 541–52.

Caramazza, A. and Hillis, A. E. (1991). Lexical organization of nouns and verbs in the brain. *Nature,* **349**, 788–90.

Caramazza, A. and Zurif, E. B. (1976). Dissociation of algorithmic and heuristic processes in language comprehension: Evidence from aphasia. *Brain and Language,* **3**, 572–82.

Connolly, J. F. and Phillips, N. A. (1994). Event-related potential components reflect phonological and semantic processing of the terminal words of spoken sentences. *Journal of Cognitive Neuroscience,* **6**, 256–66.

Coulson, S., King, J. W., and Kutas, M. (1998). Expect the unexpected: Event-related brain response to morphosyntactic violations. *Language and Cognitive Processes,* **13**, 21–58.

Crain, S. and Steedman, M. (1985). On not being led up the garden path: The use of context by the psychological parser. In *Natural language parsing* (eds D. R. Dowty, L. Karttunen, and A. M. N. Zwicky), pp. 320–58. Cambridge University Press.

Damasio, A. R. and Tranel, D. (1993). Verbs and nouns are retrieved from separate neural systems. *Proceedings of the National Academy of Science,* **90**, 4957–60.

De Bleser, R. (1987). From agrammatism to paragrammatism: German aphasiological traditions and grammatical disturbances. *Cognitive Neuropsychology,* **4**, 187–256.

Dell, G. S. (1986). A spreading-activation theory of retrieval in language production. *Psychological Review,* **93**, 283–321.

Dronkers, N. F., Wilkins, D. P., Van Valin Jr, R. D., Redfern, B. B., and Jaeger, J. J. (1998). Cortical areas underlying the comprehension of grammar. (Manuscript.)

Elman, J. L. (1990). Finding structure in time. *Cognitive Science,* **14**, 179–211.

Fodor, J. D. (1978). Parsing strategies and constraints on transformations. *Linguistic Inquiry,* **9**, 427–73.

Frazier, L. (1987). Sentence processing: A tutorial review. In *Attention and performance XII* (ed. M. Coltheart), pp. 559–85. Erlbaum, London.

Frazier, L. and Clifton, C., Jr (1996). *Construal.* MIT Press, Cambridge, MA.

Frazier, L. and Rayner, K. (1982). Making and correcting errors during sentence comprehension: Eye movements in the analysis of structurally ambiguous sentences. *Cognitive Psychology*, **14**, 178–210.

Friederici, A. D. (1995). The time course of syntactic activation during language processing: A model based on neuropsychological and neurophysiological data. *Brain and Language*, **50**, 259–81.

Friederici, A. D., Pfeifer, E., and Hahne, A. (1993). Event-related brain potentials during natural speech processing: Effects of semantic, morphological and syntactic violations. *Cognitive Brain Research*, **1**, 183–92.

Friederici, A. D., Hahne, A., and Mecklinger, A. (1996). Temporal structure of syntactic parsing: Early and late event-related brain potential effects. *Journal of Experimental Psychology: Learning, Memory, and Cognition*, **22**, 1219–48.

Friederici, A. D., Hahne, A., and von Cramon, D. Y. (1998). First-pass versus second-pass parsing processes in a Wernicke's and a Broca's aphasic: Electrophysiological evidence for a double dissociation. *Brain and Language*, **62**, 311–41.

Ganis, G., Kutas, M., and Sereno, M. I. (1996). The search for 'common sense': An electrophysiological study of the comprehension of words and pictures in reading. *Journal of Cognitive Neuroscience*, **8**, 89–106.

Garnsey, S. M., Tanenhaus, M. K., and Chapman, R. M. (1989). Evoked potentials and the study of sentence comprehension. *Journal of Psycholinguistic Research*, **18**, 51–60.

Garnsey, S. M., Pearlmutter, N. J., Myers, E., and Lotocky, M. A. (1997). The contribution of verb bias and plausibility to the comprehension of temporarily ambiguous verbs. *Journal of Memory and Language*, **37**, 58–93.

Garrett, M. F. (1980). Levels of processing in sentence production. In *Language production*, Vol. 1 (ed. B. Butterworth), pp. 133–77. Academic Press, London.

Geschwind, N. (1965). Disconnection syndromes in animals and man. *Brain*, **88**, 237–94, 585–644.

Gibson, E. (1998). Linguistic complexity: Locality of syntactic dependencies, *Cognition*, **68**, 1–76.

Gunter, T. C., Stowe, L. A., and Mulder, G. M. (1997). When syntax meets semantics. *Psychophysiology*, **34**, 660–76.

Hagoort, P. and Brown, C. M. (1994). Brain responses to lexical ambiguity resolution and parsing. In *Perspectives on sentence processing* (eds C. Clifton Jr, L. Frazier, and K. Rayner), pp. 45–80. Erlbaum, NJ.

Hagoort, P. and Brown, C. M. (1997). When syntax meets semantics: Who is doing what to whom? Poster, *Fourth annual meeting of the Cognitive Neuroscience Society*, Boston.

Hagoort, P. and Brown, C. M. Semantic and syntactic ERP effects of listening to speech compared to reading. *Neuropsychologia*. (In press.)

Hagoort, P. and Indefrey, P. (1997). De neurale architectuur van het menselijk taalvermogen. In *Handboek stem- spraak- taalpathologie*, Vol. 3. (eds H. F. M. Peters *et al.*), pp. 1–36. Bohn, Stafleu, van Loghum, Houten.

Hagoort, P., Brown, C. M., and Groothusen, J. (1993). The syntactic positive shift (SPS) as an ERP measure of syntactic processing. *Language and Cognitive Processes*, **8**, 439–83.

Hagoort, P., Brown, C. M., Vonk, W., and Hoeks, J. Syntactic ambiguity effects in coordination structures: ERP evidence. (Forthcoming.)

Heeschen, C. (1985). Agrammatism versus paragrammatism: A fictitious opposition. In *Agrammatism* (ed. M.-L. Kean), pp. 207–48. Academic Press, San Diego.

Heilman, K. M. and Scholes, R. J. (1976). The nature of comprehension errors in Broca's, conduction and Wernicke's aphasics. *Cortex*, **12**, 258–65.

Hillis, A. E. and Caramazza, A. (1995). Representation of grammatical knowledge in the brain. *Journal of Cognitive Neuroscience*, **7**, 397–407.

Indefrey, P., Hagoort, P., Brown, C. M., Herzog, H., and Seitz, R. J. (1996). Cortical activation induced by syntactic processing: A [15O]-butanol PET study. *NeuroImage*, **3**, S442.

Indefrey, P., Hagoort, P., Brown, C. M., Herzog, H., and Seitz, R. J. (1998). Specific response of the left inferior frontal sulcus to syntactic processing. (Manuscript)

Jackendoff, R. (1997). *The architecture of the language faculty*. MIT Press, Cambridge, MA.

Just, M. A. and Carpenter, P. A. (1992). A capacity theory of comprehension: Individual differences in syntactic processing. *Psychological Review*, **99**, 122–49.

Just, M. A., Carpenter, P. A., and Keller, T. A. (1996*a*). The capacity theory of comprehension: New frontiers of evidence and arguments. *Psychological Review*, **103**, 773–80.

Just, M. A., Carpenter, P. A., Keller, T. A., Eddy, W. F., and Thulborn, K. R. (1996*b*). Brain activation modulated by sentence comprehension. *Science*, **274**, 114–16.

Kempen, G. (1999). Grammatical performance in human sentence production and comprehension. (Manuscript)

King, J. and Just, M. A. (1991). Individual differences in syntactic processing: The role of working memory. *Journal of Memory and Language*, **30**, 580–602.

King, J. W. and Kutas, M. (1995). Who did what and when? Using word- and clause-level ERPs to monitor working memory usage in reading. *Journal of Cognitive Neuroscience*, **7**, 376–95.

King, J. W. and Kutas, M. (1998). Neural plasticity in the dynamics of human visual word recognition. *Neuroscience Letters*, **244**, 1–4.

Kluender, R. and Kutas, M. (1993). Subjacency as a processing phenomenon. *Language and Cognitive Processes*, **8**, 573–633.

Kolk, H. and Heeschen, C. (1992). Agrammatism, paragrammatism and the management of language. *Language and Cognitive Processes*, **7**, 89–129.

Kolk, H. H. J., Grunsven, M. J. F. van, and Keyser, A. (1985). On parallelism between production and comprehension in agrammatism. In *Agrammatism* (ed. M.-L. Kean), pp. 165–206. Academic Press, San Diego.

Kutas, M. (1997). Views on how the electrical activity that the brain generates reflects the functions of different language structures. *Psychophysiology*, **34**, 383–98.

Kutas, M. and Hillyard, S. A. (1980). Reading senseless sentences: Brain potentials reflect semantic anomaly. *Science*, **207**, 203–5.

Kutas, M. and Van Petten, C. K. (1994). Psycholinguistics electrified: Event-related brain potential investigations. In *Handbook of psycholinguistics* (ed. M. A. Gernsbacher), pp. 83–143. Academic Press, San Diego.

Levelt, W. J. M. (1989). *Speaking: From intention to articulation*. MIT Press, Cambridge, MA.

Linebarger, M. C., Schwartz, M. F., and Saffran, E. M. (1983). Sensitivity to grammatical structure in so-called agrammatic aphasics. *Cognition*, **13**, 361–92.

MacDonald, M. C., Pearlmutter, N. J., and Seidenberg, M. S. (1994). Lexical nature of syntactic ambiguity resolution. *Psychological Review*, **101**, 676–703.

Martin, R. C. (1993). Short-term memory and sentence processing: Evidence from neuropsychology. *Memory and Cognition*, **21**, 176–83.

Mazoyer, B. M., Tzourio, N., Frak, V., Syrota, A., Murayama, N., Levrier, O., *et al.* (1993). The cortical representation of speech. *Journal of Cognitive Neuroscience*, **5**, 467–79.

McClelland, J. L., St. John, M., and Taraban, R. (1989). Sentence comprehension: A parallel distributed processing approach. *Language and Cognitive Processes*, **4**, 287–335.

McKinnon, R. and Osterhout, L. (1996). Constraints on movement phenomena in sentence processing: Evidence from event-related brain potentials. *Language and Cognitive Processes*, **11**, 495–523.

McRae, K., Spivey-Knowlton, M. J., and Tanenhaus, M. K. (1998). Modeling the influence of thematic fit (and other constraints) in on-line sentence comprehension. *Journal of Memory and Language*, **38**, 283–312.

Mecklinger, A., Schriefers, H., Steinhauer, K., and Friederici, A. D. (1995). Processing relative clauses varying on syntactic and semantic dimensions: An analysis with event-related potentials. *Memory and Cognition*, **23**, 477–94.

Miceli, G., Mazzucchi, A., Menn, L., and Goodglass, H. (1983). Contrasting cases of Italian agrammatic aphasia without comprehension disorder. *Brain and Language*, **19**, 65–97.

Miceli, G., Silveri, M. C., Nocentini, U., and Caramazza, A. (1988). Patterns of dissociation in comprehension and production of nouns and verbs. *Aphasiology*, **2**, 351–8.

Mitchell, D. C. (1994). Sentence parsing. In *Handbook of psycholinguistics* (ed. M. A. Gernsbacher), pp. 375–409. Academic Press, San Diego.

Mitchell, D. C. and Green, D. W. (1978). The effects of context and content on immediate processing in reading. *Quarterly Journal of Experimental Psychology*, **30**, 609–36.

Mitchell, D. C., Cuetos, F., Corley, M. M. B., and Brysbaert, M. (1995). Exposure-based models of human parsing: Evidence for the use of coarse-grained (nonlexical) statistical records. *Journal of Psycholinguistic Research*, **24**, 469–88.

Mohr. J., Pessin, M., Finkelstein, S., Funkenstein, H., Duncan, G., and Davis, K. (1978). Broca's aphasia: Pathological and clinical. *Neurology*, **28**, 311–24.

Münte, T. F. and Heinze, H. J. (1994). ERP negativities during syntactic processing of written words. In *Cognitive electrophysiology* (eds H. J. Heinze, T. F. Münte, and G. R. Mangun), pp. 211–38. Birkhauser, Boston, MA.

Münte, T. F., Heinze, H. J., and Mangun, G. R. (1993). Dissociation of brain activity related to syntactic and semantic aspects of language. *Journal of Cognitive Neuroscience*, **5**, 335–44.

Münte, T. F., Matzke, M., and Johannes, S. (1997). Brain activity associated with syntactic incongruities in words and pseudo-words. *Journal of Cognitive Neuroscience*, **9**, 300–11.

Münte, T. F., Heinze, H. J., Matzke, M., Wieringa, B. M., and Johannes, S. (1998). Brain potentials and syntactic violations revisited: No evidence for specificity of the syntactic positive shift. *Neuropsychologia*, **36**, 217–26.

Nespoulous, J.-L., Dordain, M., Perron, C., Ska, B., Bub, D., Caplan, D., *et al.* (1992). Agrammatism in sentence production without comprehension deficits: Reduced availability of syntactic structures and/or grammatical morphemes. A case study. *Brain and Language*, **33**, 273–95.

Neville, H. J., Nicol, J. L., Barss, A., Forster, K. I., and Garrett, M. F. (1991). Syntactically based sentence processing classes: Evidence from event-related brain potentials. *Journal of Cognitive Neuroscience*, **3**, 151–65.

Neville, H. J., Mills, D. L., and Lawson, D. S. (1992). Fractionating language: Different neural subsystems with different sensitive periods. *Cerebral Cortex*, **2**, 244–58.

Ni, W., Crain, S., and Shankweiler, D. (1996). Sidestepping garden paths: Assessing the contributions of syntax, semantics and plausibility in resolving ambiguities. *Language and Cognitive Processes*, **11**, 283–334.

Nichelli, P., Grafman, J., Pietrini, P., Clark, K., Lee, K. Y., and Miletich, R. (1995). Where the brain appreciates the moral of a story. *NeuroReport*, **6**, 2309–13.

Nobre, A. C. and McCarthy, G. (1994). Language-related ERPs: Scalp distributions and modulations by word type and semantic priming. *Journal of Cognitive Neuroscience*, **6**, 233–55.

Nobre, A. C., Allison, T., and McCarthy, G. (1994). Word recognition in the human inferior temporal lobe. *Nature*, **372**, 260–3.

Ojemann, G. (1991). Cortical organization of language and verbal memory based on intraoperative investigations. *Progress in Sensory Physiology*, **12**, 193–210.

O'Seaghdha, P. G. O. (1997). Conjoint and dissociable effects of syntactic and semantic context. *Journal of Experimental Psychology: Learning, Memory, and Cognition*, **23**, 807–28.

Osterhout, L. (1997). On the brain response to syntactic anomalies: Manipulations of word position and word class reveal individual differences. *Brain and Language*, **59**, 494–522.

Osterhout, L. and Hagoort, P. (1999). A superficial resemblance doesn't necessarily mean you're part of the family: Counterarguments to Coulson, King, and Kutas (1998) in the P600/SPS-P300 debate. *Language and Cognitive Processes*, **14** (In press).

Osterhout, L. and Holcomb, P. J. (1992). Event-related brain potentials elicited by syntactic anomaly. *Journal of Memory and Language*, **31**, 785–806.

Osterhout, L. and Holcomb, P. J. (1993). Event-related potentials and syntactic anomaly: Evidence of anomaly detection during the perception of continuous speech. *Language and Cognitive Processes*, **8**, 413–38.

Osterhout, L. and Holcomb, P. J. (1995). Event-related potentials and language comprehension. In *Electrophysiology of mind* (eds M. D. Rugg and M. G. H. Coles). pp. 171–215. Oxford University Press.

Osterhout, L. and Mobley, L. A. (1995). Event-related brain potentials elicited by failure to agree. *Journal of Memory and Language*, **34**, 739–73.

Osterhout, L., Holcomb, P. J., and Swinney, D. A. (1994). Brain potentials elicited by garden-path sentences: Evidence of the application of verb information during parsing. *Journal of Experimental Psychology: Learning, Memory, and Cognition*, **20**, 786–803.

Osterhout, L., McKinnon, R., Bersick, M., and Corey, V. (1996). On the language-specificity of the brain response to syntactic anomalies: Is the syntactic positive shift a member of the P300 family? *Journal of Cognitive Neuroscience*, **8**, 507–26.

Osterhout, L., Bersick, M., and McKinnon, R. (1997*a*). Brain potentials elicited by words: Word length and frequency predict the latency of an early negativity. *Biological Psychology*, **46**, 143–68.

Osterhout, L., McLaughlin, J. and Bersick, M. (1997*b*). Event-related brain potentials and human language. *Trends in Cognitive Sciences*, **1**, 203–9.

Patel, A. D., Gibson, E., Ratner, J., Besson, M., and Holcomb, P. J. (1988). Processing syntactic relations in language and music: An event-related potential study. *Journal of Cognitive Neuroscience*, **10**, 717–33.

Praamstra, P., Meyer, A. S. , and Levelt, W. J. M. (1994). Neurophysiological manifestations of phonological processing: Latency variation of a negative ERP component timelocked to phonological mismatch. *Journal of Cognitive Neuroscience*, **6**, 204–19.

Pritchett, B. L. (1992). *Grammatical competence and parsing performance*. University of Chicago Press.

Pulvermüller, F., Lutzenberger, W., and Birbaumer, N. (1995). Electrocortical distinction of vocabulary types. *Electroencephalography and Clinical Neurophysiology*, **94**, 357–70.

Rapp, B., and Caramazza, A. (1997). The modality-specific organization of grammatical categories: Evidence from impaired spoken and written sentence production. *Brain and Language*, **56**, 248–86.

Roelofs, A. (1992). A spreading-activation theory of lemma retrieval in speaking. *Cognition*, **42**, 107–42.

Roelofs, A. (1993). Testing a non-decompositional theory of lemma retrieval in speaking: Retrieval of verbs. *Cognition*, **47**, 59–87.

Rösler, F., Friederici, A. D., Pütz, P., and Hahne, A. (1993). Event-related brain potentials while encountering semantic and syntactic constraint violations. *Journal of Cognitive Neuroscience*, **5**, 345–62.

Rugg, M. D. (1984*a*). Event-related potentials in phonological matching tasks. *Brain and Language*, **23**, 225–40.

Rugg, M. D. (1984*b*). Event-related potentials and the phonological processing of words and non-words. *Neuropsychologia*, **22**, 642–7.

Rugg, M. D. and Barrett, S. E. (1987). Event-related potentials and the interaction between orthographic and phonological information in a rhyme-judgement task. *Brain and Language*, **32**, 336–61.

Rugg, M. D. and Coles, M. G. H. (1995). The ERP and cognitive psychology: Conceptual issues. In *Electrophysiology of mind: Event-related brain potentials and cognition*. (eds M. D. Rugg and M. G. H. Coles), pp. 27–39. Oxford University Press.

Schriefers, H., Friederici, A. D., and Kühn, K. (1995). The processing of locally ambiguous relative clauses in German. *Journal of Memory and Language*, **34**, 499–520.

Shallice, T. (1988). *From neuropsychology to mental structure*. Cambridge University Press.

Shulman, G. L., Corbetta, M., Buckner, R. L., Raichle, M. E., Fiez, J. A., Miezin, F. M., and Petersen, S. E. (1997). Top down modulation of early sensory cortex. *Cerebral Cortex*, **7**, 193–206.

Stowe, L. A., Wijers, A. A., Willemsen, A. T. M., Reuland, E., Paans, A. M. J., and Vaalburg, W. (1994). PET-studies of language: An assessment of the reliability of the technique. *Journal of Psycholinguistic Research*, **23**, 499–527.

Stromswold, K., Caplan, D., Alpert, N., and Rauch, S. (1996). Localization of syntactic comprehension by positron emission tomography. *Brain and Language*, **52**, 452–73.

Tabor, W. and Tanenhaus, M. K. (1998). Dynamic models of sentence processing. (Manuscript.)

Tanenhaus, M. K. and Trueswell, C. (1995). Sentence comprehension. In *Speech, language, and communication* (eds J. L. Miller and P. D. Eimas), pp. 217–62. Academic Press, San Diego.

Tanenhaus, M. K., Spivey-Knowlton, M. J., and Hanna, J. E. In *Architectures and mechanisms for language processing* (eds M. Crocker, M. Pickering, and C. Clifton). Cambridge University Press. (In press.)

Trueswell, J. C., Tanenhaus, M. K., and Kello, C. (1993). Verb-specific constraints in sentence processing: Separating effects of lexical preference from garden-paths. *Journal of Experimental Psychology: Learning, Memory, and Cognition*, **19**, 528–53.

Vanier, M. and Caplan, D. (1990). CT-scan correlates of agrammatism. *Agrammatic aphasia: A cross-language narrative source book* (eds L Menn and L. K. Obler), pp. 37–114. Benjamins, Amsterdam.

Von Stockert, T. R. and Bader, L. (1976). Some relations of grammar and lexicon in aphasia. *Cortex*, **12**, 49–60.

Vosse, T. and Kempen, G. (1999). Syntactic processing in human sentence comprehension: An inhibition-based parser with a lexicalized grammar. (Manuscript.)

Wassenaar, M., Hagoort, P., and Brown, C. M. (1997). Syntactic ERP effects in Broca's aphasics with agrammatic comprehension. *Brain and Language*, **60**, 61–4.

Waters, G. S. and Caplan, D. (1996). The capacity theory of sentence comprehension: Critique of Just and Carpenter (1992). *Psychological Review*, **103**, 761–72.

Waters, G. S., Caplan, D., and Hildebrandt, N. (1987). Working memory and written sentence comprehension. In *Attention and performance XII* (ed. M. Coltheart), pp. 531–55. Erlbaum, London.

Waters, G. S., Caplan, D., and Hildebrandt, N. (1991). On the structure of verbal STM and its functional role in sentence comprehension: A case study. *Cognitive Neuropsychology*, **8**, 81–126.

Willmes, K. and Poeck, K. (1993). To what extent can aphasic syndromes be localized? *Brain*, **116**, 1527–40.

Zurif, E. B. (1998). The neurological organization of some aspects of sentence comprehension. *Journal of Psycholinguistic Research*, **27**, 181–90.

Zurif, E. B., Caramazza, A., and Myerson, R. (1972). Grammatical judgments of agrammatic aphasics. *Neuropsychologia*, **10**, 405–17.

Section 4

Language from a neurobiological perspective

10 Broca's language area from a neuroanatomical and developmental perspective

Harry B. M. Uylings, Lidia I. Malofeeva, Irina N. Bogolepova, Katrin Amunts, and Karl Zilles

10.1 Introduction

Broca's area and Wernicke's area are two cortical regions originally defined in patients with brain lesions. These areas are thought to be essential for language functions. Although there are other areas that are also assumed to be essential for language, such as parts of the thalamus and other regions in both the temporoparietal lobe and the frontal lobe (e.g. Nobre and Plunkett 1997; Crosson 1992; Ojemann 1994; Dronkers 1996), Broca's and Wernicke's area are classically considered to be the most directly related to language. In this chapter, we will focus on the localization, development, and function of Broca's area. We will conclude that, given its structural and functional variability, it is necessary to construct an anatomical definition of Broca's area that is different from the vague definition of the cortical regions whose lesions led to the concept of Broca's aphasia. The aspects of delineation and individual variability discussed for Broca's area are also illustrative of other language areas. Neurolinguistic studies will continue to make fundamental progress when functional imaging of healthy volunteers performing neurolinguistic tests is combined with microscopically and architectonically defined brain areas. Given the large variability between healthy individuals in the shape and size of their brains we have to move to a 3-D system providing neuroanatomical localization of functional areas, which takes into account the variability of location and size of anatomically defined areas such as Broca's area.

10.2 Localization of cortical areas for language

The earliest method (see Table 10.1) which could reveal that particular regions of the brain are essential for cognitive functions is the post-mortem analysis of restricted brain lesions that caused a deficit in a specific cognitive function during a patient's life.

Table 10.1   Insights into localization of brain functions

Gross-anatomical study of patients with restricted brain lesion due to accident, disease, or war. (Famous cases in literature: Phineas Gage, Leborgne, Lelong, H. M.)[1]	
Mapping functions interrupted by stimulation of subdural surface electrodes in preparation of neurosurgical operations[2,3] [cm]	
Functional and structural non-invasive imaging of healthy volunteers and patients with restricted brain lesions	– EEG and Event Related Potential analysis with a large set of electrodes[4] [ms] – Magnetoencephalographic (MEG) analysis[5] [ms] – Positron Emission Tomography (PET) analysis[5,6] [min] – Single Photon Emission Computer Tomography (SPECT) analysis[5,6] [min] – Functional Magneto-Resonance Imaging (fMRI) analysis[7] [s] – Structural MRI[8] [1 mm^3] – MRI fused with microscopic anatomy[9]

1: Code *et al.* (1997); 2: Penfield and Roberts (1959); 3: Ojemann (1994); 4: Gevins *et al.* (1997); 5: Thatcher *et al.* (1994); 6: Roland (1993); 7: Friston *et al.* (1998); 8: Damasio (1995); 9: Roland and Zilles (1994).
[. . .]: resolution scale of space or time.

In this way, based on Paul Broca's studies of the famous cases of patients Leborgne (also called Tan) and, especially, Lelong, one of the first descriptions of a language area arose in 1861 (see e.g. Schiller 1992, pp. 186–187; Ryalls and Lecours 1996). This macroscopically described language area was given the name Broca's area and was considered to be essential for speech production. One decade later, in 1874, also based on cases with restricted brain lesions, Carl Wernicke proposed that comprehension of speech was impaired when lesions were in a more posterior brain region than Broca's region, that is Wernicke's area. A lesion in this area was associated with a fluent aphasia of the Wernicke type. For a review, see also Hagoort *et al.*, this volume.

Originally Broca's and Wernicke's areas were restricted to the dominant half of the brain, generally the left, and were only defined by gross anatomical examination of post-mortem brains. Nowadays, the microscopically defined cortical areas 44 and 45 are considered to form Broca's area (see section 10.3 below). These areas are described in the left and in the right hemisphere (Brodmann 1909; Von Economo and Koskinas 1925; Kononova 1949). The microscopical cortical areas which make up Wernicke's area, however, have still not been defined unambiguously (Steinmetz and Galaburda 1991; Roland 1993; Aboitiz and García 1997), except for a region called area Tpt or Brodmann's area 22, which occupies a large part of the planum temporale that lies at the centre of Wernicke's area (Galaburda and Sanides 1980).

The connectivity circuitry between Broca's area and Wernicke's area in the human brain is not known precisely. The arcuate fascicle (also called fasciculus longitudinalis superior) is a large tract of fibres that curves behind the bottom of the Sylvian fissure and connects these two areas (see e.g. Gluhbecović and Williams 1980 for its location).

Subhuman primate studies indicate that it is quite likely that the circuitry is more complex (see for review e.g. Aboitiz and García 1997).

When there is a lesion in the arcuate fascicle, another type of aphasia arises, that is conduction aphasia, which is different from Broca's aphasia and Wernicke's aphasia. In conduction aphasia, speech production and comprehension are preserved but the patient is unable to repeat sentences (Damasio 1992).

The analysis of localization of function in patients with brain lesions was hampered (i) by the size of the lesion (several cases had a widespread lesion), which was frequently larger than the pertinent cortical area and often involved subcortical white matter; and (ii) by the fact that brain lesions could only be examined after the death of a patient. More data on cortical areas involved in language functions came from brain-mapping studies using electrical stimulation in preparation for neurosurgical operations. These stimulation studies were performed by Penfield in Montreal during the thirties, forties, and fifties, and Ojemann in Seattle during the seventies, eighties, and nineties. They showed the importance of Broca's and Wernicke's area, but also of other cortical regions and the thalamus for object naming and other language functions (Feindel 1994; Ojemann 1994).

In the last two decades, more precise neurolinguistic examinations of the brain using non-invasive, functional imaging techniques have provided new insights and prospects for localization of brain regions involved in particular language functions (e.g. Mazoyer *et al.* 1993, and this book). With these modern techniques we now know that Broca's aphasia can also be caused by a lesion outside Broca's region (e.g. Dronkers *et al.* 1992; Damasio 1992).

Modern, structural imaging produces beautiful, but gross (i.e. macroscopic) anatomical images. In these images, cortical regions are generally indicated by assigning Talairach co-ordinates in an orthogonal, normalized co-ordinate system referenced to the AC–PC (anterior commissure–posterior commissure) line. In relation to this line the brain is divided into 12 rectangular boxes, and standardization according to Talairach is achieved through linear transformation of a particular brain within each of the 12 boxes (Talairach and Tournoux 1988, p. 57). The disadvantage of this procedure is that in this way the cortical regions are not defined as anatomical, cytoarchitectonic cortical areas. Functional imaging of language functions, however, requires information on anatomically defined cortical areas. It is therefore mandatory to fuse the macroscopic MRI images with microscopical, neuroanatomical images and data. This will bring the description of functional localization up to a level where different neuroanatomical systems can be distinguished. In this respect, it will also be necessary to take into account the anatomical and functional variability between different individuals (e.g. Roland and Zilles 1994).

10.3 Broca's area

10.3.1 Neuroanatomical localization of Broca's area

We have already mentioned that Wernicke's area has not been unambiguously defined in anatomical terms (e.g. Roland 1993; Steinmetz and Galaburda 1991). This is to a lesser extent also true for Broca's area. There are various reasons for this situation. One reason is that the lesions of patients in neurolinguistic studies were often too large and had in many cases been examined only macroscopically. Another reason is that the functional definition of Broca's area on the basis of Broca's aphasia was rather imprecise and has been frequently reformulated (Mohr 1976; Damasio 1992).

Originally, the anatomical definition was based on gross anatomical studies of damaged brain convolutions (gyri) in patients with speech disturbances (e.g. Broca 1861; Hervé 1888). Broca deduced that the posterior third of the third frontal gyrus was the essential area from which Broca's aphasia started (e.g. Schiller 1992). This posterior third corresponds to a small gyrus called the pars opercularis of the inferior (third) frontal gyrus. Hervé (1888) extended the gross, anatomically defined Broca's area to the whole inferior frontal gyrus, which includes, besides the pars opercularis, also the pars triangularis and the pars orbitalis (see for location e.g. Williams and Warwick 1975, p. 923; Gluhbecović and Williams 1980; Nieuwenhuys *et al.* 1988).

From the beginning of this century, the lesion approach has been complemented by microscopic analysis of the cytoarchitecture and myeloarchitecture (Brodmann 1909; Vogt 1910; Von Economo and Koskinas 1925; Kononova 1949). Although the cytoarchitectonic division of the inferior frontal gyrus in three cortical areas by Brodmann, Von Economo and Koskinas, and Kononova are roughly the same, the area they allocate to Broca's region differs greatly (see Table 10.2). The reasons for these differences are partly historical and partly due to a different understanding of functional localization, and thus are not due to differences in the knowledge of the anatomy. All authors agree that there are clear resemblances between the cortical areas in the inferior frontal gyrus. These areas are comparable with cortical areas 44, 45, and 47 of the Brodmann map. However, note that although Brodmann numbers are used worldwide, Brodmann did not publish the cytoarchitectonic features to characterize and distinguish cortical areas 44, 45, and 47 (see Brodmann 1909, pp. 138–139). Detailed cytoarchitectonic characteristics of the cortical areas in the inferior frontal gyrus were published by Von Economo and Koskinas (1925), Riegele (1931), Rose (1935), and Kononova (1935, 1949). The last mentioned author is from the school of Vogt at the Brain Research Institute in Moscow and she used Brodmann numbers.

Table 10.2   Different anatomical definitions for Broca's region

Area 44	Areas 44 and 45	Areas 44, 45, and 47
Broca (1861)	Kononova (1949)	Hervé (1888)
Brodmann (1909)	Williams and Warwick (1975)	Vogt (1910)
Von Economo and Koskinas (1925)	Damasio (1992)	Riegele (1931)
Bailey and Von Bonin (1951)	Hayes and Lewis (1993)	Harasty *et al.* (1997)
Sanides (1964)	Roland (1993)	
Galaburda (1980)	Aboitiz and García (1997)	
Nieuwenhuys *et al.* (1988)		

Comparing these cortical areas with the brain sites found to be essential for object naming by surface electrode stimulation and mapping, Ojemann *et al.* (1989) showed that the most posterior part of the inferior frontal gyrus (i.e. the pars opercularis ≈ cortical area 44) is the most frequently mapped site essential for object naming (79 per cent of the cases). However, object naming can also be blocked by electrode stimulation in the middle and superior frontal gyrus in about 50 per cent of the cases, and in the superior temporal gyrus in about 36 per cent of the 117 studied cases (Ojemann *et al.* 1989). This functional test can therefore not really localize Broca's area, or the so-called anterior speech area.

Roland (1993) and Damasio (1992), who used functional imaging and structural MR imaging of healthy volunteers and patients with brain lesions, call cortical areas 44 and 45 Broca's area 'for the sake of simplicity' (Roland 1993). This was based on the observations that four types of language production tasks activate the pars triangularis and the pars opercularis, roughly corresponding to cortical areas 44 and 45 (Roland 1993, p. 285). In agreement with these functional observations and with Kononova's functional concept (1949), we call area 44 and 45 Broca's area.

It is an old concept that borders of anatomical cortical areas coincide with the bottom of sulci. If this were true, it would be relatively easy to study the macroscopic brain structures with structural MRI. In the text books, one usually sees the convolution pattern of the third frontal gyrus in which the pars opercularis, the pars triangularis, and, to a slightly lesser extent, the pars orbitalis can be easily distinguished (e.g. Williams and Warwick 1975, p. 923; Nieuwenhuys *et al.* 1988). However, the gross anatomical descriptions of the human brain convolutions of Zernov (1877), Retzius (1896), and Ono *et al.* (1990) demonstrate that the pattern of sulci is quite variable between the left and right hemisphere, and between human individuals. Photographs of human brains (e.g. in Ono *et al.* 1990, p. 54–55) show such a large gross anatomical variability that it is often quite difficult to find the pars opercularis and triangularis. Furthermore, the studies by Kononova (1949), Amunts *et al.* (1997), and our own studies (Uylings *et al.* 1997) demonstrate that the borders of the cortical areas 44 and 45 do not coincide completely with sulci. Kononova (1935) reported that area 44 roughly correlates with the pars opercularis. In general, the rostral and caudal borders of area 44 are the ramus ascendens of the Sylvian fissure and the inferior part of the precentral sulcus, respectively (Fig. 10.1). The dorsal border of area 44 is in the vicinity of the inferior frontal sulcus (Fig. 10.1). She also described that area 45 roughly correlates with a small gyrus, that is the pars triangularis, which is located between the ramus ascendens and the ramus horizontalis of the Sylvian fissure (Fig. 10.1). (In neuroanatomical textbooks the Sylvian fissure is also called the lateral sulcus.) The ventral border of area 45 frequently appears below the ramus horizontalis. From our Figs 10.2 and 10.3 it is evident that the borders are not completely determined by sulci and that especially the size and location of particularly the rami ascendens and horizontalis vary enormously. Moreover, our studies on human brains have shown that the border between areas 44 and 45 can even shift between the

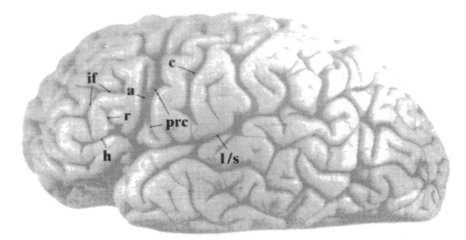

Fig. 10.1   Lateral view of a 32-year-old male brain. The indicated sulci are: if—inferior frontal sulcus; a—ramus ascendens of the Sylvian fissure; h—ramus horizontalis of the Sylvian fissure; r—sulcus radialis; prc—precentral sulcus; c—central sulcus; l/s—lateral sulcus/ Sylvian fissure.

ascending branch (ramus ascendens) of the Sylvian fissure and the sulcus diagonalis (Amunts *et al.* 1997), which is situated between the ramus ascendens and the precentral sulcus. As Kononova (1935) has already clearly stated, sulci can no longer be used as a simple criterion for cortex division.

It is outside the scope of this book to mention here all the detailed microscopic characteristics for the delineation of cortical areas 44 and 45. For these characteristics we refer to Kononova (1935, 1949), to Rose (1935), and to Amunts *et al.* (in preparation). It suffices to mention here that area 44 is dysgranular, that is layer IV is rather small and not clearly separated from the surrounding layers III and V. In area 45, the granular layer IV is more pronounced, but still less distinct and smaller than in the neighbouring frontal areas 46 and 10. In addition, area 44 has a higher cell density and a larger cortical thickness than the dysgranular cortical area 8.

In our developmental study, we mainly followed the characteristics of Kononova (1935, 1949). We noticed that a general difference between Broca's area in the left and right hemisphere was that the cytoarchitectonic differences between area 44 and area 45 are more pronounced in the left hemisphere, since in this hemisphere the granular layer IV is more obvious. In addition, we noticed interindividual differences in the extent of granularity of layer IV in our studies of adult cases (Rajkowska and Uylings, unpublished observations). Some subjects had a less pronounced granular layer IV in all the prefrontal cortical areas. In this group, the delineation of frontal cortical areas was more difficult, *casu quo* less obvious.

10.3.2 Postnatal development of Broca's area

Kononova (1949) described that the frontal cortex increased in the surface area, mainly in the first 2 years after birth. This would be true especially for the new areas

FEMALES   Right   Left

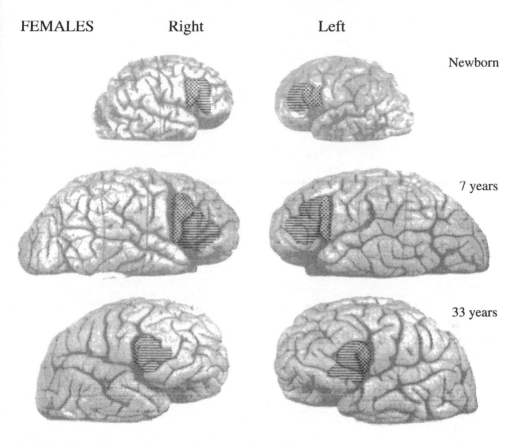

Newborn

7 years

33 years

Fig. 10.2   The lateral view of Broca's cortical areas 44 and 45 in a female new-born case, a 7-year-old, and a 33-year-old case. Area 44: dotted; Area 45: horizontal stripes.

(cortical areas 10, 44, and 45). Wada *et al.* (1975) studied the development of asymmetry in the planum temporale, but also in what they call the 'frontal operculum'. They confirmed the left-over-right asymmetry in size of the planum temporale reported earlier by Geschwind and Levitsky (1968), and, in addition, found a small but significant right-over-left asymmetry in the surface area of the frontal operculum in the group of 100 adult and 85 infant brains studied. They defined the frontal operculum as the posterior half of the third frontal gyrus, that is pars opercularis ($\approx$ area 44) and a caudal part of pars triangularis. This is not really the anatomical definition (e.g. Gluhbecović and Williams 1980; Nieuwenhuys *et al.* 1988), in which the frontal operculum is the lip of the frontal cortex over the insular cortex. This piece of cortex corresponds with the pars opercularis, the pars triangularis, and the pars orbitalis of the third frontal gyrus. In spite of the reported right-over-left asymmetry in the flat open surface of the frontal operculum, Wada *et al.* (1975) themselves left open the possibility that a left-over-right asymmetry can be found in this frontal cortex, because a large part of this cortex was hidden in the sulci and was not measured. Galaburda

MALES   Right   Left

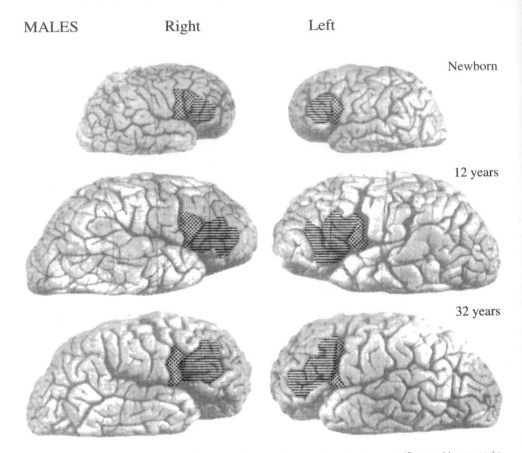

Fig.10.3   The lateral view of Broca's cortical areas 44 and 45 in a male new-born case, a 12-year-old case, and a 32-year-old case. Area 44: dotted; Area 45: horizontal stripes.

(1980) estimated the volume of cortical area 44 in 10 adult cases and reported a strong left-over-right asymmetry in six cases and only in one case a right-over-left asymmetry. In this report no specification of sex was given.

Falzi *et al.* (1982) studied the surface area of the pars opercularis and the pars triangularis in 12 consistently right-handed adult cases (age range between 50 and 60 years). They concluded that Wada *et al.*'s (1975) suspicion was correct, since they reported an overall left-over-right asymmetry in the surface area of both the open gyral regions and the regions hidden in the sulci. They did not specify the sex of the different cases, but in six of the twelve cases the left surface area was clearly larger than the right.

Since a functional asymmetry in the anterior language area is frequently reported, we wondered whether there is a structural asymmetry in volume and neuron number in Broca's area, and, if so, whether this is different for the sexes, and varies during development. In rat prefrontal cortex we have found that the asymmetry in size alternates between the left and right hemisphere during postnatal development (Van Eden *et al.* 1984).

In our study we estimated the volume of cortical areas 44 and 45 (with the Cavalieri method, e.g. Uylings *et al.* 1986) and the number of neurons (with the disector method; Gundersen, 1985) in a developmental series of 11 cases; six females and five males. These cases were all consistently right-handed. The number of cases here is relatively small due to the problem of obtaining preparations of complete Broca's areas from both the left and right hemisphere from cases without known neurological diseases or pathology, but with a known handedness. The preparations of these 11 cases are from the cytoarchitectonic collection of the *Division of Anatomy and Cytoarchitecture of the Brain* of the Brain Research Institute in Moscow.

In Figs 10.2 and 10.3, an impression is given of the variability in size and location of areas 44 and 45, although parts of the cortical areas are here hidden in the sulci. From these figures it is evident that borders are not completely determined by sulci and that asymmetry is to be expected. Asymmetry is more appropriately specified in Tables 10.3 and 10.4. From Table 10.3 we clearly see that in our relatively small group of cases the largest asymmetry in volume has been found in area 45. In the male group, with the exception of cases younger than 2 years, a consistently larger left-over-right size of area 45 is noted, and a smaller left-over-right asymmetry in area 44. The extent of left-over-right asymmetry in the female group is smaller. Also in this group we see an alteration from right-over-left asymmetry in volume in the youngest ages to left-over-right asymmetry in the older ages. These data suggest that also in human frontal cortex, alterations of structural asymmetry may occur during development. Note, however, the relatively small sample of cases examined. Further research is therefore needed to establish this finding. In Table 10.4 the percentage difference in total number of neurons is given for these 11 cases. In the lateralization of number of neurons, no obvious developmental trend is visible, neither for area 44 nor for area 45. From birth onwards a similar left-over-right asymmetry in total number of neurons in area 45 has been found for both sexes. Area 44 does not show much lateralization in number of neurons. For area 44 the male asymmetry values are only slightly higher, and some female values do not differ much from a symmetrical distribution of total number of neurons. Combining Tables 10.3 and 10.4, a tentative conclusion is that the shift of volume asymmetry in the young cases is not a reflection of a shift in asymmetry in total number of neurons. These neuronal numbers remain rather stable in all the cases examined. Apparently other factors influence the size of the neuronal trees during development. Tentatively we suggest that the adult left-over-right asymmetry in volumetric size of cortical areas 45 and 44 is 'predicted' by the rather stable asymmetry in number of neurons.

In another study of 10 adult cases (Amunts *et al.*, in preparation) a left-over-right asymmetry in volume of area 44 was found, but not for area 45 (see below section 10.3.3).

Table 10.3   Percentage asymmetry in volume of Broca's area

	Area 44	Area 45	Broca's area 44 and 45	Brain weight (g)
Female cases				
New-born	L ~ R	L ~ R	L ~ R	382
2 years	(L > R) 7%	R > L 24%	R > L 17%	935
7 years	R > L 14%	L ~ R	L ~ R	1205
12.75 years	L > R 15%	L > R 21%	L > R 19%	1360
30 years	R ~ L	L > R 10%	(L > R) 7%	1320
33 years	L > R 13%	L > R 10%	L > R 11%	1233
Male cases				
New-born	R > L 52%	(R > L) 5%	R > L 26%	524
1.6 years	L > R 12%	R > L 25%	R > L 14%	1235
7 years	L > R 12%	L > R 12%	L > R 12%	1390
12 years	L > R 10%	L > R 26%	L > R 21%	1390
32 years	L > R 10%	L > R 33%	L > R 25%	1400

Table 10.4   Percentage difference in number of neurons in left and right Broca's area

	Area 44	Area 45	Broca's area 44 and 45	Brain weight (g)
Female cases				
New-born	L ~ R	L > R 18%	L > R 14%	382
2 years	L > R 11%	L > R 19%	L > R 16%	935
7 years	(L > R) 8%	L > R 22%	L > R 17%	1205
12.75 years	L > R 12%	L > R 19%	L > R 17%	1360
30 years	L > R 12%	L > R 22%	L > R 18%	1320
33 years	(L > R) 8%	L > R 18%	L > R 16%	1233
Male cases				
New-born	(R > L) 9%	L > R 15%	(L > R) 7%	524
1.6 years	L > R 14%	L > R 20%	L > R 18%	1235
7 years	L > R 14%	L > R 25%	L > R 21%	1390
12 years	L > R 14%	L > R 24%	L > R 21%	1390
32 years	L > R 11%	L > R 31%	L > R 24%	1400

Our left-over-right asymmetry data seem to be at variance with the report of Harasty *et al.* (1997). Harasty *et al.* (1997) observed a very interesting, higher volume proportion of language-associated cortical areas relative to total cerebral volume in females. However, they did not find a hemisphere difference in the total volume of areas 44, 45, and 47, nor did they find a hemisphere difference in the volume of the planum temporale in an adult group of 10 males and 11 females aged between 46 and 93 years. This difference in results may be due to the fact that we studied the volume of individual, microscopically defined cortical areas 44 and 45 and not of macroscopical structures lacking a clear association with cortical areas, or to the fact that the resolution of our microscopic measurements was much higher than the volumetric estimations based on macroscopic photographs. Finally, it could be due to the fact that the group of Russian subjects was made up of consistently right-handed persons.

However, both studies are based on relatively small numbers of cases and further studies are therefore required to establish the pattern of hemispheric asymmetry and its variability for Broca's area and other language-associated cortical areas.

In the majority of the cases that Falzi *et al.* studied (1982), the kind of asymmetry of the anterior speech region was similar to the one of the posterior speech region. This does not necessarily mean that the whole cerebral cortex is asymmetric. Filipek *et al.* (1994) found only a minor structural asymmetry in size of total neocortex, which is, however, a right-over-left asymmetry and not a left-over-right one. In the rat brain we have found similar data. A clear-cut volumetric asymmetry in the prefrontal cortex is not reflected in a size lateralization of the whole neocortical hemispheres (Van Eden *et al.* 1984; Uylings *et al.*, unpublished data). This is due to differential asymmetry in different cortical areas of both hemispheres.

In the literature, structural asymmetry is usually supposed to form a basis for functional asymmetry (see Strauss *et al.* 1983, for a review). Indeed, we know that extra stimulation of particular functions may lead to a structural increase in size of particular brain regions involved in these functions, even in adult mammals (Uylings *et al.* 1978; Greenough *et al.* 1990; Yang *et al.* 1994; Rauschecker 1995). On the other hand, the correlation of a particular functional lateralization with structural lateralization becomes complicated when the contralateral cortex is also involved in other functions.

10.3.3 Variability in structure of areas 44 and 45 in the adult brain

Figures 10.2 and 10.3 show some interindividual variation in the extent and external shape of areas 44 and 45 during development. Is this variation caused only by biological differences between individuals in the location, extent, and microstructure of both areas or is it also influenced by the observer-dependent definition of cytoarchitectonic areas through visual inspection? The classical anatomical mapping techniques depend to a large extent on the experience and abilities of the investigator in the recognition of the typical laminar pattern of a cytoarchitectonic area.

In order to exclude the latter source of variability, we applied a new observer-independent method for the detection of cytoarchitectonic borders of areas 44 and 45 (Schleicher *et al.* 1999). These cortical areas were analysed in serial histological sections of 10 human brains, five male and five female (Amunts *et al.*, in preparation). The brains are from the collection of the *C. and O. Vogt Institute for Brain Research* in Düsseldorf. The cytoarchitecture was analysed by calculating the gray level index as a measure of cell density (Schleicher and Zilles 1990; Amunts *et al.* 1996; Zilles *et al.* 1995), followed by the new observer-independent method for the delineation of cortical areas (Schleicher *et al.* 1999). We found larger cytoarchitectonic differences of areas 44 and 45 between different individuals than between areas 44 and 45 within each individual. Furthermore, the measurements in area 44 revealed a significant left-over-right asymmetry in the cell density, which was more prominent in males than in females. Large individual differences in cortical volumes of areas 44 and 45 were

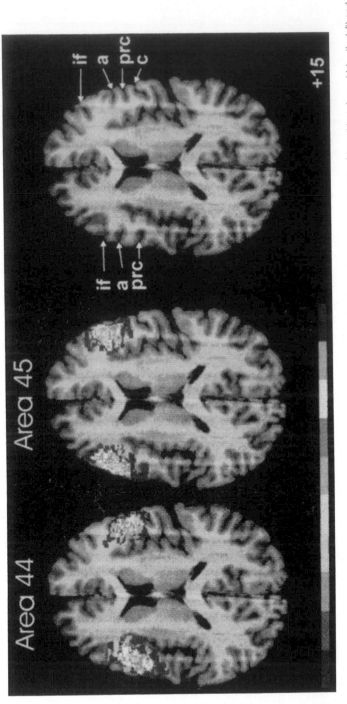

Fig. 10.4   Horizontal sections of the standard reference brain at +15 mm above the AC–PC line. Left hemisphere is on the right side of the subject. Areas 44 (on the left) and 45 (in the middle) of all 10 brains were overlaid upon the horizontal sections. The number of overlaid areas in each pixel is coded in colours ranging from blue (one brain) to red (10 brains). On the right, the same horizontal sections, but with marked sulci: if—inferior frontal sulcus; a—ascending branch of the Sylvian fissure (ramus ascendens); prc—precentral sulcus, c—central sulcus.

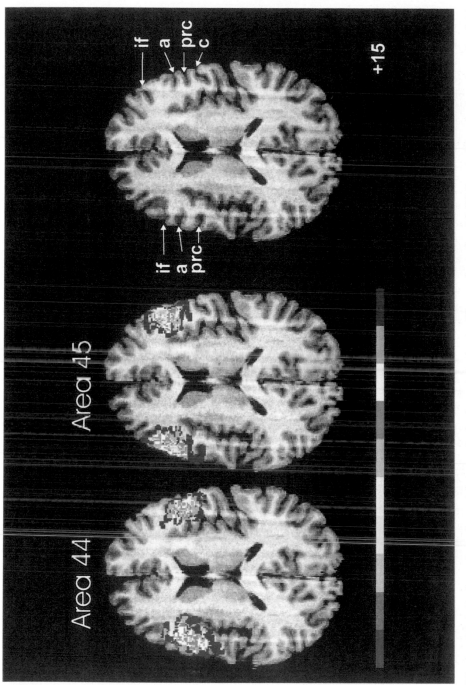

Figure 10.4 Horizontal sections of the standard reference brain at +15 mm above the AC-PC line. Left hemisphere is on the right side of the subject. Areas 44 (on the left) and 45 (in the middle) of all 10 brains were overlayed upon the horizontal sections. The number of overlayed areas in each pixel is coded in colours ranging from blue (one brain) to red (10 brains). On the right, the same horizontal sections, but with marked sulci: if – inferior frontal sulcus; a – ascending branch of the Sylvian fissure (ramus ascendens); pre – precentral sulcus, c – central sulcus.

revealed after estimation of volume with Cavalieri's method. Nevertheless, all 10 brains showed a larger area 44 on the left than on the right side, whereas left-right differences in area 45 were not significant. In area 45, 50 per cent of the cases had a left-over-right asymmetry and 50 per cent showed a reversed asymmetry in volume.

Figure 10.4 supplements Figs 10.2 and 10.3 on developmental changes in the external view of areas 44 and 45 by providing representative horizontal sections of the standard reference brain in which areas 44 and 45 of all 10 brains were mapped in the same spatial co-ordinate system. This presentation is based on a 3-D reconstruction of the areas 44 and 45 in each brain and on an alignment of these reconstructions to the format of a 3-D standard reference brain (Roland and Zilles 1994; Schormann *et al.* 1993; Schormann and Zilles 1998). The number of overlaid cortical areas in each voxel of the brain volume is coded in different colours. Figure 10.4 indicates a high individual variability in extent, size and shape of areas 44 and 45 delineated in the 10 adult brains with the observer-independent method. This has to be taken into account when interpreting data from functional imaging studies. Figure 10.4 also emphasizes that the analysis of structural–functional correlations should be based on an architectonic delineation of cortical areas.

10.4 Conclusions

The major conclusion is that for neurolinguistic functional-imaging studies it is necessary to fuse the gross anatomical (i.e. macroscopical) map of activated areas with 3-D microscopically defined cortical areas. In order to come to a correct estimation of the neuroanatomical systems involved in particular language functions, it is essential to take into account the variability in size and location of Broca's areas 44 and 45 and of other cortical areas. Given the data shown in this chapter, it is evident that we need to move to a 3-D computerized human brain atlas and database (e.g. Roland and Zilles 1994). In this way, differences in size and location of cortical areas in different persons are incorporated in the database. This prevents incorrect neurobiological hypotheses about the cortical systems involved in particular language functions. The microscopically defined cortical areas have to be characterized by features that lead to reproducible borders of cortical areas by independent observers, preferably with observer-independent analysis methods (Schleicher *et al.* 1995, 1999). Discussions about the extent of Wernicke's area etc. will be replaced by more specific and relevant discussions about the involvement of different cortical areas in specifically described neurolinguistic functions. Our results have shown that, whenever possible, sex (see also Kimura 1983, 1996) and handedness, just as age or developmental state, must be distinguished. Factors such as socioeconomic background (stimulating or impoverished environment) are likely to be confounding.

A final conclusion is that developmental shifts can occur in lateralization, and that a functional asymmetry is not necessarily correlated with a structural asymmetry.

Acknowledgements

We acknowledge the financial support of the Netherlands Organization for Scientific Research (NWO—program Russia grant 047–012–223) to H. U., L. M. and I. B.; the financial support of the European Biotech Program (BIO4-CT96–0177) to K. Z. and H. U; and the NATO grant CRG 961225 to H. U. We also acknowledge Mr. H. Stoffels for the fine compositions of Figs 10.1 and 10.2, and Ms. W. T. P. Verweij for secretarial assistance.

References

Aboitiz, F. and García, R. (1997). The evolutionary origin of the language areas in the human brain. A neuroanatomical perspective. *Brain Research Reviews*, **25**, 381–96.

Amunts, K., Schlaug, G., Schleicher, A., Steinmetz, H., Dabringhaus, A., Roland, P. E., *et al.* (1996). Asymmetry in the human motor cortex and handedness. *NeuroImage*, **4**, 216–22.

Amunts, K., Schleicher, A., Schormann, T., Bürgl, U., Mohlberg, H., Uylings, H. B. M., *et al.* (1997). The cytoarchitecture of Broca's region and its variability. *NeuroImage*, **5**, S353.

Bailey, P. and Von Bonin, G. (1951). *The isocortex of man*. Illinois Monographs in the Medical Sciences, Vol. VI, 182, University of Illinois Press, Urbana.

Broca, P. (1861). Remarques sur le siège de la faculté du langage articulé, suivies d'une observation d'aphemie (pert de la parole). *Bulletin Société Anatomique de Paris*, **36**, 330–57.

Brodmann, K. (1909). *Vergleichende Lokalisationslehre der Grosshirnrinde*. Barth, Leipzig.

Code, C., Wallesch, C.-W., Joanette, Y., and Lecours, A. R. (eds) (1997). *Classic cases in neuropsychology*. Psychology Press, Hove.

Crosson, B. (1992). *Subcortical functions in language and memory*. Guilford, New York.

Damasio, A. R. (1992). Aphasia. *New England Journal of Medicine*, **326**, 531–9.

Damasio, H. (1995). *Human brain anatomy in computerized images*. Oxford University Press, New York.

Dronkers, N. F. (1996). A new brain region for coordinating speech articulation. *Nature*, **384**, 159–61.

Dronkers, N. F., Shapiro, J. K., Redfern, B., and Knight, R. T. (1992). The role of Broca's area in Broca's aphasia. *Journal of Clinical and Experimental Neuropsychology*, **14**, 52–3.

Falzi, G., Perrone, P., and Vignolo, L. A. (1982). Right-left asymmetry in anterior speech region. *Archives of Neurology*, **39**, 239–40.

Feindel, W. (1994). Cortical localization of speech, evidence from stimulation and excision. *Discussions in Neurosciences*, **10**, 34–45.

Filipek, P. A., Richelme, C., Kennedy, D. N., and Caviness, V. S., Jr (1994). The young adult human brain: An MRI-based morphometric analysis. *Cerebral Cortex*, **4**, 344–60.

Friston, K. J., Fletcher, P., Josephs, O., Holmes, A., Rugg, M. D., and Turner, R. (1998). Event-related fMRI: Characterizing differential responses. *NeuroImage*, **7**, 30–40.

Galaburda, A. M. (1980). La région de Broca. Observations anatomiques faites un siècle après la mort de son découvreur. *Revue Neurologique*, **136**, 609–16.

Galaburda, A. M. and Sanides, F. (1980). Cytoarchitectonic organization of the human auditory cortex. *Journal of Comparative Neurology*, **190**, 597–610.

Geschwind, N. and Levitsky, W. (1968). Human brain: Left-right asymmetries in temporal speech region. *Science*, **161**, 186–7.

Gevins, A., Smith, M. E., McEroy, L., and Yu, D. (1997). High resolution EEG mapping of cortical activation related to working memory: Effects of task difficulty, type of processing, and practice. *Cerebral Cortex*, **7**, 374–85.

Gluhbecović N. and Williams, T. H. (1980). *The human brain. A photographic guide.* Harper and Row, Hagerstown.

Greenough, W. T., Withers, G. S., and Wallace, C. S. (1990). Morphological changes in the nervous system arising from behavioral experience: What is evidence that they are involved in learning and memory? In *The biology of memory* (eds L.S. Squire and E. Lindenlaub), Symposia Medica Hoechst, Vol. 23, pp. 159–92. Schattauer, Stuttgart-New York.

Gundersen, H. J. G. (1985). Stereology of arbitrary particles. *Journal of Microscopy*, **143**, 3–45.

Harasty, J., Double, K. L., Halliday, G. M., Kril, J. J., and McRitchie, D. A. (1997). Language-associated cortical regions are proportionally larger in the female brain. *Archives of Neurology*, **54**, 171–6.

Hayes, T. L. and Lewis, D. A. (1993). Hemispheric differences in layer III pyramidal neurons of the anterior language area. *Archives of Neurology*, **50**, 501–5.

Hervé, G. (1888). *La circonvolution de Broca. Etude de morphologie cérébrale.* Davy, Paris.

Kimura, D. (1983). Sex differences in cerebral organization for speech and praxic functions. *Canadian Journal of Psychology*, **37**, 19–35.

Kimura, D. (1996). Sex, sexual orientation and sex hormones influence human cognitive function. *Current Opinions in Neurobiology*, **6**, 259–63.

Kononova, E. P. (1935). The variability of structure of the cortex of the brain: Inferior frontal gyrus of adult man. Brain Research Institute, Publ. 1, 49–118. (In Russian. English translation is in preparation).

Kononova, E. P. (1949). The frontal region. In *Architectonics of the cerebral cortex* (ed. S. A. Sarkisov), pp. 309–43. Medgiz, Moscow. (In Russian. English translation is in preparation).

Mazoyer, B. M., Tzourio, N., Frak, V., Syrota, A., Murayama, N., Levier, O., *et al.* (1993). The cortical representation of speech. *Journal of Cognitive Neuroscience*, **5**, 467–79.

Mohr, J. P. (1976). Broca's area and Broca's aphasia. In *Studies in neurolinguistics*, Vol. 1 (ed. H. Whitaker and H. A. Whitaker), pp. 201–35. Academic Press, New York.

Nieuwenhuys, R., Voogd, J., and van Huijzen, Chr. (1988). *The human central nervous system. A synopsis and atlas* (3rd edn.) Springer, Berlin.

Nobre, A. C. and Plunkett, K. (1997). The neural system of language: Structure and development. *Current Opinions in Neurobiology*, **7**, 262–8.

Ojemann, G. A. (1994). Intraoperative investigations of the neurobiology of language. *Discussions in Neurosciences*, **10**, 51–7.

Ojemann, G., Ojemann, J., Lettich, E., and Berger, M. (1989). Cortical language localization in left, dominant hemisphere: An electrical stimulation mapping investigation in 117 patients. *Journal of Neurosurgery*, **71**, 316–26.

Ono, M., Kubik, S., and Abernathy, C. D. (1990). *Atlas of the cerebral sulci.* Thieme, Stuttgart.

Penfield, W. and Roberts, L. (1959). *Speech and brain mechanisms.* Princeton University Press.

Rauschecker, J. P. (1995). Compensatory plasticity and sensory substitution in the cerebral cortex. *Trends in Neurosciences*, **18**, 36–43.

Retzius, G. (1896). *Das Menschen Hirn*, Teil 1 Text. Norstedt and Söner, Stockholm.

Riegele, L. (1931). Die Cytoarchitektonik der Felder der Brocaschen Region. *Journal für Psychologie und Neurologie*, **42**, 496–514.

Roland, P. E. (1993). *Brain activation*. Wiley-Liss, New York.

Roland, P. E. and Zilles, K. (1994). Brain atlases—a new research tool. *Trends in Neurosciences*, **17**, 458–67.

Rose, M. (1935). Cytoarchitectonik und Myeloarchitektonik der Grosshirnrinde. In *Handbuch der Neurologie. Allgemeine Neurologie, Vol. 1 Anatomie* (eds O. Bumke and O. Foerster), pp. 588–778. Springer, Berlin.

Ryalls, J. and Lecours, A. R. (1996). Broca's first two cases: From bumps on the head to cortical convolutions. In *Classic cases in neuropsychology* (eds C. Code, C.-W. Wallesch, Y. Joanette, and A. R. Lecours), pp. 235–42. Psychology Press, Hove.

Sanides, F. (1964). The cyto-myeloarchitecture of the human frontal lobe and its relation to phylogenetic differentiation of the cerebral cortex. *Journal für Hirnforschung*, **6**, 269–82.

Schiller, F. (1992). *Paul Broca: Founder of French anthropology, explorer of the brain*. Oxford University Press, New York.

Schleicher, A. and Zilles, K. (1990). A quantitative approach to cytoarchitectonics: Analysis of structural inhomogeneities in nervous tissue using an image analyser. *Journal of Microscopy*, **157**, 367–81.

Schleicher, A., Amunts, K., Geyer, S., Simon, U., Zilles, K., and Roland, P. E. (1995). A method of observer-independent cytoarchitectonic mapping of the human cortex. *Human Brain Mapping*, Supplement 1, 77.

Schleicher, A., Amunts, K., Geyer, S., Morosan, P., and Zilles, K. Observer-independent method for microstructural parcellation of cerebral cortex: A quantitative approach to cytoarchitectonics. *NeuroImage*, (In press.)

Schormann, T. and Zilles, K. (1998). Three-dimensional linear and nonlinear transformations: An integration of light microscopical and MRI data. *Human Brain Mapping*, **6**, 339–47.

Schormann, T., Von Matthey, M., Dabringhaus, A., and Zilles, K. (1993). Alignment of 3-D brain data sets originating from MR and histology. *Bioimaging*, **1**, 119–28.

Steinmetz, H. and Galaburda, A. M. (1991). Planum temporale asymmetry: *In vivo* morphometry affords a new perspective for neuro-behavioral research. *Reading and Writing: An Interdisciplinary Journal*, **3**, 331–43.

Strauss, E., Kosaka, B., and Wada, J. (1983). The neurobiological basis of lateralized cerebral function. A review. *Human Neurobiology*, **2**, 115–27.

Talairach, J. and Tournoux, P. (1988). *Co-planar stereotaxic atlas of the human brain. 3-D proportional system: An approach to cerebral imaging*. Thieme, Stuttgart.

Thatcher, R. W., Hallett, M., Zeffiro, T., John, E. R., and Huerta, M. (1994). *Functional neuroimaging. Technical foundations*. Academic Press, San Diego.

Uylings, H. B. M., Kuypers, K., Diamond, M. C., and Veltman, W. A. M. (1978). Effects of differential environments on plasticity of dendrites of cortical pyramidal neurons in adult rats. *Experimental Neurology*, **62**, 658–77.

Uylings, H. B. M., Van Eden, C. G., and Hofman, M. A. (1986). Morphometry of size/volume variables and comparison of their bivariate relations in the nervous system under different conditions. *Journal of Neuroscience Methods*, **18**, 19–37.

Uylings, H. B. M., Malofeeva, L. I., and Bogolepova, I. N. (1997). Variability in cortical location of Broca's area. *NeuroImage*, **5**, S354.

Van Eden, C. G., Uylings, H. B. M., and Van Pelt, J. (1984). Sex-difference and left-right asymmetries in the prefrontal cortex during postnatal development in the rat. *Developmental Brain Research*, **12**, 146–53.

Vogt, O. (1910). Die myeloarchitektonische Felderung des menschlichen Stirnhirns. *Journal für Psychologie und Neurologie*, **15**, 221–38.

Von Economo, C. and Koskinas, G. (1925). *Die Cytoarchitektonik der Hirnrinde des erwachsenen Menschen*. Springer, Berlin.

Wada, J. A., Clarke, R., and Hamm, A. (1975). Cerebral hemispheric asymmetry in humans. *Archives of Neurology*, **32**, 239–46.

Williams, P. L. and Warwick, R. (1975). *Functional neuroanatomy of man. The neurology section from Gray's anatomy*, 53rd edn. Churchill Livingstone, Edinburgh, pp. 746–1194.

Yang, T. T., Gallen, C. C., Ramachandran, V. S., Cobb, S., Schwartz, B. J., and Bloom, F. E. (1994). Noninvasive detections of cerebral plasticity in adult human somatosensory cortex. *NeuroReport*, **5**, 701–4.

Zernov, D. N. (1877). *A guide to descriptive anatomy of the individual types of the brain sinuosity*. University of Moscow (in Russian).

Zilles, K., Schlaug, G., Matelli, M., Luppino, G., Schleicher, A., Qü, M., *et al.* (1995). Mapping of human and macaque sensorimotor areas by integrating architectonic transmitter receptor, MRI and PET data. *Journal of Anatomy*, **187**, 515–37.

11 Functional integration: methods for assessing interactions among neuronal systems using brain imaging

Christian Büchel, Chris Frith, and Karl Friston

11.1 Introduction

In the late 19th century, the early investigations of brain function were dominated by the concept of functional segregation. This belief was driven largely by the data available to scientists of that era. Patients with circumscribed lesions were found who were impaired in one particular ability while other abilities remained largely intact. Indeed, descriptions of patients with different kinds of aphasia made at this time have left a permanent legacy in the contrast between Broca's and Wernicke's aphasia. These syndromes were thought to result from damage to anterior or posterior regions of the left hemisphere respectively. Only recently more detailed lesion analyses have highlighted that the relation between lesion site and aphasic syndrome is far from perfect (Willmes and Poeck 1993). In the first part of the 20th century, the idea of functional segregation fell into disrepute and the doctrine of 'mass action' held sway, proposing that higher abilities depended on the function of the brain 'as a whole' (Lashley 1929). This doctrine was always going to be unsatisfying, however. With the resources available at the time it was simply not possible to make any progress studying the function of the 'brain as a whole'. By the end the 20th century, the concept of functional segregation has returned to domination.

The doctrine is now particularly associated with cognitive neuropsychology and is enshrined in the concept of double dissociation (see Shallice 1988, Chapter 10). A double dissociation is demonstrated when neurological patients can be found with 'mirror' abnormalities. For example, many patients have been described who have severe impairments of long-term memory while their short-term memory is intact. In 1969 Warrington and Shallice described the first of a series of patients who had severe impairments of phonological short-term memory, but no impairments of long-term memory. This is a particularly striking example of double dissociation. It demonstrates that different brain regions are involved in short and long-term memory. Furthermore, it shows that these regions can function in a largely independent fashion. This observation caused major problems for theories of memory, extant at the time, which supposed that inputs to long-term memory emanated from short-term memory systems (e.g. Atkinson and Shiffrin 1967).

Of course, we all know that the brain does not consist of 51 small independent units that just happen to cohabit the same skull. At the very least, in a task like visual object naming there must be an input from the visual system into the object recognition system and an output from the object recognition system to a verbal articulation system. The problem is that the lesion method is not very good at studying interactions between brain regions, although a few disconnection syndromes have been described.

Functional brain imaging avoids many of the problems of lesion studies, but, here too, the field has been dominated by the doctrine of functional segregation. Nevertheless, it is implicit in the subtraction method that brain regions communicate with each other. If we want to distinguish between brain regions associated with certain central processes for example, then we will design an experiment in which the sensory input and motor output is the same across all conditions. In this way activity associated with sensory input and motor output will be subtracted out. The early studies of reading by Posner and his colleagues are still among the best examples of this approach (Petersen *et al*. 1990; Posner *et al*. 1988). The design of these studies was based on the assumption that reading goes through a single series of discrete and independent stages; visual shapes are analysed to form letters, letters are put together to form words, the visual word form is translated into sound, the sound form is translated into articulation, and so on. By comparison of suitable tasks (e.g. letters vs. false font, words vs. letters, etc.), each stage can be isolated and the associated brain region identified. Although subsequent studies have shown that this characterisation of the brain activity associated with reading is a considerable oversimplification, this original report still captures the essence of most functional imaging studies; a number of discrete cognitive stages are mapped onto discrete brain areas. Nothing is revealed about how the cognitive processes interact or how the brain regions communicate with each other. If word recognition really did depend on the passage of information through a single series of discrete stages, we would at least like to know the temporal order in which the associated brain regions were engaged. Some evidence about this comes from EEG and MEG studies. In fact, we know that word recognition depends upon at least two parallel routes; one via meaning and one via phonology (Marshall and Newcombe 1973). Given this model, we would like to be able to specify the brain regions associated with each route and have some measure of the strengths of the connections between these different regions. Finally, we know from anatomical and behavioural studies that the pathways involved are not always unidirectional; information from higher order processes can be fed back to sensory regions. This is illustrated in Fig. 11.1. The two sentences are simple to read and are not problematic in any obvious way. Yet close examination shows that the visual sign for the 'ev' in *event* is identical to the sign used for the 'w' in *went*. In this example our knowledge of the meaning of the sentence has influenced our perception of the visual stimuli. In the

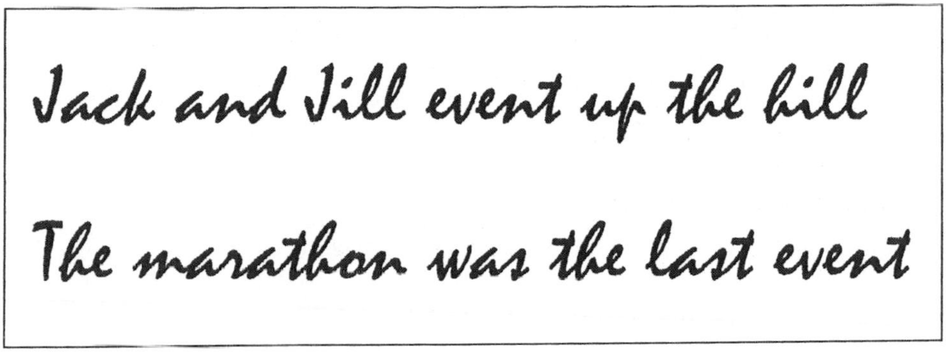

Fig.11.1 The perception of individual letters and words depends on the meaning of the whole sentence.

auditory domain there are even more striking demonstrations of how meaning and expectation can alter our perception of sound (Warren 1970).

In this chapter we shall show that new methods for measuring effective connectivity allow us to characterize the interactions between brain regions which underlie the complex interactions among different processing stages.

11.2 Definitions

In the analysis of neuroimaging time series (i.e. signal changes in a set of voxels, expressed as a function of time), functional connectivity is defined as the *temporal correlations between spatially remote neurophysiological events* (Friston *et al.* 1993*b*). This definition provides a simple characterization of functional interactions. The alternative is effective connectivity (i.e. *the influence one neuronal system exerts over another*) (Friston *et al.* 1993*a*). These concepts originated in the analysis of separable spike trains obtained from multi-unit electrode recordings (Aertsen and Preissl 1991; Gerstein and Perkel 1969). Functional connectivity is simply a statement about the observed correlations; it does not comment on how these correlations are mediated. For example, at the level of multi-unit micro-electrode recordings, correlations can result from *stimulus-locked transients,* evoked by a common afferent input, or reflect *stimulus-induced oscillations,* phasic coupling of neural assemblies, mediated by synaptic connections (Gerstein *et al.* 1989). Effective connectivity is closer to the notion of a connection, either at a synaptic (cf. synaptic efficacy) or cortical level. Although functional and effective connectivity can be invoked at a conceptual level in both neuroimaging and electrophysiology, they differ fundamentally at a practical level. This is because the time-scales and nature of neurophysiological measurements are very different (seconds vs. milliseconds and haemodynamic vs. spike trains). In electrophysiology it is often necessary to remove the confounding effects of stimulus-locked transients (that introduce correlations *not* causally mediated by direct neural interactions) in order to reveal an underlying connectivity. The confounding effect of stimulus-evoked transients is less problematic in neuroimaging because propagation of signals from primary sensory areas onwards is mediated by neuronal connections (usually reciprocal and interconnecting). However, it should be remembered that functional connectivity is not necessarily due to effective connectivity (e.g. common neuromodulatory input from ascending aminergic neurotransmitter systems or thalamo-cortical afferents) and, where it is, effective influences may be indirect (e.g. polysynaptic relays through multiple areas).

11.3 Functional connectivity

Here we introduce a simple way of measuring the amount a pattern of activity (representing a connected brain system) contributes to the functional connectivity or variance–covariances observed in the imaging data. Functional connectivity is defined in terms of correlations or covariance (correlations are normalized covariances). The point to point functional connectivity between one voxel and another is not usually of great interest. The important aspect of a covariance structure is the pattern of correlated activity subtended by (an enormous number of) pairwise covariances. In measuring such patterns it is useful to introduce the concept of a norm. Vector and matrix norms serve the same purpose as absolute values for scalar quantities. In other words they furnish a measure of distance. One frequently used norm is the 2-norm, which is the length of a vector. The vector 2-norm can be used to measure the degree to which a particular pattern of brain activity contributes to a covariance structure: if a pattern is described by a column vector (p), with an element for each voxel, then the contribution of that pattern to the covariance structure can be measured by the 2-norm of $M \cdot p = |M \cdot p|_2$. Data matrix M is mean corrected with one row for each successive scan and one column for each voxel (T denotes transposition):

$$(1)\quad |M \cdot p|_2^{\,2} = p^{\mathrm{T}} \cdot M^{\mathrm{T}} \cdot M \cdot p$$

Put simply, the 2-norm is a number that reflects the amount of variance–covariance or functional connectivity that can be accounted for by a particular distributed pattern; if time-dependent changes occur predominantly in regions described by the pattern (p) then the correlation between the pattern of activity and p over space will vary substantially over time. The 2-norm measures this temporal variance in the spatial correlation. The pattern p can be used to define the functional connectivity of interest. For example, if one were interested in the functional connectivity between left dorsolateral prefrontal cortex (DLPFC) and left superior temporal region one could test for this interaction using the 2-norm in Eq. (1) where p had large values in the frontal and temporal regions.

It should be noted that the 2-norm only measures the pattern of interest. There may be many other important patterns of functional connectivity. This fact begs the question 'what are the most prevalent patterns of coherent activity?' To answer this question one turns to eigenimages or spatial modes.

11.3.1 Eigenimages and spatial modes

In this section the concept of eigenimages or spatial modes is introduced in terms of patterns of activity (p) defined in the previous section. We show that spatial modes are simply those patterns that account for the most variance–covariance (i.e. have the largest 2-norm).

Eigenimages or spatial modes are most commonly obtained using singular value decomposition (SVD). SVD is an operation that decomposes an original time series (M) into two sets of orthogonal vectors (patterns in space and patterns in time) V and U where:

(2) $[USV] = \mathrm{SVD}\{M\}$

such that: $M = U.S.V^{\mathrm{T}}$

U and V are unitary orthogonal matrices (the sum of squares of each column is unity and all the column are uncorrelated) and S is a diagonal matrix (only the leading diagonal has non-zero values) of decreasing singular values. The singular value of each eigenimage is simply its 2-norm. Because SVD maximizes the largest singular value, the first eigenimage is the pattern that accounts for the greatest amount of the variance–covariance structure. In summary, SVD and equivalent devices are powerful ways of decomposing an imaging time-series into a series of orthogonal patterns that embody, in a step-down fashion, the greatest amounts of functional connectivity. Each eigenvector (column of V) defines a distributed brain system that can be displayed as an image. The distributed systems that ensue are called eigenimages or spatial modes and have been used to characterize the spatiotemporal dynamics of neurophysiological time series from several modalities; including multi-unit electrode recordings (Mayer-Kress *et al.* 1991), EEG (Friedrich *et al.* 1991), MEG (Fuchs *et al.* 1992), PET (Friston *et al.* 1993a), and functional MRI (Friston *et al.* 1993c).

Many readers will notice that the eigenimages associated with the functional connectivity or covariance matrix are simply principal components of the time series. In the EEG literature one sometimes comes across the Karhunen–Loeve expansion which is employed to identify spatial modes. If this expansion is in terms of eigenvectors of covariances (and it usually is), then the analysis is formally identical to the one presented above.

One might ask what the column vectors of U in Eq. (2) correspond to. These vectors are the time-dependent profiles associated with each eigenimage. They reflect the extent to which an eigenimage is expressed in each experimental condition or over time. These vectors play an important role in the functional attribution of distributed systems defined by eigenimages. This point and others will be illustrated in the next section.

11.3.2 Example: verbal fluency

To illustrate the approach, we will use a standard word generation study. The data were obtained from five subjects scanned 12 times whilst performing one of two verbal tasks in alternation. One task involved repeating a phoneme presented aurally at one per two second (phoneme repetition). The other was a paced verbal fluency task, where subjects responded with a word that began with the presented phoneme (cued word generation). To facilitate intersubject pooling, the data were realigned and spatially normalized and smoothed with an isotropic Gaussian kernel (FWHM of 16 mm). The data were then subject to an AnCova (modelling 12 individual conditions rather than two conditions with six replications, subject effects and global activity as a confound). Voxels were selected using the omnibus F-ratio to identify those significant at $p < 0.05$ (uncorrected). The adjusted time-series from each of these voxels formed a mean corrected data matrix M with 12 rows (one for each condition) and one column for each voxel.

The images data matrix M was subject to SVD as described in the previous section. The distribution of eigenvalues (Fig. 11.2, lower left) suggests that only two eigenimages are required to account for most of the observed variance–covariance structure. The first mode accounted for 64 per cent and the second for 16 per cent of the variance. The first eigenimage (the first column of V) is shown in Fig. 11.2 (top) along with the corresponding vector in time (the first column of U—lower right). The first eigenimage has negative loadings in the anterior cingulate, the left DLPFC, Broca's area, the thalamic nuclei, and in the cerebellum. Positive loadings were seen bitemporally and in the posterior cingulate. According to U, the negative loadings of this eigenimage are related to the verbal fluency task (negative bars in the lower right of Fig. 11.2). The second eigenimage (not shown) had its highest positive loadings in the anterior cingulate and bitemporal regions (notably Wernicke's area on the left). This eigenimage corresponded to a highly non-linear, monotonic time effect with greatest prominence in earlier conditions.

The *post hoc* functional attribution of these eigenimages is usually based on their time-dependent profiles (U). The first eigenimage may represent an intentional system critical for the intrinsic generation of words in the sense that the key cognitive difference between verbal fluency and phoneme repetition is the intrinsic generation as opposed to extrinsic specification of word representations and implicit mnemonic processing. The second eigenimage, that includes the anterior cingulate, seems to be involved in habituation, possibly of attentional or perceptual set.

There is nothing 'biologically' important about the particular spatial modes obtained in this fashion, in the sense that one could 'rotate' the eigenvectors such that they were still orthogonal and yet gave different eigenimages. The uniqueness of the particular solution given by SVD is that the first eigenimage accounts for the largest amount of variance–covariance and the second for the greatest amount that remains and so on. The reason that the eigenimages in the example above lend themselves to such a simple interpretation is that the variance introduced by experimental design (i.e. intentional component = verbal fluency) was substantially greater than that due to time (i.e. habituation), and both these sources were greater than any other effect. Other factors that ensure a parsimonious characterization of a time-series, with small numbers of well defined modes, include (i) smoothness in the data and (ii) using only voxels that showed a non-trivial amount of change during the scanning session. The eigenimage analysis is not independent of the categorical analysis because subject and global blood-flow effects were removed and only voxels that survived a threshold of $p < 0.05$ in the omnibus F-test were used. Therefore this analysis delivers additional information, but should not be seen as an independent validation.

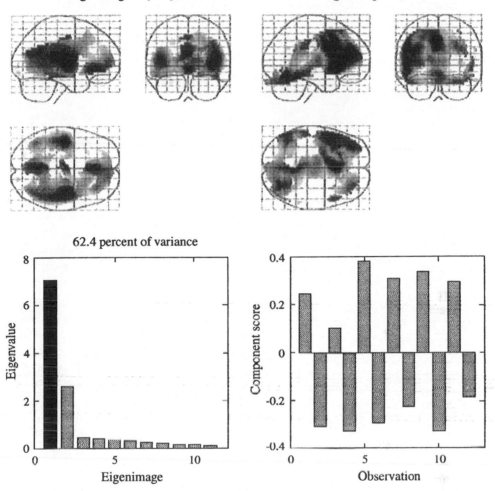

Fig. 11.2 Eigenimage analysis of the PET activation study of word generation. Top: positive and negative components of the first eigenimage (i.e. first column of V). The maximum intensity projection display format is standard and provides three views of the brain in the stereotactic space of Talairach and Tournoux (1988), from the back, from the right, and from the top. Lower left: eigenvalues (singular values squared) of the functional connectivity matrix reflecting the relative amounts of variance accounted for by the 11 eigenimages associated with this data. Only two eigenvalues are greater than unity and to all intents and purposes the changes characterizing this time series can be considered two-dimensional. Lower right: the temporal eigenvector reflecting the expression of this eigenimage over the 12 conditions (i.e. the first column of U). Conditions showing negative component scores are therefore associated with the negative loadings of the first eigenimage.

11.4 Effective connectivity

11.4.1 A simple model

Effective connectivity depends on two models: a mathematical model, describing 'how' areas are connected and a neuroanatomical model describing 'which' areas are connected. We shall consider linear and non-linear models. Perhaps the simplest model of effective connectivity expresses the haemodynamic change at one voxel as a weighted sum of changes elsewhere. This can be regarded as a multiple linear regression, where the effective connectivity reflects the amount of rCBF variability, at the target region, attributable to rCBF changes at a source region. As an example, consider the influence of other areas M on area $V1$. This can be framed in a simple equation:

$$(3) \quad V1 = Mc + e$$

where M is a $n \times m$ matrix with m regions and n observations (scans), c is a $m \times 1$ column vector with a parameter estimate for each region.

Implicit in this interpretation is a mediation of this influence by neuronal connections with an effective strength equal to the (regression) coefficients c. This highlights the fact that the linear model assumes that the connectivity is constant over the whole range of activation and is isolated from other sources.

Experience suggests that the linear model can give fairly robust results. One explanation is that the dimensionality (the number of things that are going on) of the physiological changes can be small. In fact, the distribution of eigenvalues associated with the PET study of the previous section suggested a very low dimensionality. In other words, the brain responds to simple and well organized experiments in a simple and well organized way.

Generally, however, neurophysiology is non-linear and the adequacy of linear models must be questioned (or at least qualified). Consequently we will focus on a nonlinear model of effective connectivity (Friston *et al.* 1995). Reversible cooling experiments in monkey visual cortex, during visual stimulation, have demonstrated that neuronal activity in $V2$ depends on forward inputs from $V1$. Conversely neuronal activity in $V1$ is *modulated* by backward or re-entrant connections from $V2$ to $V1$ (Girard and Bullier 1988; Sandell and Schiller 1982; Schiller and Malpeli 1977). Retinotopically corresponding regions of $V1$ and $V2$ are reciprocally connected in the monkey. $V1$ provides a crucial input to $V2$, in the sense that visual activation of $V2$ cells depends on input from $V1$. This dependency has been demonstrated by reversibly cooling (deactivating) $V1$ while recording from $V2$ during visual stimulation (Girard and Bullier 1988; Schiller and Malpeli 1977). In contrast, cooling $V2$ has a more *modulatory* effect on $V1$ unit activity. The cells in $V1$ that were most affected by $V2$ deactivation were in the infragranular layers, suggesting $V2$ may use this pathway to modulate the output from $V1$ (Sandell and Schiller 1982). Because, in the absence of $V1$ input, these re-entrant connections do not constitute an efficient drive to $V2$ cells, their role is most likely to modulate the information relayed through area 17 ($V1$).

To examine the interactions between $V1$ and $V2$, using fMRI in man, we have used a non-linear model of effective connectivity, extended to include a modulatory interaction (cf. Eq. (3)):

$$(4) \quad V1 = M \cdot c_O + \text{diag}(V1)Mc_M$$

where diag($V1$) refers to a diagonal matrix with elements of the vector $V1$.

This model has two terms that allow for the activity in area $V1$ to be influenced by the activity in other areas M (our hypothesis being that $V2$ is prominent amongst those areas). The first represents an effect that depends only on afferent input from other areas M. This is the activity in M scaled by c_O. The coefficients in c_O are referred to as *obligatory* connection strengths, in the sense that a change in areas M results in an obligatory response in area $V1$. This is similar to c in the simple linear model above. Conversely, the second term reflects a modulatory influence of areas M on area $V1$. The coefficient determining the size of this effect (c_M) is referred to as a *modulatory* connection strength, because the overall effect depends on both the afferent input ($M \cdot c_M$) and intrinsic activity in $V1$. This can be considered as a greater responsiveness of $V1$ to inputs at higher intrinsic activation of $V1$.

This intrinsic activity-dependent effect, determined by the value of c_M, provides an intuitive sense of how to estimate c_M. Imagine one were able to 'fix' the activity in $V1$ at a *low* level and measure the connectivity between the regions in M and $V1$ assuming a simple linear relationship (Eq. (3)); A value for the sensitivity of $V1$ to changes elsewhere could be obtained, say c_1. Now, if the procedure were repeated with $V1$ activity fixed at a *high* level, a second (linear) estimate would be obtained, say c_2. In the presence of a substantial modulatory interaction between regions in M and $V1$ the second estimate (c_2) will be higher than the first (c_1). This is because the activity intrinsic to $V1$ is higher and $V1$ should be more sensitive to inputs. In short $c_2 - c_1$ provides an estimate of the modulatory influence on $V1$. By analogy to reversible cooling which allows one to remove the effects of isolated cortical regions, we 'fix' activity *post hoc* by simply selecting a subset of data in which the $V1$ activity is confined to some small range (*high* or *low* activity).

The data used in this analysis were a time series of 64 gradient-echo EPI coronal slices (5 mm thick, with 64×64 voxels $2.5 \times 2.5 \times 5$ mm) through the calcarine sulcus and extrastriate areas. Images were obtained every 3 s from a normal male subject using a 4.0 T whole body system, fitted with a small (27 cm diameter) z-gradient coil (TE 25 ms, acquisition time 41 ms). Photic stimulation (at 16 Hz) was provided by goggles fitted with 16 light emitting diodes. The stimulation was off for the first ten scans (30 s), on for the second ten, off for the third, and so on. The data were interpolated to 128×128 voxels. Each interpolated voxel thus represented $1.25 \times 1.25 \times 5$ mm of cerebral tissue. The first four scans were removed to eliminate magnetic saturation effects and the remainder were realigned. The result of this preprocessing was a mean corrected data matrix M with 60 rows (one for each scan) and 2160 columns (one for each voxel).

11.4.1.1 Results

A reference voxel was chosen in right $V1$ and the effective connection strengths c_M were estimated allowing a map of c_M (and c_O) to be constructed. This map provides a direct test of the hypothesis concerning the topography and regional specificity of modulatory influences on $V1$. The lower row in Fig. 11.3 shows maps of c_O and c_M (for a

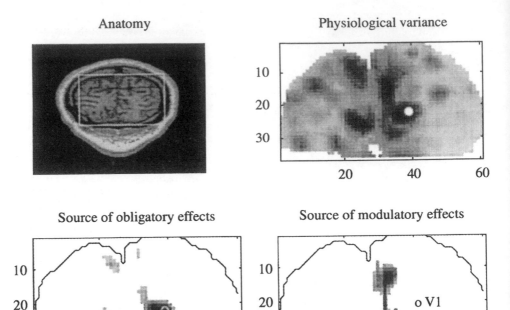

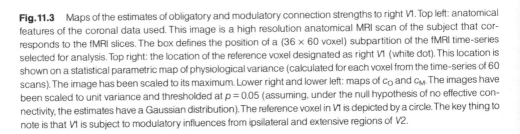

Fig.11.3 Maps of the estimates of obligatory and modulatory connection strengths to right *V*1. Top left: anatomical features of the coronal data used. This image is a high resolution anatomical MRI scan of the subject that corresponds to the fMRI slices. The box defines the position of a (36 × 60 voxel) subpartition of the fMRI time-series selected for analysis. Top right: the location of the reference voxel designated as right *V*1 (white dot). This location is shown on a statistical parametric map of physiological variance (calculated for each voxel from the time-series of 60 scans). The image has been scaled to its maximum. Lower right and lower left: maps of c_O and c_M. The images have been scaled to unit variance and thresholded at $p = 0.05$ (assuming, under the null hypothesis of no effective connectivity, the estimates have a Gaussian distribution). The reference voxel in *V*1 is depicted by a circle. The key thing to note is that *V*1 is subject to modulatory influences from ipsilateral and extensive regions of *V*2.

reference in *V*1 on the right) which reflect the degree to which the area exerts an obligatory (left) or modulatory (right) effect on *V*1 activity. These maps have been thresholded at 1.64 after normalization to a standard deviation of unity. This corresponds to an uncorrected threshold of $p = 0.05$.

The obligatory connections to the reference voxel derive mainly from *V*1 itself, both ipsilaterally and contralaterally with a small contribution from contiguous portions of *V*2. The effective connectivity from contralateral *V*1 should not be over-interpreted given that (i) the source of many afferents to *V*1 (the lateral geniculate nuclei) were not included in the field of view and that (ii) this finding can be more parsimoniously explained by 'common input'. As predicted, and with remarkable regional specificity, the modulatory connections were most marked from ipsilateral *V*2, dorsal and ventral to the calcarine fissure (note that 'common input' cannot explain interactions between $V1$ and $V2$ because the geniculate inputs are restricted to $V1$).

11.4.1.2 Functional asymmetry in $V2$–$V1$ and $V1$–$V2$ modulatory connections

To address functional asymmetry in terms of forward and backward modulatory influences the modulatory connection strengths between two extended regions (two 5×5 voxel squares) in ipsilateral $V1$ and $V2$ were examined. The estimates of effective connection strengths were based on haemodynamic changes in all areas and the subset of connections between the two regions were selected to compare the distributions of forward and backward modulatory influences. Figure 11.4 shows the location of the two regions and the frequency distribution (i.e. histogram) of the estimates for connections from the voxels in the $V1$ box to the $V2$ box (broken line) and the corresponding estimates for connections from voxels in the $V2$ box to $V1$ (solid line). There is a remarkable dissociation, with backward modulatory effects ($V2$ to $V1$) being much greater than forward effects ($V1$ to $V2$). This can be considered a confirmation of the functional asymmetry hypothesis.

11.4.2 Structural equation modelling

The simple model above was sufficient to analyse effective connectivity to one region at a time (e.g. $V1$ or $V2$). We will now introduce structural equation modelling as a tool allowing for more complicated models comprising many regions of interest and demonstrate how non-linear interactions are dealt with in this context. The basic idea

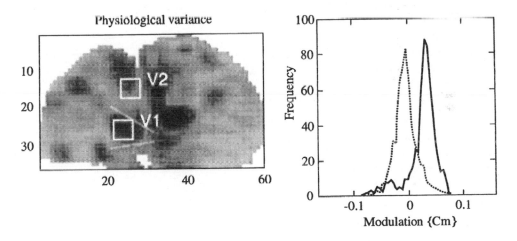

Fig.11.4 Graphical presentation of a direct test of the hypothesis concerning the asymmetry between forward and backward $V1$–$V2$ interactions. Left: a map of physiological variance showing the positions of two boxes defining regions in left $V1$ and $V2$. The broken lines correspond (roughly) to the position of the $V1/V2$ border according to the atlas of Talairach and Tournoux (1988). The value of c_M were computed for all voxels in either box and Euclidean normalized to unity over the image. The frequency distribution of c_M connecting the two regions is presented on the right. The backward connections ($V2$ to $V1$, solid line) are clearly higher than the corresponding forward connections ($V1$ to $V2$, broken line).

behind structural equation modelling (SEM) differs from the usual statistical approach of modelling individual observations. In the multiple regression or AnCova models reviewed in the previous section, the regression coefficients or the error variance derive from the minimization of the sum of squared differences of the predicted and observed dependent variables (i.e. activity in the target region). Structural equation modelling approaches the data from a different perspective: instead of considering variables individually, the emphasis lies on the variance–covariance structure. Thus, models are solved in structural equation modelling by minimizing the difference between the observed variance–covariance structure and the one implied by a structural or path model. In the past few years, structural equation modelling has been applied to functional brain imaging. For example, McIntosh and Gonzalez-Lima (1994) demonstrated the dissociation between ventral and dorsal visual pathways for object and spatial vision using structural equation modelling of PET data in the human. In this section we will focus on the theoretical background of structural equation modelling and demonstrate this technique using functional brain imaging with fMRI.

In terms of neuronal systems, a measure of covariance represents the degree to which the activities of two or more regions are related (i.e. functional connectivity). The study of variance–covariance structures in neurosciences is much simpler compared to applications in other fields: the interconnection of the dependent variables (regional activity of brain areas) is anatomically determined and the activation of each region can be directly measured with functional brain imaging. This represents a major difference to 'classical' structural equation modelling in the behavioural sciences, where models are often hypothetical and include latent variables denoting rather abstract concepts like intelligence.

As mentioned above, structural equation modelling minimizes the difference between the observed or measured covariance matrix and the one that is implied by the structure of the model. The free parameters (path coefficients or connection strengths c above) are adjusted to minimize the difference[1] between the measured and modelled covariance matrix (see Büchel and Friston (1997) for details).

An important issue in structural equation modelling is the determination of the participating regions and the underlying anatomical model. Several approaches to this issue can be adopted: these include categorical comparisons between different conditions, eigenimages highlighting structures of functional connectivity, and non-human electrophysiological and anatomical studies (McIntosh and Gonzalez-Lima 1994). A model is always a simplification of reality: absolutely exhaustively correct models either do not exist, or would be too complicated to understand. In the context of effective connectivity one has to find a compromise between complexity, anatomical accuracy, and interpretability. There are also mathematical constraints on the model: if the number of free parameters exceeds the number of observed covariances the system is underdetermined and no single solution exists.

In the context of multivariate normally distributed variables, the minimum of the maximum likelihood fit function times the number of observations minus one, follows a chi-square distribution (Bollen 1989). Therefore each estimated model will give a chi-square distributed goodness of fit measure. This measure is useful when comparing different models with each other. This 'nested model' approach can be used to compare different models (e.g. data from different groups or conditions) in the context of structural equation modelling. A so called 'null-model' is constructed where the estimates of the free parameters are constrained to be the same for both groups. The alternative model allows free parameters to differ between groups. The significance of the differences between the models is expressed by the difference of the chi-square goodness of fit statistic. Consider the following hypothetical example. Subjects are scanned under two different conditions, for example 'attention' and 'no attention'. The hypothesis might be that within a system of regions A, B, C and D, the connectivity between A and B is different under the two attentional conditions. To determine whether the difference in connectivity is statistically significant, we estimate the goodness of fit measure for two models: Model 1 allows the connectivity between A and B to take different values for both conditions. Model 2 constrains the path coefficient between A and B to be equal for 'attention' and 'no attention'. If the change ofconnectivity between 'attention'and 'no attention'for the connection of A and B is negligible, the constrained model (model 2) should fit the data equally well compared to the free model (1). Since both goodness of fit measures are chi-square distributed, we can now infer whether the difference of the two goodness of fit measures are significant, because the difference will also be chi-square distributed. Model 2 has one degree of freedom (path coefficient) less than model 1, so the difference of fit follows a chi-square distribution with one degree of freedom.

How are path coefficients interpreted? The path coefficients calculated by the minimization procedure outlined above depend upon the units in which the variables are measured. Although all variables in functional imaging procedures are measured in the same units, the direct comparison of path coefficients between two different groups might be misleading due to different scaling (e.g. global blood flow in PET). In this case standardized path coefficients are calculated. This is the path coefficient times the ratio of the standard deviations of the two connected variables (the standard deviation of the caused variable constituting the denominator). The standardized coefficient shows the mean response in units of standard deviation of the dependent variable for a standard deviation change in an explanatory variable, whilst the other variables in the model are held constant (Bollen 1989).

Non-linear models can also be accommodated in the framework of SEM by introducing additional variables containing a non-linear function (e.g. $f(x) = x^2$) of theoriginal variables (Kenny and Judd 1984). Interactions of variables can be incorporated in a similar fashion; wherein a new variable, containing the product of the two interacting variables, is introduced as an additional influence. This is similar to the approach used in the previous section, where the interaction was expressed by the influence of the product of $V1$ and $V2$ on $V1$. We will now demonstrate these ideas using an example. More details of structural equation modelling, including the operational equations, can be found in Büchel and Friston (1997).

11.4.2.1 Example: attention

Electrophysiological and neuroimaging studies have shown that attention to visual motion can increase the responsiveness of the motion-selective cortical area $V5$ (O'Craven and Savoy 1995; Treue and Maunsell 1996) and the posterior parietal cortex (PP) (Assad and Maunsell 1995). Increased or decreased activation in a cortical area is often attributed to attentional modulation of the cortical projections to that area. This leads to the notion that attention is associated with changes in connectivity.

Here we present fMRI data from an individual subject, scanned under identical visual motion stimulus conditions, while changing only the attentional component of the tasks employed. In the first stage we identified regions that show differential activations in relation to attentional set. In the second stage changes in effective connectivity to these areas are assessed using structural equation modelling. In the final stage we show how these attention dependent changes in effective connectivity might be explained by the modulatory influence of parietal areas using a non-linear extension of structural equation modelling. The specific hypothesis we addressed was that parietal cortex could modulate the inputs from $V1$ to $V5$.

The experiment was performed on a 2 Tesla whole body MRI system equipped with a head volume coil. Contiguous multislice T2* weighted fMRI images were obtained with echo-planar imaging (EPI). The effective repetition time was 3.22 s. The subject was scanned during four different conditions: 'fixation', 'attention', 'no attention', and 'stationary'. Each condition lasted 32 s giving 10 multislice volumes per condition. We acquired a total of 360 images. During all conditions the subject looked at a fixation point in the middle of a screen. In this section we are only interested in the two conditions with visual motion ('attention' and 'no attention'), where 250 small white dots moved radially from the fixation point, in random directions, towards the border of the screen, at a constant speed of 4.7° per second. The difference between 'attention' and 'no attention' lay in the explicit command given to the subject shortly before the condition: 'just look' indicated 'no attention' and 'detect changes' the 'attention' condition. Both visual motion conditions were interleaved with 'fixation'. No response was required.

Before scanning, the subject was exposed to five 30-second trials of the stimulus. The speed of the moving dots was changed five times during each trial. The subject was asked to indicate any change in speed. Changes in speed were gradually reduced over the five trials, until a 1 per cent change was presented on the last occasion. Once in the scanner, changes in speed were completely eliminated (without the knowledge of the subject), so that identical visual stimuli were shown in all the motion conditions.

Regions of interest were defined by categorical comparisons using the SPM{Z} comparing 'attention' and 'no attention' and comparing 'no attention' and 'fixation'. As predicted, given a stimulus consisting of radially moving dots, we found activation of the lateral geniculate nucleus (LGN), primary visual cortex ($V1$), motion sensitive area $V5$ and the posterior parietal complex (PP). For the subsequent analysis of effective connectivity, we defined regions of interest (ROI) with a diameter of 8 mm, centred around the most significant voxel as revealed by the categorical comparison.

A single time-series, representative of this region, was defined by the first eigenvector of all the voxels in the ROI (Büchel and Friston 1997).

Our model of the dorsal visual stream included the LGN, primary visual cortex ($V1$), $V5$ and the posterior parietal complex (PP). Although connections between regions are generally reciprocal, for simplicity we only modelled unidirectional paths.

To assess effective connectivity in a condition-specific fashion, we used time-series that comprised observations during the condition in question. Path coefficients for both conditions ('attention' and 'no attention') were estimated using a maximum likelihood function implemented in MatLab. To test for the impact of changes in effective connectivity between 'attention' and 'no attention', we defined a free model (allowing different path coefficients between $V1$ and $V5$ for attention and no attention) and a constrained model (constraining the $V1 \rightarrow V5$ coefficients to be equal). Figure 11.5 shows the free model and the estimated path coefficients. The connectivity between $V1$ and $V5$ increases significantly during attention. Note that there is also a significant difference in connectivity between $V5$ and PP.

The linear path model comparing 'attention' and 'no attention' revealed increased effective connectivity in the dorsal visual pathway in relation to attention. The question that arises is which part of the brain is capable of modulating this pathway? Based on lesion studies (Lawler and Cowey 1987) and on the system for directed attention as described by Mesulam (1990), the posterior parietal cortex is hypothesized to play such a modulatory role.

We extended our model accordingly to allow for non-linear interactions, testing the hypothesis that the PP acts as a moderator on the connectivity between $V1$ and $V5$. Assuming a non-linear modulation of this connection, we constructed a new variable 'V1PP' in our analysis. This variable, mediating the interaction, is simply the time series from region $V1$ multiplied (element by element) by the time-series of the right posterior parietal region.

The influence of this new variable on $V5$ corresponds to the influence of the posterior parietal cortex on the connection between $V1$ and $V5$ (i.e. the influence of $V1$ on $V5$ is greater when activity in PP is high). The model is shown in Fig. 11.6. Because our non-linear model could accommodate changes in connectivity between 'attention' and 'no attention' the entire time-series was analysed (i.e. attention specific changes are now explicitly modelled by the interaction term).

As in the linear model, we tested for the significance of the interaction effect by comparing a restricted and a free model. In the restricted model the interaction term (i.e. the path from $V1PP$ to $V5$) was set to zero. Omitting the interaction term led to a significantly reduced model fit ($\chi^2 = 10.8, p < 0.01$), indicating the predictive value of the interaction term.

The presence of an interaction effect of the PP on the connection between $V1$ and $V5$ can also be illustrated by a simple regression analysis. If PP shows a positive modulatory influence on the path between $V1$ and $V5$, the influence of $V1$ on $V5$ should depend on the activity of PP. This can be tested, by splitting the observations into two sets, one containing observations in which PP activity is high and another one in which

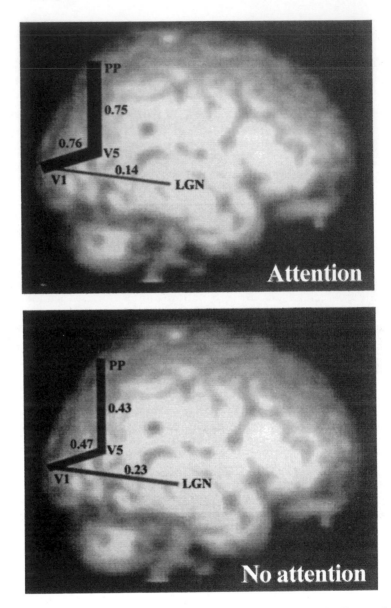

Fig.11.5   Structural equation model of the dorsal visual pathway, comparing 'attention' and 'no attention'. Connectivity between right *V1* and *V5* is increased during 'attention' relative to 'no attention'. This is also shown for the connection between *V5* and PP.

PP activity is low. It is now possible to perform separate regressions of $V5$ on $V1$ using both sets. If the hypothesis of positive modulation is true, the slope of the regression of $V5$ on $V1$ should be steeper under high values of PP. Figure 11.7 shows exactly this and provides the regression coefficients and the p-value for the difference in slope. This

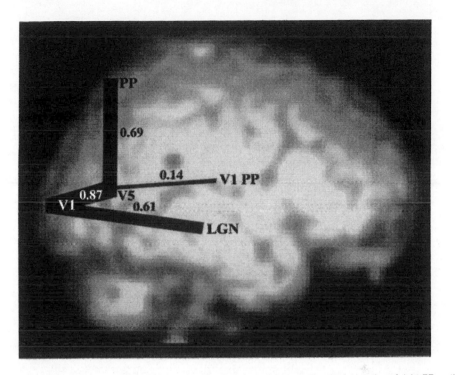

Fig. 11.6 Structural equation model of the dorsal visual pathway incorporating the interaction of right PP on the connection from right V1 to V5.

approach is comparable to the one outlined in the first section, where we used high and low values to demonstrate a modulation of $V1$ on the influence $V2$ has over $V1$.

11.4.3 Effective connectivity versus categorical comparisons

One obvious advantage of the assessment of effective connectivity is that it allows one to test hypotheses about the integration of cortical areas. For example in the presence of modulation the categorical comparison between 'attention' and 'no attention' might reveal prestriate, parietal, and frontal activations. However, the only statement possible is that these areas show higher cortical activity during the 'attention' condition as opposed to the 'no attention' condition. The analysis of effective connectivity revealed two additional results. Firstly, we showed that attention affects the pathway from $V1$ to $V5$ and from $V5$ to PP. Secondly, the introduction of non-linear interaction terms allowed us to test a hypothesis about how these modulations are mediated. The latter analysis suggested that the posterior parietal cortex exerts a modulatory influence on area $V5$.

The measurements used in all examples of this chapter were *haemodynamic* in nature. This limits an interpretation at the level of *neuronal* interactions. However the analogy between the form of the non-linear interactions above and voltage-dependent (i.e. modulatory) connections is a strong one. It is possible that the modulatory impact

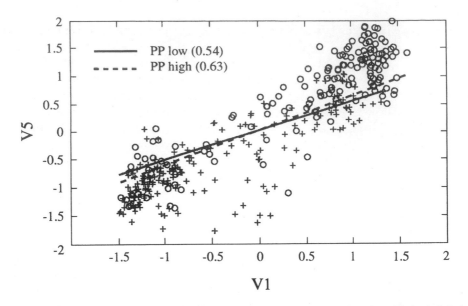

Fig. 11.7   Regression of *V5* on *V1*. The data is split in samples where PP activity is either above (dashed; circles) or below (solid; plus) the mean. A greater regression coefficient for high values of PP indicates a modulation of connection from right *V1* to *V5* by right PP ($p < 0.05$).

of *V2* on *V1* is mediated by predominantly voltage-dependent connections. The presence of horizontal voltage-dependent connections within *V1* has been established in cat striate cortex (Hirsch and Gilbert 1991). We know of no direct electrophysiological evidence to suggest that extrinsic backward *V2* to *V1* connections are voltage-dependent; however our results are consistent with this. An alternative explanation for modulatory effects, which does not necessarily involve voltage-dependent connections, can be found in the work of Aertsen and Preissl (1991). These authors show that effective connectivity varies strongly with, or is modulated by, background neuronal activity. The mechanism relates to the efficacy of subthreshold excitatory postsynaptic potentials (EPSPs) in establishing dynamic interactions. This efficacy is a function of post-synaptic depolarization, which in turn depends on the tonic background of activity. This clearly relates to the idea that sensitivity to afferent input (from *V2*) increases with intrinsic activity (in *V1*).

It is also important to clarify the terms 'excitatory' and 'inhibitory' effects in the context of effective connectivity. The conclusion that a positive path coefficient from region A to B reflects a predominantly excitatory pathway between A and B might not be true. As mentioned before, all measurements are haemodynamic in nature and one has to keep in mind that both excitation and inhibition can lead to an increase in metabolic requirement and haemodynamic response.

11.4.4 Conclusions

This chapter has reviewed the basic concepts of functional and effective connectivity in neuroimaging. Eigenimages were introduced as a parsimonious characterization of functional connectivity in imaging neuroscience. In the second half, we introduced methods to assess effective connectivity. The first example demonstrated that non-linear interactions can be characterized using simple extensions of linear models. In the second example, structural equation modelling was introduced as a device that allows one to combine observed changes in cortical activity and anatomical models. This example focused on backward modulatory influences of high order areas on lower order areas. This clearly relates to the sorts of effects illustrated in Fig. 11.1 that are probably ubiquitous at all levels of word processing. Both examples concentrated on changes in effective connectivity and allowed us to characterize the interacting areas of the network at a functional level. Although less than a mature field, this approach to neuroimaging data and regional interactions is an exciting endeavour that is starting to attract more and more attention. Currently these techniques are applied in areas where strong anatomical and electrophysiological prior knowledge from non-human primates exists. It will be a challenge to apply these techniques to imaging studies in humans, where we cannot rely on prior knowledge. This challenge will be more acute when looking at language systems in the human brain. However, the potential insight makes it a challenge that is worth taking up.

Notes

1. The free parameters are estimated by minimizing a function of the observed and implied covariance matrix. To date the most widely used objective function in structural equation modelling is the maximum likelihood (ML) function.

References

Aertsen, A. and Preissl, H. (1991). *Dynamics of activity and connectivity in physiological neuronal networks*. VCH, New York.

Assad, J. A. and Maunsell, J. H. (1995). Neuronal correlates of inferred motion in primate posterior parietal cortex. *Nature*, **373**, 518–20.

Atkinson, R. C. and Shiffrin, R. M. (1967). Human memory: A proposed system and its control processes. *Technical Report No. 110*, March 21, 1967. Psychology Series Institute for Mathematical Studies in the Social Sciences, Stanford University, CA.

Bollen, K. A. (1989). *Structural equations with latent variables*. Wiley, New York.

Büchel, C. and Friston, K. J. (1997). Modulation of connectivity in visual pathways by attention: Cortical interactions evaluated with structural equation modelling and fMRI. *Cerebral Cortex*, **7**, 768–78.

Friedrich, R., Fuchs, A., and Haken, H. (1991). Modelling of spatio-temporal EEG patterns. In *Mathematical approaches to brain functioning diagnostics* (eds I. Dvorak and A. V. Holden), pp. 45–61. Manchester University Press, New York.

Friston, K. J., Frith, C. D., and Frackowiak, R. S. J. (1993*a*). Time-dependent changes in effective connectivity measured with PET. *Human Brain Mapping*, **1**, 69–80.

Friston, K. J., Frith, C. D., Liddle, P. F., and Frackowiak, R. S. J. (1993*b*). Functional connectivity: The principal component analysis of large (PET) data sets. *Journal of Cerebral Blood Flow Metabolism*, **13**, 5–14.

Friston, K. J., Jezzard, P., Frackowiak, R. S. J., and Turner, R. (1993*c*). Characterizing focal and distributed physiological changes with MRI and PET functional MRI of the Brain. *Society of Magnetic Resonance in Medicine, Berkeley CA*, 207–16.

Friston, K. J., Ungerleider, L. G., Jezzard, P., and Turner, R. (1995). Characterizing modulatory interactions between V1 and V2 in human cortex with fMRI. *Human Brain Mapping*, **2**, 211–24.

Fuchs, A., Kelso, J. A. S., and Haken, H. (1992). Phase transitions in the human brain: Spatial mode dynamics. *International Journal of Bifurcation and Chaos*, **2**, 917–39.

Gerstein, G. L. and Perkel, D. H. (1969). Simultaneously recorded trains of action potentials: Analysis and functional interpretation. *Science*, **164**, 828–30.

Gerstein, G. L., Bedenbaugh, P., and Aertsen, A. (1989). Neuronal assemblies. *IEEE Transactions on Biomedical Engineering*, **36**, 4–14.

Girard, P. and Bullier, J. (1988). Visual activity in area V2 during reversible inactivation of area 17 in the macaque monkey. *Journal of Neurophysiology*, **62**, 1287–1301.

Hirsch, J. A. and Gilbert, C. D. (1991). Synaptic physiology of horizontal connections in the cat's visual cortex. *Journal of Neuroscience*, **11**, 1800–09.

Kenny, D. A. and Judd, C. M. (1984). Estimating nonlinear and interactive effects of latent variables. *Psychological Bulletin*, **96**, 201–10.

Lashley, K. S. (1929). *Brain mechanisms and intelligence*. University of Chicago Press.

Lawler, K. A. and Cowey, A. (1987). On the role of posterior parietal and prefrontal cortex in visuo-spatial perception and attention. *Experimental Brain Research*, **65**, 695–8.

Marshall, J. C. and Newcombe, F. (1973). Patterns of paralexia: A neurolinguistic approach. *Journal of Psycholinguistic Research*, **2**, 175–99.

Mayer-Kress, G., Barczys, C., and Freeman, W. (1991). Attractor reconstruction from event-related multi-electrode EEG data. In *Mathematical approaches to brain functioning diagnostics* (eds I. Dvorak and A. V. Holden), pp. 315–36. Manchester University Press, New York.

McIntosh, A. R. and Gonzalez-Lima, F. (1994). Structural equation modelling and its application to network analysis in functional brain imaging. *Human Brain Mapping*, **2**, 2–22.

Mesulam, M. M. (1990). Large-scale neurocognitive networks and distributed processing for attention, language, and memory. *Annals of Neurology*, **28**, 597–613.

O'Craven, K. M. and Savoy R. L. (1995). Voluntary attention can modulate fMRI activity in human MT/MST. *Investigative Ophthalmology and Visual Science (Suppl.)*, **36**, 856.

Petersen, S. E., Fox, P. T., Snyder, A. Z., and Raichle, M. E. (1990). Activation of extrastriate and frontal cortical areas by words and word-like stimuli. *Science*, **249**, 1041–44.

Posner, M. I., Petersen, S. E., Fox, P. T., and Raichle, M. E. (1988). Localization of cognitive operations in the human brain. *Science*, **240**, 1627–31.

Sandell, J. H. and Schiller, P. H. (1982). Effect of cooling area 18 on striate cortex cells in the squirrel monkey. *Journal of Neurophysiology*, **48**, 38–48.

Schiller, P. H. and Malpeli, J. G. (1977). The effect of striate cortex cooling on area 18 cells in the monkey. *Brain Research*, **126**, 366–9.

Shallice, T. (1988). *From neuropsychology to mental structure*. Cambridge University Press.

Talairach, P. and Tournoux, J. (1988). *A stereotactic coplanar atlas of the human brain*. Thieme, Stuttgart.

Treue, S. and Maunsell, H. R. (1996). Attentional modulation of visual motion processing in cortical areas MT and MST. *Nature*, **382**, 539–41.

Warren, R. M. (1970). Perceptual restoration of missing speech sounds. *Science*, **167**, 392–93.

Warrington, E. K. and Shallice, T. (1969). The selective impairment of auditory short term memory. *Brain*, **92**, 885–96.

Willmes, K. and Poeck, K. (1993). To what extent can aphasic syndromes be localized. *Brain*, **116**, 1527–40.

12 *Current approaches to mapping language in electromagnetic space*

Marta Kutas, Kara D. Federmeier, and Martin I. Sereno

'Language ... this great instrument which we have jointly built ... every word the mystic embodiment of a thousand years of vanished passion, hope, desire, thought.'

Voltairine de Cleyre

12.1 Introduction

The human species is distinguished by its tool-making abilities, and by far the most important and frequently used tool we have created is language. We use language to convey our thoughts and feelings to others via the systematic combination of spoken sounds, manual signs, or written symbols. This ability allows us to bridge the minds of others—sometimes across vast distances of time and space. Language mediates and shapes our social structure, dividing the people of the world according to the kind of sounds or signs they recognize and produce. Language is also used to bring individuals together—to reinforce emotional ties (e.g. wedding vows, business contracts), or to negotiate peace treaties.

Comprehending language requires deriving structure from a stream of auditory or visual inputs at a number of levels. From sensory signals are built phonemes/letters, morphemes, syllables, words, phrases, clauses, sentences, discourses, and, ultimately, concepts. All of these levels are structured—each in its own way—yet extremely flexible as well. Every day we are likely to hear and to produce strings of sounds or signs that we have never before heard or produced. Yet we comprehend these novel streams with ease, perhaps because they are so structured. Having comprehended language input, we can respond by converting concepts into a series of motor commands that will produce systematic changes in our vocal tract and/or our hands.

These transformations require a sophisticated set of sensory receptors and motor effectors. However, whether we comprehend or produce by hand or by mouth, by ear or by eye, the essential processes that allow concepts and feelings to be transferred over individuals, space, and time take place in the human brain. Like language itself, the human brain is structured on a number of levels. On a very gross level, the human brain is made up of two cerebral hemispheres, a thalamus, midbrain structures, a cerebellum, and a hindbrain. These, in turn, can be divided into areas—regions with gross morphological or functional differences. Areas are built from neural ensembles that are made up of neurons, that are, themselves, just the medium for a complicated set of electrochemical processes.

12.2 Using neurobiological data to understand language processes

Because, in essence, it is the brain from which human language derives, it is to the brain that many turn to discover what language is like, how it is learned and used, and how it might be learned or used more effectively. To do this requires that one look at language in new ways. This chapter describes some of these ways and outlines the improvements that have been made and need to be made in order for the brain-language mappings to yield the information we seek. First, we must begin to understand language as a set of electrochemical processes. Accordingly, we briefly overview the basis of neural communication and outline the strengths and limitations of the various psychophysiological techniques used to measure aspects of electrochemical activity in the brain. These electrochemical processes we measure take place over time and space. Already psychophysiological techniques have allowed us to monitor various aspects of language over time. What has proven harder is the use of these techniques to examine the spatial mapping of language function. We discuss, first, strategies for comparing the spatial distributions of electromagnetic data and for decomposing those distributions into subparts. We then turn to the difficult problem of linking measured distributions to underlying neural generators, outlining the kinds of models used to make this mapping and examining their assumptions.

Turning the measurements we make with our psychophysiological tools into an understanding of the flow of information over space and time and mapping that onto cognition is a difficult and delicate process. Nonetheless, progress is being made and the potential rewards are numerous. By examining the neurobiological roots of language processing, we can ask how the structure and flexibility of the brain mediates the structure and flexibility of language at various levels of both. What brain areas are involved in language processing and what are the more general functions of these areas? What is the extent and temporal order of their involvement in various aspects of language processing? The information that neurobiology has to offer theories of language is very rich and can aid our understanding in a number of different ways. First, neurobiological data can test the psychological reality of the different kinds of language representations posited by linguists and psycholinguists. For example, linguistic theories have suggested that speech is broken down into phonemes, an abstract 'sound' representation that encompasses a number of different possible physical (acoustic and articulatory) patterns. Psycholinguists and linguists also have argued for the existence of a structured lexicon, or 'mental dictionary', of words that mediates associations between their phonological, orthographic, morphological, and semantic aspects. To what extent do we find evidence for these representational levels (e.g. phonological, lexical, semantic, syntactic) and their proposed organizations in the brain?

Neurobiological data also can inform theories about how various representations are used during language production and comprehension. Some theories, for example, maintain that various language subprocesses are handled by independent, highly specialized 'modules' that are impervious to other types of information. This approach predicts that brain areas processing different types of representations will have little direct influence over one another and will become active in specific sequences (e.g. syntax before semantics). Interactionist accounts, on the other hand, maintain that lower levels of processing/representation are not entirely independent of higher levels but rather interact with them continuously during the processing of a sentence, for instance. Both accounts continue to grapple with questions regarding the domain-generality of language processing. To what extent does the structure of language arise from the functioning of language-specific neurobiological processes and to what extent does it emerge from more general cognitive constraints, such as the amount and availability of attentional and working memory resources?

Neurobiological data can help not only to sort out the nature of language representations and the processes that act on them but also to reveal how language develops, breaks down after trauma or disease, and serves individuals who know more than one. To use neurobiological data to constrain linguistic and psycholinguistic theories, however, requires us to determine what factors the brain is sensitive to and how those factors contribute to language function(s). This is especially difficult, as the concepts and terminology used to theorize about language processing do not readily map onto the terms and concepts used to understand brain functioning. Research using animal models, for example, has shown that factors such as stimulus modality and intensity, frequency (type and token, in the world and in the experimental context), spatial and temporal proximity, similarity (between two stimuli or between a stimulus and a stored representation), and context (physical, experimental, etc.) all influence neurobiological processes. When these factors are manipulated experimentally, one observes changes at various levels; here we give just a few illustrative examples.

Neuronal responses are very context-sensitive; in fact, the firing pattern of individual neurons to the same stimulus has been observed to change in response to aspects of context that are outside the neuron's 'field of view' (classical receptive field) (Zipser *et al.* 1996). When stimuli are paired together or repeated in rapid succession, the response of neurons may be enhanced for minutes to hours, a phenomenon known as long-term potentiation (LTP) (e.g. original report by Bliss and Lomo 1973); an analogous decrease in neuronal response is observed in some brain areas after inconsistent or infrequent stimulation (LTD, long-term depression) (e.g. Linden 1994). At larger scales, different neurons in a neural ensemble may become active to stimulation depending upon the similarity of the stimulus to something experienced in the distant or recent past. For example, after monkeys had been trained to associate pairs of visual stimuli, researchers noted a significant increase in the number of neurons that would respond to the learned pairs in the inferior temporal cortex of these animals (Sakai and Miyashita 1991). In fact, recent imaging studies suggest that the recruitment of entire brain areas may change with practice (e.g. Raichle *et al.* 1994). These changes can be instantiated with more permanence via the alteration of neuronal connectivity (e.g. Merzenich *et al.* 1988; Black *et al.* 1990). However, it is still relatively uncommon and often difficult to map between these kinds of data and what is known about language processing.

12.3 Electrochemical basis of neural communication

We can begin to understand how these kinds of factors influence language processing, however, by monitoring neural functioning as individuals perform various language tasks. Various kinds of signals can be monitored, of which the most direct and immediate are electrochemical. Just as humans are distinguished from other species of animals by the complexity of their communication abilities, so neurons are distinguished from other types of cells by their more sophisticated ability to communicate. Channels in the resting neural membrane make it selectively permeable to charge-bearing elements (ions) like potassium, creating a stable electrical gradient between the cell interior and the external fluid. In fact, the electrochemical potential created across the membrane for each type of ion can be thought of as a tiny battery. At rest, a neuron maintains a negative potential (ca. -77 mV) inside relative to outside the cell. Communication between neurons arises from the flow of ions across the neural membrane following changes in the permeability of the membrane. Axonal membranes contain voltage-sensitive sodium channels that open when the membrane potential reaches some threshold, thereby increasing sodium conductance and resulting in a rapid, transient depolarization of the membrane (the inside of the cell becoming more positive). This phenomenon is known as an action potential, or 'spike', and forms the basis of signal transmission in axons.

This disruption of the resting electrical potential travels in wave-like fashion along an axon (as an all-or-none spike) and can be passed on to other neurons via the release of neurotransmitters at synapses. Some neurotransmitters released from the presynaptic terminal open ion channels on the receiving postsynaptic cell that increase the permeability of the postsynaptic membrane to sodium ions, making the inside of the cell more positive. This depolarization of the neuron is called an excitatory postsynaptic potential (EPSP). Similarly, neurotransmitters which increase the permeability of the membrane to potassium and chloride and make the inside of the cell more negative generate inhibitory postsynaptic potentials (IPSPs). Over the past 10 years, a lot of voltage-sensitive channels have been found on dendrites too—perhaps most notable being NMDA channels which need both glutamate and depolarization to open.

The neural communication that underlies human communication thus involves the flow of charged particles across the neural membrane, which generates an electric potential in the conductive media both inside and outside the cell. These transmembrane current flows are the basis both for the electrophysiological recordings in the brain and at the scalp and for the magnetic fields recorded outside of the head for the magnetoencephalogram. These magnetic changes occur in a direction perpendicular to the direction of intracranial current flow, as given by the right-hand rule (if the thumb points in the direction of current flow, the magnetic field points in the direction of the curled fingers). Viewed from outside the neuron, each patch of membrane acts as a tiny current source or sink, depending on whether the net local current flow is outward or inward, respectively. Both the electric potential and the magnetic field at time *t* depend on the membrane currents only at that time. This is important for inferences about the timing of electrical and magnetic events at different scalp locations. Moreover, the electric potential field generated by a particular spatial distribution of sources and sinks is the simple linear sum of the individual contribution of each current source and sink in the entire source space.

The development and improvement of psychophysiological tools such as the electroencephalogram (EEG), event-related brain potentials (ERPs), and the magnetoencephalogram (MEG) that are sensitive to these electromagnetic changes is making it possible to begin understanding the flow of information through the brain over time and space. These measures are sensitive to primarily postsynaptic currents, as opposed to the spikes recorded via extracellular single unit recordings[1] (Ilmonicmi 1993), in brain regions where (i) the average distribution of current sources and sinks within the neurons is distributed in a non-radially symmetric fashion, (ii) the neurons are aligned in some systematic fashion, and (iii) the neurons are activated in local synchrony (see Fig. 12.1).

The neocortex satisfies these constraints. It is organized as a large folded sheet a few millimeters thick wherein about 70 per cent of the cells are pyramidal cells with apical dendrites extending from the soma towards the surface of the cortical sheet. When the proximal parts of these apical dendrites of a cell are activated, current flows preferentially along the length of the dendrite and out of the cell at more distal sites, thereby creating an approximately dipolar source/sink configuration oriented perpendicular to the cortical sheet. Similarly, if the distal parts of a dendrite are activated a dipole field of the opposite orientation is generated. The extracellular currents generated by any single pyramidal neuron are weak, but a cortical region containing hundreds of thousands of such cells activated in synchrony produces a signal strong enough to be detected at the scalp (for more detail, see Kutas and Dale 1997).

EEG, ERP, and MEG techniques measure somewhat different aspects of neural activity, but as a group are among the most direct, non-invasive methods available for the study of neural processing during natural language processing. The EEG measures spontaneous rhythmic electrical activity occurring in multiple frequency bands. Event-related synchronizations in the alpha (8–12 Hz) and lower beta (18–30 Hz) bands are taken as electrophysiological correlates of resting or idling cortical areas. Thus, by examining these together with localized, transient attenuation of the EEG activity in the same frequency bands to an event (event-related desynchronizations, or ERD), one can make inferences about the fine structure of neural processing (e.g. Pfurtscheller *et al.* 1994; Krause *et al.* 1996). Another approach examines the average event-related potentials (ERPs) elicited in response to specific events (where 'event' is loosely defined and in some cases refers to preparation for movement or the absence of a stimulus). These are generally measured as a series of positive and negative potential deflections ('components') that can be characterized with respect to their amplitude and latency

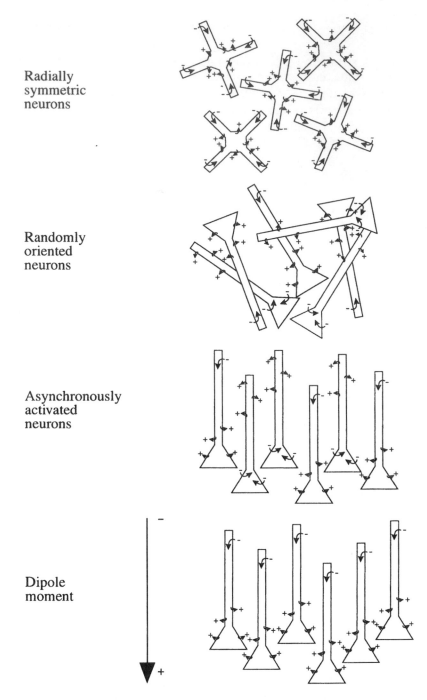

Fig. 12.1 Examples of closed and open source field configurations. Radially symmetric neurons (top), randomly oriented neurons (second from top), and asynchronously activated neurons (third from top) do not produce externally observable electric or magnetic fields; rather, they produce 'closed fields'. In contrast, neurons that are non-radially symmetric, are spatially aligned, and are activated in synchrony (bottom) produce 'open fields', externally observable electric and/or magnetic fields. (From Kutas and Dale (1997). Copyright © 1997 Psychology Press, reprinted by permission.)

across the scalp, although in principle every time point in an ERP waveform can provide valuable information about the ongoing brain activity (e.g. because the surface potential reflects the sum of many differently oriented local sources, a zero potential at a scalp electrode may arise from activity peaks in nearby cortical regions).

12.4 Relationship between EEG and MEG

MEG provides a different, but complementary, picture of the same neural activity measured with EEG/ERPs. As previously mentioned, each local current flow generates a magnetic field orthogonal to the flow (Fig. 12.2). The magnetic fields generated by all active areas add linearly to each other to create the field observed outside the head. The EEG and MEG are affected differently by head shape, dipole location, and dipole orientation. Since so little current flows through the skull, the small magnetic fields generated there can be ignored. Magnetic fields are therefore largely unaffected by inhomogeneities in the skull and intervening tissue (Hämäläinen 1995). With EEG, the skull and the skin must be modelled since the electrical signals we measure pass through them. However, magnetic field strength falls off more rapidly with depth than does the electric potential strength, so MEG is less sensitive to deep sources; furthermore, MEG is insensitive to radial sources (Mosher *et al.* 1993). In practice, this means that the MEG is more sensitive to activity on the banks of sulci and much less sensitive to activity on the crowns of gyri. The EEG is sensitive to both tangential and radial sources, although the electric field due to tangential sources in the fissures may be masked by superficial radial sources (Ilmoniemi 1993).

12.5 Language-related ERP effects

Thus, EEG, ERPs, and MEG allow one to monitor changes in electromagnetic activity coming from various cortical (and some subcortical) areas. By examining how these changes are correlated with behaviour of interest—recognizing a visual stimulus as a

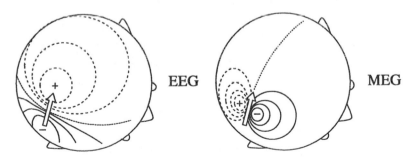

Fig.12.2 Diagram of hypothetical EEG and MEG field patterns over the scalp produced by a tangential superficial cortical dipole (arrow). Dashed lines indicate positive electrical potential and magnetic flux out of the head while solid lines indicate negative electrical potential and magnetic flux into the head. Magnetic fields are observed perpendicular to electric fields and are less affected by intervening (e.g. skull, scalp) tissue.

word, accessing its meaning, determining its role in the sentence structure—we can begin to map out how cognitive processes are instantiated in the electrochemical medium of the brain. A number of ERP components that change systematically with different aspects of language processing have already been described. Some of these are sensitive to factors (like those already mentioned) that are known to be important for neurobiological processes. Others correlate with variables in language processing that are just beginning to be put in neurobiological terms. Between 200 and 400 ms the ERP to written words over left frontal electrode sites shows a sensitivity to the eliciting word's frequency of occurrence in the language (King and Kutas 1998). The highest correlation ($r = 0.96$) is shown by the latency of a left anterior negativity, referred to as the lexical processing negativity (LPN);[2] this component peaks earlier to the extent that a word is frequent in daily usage. As it overlaps other components in the same time range, it is best seen after digital filtering to remove lower frequency components such as the P2 and N400 (see below). The so-called N280, which has been specifically linked to closed-class or function words (Neville *et al.* 1992), seems to be an instance of an early LPN due to the disproportionately higher average frequency of this class (which includes articles, prepositions, conjunctions, auxiliaries) relative to members of the open class (including content words such as nouns, verbs, adjectives, and adverbs). While other parts of the ERP vary their amplitude as a function of word frequency, none show a variation in latency. Within the same latency range, the potentials at nearby recording sites show a sensitivity to word length (i.e. number of letters).

The most heavily investigated of the language-related (though not necessarily language-specific) ERP components is a negativity between 250 and 600 ms, peaking around 400 ms post-stimulus onset, with a posterior, right-hemisphere distribution. First described by Kutas and Hillyard (1980) to lexical semantic anomalies, the N400, like the LPN, is a part of the response to every word; in fact without special analytic procedures the two may be difficult to tease apart even though they have different spatial distributions. The N400 seems to be the default response to words whether they occur in auditory speech, in sign language, or in written text (as long as they are orthographically legal). The amplitude of the N400 to content words in lists is smaller for those that are abstract than concrete and decreases with word frequency, repetition, and orthographic, morphological, phonological, and semantic priming; in sentence contexts, its amplitude decreases as the predictability of the word in the context increases ('cloze probability', usually due to increasing contextual constraint) (see Kutas and Van Petten 1994, for more detail, Fig. 12.3 gives an example). The reduction in N400 amplitude across the course of a sentence has been interpreted as reflecting a reduction in the difficulty of sentential integration due to the build-up of semantic constraints (Van Petten and Kutas 1990).

Note that the presumed equivalence of N400s across sensory modalities is based on functional rather than spatial similarity. For instance, while the amplitude of the N400 to both a written and spoken word is reduced by a preceding semantic associate, the visual N400 is later and more prominent over the right posterior areas than the auditory N400. In fact, even within a sensory modality, the apparent distribution of an

They wanted to make the hotel look like a tropical resort.
So along the driveway they planted rows of . . .

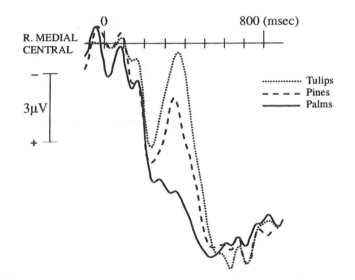

Fig. 12.3 ERPs to visually-presented sentence-final words, shown at a right, medial electrode site. The response to words expected in the context (solid line) is characterized by a sustained positivity. In contrast, ERPs to words unexpected in the context (dashed and dotted lines) are characterized by a negative-going potential peaking approximately 400 ms post-stimulus onset (N400). In addition to its sensitivity to sentential context, the N400 effect reflects long-term memory structure; responses to unexpected words from the same category as the expected word (dashed line) show a reduced N400 response relative to equally unexpected words from a different semantic category (dotted line). (Data from Federmeier and Kutas, submitted.)

N400 effect (difference between responses to congruent and incongruent words, for example) may change with factors such as speed of presentation; faster presentation rates are associated with more frontal negativity in the N400 region than slower rates (e.g. Kutas 1987). Such changes in the surface distribution of the potential imply a change in the orientation or location of the active neural sources, which implies that different parts of the cortex are generating the signal.

Electrophysiological researchers have identified two ERP components that seem to be sensitive to syntactic manipulations (for a more complete review, see Hagoort *et al.* Chapter 9). One is a negativity, called the left anterior negativity or LAN, whose latency range is similar to that of the N400 but which has a more anterior distribution and left hemisphere bias (Neville *et al.* 1991; Osterhout and Holcomb 1992; Rösler *et al.* 1993). Münte *et al.* (1993) used distributional as well as functional differences to argue that the LAN effects are distinct from the N400 component, are produced by different underlying generators, and index syntactic aspects of processing. Kluender and Kutas (1993*a*; 1993*b*), however, have suggested that the LAN elicited by certain syntactic violations actually indexes some aspect of working memory usage. Even in grammatically correct sentences, Kluender and Kutas find a LAN effect that is associated with entering a filler in working memory, storing it, and subsequently retrieving it to assign fillers to gaps. King and Kutas (1995) likewise observed a LAN effect in ERPs elicited by verbs that tax working memory; specifically, they recorded a LAN to a main-clause verb immediately following the gap in object-relative clauses in comparison to the corresponding verb in subject-relative clauses, which in turn had a larger LAN than verbs in unembedded sentences. As this class of negativities does show some variation in distribution, timing, and especially in its degree of lateralization, it may not reflect a unitary process.

The syntactic effect that has received greater attention is a slow, positive shift observed in response to violations of a range of syntactic phenomena, including agreement, phrase structure, subcategorization, and subjacency (Neville *et al.* 1991; Osterhout and Holcomb 1992; Hagoort *et al.* 1993; Münte *et al.* 1997; Coulson *et al.* 1998). This positivity has variously been labelled the P600, or the syntactic positive shift (SPS). The nature of the P600 component has not been wholly consistent across studies. For example, Osterhout and Holcomb (1992) report a P600 in response to both phrase structure and subcategorization violations, but they vary in scalp distribution. Moreover, for the same sort of phrase structure violations that yield a positivity with right anterior distribution, Neville *et al.* (1991) report a laterally symmetric positivity largest over occipital regions, Likewise, for the violation of subcategorization constraints to which Osterhout and Holcomb (1992) report a positivity with symmetric posterior distribution, Hagoort *et al.* (1993) find no effect. This variation may reflect the existence of more than one late positivity with different scalp distributions in this time interval, or the overlap of other components (such as the LAN or N400) which may alter the apparent distribution at the scalp. The P600 is typically described as beginning around 500 ms and having its midpoint around 600 ms, with a somewhat posterior maximum. This component, or set of components, seems to be sensitive to grammatical violations, both locally (e.g. agreement) and more globally (e.g. phrase structure). The fact that it is also sensitive to the probability of the violation in the experimental context suggests that it may be related to the family of positivities that includes the P300 (see Coulson *et al.* 1998).[3]

In addition to analysing these transient ERP effects elicited by linguistic violations or regions of lexical, semantic, or syntactic ambiguity, researchers have begun to monitor potentials time-locked to entire clauses or sentences, or larger parts than individual words therein. Moreover, many of these investigations have focused on wholly congruent sentences (i.e. without linguistic violations of any sort) that vary only in their structure (e.g. number of embeddings). These cross-clause potentials tend to be of a lower frequency than the transient effects and are often best seen after a low-pass digital filter is applied to the raw ERP data. Such filtering reveals that there are electrophysiological measures that emerge across sentences that are more than the responses to the individual words lined up one after another (Kutas and King 1996).

These slow potentials show systematic variation in time across the extent of the clause and in space across the scalp in both the anterior–posterior and lateral dimensions (for review, see Kutas and King 1996). For example, a sustained negativity over occipital regions is insensitive to word class but is specific to the processing of visual (as opposed to auditory) features. Anterior temporal sites, by contrast, do show a sensitivity to lexical class. A phasic positivity primarily over the left hemisphere is observed coincident with a verb's occurrence in a sentence, both in word by word reading and natural speech. It has been hypothesized that this positivity reflects some aspect of thematic-role assignment based on information contained in the lexical representation of the verb. Associated with clause endings during reading and listening, these slow potentials are characterized by a clause ending negativity (CEN), which is also somewhat better defined over the left than right temporal and central sites; these have hypothetically been linked to working memory operations at clause boundaries, so-called wrap-up processes. Perhaps, the most striking effect in these cross-clausal data is an extremely slow (< 0.2 Hz), cumulative positivity over (especially left) frontal recording sites. It has tentatively been linked to some executive function(s) of working memory such as the integration of items in working memory with information from long-term memory. Thus it might reflect the use of long-term memory to build a mental model, schema, or frame (message level representation) of the incoming sentence in working memory.

We examined this hypothesis further by contrasting two sentence types that vary in working memory demands by virtue of the differences in conceptual knowledge activated by their initial words (*before* vs. *after*) (Münte *et al.* 1998). Our real world experiences suggest to us that time unfolds sequentially, with current events sometimes causing future events. Our linguistic knowledge tells us that temporal conjunctions often draw attention to the sequence of events in a discourse. Moreover, whereas *after* signals that events will be expressed in their actual order of occurrence, *before* signals that events will be expressed in reverse order. We believe that there should be processing consequences of this. In a sentence beginning with *before*, the first clause cannot be fully integrated in a message level representation until after the second clause. In a sentence beginning with *after* the first clause can be integrated upon its completion. The former clearly places more demands on working memory. As can be seen in Fig. 12.4, the ERPs to the two sentence types diverge soon after the initial words; the waveform to the less-demanding or easier to integrate *after* sentences goes positive whereas that to the more taxing *before* sentences stays negative (see also King and Kutas 1995 for a similar effect comparing subject- versus object-relative sentences).

The different spatial distributions of these various effects also point to the distributed nature of aspects of sentence processing. By continuously recording across clauses and applying low-pass digital filtering, it is possible to monitor some of the overlapping but different processes that take place in multiple brain regions at the same time, albeit with different time courses. Also of note is that many of these slow potential effects associated with reading of, or listening to, sentential clauses differ reliably as a function of the comprehension skill of the reader or listener. Good comprehenders, for instance, show larger occipital negativities and smaller ultra-slow frontal positivities than poorer comprehenders. In summary, there are a number of fast and slow ERP responses to word- and clause-level effects that vary systematically in their timing and

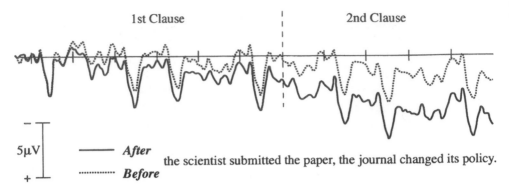

Fig. 12.4   Over-sentence ERPs to two sentence types recorded at a left frontal electrode site as volunteers (*n* = 8) with high verbal working memory span scores read sentences one word at a time for comprehension. The clause boundary is marked. Single word responses (repeated, higher-frequency activity) can be seen riding on top of a slow, sustained difference in which responses to sentences beginning with 'after' (solid line) are progressively more positive than (otherwise identical sentences) beginning with 'before' (dotted line). (From Münte, *et al.* (1998). Copyright © Macmillan Magazines, reprinted with permission.)

spatial distribution in ways that can be used to answer psycholinguistic questions at the level of word recognition as well as discourse.

12.6 Issues in ERP signal analysis

12.6.1 ERPs and the time course of processes

Thus, language components have been differentiated from one another and tied to cognitive processes via both their temporal and spatial properties. Of the two, the measurement of time using EEG/ERPs/MEG is more straightforward. Because these are direct, real-time measures of neural electrical activity, their temporal precision is quite high, with an upper limit at the sub-millisecond level. This precision is given by the fact that both the electric potential and the magnetic field at time *t* depend on the membrane current at time *t* only; in other words, the propagation of the potential and magnetic field is essentially instantaneous. Thus, if *t* is the earliest time at which ERPs from the two conditions differ significantly, it can be concluded that the brain activity differs between the two conditions at that time. The onset of the latency of the ERP difference between two conditions can thus be taken as an upper limit on the time by which the brain must have processed the stimuli sufficiently to distinguish them. Note that the converse does not hold; there are many reasons why one might fail to detect a difference between two conditions.

The order of processes for some language function and the duration of any given process can be critically important given the long-range dependencies that characterize language comprehension. In fact, many of the current debates about language processing revolve around issues of timing such as when some information becomes available or when it is used. Timing is of the essence when considering, for example, the nature of lexical access (is it automatic or controlled?), the extent to which syntax is autonomous, and the influence of context. Many language processes are extremely fast—individuals are able to produce words at a rate of two to three words per second (Levelt 1989)—and to follow these processes it is necessary to have a real-time measure that has a temporal resolution on the order of milliseconds. Other language processes, however, are quite slow because they must span a long discourse, a lengthy passage, or a sentence, which, given the recursive nature of language structures, could also be quite long. Indeed, the practical beauty of the ERP methodology is its applicability to language processes of any duration. Electrophysiological techniques thus provide the only dependent variables that can span both the crucial milliseconds determining what phoneme has been uttered and the seconds or minutes that may be needed to determine who did what to whom in a wh-question or a sentence with one or more embeddings (e.g. *The cat the rat the bat bit saw lunged and all hell broke loose temporarily*).

12.6.2 ERPs and functional independence

Since the electromagnetic activity associated with different generators adds linearly, ERP and MEG methods can also be used to determine the extent of functional independence between different brain mechanisms. If two conditions/processes are completely independent—that is do not share neural resources—then the activity generated when the two processes occur and overlap in time will be the sum of the activity generated by each process alone. If a given source is involved in both conditions, there may be non-linear interactions; for example, one condition may already drive a source to its maximum output. Nevertheless, we can count on the output of any given source adding linearly to the signal we observe from other sources.

Thus, the ERP can be used to examine when and how the brain subdivides complex cognitive tasks. For example, Besson and her collaborators (manuscript) performed a series of experiments to determine if musical lyrics and musical tones are processed independently or form a single percept. While semantically incongruous words within sentences elicit an N400 component (e.g. Kutas and Hillyard 1980), harmonically incongruous notes are associated with a positivity (the late positive complex, LPC) in a similar time window (Besson and Faita 1995). To examine whether these differences reflect independent processing of musical tones and musical lyrics, Besson *et al.* recorded ERPs as professional musicians listened to four types of operatic excerpts: (i) semantically congruous and sung in key, (ii) semantically congruous but sung out of key, (iii) semantically incongruous but sung in key, and (iv) semantically incongruous and sung out of key. As noted in previous studies, semantically incongruous items elicited an N400 while out-of-key notes elicited an LPC. Results in the double incongruity condition were consistent with an additive model of these two components, arguing for a complete independence of semantic and harmonic processing.

12.6.3 The value of multiple recording sites

Determining that the brain is sensitive to a particular factor and following this sensitivity over time could, in principle, be done by recording from only a single electrode.

Since electrical and magnetic fields are generally very small (electrical activity at the scalp is on the order of tens of microvolts and the magnetic fields recorded are nine orders of magnitude weaker than the earth's magnetic field), at times it proves useful to record from multiple sites to verify the reality of the measured signal change (though, in principle, an effect can be limited to one location and still be real; the LPN, for instance, is quite focal). Replication and averaging, however, can be as effective as more recording sites for this purpose. On the other hand, if the data suggest that some variable has no effect then more channels may be needed to verify this conclusion, since it is always possible that recordings were made at the wrong sites and/or that the effect has been missed for some other reason.

Traditionally, EEG recordings have been based on the 10–20 system of electrode placement (Jasper 1958; also see Böcker *et al.* 1994). It has the advantage of being standardized (and has been routinely used in the clinic). However, electrode placements are relatively sparse, with interelectrode distances on the order of 7 cm (for reference, the distance between two adjacent cortical gyri is on the order of 1 cm). The Nyquist distance[4] for cortical generators of electrical signals dictates interelectrode distances on the order of 3 cm or less (closer to the spacing of gyri) (Spitzer *et al.* 1989). Yvert *et al.* (1996) found significant improvements in dipole localization accuracy in simulated data by increasing the number of electrodes from 19 to 63. Equally as important as the high density of recording sites is that they be systematically placed on the head. The best would be an equidistant placement of the electrodes covering the entire surface of the head (including the bottom portions). A subtesselated icoscahedral configuration provides excellent uniform coverage of the top of head. It is also critical, however, that electrode impedances at the scalp be low (below 3 kOhms) and identical to one another.[5] For some uses (related to increasing spatial resolution), it is also important to know the exact locations of the electrodes. The average error in standard electrode placement is estimated to be on the order of 1–2.5 cm (Kavanagh *et al.* 1978). Methods for direct localization of electrode co-ordinates, such as with three-dimensional digitizers, are available (e.g. Echallier *et al.* 1992). Under conditions of high spatial sampling and appropriate recording conditions, the absence of an effect may form the basis of a working hypothesis that the generators of the scalp potentials are probably not differentially sensitive to the variable in question.

Determining that the neurons creating the activity measured by the dependent measure are not sensitive to some variable, however, is not the same as determining that the brain is insensitive to that variable. Not all brain events can be seen at the scalp surface. For example, active neurons may be radially symmetric, or may be arranged in a closed field, or may become active too asynchronously to signal their involvement at the scalp (see Fig. 12.1). Since not all brain activity can be seen at the scalp's surface, it is always more difficult to interpret the absence than the presence of an effect. Nonetheless, given what is known about the primary generators of the ERPs, the lack of an effect in clean, replicable data could lead to the hypothesis that at least the pyramidal cells in much of the neocortex are probably not sensitive to the manipulated factor. The fact that some brain activity cannot ever be seen at the surface adds to the inherent limitations in using the ERP to localize, given that the same spatial pattern of potentials at the scalp can be consistent with an infinite number of source configurations in the brain. We will discuss this so-called inverse problem and ways to deal with it in more detail later.

In most cases, when we do find an effect we are not merely interested in its existence or even just its timing. Rather, we would like to be able to identify it—to link it to and differentiate it from other known ERP effects. For this purpose, data from one recording site definitely will not suffice. An effect can vary in latency as a function of stimulus, response, and cognitive variables and still be generated by the same source configuration. Thus, many components/effects can only be definitively identified by virtue of their scalp distribution, although this is not easily accomplished. The N400, LPN, and LAN all have known characteristic distributions, and it is as much their different distributions as their different timings/temporal courses and sensitivities to experimental variables that identifies a negativity as an N400 and not an LPN or an LAN, for example. If we could assume that the mind was a serial stage processor, it would be relatively easy to characterize the spatial distribution of the associated ERP effect by measuring the amplitude of the potential at all recording locations at a given time point (peak amplitude) or within some range (area or mean amplitude). In reality, however, there is enough empirical evidence for the existence of cascade-like and parallel cognitive processes to render this simple serial assumption invalid. Mental processes and the associated ERP effects overlap in time and therefore in space, making it analytically quite difficult to define the spatial distribution of an effect unequivocally.

12.6.4 Comparing ERP scalp distributions

Given the importance of distributional analyses for many kinds of questions, it is a major analytic shortcoming in the field that there are no commonly agreed upon, objective techniques for comparing scalp distributions. These comparisons are typically made using electrode as a variable in a repeated factors ANOVA or by breaking down electrode locations into laterality (left vs. right, sometimes also including medial vs. lateral vs. midline) and anteriority (anterior–posterior with several levels) and using those as variables. McCarthy and Wood (1985) addressed the potential problems raised by such comparisons when the amplitudes of the effect for which distributional differences are being assessed are unequal. They pointed out that amplitude differences can be misinterpreted as differences in distribution and suggested normalizing the measures and performing the ANOVAs on normalized data. If a reliable interaction between some experimental manipulation and an electrode factor remains after such normalization, the inference that there is a distributional difference is justified.

The better the characterization of the spatial distribution, the more accurate our ability to differentiate two components at the level of scalp distributions or to determine that different neural generators are involved in different experimental conditions. A number of factors have led to the poor spatial resolution of conventional EEG/ERP methods at the scalp and in the brain. These include limited spatial sampling, reference electrode contamination, and failure to use inverse methods including information about the volume conductor (see Nunez *et al.* 1993). All of these shortcomings have been addressed in the recent past, however, and the current spatial resolution of the EEG/ERP is much better than it is typically characterized as being.

As already mentioned, the use of more electrodes, under the right conditions, can lead to a much improved characterization of the spatial distribution of the signal (also see later section on the forward solution). However, the utility of increased spatial sampling is ultimately limited by the distortion of the neuronal potentials as they are conducted through the highly resistive skull. The appreciably larger resistivity of the skull than the brain leads to current flow parallel to the skull for a distance, effectively smearing the image of a cortical source. The practical consequence of this is that the use of more than 256 electrodes (approximately intergyrus spacing) is unlikely to provide much additional information. The smearing of the potential distribution by the skull differentiates the EEG from the MEG. Because of the nature of the MEG forward solution (cancellation of magnetic fields generated by return currents in a spherical conductor), MEG field maps typically contain somewhat higher spatial frequencies than corresponding EEG potential maps; it has been suggested that this may be an advantage for recovering more information about multiple or distributed neural electromagnetic sources.

12.6.5 The Laplacian or current source density

One common deblurring or spatial enhancement technique is the Laplacian operator, which is the second spatial derivative of the potential field at each electrode.[6] The Laplacian is also called the current source density (CSD) and is proportional to the current entering and exiting the scalp at each electrode site (if the cortex was actually on the surface of the head and there were no deep sources, a high resolution CSD map would exactly describe the pattern of current flow into and out of the cortex) (e.g. Nunez 1981; Perrin *et al.* 1987). The Laplacian measures the curvature of the potential field, which is often not easy to see by inspecting the potential map. For example, a generally positive region in the potential map may signify either a source, a sink, or no current flow depending on its curvature. In a potential map, a small source or sink can easily be overwhelmed by a more broadly distributed potential on which it rides. By contrast, these functionally significant changes in the field are revealed in a CSD map (e.g. Fig. 12.5). Laplacian estimators of scalp current density are reference independent and converge on the true spatial pattern of scalp current sources and sinks as the density of electrodes increases.

However, because the Laplacian is a derivative operator (i.e. based only on nearest neighbour differences), it is sensitive to noise. Typically, the potential field is first interpolated with a smooth function before the derivative is taken. One typical function for this purpose is a spherical spline, which allows interpolation of data from irregularly spaced electrodes (Perrin *et al.* 1989; also see Nunez and Westdorp 1994). The CSD is relatively insensitive to signals that are common to the local group of electrodes used to compute it; thus it is more sensitive to cortical potentials of higher

Voltage   Current density

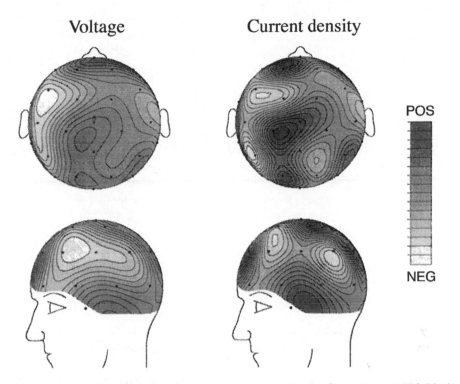

POS

NEG

Fig 12 5 Comparison of interpolated voltage and current source density maps. Shown are top and left side views of electrical activity recorded as a group (*n* = 24) of individuals read sentences one word at a time for comprehension. Plotted is the mean amplitude of difference in activity recorded across two sentence types that differ only in their initial word (e.g. 'Before/After the scientist submitted the paper, the journal changed its policy.') Note that the *Before* sentence is associated with greater negativity over left frontal sites. (From Münte *et al.* unpublished data.)

spatial frequency than to signals conducted from sources (subcortical) further away (e.g. Gevins 1996).

Although accurate distributions are important, at times inappropriate inferences are drawn from these distributional analyses. For example, when it is said that the visual N400 has a posterior, right hemisphere dominance, this means that it is generally larger over posterior rather than anterior electrode sites and generally larger over the right than the left hemisphere (at least when certain references are used, such as linked or average mastoids or non-cephalic reference). While this description has some heuristic value, it can be misleading—first because people may tend to believe that the N400 effect at the scalp represents the activity of some single source (neural generator) within the brain and second because they might assume that the fact that an effect has the largest amplitude over some scalp location reveals the source of its underlying generator in some transparent way. However, the scalp N400, for example, is likely to reflect activity from several neural generators (see intracranial discussion below). Additionally, very deep, midline sources can have quite broad distributions at the scalp, from which little information can be gleaned about the actual location of the generator(s). Moreover where on the scalp a potential is maximal depends very much on the orientation of the generator. For example, it is well known that generators on the medial surface of a hemisphere can be 'paradoxically' lateralized—that is, be larger over the contralateral hemisphere (e.g. Regan 1989).

Neural activity in a particular location in the brain produces a potential field with a characteristic scalp distribution. Simultaneous neural activity in two different locations would result in a scalp distribution that would be the sum of the characteristic scalp distribution of each alone, and so on. Thus, the distribution of activity at the scalp at any given moment is not a pure measure of any process unless we can be certain that only one generator is active. It is often assumed that a peak reflects the same process at all electrodes, and that differences in peak latency across the scalp reflect propagation of the process from one side of the head to the other. In fact, changes in scalp distribution over time necessarily imply that several generators with different time courses are involved. Because of the nature of electrical field propagation, neural activity that overlaps in time will also overlap in the spatial distribution of the effect and be quite difficult (if not impossible) to identify without quantitative modelling.

12.6.6 Extracting signals

Since different brain generators produce widespread, overlapping potential distributions, it is essential to have a method for extracting the signal produced by each generator. If the scalp distribution of each generator were known, then the contribution of each could be determined using a weighted sum of the potentials recorded at each electrode, with weights given by a least squares solution. In other words, at any given moment the signal recorded in, for example, an ERP experiment can be thought of as composed of the sum of a number of independent electrical processes. For instance, an individual may be simultaneously processing a semantic incongruity, processing a harmonic incongruity, shifting position in her chair (generating muscle activity), and blinking her eyes. These signals may be independent, but because they overlap in space and time it can be quite difficult to determine which aspect of the measured waveform is due to which of the possible sources.

In a recent paper, Bell and Sejnowski (1995) describe a new unsupervised learning algorithm that maximizes information transfer from input to output through a network consisting of non-linear units. Because the units that implement the input–output transfer function are non-linear, the system is able to pick up on higher-order moments of the input distributions (that is, non-linearities) and reduce redundancy between units in the output representation. The consequence is that the network separates statistically independent components in the inputs. This technique, used on the hypothetical data described in the previous experiment, would return the independent components of the original waveform—dividing them into a waveform due to the processing of semantic incongruity alone, that due to the processing of the harmonic incongruity alone, that due to the muscle activity alone, and that due to the blink. These independent components can be linearly recombined to reconstruct the original input, or they can be manipulated independently—used, for example, as templates for removing muscle and eye blink artefact from the original waveform.

This procedure is related to PCA—principal components analysis—as well as other separation methods such as generalized eigen vector analysis (Dale 1994) that use spatial filters to reduce the dimensionality of ERP data to a smaller set of uncorrelated or independent components. At a minimum, these procedures make it easier to separate the signal of interest from artefacts (such as the electrical signals caused by blinks or heart and striate muscle activity). But such procedures also may be quite effective at separating signals with distinct spatial distributions and therefore useful for decomposing waveforms in terms of informative experimental manipulations (for spatial PCA see, e.g. Skrandies and Lehmann 1982). Note, however, that blind application of such methods without due concern for experimental manipulations and/or the associated neurophysiology can be misleading.

Another new technique involving iterative deconvolution, first introduced by Woldorff (1993), can also be used to tease apart overlapping responses (for example, that to a stimulus versus that to a response). Such overlap is commonplace, occurring whenever the interval between adjacent events is smaller than the duration of the event-related response. Overlap of this sort can lead to significant distortion of the average event-related ERPs. Woldorff's procedure works only with moderate amounts of overlap and does not provide an exact solution. Dale *et al.* (in press) have provided a general exact solution to the overlap problem called DOC a direct method for overlap correction (also see Hansen 1983).

12.7 Localizing ERP generators

Although a better specification of an ERP effect's distribution can help resolve some kinds of issues and answer some kinds of questions, for the purposes of functional brain mapping we are often interested in determining where in the brain an effect is taking place. ERP data can contribute to this process in several ways. First, while it clear that ERPs can provide useful information about the temporal course of language-related processing, it may be much less obvious that timing information can also be very important for the purposes of localization. It is generally assumed that localization of active language areas requires a brain measure with high spatial resolution such as PET or fMRI. But spatially contiguous activity may be hard to tease apart except by temporal course differences. Moreover, it may be that some functional activity (e.g. phase-locked oscillatory activity) can only be defined by its temporal characteristics and thus requires methods such as ERPs/MEG (or fMRI) for its resolution. Since electromagnetic measurements are also sensitive to the orientation of current flow, they can aid in distinguishing nearby, but functionally distinct, regions of cortical activation.

12.7.1 Intracranial recordings

In some cases, the localization of ERP components recorded at the scalp has been aided by intracranial recording in humans. In these experiments, recordings are made via subdural electrode grids or depth probes in patients undergoing evaluation for medically intractable epilepsy (e.g. Lesser *et al.* 1994; Fried *et al.* 1981). Relatively few intracranial experiments have been done looking at language sensitive components; recently, however, a handful of studies examining word repetition, semantic priming, and sentence context effects have been reported. Building on earlier work by Smith *et al.* (1986), McCarthy *et al.* (1995) examined intracranial responses to congruent and anomalous words in sentence contexts. Anomalous words were associated with a bilateral negative field potential in the anterior medial-temporal lobe with peak latency near 400 ms (Fig. 12.6). Electrodes near the collateral sulcus recorded positive field potentials at the same latency. Because a potential arising from a particular source will be positive when measured from one direction and negative when measured from the other, this kind of 'polarity reversal' can be used to narrow down the spatial location of a source; in this case, the authors suggest that the voltage pattern is consistent with a source in or near parahippocampal and anterior fusiform cortices.

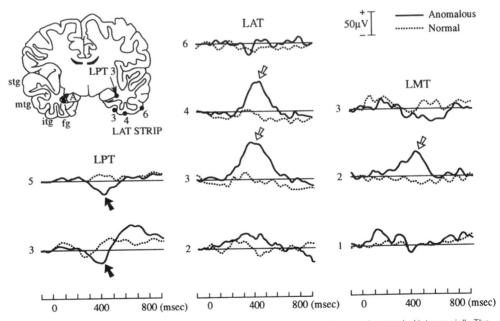

Fig. 12.6   ERPs elicited by anomalous (solid line) and normal sentence-ending words recorded intracranially. The black arrows point to the anterior medial temporal lobe (AMTL) N400, which was recorded from the left posterior temporal (LPT) probe. LPT3, shown on the MRI tracing, was located on the lateral border of the amygdala and is indicated by the labelled arrow. The white arrows point to AMTL P400s which were recorded from left anterior temporal (LAT) and left medial-temporal (LMT) subdural strips. Polarity inversions like these can be used to determine approximate locations of the neural generators of the measured response. (From McCarthy *et al.* (1995). Copyright © 1995 Society for Neuroscience, reprinted by permission.)

The component observed in the anterior medial-temporal lobe to anomalous words in sentences shares several important properties with the scalp-recorded N400 component already described. Isolated words generate these potentials, but only if they are orthographically legal (Nobre and McCarthy 1995). An earlier intracranial component called the N200 recorded in the posterior fusiform gyrus is sensitive to letter strings regardless of their legality (Allison *et al.* 1994; Nobre *et al.* 1994). The later potential, like the N400, is larger to content words than to function words and is diminished by semantic priming (Nobre and McCarthy 1995). Like the N400, this component also seems to be associated with memory, though the potential generated during, for example, continuous recognition tasks may be more widely distributed among medial temporal structures including hippocampus and amygdala (Guillem *et al.* 1996). Some have argued for a functional dissociation across structures for the roles played in memory-related processing by potentials in this time window, with left medial-temporal N400s predicting immediate recall performance and left anterior medial-temporal N400s predicting delayed verbal recall (Elger *et al.* 1997).

Even with intracranial recordings, however, precise localization can be difficult and the mapping between depth potentials and surface potentials is not straightforward because of the infoldings of the cortex. Volume conduction is also a problem for localization in depth, and, in the absence of a dense three-dimensional grid of recording sites, it can be difficult to know from where the source of the electrical activity recorded at a particular electrode emanates. That is, depth recordings are also subject to the inverse problem, discussed below. Additionally, electrical activity recorded at the scalp may arise from the summation of many, divergent brain sources. For example, while the anterior medial-temporal component behaves much like the scalp-recorded N400, the authors note that anomalous endings are frequently, though not consistently, associated with activity that seems to be generated in the hippocampus proper (McCarthy *et al.* 1995). Studies of memory have noted activity in the N400 latency range in the frontal, parietal, and occipital lobes, as well as the temporal lobe (Guillem *et al.* 1995), and it is unknown whether these findings suggest a distributed source for the N400 or merely reflect volume conduction of more localized electrical sources. Thus, while intracranial studies provide valuable information, they do not, in and of themselves, allow for exact localization.

While ERP/EEG data can contribute to localization via temporal information and while intracranial techniques can bring us closer to the source of scalp-recorded potentials, we would ultimately like to use our EEG/MEG measurements to specify the current distribution throughout the brain volume. In other words, we would like to know the number, location, spatial configuration, strength, and time course of neuronal currents that give rise to the potential distribution or magnetic field we record at the scalp (or in some cases in the depths). In short, we are faced with the problem of calculating current distributions inside the brain given magnetic field and/or scalp potential measurements on the outside; this is known as the electromagnetic inverse problem.

12.7.2 The forward solution

Before discussing why the inverse problem is inherently insoluble, let us quickly examine the electromagnetic forward problem, whose solution is limited only by the suitability of the source and head models chosen. Calculating the electrical potential and/or magnetic fields outside the head given a particular distribution of current inside is known as the forward problem. Its solution depends on a source model of the properties of the current sources (including location, orientation, and amplitude) and a volume or head model of the electromagnetic properties of the brain, skull, and other tissues as electrically conductive media (Fig. 12.7 gives an example). A variety of source (single point current dipoles, dipole sheets, and realistic current distributions) and head (single homogeneous sphere, multicompartment spherical shells, realistic) models have been tried.

12.7.2.1 Head models

A commonly used head model consists of three concentric spheres representing the boundaries between the air/skin, skin/skull, and skull/brain (sometimes the brain and cerebrospinal fluid are distinguished using another sphere). Such shell models do not provide variations in the conductivity of the scalp, skull, and brain and assume a single value for electrical conductivity. Thus, spherical shell volume conduction models are only a first approximation for electrical measurements, as the shape and thickness of the low-conductivity skull and, actually more importantly, the skin (on which the electrodes are placed) can have significant effects on the surface potential data (Cuffin *et al.* 1991). Finite element models take into account various geometric factors such as the shape of the skull, variation in its thickness, presence of skull openings (foramina and sutures), as well as the location, size, and shape of the ventricles. They use a large number of finite volume elements to create a head model which is anatomically accurate to any arbitrary level of precision.

Using high resolution MRIs, some have demonstrated three-dimensional finite element methods that can model the entire head volume at several millimetre resolution, accounting for fluid-filled spaces, local inhomogeneities, and anisotropies arising from white matter fibre tracts (George *et al.* 1995). While finite element deblurring (FED) methods can clearly increase the available spatial detail, the improvements do not come without a price. They require considerably more knowledge about the electrical (resistivities) and geometric (tissue boundaries) properties of small parts of the head. This information is not available from MRI without additional assumptions about the relation between MRI contrast and conductivity. Direct methods for measuring local conductivities (electroimpedance tomography) have extremely course resolution, for now. Finally, FED becomes computationally intractable with small elements.

A compromise between spherical analytical solutions and finite element methods is the boundary element method. Like the spherical shell model, it assumes that the

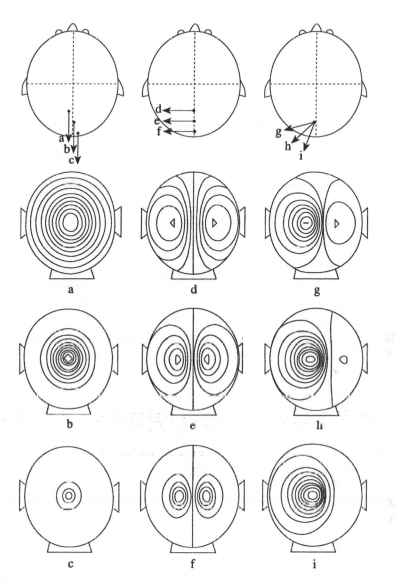

Fig. 12.7   Hypothetical scalp topographic maps, seen from the inion, for the dipoles shown at the top of each column. (From Fender (1987). Copyright © 1987 Elsevier, reprinted by permission.)

conductivity within one shell (skin, skull, or brain) is constant. But the surfaces defining the shells are broken up into many surface elements. These non-spherical surfaces can be extracted from MRI scans. Boundary element methods are more computationally tractable than three-dimensional finite element methods. While the accuracy of the forward calculation depends on the realism of these models, the important point is that it can, in principle, be solved.

12.7.3 The inverse problem

By contrast, the reverse of the forward problem, namely the inverse problem, cannot be solved in principle. The inverse problem (of estimating current sources in the brain from surface EEG and MEG measurements) is mathematically ill-posed, which means that there is no unique solution in the most general, unconstrained case. The solution is ambiguous because different source configurations can give rise to identical scalp potential and external magnetic field distributions. There are infinite mathematical solutions that are mathematically correct.

While the general inverse problem is ill-posed, it is possible to arrive at a unique solution by restricting the number of possible neural sources or by adding assumptions about the expected form of a many-dipole solution. These general approaches to the inverse problem are the dipole modelling approach, which assumes a small number of dipoles with unknown locations, and the imaging approach, which assumes a large number of (distributed) sources of known locations. The distribution of sources and sinks within a patch observed at a distance greater than the linear extent of the patch can be well approximated by a single so-called 'equivalent dipole' located in the middle of the patch.[7] A local current dipole is characterized by an amplitude (strength), a position, and an orientation. Simply rotating the orientation of the source at a fixed location can have a major impact on the scalp topography of its field. Deeper sources are generally associated with less compact patterns (less separation between negativity and positivity) and lower signal amplitudes than are shallower sources. Dipole position is defined relative to a three-dimensional co-ordinate system—for example, a Cartesian co-ordinate system (x, y, z) with the origin at the centre of the sphere serving as a head model. The orientation of a source can be described by two angles—for example, its angle relative to a chosen axis (e.g. X-axis), and its angular elevation from the X–Y plane. Each dipole source thus requires six parameters to characterize its activity at one time point: three corresponding to dipole location and three components representing dipole moment (two for angular relations, one for amplitude).

In the few dipole modelling approaches, a small number of equivalent current dipole sources are combined with a head model, and a non-linear least square minimization technique is used to find the six parameters of each of the dipoles that best generates the observed field distribution (e.g. Scherg 1990; Scherg and Ebersole 1993). Non-linear minimization techniques must be used because surface electrical and magnetic fields are non-linear functions of the source location and angle parameters. In this approach, the forward problem is calculated iteratively as dipole parameter values are adjusted until a minimum is found in the error between the recorded data and the values generated by the model.

While it is possible to achieve excellent fits to recorded data using these techniques, there are several problems in interpreting the resulting solution dipoles. One problem has to do with the order of the model. If one assumes there is only one dipole and there is only one dipole, it is possible to localize it with precision. However, if the assumed number is incorrect (e.g. too low), the solution may be misleading. The second problem has to do with local minima in the non-linear fitting procedure. Different starting points for the fitting procedure (i.e. different initial dipole locations and orientations) can result in different solutions, each of which minimizes error (in the sense that small changes in any of the dipoles lead to higher error). When there are more than two dipoles, it is not practical to exhaustively search the space of solutions. On the positive side, many source configurations, including extended sheets, can be well approximated by a single dipole. And the number of different spatial patterns observed in a typical ERP experiment (as estimated by spatial principal components, for example) is usually not large, indicating that it is possible to describe the activity accurately with a small number of sources.

An alternative to the few moveable dipoles model is a many fixed dipole approach (De Munck *et al.* 1988). Like the few dipole modelling approach, this method requires a mathematical formulation of the forward problem. Unlike the dipole modelling approach, which assumes a small number of dipoles or other current sources the current modelling approach assumes a surface or volume of a large number of possible current elements whose values are to be estimated. It is necessary to calculate the non-linear forward problem for each assumed current element in the volume only once. The most unconstrained of these reconstructions assume a three-dimensional grid of locations, with three orthogonal dipoles at each location. Determining the amplitudes of these dipoles is a linear problem.

The main problem with this approach to source localization is that the number of locations needed to represent the surface or volume of tissue is typically so large that it results in a severely underdetermined linear problem; that is we are faced with a system of linear equations where the number of unknowns far exceeds the number of measurements. Recording data from more electrodes distributed evenly across the volume surface is thus critical for providing a good estimate of the field for which the sources are sought. However, with no additional constraints, it is not possible to recover more dipoles than the number of electrodes divided by three (Fernandez *et al.* 1995).

One way of helping with the underdetermination problem is to use our knowledge of the sources of electrophysiological currents to constrain the reconstruction volume. Restricting the dipolar sources to the cortex, for example, reduces the number of possible locations in x, y, z but still requires solution for the three amplitudes of the three orthogonal dipoles at each of these locations. Additional constraints are provided by arguments based on architecture of the cortex and on invasive recordings suggesting that the primary axis of current flow is normal to the local cortical surface. With dipole locations and orientations fixed, it is possible to estimate as many dipoles as there are recording electrodes. Unfortunately, it takes on the order of 10 000 dipoles to adequately 'tile' the cortex. The resulting underdetermined inverse problem is typically solved by assuming that both the noise at each sensor and the strength of each dipole are independent and of equal variance (which is equivalent to the so-called minimum norm solution) (Dale and Sereno 1993). This solution has well understood properties when applied to the cortex (e.g. it tends to underestimate the depth of sources, but more accurately recovers their tangential location).

Functional MRI could potentially be used to further constrain the inverse problem. Functional MRI has superior and more uniform spatial resolution than EEG/MEG, but its temporal resolution is at least three orders of magnitude coarser. However, using fMRI to constrain EEG/MEG only makes sense to the extent that they measure the same thing. One way to test this is to present stimulus sets that are as similar as possible (given the constraints of the traditional fMRI block design versus event-related designs with EEG and MEG)[8] and then determine to what extent the independent results are similar to each other. Preliminary studies of this kind suggest that these very different techniques appear to detect activity in similar spatial locations (Barinaga 1997).

To achieve the best combination of spatial and temporal resolution, the techniques could be combined to provide mutual formal constraints upon each other. For example, a weighted linear inverse solution could be calculated where cortical locations with significant fMRI activity would be given a higher prior probability of being EEG or MEG sources (but without completely preventing sites inactive in fMRI images from contributing to the solution) (Dale *et al.* 1996). With this technique, it is essentially possible to extract the time course of activity of an fMRI site, improving upon the lower intrinsic spatial resolution of EEG and/or MEG. It is worth noting that this combination technique is not capable of specifically assigning activity to sources detected with fMRI that are close enough to each other so as to be indistinguishable with MEG and or EEG alone (e.g. two nearby visual areas). Nevertheless, the technique is excellently suited to detecting and localizing overlapping time courses of activity in motor, occipital, parietal, and temporal cortices—which are far enough apart.

12.8 The theoretical power of increased spatial resolution

Improved technology and improved models for looking at data, therefore, have combined to increase significantly the spatial resolution of electrophysiological techniques—both for voltage over the scalp and for determining the underlying spatial distribution of sources. But how much theoretical power does this increased spatial resolution afford? It is important when faced with new or improved technology to remember that increased spatial and temporal resolution does not, in and of itself, provide one with more inferential power. Only if the question asked dictates high spatial resolution does high spatial resolution become an advantage; if a question can be answered using a single electrode, it is easier and more economical by far to use a single electrode rather than a hundred or more. Furthermore, as our ability to resolve differences becomes better, we must be even more cautious about assigning meaning to any difference.

As stated earlier, both cognitive and neurobiological processes are structured at multiple levels. One can define differences at all of these levels—different processes within a given neuron, different neurons, different groups of neurons with or without different connectivity patterns, different areas, different hemispheres, different brains ... all acting on the same or different inputs to create the same or different outputs, also at multiple levels. Differences at one level are not necessarily indicative of differences at another level, and differences in neurobiological processing are not necessarily indicative of differences in cognitive processing (and vice versa). This becomes especially clear if we examine simple examples from neurobiology.

The visual system is divided across the two cerebral hemispheres such that input in the right visual field influences processing in the left primary visual cortex via the left lateral geniculate nucleus (LGN), and input in the left visual field influences processing in the right visual cortex via the right LGN. No gross anatomical or physiological differences have been reported between the hemispheres for this early stage of perceptual processing; both at a macrostructural and at a microstructural level, striate cortex in the two hemispheres seems to be equivalent in its processing of visual input. Most would agree that the processes going on in the two hemispheres at this level, then, are 'the same' at some important level. Obviously, different neurons are involved, but those neurons seem to be connected the same way and they operate on the same type of input to create the same type of output (cf. other sensory and motor areas). One would not want to say that different 'mechanisms' are responsible for processing right and left hemifield stimuli just because these stimuli create different patterns of neural activity. Yet, clearly, the spatial pattern of electrical activity that will be picked up at the scalp for the same stimuli flashed to the right and the left visual fields will be substantially different. Most investigators would not misinterpret this difference, but that is because we are aware of the physiological and anatomical underpinnings of the process being measured in this case. Without that knowledge, we would not be certain of whether the different pattern we record reflects a theoretically significant difference.

So different patterns of neural activity—patterns arising from different neurons and even different ensembles—do not always reflect true processing differences from a cognitive point of view. Even processing in different brain areas may be psychologically uninteresting. Stimulus intensity, for example, seems to have similar effects across a variety of sensory areas—increased brightness, loudness, or pressure all create similar changes in the neural activity evoked in their respective primary sensory areas, namely an increase in firing rate. The neurons, neural ensembles, and even areas involved are different; however, at another level there seems to be something remarkably similar about the coding of sensory intensity across modalities.

When do differences become theoretically important, then? In the absence of theory, this can be quite difficult to determine. Take the case of determining stimulus location in the visual and the auditory modalities. In the visual modality, stimulus location is represented directly; contiguous points in visual space create activity in contiguous points of the retina and this mapping is maintained across early cortical visual processing areas. Determining a visual stimulus' spatial location, therefore, is simply a matter of 'looking' at its position on the visual map. Deriving stimulus location from auditory signals, however, is not so easy. The cochlea orders information by frequency rather than spatial location. Stimulus location information must be derived from the input via comparisons of intensity and phase between the two ears; this information only emerges after several stages of neural processing. Clearly there is an important mechanistic difference between visual and auditory localization—neurons in different areas with different patterns of connectivity process very different types of information in computationally distinct ways in order to obtain the same conclusion (and possibly to elicit the same motor programmes, such as pointing). Yet even in this case, there is a level at which these two processes are the same—they are both involved in stimulus localization.

These examples serve to illustrate that using spatial information alone—differences in distributions or in neural sources—to answer cognitive questions or to decide between competing psychological or linguistic theories is a difficult endeavour. What a difference *means* depends on the question being asked, the task(s) used, the measure and its sensitivities, and a clear understanding of the levels of both psychology and neurobiology that are relevant. Especially because any purely spatial distribution is a slice through a process distributed in time, interpreting an observed spatial difference as a meaningful neurobiological, let alone functional/cognitive, difference is problematic regardless of a measure's resolution. However, the increased spatial resolution provided by new methodologies and new analysis techniques does open up new ways of using spatial information to aid our understanding of language processing. Instead of simply looking for a difference—any difference—we may begin to be able to examine how and how much two processes or representations are similar or different. We may, for example, begin creating 'similarity spaces' for the spatial distributions we measure during language tasks and from this gain a picture of the extent to which different cognitive processes use the same neurobiological resources or the extent to which different cognitive processes can be mediated by the same neural connections. More importantly, increasing the spatial resolution of techniques that already have good temporal resolution (and vice versa) increases our ability to resolve the real *spatiotemporal* signal that forms the basis of cognitive processing. In order to truly understand the processes underlying language, we need to know both when and where information becomes available in the brain, and our theories need to recognize the essential links between space and time for neural information processing. Ultimately, then, an increase in our ability to resolve spatial distributions is most exciting not because it gives us more power to test our current theories but because it provides us with an increased ability to create and test new theories that explore language in neurobiologically meaningful terms.

Acknowledgements

The authors gratefully acknowledge support from NIMH (MH52893), NIA (AG08313), and NICHD (HD22614) to M. K. and a predoctoral fellowship from the Howard Hughes Medical Foundation to K. D. F.

Notes

1. Spikes are generally not 'visible' at a distance because the sources and sinks generated by them are so close to each other.

2. Also known as the frequency-sensitive negativity (FSN); it is not yet known whether a similar negativity would be elicited by different (e.g. pictoral) information as a function of its frequency of occurrence.

3. For a different conclusion, see Osterhout *et al.* (1996).

4. The Nyquist frequency (distance) refers to the critical sampling rate needed to resolve the highest frequencies (in this case spatial frequencies) in the data—namely, twice the highest frequency in the signal. Sampling at a lower rate will result in aliasing, which is the artefactual appearance of a lower frequency (a misestimate of the spatial distribution and its peaks) (Blackman and Tukey 1959).

5. The saline/sponge/silver chloride electrodes in commercially available geodesic nets have higher and more variable impedances than standard cup and gel electrodes.

6. The discrete approximation of the Laplacian—subtract the average of the potentials of surrounding points from the current point—provides an intuitive understanding of how it measures curvature.

7. The use of equivalent current dipoles is justified in that the dipole term of a multipole expansion accounts for the largest proportion of variance in surface data. The potential produced by any arbitrary collection of sources and sinks can be expressed in terms of a multipole expansion (monopolar, dipolar, quadropolar, and other higher-order terms). The potential produced by a source or sink (monopole) falls off as the inverse of the distance from the measuring point, the potential produced by a dipole falls off more rapidly (the inverse of the distance squared), and higher-order terms fall off even faster (inverse of the distance cubed). Hence, the electric potential produced by a set of current sources and sinks within a region can be approximated closely by the monopolar and dipolar terms as long as the size of the region is small relative to the distance at which the measurements are made. Moreover, since the total amount of current leaving a cell must equal that entering a cell, the monopolar term in the multipole expansion must equal zero.

8. Recently, however, a number of approaches for collecting and averaging event-related fMRI activity have been described (Dale and Buckner 1997; Zarahn *et al.* 1997; Buckner *et al.* 1996). Approaches like these significantly improve the possibilities for setting up experimental designs that can be used with both methodologies without modification.

References

Allison, T., McCarthy, G., Nobre, A., Puce, A., *et al.* (1994). Human extrastriate visual cortex and the perception of faces, words, numbers, and colors. *Cerebral Cortex*, **5**, 544–54.

Barinaga, M. (1997). New imaging methods provide a better view into the brain. *Science*, **276**, 1974–6.

Bell, A. J. and Sejnowski, T. J. (1995). An information maximization approach to blind separation and blind deconvolution. *Neural Computation*, **7**, 1129–59.

Besson, M. and Faita, F. (1995). An event-related potential (ERP) study of musical expectancy: Comparison of musicians with nonmusicians. *Journal of Experimental Psychology: Human Perception and Performance*, **21**, 1278–96.

Besson, M., Faita, F., Peretz, I., Bonnel, A. M., and Requin, J. (1998). Singing in the brain: Independence of lyrics and tunes. *Psychological Science*, **9**, 494–8.

Black, J. E., Isaacs, K. R., Anderson, B. J., Alcantara, A. A., *et al.* (1990). Learning causes synaptogenesis, whereas motor activity causes angiogenesis, in cerebellar cortex of adult rats. *Proceedings of the National Academy of Sciences, USA*, **87**, 5568–72.

Blackman, R. B. and Tukey, J. W. (1959). *The measurement of power spectra, from the point of view of communications engineering*. Dover, New York.

Bliss, T. V. P. and Lomo, T. (1973). Long-lasting potentiation of synaptic transmission in the dentate area of the anaesthetized rabbit following stimulation of the perforant path. *Journal of Physiology*, **232**, 3331–56.

Böcker, K. B. E., Van Avermaete, J. A. G., and Van den Berg-Lenssen, M. M. (1994). The international 10–20 system revisited: Cartesian and spherical coordinates. *Brain Topography*, **6**, 231–5.

Buckner, R. L., Bandettini, P. A., O'Craven, K. M., Savoy, R. L., Petersen, S. E., Raichle, M. E., *et al.* (1996). Detection of cortical activation during averaged single trials of a cognitive task using functional magnetic resonance imaging. *Proceedings of the National Academy of Sciences, USA*, **93**, 14878–83.

Coulson, S., King, J. W., and Kutas, M. (1998). Expect the unexpected: Event-related brain response to morphosyntactic violations. *Language and Cognitive Processes*, **13**, 21–58.

Cuffin, B. N., Cohen, D., Yunokuchi, K., Maniewski, R., Purcell, C., Cosgrove, G. R., *et al.* (1991). Tests of EEG localization accuracy using implanted sources in the human brain. *Annals of Neurology*, **29**, 132–8.

Dale, A. (1994). Source localization and spatial discriminant analysis: Linear approaches. Unpublished Ph.D. thesis. University of California, San Diego.

Dale, A. M. and Buckner, R. L. (1997). Selective averaging of rapidly presented individual trials using fMRI. *Human Brain Mapping*, **5**, 329–40.

Dale, A. M. and Sereno, M. I. (1993). Improved localization of cortical activity by combining EEG and MEG with MRI cortical surface reconstruction—a linear approach. *Journal of Cognitive Neuroscience*, **5**, 162–76.

Dale, A. M., Ahlfors, S. P., Aronen, H. J., Belliveau, J. W., Huotilainen, M., Ilmoniemi, R. J., *et al.* (1996). Spatiotemporal imaging of motion processing in human visual cortex. *NeuroImage*, **3**, S359.

Dale, A. M., Ganis, G., and Kutas, M. A direct method for overlap correcting selectively averaged ERP and fMRI waveforms. (submitted.)

De Munck, J. C., Van Dijk, B. W., and Spekreijse, H. (1988). Mathematical dipoles are adequate to describe realistic generators of human brain activity. *IEEE Transactions in Biomedical Engineering*, **35**, 960–6.

Echallier, J. F., Perrin, F., and Pernier, J. (1992). Computer-assisted placement of electrodes on the human head. *Electroencephalography and Clinical Neurophysiology*, **82**, 160–3.

Elger, C. E., Grunwald, T., Lehnertz, K., Kutas, M., *et al.* (1997). Human temporal lobe potentials in verbal learning and memory processes. *Neuropsychologia*, **35**, 657–67.

Federmeier, K. D., and Kutas, M. (1998). A rose by any other name: Long-term memory structure and sentence processing. (submitted.)

Fender, D. H. (1987). Source localization of brain electrical activity. In *Handbook of electroencephalography and clinical neurophysiology, Vol. 1: Methods of analysis of brain electrical and magnetic signals* (eds A. S. Gevins and A. Remond), pp. 355–404. Elsevier, New York.

Fernandez, D. C., de Peraita Menendez, R. G., and Gonzalez Andino, S. L. (1995). Some limitations of spatio temporal source models. *Brain Topography*, **7**, 233–43.

Fried, I., Ojemann, G. A., and Fetz, E. E. (1981). Language-related potentials specific to human language cortex. *Science*, **212**, 353–6.

George, J. S., Aire, C. J., Mosher, J. C., Schmidt, D. M., Ranken, D. M., Schlett, H. A., *et al.* (1995). Mapping function in the human brain with magnetoencephalography, anatomical magnetic resonance imaging, and functional magnetic resonance imaging. *Journal of Clinical Neurophysiology*, **12**, 406–31.

Gevins, A. (1996). High resolution evoked potentials of cognition. *Brain Topography*, **8**, 189–99.

Guillem, F., N'Kaoua, B., Rougier, A., and Claverie, B. (1995). Intracranial topography of event-related potentials (N400/P600) elicited during a continuous recognition memory task. *Psychophysiology*, **32**, 382–92.

Guillem, F., N'Kaoua, B., Rougier, A., and Claverie, B. (1996). Differential involvement of the human temporal lobe structures in short- and long-term memory processes assessed by intracranial ERPs. *Psychophysiology*, **33**, 720–30.

Hagoort, P., Brown, C., and Groothusen, J. (1993). The syntactic positive shift (SPS) as an ERP measure of syntactic processing. *Language and Cognitive Processes*, **8**, 439–83.

Hämäläinen, M. S. (1995). Functional localization based on measurements of a whole head magnetometer system. *Brain Topography*, **7**, 283–9.

Hansen, J. C. (1983). Separation of overlapping waveforms having known temporal distributions. *Journal of Neuroscience Methods*, **9**, 127–39.

Ilmoniemi, R. J. (1993). Models of source currents in the brain. *Brain Topography*, **5**, 331–6.

Jasper, H. H. (1958). The 10–20 electrode system of the International Federation. *Electroencephalography and Clinical Neurophysiology*, **10**, 370–5.

Kavanagh, R. H., Darcey, T. M., Lehmann, D., and Fender, D. H. (1978). Evaluation of methods for three-dimensional localization of electrical sources in the human brain. *IEEE Transactions in Biomedical Engineering*, **25**, 421–9.

King, J. W. and Kutas, M. (1995). Who did what and when? Using word- and clause-related ERPs to monitor working memory usage in reading. *Journal of Cognitive Neuroscience*, **7**, 378–97.

King, J. W. and Kutas, M. (1998). Neural plasticity in the dynamics of human visual word recognition. *Neuroscience Letters*, **244**, 1–4.

Kluender, R. and Kutas, M. (1993*a*). Bridging the gap: Evidence from ERPs on the processing of unbounded dependencies. *Journal of Cognitive Neuroscience*, **5**, 196–214.

Kluender, R., and Kutas, M. (1993*b*). Subjacency as a processing phenomenon. *Language and Cognitive Processes*, **8**, 573–633.

Krause, C. M., Lang, A. H., Laine, M., Kuusisto, M., *et al.* (1996). Event-related EEG desynchronization and synchronization during an auditory memory task. *Electroencephalography*, **98**, 319–26.

Kutas, M. (1987). Event-related potentials (ERPs) elicited during rapid serial visual presentation of congruous and incongruous sentences. In *Current trends in event related brain potential research* (eds R. Johnson, Jr, J. W. Rohrbaugh, and R. Parasuramen), pp. 406–11. Elsevier, Amsterdam.

Kutas, M and Dale, A. M. (1997). Electrical and magnetic readings of mental functions. In *Cognitive neuroscience* (ed. M. D. Rugg), pp. 197–242. University College Press, London.

Kutas, M. and Hillyard, S. A. (1980). Reading senseless sentences: Brain potentials reflect semantic incongruity. *Science*, **207**, 203–5.

Kutas, M. and King, J. W. (1996). The potentials for basic sentence processing: Differentiating integrative processes. In *Attention and performance XVI.* (eds I. Ikeda and J. L. McClelland), pp. 501–46. MIT Press, Cambridge, MA.

Kutas, M. and Van Petten, C. K. (1994). Psycholinguistics electrified: Event-related brain potential investigations. In *Handbook of psycholinguistics* (ed. M. A. Gernsbacher), pp. 83–144. Academic Press, San Diego.

Lesser, R. P., Arroyo, S., Hart, J., and Gordon, B. (1994). Use of subdural electrodes for the study of language functions. In *Localization and neuroimaging in neuropsychology* (ed. A. Kertesz), pp. 57–72. Academic, San Diego.

Levelt, W. J. H. (1989). *Speaking: From intention to articulation*. MIT Press, Cambridge, MA.

Linden, D. J. (1994). Long-term synaptic depression in the mammalian brain. *Neuron*, **12**, 457–72.

McCarthy, G. and Wood, C. C. (1985). Scalp distributions of event-related potentials: An ambiguity associated with analysis of variance models. *Electroencephalography and Clinical Neurophysiology*, **62**, 203–8.

McCarthy, G., Nobre, A. C., Bentin, S., and Spencer, D. D. (1995). Language related field potentials in the anterior-medial temporal lobe: I. Intracranial distribution and neural generators. *Journal of Neuroscience*, **15**, 1080–9.

Merzenich, M. M., Recanzone, G., Jenkins, W. M., Allard, T. T., *et al.* (1988). Cortical representational plasticity. In *Neurobiology of neocortex* (eds P. Rakic and W. Singer), pp. 41–67. Wiley, New York.

Mosher, J. C., Spencer, M. E., Leahy, R. M., and Lewis, P. S. (1993). Error bounds for EEG and MEG dipole source localization. *Electroencephalography*, **86**, 303–21.

Münte, T. F., Heinze, H., and Mangun, G. R. (1993). Dissociation of brain activity related to syntactic and semantic aspects of language. *Journal of Cognitive Neuroscience*, **5**, 335–44.

Münte, T. F., Matzke, M., and Johannes, S. (1997). Brain activity associated with syntactic incongruities in words and pseudowords. *Journal of Cognitive Neuroscience*, **9**, 318–29.

Münte, T. F., Schiltz, K., and Kutas, M. (1998). When temporal terms belie conceptual order: An electrophysiological analysis. *Nature*, **395**, 71–3.

Neville, H. J, Nicol, J. L., Barss, A., Forster, K. I., *et al.* (1991). Syntactically based sentence processing classes: Evidence from event-related brain potentials. *Journal of Cognitive Neuroscience*, **3**, 151–65.

Neville, H. J., Mills, D. L., and Lawson, D. S. (1992). Fractionating language: Different neural subsystems with different sensitive periods. *Cerebral Cortex*, **2**, 244–58.

Nobre, A. C. and McCarthy, G. (1995). Language-related field potentials in the anterior-medial temporal lobe: II. Effects of word type and semantic priming. *Journal of Neuroscience*, **15**, 1090–8.

Nobre, A. C., Allison, T., and McCarthy, G. (1994). Word recognition in the human inferior temporal lobe. *Nature*, **372**, 260–3.

Nunez, P. L. (1981). *Electric fields of the brain*. Oxford University Press, New York.

Nunez, P. L. and Westdorp, A. F. (1994). The surface Laplacian, high resolution EEG and controversies. *Brain Topography*, **6**, 221–6.

Nunez, P. L., Silbestein, R. B., Cadusch, P. J., and Wijesinghe, R. (1993). Comparison of high resolution EEG methods having different theoretical bases. *Brain Topography*, **5**, 361–4.

Osterhout, L. and Holcomb, P. (1992). Event-related brain potentials elicited by syntactic anomaly. *Journal of Memory and Language*, **31**, 785–806.

Osterhout, L., McKinnon, R., Bersick, M., and Corey, V. (1996). On the language-specificity of the brain response to syntactic anomalies: Is the syntactic positive shift a member of the P300 family. *Journal of Cognitive Neuroscience*, **8**, 507–26.

Perrin, F., Bertrand, O., and Pernire, J. (1987). Scalp current density: Value and estimation from potential data. *IEEE Transactions in Biomedical Engineering*, **34**, 283–8.

Perrin, F., Pernier, J., Bertrand, O., and Echallier, J. F. (1989). Spherical splines for scalp potential and current density mapping. *Electroencephalography and Clinical Neurophysiology*, **72**, 184–7.

Pfurtscheller, G., Neuper, C., and Berger, J. (1994). Source localization using event-related desynchronization (ERD) within the alpha band. *Brain Topography*, **6**, 69–275.

Raichle, M. E., Fiez, J. A., Videen, T. O., MacLeod, A. K., *et al.* (1994). Practice-related changes in human brain functional anatomy during non-motor learning. *Cerebral Cortex*, **4**, 8–26.

Regan, D. (1989). *Human brain electrophysiology*. Elsevier, New York.

Rösler, F., Pütz, P., Friederici, A. D., and Hahne, A. (1993). Event-related brain potentials while encountering semantic and syntactic constraint violations. *Journal of Cognitive Neuroscience*, **5**, 345–62.

Sakai, K. and Miyashita, Y. (1991). Neural organization for the long-term memory of paired associates. *Nature*, **354**, 152–5.

Scherg, M. (1990). Fundamentals of dipole source potential analysis. In *Auditory evoked magnetic fields and electric potentials* (eds F. Grandori, M. Hoke, and G. L. Romani), pp. 40–69. Karger, Basel.

Scherg, M. and Ebersole, J. S. (1993). Models of brain sources. *Brain Topography*, **5**, 419–23.

Skrandies, W. and Lehmann, D. (1982). Spatial principle components of multichannel maps evoked by lateral visual half-field stimuli. *Electroencephalography and Clinical Neurophysiology*, **54**, 662–7.

Smith, M. E., Stapleton, J. M., and Halgren, E. (1986). Human medial temporal lobe potentials evoked in memory and language tasks. *Electroencephalography and Clinical Neurophysiology*, **63**, 145–63.

Spitzer, A. R., Cohen, L. G., Fabrikant, J., and Hallett (1989). A method for determining optimal interelectrode spacing for cerebral topographic mapping. *Electroencephalography and Clinical Neurophysiology*, **72**, 355–61.

Van Petten, C. and Kutas, M. (1990). Interactions between sentence context and word frequency in event-related brain potentials. *Memory and Cognition*, **18**, 380–93.

Woldorff, M. G. (1993). Distortion of ERP averages due to overlap from temporally adjacent ERPs: Analysis and correction. *Psychophysiology*, **30**, 98–119.

Yvert, B., Bertrand, O., Echallier, J. F., and Peruier, J. (1996). Improved dipole lateralization using local mesh refinement of realistic head geometries; An EEG simulation study. *Electroencephalography and Clinical Neurophysiology*, **99**, 79–89.

Zarahn, E., Aguirre, G., and D'Esposito, M. (1997). A trial-based experimental design for fMRI. *NeuroImage*, **6**, 122–38.

Zipser, K., Lamme, V. A., and Schiller, P. H. (1996). Contextual modulation in primary visual cortex. *Journal of Neuroscience*, **16**, 7376–89.

Index